HAMLET ON SCREEN

EDITORIAL ADDRESSES:
The Edwin Mellen Press
PO Box 450
Lewiston, NY 14092, USA

General Editor
Holger Klein
Institut für Anglistik
und Amerikanistik
Universität Salzburg
A-5020 Salzburg
Austria
Fax: 0043-662-8044-613

Reviews Editor
C. N. Smith
School of Modern Language
and European Studies
University of East Anglia
Norwich NR4 7TJ
England, UK
Fax: 01603-250599

The *Shakespeare Yearbook* is an annual dealing with all aspects of Shakespeare and his period, with particular emphases on theater-oriented, comparative, and interdisciplinary studies. From Volume IV (1993) onwards each volume has a main theme, but there will always be space for some independent contributions on other issues. As a rule, articles are double-read before acceptance.

Members of the Editorial Board
Dimiter Daphinoff (Fribourg)
Péter Dávidházi (Budapest)
James Harner (Texas A&M)
Joan Hartwig (Lexington)
André Lorant (Paris)
Peter Milward, S.J. (Tokyo)
Helen Wilcox (Groningen)
Simon Williams (Santa Barbara)
Rowland Wymer (Hull)

Contributions: Please type 60 digits per line, use line-spacing 1.5, employ MLA style and send in hard copy plus a disk (MS DOS, Word 6 or 7 for Windows, or WordPerfect, *both geared to IBM*). **Reviews** (not usually longer than 1000 words; one hard copy plus disk): **send to** Dr. C. N. **Smith**, University of East Anglia, School of Modern Languages and European Studies, Norwich NR4 7TJ, England, Fax: 01603-250599, Tel. 01603-56161. **Articles** (under 30 pages including notes; two hard copies needed plus disk): **send to** Professor H.M. **Klein**, Institut für Anglistik und Amerikanistik, Universität Salzburg, Akademiestraße 24, A-5020 Salzburg, Austria. Fax: +43-662-8044-613: The General Editor also welcomes **announcements, ideas** and **suggestions**.

Published annually. Subscription price $ 49.95 (hardcover). To order please contact the Order Fulfillment; The Edwin Mellen Press; P.O. Box 450; Lewiston, NY 14092-0450; (716)754-2788; FAX: (716)754-4056.

HAMLET ON SCREEN

Edited by
Holger Klein
and
Dimiter Daphinoff

A Publication of the Shakespeare Yearbook
Volume 8

The Edwin Mellen Press

Library of Congress Cataloging-in-Publication Data

This volume has been registered with the Library of Congress.

ISBN 0-7734-8502-3

> This is volume 8 in the continuing series
> Shakespeare Yearbook
> Volume 8 ISBN 0-7734-8502-3
> SY Series ISSN 1045-9456

A CIP catalog record for this book is available from the British Library.

Copyright © 1997 The Edwin Mellen Press

All rights reserved. For information contact

    The Edwin Mellen Press   The Edwin Mellen Press
    Box 450   Box 67
    Lewiston, New York   Queenston, Ontario
    USA 14092-0450   CANADA L0S 1L0

The Edwin Mellen Press, Ltd.
Lampeter, Dyfed, Wales
UNITED KINGDOM SA48 7DY

Printed in the United States of America

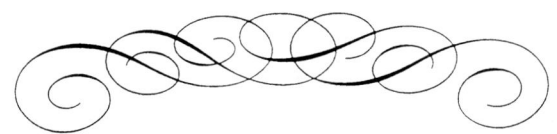

CONTENTS

HAMLET ON SCREEN

NEIL FORSYTH (Lausanne)
Ghosts and Courts: The Openings of *Hamlets* — 1

PATRICK HUNTER (Northridge)
Hamlet's Ghost on the Screen — 18

DEBORAH CARTMELL (Leicester)
Reading and Screening Ophelia: 1948 - 1996 — 28

THOMAS L. WILMETH (Meguon, Wisconsin)
Fortinbras on Film: Safe Passage for the Prince — 42

LEIGH WOODS (Ann Arbor, Michigan)
"Abstract and Brief Chronicles" on Film:
The Players' Scenes in *Hamlet* — 56

DAVID G. HALE (Brockport, New York)
"Didst Perceive?": Five Versions of the Mousetrap in *Hamlet* — 74

JAMES RIGNEY (London)
Hamlet and the Jester's Skull: The Graveyard Scene on Film — 85

JOHN OTTENHOFF (Alma, Michigan)
Hamlet and the Kiss — 98

EMMA SMITH (Oxford)
'Remember Me': The Gaumont-Hepworth Hamlet (1913) — 110

THOMAS KOEBNER (Mainz)
Hamlet as a Woman: Asta Nielsen's Shakespeare Film of 1921 — 125

LAWRENCE GUNTNER (Braunschweig)
A Microcosm of Art: Olivier's Expressionist *Hamlet* (1948) — 133

STEPHEN J. PHILLIPS (Plymouth)
Rotten States: Shakespeare's *Hamlet*
and Kurosawa's *The Bad Sleep Well* — 153

PATRICK BURKE (Dublin)
'Hidden Games, Cunning Traps, Ambushes': The Russian *Hamlet* — 163

PATRICK MCCORD (Athens, Georgia)
A Worthy Dane: Richard Chamberlain's *Hamlet*   181

EVGENIA PANCHEVA (Sofia)
O That This Too Too Solid Play Would Melt:
Coronado's *Anti-O(edi)pus*   197

STEPHEN M. BUHLER (Lincoln, Nebraska)
Antic Dispositions: Shakespeare and Steve Martin's *L. A. Story*   212

CHRIS LAWSON (Bristol)
"A Palpable Hit": Franco Zeffirelli's *Hamlet* (USA, 1990)   230

MARY Z. MAHER (Tucson, Arizona)
"Neither a Borrower, Nor a Lender Be": Zeffirelli's *Hamlet*   250

MICHAEL SKOVMAND (Aarhus)
Melodrama at Elsinore: Zeffirelli's *Hamlet*   262

PHILIP H. CHRISTENSEN (Suffolk)
"Shakespeare in Tombstone": Hamlet's Undiscovered Country   280

PARK BUCKER (Columbia, South Carolina)
The "Hope" Hamlet: Kenneth Branagh's Comic Use of
Shakespeare's Tragedy in *A Midwinter's Tale*   290

H. R. COURSEN (Augusta, Maine)
Words, Words, Words: Searching for *Hamlet*   306

DAVID KENNEDY SAUER (Mobile, Alabama)
Suiting the Word to the Action:
Kenneth Branagh's Interpolations in *Hamlet*   325

ANNY CRUNELLE VANRIGH (Valenciennes)
All the World's a Screen: Transcoding in Branagh's *Hamlet*   349

HARDY M. COOK (Maryland)
Reformatting *Hamlet*: Creating a Q1 *Hamlet* for Television   370

OTHER CONTRIBUTIONS

PATRICIA L. CORNETT (Southfield)
Some Poetic and Dramatic Uses of Cookery in Shakespeare's Plays   383

WILL and MIMOSA STEPHENSON (Brownsville)

IAN WARD (Dundee)
Issues of Kingship and Governance in *Richard II*,
Richard III and *King John*   403

JULIE D. CAMPBELL (College Station, Texas)
"And Yet a Maiden Hath No Tongue But Thought": Shakespeare's
Subversion of the *Querelle Des Femmes* in *The Merchant of Venice*   430

PETER CUMMINGS (Geneva, New York)
Verbal Energy in Shakespeare's *Much Ado About Nothing*   448

HEE-WON LEE (Seoul)
Helena's Tricks: Transgression and Negotiation in
All's Well That Ends Well   459

EDWARD M. MOORE (Grinnell, Iowa)
Bradley's Ending of *King Lear*   479

REVIEWS

James Harner, ed. *The World Shakespeare Bibliography,
1990-1993, on CD-Rom.*
(Christopher N. Smith)   496

Joseph Candido, ed. *Shakespeare: The Critical Tradition: 'King John'*.
(Sandra Clark)   499

Andrew Gurr. *The Shakespearean Playing Companies.*
(Martin Dodsworth)   502

Gordon Williams. *Shakespeare, Sex and the Print Revolution.*
(Jane Dowson)   506

CONFERENCE REPORT   509

EDITORIAL

The *Shakespeare Yearbook* was founded in 1990. I agreed, in autumn of 1992, to take over responsibility from Volume IV (1993) *The Opera and Shakespeare* (co-editor: C.N. Smith) onwards.

In the process of transition, the concept of the journal was redefined. It seemed particularly apposite to try and put the *Shakespeare Yearbook* on a broader international basis, and to place particular emphasis on the studies dealing with aspects of the theatre, with comparative literary issues and interdisciplinary question, as well as with Shakespeare reception in specific countries and regions, thus in some ways narrowing down the original conception, in others enlarging it.

It also seemed useful to focus on particular themes for each issue, while reserving some space for free contributions on any subject within the journal's scope. For most volumes co-editors have been won, as in the example of the present Vol. VIII, Dimiter Daphinoff (University of Fribourg), to whom I express my particular gratitude for all the work he has done.

Future volumes planned are:

No. IX (1998) *Shakespeare and Japan* (co-editor: Peter Milward)

No. X (1999) *Shakespeare and Italy* (co-editor: Michele Marrapodi)

No. XI (2000) *Shakespeare in the Visual Arts* (co-editor: James Harner)

I will gladly consider suggestions for later volumes, and also invite items of News and Announcements to be inserted.

Salzburg, Autumn 1997   Holger Klein

GHOSTS AND COURTS:
THE OPENINGS OF *HAMLETS*

Neil Forsyth
(University of Lausanne)

From its beginnings, the art of film has always pulled in two different directions, towards magic and towards realism. One is the tradition of Georges Méliès, a stage magician turned *cinéaste*, many of whose films had the words *nightmare* or *dream* in their titles: it is still at work in Griffith, and spreads out into the grand guignol inheritance of Eisenstein's *montage of attractions* or Cocteau's surrealism; it is still alive in animations, in the horror movie and in "special effects". The other direction derives from the Lumière brothers, who came to film from photography, and who at first simply tried to reproduce time and events accurately – a train leaving a station or the famous shot, widely reproduced during the 1995 centenary, of workers leaving the Lumière factory. The trend was seriously restricted by the Hollywood conventions that came to govern the industry, based as they were like Castelvetro's Aristotle on a distrustful sense of the spectators' limitations: what will the poor sap be able to understand? But it reappears in many more appealing ways, as in the documentary impulse, in Direct Cinema, or in the contemporary hyperrealism of a Mike Leigh. What brings the two contradictory traditions together and makes them both present or potential in any film is the idea of illusion: magic depends on illusion, but so does the representation in sequences of still frames of moving images and familiar, recognizable settings.[1] The basic hypothesis of this essay is that *Hamlet* films can be read according to how they exploit this informing doubleness of film. In particular I want to read the beginnings of the films, on the assumption that a film's interpretive stance will be clearly established during the opening sequences.

The first two scenes of *Hamlet* establish the basic division of the play between ghost and court. The rivalry of two brothers continues even after one of them has murdered the other, and Hamlet, despite his predominance in the play's action, is caught as a pawn in this ancient battle. But the rivalry extends to larger issues: the state of Denmark obviously, since both have been kings and one of them has usurped the other's throne; fatherhood, since both claim Hamlet as their son, and the play reiterates this claim several times; past and present, which Hamlet soon discovers means tradition and treason.[2] These two worlds are thus opposed early: the everyday world of the court, required by affairs of state to reassert its ordinariness in spite of official mourning for the previous king, and that other world, the supernatural, or the world of the dead, strangely insistent in this play and from whose bourne no traveller returns (even though at least one surely seems to). The two worlds also contrast as linguistic styles: 1.1. is full of questions and darkness and hesitations, misunderstandings in which the wrong guard asks the crucial "who's there?", and the appearance of the strange ghost is signalled by Horatio's sequence of if-clauses, whereas 1.2. is smooth, elaborately rhetorical, organized (by Claudius), structured, like the world Claudius is trying to construct. How these worlds are presented at the beginning of the play determines how the rest of the action is to be interpreted, and the various films of *Hamlet* all do it quite differently. Thus early on they establish themselves as not what the previous films had been. And even though the first two scenes may be quite radically altered, one of them even suppressed, the basic contrast, "Hyperion to a satyr" as Hamlet puts it (1.2.140), still needs to be made if the film is to be a film of *Hamlet* at all.

Take first the progenitor of all the subsequent performances, Lawrence Olivier's 1948 film. Notoriously the film begins with that pretentious banality which tries to make an Aristotelian out of a Shakespearean tragedy: Olivier lifts Hamlet's speech about "one particular fault" from 1.4.23-38, where it occurs as a general musing on the effects of drunkenness, and inserts it as a prologue, the words written carefully on the screen so we remember with respect where we are, not just at a movie but at a classic text, a "Shakespeare". These special words in this new exposed position unmistakably signal Aristotle's theory of *hamartia* as the key to a tragic hero.[3] Olivier then follows this fine but displaced speech with the bathetic voice-over "This is the tragedy of a man who could not make up his mind". The film can only get better now, and indeed it does. We are immediately where Shakespeare would have wanted us to be, in the midnight darkness that is so appropriate yet so impossible for the afternoon Globe stage to represent. Out of the darkness come those questions fired from unseen bodies: "Who's there?", "Have you had quiet guard?", etc.

The ghost's appearance is carefully staged. He arises first in the awed conversation of the guards with the sceptical Horatio, then as a rhythmic beat on the sound track, before at the startled cry of "Lo where it comes again"; as Walton's now harsh music builds a crescendo, we cut to a bearded helmet in the mist, and a sudden silence. Cut back to a medium shot of a full but indistinct cloaked figure in the mist, surrounded by an eerie light, as the sound track says "it is in the same figure as the dead king Hamlet". Cut back to the watching soldiers, including Horatio, to whom, since he is a scholar, the men now appeal. Cut now to the first establishing shot, backs of the men in close-up and we look through their two raised lances to the ghost in the medium distance. "Looks it not like the king, Horatio?" "Most like". (We must assume the men can see better than we can through the dry ice. But there is no time for this thought to form.) The ghost gestures and the men urge Horatio again to speak. As we cut back to a medium shot of the men facing slightly upwards, Horatio does speak. Cut back to a full frame image of the misty ghost, as Horatio urges it to speak. Instead there comes the crow of the cock and in spite of the men's cries of "Stay!" the helmet disappears, fading into the mist. Cut back to the men, but now in a long shot and way below, as if the camera is now where the ghost was, looking back down as it floats off into the cloud. The three men are left to react and to recount their ghost-lore.

The film has done what it can, mostly with sound track, dry ice and back lighting, to evoke the mysterious otherness that is the ghost: the space of the sequence has not changed from the battlements of the castle, and yet the ghost is shot slightly from below, and so distanced from the watching men. Horatio (that'll teach him to be a sceptic!) guarantees the truth of the experience by "the sensible and true avouch of my own eyes" – a line which in this context refers to the cinematic experience, to the whole idea of a magical vision. The motif of the sceptic convinced guarantees not simply the reality of the ghost but the authenticity of what might otherwise seem to the audience like a hokey horror film, not high classic art. So the film does exploit, but is at the same time careful to disavow, the Mélies tradition. This ambivalence is characteristic of much cinema that tries to reach a popular audience but is uncertain of its own aesthetic.

The scene concludes on another line that is moved up here from 1.4.90, "Something is rotten in the state of Denmark". The camera pauses on the three men, who now look off right out of the frame, in fact to the direction in which the camera now moves us away in its exploratory journey through the castle, that symbolic and claustrophobic Denmark, to find what is rotten. It travels down the stairs across various disparate objects, including an empty chair that we are soon to identify as Hamlet's, but settles on the famous canopied bed, which then zooms forward toward us ("so that's what's rotten!") before dissolving into the close-up of Claudius's face, fully lit unlike the ghost's, with a raised cup, drinking. ("So that's what's rotten!") Trumpets sound out from the balcony above, before the king's voice, slurred but speaking a perfectly clear and logical speech, continues with permission to Laertes to leave, and introduces Polonius briefly to give his consent. Still on Claudius's speech the camera withdraws till it allows us to find Hamlet now sitting in that chair, silent and turned sideways away from the court group, very clearly downstage and in the forefront of the audience-camera's vision. A brief silence falls as Hamlet refuses to answer until Gertrude intervenes and speaks, moving across away from Claudius and down along the table side toward Hamlet to take her position behind him. Finally Hamlet speaks his first words: "Ay, madam, 'tis [it is] common" (1.2.74).

Now Claudius starts up again and as he delivers his own rather callous speech about fathers losing fathers moves downstage to the group which is framed in the final shot of his speech, mother and son on the left, Claudius on the right. Gertrude speaks again, and provokes Hamlet's inky cloak speech: "seems, madam,

The Openings of *Hamlets*

nay I know not seems". Then after Hamlet agrees to her urging that he should not go to Wittenberg, Claudius again tries to take back control, but in another famous moment, the 34 year-old Gertrude bends down to kiss her 40 year-old son on the mouth. The kiss lasts and lasts, and Claudius is forced to mutter "Come, madam", and to take her roughly by the hand and draw her back to the other end of the long table.

Hamlet's first words then ("A little more than kin and less than kind", "Not so, my lord, I am too much i' the sun", 1.2.65/67) have been suppressed. No stage asides now, and the punning wit has been sacrificed to the clarity of a dramatic confrontation and the sexually explicit mother-son-substitute father scene. By making filmicly explicit (through its dramatic blocking based on Claudius's "Come, madam" line) this struggle for Hamlet's attention and for the service of his body, Olivier loses the complexity in the language, the mixed-up relations in kin and kind, the problem of the sun/son idea confusing kingship and kinship. Yet it is enough, that the camera lingers while Claudius pauses in saying "our sometime sister [...], now our queen". The film shows explicitly what Hamlet's first words in Shakespeare imply. And it is also important that throughout the scene Hamlet has not moved from the chair: the others are forced to come downstage to address him, and, apart from looking back and slightly upward towards but not at his mother behind him, he never looks at either parent. This demonstrates both his dominance of the film stage and the potential passivity in Olivier's interpretation of the action of the play.[4] The first two scenes are quite different (outside and inside, dark and light, mysterious and formally ordinary) and yet deliberately linked as that moving camera travels inside and down the stairs of the castle, symbolically looking for the rotten part of Denmark but also descending into the Hamlet-Olivier personality, which Elsinore comes more and more to represent.

The Russian director Grigori Kozintsev's splendid 1964 film opens with a clear allusion to Olivier, since once again the sea (and a castle on the sea-coast) defines part of the atmosphere: there is a long shot of the sea from above, recalling the setting for Olivier's "To be or not to be" soliloquy. On the sound-track a funeral bell tolls, linking the sea with death and establishing a recurrent image. But the opening scene turns out to be radically different, since it skips the scene that Shakespeare and (more or less) Olivier put first. Soon, as the bell continues to toll, fire replaces water: the credits roll over what we realize must be Hamlet senior's funeral pyre in the middle distance, though by a slight camera shift it is still clearly located in the movie's time-space above the sea. The music credit to Shostakovitch soon follows and it coincides with the first chords of the sombre music score: the bell has faded and the camera now shows us the castle exterior, then through an opening in the stone wall a flag fluttering in the breeze. Men on horseback arrive outside, more flags are seen, and in a very disconcerting cut, suddenly more horse-riders are galloping along a beach from right to left. Where are we? Quickly we see the castle again, relieving the anxiety produced by the galloping horsemen. And now we see that the main rider must be Hamlet himself, returning for the funeral to Elsinore, since as soon as he enters the castle he embraces his mother, and we hear the funeral guns. We watch the machinery being turned that closes the castle door (on us too) as more sombre Shostakovitch accompanies the action. As in Olivier the castle is becoming both a prison and a film-space of its own, an artificial construct related to, yet unlike any realistic space, and in which we cannot find our way. And as in Olivier, Kozintsev's castle is a place of glimpses, of narrow openings, of doors and windows "the better to spy from", as he puts it. "The walls are made up of guards".[5]

A dramatic cut now to drums and then into Claudius's opening speech in 1.2. The first part is done by a herald addressing the crowd outside in a loud town crier-like voice, reading the speech as if it were (and indeed it is) a proclamation. Cut again for the rest of the speech to be done by Claudius himself, inside the court, once the setting is established by two pairs of ambassadors who cross in front of the camera speaking German and French. Claudius now addresses those assembled round the long table as at a board meeting (longer than Olivier's table but clearly echoing it), and then, as they all stand, the camera shifts aside slightly to allow a brief glimpse of Hamlet sitting alone in almost the same chair he occupied for Olivier.

The Openings of *Hamlets*

What Claudius actually says, though, is to announce the claims of Fortinbras to the throne of Denmark, an essential difference from Olivier, who eliminated entirely the third of the play's three young men, parallel sons of important fathers, and thus at a stroke eliminated the play's politics. For Olivier what is rotten in the state of Denmark may well be Claudius, but as paternal, not really as political figure. Here, however, Fortinbras is a genuine threat, and the moment is stressed as marching music is heard and we all draw to the window to see outside the parade of men presumably accompanying the ambassadors. Kozintsev indeed says that "Olivier cut the theme of government, which I find extremely interesting" (p. 234). He does not need to explain that he has lived through the revolution and Stalin for us to see what he means.

Then we return inside to deal very rapidly with Laertes' request to go to Paris, and Claudius turns immediately to Hamlet. But he is not there. The camera cuts to a new shot in which we quickly find him going down wide straight stairs (unlike Olivier's) outside the court chamber, followed, chased even, by Gertrude, then Claudius and other members of the court. As Gertrude goes up to Hamlet, her character is given by her gesture: she looks at herself in a mirror, and preens. This gives extra point to Hamlet's first words: "Ay madam, tis common". Once again, the initial puns on "sun" and "kin" have gone, and the pun on "common" bears all their weight. Once again, we can sense Olivier's film behind this one, even in the radical variant of the staging whereby Hamlet rushes out instead of staying seated.

Now a public and oily Claudius congratulates Hamlet on his acquiescence in his mother's request, ignoring what we have all noticed, that Hamlet paid no attention to Claudius, only to Gertrude, and then the court begins to break up as Hamlet strides though the crowd with the first soliloquy, "How weary, stale, etc." (1.2.129 ff.) in voice-over. For the first time we see his face fully in medium close-up and we begin to establish our intimacy with him. At the end of the soliloquy, he meets Horatio and the two soldiers, and the discussion turns to Hamlet senior, and – also for the first time in the film, as harsh music plays behind – Horatio tells of the ghost. The camera again sees fire in the background, this time through an archway, and after the story is told, we cut to the fire again, then to Hamlet as he walks up and into the court room and sits alone at the table, first in rear-angle shot, then from the front.

Now comes strange but lively dance music as we cut to see Ophelia already weirdly moving in an inappropriate space for such a dance. The Laertes scene follows, then Polonius warns Ophelia against Hamlet, and she returns oddly to that forlorn and unsettling dance. A *glockenspiel* with mechanical, disconcerting figures, as weird as the Ophelia dance, strikes twelve, wind blows the clouds across the dark sky, and sudden noise intervenes as the court revelry spills out into the courtyard, while the camera watches Claudius and Gertrude stride through it all – a transparent allusion this to the revelry scenes in *Ivan the Terrible*, with Shostakovitch's music deliberately imitating Prokofiev's. Then the camera recedes and we find ourselves outside, just as horses burst loose, disturbed in some way by the night or the elements, or their extra sense of danger or the supernatural – it is not clear, but the horses are powerful images in the scene, here and later[6] – and men emerge, but then the camera over blaring music focuses on the vast sign in the heavens (the Aurora Borealis) as the soundtrack says "Look where it comes again".[7] We see a ruin, battlements, and the camera leads Hamlet to the seashore, from where he looks up to see the indistinct figure above. As the long scene develops (5 minutes) and the ghost tells his story, he becomes more and more distinct as a cloaked figure in full armour, but thus unrecognizable as any particular human being. The up/down relation is maintained between father and son, and the winds blow his cloak about throughout. Finally, as he says he must go because of the coming dawn, and cries "Remember me" (1.5.91), the camera shows Hamlet looking for him, and then itself searches, sweeping down and around as the clock strikes five.

Two things are remarkable about this sequence. First we never see Hamlet senior and junior in the same shot, and so never get a sense of their related size, except that Hamlet is always looking upwards from the beach to the castle walls. The ghost himself is never shown in relation to any recognizable element of the scene and remains, therefore, in a space of his own, always separate from that of the other characters. This might be expected, since he is after all a ghost, but the effect is both disturbing and impressive: he might well be enormous as we look up at him, we can't tell – and Shostakovitch gives it his most disturbing and moving music. The visual details of the scene are also disturbing. The ghost's cloak waves and billows in the wind, for example, a movement which is picked up[8] in movements of curtains, but also of flames, waves and clouds, everything, in short, which is other than the world of Claudius' earthbound and imprisoning court ("Your intent to go to Wittenberg is most retrograde to our desire" (cf. 1.2.113-14) – a turn of phrase that typifies Claudius's pompous but menacing language. What it means is: "No, you can't escape"). Kozintsev's background is in the Constructivism of the revolutionary period. In particular, he founded FEKS, the Factory of the Eccentric Actor, in 1922, the main goal of which was to subvert bourgeois realism by new techniques, by reassembling images, as in the disturbing horsemen sequence, and above all by following Eisenstein and the other founders of Russian cinema to insist on educating the new public to the provocative, mysterious otherness of this filmic world.[9] Hence he was supremely well prepared for this strange and compelling ghost.

Secondly, this ghost scene has been given extra prominence as the only one: the first scene of the play is missing entirely. This makes the ghost appear in the development of the film only once we have experienced the full impact of the public style of the new regime – oily, showy, superficial. The ghost, insistent and implacable in his demands, gets extra credibility from this transposition, almost as if he appears in response to our distaste at Claudius, as if he comes as much to set right the politics of this corrupt court as to avenge his own murder. And the result is that, in the absence of the first scene, the ghost appears especially and indeed only for Hamlet, who receives his message as a political challenge as well as a psychologically disturbing appeal to his dynastic and family loyalty.

In spite of Kozintsev's obvious debt to Olivier, an important difference, then, lies in the insistence on Freudian depth in Olivier, on court politics in the Russian version. Stalin had died in 1953, and ten years later when the film was made, Khrushchev was still promising a more open political style. Yet most of the overt politics of the film can still be referred, not to the contemporary world (as everyone had imagined Eisenstein had done in *Ivan the Terrible*, to Stalin's great displeasure), but to an autocratic and corrupt monarchical past from which the new Soviet world had emerged. The dark brooding quality of the film, the sombre soundtrack, may in retrospect look like covert critique of the communist regime, but that is apparently not how they were received at the time. Indeed Kozintsev called Hamlet a "tragedy of conscience" (p. 243), and this is revealing of how he saw himself and his work. He might have said "consciousness" as well, to underline the difference from Olivier (where it is the unconscious that the film finds ways to show at work). Clearly one of the things of which Hamlet is conscious is politics, but Kozintsev is careful to see the relation of ghost to king, or past to present, of dream-world to waking self, as primarily a moral one.

There is little of this, certainly none of the politics, in that odd and whiny sixties Hamlet of Nicol Williamson in Tony Richardson's 1969 version (nor in the more recent and upbeat Zeffirelli, as we shall soon see). The Richardson version (based on his Round House production and using no identifiable sets beyond that enclosed world)[10] went as far as possible into making Claudius (a splendid Anthony Hopkins performance) sympathetic. He is thoughtful, mature, sensitive, secretly troubled. This is close to the Wilson Knight view that Hamlet is diseased, the sick soul of William James, and Claudius "a good and gentle king".[11] You almost begin to wonder, as indeed the play requires in some measure, whether he really did murder his brother. Shakespeare has the Murder of Gonzago-Mousetrap play set up for exactly that reason, but none of the other films really make us question the ghost's version of events: certainly neither Olivier's drunken Claudius, nor Kozintsev's smooth operator statesman is any match for a genuine ghost in our minds. But Hopkins manages it, and conversely Williamson's complaining and unpleasant Hamlet, intelligent though he is, gets little emotional sympathy. This is all the more significant in that Richardson gives us no ghost, merely a light which is usually reflected in Williamson's face. So the confrontation at the basis of the plot is between a voice off and Anthony Hopkins – an uneven struggle. Conversely the effect of the odd light in Williamson's face is not to make us

The Openings of *Hamlets* 11

experience the ghost as a projection of Hamlet's conscience or consciousness, although of course we wonder, but rather to make us dislike that face and the extra attention we have to give it. The balance has been drastically altered between the two father-figures, and the film thus makes no use of the Méliès tradition of fantasy, in spite of its potential relevance to the Richardson interpretation.

This is also true for Franco Zeffirelli, in his underestimated 1990 version. He copies Kozintsev's reordering of the events (funeral, court scene, Ophelia-Laertes-Polonius, then Horatio and the news of the ghost, then and only then the ghost scene), but this time, oddly but understandably, given his ideological bent, without the politics. The opening sequence is extraordinarily good, I think, but not for these reasons, rather because it attempts, as Branagh has now done also with more glamour but perhaps less clarity, resolutely to undo that Gothic castle idea of Elsinore.[12] There are three main techniques for doing this. First, Zeffirelli has the ghost played by Paul Scofield, not at all as if he were a ghost who must leave as dawn approaches, but rather as if he were a man pressed for time, and the dialogue with Hamlet is intimate, in close-up, man to man, belonging entirely, and rather oddly if you think about it, to the realistic side of film tradition. Any sense of Scofield's otherness is quickly erased or domesticated. Secondly, Zeffirelli floods everywhere with light. This makes sense, of course, in the court scene itself, and especially when Hamlet and his friends look down into the revelry from outside, so the scene is framed by the window. But in fact every possible scene either takes place outside, in the bright sunlight, or moves as quickly outside as it can. Exteriors dominate the film. The first shot of all is the outside of the castle, with close-ups of anonymous soldiers' faces, and it is already a colourful world as the words "The Royal Castle of Elsinore, Denmark" appear on the screen – as in a travelogue.

The first scene is the funeral, with its early close-up of a Glenn Close who weeps copiously, and then an Alan Bates who clearly wishes she wouldn't. Then a hand picks up dirt and pours it over the embalmed body of Hamlet senior: it runs off ineffectually. A brief shot shows who the hand belongs to, a hooded Hamlet, and Claudius tries in voice-over to persuade him not to grieve since he is "nearest to our throne". Hamlet is not impressed, but a further sequence of shots shows he has apparently the same distaste for his mother's tears. This is man's stuff. The scene takes place in a kind of crypt – but we have no trouble in seeing it all, and very clearly too. And quickly Hamlet walks outside into the light. No black-and-white gloom for Zeffirelli. Even – and most oddly – the night outside on the castle battlements is extraordinarily bright. As the ghost appears we see it in close-up, not spatially defined, then quickly we see all the men facing it, so we locate its position without trouble (an important consideration for Zeffirelli, that the audience be given little trouble), then Hamlet strides eagerly forward into the light. Never mind that it is moonlight, and therefore white light. It is bright light. And the whole scene is lit by this bright and obviously artificial moon, such that one understands it when Scofield shelters under the wall – he is trying to find some shade. The swearing scene, even though it concludes the same sequence as in Shakespeare, takes place at a run outside on the battlements, but now in broad daylight again: nights are brief as woman's love in Zeffirelli's Elsinore, and with the night has gone any sense of the dreamlike or the inexplicable associated with the ghost.

The third technique for unpicking the Gothic idea of *Hamlet* is the casting. Alan Bates is a strong and even likeable Claudius, Glenn Close is a lively, girlish, shallow but centrally important Gertrude, and above all, there is the Lethal Weapon Mel Gibson himself. Hardly the man to pick if you want a brooding, introspective Hamlet. Gibson is very good indeed, I think, but he makes the film what many of his previous films have been, an action spectacular – appropriate enough, if you think about it, for a revenge play. It is possible, for example, that Shakespeare's Hamlet is already supposed to draw his sword and threaten the soldiers when they try to stop him following the ghost, but Gibson's "I'll make a ghost of him that tries to stop me" (1.4.85) has real conviction: his companions stand cowed like bureaucrats or extras waiting for the next cue. And it is the second brawl he has got involved in already (the first was just before, when

The Openings of *Hamlets*

Horatio for Hamlet's own good tried to warn him). Gibson's willingness to retaliate violently contrasts obviously enough with Olivier's hangdog Hamlet, and indeed this is part of Zeffirelli's purpose. He invokes that recent movie trend to have a "slightly anti-social, often humorous, male hero (or pair of buddies) challenge a corrupt and evil male villain, finally outwitting and then killing him after scenes of extraordinary violence".[13] The film makes us close to Gibson in various ways, not least because most of his fans can be presumed to be cheering him on to make a success of this difficult challenge, as well as to "get" that evil Claudius, and at the same time teach his mom a lesson.

But let us not make too much fun of this star-crossed direction.[14] Zeffirelli, after all, risks what the other hadn't, he puts back Hamlet's puns. They are in fact Gibson's first words, as in Shakespeare, but now they come out as unusually sly for Mel Gibson and momentarily at least contrast rather unfavourably with the direct and reasonable public speech of Claudius. And when the first soliloquy soon follows, not in voice-over but spoken out directly to the space around, it is pretty hard to believe this vigorous and good-looking, heroic young man could possibly mean it when he wishes "the almighty had not fixed his canon gainst self-slaughter" (cf. 1.2.131-2). There is nowhere for the sentiment to have come from. Then, quickly, he moves across the room and looks outside. He sees Glenn Close kissing Claudius, and makes up the "Hyperion to a satyr" line on the spot – and for the first time we see some jealousy. This is not a psychologically troubled Hamlet, like Olivier's, but he does have emotions, clean straightforward manly emotions though they obviously are. "Frailty thy name is woman" he says and closes the window almost angrily. Gibson's own comment on the sexual complications of the mother-son jealousy typically smoothes it out: "When she abandons him and runs off with his uncle [...] He's lost his gal, in a way".[15]

Nonetheless, the main thing that has emerged about Hamlet so far is that he is alone. Everyone else is in company, even jovial company, but Gibson as Hamlet is alone. Like all good Western heroes. Even the Ophelia-Laertes-Polonius scene which follows confirms this, since Zeffirelli chooses to have Hamlet look down from the battlements into the bright sunny courtyard where they are seeing off Laertes. Hamlet can, we gather gradually from the shot sequence, overhear what Polonius is saying as he warns Ophelia against him. Olivier's Hamlet reacts by subtle body language as Polonius calls Ophelia back inside, away from Hamlet's line of vision in that famous deep-focus shot,[16] but Zeffirelli does it by stressing even further the spying, eavesdropping motif in the play. Eventually and right at the end of the sequence, Polonius notices Hamlet watching (but does not, I think, realize he heard). Hamlet immediately withdraws and disappears from view. It is a brilliant and unsettling sequence. But we stay on the sunny battlements now for Horatio to come and tell Hamlet his story of the ghost, then, as the story unrolls we move inside, following Hamlet, and finally into his Dürer-like study, which has the classic objects of the student-loner of the time, an orrery and other scientific instruments, a book or two. Zeffirelli ends the scene characteristically – as Gibson swears the oath, he draws his sword.

There is, of course, something swashbuckling about Olivier's performance, but the contrast could not be greater between that gloomy 1948 version and Zeffirelli's "*Hamlet* for a new young audience that would normally approach Shakespeare with deep suspicion" (in the language of the promotional literature). As Annick Monod puts it in a fine unpublished essay comparing the two films,

> Olivier's *Hamlet* emphasizes the Prince of Denmark's inability to take revenge on Claudius, whereas Zeffirelli's version insists on how the hero succeeds. Two films based on the same plot but telling opposed stories, the story of a failure and the story of a successful revenge. On the one hand, that of 'a man who could not make up his mind', and on the other hand that of a prince determined to carry out what he has decided to do, whatever the obstacles.

Given that emphasis, it is hardly surprising that Zeffirelli resolutely ignores what Kozintsev had exploited so well, both the murkiness of the political world and the mysterious qualities of cinema for the ghost.

It was only Kozintsev's film, then, that made anything of the politics of *Hamlet*, at least until Branagh's 1996 "complete" *Hamlet*, about which I want here to add a

The Openings of *Hamlets*

brief comment. He has transposed it into the nineteenth century and deliberately evoked that century's major revolutions. He signals by the arrival of Fortinbras' elaborate army at the end that one more petty and corrupt little European state has proved easy pickings for a Napoleonic or Bismarckian invader. Such a reading, however, leaves almost no place for a ghost, who as a result of the unflinching use of realistic wide-screen conventions and high-definition 70-mm photography seems like a fish out of water. It doesn't really help that Brian Blessed tries to play him as a throwback to a more heroic era: he is largely irrelevant.

One final illustration, this time from the soliloquys, will fix our sense of the differences among the three main films I have been discussing. Mel Gibson's soliloquies enable Hamlet to release some of his vitality and craving for vengeance. But Olivier's reveal Hamlet's state of deep depression, his weakness, almost his pusillanimity. This appears clearly in the "Remember thee, ay thou poor ghost" speech (1.5.95ff) which follows Hamlet's first encounter with his dead father. Zeffirelli's Hamlet speaks these lines while jumping to his feet and running down from the dungeon to the platform, his sword drawn. Then he looks down at the king and the queen carousing in the hall (crosscuts of Hamlet speaking and king and queen drinking and laughing), and, mad with anger, he hits the low wall with such violence that sparks shoot up. Olivier's Hamlet, on the other hand, begins this same soliloquy kneeling. He then collapses onto the floor and lies on his back, weeping. He draws his sword for a solemn oath, then drops it and lies down again. He finally holds up his sword as a cross to sanctify his vow of remembrance, but his strength is still faltering. Such bursts of energy, such solemn words leave Olivier's Hamlet in a state of utter exhaustion, which prevents him from actually putting his words into acts. This process of self-sabotage has been described by Olivier himself as Hamlet's "weakness for dramatics":

> This would be reasonable if the dramatics spurred him to action, but unfortunately they help to delay it. It is as if his shows of temperament not only exhaust him but give him relief from his absorption in his purpose, like an actor who, having spent all in rehearsal, feels it almost redundant to go through with the performance.[17]

Branagh's performance seems to hover uncertainly between the Olivier and Gibson readings.

But what happens in Kozintsev? The entire speech is dropped. It is, in a way, unnecessary, at least if the primary dramatic purpose of the speech is to show Hamlet's reaction and so judge the significance of the ghost. With the Kozintsev ghost, we have been way beyond that world of swords and stone, or shows of temperament. We have watched that strange isolated helmet move and turn against the lightening sky: it has seemed empty at one point, though still somehow speaking, and then we have finally seen its eyes, the rest of the face masked. At the end of the scene it has merged into the sky and on this wide screen the dawn sky is enormous and serene and utterly beautiful. Hamlet is then seen looking up at that dawn, dwarfed but resolute. The words of the speech, so necessary to Gibson's anger and frustration, or to Olivier's now serious neurosis, are all done with that look, and that sky. "Remember?" How indeed could one forget that overwhelming image?

Among these various films, then, all are more than willing to use the central realist tradition of film in their various ways for the court scenes, but only Kozintsev is sufficiently confident to exploit the illusionist mysteriousness that is also at the heart of film. Perhaps this is one reason why his film remains for most cinema-lovers the most powerful *Hamlet* film, not simply because of its ghost, of course, but because of the way the images and movements within the ghost scene prepare for and connect with everything else in the film that is disturbing and determinedly strange.

Notes

1. A brief restatement of this common view of film aesthetics will be found in James Monaco, *How to Read a Film* (London: Oxford UP, 1981), p. 236.

2. *Tradition* and *treason* are etymologically the same word, which brings these two apparently opposite worlds together, and surely complicates Hamlet's difficulties. See my "Rewriting Shakespeare: Travesty and Tradition" in *On Strangeness*, SPELL 5, ed. Margaret Bridges (Tübingen: Gunter Narr, 1990), pp. 113-31.

The Openings of *Hamlets*

3. Printing of text over, in or as image during the credits sequence is a common technique at the opening of Shakespeare films: compare Olivier's wartime *Henry V* with its famous dedication, or Branagh's *Much Ado About Nothing*, with its frontal presentation of "Sigh no more". I am indebted to Peter Holland for this point.

4. A fine treatment of the film's Freudian implications is Peter Donaldson's in *Shakespeare Films/Shakespeare Directors*. (Boston: Unwin Hyman, 1990).

5. Grigori Kozintsev, *Shakespeare, Time and Conscience* (New York: Hill and Wang 1966), p. 255.

6. Horses are important also in Kozintsev's *King Lear*, and in both cases recall the wonderful scene in Kurosawa's *Throne of Blood*, when Banquo and Fléance discuss whether to go the banquet since the horses don't want to.

7. Or I suppose it does: Pasternak's Russian translation is rendered back into Shakespeare by the English subtitles.

8. See Raymond Ingram, "Angles of Perception", in *As You Like It: Audio Visual Shakespeare*, ed. Cathy Grant (London: British Universities Film and Video Council, 1992), p. 17 and Neil Taylor, "The Films of Hamlet", in *Shakespeare and the Moving Image*, ed Anthony Davies and Stanley Wells (Cambridge UP, 1994), p. 185.

9. John Collick, *Shakespeseare, Cinema and Society* (Manchester UP, 1989), p.127-40, makes a case for Bakhtinian carnival as the dominant idea. Perhaps so, but surely the Méliès tradition of spectacular illusion (carnivalesque in its own way) is more important. And one sees it at work in Eisenstein's essay on "Dickens, Griffith and the Film Today", *Film Form* (Cleveland, Ohio: Meridian), pp. 195-255.

10. Roger Manvell, *Shakespeare and the Film* (New York: Praeger, 1971), p. 127.

11. G. Wilson Knight *The Wheel of Fire* (London: Methuen, 1930), pp. 32, 39.

12. In an interview on BBC Breakfast News the day of the film's London release, 15.2.97, Branagh said he chose the nineteenth century because it was "glamourous and opulent so the film would seem to be those things too, [...] and away from the kind of gloomy Gothic castle kind of setting [...] that is lowering and black and white and where you think the entire court is peopled by manic-depressives". This is a transparent allusion to Branagh's onlie begetter, Olivier once again, but also probably to Kozintsev.

13. Neil Taylor, in *Shakespeare and the Moving Image*, op.cit., p. 192.

14. Zeffirelli had done the same thing, and with a similar point, for his Burton-Taylor *Shrew*: here Glenn Close stars shortly after her sexy leads in *Fatal Attraction* and *Dangerous Liasons*. Opposite her nominal son, she and Gibson nonetheless play out a screen romance.

15. Quoted from the promotional *Classic Mel Gibson: The Making of Hamlet*, 1991, in Ace Pilkington, "Zeffirelli's Shakespeare", *Shakespeare and the Moving Image*, ed. Anthony Davies and Stanley Wells (Cambridge UP, 1994), p. 175.

16. Brilliantly analyzed by Anthony Davies in *Filming Shakespeare's Plays* (Cambridge UP, 1988), pp. 48-9.

17. Quoted in Donaldson, p. 32.

HAMLET'S GHOST ON THE SCREEN

Patrick Hunter
(California State University, Northridge)

Pathetic victim. Irate Jehovah. Stern Father. Compassionate Father. Demon. Warrior. Each of these has served as an interpretation of the Ghost, among many others. Although Hamlet is the more substantial character, the Ghost arguably lends itself to as many varied interpretations. Compare the character of Hamlet in Olivier's film version with the one in Zefferelli's; each actor essentially plays the character as primarily Oedipal, and, psychologically speaking, they are very similar. On the other hand, compare the Ghost in each of these two versions; not only does each actor present a different appearance, but also different – even opposite – motivations, as we shall see. In fact, surveying the various film and TV versions of Shakespeare's play can serve to show just how multifaceted the character of the Ghost can be.

Produced by the English Two Cities Films in 1948, Olivier's version of Shakespeare's *Hamlet* has been highly regarded ever since, despite its shortcomings. Many today find the acting too theatrical and the long roaming camera shots purposeless. The movie opens with Olivier telling the audience that "This is the story of a man who could not make up his mind", and then proceeds to perform the character as everything but wishy-washy or even vacillating.[1] However, despite these and other weaknesses, the film stands out as certainly the first major cinematic version of Shakespeare's play, and it has its defenders; few, if any, have criticized its black and white cinematography, which always has been ideal, of course, for shadows and scenes of horror. It also ideally suits a traditionally horrific interpretation of the Ghost.

The Ghost in this version, with his long gray beard, looks wizened enough to be both Hamlet's and Gertrude's father.[2] Often expressionately filmed within shadows and mist, with a slightly blurred face, the unaccredited acoter costumed is hardly visible; when we do see him, his face seems dolorous and agonized, as if the armor were too heavy to bear. Indeed, Olivier's interpretation of the Ghost largely coincides with how Horatio describes him: armored with a visor raised and a countenance more in sorrow than in anger. Beyond this, however, Olivier also presents a strange bond between Hamlet and the Ghost. In 1.4, Shakespeare indicates that the first one to spot the Ghost is not Hamlet, but Horatio, who cries out, "Look, my lord, it comes." (ll 38). Olivier, however, directs this moment with Hamlet being the first to sense the approaching spirit, by having the camera close in on the Prince, blurring slightly in and out of focus to a booming heartbeat on the soundtrack. To further emphasize the connection between Hamlet and his father's spirit, Olivier used his own voice, electronically slowed down and deepened, for the voice of the Ghost. Obviously, Olivier, reinforcing his Oedipal interpretation, presents the Ghost as a personification of a side of Hamlet himself, a projection of the Prince's own sub-conscious.

More than one shot visually discloses that this Ghost ambiguously both appeals to as well as extends from Hamlet's chaotic mind. When the Ghost relates his murder, he is largely framed in the center of a long shot with Hamlet's back to the audience. All that can be seen of the Danish Prince is the back of his head at the bottom of the frame, appearing as if the Ghost were directly hovering above, as if emanating from Hamlet's brain. That his brain interrelates with the Ghost is shown again with the line "To be or not to be." Olivier presents the back of this head in full close-up, closes in on it and then blurs the image into that of the violent ocean, "when the eyes of the Ghost appear briefly in the waves" (Davies, 57). In both these shots, Olivier shows swirling imagery surrounding the back of Hamlet's head: in the first one, he uses mist; in the second, ocean waves. In both cases, the surrounding swirling images reflect the disorder of Hamlet's mind, and the Ghost's influence upon it. In addition to this, by associating the Ghost with the line contemplating suicide, Olivier also connects the Ghost with Hamlet's death-wish.[3]

That the Ghost serves as a deadly influence is indicated earlier in the film. When Hamlet follows it, he does so holding his sword with the handle raised up, like a protective cross. Despite the many cuts to the text, Olivier retains Horatio's warning:

> What if it tempt you toward the flood, my lord,
> Or to the dreadful summit of the cliff (1.4.69-70)

In this film version, the lines increase their power as Hamlet treads up the castle steps. The camera closes in on his feet as each one slowly and cautiously climbs up, and as it's so dark and foggy, who knows what lies beyond the next step? When finally Hamlet reaches the top of the tower, he stops for a moment and says, "Whither wilt thou lead me? Speak, I'll go no further." Obviously, he remembers Horatio's words and realizes that the Ghost could be a hellish specter attempting to lead him to his death. Such moments accentuate that so much of the main character's conflict in Acts 2 and 3 is deciding whether the Ghost is really "a spirit of health or a goblin damned" (1.4.40). The matter is not one lightly to dismiss. As Northrop Frye states

> Hamlet's real difficulty with the Ghost is: if purgatory is a place of purification, why does a ghost come from it shrieking for vengence? And why does purgatory, as the Ghost describes it, sound so much as though it were hell? The Ghost's credentials are very doubtful, by all Elizabethan tests for such things, and although Hamlet is in a state close to hysteria when he calls the Ghost "old mole", "this fellow in the cellarage", and the like, it is still unlikely that he would use such phrases if he had firmly identified the Ghost with his father at that point. (86)

Despite his simplifying claim that the Prince is "a man who could not make up his mind", Olivier visually indicates that Hamlet's conflict doesn't stem from an indecisive nature; Hamlet's conflict is that he has excellent reason to doubt this ghost, especially with its appearance so unsettling. Of the many English film versions of *Hamlet*, Olivier's Ghost is the one most like a phantom and the one with the most mystery.

Olivier's version has influenced others. One example is a TV production, *Hamlet at Elsinore*, broadcast in 1964, and starring Christopher Plummer, an actor whose classically heroic persona compares with Olivier's. The production was taped at Elsinore castle, with its raging coast, and it contained comparable camera tracking shots wandering through a dark castle; however, this time the shots seem more purposeful, because, as is soon revealed, the Ghost is not a visible actor but the camera itself. For the scene when he meets the Ghost, Plummer spoke directly to the camera with an off-screen voice answering. The moment is well-described by Bernice W. Kliman:

> For the scene with the ghost, we see Hamlet in close-up, out of focus, behind him, and we hear the ghost's hoarse whisper and then more normal-sounding voice for the revelation. The shot remains in effect virtually throughout the whole scene, varying only in distance from the camera, from medium to extreme close-up – movement being provided by the wind blowing Hamlet's cape, the waves behind him, and his features. The use of the shot is unmistakable: the sea represents the turmoil in Hamlet's heart ...(156)

As mentioned above, a comparable use of ocean waves was made to visualize Hamlet's mental turmoil in Olivier's movie version; however, the device of presenting the Ghost as only an off-screen voice inevitably reduces it as a character. Indeed, he becomes less a character and more an abstract presence, with hints of omnipresence, omniscience, and other qualities associated with God. This also can be seen in another film version made the same year: Richard Burton's Broadway production, which used the off-stage recorded voice of John Gielgud for the Ghost. All that is seen on-stage is a shadow of a slightly bearded man with a Renaissance bonnet on his head; however, as the shadow stands about eighteen feet high, it darkens most of the set, almost dwarfing Richard Burton. The Ghost becomes less a character and more of a force of almost God-like power, as with the Plummer *Hamlet at Elsinore*. Also like the Plummer version, the Burton version is difficult to locate on video, and one fears that the original negative is either deteriorating or missing.

To realize how fragile motion pictures can be, one has to only view the Nicole Williamson version. The film, on the existing videotape release, seems at times to crumble apart and suffers from scratches and faded color. While mostly a film of the acclaimed stage production directed by Tony Richardson in the late sixties, this version benefits from Williamson's vigorous portrayal of both Hamlet and the Ghost. Like the above-mentioned productions of the sixties, the Ghost is again a disembodied voice, and, like the Olivier film, the voice is Hamlet's (or actually Nicole Williamson's). Electronically recorded to simulate an echo-like effect, it offers more mystery than the other off-screen Ghosts, and, because of the actor's stentorian vocal powers, it also suggests more authority. As with the Olivier version, using Hamlet's voice accentuates that the Ghost personifies an aspect of Hamlet himself. Whatever its positive qualities, however, presenting the Ghost as an off-screen voice ultimately doesn't serve the Ghost as much as it serves Hamlet. In an article examining the various films of *Hamlet*, Neil Taylor states that making the Ghost a light shining on the characters who see it "might encourage in us Gertrude's opinion that Hamlet is deluded [... but] its chief effect is to put the spotlight literally on to Hamlet" (189).

In emphasizing Hamlet, the off-screen interpretation inevitably avoids the elements that distinguish the Ghost as a character: his armor, his facial expressions, and – for most film versions – the use of special effects. Not surprisingly, subsequent film and taped productions have avoided utilizing the off-screen Ghost. The next TV version, a 1970 Hallmark Hall of Fame presentation, starred Richard Chamberlain as Hamlet. Set in the Age of Enlightenment, the production, like other Hallmark shows of the time, fully exploited the then-new popularity of color televisions by presenting lividly pigmented costumes, photography, and even make-up. Here, for once, is a Hamlet who is neither blond nor dark-haired, but a redhead. Standing apart from all the bright colors is John Gielgud as the Ghost, appearing completely white. As with Melville's whale, the color white proves a strikingly neutral color, lending itself to a variety of interpretations. However, Gielgud, with an impassive and mournful voice, presents a largely pitiful appearance, completely lacking any hint of power or brutality. Instead of armor, he is dressed as an eighteenth-century general, including a three-corner hat. Little else

Hamlet's Ghost on Screen

can be offered as the production cut the play to less than 100 minutes, perhaps the most butchered sound version ever recorded on film or videotape.

On the other hand, the next televised version, which came in 1980, contained so few cuts it ran well over three hours. Produced by Cedric Messina as part of the BBC Shakespeare Series, it starred Derek Jacobi as Hamlet and Patrick Allen as the Ghost. Allen, whom Messina had previously cast as General Sir Claude Auchinleck for the docudrama *Churchill and the Generals*, possesses traits ideal for military roles, and his Ghost remains the most warrior-like of all screen characterizations. When first seen, he is dressed in full armor, striding in an upright, military march. When Jacobi cries out, "Alas, poor Ghost!" Allen angrily retorts "Pity me not!" Stern-faced and angry, Allen totally embodies the king-as-a-soldier, and only occasionally allows moments of pathos. He gazes off toward the horizon, his voice trailing off, when he speaks the lines:

> The glow worm shows the matin to be near
> And gins to pale his uneffectual fire.
> Adieu ...(1.5.89-90)

He emphasizes not only that he must leave, but also what he now is denied by death, his first "adieu" directed not at Hamlet but at the approaching daylight, which he could enjoy only when alive. Then abruptly, as if catching himself at his own vulnerability, he darts back to down to Hamlet, returning to his stern brow look and finishing the remaining "adieus" with a tone that implies "Get to work". Allen's other moments of pathos also center on what the former king has lost. When he visits the bedchamber, his final moment shows a close-up of agonized longing for his queen wom he can no longer reach. Despite such moments of pathos, all in all, Allen's Ghost comes across as a warrior, much the way Hamlet describes him. Frequently, productions will interpret the Ghost as Horatio describes him, as mournful and sorrowful, but it is Hamlet who insinuates that his father normally looks "frowningly" (1.2.230), and even after seeing the Ghost, describes him as possessing an "eye like Mars to threaten and command," (3.4.57).

If the Ghost in Olivier's version approximated Horatio's description, then this Ghost approximates Hamlet's.

With most of the film and taped versions, the directors presented the Ghost using devices available only to the camera. Whether using double exposure to create a diaphanous appearance or with other special effects, they often have shown the Ghost in a manner comparable to ghosts in fairy tales or early nineteenth century stories. They often neglect what experts in the paranormal have consistently repeated: that when people claim to have seen a dead relative's spirit, they claim to have seen them appearing as ordinary as in real life. Realism may or may not suit a Shakespeare adaptation, but if it does, by far the most realistic of the many film versions remains the Zefferelli *Hamlet*, in terms of its acting, its set design, and its treatment of the Ghost. No expressionistic shadows, no special effects, not even any alteration in make-up, and when he first appears, he seems to walk quietly out of a corner.

He is also lacking in cruelty, despite his asking Hamlet to commit an act of revenge. Unlike the Ghost in Olivier's and most other versions, he does not wear armor (although he is buried in it). Dressed in what looks like a monk's robe, Paul Scofield emphasizes all the Ghost's agony and sorrow.[4] When he speaks of his death, he says "... but by a brother's hand ..." accentuating "brother" to stress the unnaturalness of the murder, and perhaps even his own despair at acknowledging it. By the scene's end, Scofield mournfully intones "Adieu, adieu ..." and then comes directly to the camera with his sad-eyed face in full close-up as he says, "Remember me". Who could forget? Scofield's is the most compassinate, most vulnerable Ghost on film, even crying tears at one point. Not surprisingly, the instance when the Ghost enters the Queen's bedchamber – the moment that most often serves for pathos for this specter of the night – is cut, because any further attempt at pathos would be redundant or maudlin. In the Olivier version, the Ghost leads Hamlet to the castle's topmost tower, possibly wanting him to plunge to his death; in this version, Hamlet and the Ghost sit down together on a castle tower for a close father/son chat. A viewer cannot possibly doubt that this spirit suffers

Hamlet's Ghost on Screen

daily, not in hell, but in purgatory, so piteous and dolorous is he, the question of his being a demon in disguise becomes irrelevant.

Screen portrayals of the Ghost culminate with the most recent film version, starring and directed by Kenneth Brannagh. For decades, the view that a Shakespeare play *must* be hacked up when adapting it has gone unquestioned by filmmakers. Brannagh's motion picture attempts to adapt the complete text and at the same time make it cinematic. Whatever its shortcomings, the movie is unprecedented in film history, and shows a filmmaker admirable in his audacity. Because Brannagh uses the play's complete text, his motion picture stretches to over four hours. Such a duration can try the patience of the audience, but it allows Brannagh to incorporate all the elements Shakespeare provides for the Ghost, the warrior-like aspects as well as the pathetic ones. This movie version even clarifies what other versions have either overlooked or neglected: that the Ghost, when human, had been a tyrant. For the many long speeches, Brannagh relies – perhaps too predictably – on visualizations of the words being spoken; as a result, this version not only has Fortinbras, but also his father Norway, played by gentle-faced John Mills. To actually see, if even briefly, Norway futilely writing his appeals only underscores that this Ghost, while ruling as king, had stolen lands. Like a Rameses II or a Stalin or many another tyrant, this King Hamlet has also proliferated his state with statues of himself, reinforcing his authority and dominion.

Opening the film with shots of the statue not only clues the audience that Hamlet Sr. has acted as a despot; it also prepares the audience for a remarkable introduction. When Horatio, Bernardo, and Marcellus first spot the Ghost, they see what appears to be the statue brought to life! In this version, the statue and the Ghost are virtually one. Immobile and burly, with his arms still, his body erect, and his face glaring, he is reminiscent of the statue at the climax of Joseph Losey's film of Mozart's *Don Giovanni*. Perhaps this is intended, for like that statue, which summons the main character's soul to damnation, this Ghost also seems like an outrider from the underworld. Of all the Ghosts on film, this one is the most demonic. When Hamlet first follows him into a dark forest, crevices spring open, the earth coughs up foggy mists, and the ground shakes as if in a major earthquake. Such effects can inspire wisecracks from a modern audience, but they also present the Ghost with a hellish savagery that Elizabethans would have understood. At the film's end, after Fortinbras has reclaimed the lands lost by Norway and all scores have been settled, Brannagh concludes with shots of the statue at the start being pulled down. The demon has been exorcised.

Like Kenneth Brannagh's other work (i.e., *Mary Shelley's Frankenstein*), this film also suffers from effects that do not fully work. Brian Blessed, whom Brannagh had cast as the Duke of Exeter in *Henry V*, is a powerful-looking, burly man, completely convincing as a warrior, and certainly intimidating as the Ghost, but his moments of pathos in the bed chamber scene become ineffectual. Obviously, Brannagh aimed for pathos at this moment, as he replaces the Ghost's armor with what appears to be a shroud or a monk's habit (wisely, Brannagh does not dress the Ghost in a nightgown as the first Quarto specifies). By removing the armor, Brannagh attempts to disassociate the Ghost from the tyrant/statue image evoked not only earlier, but referred to again with the movie's final scene. Blessed looks appropriately mournful and longing, but the green contact lenses, which previously contributed to his demonic appearance, look out-of-place, even silly at this moment.

The problem may reside with aiming too high, with attempting to incorporate too many interpretations at once. It is difficult, perhaps impossible, to represent the Ghost as both demonic and pitiable. The character, as written by Shakespeare, does possess these conflicting characteristics, but the problem for a director and actor lies in believably conveying them. Has any one actor ever incorporated to the fullest *all* the qualities of Hamlet, who is at times logical yet spontaneous, intellectual yet passionate, tender yet virile, princely yet coarse? Shakespeare often employs ambiguous and paradoxical qualities for his best characters, but the director or actor who tries to combine all possible and even clashing interpretations often aims too high for human possibility. In order to fully develop our understanding of Hamlet as a character, we would do better to reject assuming that only one performance or interpretation is definitive, and would instead benefit from seeing a variety of performances, by a variety of actors, served by a variety of interpretations. I would argue the same for fully developing an understanding of the Ghost.

Notes

1. Olivier has been quoted with dismissive statements toward other Shakespearean characters. He once called King Lear "just an old fart", and then proceeded to play the character with a complexity that suggested anything but. While on may criticize Olivier for such statements, many Shakespearean actors know that such claims are necessary to guard against being intimidated by the part. Unlike other actors, such as Charles Laughton or John Barrymore, Olivier was never too intimidated to tackle innumerable classical roles.

2. The film emphasized – overemphasized for some – the Oedipal complex, and so Eileen Herlie, an actress thirteen years younger than Olivier, was used for Gertrude. Though some have criticized Olivier for this, few have criticized Zefferelli for casting a Gertrude (Glenn Close) who looks virtually the same age as Hamlet (Mel Gibson).

3. Anthony Davies expands on this further in *Filming Shakespeare's Plays*, bringing out how the Topmost Tower serves as a symbol of death. It is not only where the Ghost first leads Hamlet, but also where the Prince utters "To be or not to be" with thoughts of jumping over, and finally where his funeral march journeys at the film's end.

4. When consulting on the casting for the lead of a film version of Brecht's *Galileo*, Kenneth Tynan rejected Paul Scofield because he "would look as if he had been through the Inquisition before the film began" (Caute 176).

Works Cited

Caute, David. *Joseph Losey: A Revenge on Life*. New York: Oxford UP, 1994.

Frye, Northrop. *Northrop Frye on Shakespeare*, ed. by Robert Sandler. New Haven: Yale UP, 1986.

Davies, Anthony. *Filming Shakespeare's Plays*. New York: Cambridge UP, 1988.

Kliman, Bernice W. Hamlet: *Film, Television, and Audio Performance*. London and Toronto: Associated UP, 1988.

Young, Neil. "The Films of Hamlet" in *Shakespeare and the Moving Image*, ed. Anthony Davies and Stanley Wells (New York: Cambridge UP, 1994), pp. 180-96.

READING AND SCREENING OPHELIA: 1948 - 1996

Deborah Cartmell
(De Montfort University, Leicester)

This paper takes Bernice Kliman's statement that "some films have found their inspiration, and perhaps their legitimacy in scholarly research and criticism"[1], a stage further, examining the interplay between film adaptations and literary criticism. A film adaptation is, as John Collick has argued, a reading in its own right: "... the task of the director is to understand and articulate the values and truths that are supposedly embodied in the poetry".[2] The original text becomes of interest for generating a plurality of meanings - values and truths - which Catherine Belsey describes as "... not fixed or given, but [...] released in the process of reading".[3] What is often shockingly apparent in cinematic readings lurks dangerously beneath the surface in literary criticism. Until recently, Shakespeare-on-screen studies tend to be either director or film-centred; but by comparing film adaptations to critical readings synchronically, students can learn to question readings of Shakespeare which they accept uncritically as authoritative. The study of Shakespeare on screen should be a study of readings, readings which ultimately need to be viewed as Baudrillard's 'simulations' where the existence of the duplication or adaptation renders the 'original' Shakespeare text itself artificial.

Ophelia, especially, is a victim of the critic's and director's gaze, above all in the 'nunnery scene', probably the most filmed of all scenes in Shakespeare. As most critics of the mid-century invariably remind us, the initial question a director must ask when staging this scene is: does Hamlet look behind the arras and is he aware of his audience and therefore acting the part of madman? In performance the point of revelation normally comes when Ophelia lies to Hamlet when she responds to his question: "Where's your father?" If she lies convincingly with, "At home, my lord" (3.1.132-3),[4] then she is a natural-born liar and if she lies falteringly, then Hamlet knows he is being deceived. In *What Happens in Hamlet*

(1935) John Dover Wilson initiated interest in the dilemma as to whether or not Hamlet sees (or, at least, knows about) his on-stage audience - a dilemma which intrigued critics of the 40s and 50s (who almost never fail to refer to the problem) and which doomed Ophelia to being regarded as a traitor by both Hamlet and the play's critics. Undoubtedly, this scene embodying the problem of who is looking at whom provides an ideal opportunity to disclose the ways in which literary criticism, like film, directs our gaze.

Olivier's film of the play came after his great success with *Henry V* (1945) in which film and theatre were playfully merged; the earlier film begins with a reconstruction of the Globe Theatre, and gradually moves out from a painted film set, to an impression of real space. *Hamlet,* as Bernice Kliman observes, is in a similar tradition, seeming to work "against the inherent naturalism of film";[5] so we are aware that this is a theatrical space as well as a film space. The tension between film set and theatrical space is best summarised in Olivier's famous prologue to the film, ' This is the tragedy of a man who could not make up his mind". But the tension conveyed by the space defamiliarlises the audience, making them unsure as to what is real and what is not. This is the critical tradition out of which Olivier's *Hamlet* emerged, typified by A.C. Bradley's interpretation of Hamlet in 1904 as suffering from ... an unconscious weaving of pretexts for inaction'[6] and T.S. Eliot's famous account of Hamlet's procrastination in 1919 according to which Hamlet is searching for an "objective correlative" defined as "the complete adequacy of the external to the emotion".[7] There is an obvious tension conveyed by Olivier's *mise en scene* in the uneasy mixture of film and theatre space; the set, dominated by staircases and closed spaces, evokes a sense of claustrophobia . It also impresses upon the audience that this is a domestic tragedy; most of the action takes place indoors, the interiors being cold and labyrinthine. The film set is most likely influenced by Caroline Spurgeon's influential study of the drama's imagery, published in 1935, in which she describes the atmosphere of the play as due to the numerous images of sickness and disease.[8] The disease or unease of the play is reflected in the film by the complexity of the set - the monochromatic film is both theatrical and filmic - which simultaneously closes in on the individual while tantalising us with glimpses of spaces beyond itself conveyed by medieval paintings, windows and views from the castle. It's hard to miss the Freudian interpretation which dominates Olivier's film, carried over from his 1937 Old Vic production. This is a film with a woman-centred domination, as Ernest Jones's reading (which Olivier had consulted in the 30s)[9] also suggests.[10]

Olivier was 40 when he played Hamlet, Eileen Herlie was 27 when she played Gertrude; although she looks older, her attraction to her son is immediately apparent in the passionate kiss she gives him when we first see her. Jean Simmons is, at 16, more like Hamlet's daughter than his future wife: a pitiable rather than admirable Ophelia, visually far too young to be taken seriously. This Ophelia is incapable of the rational "O what a noble mind" speech and, accordingly, Olivier eliminates her one moment of glory. Ophelia's speech, as commented on by critics in the first half of the century, is only of interest insofar as it sheds light on *Hamlet's* character. Although Olivier clearly considered the possibility of Hamlet's having slept with Ophelia in the past, this Ophelia seems too young to match Hamlet's powerful presence, and as such is blameless.

If we are to blame her at all, it is for being a woman (and therefore stupid); and Olivier's reading is in accordance with that of his contemporaries' phallocentric views of the play. Jones sees Hamlet as understandably inflamed by Ophelia's complicity with father and king, complaining of "the hypocritical prudishness with which Ophelia follows her father and brother"[11] while Dover Wilson blames Ophelia "narrowness of vision and over-readiness to comply with her father's commands",[12] and his catalogue of her faults suggests that Hamlet has no option but to blame her: '... she had refused to see him and had returned his letters; she could not even speak a word of comfort when in deep trouble he forced his way into her room with mute pitiable appeal".[13] Implicit in these remarks is the rhetorical question: what do you expect a guy to do? Both critics fail to take into account the overwhelming power fathers held over their daughters in the early seventeenth century. In the tradition of Wilson and Jones, Olivier intimates that she is both a liar and selfish in the change in line from, "O help *him* sweet heaven" to "O help *me*". Ophelia's duplicity is further suggested by the fact that Jean Simmons' Ophelia bears an unnerving resemblance to the boy actor in the film, especially when Hamlet puts on his/her wig; this shorthand gesture succinctly brings the love and theatre interests together in the minds of the film audience. Olivier places a long blond wig on the boy and is momentarily overcome with dismay at the transformation of the young boy into Ophelia. But Jean Simmons' Ophelia can't even 'act' her part, as Olivier makes clear. This is a Hamlet who comprehends the situation he is in; he overhears Polonius talking to Gertrude and Claudius and he immediately spots his guilty spectators behind the arras, turns the book Ophelia is reading right-side-up and continues to address the spectators in a loud voice, Ophelia in a softer tone.

That it is Hamlet rather than Polonius's death that causes Ophelia's madness is intimated by the film; the camera pans away from her distraught figure on the stairs and she becomes increasingly insignificant - the tiny Ophelia is juxtaposed with the close-up of the back of Hamlet's head (which fills the screen) in the subsequent sequence, reflecting their relative importance . Ophelia's dishevelled appearance, abandoned on the staircase, is evocative of a rape victim and, as such, she becomes no longer of any use to the males present. The movement away from Ophelia at the bottom of the stairs is accompanied by Claudius speaking the line aimed at Hamlet but now applicable to Ophelia clearly on the verge of insanity herself: "madness in great ones must not unwatched go".[14] It is Ophelia's loveplight which is tragically neglected. The love plot is magnified by Olivier, who shows Hamlet's remorse for his overly harsh treatment of Ophelia as reflected in the transposition of the "To be or not to be" speech; it comes at the end rather than the beginning of the scene, suggesting that it is a result of his confrontation with Ophelia that he has come to contemplate suicide.

It is Ophelia's love (rather than Gertrude's) which ultimately holds sway as in the final scene, the Freudian overtones are abandoned for a return to post-war family values. The Queen, acting on Hamlet's advice, deeply suspicious of

Claudius, knowingly drinks the poison in an act of supreme self-sacrifice. For a post-war audience, familiar with sons sacrificing themselves in the war, this would perhaps touch a chord - a mother here lovingly watching her swashbuckling son takes the poison in the hope that the act will save him and he will survive her. Cunningly, Olivier ultimately places the women in the play in relation to Hamlet: Ophelia is Hamlet's beloved, Gertrude, Hamlet's mother: they are defined in relation to the dominant man in their lives.

What is also noteworthy about the Olivier version of *Hamlet* is the absence of Fortinbras, Rosencrantz and Guildenstern; the political elements eliminated from Olivier's film are precisely those that the Russian director Kosintsev found so interesting.

Maynard Mack's observation made in 1952 of the time being out of joint throughout *Hamlet* can be traced in film versions which follow:

> The whole time is out of joint, he feels, and in his young man's egocentricity he will set it right. Hence he misjudges Ophelia, seeing in her only a breeder of sinners. Hence he misjudges himself, seeing himself a vermin crawling between earth and heaven. Hence he takes it upon himself to be his mother's conscience ...[15]

In Kozintsev's film, the time is genuinely out of joint as the director invites us to make comparisons between Claudius's and Stalin's dictatorships. The castle is literally rendered as a prison; once Hamlet enters, he is doomed to the death sentence. Ophelia, as Bernice Kliman observes, is not the repulser but the repulsée of this film.[16] Hamlet, played by Innokenti Smukhtunovski, is too busy for women - his motivation is political rather than woman-centred, and the sweeping aside of Ophelia is seen as evidence of Hamlet's self-denial rather than his misogyny. The overtly political and topical aspect of this film can be likened to the criticism of Jan Kott, Kozintsev's contemporary, who writes about *Hamlet* in the context of the experience of totalitarian Poland. He describes a production of the play in 1964 which opens up new political readings:

> The *Hamlet* produced in Cracow a few weeks after the Twentieth Congress of the Soviet Communist Party lasted exactly three hours. It

> was light and clear, tense and sharp, modern and consistent, limited to one issue only. It was a political drama *par excellence.* Something is rotten in the state of 'Denmark' - was the first chord of *Hamlet's* new meaning [...] Ophelia, too, has been drawn into the big game. They listen in to her conversations, ask questions, read her letters. It is true that she gives them up herself. She is at the same time part of the Mechanism and its victim. Politics hangs here over every feeling, and there is no getting away from it. All the characters are poisoned by it. The only subject of their conversation is politics. It is a kind of madness.
> Hamlet loves Ophelia. But he knows he is being watched; moreover - he has more important matters to attend to. Love is gradually fading away. There is no room for it in this world. Hamlet's dramatic cry; "Get thee to a nunnery!" is addressed not to Ophelia alone, but also to those who are overhearing the two lovers. It is to confirm their impression of his alleged madness. But for Hamlet and for Ophelia it means that in the world where murder holds sway there is no room for love.[17]

(It is worth mentioning that this reading of the film follows closely Kott's own interpretation of Kozintsev's *Hamlet* in 1979).[18]

Tony Richardson's television production of 1969 is largely a filmed play, portraying an exceptionally epicurean court. The casting of Marianne Faithfull as Ophelia raises the question of her innocence - her pop star status and relationship with rock star Mick Jagger could not fail to influence viewers. In the nunnery scene, she is made to recline on a hammock, and the camera teases us with a close-up of her decolletage. Visually, Richardson signals to us that she is a closet whore: her father's containment of her is a necessary one. She has what Milton calls an "excremental innocence", an untried innocence which is, in reality, ignorance. This is an Ophelia who can only be innocent in madness when she sheds the hypocrisy of innocence and reveals the sexual awareness which she has concealed for so long. Unlike Jean Simmons' Ophelia, Marianne Faithfull's Ophelia is excellent at pretence; she convincingly pretends to be asleep and Eve-like, she is awoken by a deceived and vulnerable Hamlet who falls into her hammock as into a spider's web.

This view of Ophelia is implicitly offered by John Bayley in 1981:

> Conditioned to goodness and docility [Ophelia] is the exact foil to Hamlet's wildness, which means his native - though also indulged and princely - immediacy of behaviour. There is no guile in Ophelia.[...] But

there is a continuity, so justly imagined as to be taken for granted, between the girl who endures with suffering but stoical decorum the tasteless gibes of the man on the edge and climax of his own private nightmare - the man whom she thought was paying his attentions to her - and the girl who reveals in her breakdown just how naturally familiar she is with the world of sexual innuendo and speculation [...] But schooled in proper behaviour as she is, and without much individuality of her own, Ophelia can still suffer as much as any girl, and she does suffer horribly from the cruelty of Hamlet, who understandably if mistakenly associates her behaviour with cunning and concealment.[19]

Bayley intimates Ophelia's hypocrisy (Hamlet *understandably* blames Ophelia for duplicity - after all her 'innocence' in the nunnery scene is called into question after her breakdown). Bayley's reading, which denies Ophelia of individuality and which endorses the stereotype is typical of Ophelia representations: she is either innocent in the sense of ignorance, or she coyly pretends innocence. Bayley sides with the view of Polonius and Hamlet, assuming women to be both inferior and corrupt. Critics, like directors (perhaps, like Hamlet himself), find her most perfect in death where she is sexually passive and speechless. This is Ophelia's finest hour, where we, as spectators, like Hamlet and Laertes, can lavish attention on her passive body, untroubled by what she has to say about it.[20]

Rodney Bennett's BBC version of the play, televised in 1980 starring Derek Jacobi as Hamlet, falls in with Bayley's reading, which focuses on Hamlet's isolation. Both Bayley's and Bennett's reading are markedly apolitical (for instance, Claire Bloom's Gertrude and Patrick Stewart's Claudius are essentially well-intentioned and only, to quote from *Measure for Measure,* "a little bad" - 5.1.347); and both readings de-emphasise the women's parts. In casting Lalla Ward, Dr Who's former assistant, as Ophelia, Bennett ensures that she will not be taken seriously. Jacobi speaks to her, and looks at her throughout with a degree of sarcasm which the viewer, implicitly, shares.

Undoubtedly, *Hamlet* film-makers between 1948 and 1980 confirm the theory that in the cinema the female is simply "the object by which the patriarchal subject can define himself".[21] In considering representations of Ophelia, it is clear

Reading and Screening Ophelia

that it is not just Shakespeare who deprives her of a voice and an identity – it is both film-maker and literary critic alike.

These male-centred (or Hamlet-centred) readings of the play are increasingly challenged in the 80s, inspired by Lisa Jardine's *Still Harping on Daughters* (1983); Jardine is among the first to articulate Ophelia's dilemma:

> Ophelia is honest (chaste) or a bawd (a whore) depending on how Hamlet now chooses to describe his own behavior towards her. If he loved her, declared that love to her, and she accepted his gifts and embraces, then she is chaste. If he never loved her, but attempted to seduce her only, then *she* is lewd and lascivious, because *Hamlet* trifled with her. Either way she should "get [her] to a nunnery" – "nunnery", as all modern editions of the play hasten to tell the reader, meant both a convent and a brothel in Elizabethan colloquial expression.[22]

Conversely, rather than condemn Shakespeare as a spokesman for the dominant culture, Juliet Dusinberre argues that "the drama from 1590 to 1625 is feminist in sympathy" and that Shakespeare is questioning the stereotypes his society imposed on women.[23] More recently Elaine Showalter moves away from feminist critiques of Shakespeare's patriarchal discourse where Ophelia can only satisfy father, brother and lover in death (that is once she becomes truly 'nothing') and suggests that Ophelia has "a story of her own":

> To liberate Ophelia from the text, or to make her its tragic center, is to reappropriate her for our own ends; to dissolve her into a female symbolism of absence is to endorse our own marginality; to make her Hamlet's anima is to reduce her to a metaphor of male experience. I would like to propose instead that Ophelia *does* have a story of her own that feminist criticism can tell [...] it is [...] the *history* of her representation.[24]

Showalter combines feminist and cultural criticism, showing how our perception of Ophelia is shaped by popular culture - her evaluation of the play depends not on a reconstruction of the original conditions of production but on an analysis of the play's reproductions.

Although this is a vast simplification of developments in feminist Shakespeare criticism, these accounts of the play are not perceptible in earlier film versions. Zeffirelli's version of *Hamlet* stands apart from the previous productions discussed here and clearly reflects the cross-influences of film and literary criticism. Zeffirelli's *Hamlet* starring Mel Gibson and Glen Close can be regarded as a textual realisation in the same way as we regard the textual realisations of Showalter or Jardine.

The first impression we have of this film is that we are unsure as to who the star is: Mel Gibson or Glen Close. The latter's Gertrude dominates the film; she brings to the role shades of her earlier *femme fatale* roles from Adrian Lyne's *Fatal Attraction* (1987) and Stephen Frears' *Dangerous Liaisons* (1988). Indeed Close's role as the sexy homewrecker of *Fatal Attraction*, whose extreme sexuality justifiably leads to her death, invariably influences readings of her Gertrude. Similarly, Gibson's Hamlet is influenced by his earlier action-man roles, and the film accordingly moves quickly, the scene changes are uniquely fast for the normally slow pace we expect from the play. Although the part of Fortinbras is eliminated, Hamlet's political ambitions are made clear from the outset. The funeral of Hamlet Senior opens the film with the announcement by Claudius that young Hamlet is heir apparent. This Hamlet overhears/overlooks everything - and thus we don't doubt his clear-headedness throughout. The casting of Paul Schofield as the ghost visually brings to mind Schofield's role as Lear in Peter Brook's film - in fact, Zeffirelli's film is 'haunted' by images from Brook's *King Lear* of 1970 in the stark Bergmanesque exteriors. The casting of Ian Holm as Polonius gives the film further theatrical authenticity whereas Glen Close as Gertrude and Alan Bates as Claudius bring a host of filmic associations to their parts.

Ophelia, played by Helena Bonham Carter, conveys the impression of a woman who thinks for herself. She manages to oppose the prescriptions of her father through her defiant looks and also interacts with Hamlet in the nunnery scene in a manner which challenges what the men expect of her. While Olivier's Hamlet and Ophelia were dressed in black and white respectively, Zeffirelli dresses both figures in muted colours, visually signalling their equality. The nunnery scene is drastically - almost bewilderingly - cut (some of the lines are transposed to the Mousetrap sequence). When Ophelia is abandoned by Hamlet, the camera, as in

Reading and Screening Ophelia

Olivier's film, pans away, making her incrementally small as she stoops to reclaim Hamlet's gifts, while the space around her becomes enlarged; but Hamlet seems diminished too, both are pawns, small figures against a massive system. In Olivier's film, the smallness of Ophelia is juxtaposed in the following sequence by the hugeness of Hamlet's head, once again alluding to Hamlet's vast superiority over the helpless, insignificant Ophelia.

Zeffirelli creates a *Hamlet* which is watchable and entertaining. He animates the play by making Hamlet excessively mobile and by a succession of short sequences. In a sense, this is a cartoon version of *Hamlet* and bears comparison with the animated version of the play. When set before children, of all the plays in the animated series, it was *Hamlet* which I found generated the most enjoyment and discussion. This version depicts Hamlet as a child himself, unnaturally thrown into the dark world of adulthood. In 1994, Disney's *Lion King* was released, seemingly the only Disney film without a literary source. But of course, if we look closely, we see the most discussed of all literary texts lurking beneath the playful surface: *Hamlet* is present in the story of an Uncle's murder and usurpation of his brother the King and in the son's gradual realisation of his position through the intervention of the supernatural. The hero's song before he reaches adulthood - "I Just Want to be King" - is revised through the process of the film as he learns to accept the heavy responsibilities of life at the top of the food chain. Significantly, this version of *Hamlet* does not doom Ophelia to a nunnery, but it is the lioness and future wife of the hero who advises him to act and helps him achieve his goal. As *The Lion King* and Zeffirelli's action-man *Hamlet* reveal, a move away from 'authenticity' is necessary in order to produce a 'politically correct' Ophelia; yet Kenneth Branagh's 1996 version sets out to preserve the text, and it is interesting to see whether or not this damns or redeems Ophelia.

Kenneth Branagh's *Hamlet* cannot be accused of producing a 'politically correct' reading of the play, perhaps because (unlike *The Lion King*) it sticks so closely to the text. Set in Blenheim Palace (and filmed at Shepperton Studios), sometime in the nineteenth century (with shades of *War and Peace*), it includes two interpolations of Hamlet and Ophelia (played by Kate Winslet) in bed. With this addition, her choice of her father (played by Richard Briers, who has an uncanny resemblance to Robin Cook , then a member of the Shadow Cabinet), over Hamlet seems disturbingly hypocritical (reminding us of Brabantio's lines in *Othello*, "She has deceiv'd her father, and may thee" [1.3.293]). As Alexander Walker, writing for *The Evening Standard*, put it: "the movie makes it official: Ophelia was definitely no virgin".[25]

In this light, Hamlet's feelings of betrayal are all the more understandable. Unlike Olivier's dark, claustrophobic sets (the only allusion to Olivier's film seems to be in Branagh similarly dyed blond hair), Branagh's set is brightly lit, described by Owen Gleiberman as producing the "'objective' glare of what could almost be a surgeon's operating theater".[26] This 'glare' (although not as apparent on video) is particularly hard on the women in the play - not just in making them look old before their time (the lighting sometimes makes Julie Christie's Gertrude look more like Hamlet's grandmother than mother), but in making them look guilty. This contrasts strikingly with Zeffirelli's positive images of women, especially Glen Close's Gertrude (who visited Branagh's set when filming *101 Dalmatians* next door at Shepperton Studios).

While Hamlet is genuinely hurt with Ophelia's answer to the question, "Where's your father", his gaze throughout the scene is directed more at Claudius (than at Ophelia), who, he comes to know, is concealed behind one of the many mirrored doors. Unknowingly, Hamlet comes face to face with Claudius (played by Derek Jacobi, significantly, a well-known Hamlet of the past)[27] during the "To be or not to be" soliloquy. Branagh draws our attention to their visual similarities (especially in their closely cropped light hair and trimmed beards - a similarity also noted by Gérard Depardieu arriving on the set to play Reynaldo);[28] the simultaneous attraction and repulsion Hamlet feels for Claudius, he also feels for himself as he seems to wince at his (or is it Claudius's?) image in the mirror. The mirroring of Claudius and Hamlet anticipates Hamlet's advice to the players (who look as if they were out of Dickens' *Nicholas Nickleby*) in the following scene: "hold as 'twere the mirror up to nature, to show virtue her own feature, scorn her own image, and the very age and body of the time his form and pressure" (2.2.21-3). Thus his contemplation of his reflected image is, importantly, also a contemplation of Claudius (who similarly sees Hamlet through the double glass as an image of himself). Branagh chooses to focus on this pair, blurring the boundaries between observed and observer, actor and spectator, as we are not sure who is looking at whom.

In his introduction to the Arden text (1982), Harold Jenkins identifies a pattern of analogies between Claudius and Hamlet; certainly in killing Polonius, Hamlet becomes a Claudius figure in that he makes himself an object of revenge. Jenkins observes that Hamlet, like Claudius has "'hurt' his 'brother' [5.2.237-40), and that the prince who reveres Hyperion and aspires to redeem his kingdom has also the satyr in him".[29] Philip Armstrong has also concentrated on the mirroring devices in the play and comments that - even when they involve women - they are still masculine.[30] The focus on Claudius and Hamlet (at the cost of Ophelia) almost makes this a 'buddy movie' gone wrong.

Even though Ophelia is allowed the "O what a noble mind" speech, the inclusion of her lines revealing Hamlet as the "glass of fashion and the mould of form" (3.1.156) redirects the film audience's attention to Hamlet, Claudius and the mirrors. Finally, Ophelia and Polonius fade as the camera directs our gaze squarely at Jacobi whose "Madness in great ones" is spoken self-reflectively, and seems now to apply as much to himself as to Hamlet. Ophelia is hurt but ultimately unscathed by Hamlet's brutal accusations - there is a sense in Winslet's performance that she feels she deserves what she gets. In the Mousetrap scene, Hamlet looks askance at Ophelia during the Player Queen's (uncomfortably lengthy) speech, a speech which is an exemplification of female inconstancy. The camera shifts between Ophelia and the Player Queen, while Hamlet looks accusingly at Ophelia during the false protestations of the grotesquely painted (and false) Player Queen (Rosemary Harris):

A second time I kill my husband dead
When second husband kisses me in bed. (3.2.175-6)

The Player Queen is the embodiment of Claudius's nightmare image of the harlot, "beautied with plast'ring art" (3.1.53) and a visualisation of Hamlet's rebuke to Ophelia: "God have given you one face, and you make yourself another" (3.1.146-7). Ophelia's visible nervousness during the performance clinches her guilt as Hamlet uses the play to catch her as well as the king. After the theatrical (and real?) display of female inconstancy, it is no wonder that Hamlet rails at his mother in the following scene in a tone which echoes Polonius' and Laertes' earlier warnings to Ophelia to preserve her chastity ; it seems that female sexuality is a dangerous thing.

Reading like filming is a form of 're-membering' the past as Susan Bennett has outlined in *Performing Nostalgia: Shifting Shakespeare and the Contemporary Past* (1996).[31] Each film adaptation of *Hamlet*, like each reading, is a re-enactment of the past with an eye to its present-day consumer culture. What is disturbing about Branagh's 'nostalgia film' is its seeming desire to return to a time when women were expected – and to an extent deserved – to take the blame. Undoubtedly, the most striking thing about this *Hamlet* is its length; and, as Adam Mars-Jones remarks, the film is "redeemed by the one decision that seems perverse, even indefensible, the decision that is never made in cinema: trusting the author"[32] A question open for debate is whether it is the full Shakespearean text or Branagh's interpolations which doom Ophelia here. Alarmingly, in a post-feminist era, it is acceptable to blame Ophelia as – at least, in part – a traitor to the man she seems to have loved.

Notes
1. Bernice Kliman, *Film, Television and Audio Performance* (London:AUP, 1988), p. 297.
2. *Shakespeare, Cinema and Society* (Manchester UP, 1989), p. 4.
3. *Critical Practice* (London: Methuen, 1980), p. 20.
4. All quotations from Shakespeare are taken from *The Complete Works*, ed. Stanley Wells, Gary Tayor, John Jowett and William Montgomery (Oxford: Clarendon Press, 1988).
5. Kliman, p. 26.

Reading and Screening Ophelia 41

6. *Shakespearean Tragedy* (1904, reprinted in John Jump, ed. *Shakespeare: Hamlet* (London: Macmillan, 1968), p. 39.

7. "Hamlet" (1919) printed in Jump, p. 39.

8. Spurgeon, *Shakespeare's Imagery and What it Tells Us* (1935, repr. Cambridge UP, 1993), p. 316.

9. Laurence Olivier, *Confessions of an Actor: An Autobiography* (New York: Simon, 1982), p. 79.

10. Ernest Jones, *Hamlet and Oedipus* (1949; repr. New York: Norton, 1976), p. 86.

11. Ibid. p. 84.

12. J. Dover Wilson, *What Happens in Hamlet* (Cambridge UP, 1937), p. 131.

13. Ibid. p. 131.

14. Olivier cunningly replaces the irony implicit in Ophelia's "O, What a noble mind is here o'erthrown" in the play text; cruelly, it is Ophelia's 'noble mind' which is in peril, not Hamlet's.

15. Maynard Mack, *The World of 'Hamlet'* (1952), in Jump, p. 105.

16. Kliman, p. 91.

17. Jan Kott, *Shakespeare Our Contemporary* (1964) in Jump, pp.197-9.

18. *The Literary Review* 22:4 (1979), pp. 385-90.

19. John Bayley, *Shakespeare and Tragedy* (London: Routledge & Kegan Paul, 1981), p. 173.

20. Surveying the BFI holding of stills for the Olivier production, I was struck at how many there were of the making of Ophelia's death - a scene, unfortunately rather laughable in the Olivier film, obviously put together with enormous care in its reconstruction of the famous Millais portrait where Ophelia is portrayed in death as a virgin ready to greet her lover.

21. E.D. Pribam, ed. *Female Spectators* (London: Verso, 1988), p. 1.

22. Jardine, *Still Harping on Daughters: Women and Drama in the Age of Shakespeare* (1983) 2nd edn (New York, London, Toronto: Harvester, 1989), p. 73.

23. Dusinberre, *Shakespeare and the Nature of Women* (London: Macmillan, 1975), p. 5.

24. Elaine Showalter "Representing Ophelia: Women, Madness, and the Responsibilities of Feminist Criticism" 220-240, in *Hamlet*, ed. Susanne L Wofford Case Studies in Contemporary Criticism, (Boston, New York: St. Martin's Press; Basingstoke: Macmillan, 1994), p. 233.

25. 13 February, pp. 26-7.

26. *Entertainment,* http://us.imdb.com/cache/urls/title +45530, nd.

27. Jacobi's Hamlet was a strong influence on the young Branagh - see Branagh's introduction to the screenplay (London: Random House, 1996), p. 5; and Jacobi directed Branagh as Hamlet for Branagh's company.

28. Russel Jackson, 'Film Diary', in Branagh, *Hamlet*, p. 187.

29. *Hamlet* (London: Methuen, 1982), p.146.

30. "Watching *Hamlet* watching: Lacan, Shakespeare and the mirror / stage", *Alternative Shakespeares* vol. 2., ed. Terence Hawkes (London: Routledge, 1996), pp. 216-37, (here p. 235).

31. (London: Routledge, 1996).

32. *The Independent Tabloid,* 13 February, 1997, p. 5.

FORTINBRAS ON FILM:
SAFE PASSAGE FOR THE PRINCE

Thomas L. Wilmeth
(Concordia University Wisconsin)

In Shakespeare's *Hamlet*, the role of Fortinbras often creates problems for a director because of the character's "enigmatic" qualities.[1] Fortinbras, and the accompanying military subplot, are thought by some critics and directors as an "expendable distraction" to *Hamlet*.[2] Robert Willson is accurate, and only partly jesting when he states that "it is a time honored custom [...] to cut the story of Fortinbras" from productions of the play.[3] The off-stage plottings of Young Fortinbras, first planning an attack on Denmark, followed by descriptions of his uncle's reprimand and subsequent request for safe passage, is rarely at the center of an audience's thoughts.

Gregg Dion speculates, "Throughout most of the stage history of *Hamlet*, audiences were untroubled by either the appearance [or absence] of Fortinbras".[4] Audience neutrality is understandable on this point, for there is so much fascinating on-stage strife at Elsinore to consider. Opinions of critics, however, are less passive, ranging from viewing Fortinbras as a "minor plot element" to his presence as "central" to the play.[5] The directoral decisions concerning what to do with this subplot centers on one large question: how does the exclusion or modification of Fortinbras effect (or defect) film treatments of *Hamlet*.

A comprehensive examination of directors' interpretations of the Fortinbras material in all extant cinematic adaptations of *Hamlet* would warrant a book-length study. This paper focuses upon several widely seen English language film versions of the play which are representative of various directors' approaches to the work. These examples are drawn from as wide a time frame as the form permits, beginning with Sir Laurence Olivier's first feature length film adaptation of 1948, and continuing through Kenneth Branagh's production of the complete text in 1996.

Modern critics are filled with righteous indignation when recalling how The Fool was omitted from acting versions of *King Lear* for well over 100 years.[6] Similarly, scholars smile knowingly when recounting how a tragicomedy version of *Romeo and Juliet* was regularly staged, ending with the lovers surviving and happy.[7] These drastic transformations of Shakespeare's text are now dismissed as mistakes of the past, the assumption being that a current production would never be guilty of such a textual sin or invalid adaptation. Why, then, is this Fortinbras subplot so easily dismissed by most film directors?

With a performance time of over four hours, it is little wonder that almost all who attempt to film the play appeal to their "director's privilege" to trim its sheer length. The story of Fortinbras, along with most of *The Murder of Gonzago*, is often among the first material circled by the director's blue pen for deletion. The central reason for cutting *Gonzago* is self-evident. It is lengthy and has the effect of bringing the action to a complete stop, in spite of the scene's larger importance to "catch the conscious of the king".[8]

In comparison, the Fortinbras subplot takes almost no time at all. The character himself has a mere 18 lines, delivered in four speeches over the course of two scenes. Even the references to Fortinbras, his army, his deceased father's battles, and Old Norway taken together scarcely divert an audience from the focus of Hamlet's quest. Further, this exclusion robs the play of "the successor to the throne" of Elsinore, to whom "Hamlet gives his dying voice".[9]

Olivier: Setting the Scene

The "common reference point" for more than a generation, Laurence Olivier's film of *Hamlet* was created for a "larger and more mixed audience" than attempted by any previous producer.[10] But Laurence Kitchin, in an early essay on screen adaptations, reminds us that "it is a mass audience which demands concessions".[11] One such concession was Olivier's belief that for his film to be "marketable," it needed "to conform to [...] a conventional maximum length" of "less than three hours"[12] At 155 minutes, Olivier succeeded in this goal, and was able to fill the screen with images which continue to serve as a touchstone for studies of *Hamlet* on film.

However, these "concessions" introduce complicating difficulties of their own. Throughout his film career, Olivier demonstrated that he was not opposed to altering Shakespeare's plays for the sake of perceived clarity, or what Jack J. Jorgens correctly terms his "conscious simplification" of the plot.[13] For example, early in his film adaptation of *King Richard III*, soldiers enter with a corpse. But they do not carry the body of King Henry VI, as Shakespeare's text indicates; Olivier has instead killed Anne's husband Edward. The body has been recast for the sake of a streamlined plot, and presumably to lessen potential confusion over relationships. Olivier apparently felt that a dead husband would make more immediate sense to an audience than introducing Anne's connections to this dead monarch from another play. The point of this scene, after all, is the ensuing seduction.

It should come as no surprise that Olivier adapted his film of an even more complex story with an equally free hand. In his effort to clarify plot subtleties (and reduce the film's running time) Olivier has completely omitted the Fortinbras material, beginning with Horatio's speech at 1.1.63-7, which describes King Hamlet's victory at the Pollack battle, thirty years before. The Clown in 5.1 will again remind the audience of the importance of this battle with King Fortinbras, and how it lives in the memory of all Denmark, but this too is deleted. Also gone are Marcellus' references to Denmark's "daily cast of blazen canon [...] for implements of war" in the first scene, and Horatio's following speech of 27 lines (1.1.76-7; 1.1.82-110). Together, these comments comprise exposition about the defense of Denmark and, more specifically, Young Fortinbras' tenuous relationship to the past and present of Elsinore.

Lorne Buchman expresses the concerns of many when he says that through cuts such as these, Olivier "obliterates the details" of the play.[14] But Bernice

Fortinbras on Film

Kliman defends the director, saying that the omission of Fortinbras "serves Olivier well", and argues that inclusion would "detract from his interpretation [of] woman-centered motivation".[15] More widely held, however, is Jack Jorgen's view that when "the conflict between Denmark and Norway is thrust to the background," this causes an "imbalance between Hamlet and his world".[16] Willson also thinks that by deleting Fortinbras the play's focus shifts away from Shakeapeare's intentions, "tend[ing] to place too much weight on Hamlet's death and not enough on the restoration" of order and a moral value system.[17]

As with the beginning of the film, Olivier ends his *Hamlet* with a liberal amount of textual freedom. Fortinbras does not appear in 5.2, nor does Hamlet ask about the "warlike noise" he hears as he dies (5.2.354). Olivier includes Fortinbras' final speech concerning Hamlet's probable worthiness as a leader intact, but reassigns it to Horatio (5.2.400-8). Then, in a further directorial rearrangement, Horatio speaks his own earlier line, "Good night sweet prince / And flights of angels sing thee to thy rest," which concludes the film's dialogue (5.2.364-5). While a touching conclusion, these changes conspire to rob the play of the close Shakespeare has provided. Olivier has summarily dropped all aspects of Fortinbras from his film.

Film Productions of the Sixties: Aborted and Abused

The most famous production of *Hamlet* during the 1960s undoubtedly belonged to director Sir John Gielgud, and featured Richard Burton. This production broke new ground for its seemingly casual approach – treating the actual performance as if the cast were still at work preparing the play. By having actors in rehearsal clothes, using limited scenery and few props, attention would be most focused on the play's language.[18]

Although parameters here are limited to those films which have been available to a wide audience, this one exception must be made. Gielgud's stage production was filmed for cinematic release during two nights' performances. The film had a very brief run of two days in movie houses before Burton decided that

Hamlet should be experienced on the stage of a theatre, and immediately pulled the film from distribution. Going further, Burton ordered all prints of the film destroyed.[19]

However, early in 1997 newspapers reported that Burton's widow had found a deteriorating print of the film in the basement of the couple's home in Switzerland some three years earlier. Since the discovery of this only known copy, Gielgud's adaptation has been digitally restored and was premiered on the Internet on 6 April 1997. It is currently making its way into wider circulation through video tape and limited theatrical release, adding a very famous and important film adaptation to the canon.[20]

While in many ways revolutionary, this adaptation stays quite close to Shakespeare's text. Here it is largely the "trappings, and the suits" of the actors which are altered (1.2.86). And while some sections of the play are truncated, Gielgud includes nearly all of the Fortinbras material, with the character's scripted stage appearances at 4.4 and 5.2. Also, the playwright's references to Fortinbras are retained in 1.1, 1.2 and 2.2 in order to prepare for his subsequent role.

Gielgud's Fortinbras does not call much attention to himself in 5.2. He arrives simply to put things right after Hamlet's death, with little hostility or purpose of revenge evident in this characterization. Instead, the director underscores those lines which stress the sadness of the concluding situation. Fortinbras appears as a thoughtful ally, merely taking the safe passage through Denmark that he had promised his uncle. Hamlet's own adjectives describing Fortinbras as "delicate and tender" seem to have been taken to heart by Gielgud, for calm and order are restored at his arrival (4.4.48).

Since Burton quickly pulled the 1964 film from theatres, it was not until 1969 that the first new version of Hamlet since Olivier played uninterrupted in traditional movie houses. Instead of filming in the theatre during actual performance, director Tony Richardson brought his stage version of *Hamlet* into the sound studio and stripped it to less than two hours. If Olivier could be accused of an "undeniable [...] sense of staginess" in his production, Richardson leans the other way, depicting Gertrude and Claudius as unrepentantly slovenly and decadent.[21] In fact, Anthony Hopkins' squalid Claudius provides some of the most interesting and entertaining scenes in this film.

Richardson combines elements of both Gielgud and Olivier, but the result is woefully inferior to either. All background speeches concerning Fortinbras are cut from 1.1 and 1.2. Subsequent references are introduced at two junctures, but the character never appears and the subplot is in no way developed. A speech of Claudius' describing the condition of Old Fortinbras is retained in 2.1, but only in order that the description of the aged ruler as "impotent" be included, which stops the scene (in mid-line) for all present at court to laugh at this labored sexual reference (1.2.29).

It seems that Richardson had no overall vision for his film. Lines are retained and cut apparently at random, with no sense of a unifying view for the play's themes. Fortinbras does not appear in 4.4 but, oddly, his name is mentioned by the Captain in relationship to the army about which Hamlet inquires. Earlier, this same incongruity exists when in 2.2 Polonious announces the return of Voltemand and Cornelius from Norway, but the ambassadors never appear and their message concerning Fortinbras remains undelivered. Richardson's film ends with Hamlet's line "the rest is silence" (5.2.363). There are no sounds of warfare, no entrance of Fortinbras, and no final words by Horatio.

Zeffirelli: In the Tradition of Sir Laurence
Mel Gibson played Hamlet in Franco Zeffirelli's 1990 film adaptation. This version is noteworthy, in part, for its bold rearrangement of scenes. The film opens, for example, with Claudius' pronouncements concerning his new wife and recently acquired kingdom. The two battlement scenes are combined into one, with the film completely bypassing 1.1. This allows the director to streamline Act One, and begin the film with greater action that an expository discussion by underlings awaiting a ghost.

Although Neil Taylor says this is perhaps "the slightest" of the films and complains about the "cavalier" reorganization of the text, Zeffirelli does an admirable job of following Olivier's idea of making his Hamlet "marketable" to a wide audience.[22] With Mel Gibson in the lead role, younger audiences could be exposed to Shakespeare through the drawing power of a true Hollywood movie star. Zeffirelli follows his predecessor's lead in more than his intention of garnering a broad audience for, as in Olivier, the Fortinbras subplot is completely cut from this film.

This version provides a good entry point for students and the uninitiated. It is fast-paced, and the entire cast is excellent. Gibson is a surprisingly able Hamlet, allowing the audience temporarily to forget the persona as a movie star. And although Zeffirelli's adaptation offers no Fortinbras, the cinema had only a few years to wait until this character would emerge fully formed, and stronger than ever.

The Complete Text, and then some
Kenneth Branagh, true to his promotional word, offers a "full-length version" of the play with the director in the title role.[23] Unlike Olivier, Branagh includes Fortinbras intact, and does not reassign speeches. And unlike Richardson, Branagh has a clear concept of this character and his role in the play. Branagh is most similar to Gielgud, but is willing to take the 'enigmatic' qualities of Fortinbras into his own hands and, remaining true to the text, validly molds this character toward his own interpretation.[24]

Rebecca West has argued that many speeches in *Hamlet* can be interpreted in two ways, "with or without irony; each reading equally faithful to the text".[25] While perhaps a bit hyperbolic, this idea is certainly true of the Fortinbras speeches. Although speaking a mere 18 lines, this character can legitimately be seen in more than one light. Grigoriy Kozintsev, in his Russian language film adaptation of 1964, demonstrates this point visually by showing Fortinbras' army simultaneously marching in two different directions.[26]

Fortinbras on Film

Part of the difficulty in interpreting Fortinbras' significance is that most information relating to him is acquired from second-hand sources. The audience is merely *told*, for example, of the generous stipend that Fortinbras' uncle has bestowed on his nephew for not attacking Denmark. And while there is no textual reason to doubt this news, there is also no way to judge if Fortinbras is honoring his word. Additionally, even if a director decides to include all lines and references to Fortinbras, this character's first stage entrance late in the play can cause confusion. The audience has never seen him prior to 4.4, and the Fortinbras subplot has not been mentioned during the two previous acts.

Branagh's portrayal of Fortinbras as the avenging son is a defendable interpretation, and demonstrates a director's prerogative that differs markedly from the other directors under discussion. Yet to make his vision more pointed Branagh chooses to include several shots which, although logical and effective, fall outside the realm of the text. While certainly not originating the technique, Branagh makes fine use of a film's capabilities to solve the dual problem of character recognition and motivation.

During appropriate points of Horatio's expository speeches in 1.1, Branagh shifts his camera to show a "hot and full" Young Fortinbras advising his military leaders about his obvious unhappiness (1.1.99; 1.1.98-107). The words of Horatio continue in voice-over as the audience sees Fortinbras silently and violently gesturing toward a map of presumably lost territory. The meaning is clear – the son wants his father's lands returned. By showing this scene Branagh not only allows the audience to connect a face with the name Fortinbras, but it also illustrates this prince's hostile attitude toward Denmark. Branagh used this same technique to show several unstaged narratives in his film, including the reprimand and reconciliation between Fortinbras and his uncle, as described in 2.2 (2.2.61-80).

After introducing Fortinbras through silent images, Branagh continues to reinforce his specific interpretation of this subplot. Two arguably valid, if textually ambiguous aspects make interesting additions to 5.2. When Osric announces that

"Young Fortinbras [...] gives / This warlike volley", Branagh shows that the speaker has been shot in the stomach, mortally wounded (5.2.356-7). The "warlike volley" in this context refers to Osric's injury, where the accepted and logical interpretation has the pronoun "this" referring to Hamlet's previous question about the sound of "warlike noise" (5.2.354). Branagh has not changed a line of text, but through this reading he stresses that Elsinore is under life-threatening attack.

Adding to this interpretation is the reaction Branagh gives to the First Ambassador from England only 15 lines later. After learning that the court's commands for Rozencrantz and Guildenstern to be executed were fraudulent, and that the situation at Elsinore "shows much amiss", the Ambassador is shown nervously glancing around, then slipping away unseen (5.2.407). Although Fortinbras will undeniably bring order to Denmark, this representative from England is uncertain how he will fare under the new command and departs while attention is focused elsewhere. This silent piece of business, like Osric's wound, speaks to the "warlike" quality of the army's entrance at court. Once this position is established, it is not surprising to see Fortinbras' men violently dismantling the statue of King Hamlet before the film's credits begin.

Branagh takes a firm stance on a difficult character to interpret. Shakespeare gives Fortinbras no soliloquies to clarify his intentions. Instead, we are presented with a series of short speeches, nearly all of which could be taken various ways. However, a few lines of Fortinbras' sound unambiguous: "I have some rights of memory in this kingdom, / Which now to claim my vantage doth invite me" (5.2.394-5). This seems quite clear: Fortinbras has not forgotten the defeat and death of his father, lawful or not, and is at Elsinore to take what he believes to be his, perhaps with interest due.

Fortinbras' most unnerving line occurs in this same speech, and when it is cut the play is robbed of its multiple layers of complexity. He declares, "For me, with sorrow I embrace my fortune" (5.2.393). As this new leader takes control of Elsinore, one can perhaps hear the echo of Claudius' words when standing on the same precipice of accumulation in Act One, supposedly accepting his new role with "a defeated joy [in] this warlike state" (1.2.9-10).

Words, Words, Words
In his published screenplay's "Choice of the Text" commentary, Branagh states that he uses the Folio version, with the usual inclusion of scenes found only in the Second Quarto (Q2).[27] But if Branagh was so intent on demonstrating Fortinbras had a violent takeover in mind, which seems evident, a slight variance from the Folio could have served him well. It is clear that Branagh had studied Q2 for this production and was not opposed to making substitutions in his copy text. He acknowledges making this type of editorial decision when adopting an alternate reading from Q2 for a line in 1.4.

In 4.4 Fortinbras instructs his Captain to tell Claudius that he "*craves* the conveyance of a promised march / Over his kingdom". Had Branagh adopted the Q2 for this brief passage, the Captain would be ordered to report that Fortinbras "*claims* the conveyance ..." (4.4.3). Claims is the stronger verb, and would demonstrate Branagh's interpretation of not an intense wish, as "craves" suggests, but the delivery of an ultimatum, based on "rights", which he will later "claim", as he articulates in 5.2.[28] Also, "claims" would link these two scenes and provide foreshadowing in a spoken form, to buttress the attitude of Fortinbras' aggressions, emphasized by Branagh's cinematography.

Fortinbras concludes his speech to the Captain in 4.4 by instructing him to "go softly on" (4.4.8). Had Branagh also adopted Q2 for this line the admonition would have the Captain "go safely on".[29] The idea of an army going "softly" on could mean that Captain should try to keep the army's movements as covert as possible in order to surprise the court at Elsinore, as does occur in this film. But the concept of going "safely on" seems more of a warlike mind set. The Q2 term suggests that there is a reason to be mindful of the army's safety, as if heading toward a potentially dangerous situation. Fortinbras knows there is such a battle ahead, because he is about to instigate it. Both of these specific word choices would have added greater force to what Branagh portrays as a significant character, and both have textual authority.

Or is this entire passage ironic, as West might suggest? When Fortinbras tells the Captain to "greet the Danish King", has his attitude been so transformed by his uncle's reprimand that he means merely to be formally received at court (4.4.1)? Or is he talking about the greeting which will be represented by the approaching "warlike volley[s]" of his army's attack (5.2.357)? Certainly the latter is how Branagh reads the situation.

Clearly, Branagh's screen adaptation focuses more on Fortinbras and the surrounding turmoil than any other. The director must be credited with this full-text production and for taking a stand on various interpretations within the play. Branagh chooses to portray Fortinbras in a particular "warlike" manner, while Olivier finds in to his advantage to eliminate the question of characterization entirely. Gielgud includes Fortinbras, but through his calm and often flat approach to the lines, the prince's role is diminished to that of a reprimanded *deus ex machina* device, with all purpose of revenge drained from his motivation.

Is This the Promised End?
The "enigmatic" aspects of the this character, as Jorgens rightly calls them, make Fortinbras a logical candidate for exclusion.[30] It will remain a director's decision whether to include Fortinbras, and how to portray him, once engaged. But this question of what to do with Fortinbras offers no simple solution. Without him the play is less then what is written. Yet in a play already full of staging difficulties, his presence forces the director to make several important decisions.

Difficult decisions notwithstanding, this Fortinbras subplot must not be excised from *Hamlet*. It is an important element just beyond the apron of the stage, "lurking on the Danish border" to remind the audience that problems other than those within the court loom large for Elsinore.[31] Like vultures in attitude, "holding a weak supposal of [their] worth", other powers are always interested in seizing a

Fortinbras on Film 53

kingdom in turmoil – particularly when remembering, as Claudius tells Laertes, that "revenge should have no bounds" (1.2.18; 4.7.127).

Whatever his arrival portends, whether staged as a violent takeover or an orderly restoration of power, the play needs Fortinbras; without this character's apearance Hamlet simply ends in corpse-strewn disarray. Seen either vengeful and power-hungry or a "tender-prince", this character provides needed stability for Elsinore and for Norway. Remembering that Laertes' mob of supporters could be incited by both his death and the death of Hamlet (whose popularity with the commoners is mentioned twice by Claudius), Hortaio's speech will help calm the citizens by explaining the effects of the recent treachery at court. Fortinbras will assert leadership to maintain order (by force, if necessary) and make certain that the former supporters of Laertes find no Jack Cade figure around which to rally.

The Future

This paper has primarily focused upon three approaches to the Fortinbras material when adapting *Hamlet* for film. A director's decision over what to do with this character and subplot will remain problematic. And while a director's privilege must be respected, so must the play which is being directed. Olivier could be accused of omission for the sake of time and simplicity. He represents the decision of many when he completely cuts material from his production. Gielgud offers what might be viewed as the traditionally accepted handling of the material when included – using Fortinbras largely as a plot device to wrap up loose ends. Richardson straddles interpretations, and seems uncertain about how he views the intricacies of Shakespeare's story.

Branagh, like others before him, must be congratulated for bringing a valid interpretation of *Hamlet* to the screen. And like all directors, stage or cinema, Branagh had to decide what to do with the character of Fortinbras. A complete text adaptation will undoubtedly remain the exception for the film versions of this play yet to be produced.[32] But director's privilege notwithstanding, the omission of the Fortinbras subplot will, one hopes, be a thing of the past – just as no respectable director would today consider filming adaptations of *Romeo and Juliet* with a happy ending, or *King Lear* without his Fool.

Notes

1. Jack J. Jorgens, *Shakespeare on Film* (Bloomington: Indiana UP, 1977), p. 233.
2. Gregg Dion, "Fortinbras Our Contemporary", *Theatre Studies*, 38 (1993), p. 18.
3. Robert F. Willson, Jr., "The Unkindest Cut", *Upstart Crow*, 6 (1986), p. 105.
4. Dion, p. 17.
5. Dion, p. 18; Willson, p. 107.
6. Bevington, David, "*King Lear* in Performance," in Shakespeare, *Four Tragedies* (Toronto: Bantam, 1988), pp. 409-11.
7. Bevington, David, "*Romeo and Juliet* in Performance," in Shakespeare, *Romeo and Juliet*, (New York: Bantam, 1988), p. xxix.
8. William Shakespeare, *Hamlet*, ed. Harold Jenkins (Arden Shakespeare, London: Methuen, 1987), 2.2.601. All line citations refer to this edition of the text.
9. Willson, p. 105.
10. Peter Alexander, "From School in Wittenberg" in *Focus on Shakespearean Films*, ed. Charles W. Eckert (Film Focus. Englewood Cliffs, NJ: Prentice-Hall, 1972), p. 67.
11. Laurence Kitchen, "Shakespeare on the Screen", *Shakespeare Survey*, 18 (1965), p. 70.
12. Neil Taylor, "The Films of Hamlet", in *Shakespeare and The Moving Image: The Plays on Film and Television*, ed. Anthony Davies and Stanley Wells (Cambridge UP, 1994), p. 155.

Bernice W. Kliman, *Hamlet: Film, Television, and Audio Performance* (Cranbury, NJ: Associated UP, 1988), p. 30.

13. Jorgens, p. 208.
14. Lorne M. Buchman, *Still in Movement: Shakespeare on Screen* (New York: Oxford UP, 1991), p. 100.
15. Kliman, pp. 29-30.
16. Jorgens, pp. 208, 215.
17. Willson, p. 109.
18. Gielgud, Sir John, "A Note on Hamlet" in *Hamlet 1964* (New York: Dunetz & Lovett, 1964), p. 4. [Booklet accompanying 4 LP set of the complete audio recording of Gielgud's production, by Richard Burton and the Broadway Cast, Columbia Records DOS 702.]
19. *Detroit News*, C-6, 20 March 1997.
20. Taylor, p. 180. *Detroit News*, C-6.
21. Buchman, p. 98.
22. Taylor, p. 193, 155
23. Kenneth Branagh, *Hamlet by William Shakespeare* (New York: Norton, 1996), p. xiv.

24. Jorgens, p. 233.
25. Rebecca West, *The Court and The Castle* (The Terry Lectures. New Haven, CT: Yale UP, 1957), p. 30.
26. Jorgens, p. 225.
27. Branagh, p. 174.
28. *Hamlet*, textual note to the Q2 reading of 4.4.3 (p. 343).
29. *Hamlet*, textual note to the Q2 reading of 4.4.8 (p. 343).
30. Jorgens, p. 233.
31. Willson, p. 105.
32. Branagh is realistically aware of the difficulties inherent in marketing such a production, and even mentions plans to edit an "abridged version" of his own film available "at a more traditional length" (xiv).

"ABSTRACT AND BRIEF CHRONICLES" ON FILM: THE PLAYERS' SCENES IN *HAMLET*

Leigh Woods
(University of Michigan)

For all the preoccupation with filmic technique suffusing the criticism of *Hamlet*-films, images of *theatrical* performance cluster together if not conspicuously, then in disparate and highly suggestive forms in the various versions. This is hardly surprising in a play full of questions about the theatre as a living institution. Shakespeare's invocations of a kind of theatre he rendered as antique four hundred years ago problematized the institution in which he worked. Such invocations, and the ways they have struck modern interpreters, have continued to objectify theatre through the medium of film.

I shall examine three films made from *Hamlet*: Laurence Olivier's in 1948; Tony Richardson's, with Nicol Williamson as the title character, in 1969; and Franco Zeffirelli's, with Mel Gibson as Hamlet, in 1990.[1] In each one the players' scenes are crucial, as they are in the play, for their part in revealing Claudius' guilt in the murder of King Hamlet.[2] Those who have seen the play in more than one stage production will also know that images of performance have much broader resonance than their workings merely in Act 2, Scene 2 and Act 3, Scene 2 from Shakespeare's text, in which the players actually appear.

Moreover, differences among players' scenes in the various film-versions suggest that particularly unstable attitudes toward theatrical performance have prevailed during the postwar period – more, perhaps, than at any other time since *Hamlet* began to be produced. Over the last half century in films of *Hamlet*, the theatre and its practitioners have sometimes been endowed with uncanny power in influencing events, while at others been captured as marginal or outdated entirely. I

The Players' Scenes in *Hamlet* 57

shall examine each film for the uses it makes of theatrical performance as these relate to other elements of production, including adaptation and the depictions of the court and title character. Somewhat more briefly, given the elusiveness of the subject, I shall also be considering how *filmic* images of theatrical performance can suggest broader assumptions regarding the performance of sociability and the social utility of performance.

Olivier's *Hamlet*

The players in this film evince a brand of professionalism that is warm in its personal attachment to Hamlet, but cool in its innocence of any role it might find in the political life of the court. The theatre is captured as an institution sanctified and protected precisely by its removal from narrow partisan interests. The acting company's performance of "The Mousetrap" here frees Hamlet from the obligation – captured as demeaning in the terms of Olivier's characterization – to exercise his character's prerogatives as a 'player' himself. Not surprisingly, those elements that affiliate Hamlet with the artificial nature of acting, such as his "O, what a rogue and peasant slave am I" speech and his interactions with Rosencrantz and Guildenstern, are cut (as are the characters of Rosencrantz and Guildenstern themselves).

Consistent with this Hamlet's statuesque demeanor and the rather highly refined Danish court in this version, the visible world into which the players enter is more handsome than in the later films of *Hamlet*. Olivier captures a court fairly bathed in luxury, with shiny floors and Byzantine tapestries that contrast sharply with the hulking gloom of the battlements he uses for certain 'exterior' shots. The actors, when they enter, conform largely to the court's polish. Once their arrival is announced by Polonius (faithful to Shakespeare's 2.2), they first show themselves in a practiced communal tumbling run, executed crisply down a short set of stairs. The troupe is large, numbering about 15 at their first entrance,[3] well-fed and smartly dressed. Company members range in age from prepubescent boys to the venerable First Player, who eventually speaks the prologue to "The Mousetrap." Their number and range of ages suggest nothing so much as a well-established, generous, and all-male commercial guild.[4]

Olivier's Hamlet brightens at the sight of this solid company in a way that contrasts with his previously restrained and reclusive demeanor, even with Horatio. There is a certain unselfconscious frivolity to these players' tumbling entrance, which seems like 'playing' indeed in contrast to Hamlet's more austere behavior and the stuffiness that prevails at this court. However, such practiced spontaneity as the players demonstrate with their first entrance gives way quickly to their respectful collective response to Hamlet when he greets them: and this deference, in turn, culminates in their not previewing for him the play they are to perform, as Shakespeare has them do in the latter part of 2.2. In this and other moments, these players seem to exist not as much for their own sake, nor for the sake of the art they practice, as for the levity and inspiration they provide for this Hamlet.

Accordingly, they stand at polite attention as a stern Olivier delivers the "Speak the speech" passages. Their appearance is entirely static as Olivier speaks and moves among them in the manner of a modern stage director. His very presence, indeed, is sufficient to cause the players to group themselves into balanced and ordered clusters – mirroring this Hamlet's previous tendencies of movement while indicating, by contrast, his quickening engagement with the prospect of certifying Claudius' role in his father's death. In this film, the players seem to liberate Hamlet, letting him become a different kind of 'player' in his demonstrative behavior around them, tracing its sources to motives so much more pregnant than theirs are. Olivier's domination of both space and dialogue as, first, he greets the players and, later, dispenses advice to them, reinforces the disparity between his social standing and the company members', and between his methods of taking action and their own more innocent, though more practiced ones.[5]

By cutting the players' preview/rehearsal, and by including only Hamlet's plan to "catch the conscience of the king" (2.2), Olivier's film collapses 2.2 and 3.2 from Shakespeare's play into a single, continuous sequence. This alters Shakespeare's two players' scenes into a single ur-scene that furnishes the second major climax in the film, following the revelations of Hamlet's ghostly father. Olivier also achieves this compression by repositioning Shakespeare's 3.1, containing Hamlet's "To be or not to be" soliloquy and his exchange with Ophelia (ending with "Get thee to a nunnery"), so that these occur before the players enter. Olivier's delivery of "catch the conscience of the king", then, leads directly into his authoritative reading of "Speak the speech" to the players (3.2) and then directly, again, into the ceremonial entry of the court and the performance of "The Mousetrap."[6]

Entirely absent in Olivier's version is the First Player's "rugged Pyrhhus" speech, containing the reference to Hecuba that precipitates Hamlet's "O, what a rogue" soliloquy at the end of 2.2. Given no chance either to rehearse or perform between the time of their first light-hearted entrance and their much more formal appearance before the court, these players' exposure to artistic process comes in the form of Hamlet's instructions to them rather than from their own exertions. His instructions, moreover, are of a general theoretical nature, bearing no direct relationship to the particular demands of "The Mousetrap." The players' self-sufficiency is left to stand analogous to Hamlet's own independence and isolation from the court – although the players, at least, have each other for company.

Another moment that works to distinguish between this solitary, reflective Hamlet and the jolly, collegial company comes when the prince helps the boy-actor who will become the Player Queen put on a long-braided blond wig just prior to the performance of "The Mousetrap." Having done this, he is overcome by the young actor's resemblance to Ophelia. He lingers for a moment on the boy's face, puzzled by the transformation he himself has helped to effect, and then he lets the boy go off to make further preparations. In this moment, Hamlet is caught between his dominion over the players and his sense of them as barely controllable versions of his own life. The theatre here, although seen as obligated to its patrons and the society they inhabit, discharges its duties by rules known only to itself, that baffle even such an assured expert as Olivier makes his Hamlet out to be.

The royal entry preceding the performance of "The Mousetrap" is full of pomp and splendor, its formality and heraldic music contrasting with the players' more blithe and gamesome entrance earlier. However, the parallel nature of these two entrances, made as they are into the same stateroom, calls attention to the discipline and concern for appearances that the players share with this particular court, and with this particular Hamlet, too. The degree of courtly protocol in this version also makes Claudius' troubled departure seem even more out-of-place than it might have done otherwise. Hamlet caps this moment by abandoning his previous repression to sing his lines, "Why let the strucken deer go weep", the only time during the play he breaks into song.

Such a climactic and uncharacteristic moment is consistent with Olivier's larger design. He builds the players' scenes so that his Hamlet can be inspired into a different register of engagement by witnessing an unabashed performance, as opposed to the more guileful machinations of the court. "The Mousetrap" stands, as Lorne M. Buchman has pointed out, as "a stage enactment of Hamlet's subjective picture" of the "[murder of his father ...] a product of Hamlet's visual imagination".[7] Olivier's version of this moment stands quite consistent with his pronounced interest in suggesting Hamlet's state of mind, and with the many other ways he finds to do so.

The use Olivier finds for the players seems more dignified and, at the same time, less metaphorical than those in the later films. The theatre is granted a proud

The Players' Scenes in *Hamlet*

and clearly institutionalized place in Olivier's Hamlet, much as it enjoyed in postwar Britain.[8] However, the relatively narrowly defined and largely utilitarian functions Olivier assigned his players largely evaporated by the time the next major film version of Hamlet appeared. By then, Olivier's notion of performers as naive to the exercises of power seemed sufficiently unrealistic to dictate a different set of choices around the players' scenes.

Richardson's *Hamlet*

The players in this film first show themselves neither so cohesive nor so practiced as in Olivier's. They enter first to dissonant music on pipe and drums, which they play themselves, and badly. This stands in striking contrast to the more heavily orchestral, and as it turns out, recurrent musical theme William Walton provided for the players, who only mime playing their instruments in Olivier.[9] Richardson's company numbers only five, or about one-third the size of Olivier's better established and more monied troupe.

As this Hamlet wears on, however, a much looser and more capacious definition of performance insinuates itself into the action. Here, the players prove as skilled and devious as improvisers as Olivier's company were polished and well-rehearsed.[10] However, the appearance of Richardson's First Player, acted by Roger Livesey, belies the company's later versatility even as their initially slipshod appearance does. A distinguished looking man with long grey hair, Livesey's leading attribute lies in his reedy, ruined voice. The first view of him suggests a broken-down actor heading a very small troupe apparently down on its luck. His shopworn visage and straining voice initially lend these performers a pathetic air in comparison to the more numerous and better-appointed group in Olivier's *Hamlet*.

Livesey's distinctive vocal quality also leaves him ill-adapted to transform himself between one and another of his roles, first as the leading player, next as Lucianus the poisoner in "The Mousetrap", and finally and most surprisingly as the

Gravedigger in Act 5. He stands, rather, as one whose voice and identity mark him as a recurrent and familiar presence, almost with the quality of a chorus.[11] Livesey practices an apparently static kind of acting; and when Richardson also has him play the poisoner (opposed to the prologue as taken by the leading actor in Olivier's company), it supports momentarily the notion that impersonation can be multivalent in its moral associations because it is so reiterative in Livesey's own person.

Livesey, indeed, seems rather more fixed than Hamlet is, as Williamson plays him, who scorns the dignity and singular tendency Olivier displayed in moving from the rigid self-control of the early scenes to more animated behavior as the play goes on. Williamson's Hamlet lacks the maturity or patience to calculate the effects of his actions in advance, rendering the character much more exhibitionistic and volatile than Olivier's. In this connection, Williamson is constantly changing 'characters' himself, although bound in considerable measure by his distinctively nasal voice and lanky, awkward frame in something of the way Livesey is by his own distinctive qualities.

This Hamlet's flightiness, though, stands in sharp contrast to Livesey's affable fixity; and Livesey's fixity, in turn, works to complement the striking transformations his company eventually makes. These players are given an especially wide range of opportunities, partly in the form of much more dialogue than in Olivier. In this film, they range between pantomime and spoken exchanges, and between the antic quality of a prologue complete with attached clown-noses, and the antique and dignified style of "The Mousetrap", with full and elegant costumes and a handsomely painted screen of ornamental birds to decorate the action. Livesey as the poisoner is made up obviously to resemble the dark- and curly-bearded Anthony Hopkins as Claudius.

When they evoke Claudius in this way, it is as though this company feels an especial need to challenge their courtly audience, granted as they are a single, very

The Players' Scenes in *Hamlet*   63

brief prefatory fanfare before they perform, and given the rather casual attention of a very self-absorbed group of courtiers. Such lack of respect turns out to be mutual when, having made such a sorry sight at their first entrance, playing bad music, carrying only a battered trunk and two crudely-painted banners – and having recapitulated this with the laughable appearance they make in masks and states of partial undress during Hamlet's desperate and apparently superfluous enjoinders to them to merely "Speak the speech" – these players emerge for the dialogue portion of "The Mousetrap" suddenly crisp in execution and handsomely fitted out. The prologue speaks his lines through a mask of metal texture much larger and more fully executed than the half-masks and ridiculous noses seen previously.

These players' attitude toward Hamlet during his "Speak the speech" has been good-humored and indulgent rather than reverential, as in Olivier. Williamson plays the moment as a kind of amateur theatre-lover backstage for the first time, in a far cry from Olivier's disciplined and highly professional bearing during the scene. In Richardson's film, the players are seen to share Hamlet's anticipation at the prospect of the performance instead of receiving Hamlet's instructions passively and showing every intention of following them to the letter. Richardson's players also seem purposely to mislead their viewers – *including* Hamlet – as their initial disorganization gives way to the subversive disposition they show during their actual performance.

In this regard, the players appear to share their Hamlet's fondness for challenging authority. Perhaps this is because they have guessed the purpose behind his altering their little play – which here we *see*, as distinct from Olivier's version – or because they have brought their own hostility with them toward the more patronizing, distracted, and unfamiliar ones among their royal audience. By the time they have finished with this court, the players have aligned themselves with a Fortinbras posing a revolutionary threat in this film,[12] as well as with an especially angry and vengeful Laertes. Revolution is in the air in Richardson's Hamlet, and the players stand central in fomenting it.

Their clowning before the play seems calculated to lull Claudius into reading only harmlessness into the prospective contents of "The Mousetrap". This subterfuge gives way in stages, through both dumb show and spoken dialogue, until the courtly audience finally turns its collective gaze upon Claudius to observe his tortured reaction. At this moment, the players' performance becomes much less important than its effect in riveting the attention of a king and court practiced so patently in denial.[13] When Hamlet sings at the end of this "Mousetrap", he sings off key, echoing the dissonance and apparent artlessness that marked the players at their first entrance. The theatre, which had appeared only moth-eaten in the person of First Player Roger Livesey and his rag-tag company, shows vigor by imposing itself in a way that amazes both Hamlet and the rest of the Danish court. It offers up a model for transformation, and for disorder, too, quite different from the equable and deferential group Olivier captures.

The politicized players and utopian images of performance in this *Hamlet*, however, proved as much the products of their time as Olivier's more staid, predictable, and legitimated troupe. With the passage of another generation, a more media-ridden culture worked to undercut the possibilities of theatre as a politicized institution, and to render it peripheral to climactic events in the play itself. By the final decade of the century, the institutional efficacy of the theatre would be called into question, together with its capacity to effect transformations of any kind. Not surprisingly, the next major Hamlet presents a much more equivocal view of the capacities of live performance than does either Olivier's or Richardson's version.

The Players' Scenes in *Hamlet*

Zeffirelli's *Hamlet*

Zeffirelli's players struggle first to reach their place of performance, later simply to produce their play, and in our final image of them, to grasp that play's impact on their audience. They emerge from outside the castle, quite literally from the world of nature, but expressing nature's more entropic and devolutionary effects. Hamlet glimpses them first in the aftermath of his bitter exchange with Rosencrantz and Guildenstern, as the company wrestles with their wagon in order to keep it upright on a muddy road leading to the castle. They are emaciated. They do not exhibit their craft when first seen but try, as the less privileged Hamlet of this film does, to deal with the harsh realities of daily life in surroundings more evocative of the middle ages than of the Renaissance, as in the other two films.

Their actual entry into the castle, *sans* dialogue, is triumphal and crude as well, as they are mobbed by courtiers and peasants alike. They appear clearly here as *popular* entertainers; and this, too, departs from the more privileged and manifestly patronized existences suggested for them in the other two film versions. These players are worn and bedraggled, dressed in rough clothing corresponding to this Hamlet's rougher dress. Having made them welcome, Gibson's Hamlet watches the players disembark into the castle, and in very short order – without drawing any direct inspiration from them (much in Olivier's way) – hatches his plan that omits their rehearsal and moves without it, directly, to "The play's the thing ...".

In this film, alone among the three, no single player is given the chance to emerge as company-leader, given this Hamlet's precipitous and self-generated response to them. So, when they do perform their play, these actors remain virtually anonymous. In the absence of more elaborate and personalized greetings from Hamlet, and lacking the sight of the First Player weeping as he speaks of Hecuba, Gibson's Hamlet has not seen the players perform at all (apart from his previous knowledge of them) prior to witnessing "The Mousetrap" with the rest of the court.[14] So far, this adaptation bears great resemblance to Olivier's, although both the players themselves and the visible world they inhabit are set into much less opulent surroundings than in the earlier film.

This company's role is reduced still more than Olivier's was when the "Speak the speech" scene was omitted. Here, instead, Gibson is shown speaking only a single coined line, "'Tis almost time", as he moves nervously among the actors backstage just before they begin their performance. This troupe numbers about eleven, somewhere between Olivier's larger and Richardson's smaller one. Only in this film, however, are there no young boys in the company, although children too young to be actors (but with no women visible) appear initially in the wagon. Lacking here is any image of the *future* of acting, to complement those of the past that appear in the other two films, suggesting that this company is retrograde not merely in its style but in its personnel, too. The role of the Player Queen is taken by a man in his fifties, heavily rouged, red-wigged, and grotesque in the way of someone trying too hard to look younger and more attractive than he is. He offers the first view of the players as they ready themselves backstage, his gaunt appearance recapitulating this company's depleted state when first seen on the road.

Rough tumbling, joining two actors head-to-buttocks, and torch-juggling precede the performance, only a bit more crude than the by-play before "The Mousetrap" in the other two film versions. This company, however, does not elevate the tone of its acting once it leaves clowning aside; and the prologue here is delivered by an actor of grotesque appearance who, as he speaks, grins grotesquely and almost idiotically through a set of highly unusual teeth. The stage is backed by a handsome screen, but this decoration belongs to the castle and not the players. Otherwise, the stage is bare, except for a bench that calls for practical rather than decorative use when the Player King reclines and dies on it.

The Players' Scenes in *Hamlet*   67

In fact, everything about this troupe seems impoverished and cut-rate. Even the space where they perform calls attention to their lack of means and slender ability to adapt. Polonius speaks his "Best actors in the world [...] tragical-comical-historical-pastoral" to introduce the company in lines transposed from 2.2. Here, however, he seems only to be hyperbolizing about a troupe so little able to present itself to advantage. The Player Queen, when speaking, sounds a bit like a woman, but is marked as a man by his awkwardness and angularity. There is nothing in the way of magic when this company performs once they have dispensed with their *commedia* stunts, and the stunts themselves continue until they become labored.

When the poisoner Lucianus enters into this "Mousetrap", he wears a black cloak with a cowl; and when he turns to face the audience just after poisoning Gonzago, his face resembles a medieval death's head rather than showing any particular likeness to Claudius. At the very end of the play, the three leading actors are shown reacting with puzzlement to Claudius' abrupt exit, and Hamlet joins them in a little dance for his singing of "Why, let the strucken deer go weep ...". Once he has sung, though, this Hamlet adds an aside to the amazed Ophelia, enjoining her to "Believe none of us, we are errant knaves all" (relocated here from the "Get thee to a nunnery" scene in 3.1). In both these moments, Gibson's Hamlet aligns himself with the actors in the results they have achieved, even though he has taken little direct part in their performance. Counter to the perfidy they have helped reveal, Gibson's Hamlet is frank in affirming that he is, like the players, only an "errant knave" in sharing the simulation, and the dissimulation, of the court itself.

Zeffirelli's acting company evokes a sort of populist nostalgia in the appeal it holds for the mob that welcomes it to the castle. Such appeal, however, seems to exist largely in anticipation of their performance, especially of their *lazzi*, rather than in any more substantial interest in their serious acting. These players show only concern at Claudius' exit because they have no idea what angered him or, for that matter, where their next patron lies: the road they were seen travelling is a long and winding one, with no other buildings, much less castles, in sight. "The Mousetrap" they perform, unlike those in the other versions, seems to represent a failure in their own eyes, and they show only puzzlement at Hamlet's enthusiasm for its outcome.

Instead of demonstrating any capacity to transform themselves for "The Mousetrap", they remain resolutely who they are, strange teeth, wrinkles, wrong gender, and all. They emerge from abjection, straight off the road, but this seems only to endear them to their fellow working-folks and sparks an initial interest among the courtiers, too. But in this film they stay poor and disadvantaged right through "The Mousetrap", seeming barely aware by its end of their impact on the court. Moreover, they are given so little chance to prepare themselves for the play that their puzzlement at their play's aborted ending extends even to Gibson's crazed dancing with them. This sequence conforms to what is, apparently, their general wariness when performing, in haste and under less-than-ideal circumstances, before audiences comprised of unstable and ever-shifting mixtures of privileged and poor, who respond to their efforts in only the most capricious and superficial of ways.

These players are seen as relics. In this version among the three, the theatre is made to seem out of touch. Even the players' appeal to rich and poor is viewed as nostalgic, measured against the modern theatre and its affiliation with high culture. It is not coincidental that the primary visual image to emerge from the performance – that of Lucianus/Claudius as a death's head – suggests medieval origins rather than more hopeful and sophisticated ones from the Renaissance. The theatre as these players practice it betokens the past. Their performance is efficacious, but more by accident – or by numbed habit – than because of anything the actors do wittingly.

Conclusions

I think it fair to say that more of the original viewers of Olivier's *Hamlet* were familiar and engaged with the theatre than the audience that greeted Zeffirelli's film. Indeed, the casting of Mel Gibson represents Zeffirelli's attempt to attract viewers whose main exposure lies with film rather than theatre. Zeffirelli seems to have sought to enlarge the contemporary appeal of his filmed *Hamlet* by drawing out more crude and antique qualities in the players' scenes. He makes Gibson's performance seem more up-to-date by affiliating it more steadily with visual values, in architecture and nature, than with historical ones, at least as these are encapsulated in the players.

Richardson's *Hamlet* is the film version that uses the players most extensively and invokes performance in the most sweeping of ways. Not only does performance resonate in the multiple casting of its First Player, but it surfaces in the court scenes, too, in a Claudius and Gertrude who want to show themselves having fun and in the flamboyant queerness of Osric as well. The players themselves are more politically aware in this film than they are in the other two, and more capable of discerning between true and false performances. They enlist themselves actively and presciently on the side of good, as they do not in either of the other films.[15]

Among the three films, Olivier's uses the players' scenes to present the most stable and historically-legitimated view of performance. His is also the version of *Hamlet*, however, that leaves the players least 'voiced', and so reserves a more pristine kind of self-representation for Hamlet alone. The effect of the players on the action of the play is seen as beneficent, but it is achieved only with Hamlet's firm guidance. The role of the players is more heavily aestheticized by Olivier than in the other films, too, and the theatre proclaims its innocence as a politicized entity in the spectacle of Hamlet's unchallenged authority over it. Olivier's players don't need to speak in order to claim a significant role in society: his Hamlet assures that they will do so in the difference between their largely unvoiced performance and the sort of graceful, loquacious glosses on their efforts he makes to their faces and, later, before the court.

Among the three Hamlets, Williamson's is the least focused and efficacious character, and Olivier's the most capable and efficient.[16] This would suggest that the more ways performance is allowed to body forth in the play and to surround Hamlet – with the players themselves as indexes of this factor – the more Hamlet is apt to be rendered passive and self-conscious by his subordination to kinds of acting he neither practices nor can control. Such a choice also helps explain the long delay he makes before taking his revenge, more plausible in Richardson than in either of the other two films. In this connection, exfoliations of performance in *Hamlet* may leave the title character with less glamour and dignity (as they do in Williamson's characterization), while endowing the play with a more social dimension than it has found, generally, since the advent of starring-traditions beginning in the late eighteenth century. The more broadly the players are allowed to figure, together with acting as a metaphor for social interaction, the more the piece treats a *group* of characters rather than a single one among them.

Set into film, images of the theatre in its historical practice question implicitly the authority of older as against newer forms of entertainment. Such questioning may not always dispose an audience to favor the theatre over film, but it suggests nostalgia for a time when performance was more narrowly confined and simply produced than films have come to be. Invoking the theatre in films contrasts the qualities of live performance with those attending a form that is already history, in a sense, when it appears on the screen – even though the 'live' performance of "The Mousetrap" is, by nature in films, enshrouded in the illusion of immediacy conferred by cinema.[17] Given this paradoxical quality, theatrical performance can be rendered in more contemporaneous and vital ways, as in Richardson's *Hamlet*, or in more clearly nostalgic or quiescent ones as in Olivier's and Zeffirelli's

The Players' Scenes in *Hamlet*   71

versions. Even when it is depicted as antiquated, though, the theatre can take on strikingly different functions, as it does in the distance between the solidly enfranchised players of Olivier's film and the much more marginal group captured by Zeffirelli.

There is yet another paradox lying among the players' scenes. In each film version, the players appear not merely as quaint figures, but as ones whose very *brands* of quaintness suggest the attitudes of the filmmakers toward performance and performing. In a more general way, perhaps, the players' scenes serve also as a sort of index to the social histories of those periods when the films were produced. Various images of players and playing have worked in films even as they did on the stage during the three centuries prior to our own: to extend the signifying power of the players scenes' well beyond the theatre into realms of human interaction more subtly and richly realized in images than in words. This suggests the range of capacities in a play – and more lately in its filmic versions – that has been considered in modern times to revolve more around anti-sociability than its opposite.

Notes

1. I have chosen English-language films of *Hamlet* available in videocassette format and which, in the United States, at least, are relatively easy to obtain. Although these films have adapted the play in quite different ways, and the players' scenes within them, I shall deal with such differences only in passing. The matter of adaptation has been treated fully elsewhere, by Roger Manville, *Shakespeare and the Film* (New York: Praeger Publishers, 1971), pp. 40-7, 53-4; Lorne M. Buchman, *Still in Movement: Shakespeare on Screen* (Oxford UP, 1991), pp. 100-3; Ace G. Pilkington, "Zeffirelli's Shakespeare" and Neil Taylor, "The Films of Hamlet," both in *Shakespeare and the Moving Image: The Plays on Film and Television*, ed. Anthony Davies and Stanley Wells Cambridge UP, 1994), pp. 163-95. Adaptations of *Hamlet*, apart from their being highly variable, are almost inevitable as well – a state of affairs hardly surprising given that the play is rarely performed at full length on stage. Allowing the play to take up four hours on the screen, or more lately, on television, is rarer still, although not unknown. The BBC videotape version of *Hamlet*, directed by Rodney Bennett and starring Derek Jacobi, contains much more text than any of the film versions. It was released in 1980 and runs 222 minutes, as compared to 155 minutes for Olivier's film, 113 for Richardson's, and 135 for Zeffirelli's. I shall not deal with the BBC *Hamlet* because it was made for television, though quite worthy of attention on its own merits. I shall also ignore Kozintsev's Russian *Hamlet* which, if anything, integrates the players

more fully into its action than any of the English-language films other than Richardson's (see Buchman, pp. 119-20).

2. In a play replete with references to actors and acting, the 'feigning' connotations of acting are invoked repeatedly by Hamlet himself, both in soliloquy and in exchanges with those characters he trusts least, including Polonius, Claudius, and Rosencrantz and Guildenstern. Performance, its jargon, and its uses, assume an ambiguous role in the play in their associations sometimes with authenticity ("What's Hecuba to him or he to her/ That he should weep for her?" [2.2]), and sometimes with duplicity ("... one may smile and smile, and be a villain" [1.5]).

3. Marvin Rosenberg has noted that the folio edition specifies only four or five players, but that modern productions have often enlarged this number in the name of spectacular effect. See Rosenberg, *The Masks of Hamlet* (Newark: Delaware UP, 1992), pp. 423-4.

4. These players' banter and *camaraderie* suggest certain parallels to military service, an experience still fresh in the minds of many of the film's intended audience, female and male.

5. Peter S. Donaldson has noted that Olivier's standing alone, spotlit in an empty chamber at the end of this scene, climaxes "the sequence between Hamlet and the players ... [in] a moment of mastery." See Donaldson, *Shakespearean Films/Shakespearean Directors* (Boston: Unwin Hyman, 1990), p. 56.

6. By such means, Olivier avoids playing the two major soliloquies, beginning "To be or not to be" and "O, what a rogue and peasant slave am I", too close together, as they have sometimes been thought to be in a play which allows only a little more than fifty lines between the speeches at the end of 2.2 and the opening of 3.1. Rosenberg quotes Richard Burton on this point, who complained that "It's very difficult for an actor to realize the change between 'The play's the thing/ Wherein I'll catch the conscience of the king', and then within three minutes, he's back on stage contemplating suicide. That kind of inconsistency is enormously difficult for the actor to smooth over" (p. 477).

7. Buchman, p. 103.

8. In the United States, a postcolonial deference to such derivative royalty as Olivier's Hamlet signifies figured when the film won an Academy Award as Best Picture.

9. This choice is consistent with the players' entirely *unvoiced* performance of "The Mousetrap" in Olivier's version.

10. Richardson gives his players more scenes as well, with both the rehearsal scene (in which the First Player mentions Hecuba) and the dialogue-portions of "The Mousetrap" maintained in large measure.

11. By the time he appears as the Gravedigger, it is as if Livesey, as the leading actor, has stood watch over a number of the play's pivotal events and affected them in beneficent ways. In this respect, Richardson's film endows the theatre with a kind of presence and authority that supersede its narrow manifestations in Acts 2 and 3.

12. Fortinbras, in fact, is only *mentioned* in Richardson's film. The character's presence this way exceeds that in Olivier's and Zeffirelli's versions, where Fortinbras is neither mentioned nor appears.

13. In this connection, the sort of frivolity attaching to the players in Olivier's film is translated into the *court* in Richardson's.

14. This adaptation, like both Olivier's and Richardson's, relocates Shakespeare's 3.1, with "To be or not to be" followed by Hamlet's confrontation of Ophelia, so that it falls *before* the players'

The Players' Scenes in *Hamlet*

scenes – a measure that bestows a kind of gathering speed and urgency to these scenes similar to the other films'.

15. The casting of pop singer Marianne Faithfull as Ophelia also had the effect of enlarging performance in Richardson's film from its relatively narrow applications in the work of the players themselves, into larger concentric circles embracing Hamlet's romantic life and the court as well, in Faithfull's associations with the 'royalty' of popular culture including her sometime lover, Mick Jagger of the rock music group, the Rolling Stones. Such elements, in aggregate, suggest that performance was entrusted more to lively events during the 1960s than it has been recently in the sort of heavily theorized notions that have dominated discourse, enlarging definitions of performance while making them more vague and, in some ways at least, less practicable.

16. Gibson's Hamlet lies somewhere between these two in the degree of the character's effectiveness in finding a course of action and in sticking to it. His Hamlet is also more muscular and funnier, too, than either of the other two Hamlets, substituting sincerity for the wit and subtle transitions evident in both Olivier's and Williamson's acting. In short, Gibson's performance is more heavily endowed with the attributes of the action-heroes he has played in other films. Zeffirelli seems to have looked for ways to capitalize on this quality, and found them in the spectacular visual style of the film and in his use of the players, antique as they are, to render Gibson's Hamlet more contemporary and vital.

17. It will be interesting to see whether added skepticism greets the capacities conceded to live performance, continuing the tendency of Zeffirelli's *Hamlet*, or whether the theatre may find more hopeful incarnation in the hands of Kenneth Branagh, an actor-director working closer to the model of Olivier. This is especially difficult to predict (as this article goes to press), given the ways that Branagh has recapitulated, and at the same time challenged, Olivier's career. Branagh, of course, confronted Olivier's legacy when he mounted his own *Henry V* (1989), as a revisionist response to Olivier's more purely patriotic *Henry V* (1944). I hope this essay, together with some others in this volume, offers a useful perspective on what will stand as only the latest film version of a play that has long prompted its interpreters to struggle with balancing Hamlet against the courtly and performative worlds surrounding him. Kozintsev's *Hamlet*, in fact, has often been praised for its interest in rendering the political and social worlds of the play, more than do the English-language films which have tended to stress the starring performance and so implicated themselves in the values of 'bourgeois individualism'. His distaste for such traditions and the values they represent may explain Kozintsev's interest in using the players' scenes in the full and detailed ways he did.

"DIDST PERCEIVE?":
FIVE VERSIONS OF THE MOUSETRAP IN *HAMLET*

David G. Hale
(State University of New York, Brockport)

Staging multiple perceptions of an event is a common theatrical practice, though few are as complex as the "Mousetrap", the play-within-the play in *Hamlet*, Act 3, Scene 2.[1] After the arrival of the players at Elsinore, Hamlet arranges for them to "Play something like the murther of my father / Before mine uncle" (2.2.595-6).[2] The drama may so strike the soul of the guilty King that his crime will reveal itself, confirming the story told by the Ghost and thereby establishing whether or not the spirit is a devil who has assumed a pleasing shape. "I'll observe his looks," Hamlet says (2.2.596), beginning a series of onlookers for the play-within-the-play and its on-stage audience. Just before the play, Hamlet involves Horatio by describing its plot, Hamlet's purpose, and Horatio's potential contribution:

> Give him heedful note,
> For I mine eyes will rivet to his face,
> And after we will both our judgments join
> In censure of his seeming.
> [...]
> Get you a place. (3.2.84-7, 91)

Now two characters are set to pay more attention to the King than to the play. With a flourish and a "Danish march", the court – including "other Lords attendant, with [the King's] Guard carrying torches" – enters for the play (3.2.89, s.d).[3] It proceeds until interrupted by the King's call for light, from which Hamlet concludes – for better or worse – that he should "take the ghost's word for a thousand pound. Didst perceive?" (3.2.286-7). Horatio replies, "I did very well note him" (3.2.290), but does not say if he agrees with Hamlet.

A recent essay by Michael Shurgot addresses the question of the placement of the actors during *Hamlet* 3.2 as it determines what the various actors and the audience see during "The Murder of Gonzago" and how they respond to their

The Mousetrap in *Hamlet*

observations.[4] Shurgot hypothetically reconstructs a performance at the Globe to illustrate his points. Briefly, he suggests that Claudius, Gertrude, and Polonius are upstage center, Hamlet and Ophelia stage right forward of the royal group, the Players center stage, and Horatio far down stage left.[5] Their physical positions on stage indicate their emotional involvement in the action and incidentally their chances for surviving at the end of *Hamlet*. Another analytical approach is made possible by the increasing availability of multiple versions of the play on videotape.

In five generally available film or recent television performances there is considerable variation in how Hamlet, Horatio, Claudius, Gertrude, and Ophelia are placed in relation to each other, to the players, and to the attendant Lords and Guards, and how the camera presents them to us. What do they, and we, see, and when do we see it? The five versions to be considered are the films directed by and starring Laurence Olivier (1948), Tony Richardson with Nicol Williamson (1969), and Franco Zeffirelli with Mel Gibson (1990), and the television productions by Rodney Bennet with Derek Jacobi (BBC Shakespeare Plays, 1980), and Kevin Kline in modern dress (1989).[6] These performances are at varying distances from theatrical production, the closest being Kline's "translation" of his performance at the New York Shakespeare Festival.[7]

In past and present theatrical performances including those imagined by Shurgot and other critics, everyone in the audience sees everything, but from a different though fixed perspective. Performances recorded by multiple cameras, however, give us all the same viewpoint, but one which is usually selective and which changes frequently through crosscutting, varying distance and focus, and camera movement. Only Olivier, for example, has a high-angle-shot containing all the major characters, what a spectator in a balcony would see. The result is substantial difference in the presentation of the psychological and political dynamics at the climax of the play, and substantial opportunity for critical controversy.[8]

On the surface the new regime of King Claudius is far more stable, more free of internal or external challenge, than those of, say, Richard III or Macbeth.

Prince Hamlet is the main disruptive element, seen by his language, behavior and costume in the first court scene (1.2). The threat of Fortinbras's invasion from Norway has been handled by diplomatic negotiation or, in the Olivier and Zeffirelli films, by eliminating all mention of him. While the first part of Act 1, Scene 2 is for the formal transaction of public business, the second court scene, Act 3, Scene 2, is ostensibly for public entertainment, the play, as is the third court scene, Act 5, Scene 2, the fencing match. Both of the latter scenes have complex undercurrents established earlier. In addition to Hamlet's using the play to test the Ghost's story, Claudius has already determined to send Hamlet to England, and Claudius and Polonius have planned a meeting between Hamlet and Gertrude after the play to test again Polonius' theory that Hamlet's grief springs "from neglected love" (3.1.163-88). The Mousetrap scene also returns to the question of just how publicly disruptive Hamlet is and the extent, if any, to which his challenge is recognized as political by the King and those on whose support the King depends. Comparison of these five versions exemplifies the increasingly accepted view that studying multiple performances of Shakespeare leads to an appreciation of the rich texture of possible meanings in his plays. As Jack Jorgens said of the Olivier film, they graphically illustrate the subjective nature of Shakespearean reality.[9]

The placement of the major characters as audience to "The Murder of Gonzago" contains both common elements and major differences. None closely approximates the various blockings for Globe performance proposed by J.L. Styan, C. Walter Hodges, or Shurgot.[10] Claudius and Gertrude are usually seated in the most elaborate chairs or thrones, and in the most prominent location facing the Players. The exception is Zeffirelli, who places them (Alan Bates and Glen Close) and others on a raised dais at the back of the hall with the Lords and servants on rows of benches in front of them. With their backs to the royal party, these spectators are not positioned to hear the dialogue among the major characters or to see the King's reaction to the play. Olivier has Basil Sydney and Eileen Herlie at the center of a large U-shaped formation. They sit on the same chairs on a small raised platform used in the other two court scenes, here moved to the center of the great hall. Polonius (Felix Aylmer) stands behind them. Richardson places Anthony Hopkins and Judy Parfitt in a smaller, less distinct grouping with Polonius (Mark Dignam) and others behind and beside. The BBC version seats them (Patrick Stewart and Claire Bloom) and Polonius (Eric Porter) on wood arms chairs at the end of a rectangular formation of seated and standing courtiers, smaller than Olivier's group.

The exception is Kline, in which the King and Queen (Brian Murray and Dana Ivey) have simple chairs with white slip covers, like everyone else's, on a platform facing the Players and the rest of the court, which sits in a row around the stage. The King and Queen are more distanced, perhaps more alienated, from the court. Polonius (Josef Sommer) stands behind them only until the beginning of "Gonzago", when he leaves the platform and is off camera until the entrance of Lucianus when he appears standing among the courtiers opposite Hamlet and Ophelia. Much of the play is shot over the heads of the courtiers through the Players to the King and Queen, reinforcing the parallel between the play and two of its on-stage audience. The camera records approximately what Horatio and the courtiers observe. Olivier creates the same parallel through a reverse angle as the tracking camera passes behind the King and Queen three times, briefly showing us what they see of "Gonzago." The camera pauses during the poisoning to emphasize the identification of what Claudius has done and what Lucianus is doing. The BBC version also uses the reverse angle but without camera movement, shooting to the Players between the shoulders and clasped hands of Claudius and Gertrude.

Hamlet and Ophelia, "metal more attractive" (3.2.110), are at some distance from Claudius and Gertrude, and usually not in the same line, a social distancing noticed by Polonius in a tone emphasizing his view that Hamlet's madness derives from rejected love: "O ho, do you mark that?" (3.2.111) All but Zeffirelli seat Ophelia away from the King and Queen, closer to the players. Olivier has Jean Simmons to the left in the same chair Hamlet occupied in Act 1, Scene 2, and in front of the courtiers. Hamlet kneels before her to ask "Lady, shall I lie in your lap?" (3.2.114); during the play he sits on the floor by her.

Richardson provides Hamlet with a stool, on which Hamlet sits after his lines with his head on Marianne Faithfull's lap. A woman and a man stand behind them, displaying little reaction to Hamlet's statements. Bennet has Hamlet and Ophelia (Lalla Ward) on two stools to the right of the King and in front of the courtiers, who ignore Hamlet's dialogue with her about "country matters" (3.2.116). To watch the play and its audience, Hamlet moves from his stool to the floor, a position echoing Olivier's treatment. Kline responds to Gertrude's request by humorously pretending to sit on a nonexistent chair, then takes Ophelia (Diane Venora) by the hand from the row of courtiers and leads her to a chair at the side of the King's platform. Zeffirelli cuts Polonius' line and substitutes a reaction shot of a disappointed Glen Close. He seats Hamlet and Ophelia (Helena Bonham-Carter) on less elaborate chairs in the same row as the King, Queen, Rosencrantz, and Polonius, but most of Hamlet's commentary on the play and other subjects is heard only by Ophelia and the camera through a series of alternating head-and-shoulders shots.

Horatio's different "place" is variously established away from the four main characters and the players, indicating less emotional and political involvement, as Shurgot argues.[11] Differing amounts of attention are given to his observing the King, thereby emphasizing observation as a motif of the scene, as it is in much of the first half of *Hamlet*. In four versions he is well placed to observe the King and the camera shows him watching. Only Kline seats him inconspicuously with Rosenkrantz, Guildenstern and others around the stage; there are no reaction shots. Zeffirelli stands him at the right side of the seated courtiers, positioned to watch in three shots the play and the King. Horatio's position in the Richardson film is difficult to establish, although he is clearly by himself, and three shots show him observing the King through torchlight. Gordon Jackson's glasses further indicate his scholarly nature and his role as observer. The BBC version places him close to the acting area to the left of the King, echoing Olivier's blocking, but only two shots show him watching anyone. Curiously, he holds two swords, foreshadowing the fencing match of Act 5, Scene 2.

Olivier's film gives the most attention to Horatio's role as observer. He is

The Mousetrap in *Hamlet*

prominently at the King's right, and at the greatest distance, by a column at the end of the semicircle of spectators. The camera emphasizes his observing the King through at least five reaction shots; some shots of the King are from Horatio's perspective or over his shoulder. He shifts his position twice during the scene, the only character to move during the performance. His movement is amplified by three long tracking shots behind the spectators including the King and Queen; the camera doubles Horatio's function as a serious observer. As the King reacts to the play, the other spectators are shown shifting their eyes from the Players to the King, whom Horatio has been watching all along, and commenting among themselves.[12]

Major differences appear in the staging of "The Murder of Gonzago". The area in which the Players act, their props and costumes, stage business, and cuts in the dumb show and their speeches provide great variation in representing the artificiality of the play, just how it is like the murder of the old King, and what provokes Claudius to rise and cry "Give me some light!" (3.2.269). Only Bennet's BBC version gives the Players much of a theatrical set, a painted Italian scene with radical perspective creating a sense of depth. The other troupes make do with little or nothing in the way of scenery. Olivier and Zeffirelli have them act in boxlike areas suggesting proscenium arches with musicians on an upper level. Kline has most of the play on the same floor as the audience, with a little action at the front and side of the platform on which the King and Queen sit.

Bennet's BBC version uses fairly full versions of the dumb show, prologue, and play. Although Gertrude looks a little distressed, Claudius just laughs at the dumb show, a possible answer to the question why the mousetrap does not spring prematurely. Richardson also uses all three parts of the play, but makes the dumb show less like the death of King Hamlet by having the Player King strangled in a Maypole, suggested by Hamlet's "poesy of a ring" (3.2.152). Richardson's garishly acrobatic and erotic dumb show with drum and slide whistle draws some laughter from the King and others, and most explicitly suggests that Gertrude's relationship with Claudius began well before the death of King Hamlet.[13] The treatment is developed from Hamlet's scorn for "inexplicable dumb shows and noise" in his directions to the Players (3.2.12). Zeffirelli introduces another comic note by using Polonius' description of "The best actors in the world" (2.2.396-402) as an introduction of the Players, evoking much on-camera laughter from the spectators. A further humorous touch in Zeffirelli is Polonius' dozing during "Gonzago," illustrating Hamlet's "he's for a jig or a tale of bawdry, or he sleeps" (2.2.500-1). Zeffirelli replaces the dumb show and prologue with music, tumbling, and juggling; this is much laughed at by the audience, including the King and Queen, crosscut with quiet, serious conversation between Hamlet and Ophelia. This Claudius intends to enjoy the show. Olivier uses only the prologue and the dumb show, in that order, which is enough to catch the conscience of the King.[14] Kline cuts both the dumb show and prologue, beginning with the stately entrance of the Player King and Queen. No one in Olivier's or Kline's versions finds anything to laugh at before or during "The Murder of Gonzago".

Hamlet's behavior during the play provides the greatest variation. Bits of costume and gesture implement "I must be idle" as an example of Hamlet's "antic disposition" (3.2.90). Jacobi uses a cloak and a skull mask, foreshadowing Yorick's skull; Kline briefly wraps himself in a red curtain. Mel Gibson earlier borrowed a hat, cloak, and horn from the players as he rode to Elsinore with them. His interactions with Ophelia retain varying amounts of the tension or hostility of the preceding nunnery scene. Olivier is a bit brusque as he leads Ophelia to a chair, sits her down, and embarrasses her with fair thoughts of lying between maid's legs. Zeffirelli's Ophelia is confused and upset by Hamlet's words, some of which are brought in from the nunnery scene (3.1). She applauds the players very weakly, foreshadowing her next appearance as mad (4.5). Jacobi and Kline have Ophelias whose behavior on this public occasion is restrained, uneasy rather than embarrassed. Richardson's sensuous Ophelia doesn't mind Hamlet's putting his head in her lap and kisses him on the cheek to accompany "You are as good as a chorus" (3.2.245).

The extent to which Hamlet observes and otherwise interacts with his uncle and the players varies from little in Olivier to substantial in Bennet's BBC version.

Olivier just sits on the floor and watches, alternating between the players and the King. Three others are more controlled ironists: "It touches us not" (3.2.242). Kline similarly moves from Ophelia to behind the King and Queen to introduce Lucianus. Gibson also moves, standing between the royal thrones for his dialogue with Claudius and Gertrude about the play, mostly a series of two-shots. Part of Williamson's dialogue with Claudius is accompanied by approaching to pour wine for him, recalling his extensive drinking earlier and foreshadowing the poisoned cup of Act 5, Scene 2. Williamson also makes a revealing verbal slip as he introduces "one Lucianus, brother / nephew to the king" (3.2.244). As H.R. Coursen has usefully analyzed the business, Jacobi moves away from the King, entering the Players' space for some of his comments on the play and to give Lucianus some very agitated direction.[15] This Hamlet more obviously identifies himself with the play, which Claudius presumably notices.

The consequence is great variation in the extent to which the King's responds to "The Murder of Gonzago" or to the behavior of Hamlet. In Olivier, Kline, and Zeffirelli the play itself produces what Hamlet will regard as confirmation of the King's guilt. His "Give me some light" (3.2.269) is preceded by a series of shots of the King and reinforced by a wide variety of stage business. Olivier has two head and shoulders shots of the King reacting to the play and a longer shot including Polonius. Olivier laughs as he waves a torch in the King's face, giving him light and precipitating his hasty exit. In addition to showing the King and Queen behind the Players for most of "The Murder of Gonzago", Kline cuts to five two-shots of the rulers, the last of which zooms in to Claudius's face. He drops his glass at "how the murtherer gets the love of Gonzago's wife" (3.2.263-4). Bennet punctuates the performance with eleven two-shots of Claudius and Gertrude, with six head-and-shoulders shots of the King near the end. Zeffirelli builds through nine head-and-shoulders shots of the King, whose face indicates his increasing distress. Alan Bates leaves his chair and moves through the spectators towards the players, followed by Gibson. Bates laughs nervously in an unsuccessful attempt to restore his earlier mood.

Jacobi and Williamson themselves provoke the King, effectively indicating to him that they know the truth of the murder and are therefore more threatening morally and politically, even before the killing of Polonius in Act 3, Scene 4.[16] They provide clearer explanations for Claudius' plan to have Hamlet killed in England. During the play Richardson cuts to eight two-shots of the King and Queen interspersed with four head-and-shoulders shots of the King; these show attention to the play, but little emotional distress on the King's part. The King's conscience is so little engaged that the confession of his rank offense (3.3.36-72) follows the murder of Polonius and the decision to send Hamlet to his death in England (4.3). Richardson illustrates "frighted with false fire?" with a tableau of Claudius and Hamlet facing each other over a torch, with Horatio watching in the background (3.2.266). In a reversal of Olivier, the BBC Claudius asks for "some light" in a very controlled voice, then coolly holds the torch to Hamlet's frighted face.

The Queen and the courtiers generally do not perceive or understand the political situation beyond variously participating in the disorder which accompanies the King's departure. Bennet's exit sequence is the most orderly, following Claudius' apparent calm. Hamlet's occulted feelings are the ones which have unkenneled themselves. In Kline and Richardson there are simply blurs of hurrying figures, more so in Richardson. In Olivier, the entire semicircle of spectators gradually turns from the players to the King. Olivier has groups of panicked characters going in all directions. Ophelia leaves nervously with two women; there are two quick shots of groups of women clutching each other, and a quick shot of a frowning Gertrude, anticipating her "thou hast thy father much offended" (3.4.9). We also notice that the King's chair has been tipped over in the tumult. A small exception is in Zeffirelli's film, where Polonius, Rosenkrantz, and Guildenstern all notice that something ominous is going on before the King rises, although the rest see nothing until Claudius and Hamlet move forward from the rear of the hall.

These five performances reveal great and subtle variety in the presentation of "The Murder of Gonzago", reactions to it, and on-stage and on-camera perceptions of these reactions. While each is filled with tensions, they generally emphasize individual personalities and emotions rather than the social and political consequences of these events. The scene culminates Hamlet's disruption of the court through his "antic disposition", his madness which is partially or wholly "put on" (1.5.172). The text does not state and the camera does not suggest through reaction shots that "Gonzago" or Claudius' response have raised doubts about the King. Consequently he continues to enjoy enough support from Gertrude and the courtiers to cope through Act 4 with the difficulties following from Hamlet's murder of Polonius, including public reaction to Polonius' hugger-mugger burial, Ophelia's madness and suicide, and Laertes' abortive rebellion. Not until the final scene, when Laertes reveals the "foul practice" of the fencing match, does Claudius's rule collapse. "O, yet defend me, friends", he pleads, "I am but hurt" (5.2.324); no one does.

Notes

1. A version of this essay was read at the 1995 Ohio Shakespeare Conference at Ohio University.

2. All quotations are from *The Riverside Shakespeare*, ed. G. Blakemore Evans (2nd edn, Boston: Houghton Mifflin, 1977).

3. Only Olivier's film fully stages this ceremonial entrance, although Richardson uses torches to considerable effect.

4. Michael Shurgot, "'Get you a place': Staging the Mousetrap at the Globe Theatre", *Shakespeare Bulletin*, 12:3 (1994), pp. 5-9.

5. Shurgot, pp. 6, 9.

6. *Hamlet*, dir. Laurence Olivier (Rank / Twin Cities, 1948; Hollywood, CA: Paramount, 1989); dir. Tony Richardson (Woodfall, 1969; Burbank, CA: RCA / Columbia Pictures Home Video, 1988); dir. Franco Zeffirelli (Warner, 1989; Burbank, CA: Warner Home Video, 1990); dir. Rodney Bennet (BBC Shakespeare, 1980; New York: Time / Life Video); dir. Kevin Kline (New York: WNET / PBS, Nov. 2, 1990). This essay was completed before the release of Kenneth Branagh's *Hamlet* (Castle Rock, 1996). Generally the placement of the actors follows Zeffirelli, and the interaction of Hamlet (Branagh) and Claudius (Derek Jacobi) draws much from the BBC production. See Branagh, *Hamlet: Screenplay and Introduction* (New York: Norton, 1996), pp. 86-95.

7. On Kline, not commercially available, see Mary Z. Maher, "Kevin Kline's American *Hamlet*: Stage to Screen", *Shakespeare on Film Newsletter* 15:2 (1991), pp. 11-12, and "At Last, An American Hamlet for Television", *Literature / Film Quarterly*, 20 (1992), pp. 301-7; H.R. Coursen, *Watching Shakespeare on Television* (Rutherford, NJ: Fairleigh Dickinson UP, 1993), pp. 80-92.

8. Anthony Davies, *Filming Shakespeare's Plays: The Adaptations of Laurence Olivier, Orson Welles, Peter Brook, and Akira Kurosawa* (Cambridge UP, 1988), p. 61.

9. Jack J. Jorgens, *Shakespeare on Film* (Bloomington: Indiana UP, 1977), p. 123.

10. Shurgot, p. 9.

11. Shurgot, p. 6.

12. Jorgens, pp. 212-13; Davies, p. 61; Bernice W. Kliman, Hamlet: *Film, Television, and Audio Performance* (Rutherford, NJ: Fairleigh Dickinson UP, 1988), p. 27.

13. Glenn Litton, "Diseased Beauty in Tony Richardson's *Hamlet*", *Literature / Film Quarterly*, 4 (1976), p. 116.

14. Lorne M. Buchman, *Still in Movement: Shakespeare on Screen* (New York: Oxford UP, 1991), p. 101.

15. H.R. Coursen, *Shakespearean Performance as Interpretation* (Newark: Delaware UP, 1991), pp. 103-21.

16. Kliman, pp. 196-7.

HAMLET AND THE JESTER'S SKULL: THE GRAVEYARD SCENE ON FILM

James Rigney
(Roehampton Institute, London)

The relation of film versions of Shakespeare to their theatrical sources is such that for all its potential and realised powers of experimentation film frequently fails to liberate the play in its new medium from the influences that have shaped its theatrical form. This is particularly so in the way in which film conserves features of theatrical performance that have acquired an iconographic function and a cultural significance that determines and disciplines the way they appear on stage. In consequence the relation of Shakespeare on film to the theatre is often that of a medium of commentary rather than one of re-interpretation.

In the following pages I wish to examine the way in which films of *Hamlet* represent a conservative tradition in the interpretation of the play, and to do so by examining the cinematic history of one scene, the graveyard scene corresponding to Act 5 scene 1 of the play text. Initially this paper will examine the stage history of this dramatic moment to establish the cultural circumstances that laid down the style and meaning of this scene, creating an authority to which later cinematic realisations almost inevitably defer.

Neil Taylor, in his study of the film versions of *Hamlet* speaks of a 'pure core' of films and a reflective periphery of cinematic allusions.[1] In what follows I have tried to touch on both the core and the periphery (including in the latter cinematic allusions to the play as a whole and the graveyard scene in particular). Part of the interest of looking at the same scene in different film versions is the opportunity this exercise offers to examine the artistic choices made during the process of envisioning the play on film. The conclusion that the history of this scene reveals is how rarely the choice involved has entailed a departure from the dominant tradition of representation.

Certain scenes or pieces of action in Shakespeare's plays (such as the balcony scene from *Romeo and Juliet*) have acquired a significance and function that is far richer than any function they may serve within the text of a play. By far the richest of such scenes in terms of its range of reference and its cultural after-life is Hamlet's business with the skull of Yorick in Act 5, scene 1 of *Hamlet*. In *Day Dreams* (1922) Buster Keaton plays a dreamy country youth who imagines a romantic future for himself in the city. Among the roles in which he envisages himself is Hamlet, recognisable by the skull held meditatively in his hands. This image of Hamlet holding and addressing the skull of Yorick has come to possess a range of meanings both allusive and ironic; signifying the particular play, the idiom of tragedy, the *persona* of the actor (and particularly of the tragic actor), and all the works of Shakespeare, represented in a shorthand form through this, the most instantly and universally recognisable scene in the most famous of his plays. As Elizabeth Maslen comments, in terms of one particular tradition of reference:

> For nearly two hundred years (since the graveyard scene, cut by Garrick towards the end of his career, was restored to performance), Yorick's function in the popular view of *Hamlet* has been as an object in the prince's hand, the focal point of his melancholy. Hamlet with the skull has been used by a long succession of artists as a visual image central to the play. To mention only a few examples, there was an *Illustrated London News* portrayal of Macready in 1846, head jetting funeral plumes, morosely addressing Horatio over the skull; there was Sandor Jary's sculpture at the turn of the century, where Hamlet leans against a draped tombstone, head bent pensively and privately over the skull; while London Transport's *Theatre London* (1980) has on its front cover Ken Cox's flamboyant variation on the same theme. So the skull in Hamlet's hand has become a symbol of latterday melancholy, visually linked to the skulls of the Romantic Gothick tradition.[2]

From a celebration of one actor in character, to an allusion to Shakespeare's monument in Westminster Abbey and thereby to his role in national culture, to a celebration and advertisement of London theatre the prince and the skull are endlessly adaptable. However, more than mere cultural appropriation is entailed in the history of this allusion. For the image operates not only on the level of adaptable cultural reference, but it dominates critical interpretation of the particular scene and the re-presentation of that scene in different *media* such as the film.

The roots of the potency of this particular image lie in the eighteenth-century theatre. David Garrick's 'revolution' in acting brought a new authority to the actor's art of non-verbal expression; in the process celebrated, specially framed moments that revealed these arts, were cultivated. In his study of the contemporary relation of acting and portraiture Michael Wilson describes these moments:

> Designated variously as 'points', turns, or, by William Hazlitt in the term I shall employ, as 'hits', these pantomime sequences were extended, elaborated and frequently repeated for as long as the notoriously demonstrative audience showed signs of appreciation. Among the reasons the repertory became increasingly stable during the century must be included the growing visual literacy of the theatre's patrons, familiarity with the poetic text enabled their appetite for striking exhibitions of the passions to serve as the primary test of performer's powers of invention.[3]

It is in *Hamlet*, and particularly in the graveyard scene that this process is seen at its most active and where the force of theatrical iconography has been applied to shape performance history and critical interpretation both of the individual scene and of the play as a whole.

We will look in vain for the skull's presence in any edition of Hamlet prior to that of Edward Capell in 1768. Early editions of *Hamlet* do not explicitly call for a skull to be present on the stage: both Quartos and Folios speak only of the gravedigger's spade as the appropriate property. It was Capell who introduced the skull and made Hamlet handle it in an effort to clarify the meaning of Hamlet's words "Let me see." (5.1.179) in this scene.[4] While it is possible that Capell was responding to current theatrical practice by including the direction, it is certain that his decision influenced subsequent performance, and with it the critical history of the scene and the play.

The catalyst for this influence was Sir Thomas Lawrence's portrait of John Philip Kemble in the role of Hamlet, which was exhibited at the Royal Academy in 1801, eighteen years after Kemble had first appeared in the role. Lawrence's portrait highlights the melancholy side of Hamlet's character which Kemble's acting style had emphasised, and locates its essence in the graveyard scene. Hamlet holds Yorick's skull in his left hand while a pick axe lies by his feet and, in the background, the church towers indicate the direction from which Ophelia's cortege will intrude on him. This sombre portrait was an immensely popular image in the nineteenth century, and prints from it continued to be published as late as 1855.[5] This trade helped to establish this particular view of Hamlet in the public mind, and both the pose and the mood it conveyed became an authoritative tradition in theatrical and ancillary interpretation. This image of Hamlet, and its circulation, was as intimately bound up with Kemble's career as with the propagation of Kemble's characterisation. The first print of the painting was produced by Boydell in 1805, two years after Kemble had revived the role of Hamlet to launch his first season as manager and proprietor at Covent Garden.

Kemble's characterization marked a decisive turn in the theatrical and critical history of the graveyard scene. The performance and production conventions of *Hamlet* are a barometer of English theatrical taste. The restoration of the advice to the players in a 1718 acting text of *Hamlet*, for example, reflects the eighteenth century's taste for moral and instructive reflections. At the same time the early eighteenth-century's neo-classical regard for the unities led to the condemnation of the graveyard scene. In 1755, the critic Paul Hiffernan objected to this scene; addressing Eugenius, the man of straw in his critical dialogue he observed:

> You agree, that [...] Water represented is a Fault; and further add, that you have always been offended at the real Skulls and bones in the Grave-digging Scene of *Hamlet*, to which a wooden Substitution might be easily made by a Carpenter, I join with you.[6]

Hamlet and the Jester's Skull

Was such views as these led David Garrick to cut the graveyard scene from his version of the play, a decision which kept the scene off the stage until the beginning of the nineteenth century.

Speaking of the gravedigger's part, John Gielgud wrote: "The part does not seem to amuse an audience very much as a rule, but children love it and roar at the jokes and the business with the skull, which seems rather surprising."[7] And an early nineteenth-century commentator had deemed the scene in performance generally unacceptable:

> The scene between Hamlet, Horatio and the Grave-digger, though it has ever been a stumbling-block to the French critics, is not only a beautiful scene, but one of the most beautiful that came from the pen of genius; of course we speak of it as it is written, not as it is acted, which is in direct opposition to the author's meaning, and rather seems intended for a burlesque than a just representation.[8]

The restoration of the scene at the beginning of the nineteenth century became crucial to the characterization of Hamlet as presented by Kemble: the melancholy prince whose meditation on mortality deflects the vulgar meditations of the comic gravediggers. Edmund Kean's production of *Hamlet*, which opened on March 14, 1814, was offered as a direct challenge to what Kean saw as the passionless style of Kemble. However, the mood established by Kemble in Act 5 scene 1 was fundamentally unaltered as Kean fed a taste prepared by Kemble's image. F.W. Hawkins recorded Kean's performance with the skull:

> [it] comprehended everything that could be wished for, and when he took up the skull he gave the words "Alas! poor Yorick", with a degree of tenderness and feeling which touched every heart. A fine retrospective glance pervaded his utterance as he dwelt upon the association of the relic with the scenes of his early childhood, - the remembrance of innocent pleasures, of transient happiness, vague indeed and undefined, being recalled to memory in a pristine brightness which rendered its contrast with the present gloom - dark, forlorn and dreary.[9]

Finally, Dover Wilson, in *What Happens in Hamlet* (1935) summarised this traditional impression:

> Shakespeare never lets us forget that he [Hamlet] is a failure, or that he failed through weakness of character. And as all failures will, he becomes a sentimentalist in his last phase. He stands by the newly made grave with the skull of Yorick in his hands, and the world, itself ever sentimental, loves to picture him thus.'[10]

As Dover Wilson's remarks reveal, it is the predisposition to "picture him thus" that is crucial to the effective operation of the scene.

The influence of actors and the theatre as subjects for the visual arts has been thoroughly examined.[11] Somewhat less attention has been paid to the extent to which the visual presentation of certain scenes creates a tradition of performance or a type of theatrical expectation that influences the way in which a scene is played during its history.[12] On most encounters with Shakespeare's plays in performance audiences could be said to get what they expect and to expect what they have been led to expect. The visual arts of the eighteenth century were powerful forces in shaping these expectations, and the power of the expectations reached into later centuries, and into later mediums such as the cinema.

An early Italian production of *Hamlet* by the CINES company (1908/1910), though it displays in its early scenes an invigorating freedom in its aproach to the play and its use of the medium, abandons this in the graveyard scene for a studio shot projected against a painted background filmed by a stationary camera. Although the first film record of *Hamlet*, that of Sarah Bernhardt in 1900, reflects her production's emphasis on the resolute and heroic aspects of the prince's character by recording the duel scene, by the time George Méliès produced his ten-minute film of *Hamlet* in 1907 he is preserved holding and contemplating the skull in a posture reminiscent of Kemble, and – as the remarks of Méliès' brother Gaston show – the pose is eloquent of a recognised meaning:

> The melancholy disposition of the young prince is demonstrated to good advantage in the grave-yard scene where the diggers are interrupted in their weird pastime of joshing among the tombstones by the appearance of Hamlet and his friend. After questioning them he picks up one of the skulls about the newly dug grave, and is told that it is the skull of a certain Yorick who was known to Hamlet in his natural life. Hamlet slowly takes

up the skull, and his manner strongly indicates 'Alas poor York [sic], I knew him well.'[13]

The centrality of this scene and this pose is also revealed in an uncatalogued list of Méliès' films in the Museum of Modern Art in which the film is entitled *Hamlet and the Jester's Skull*.

The capacity of this scene to convey the importance of the role and the actor is revealed in Mounet-Sully's (Jean-Sully Mounet's) film of *Hamlet*, made sometime before the First World War. Only one scene survives, and perhaps only one scene was ever shot and this is the graveyard scene. A monumental Mounet-Sully is shot with a gravedigger and Horatio on an outdoor location; an indistinct background of trees and gravestones. Just behind Mounet-Sully are the grave and the gravedigger, a scattering of bones lying in front of the grave and Yorick's broken grave-stone. The latter motif is taken up by Grigori Kozintsev (at once the most masterful of filmmakers and at the same time one of the most pious in his replication of traditional features of this scene) in the choreography of Hamlet's death against a background of one-armed crosses. Though Mounet-Sully, unusually, holds Yorick's skull in both hands, and at the conclusion of the scene he rolls it along the ground, the locational devices of the setting derive from the pictorial tradition outlined above.

Johnston Forbes Robertson's *Hamlet* (1913) is simultaneously a film reproducing a stage play while at the same time seeking to exploit some of the facilities of the film medium and the opportunities of film production. So a wooden Norman church was apparently built in the grounds of Hartsbourne Manor, in Hertfordshire (which, according to the *Bristol Evening News* of June 23, 1913, served as the location for the graveyard scene) to supply a realistic location; yet it is hardly evident, since the camera is static; focussed solely on Forbes Robertson who holds the skull at arm's length above his head, creating an apex from S.A. Cookson as Horatio to Robertson (who points with his right hand towards the skull) while his cloak spreads out darkly in a wing below the skull, down to the grave-digger, in contrasting pale colours, half visible in the earth. What Roberston hoped to achieve here is what G. Wilson Knight described with reference to a similar formal staging of the scene as "...the apex of imaginative intensity."[14]

Forbes Robertson wanted to preserve a fair representation of *Hamlet* as played on stage, a mirror of a great performance, part of the greatness of which derived from its fidelity to a performance tradition. The director of Robertson's film, Cecil Hepworth, wrote that "In filming well-known actors in plays they have become famous in, I have always found it difficult to persuade them of the necessity for slight additions."[15] The difficulty cinema has in separating itself from theatrical sources in the filming of Shakespeare reveals itself nowhere so strongly as in its preservation of moments of theatrical business that have of themselves represented an inaliable force in the performance.

Prior to his 1937 Old Vic production of *Hamlet* Laurence Olivier had visited the Freudian Ernest Jones to discuss the psychological interpretation of Hamlet's character.[16] In the same year that Olivier's film premiered Jones published an edition of *Hamlet*, with psychoanalytical comments, illustrated with drawings by F. Roberts Johnson.[17] One of the most striking of these drawings is that of a naked, endomorphic figure, representing Hamlet, crouched with the skull of Yorick in his hands placed in front of his genitals. The skull with its mouth full of serrated teeth clearly represents the toothed vagina of Freudian nightmare that is explored in Olivier's reading of the play. Olivier's film treatment of the story and his interpretation of Hamlet's character allow him to place the skull scene at the centre of his reading of Hamlet's character just as Kemble had. Olivier's film focuses on Hamlet's mental state, and as a result it cuts many of the public occasions and characters with whom Shakespeare brings Hamlet into contact. Using devices such as voice-over to stress introspection and isolation, Olivier exploits the film's apparent advantage over the stage in delivering psychological information and effects. Almost all the action of Olivier's film was to take place inside the Kafkaesque castle, a dream-like setting for a drama "centred on the shadowy regions of the hero's mind."[18] The graveyard is, therefore, one of the few releases from the expressionist castle, though it is also an embodiment of the unweeded garden to which Hamlet refers (1.2.135)

Where a film chooses to cut a lot of text, as Olivier does, it must compensate with images: it was this imagistic feature of the film medium that Harley Granville Barker attacked as "pictorial indulgence."[19] Olivier's preferred technique for generating meaning is to do so within shots, rather than, for example, through the use of montage: in a famously striking effect Hamlet's shadow advances over the earth of the graveyard until the shadow of his head falls exactly over the shape of the skull lying where it has been thrown onto the ground by the grave-digger. Hamlet remains off-screen until after the line "Whose grave is this?", and the shot is held long enough to make its meaning unambiguous, foreshadowing Hamlet's death and linking the prince with his dead fool. Throughout the film Olivier makes a great deal of use of the shadow effect and its opposition of light and darkness. Thus, for instance, the approach of Horatio and Bernardo and Marcellus is heralded by their shadows falling onto the scene of Hamlet's introspection in Act 1. In Act 5 Scene 1 Hamlet holds the skull against his own cheek, and its shadow darkens the side of his face, on the line, "Make her laugh at that." The skull gives physical form to Hamlet's own pervasive preoccupation with mortality and corruption.

In Kosintzev's film "Gesture leads", according to Jack J. Jorgens, "straight to the heart of character."[20] Innokenti Smoktenovsky recoils from Polonius' blood and gags at the sight and smell of Yorrick's skull. Having sand pour out of Yorick's skull allows it to stand unambiguously as a symbol of decay and passing time (including the time that is passing before Hamlet acts on his obligation to his father's ghost). Kozintsev's production is one which removes most of the humour in the play, cutting, for example, Osric and Polonius. The only clown remaining to throw light on Hamlet's somberness is Yorrick, whose skull still wears its jaunty cap and bells. This device originated in the theatrical practice of Edwin Booth who

"... caused him [the gravedigger] to pause in his labor, to look carefully at one of the skulls, to which had adhered a fragment of soiled leather, - the tattered remnant of a fool's cap, - to pat it in a kindly, jocose way, and to lay it aside..."[21]

Stage properties and their use constitute, as Francis Teague has pointed out in *Shakespeare's Speaking Properties* (1991), a form of visual language, but the meaning conveyed by this language can become proverbial rather than fluent and vital. Drawing a parallel between Act 5, Scene 1 and Act 2, Scene 1, lines 88-92, in which Ophelia recounts a meeting with Hamlet in which :

> He took me by the wrist and held me hard,
> Then goes he to the length of all his arm,
> And with his other hand thus o'er his brow
> He falls to such perusal of my face
> As 'a would draw it.

Kent Cartwright has described this as Hamlet's "signature gesture".[22] Here an actor's gesture, a piece of stagecraft unscripted in the original texts, becomes an essential and defining feature of the play's meaning. Likewise, following the assertion of Tadeuz Kowzan that "Everything is a sign in a theatrical presentation", Teague interprets the various and interrelated meanings of the scene *via* the significance of one property - the skull:

> The skulls' initial function is to remind the audience that the scene's setting is a graveyard. While the skulls begin as place markers they soon take on other functions. When Hamlet first talks of them, they trigger a series of dark jokes about mortality and circumstance. The skull property thus functions to indicate Hamlet's character and his recovery from melancholia - still fascinated by death he is serene enough now to joke about it. It also serves as a focus for his amusing, if conventional remarks. As well as marking place, the skulls illuminate character and situation.[23]

In his paper '*Hamlet* as a *memento-mori* poem' Harry Morris argues that the skull serves as a reminder: it is one of the most important components of the *memento-mori* episode; and all of Hamlet's speculations grow out of it.[24] In this and in Elizabeth Maslen's paper where the skull performs an ironic function, appropriate to its former owner, counterbalancing the ghost as a *memento mori* consolation and enabling Hamlet to finally understand the nature of death, the skull must be physically present, though a long performance and textual history exists in which this was quite likely not the case.[25] Film has helped to preserve this contingent tradition.

Film ought in theory, and often can in practice, extend the meaning and function of imagery thanks to its situation at a shifting point in the relationship between word and image. Jorgens' taxonomy of filmed plays divides them into theatrical, realistic and filmic. Yet this taxonomy simplifies one feature of the process by which Shakespeare's plays are filmed. Cinema engages not merely with the text of the plays but also with the history of their representation. In his study Jorgens speaks of the "eloquent gestures" in which Shakespeare thought; for none of the examples that he gives is there an explicit textual authority: there is, instead, a contingent theatrical authority to which all forms of the play on stage and film do homage.

In 1911 Ernst Lubitsch played the Second Gravedigger in Max Reinhardt's Deutsches Theater production of *Hamlet*. When, thirty-two years later, he directed Jack Benny in the role of Josef Tura in *To Be or Not to Be*, his treatment of the graveyard scene may contain some gentle mocking from the ex-gravedigger to the classical actor Alexander Moissu, who played the prince in Reinhardt's production. The theme of Lubitsch's film is the indestructibility of the actor's ego; it is this power that allows Josef Tura to fulfill his heroic function, aspiring, like Buster Keaton, to the heroic persona represented by the prince with the skull. The graveyard scene, though it may briefly set the actor free, significantly constrains the medium of film when it comes to the treatment of *Hamlet*.

Notes

1. Neil Taylor, "The Films of *Hamlet*" in *Shakespeare and the Moving Image: The Plays on Film and Television*, ed. by Anthony Davies and Stanley Wells (Cambridge UP, 1994), pp. 180-95; p. 180.

2. Elizabeth Maslen, "Yorick's Place in Hamlet" *Essays and Studies*, ns. 36 (1983), pp. 1-13, here p. 1.

3. Michael Wilson "Garrick, iconic acting, and the ideologies of theatrical portraiture", *Word and Image* 6:4 (1990), pp. 368-94; p. 369.

4. References to the text are to William Shakespeare, *The Complete Works*, ed. Stanley Wells and Gary Taylor (Oxford UP, 1988). The editorial implications of this scene have been examined by Bryan Loughrey in "Editorial Skullduggery" Society for Textual Scholarship New York, April 1995.

5. See Geoffrey Ashton, *A Catalogue of Paintings at the Theatre Museum London*, ed. James Fowler (London: Victoria and Albert Museum, 1992), pp. 26-7.

6. Cited in Arthur Colby Sprague, *Shakespeare and the Actors: The Stage Business in his Plays, 1660-1905* (Cambridge, MA: Harvard UP, 1945), p. 173.

7. Rosamond Gilder, *John Gielgud's Hamlet: A Record of Performance by Rosamond Gilder, with the Hamlet Tradition: Some Notes on Costume, Scenery and Stage Business by John Gielgud* (London: Methuen, 1937), p. 164.

8. W.H. Oxberry, ed., *The New English Drama* (London, 1818), quoted in Yvonne Warburton, *The Stage-History of Hamlet, in Relation to the History of the Plays Criticism, from 1660 to 1830* (B.Litt. thesis, Oxford University, 1976), p. 144.

9. F.W. Hawkins, *The Life of Edmund Kean* 2 vols. (London, 1869), Vol. I, pp. 188-9.

10. J. Dover Wilson, *What Happens in Hamlet* (Cambridge UP, 1935), p. 263.

11. W. Moelwyn Merchant's *Shakespeare and the Artist* (Oxford: Merchant, 1959) remains a valuable work despite its age, as does T.S.R. Boase's "Illustrations of Shakespeare's plays in the seventeenth and eighteenth centuries" *Journal of the Warburg and Courtauld Institutes*, 10 (1947), pp. 83-98; likewise Geoffrey Ashton's *Shakespeare and British Art* (New Haven: Yale, 1981) has an importance beyond its scope as an exhibition catalogue. Michael Fried's *Absorption and Theatricality: Painting and the Beholder in the Age of Diderot* (Berkeley and London: California UP, 1980) situates the relation of theatre and the visual arts at the time within a broad cultural setting. Shearer West's *The Image of the Actor: Verbal and Visual Representation in the Age of Garrick and Kemble* (London: Pinter, 1991) reveals the changing function of the theatrical portrait and its manipulation as a commercial and allegorical product, questioning in the process the evidential uses to which portraits have been put by theatre historians.

12. An exception to this neglect is provided by three stimulating papers by Alan Hughes in the 1987 volume of *Theatre Notebook*: "Art and eighteenth-century acting styles, part I: aesthetics" *Theatre Notebook* 41:1 (1987), pp. 24-31; "Part II: attitudes" 41:2 (1987), pp. 79-89, and "Part III: passions" 41:3 (1987), pp. 128-39.

13. Quoted in Robert Ball, *Shakespeare on Silent Film. A Strange Eventful History* London: Allen and Unwin, 1968, p. 34.

14. G. Wilson Knight, *Principles of Shakespearean Production* (London: Faber, 1936), p. 170.

15. Ball, p. 190.

16. See Murray Biggs, "'He's going to his Mother's Closet': Hamlet and Gertrude on Screen" *Shakespeare Survey*, 45 (1993), pp. 54-7.

17. *Hamlet, by William Shakespeare with a Psychoanalytic Study by Ernest Jones Drawings by F. Roberts Johnson* (London: Vision, 1947).

18. Roger Furse, "Designing the Film *Hamlet*" in *Hamlet: the Film and the Play*, ed. Alan Dent (London: World Film Publications, 1948), unpaged.

19. Harley Granville Barker, "Alas Poor Will" *Listener*, 3.3.1936, pp. 448-50; p. 448.

Hamlet and the Jester's Skull

20. Jack J. Jorgens, *Shakespeare on Film* (Bloomington and London: Indiana UP, 1977), p. 220.

21. William Winter, *Shakespeare on the Stage* (New York: Moffat, Yard and Co., 1911), p. 347.

22. Kent Cartwright, *Shakespearean Tragedy and its Double. The Rhythm of Audience Response* (University Park: Pennsylvania UP, 1991).

23. *ibid.*

24. Harry Morris, "Hamlet as memento-mori Poem", *PMLA* 85 (1970), pp. 1035-1100.

25. Maslen, *op. cit.*

HAMLET AND THE KISS

John Ottenhoff
(Alma College, Michigan)

> Apparently for the sake of interest, stories often ignore, in a way films do not, the fact that the kiss itself is a story in miniature, a subplot.[1]

Shakespeare uses the word only a few times in *Hamlet*, yet 'the kiss' has been an important indexical symbol in the many film versions of the play. The kiss in *Hamlet* is indeed a story in itself, just as the kiss can be a "revealing sequence containing a personal history", or "the publicly acceptable representation of private sexual life, a performed allusion to it", or "a threat and a promise, the signature as cliché of the erotic".[2] In studying the kiss, we can discern the distinctive choices available to the cinematic interpreter of *Hamlet*, particularly as they relate to gender construction and interaction.

Hamlet uses the word 'kiss' or a variation thereof four times in the play. Most importantly, he warns Gertrude against Claudius's "reechy kisses" (3.4.184) in the 'closet scene'.[3] Later, in reflecting on Yorick, he recalls "those lips that I have kissed I know not how oft" (5.1.188). Hamlet also anticly says to Polonius, "For if the sun breed maggots in a dead dog, being a good kissing carrion ..." (2.2.181) in the 'fishmonger' scene and idealistically refers to his father as "a station like the herald Mercury / New lighted on a heaven-kissing hill" (3.4.58-9) in the closet scene. Two other uses of the word occur in the play-within-the-play, as the player king kisses his crown and as the player queen protests "A second time I kill my husband dead, / When second husband kisses me in bed" (3.2.184-85). Shakespeare's text, then, does not itself produce a lot of kissing, and on this very slight textual authority film directors have hung rather significant interpretive gestures. Except for the play scenes, none of the uses of 'kiss' calls for the actions we see in films.

In speaking of the kiss as an 'index', I draw upon the semiotic frameworks of C. S. Peirce and Peter Wollen. In their terms, an index occupies a middle ground between icons and symbols. With icons, "The relationship between signifier and signified is not arbitrary but is one of resemblance or likeness".[4] An index, on the other hand, "is a sign by virtue of an existential bond between itself and its object"; and Peirce offers examples such as a man with a rolling gait indicating that he's a sailor or a weathercock indicating wind direction.[5] A symbol, on the other hand, is "an arbitrary sign in which the signifier has neither a direct or an indexical relationship to the signified, but rather represents it through convention".[6] Thus, for Wollen and Peirce, a cinematic index lies "halfway between the cinematic Icon and the literary Symbol, in which cinema can convey meaning. It is not an arbitrary sign, but neither is it identical. It suggests a third type of denotation that points directly toward connotation".[7]

As Monaco suggests, the index is "most intriguing", for it allows for great flexibility and expressiveness. "It is here that film discovers its own, unique metaphorical power, which it owes to the flexibility of the frame, its ability to say many things at once".[8] In speaking of the kiss as a cinematic index, we open up a wide range of cinema history and symbology and raise interesting psychoanalytic questions, most of which cannot be addressed in this essay. But, again drawing on Phillips, we might note how film both records and sets conventions for kissing:

> ... ostentatious kisses are usually represented in the most popular and once intellectually disparaged genres, romantic novels and films. And although there are clearly conventions in literature and life governing the giving and getting of kisses, it is really only from films that we can learn what the contemporary conventions might be for kissing itself.[9]

Kissing in *Hamlet*, then, can be seen not only as indexical commentary on Shakespeare's play but as participating in a long intertextual cinematic conversation about the conventions and images of kissing extending from Edison's 1896 kinetoscope loop *The Kiss* through Andy Warhol's *Kiss* (1964) and countless Hollywood romances – and through the performance history of the play. Further, for Freud, kissing "links us to our earliest relationship with ourselves and other people"; the kiss, "blurring the boundary between the normal and the perverse is – perhaps for that same reason – the publicly acceptable representation of private sexual life, a performed allusion to it. [...] Kissing is indeed a 'softened hint' at the sexual act".[10] Representing kissing in *Hamlet* films, then, is one means by which directors might exploit various psychoanalytic readings of the play and can convey symbolic interpretations with economy and power. Cinematic kissing can both be about kissing – lips meeting lips – but also about power, sexuality, and the self.

The cinematic kiss is an extraordinarily complex index and cannot be easily reduced to a single meaning. How, then, might we develop a grammar of kissing in *Hamlet* films? One approach might be to analyze the various 'stories' told by the variety of kisses in five of the most significant cinematic versions of the play: Laurence Olivier's 1948 "oedipal" version, Tony Richardson's 1969 performance with Nicol Williamson as Hamlet, Rodney Bennett's 1979 BBC production with Derek Jacobi as Hamlet, Franco Zeffirelli's 1991 version starring Mel Gibson, and Kenneth Branagh's 1996 "full-text" version.[11] The range of interpretation is indeed strikingly varied and the stories of kissing give us a surprisingly economical means of differentiating the films.

THE OEDIPAL KISS

The most famous Hamlet kiss, of course, belongs to Olivier's "oedipal" film version of the play. Neither Olivier nor Alan Dent discuss the issue in their introductions to the film script, but the kiss carries much of the weight – along with obvious tunnels, protruding cannons, and a labia-like bed – for Ernest Lloyd Jones's Freudian reading.

More-than-motherly kisses occur on more than one occasion, and these kisses index different meanings. First, in 1.2, Eileen Herlie as Gertrude delivers her "good Hamlet" speech (1.2.68-73) standing behind Hamlet, hands on his shoulders; he looks up and back to her with "Seems, madam!" (1.2.76). She bends over him, hands under his chin. As Claudius (Basil Sydney) begins his "Tis sweet and commendable in your nature" speech (1.2.87), she backs off but remains with her son, then moves to the front of the seated Hamlet and places her hands on his chin for "Let not thy mother" (1.2.118). As he assures her "I shall in all my best obey you madam" (1.2.120), she bends to kiss him farewell – and does so for nearly four seconds of screen time. The kiss is halted only when Claudius, having already praised Hamlet for his "loving and a fair reply", rather obviously interrupts this unseemly kiss with "Madam, come" (1.2.122). This kiss seems clearly to enact Jones's questionable judgment about the queen's "markedly sensual nature and her passionate fondness for her son". The former, says Jones, is "indicated in too many places in the play to need specific reference, and is generally recognized. The latter is also manifest".[12] She is a seductive mother, "willing to use a passionate, lover's kiss as part of her plea that Hamlet remain in Elsinore".[13]

The second kiss occurs in 3.4, in the 'closet' scene. Olivier's Hamlet has been rough with his mother, throwing her on the bed – the very prominent and suggestive bed. After the ghost has appeared to Hamlet, he embraces Gertrude and kisses her on the forehead; she kisses him on the cheek, then on the lips as he tells her he must be "cruel only to be kind". They embrace, he puts his head on her breast, then on her lap. As he leaves her, they engage in another three-second kiss on the lips.[14] Olivier uses "a romantic, circling movement of the camera in keeping with a cinematic convention reserved for lovers".[15] Here again, Gertrude is shown as the erotic mother, but "we also see how closely intertwined are the violence expected of Hamlet and the desire for his mother from which he cannot dissociate that violence. For him, to approach his revenge is also somehow to approach his mother's bed".[16]

Olivier's mother and son kiss again briefly at the dueling scene – twice on the cheeks at the beginning of the scene. He kisses her on the cheek after she wipes his face – after she has knowingly drunk the poisoned wine, a sort of sacrifice for her beloved son. As Roger Manvell describes it, Hamlet and Gertrude share "a somewhat enigmatic relationship", made more so in that Eileen Herlie "appears rather to be Hamlet's sister than a woman a generation older".[17] As Peter Donaldson has shown, Olivier's use of Jones's and Freud's readings is complex, "informed by autobiographical pressures" and not wholly conforming to orthodox Freudian interpretations.[18] As an index, the 'oedipal kiss' in Olivier's film speaks obviously to the Jones thesis, to the manifest love of son for mother and mother for son. Yet, as Donaldson suggests, that thesis is somewhat muddled and "self-canceling", "offering an undeniably Freudian reading while proclaiming that 'this is the tragedy of a man who could not make up his mind'".[19]

Every film director since Olivier has had to wrestle with the impact of 'the kiss'. Few have followed him as explicitly as Franco Zeffirelli. He, however, moves the 'court' scene kiss to a private setting, presumably Hamlet's room. It follows an intimate interview between Mel Gibson's Hamlet and Glenn Close's Gertrude, during which she lays her hands, then her head on him; she hugs him, caresses him; he kneels before her, head at her waist. She kisses him three times – on his forehead, eyes, lips – and is interrupted by a hunting horn from outside; she kisses him once more on the lips and departs. Like Olivier, Zeffirelli pairs a very youthful looking actress with his Hamlet, accentuating the erotic elements of the kiss and perpetuating the Oedipal dimensions. Here, too, Gertrude seems the 'sensualist' Jones and others have described, yet her golden-white braids bespeak a girlish innocence.

Zeffirelli also follows Olivier (and Jones) in staging the 'closet' scene in Gertrude's bedroom. Gibson's Hamlet is rougher and more physical than Olivier's; paralleling Derek Jacobi's actions in the Bennett film, he throws Gertrude on the bed and jumps on top of her. As Hamlet rants and rails about "a king of shreds and patches" (3.4.102), Gertrude interrupts Hamlet with an extraordinarily passionate and lengthy kiss, six seconds in duration, as a means of stopping his words. The kiss seems to be interrupted, to be halted, only by the appearance of the ghost – paralleling Claudius's husbandly intrusion in the Olivier filming of the court scene. They embrace again after the ghost recedes, Hamlet kisses her on the head; Glenn Close's Gertrude looks sultry – her hair down – and submissive before her dominating son. This affectionate son and mother also share a romantic kiss on the lips again at the end of 4.3, as he's off to England, and another brief kiss in the duel scene in 5.2. While Zeffirelli's *Hamlet* lacks the overt physical signs and the underlying philosophical grounding of Olivier's oedipal version, the kisses between Hamlet and Gertrude do much to index that interpretation. By and large, the very physical Mel Gibson, a Hamlet who shows little irresolution and constant awareness of his political place, belies the connotations of this index. If, as Jones suggests, the oedipal interference keeps him from acting on his need to kill, Gibson is not a convincing sufferer. Zeffirelli, one could argue, pursued the Olivier line more for its box-office appeal than to make good intellectual sense of the text or to clarify Olivier's explorations.

Quite strikingly, Kenneth Branagh has thoroughly avoided this index of Hamlet's longing for his mother. While he too shows his Hamlet and Gertrude (played by Julie Christie) in a bedroom in 3.4, and mother and son embrace at the end of the scene, they never kiss, and Branagh has gone to some lengths to avoid the suggestions Olivier works so hard to develop. At the end of the closet scene, he describes them in the screenplay as sitting side by side, "like two lost children".[20] Branagh's choices most resemble those enacted by Nicol Williamson in Tony Richardson's 1969 and Derek Jacobi in the Bennett BBC version. Both of these Hamlets set a tone of coldness between mother and son, eschewing all kissing and hugging. While Jacobi depicts a nearly violent physical interaction in 3.4, showing some of the connections between sex and violence in Olivier's film, the focus seems to be on Hamlet's disgust with his mother's sexuality. Indeed, the appalling image Hamlet produces of King Claudius's "reechy kisses" and "paddling in [the] neck with his damn'd finger" seem to control the interaction of these three Hamlets regarding this index.

THE COURTLY KISS

Virtually all film versions depict intimacy between the newly married Claudius and Gertrude, and all play up in one way or another the unseemly nature of this 'incestuous' marriage, or the "increase of appetite [...] grown / [...] within a month" (1.2.144-5). In this sense, the kisses of Claudius and Gertrude can index several connotations, ranging from the innocent love of newlyweds to the corrupted lust of co-conspirators in old Hamlet's murder.

Richardson's Claudius and Gertrude, played by Anthony Hopkins and Judy Parfitt, most clearly index with their kisses the corruption of this royal couple. This court is "a barbaric community steeped in alcohol",[21] symbolized by the royal bed, a "nasty sty" in which "overweight Claudius and pallid Gertrude drink blood-red wine and feast with their dogs on greasy chicken and fruit".[22] Richardson announces this interpretation from the start of the 'council' scene, as Hopkins and Parfitt kiss ostentatiously, passionately, for three seconds as they hold forth in front of the assembled throng. The camera lingers in close-up on their kiss (indeed, the camera lingers in close-ups throughout the film), accentuating Claudius's prominent earring, his elaborate crown, and his rough, ruddy manner. The royal kiss is surrounded by much laughter, drinking, and loud talk. They have no shame or modesty about their 'incestuous' marriage.

Richardson makes the same point about royal corruption even more forcefully with a second 'courtly' kiss. In a novel interpretation, Richardson stages the king and queen's initial reception of Rosencrantz and Guildenstern (2.2.1-57) in the royal bedroom. The "nasty sty", as Jorgens describes it, indicates corruption, excess, hedonism. And quite pointedly, this royal kiss comes as Gertrude admits that the cause of Hamlet's "distemper" is "no other but the main, / His father's death and our o'erhasty marriage" (2.2.56-57). This five-second kiss – an embarrassingly long and public smooch – indexes Gertrude as complicit in Claudius's crimes and cynically indifferent to Hamlet's pain. The kiss ends only as the officious Polonius (Mark Dignam) clears his throat, reminding them of continuing official business and public observers.

Zeffirelli's Claudius (Alan Bates) and Gertrude are also lusty and sexy, displaying an intimate, affectionate sexuality. They share a public, four-second kiss in the opening 'court' scene, although Zeffirelli has chopped up the scene and cut most of its public nature. They kiss again, more passionately, after Gertrude leaves Hamlet following the "I pray thee stay" speech (1.2.119); as Hamlet watches from an upper window, Gertrude reaches up to Claudius on his horse and gives him a big kiss – in perfect synchronization with Hamlet's soliloquized words, "So excellent a king, that was to this /Hyperion to a satyr" (1.2.139-40). The effect is not as devastatingly critical as the Richardson "sty" scene, but Zeffirelli rather obviously – and heavy-handedly – indexes Hamlet's view of "reechy kisses" and courtly corruption. Both Richardson and Zeffirelli use other incidental royal kisses – at dinner, at the play – to show the queen's intimacy with her second, "satyr" husband. And both use the increasingly rare indexes of intimacy after the 'closet' scene to suggest that Gertrude has put away the "worser part" (3.4.157) of her heart and turned from Claudius.

Branagh, as is generally true of his film, navigates a moderate course in depicting the royal couple. Claudius and Gertrude, played with great strength by Derek Jacobi and Julie Christie, are shown as an "irresistibly sexy, confident couple",[23] and their kissing is presented as rather innocent. In kissing before the massed audience in the 'court' scene following Hamlet's "I shall in all my best obey you madam" (1.2.120), they are "happily letting the Court share their obvious intoxication with each other".[24] Similarly, at the play scene, Claudius and Gertrude happily kiss, but "then feign embarrassment at being 'caught out', but the moment is delicious for all".[25] While Branagh presents a court full of corruption and a Claudius as mean and ruthless as any depicted on screen, he chooses to index these features through means other than the kiss. Similarly, Olivier does not lean heavily on this index of courtly corruption; rather, he shows Claudius in the opening court scene enjoying his wine, then kissing Gertrude forcefully several times. The aged Basil Sydney and youthful Eileen Herlie are hardly the "sexy" couple Branagh depicts. Bennett's Claudius (Patrick Stewart) and Gertrude (Claire Bloom) are even more neutral in the depiction of sexuality.

THE INCESTUOUS KISS: LAERTES AND OPHELIA

Several film directors have seemed preoccupied with the relationship between Laertes and Ophelia. One might argue that the text encourages such preoccupation with Laertes's words of caution for his sister and his extraordinary display at her funeral. Yet several directors have gone far beyond those hints, using the kiss as a suggestive, yet finally ill-defined, index. Richardson goes the farthest down this road. His Ophelia and Laertes share an extremely long, seemingly passionate kiss – four seconds in duration – at the opening of their scene in 1.3. Marianne Faithfull, clad in a low-cut dress, portrays an alluring Ophelia as she leans back on a pillow while Laertes (Michael Pennington) speaks his brotherly warning. She laughs as he speaks, and brother and sister lie cheek to cheek. They begin another serious kiss when interrupted by Polonius. They share a more chaste kiss – one more appropriate under the watchful gaze of their father – as they depart after hearing Polonius's fatherly wisdom. Richardson does little to follow up on this scene, merely using it to show "how the disease of incest has spread outward in the court from the King and Queen".[26] And, indeed, the moment is both jarring and a visual foretaste of the 'sty' kiss and Polonius's interruption of that unseemly display.[27]

Branagh cautiously suggests a similar interpretation; in 1.3, Laertes and Ophelia walk with arms around each other. According to Branagh's screenplay, "they are very, some might say unnaturally, close",[28] but the script does little more than call for some brief kisses between them, and the lack of accompanying courtly corruption reduces the connotations that we noted in Richardson's film. Similarly, Bennett's BBC version of Ophelia and Laertes shows them kissing at the end of 1.3 – on the lips and perhaps too passionately. Bennett, however, follows up by strikingly showing Ophelia (Lalla Ward) in the mad scene greeting Laertes (David Robb) with a passionate, unsisterly kiss – an index here of her madness and a clearly unnerving gesture for Laertes; the scene parallels and intensifies a similar kiss from 'mad' Ophelia in Olivier's film.

Olivier and Zeffirelli seem least interested in this relationship, in part, perhaps, because both have cast extremely young-looking, asexual Ophelias. In Olivier's film, the brother and sister kiss chastely several times in 1.3, but more oddly, as Polonius gives his famous fatherly advice to Laertes, Ophelia embraces her brother from behind, reaching around to a pouch hanging in front, below his belt. The gesture could be seen as sexual, but Manvell describes this as indicating her "child-like behavior" and "extreme youth".[29] Zeffirelli alone suggests some tensions between brother and sister, and their kisses, although briefly on the lips and with the same relative positioning as Gertrude and Claudius's passionate kiss in the prior scene – he on horseback, she standing below – are hardly indexes of spreading incest.

THE LOVERS' KISS

One of the most striking of Branagh's cinematic innovations with his Hamlet is to show him as Ophelia's lover. Through a series of flashbacks, through both Ophelia's and Hamlet's points of view, Branagh establishes a sexual relationship, presumably originating after the death of old Hamlet. Alone of the *Hamlet* films we are considering, Branagh's films shows the couple naked and in the embrace of love. "We want this relationship to be as serious as possible", asserts Russell Jackson in his "Film Diary" in justifying the scenes.[30] These scenes of love-making establish a seriousness that radiates in several directions: this Hamlet (Branagh) is 'normal', afflicted with no unnatural longings for his mother, and his love interest, Ophelia (Kate Winslet), is attractive, mature, and only moderately infected by the corruption of Elsinore. And the cinematic conventions of romance help to further Branagh's overall ambition to reach a wide audience, signaled by other choices such as the use of American movie stars like Robin Williams, Jack Lemon, and Billy Crystal.

Branagh's depiction of Hamlet and Ophelia as lovers has no precedent in the recent *Hamlet* films. Richardson's 1969 version presents some tender kisses between the two in the 'nunnery' scene, but Nicol Williamson's stuffy Hamlet produces little passion and the little that emerges quickly gives way to anger. Olivier's Hamlet is very circumspect with Ophelia. In the nunnery scene, she tries to embrace him, but he angrily throws her to the floor. After throwing her down a second time on a stairway – as he begins his run up to the tower where he will deliver his interpolated "To be" speech – Olivier's Hamlet briefly bends over her and kisses her gently on a lock of her blonde hair, muttering "to a nunnery". Jean Simmons' doll-like Ophelia combines with Olivier's mother-fixated Hamlet to suggest a relationship that is asexual and chilly. Mel Gibson's Hamlet is even colder – there is no kiss, no suggestion of love making, no embrace. But at the play scene, he plants four kisses on Ophelia as he recites the interpolated "get thee to a nunnery" lines; Gibson's Hamlet seems in antic disposition. Similarly, Jacobi's Hamlet strikes a chilly tone with Ophelia throughout most of the film. Both Gibson and Jacobi seem to believe that Hamlet's forcefulness, even his madness, would be compromised by the depiction of a romantic relationship with Ophelia.

The use – and avoidance – of the 'lovers' kiss' in *Hamlet* indexes a host of issues for the director: Hamlet's 'manliness', his resolution, his attraction for his mother, his madness. The 'lovers' kiss', as depicted most forcefully by Branagh, works at cross purposes with the 'incestuous kiss' and the 'oedipal kiss', or, more positively, establishes this Hamlet's and Ophelia's heterosexual vitality and independence from the corruption at Elsinore. Richardson, as we have seen, offers strong readings of the 'courtly' and 'incestuous' kisses, while largely keeping Hamlet out of the kissing action, and other directors have chosen different combinations. While I have considered each of the kissing modes separately, they are obviously connected. Similarly, although I have considered only the most obvious exhibitions of the kiss, other modes of affection and interaction work to form larger symbolic meanings.

Kisses, as we have seen, can work quite effectively to bolster strong and various interpretive claims, but the kiss is only and always part of a complex network of symbols and images, icons and indexes, nuances and connotations. Sometimes, of course, a kiss is just a kiss – in life and in the cinema. But that is a different sort of story and one that Hamlets on film rarely realize.

Notes

1. Adam Phillips, *On Kissing, Tickling, and Being Bored* (Cambridge, MA: Harvard UP, 1993), p. 96.
2. Phillips, pp. 96-100.
3. All references to the play are from *The Riverside Shakespeare*, ed. G. Blakemore Evans, (Boston: Houghton Mifflin, 1974).
4. Peter Wollen, *Signs and Meaning in the Cinema* (Bloomington: Indiana UP, 1969), p. 122.
5. Wollen, p. 120.
6. James Monaco, *How to Read a Film* (New York: Oxford UP, 1981), p. 133.
7. Monaco, pp. 133-4.
8. Monaco, p. 134.
9. Phillips, p. 95.
10. Phillips, p. 97.

Hamlet and the Kiss

11. Laurence Olivier, dir., *Hamlet* (1948; video: Princeton, NJ : Films for the Humanities, 1986); Tony Richardson, dir., *Hamlet* (1969; video: Burbank, CA: RCA/Columbia Pictures Home Video, 1988); Rodney Bennett, dir., *Hamlet* (1979; video: New York: Time-Life Video, 1979); Franco Zeffirelli, dir., *Hamlet* (1990; video: Burbank, CA: Warner Home Video, 1991); Kenneth Branagh, dir., *Hamlet* (Castle Rock Entertainment, 1996).

12. Ernest Jones, "The Problem of Hamlet and the Oedipus-Complex", in Shakespeare, *Hamlet*, (London: Vision Press, 1947), pp. 22-3.

13. Peter Donaldson, *Shakespearean Films / Shakespearean Directors* (Boston: Unwin Hyman, 1990), p. 48.

14. Interestingly, Olivier's film text of the play omits 3.4.184-5: "And let him, for a pair of reechy kisses, / Or paddling in your neck with his damn'd finger...." Olivier does not indicate the lines as a conscious cut (as he signals other cuts) and seems to lack textual authority for the omission. However, Hamlet's concern for soiled, unseemly kissing between the king and queen would seem to conflict with Olivier's creation of such kissing between mother and son.

15. Donaldson, p. 49.

16. Ibid.

17. Roger Manvell, *Shakespeare and the Film* (London: A.S. Barnes, 1971), p. 44.

18. Donaldson, p. 34.

19. Donaldson, p. 38.

20. Kenneth Branagh, *'Hamlet': Screenplay, Introduction and Film Diary* (New York: Norton, 1996), p. 112.

21. Manvell, p. 129.

22. Jack Jorgens, *Shakespeare on Film* (Bloomington: Indiana UP, 1977), p. 27.

23. Branagh, p. 11.

24. Branagh, p. 16.

25. Branagh, p. 86.

26. Jorgens, p. 21-2.

27. In *The Masks of 'Hamlet'* (Newark: Delaware UP, 1992), p. 267, Marvin Rosenberg argues that "An incestuous drive doesn't seem to fit Laertes. He is speaking for a puritanical double standard. [...] However much he might be felt to be sexually attracted to his sister, all he says, including his heartfelt grief for her in her mad scene, proclaims his conscious care for her innocence and virginity."

28. Branagh, p. 23.

29. Manvell, p. 43.

30. Branagh, p. 177.

'REMEMBER ME':
THE GAUMONT-HEPWORTH *HAMLET* (1913)

Emma Smith
(All Souls College, Oxford)

As the first feature-length film of *Hamlet*, the Gaumont-Hepworth production of 1913 starring Johnston Forbes-Robertson can claim a certain originary status in the history of the play on film. Its prototypical position in the history of Shakespearean film itself has been argued. In his book on filmed Shakespeare in the silent era, Robert Hamilton Ball suggests that "if silent film could not encompass Shakespeare, Forbes-Robertson's *Hamlet* reaches toward a fuller recognition of the possibility".[1] As a film repeatedly described as the record of a stage production, however, this *Hamlet* instances many of the difficulties of the relationship between cinema and theatre which have continued to dominate discussion of Shakespeare films. The following analysis of the film and its reception suggests that contemporary unease about its status can offer a fruitful commentary on the play itself. Both film and play will be seen to be concerned with the cognate ideas of representation as repetition and memorial, and as absence and presence.

In employing a recently-knighted Edwardian actor-manager and the entire cast of a long-running stage production, the film emphasised its theatrical associations. This can be seen as a strategy to import the cultural lustre of traditional theatre into the fledgling and largely disprized medium of cinema, associated in its first decades with end-of-pier peep shows and down-market spectacle for the masses. As Harry Furniss wrote in his mock-heroic apologia for the medium, *Our Lady Cinema* (1914), "it is the fashion among a certain society set to sneer at cinematograph theatres as something entirely derogatory and *infra dig*".[2] Drawing on the unimpeachable reputation of contemporary Shakespearean theatre, the cinema attempted to clean up its act and to appeal to a wider audience and appease an increasingly censorious regulatory system. There was a higher concentration of Shakespearean films in the years before 1914 than at any other time in the history of cinema. As such, the efforts of two American companies, the Thanhouser Film Company and the Vitagraph Company of America, which between them produced more than a dozen fifteen- to thirty-minute films of Shakespeare plays in the period 1908-1916, was the production companies' equivalent of the exhibitors' expenditure on upgrading cinemas to make them more elegant. From about 1908, the refurbishment and redecoration of many cinemas was intended to attract better-class audiences. Rachel Low describes how "red plush and marble, ferns in brass pots, and plenty of electric light were guaranteed to give that air of cosy refinement which was wistfully sought by a trade anxious to disclaim its low birth"[3].

Hamlet opened in a West End cinema which exemplified this process of gentrification. The New Gallery Kinema had opened only months earlier, in January 1913, on the site of an old private art gallery in fashionable Regent's Street. Designed by Frank Verity, an experienced theatre architect, it seated 800 - on the large side of West End cinema capacities in its time.[4] It was clearly a venue with aspirations. A fulsome description of its attractions in the January 1913 edition of *The Cinema* praised its tasteful decor, including "thick pile carpet of apple green", "comfortable, roomy armchairs", "dainty allegorical frescoes", with temperature regulated to "the ideal 68 deg. - which sanitary science enjoins". The cinema boasted the facilities to function as "a sort of West-End club", with a restaurant and a programme of scientific lectures accompanied by animated pictures. Its opening, the magazine concludes, "will mark a new epoch in the history of cinematography in its highest artistic flight".[5] Patrons in the New Gallery's early months had already had a chance to see such educational adventure films as *Big Game Hunting in the North Ice Polefields*, a record of a Carnegie Museum expedition to Alaska and Siberia, and Edward Bulwer Lytton's *The Last Days of Pompeii*. It was an obvious venue for the opening of the prestige Gaumont-Hepworth *Hamlet*.

In borrowing style and material from respected theatre traditions the cinema was not only the poor relative of its longer-established dramatic counterpart. The idea that the rapid increase in the number of cinemas posed an actual threat to the survival of theatre was frequently raised. In April 1913 *The Times* reported on a lecture given by Dr William Martin at King's College, under the joint auspices of the Shakespeare Reading Society and the London Shakespeare League, at which the noted Shakespearean scholar Sir Sidney Lee presided. In his lecture "The Cinema in its Relation to the Drama", Martin referred to "fears [which] might exist regarding cinematography's becoming a serious competitor of the playhouse" but argued that "in the main, it was complementary, having a sphere of its own". Lee added that "all had watched this enormous growth, this eruption of picture palaces that now covered the earth - he would not say encumbered it (laughter)", judging that "their omnipresence justified consideration of the theme dealt with by Dr Martin".[6] Johnston Forbes-Robertson was asked for his views in an interview with *The World* magazine in May 1913:

> Touching on the various forms of competition with which the theatre is nowadays threatened, Mr Forbes-Robertson declares his adhesion to a policy of unrestricted free trade in amusements. Neither variety theatres, nor picture palaces, nor any other form of rivalry can ever avail, in his opinion, to thrust the drama, worthily presented, into subordinate place.[7]

A prologue to *Masks and Faces* (1917), a film made to make money for the flagging finances of the Royal Academy of Dramatic Arts (RADA), shows early twentieth-century theatre grandees, including George Bernard Shaw and Johnston Forbes-Robertson, discussing the relation of the theatre to the cinema. J. M. Barrie's proposal that an "All-Star Film" could be the answer to RADA's difficulties is eagerly taken up by Arthur Pinero, who deems it "a most excellent suggestion" as "the 'Pictures' owe much to the stage. It shall repay". John Hare takes up the theme, arguing that "there should be no caste-prejudice. The film is the sister to the stage". Such a film would, adds Sir George Alexander, "be a worthy memory of the stage today".[8] In choosing to make a film to raise money for the theatre arts, the Council of the academy implicitly recognised the profitability and popularity of the cinema over the theatre, whilst simultaneously asserting that the two media are equal sisters. Furniss went so far as to reverse the conventional relationship, arguing that "in truth a theatrical play is nothing more nor less than a moving picture on the stage" and that the only person

The Gaumont-Hepworth *Hamlet* 113

really qualified to adjudicate between them would be someone "stone deaf". "I have no doubt whatsoever", Furniss added mischievously, "that the verdict would be in favour of the cinema show".[9] Given the close relationship of British Shakespeare films of the period to the theatre - all were adaptations of existing stage productions using their costumes, decor and stage directions with little alteration - Susan Sontag's question "is cinema the successor, the rival, or the revivifyer of the theatre?"[10] was already implicit in much of the early discussion about the relationship between the arts.

While subsequent film criticism has reinvented the term 'theatrical' as a condemnation, for a film of 1913 the association with the theatre was to be exploited. This was a key tactic in the marketing of the Gaumont-Hepworth *Hamlet*, which drew heavily on the established stage reputation of its major star, and particularly on his widely publicised farewell to the stage in the early summer of 1913. Hamlet was the dramatic role on which Forbes-Robertson's career was built. When, having taken over the management of the Lyceum Theatre in 1895, the actor was looking around for a new play for the 1897 season, he was persuaded by Henry Irving, who promised to loan scenery and costumes, to try *Hamlet*. The play was to prove a mainstay, both aesthetic and economic, of his repertoire for the next twenty years. Reminiscing in his autobiography published in 1925, Forbes-Robertson recalled:

> I had played the part many hundreds of times pretty regularly for over nineteen years, beginning at the mature age of 44, and ending in my 64th year. A revival of *Hamlet* had saved my financial position on many occasions. Over and over again both in England and America, when the production of a new play had spelt failure, a revival of *Hamlet* had always set on my feet again.[11]

These successful revivals culminated in Forbes-Robertson's three-month valedictory season at Drury Lane in 1913, alternating performances of his greatest roles, including his productions of a dramatisation of Kipling's *The Light that Failed* and Jerome K. Jerome's quasi-religious play *The Passing of the Third Floor Back*. The run began and ended with *Hamlet*. The farewell season was a huge commercial success: a newspaper report put ticket receipts for the first week at £4000, reassuring the public at the same time that this 'is a real and not a faked farewell".[12] *Punch* also alluded to this Frank

Sinatra syndrome, noting wryly that "Sir Johnston Forbes Robertson has been persuaded to give another farewell performance in London. It was felt that to break with precedent by giving only one final performance would scarcely be in the best interests of the profession"[13]. These June dates were, however, his last appearances in London, and the 3,700 seat Drury Lane theatre was apparently filled to capacity.

The very last of these last appearances was as Hamlet on June 6th, in the week of Forbes-Robertson's knighthood. *The World* magazine reported his oddly circumlocutory farewell speech to the audience that night:

> How can I be sad when to this great London theatre people have crowded to bid me farewell? How can I be sad when at a dramatic moment of my life my King honours me? I bid you all farewell. It is really my farewell. And yet I will not say that now. I would rather say just frankly, God bless you, and good-night.

"With these words on his lips", *The World* report concluded, "the great actor passed from public gaze".[14] Forbes-Robertson's marked reluctance to announce his goodbye may seem to endorse *Punch's* cynicism about the finality of his farewell. A week later, the sceptics were vindicated. On June 12th, the *Kinematograph and Lantern Weekly* proudly announced that "the Gaumont Company were able to persuade the eminent actor, Sir J. Forbes-Robertson, on the eve of his retirement, to allow his magnificent performance of Hamlet to be perpetuated on the screen".[15] So it was goodbye, and not goodbye. The great actor's farewell had been indefinitely postponed with the prospect of his perpetuated *Hamlet*.

The *Kinematograph and Lantern Weekly* announcement inaugurates the idea of the film as a record of the stage production, a memorial at the end of Forbes-Robertson's career. Even before its release, "Stroller" in the *Kinematograph and Lantern Weekly* assured readers that the film was "a worthy souvenir of a great actor's farewell to the stage".[16] As Bernice Kliman observes, "for those who had seen him, it would be a souvenir [...]: for those who had not, it would substitute for the real thing"[17], alongside the numerous other souvenirs and mementoes which were marketed as remembrances of Forbes-Robertson. Visual representations featured prominently in this material. A shilling book of the film, *Shakespeare's Hamlet: The Story of the Play Concisely Told*, announced itself as "a delightful souvenir of Sir Johnston Forbes-Robertson's remarkable career. All who have seen this great actor will treasure these 54 excellent photographs of him in his most famous part".[18] A special commemorative issue of *The Theatre* magazine boasted several photographs, and fans of the actor were encouraged to apply to Drury Lane for copies of his portrait.

When the film opened in September 1913, contemporary reviews tended to refer to it as a record of the stage production, albeit for some an inadequate one. *The Times'* notice acknowledged the value of "the preservation of this record of the performance" while contending that "few could have failed to feel last night how in its somewhat audacious effort the cinematograph has exposed its limitations".[19] The *Literary Digest* also distinguished between the film as a record and as an aesthetic event: "to the historian of drama it may be useful to possess these records of a performance but to suggest that the affair from any point of view does justice to the tragedy would be an outrageous absurdity".[20] The *Manchester Courier* proposed that it is "by means of the camera that posterity will judge the merits of Sir J. Forbes-Robertson's Hamlet", and *Moving Picture World* called the film "a valuable contribution to stage history". A review in *The Morning Advertiser* describes the audience for the film in theatrical terms as "playgoers drawn from all quarters. Indeed, a proportion of the audience consisted of persons who usually pay attention only to what might be termed the theatre proper. Their applause, it was noted, was even longer than that of the regular habitues".

Relatively few reviews emphasised the film as specifically cinematic achievement, although the *Daily Chronicle* called it "perhaps the most completely artistic picture which has so far been seen". "Stroller" in the *Kinematograph and Lantern Weekly* described the film as a triumph for everyone involved, beginning with the evidence of record houses, then going on to report that "every paper is speaking in the highest terms of the clearness, steadiness and altogether magnificent quality of the picture, and of the beautiful and effective settings that have been chosen".[21] Despite this appreciation of the particular qualities of the autonomous film artifact in this review, there is no contemporary notice for the film which does not mention the stage production. Its reception was inseparable from its previous life on the stage - a subordination continued by, among others, Susan Sontag, who illustrates her contention that film can record an event so that the film itself is "a transparency" with reference to the "filmed play" of Forbes-Robertson's performance.[22]

This sense of the film's ultimately derivative status was emphasised in advertisements. For a film to be mentioned in *The Times* in 1913 was unusual, though not unprecedented. When readers of the newspaper were directed towards the cinema *Hamlet* on September 22 1913, the entry was in the column entitled "The Theatrical Season". On subsequent days the advertisement for the film showing at the New Gallery Kinema was inserted under "Entertainments" and "Varieties", demonstrating the difficulty of classifying its appeal. In describing film showings as "performances" the paper further blurred the distinction between cinema and theatre, and in the announcement of the film's opening night this confusion is highlighted:

> The first performance of the pictorial representation of Sir J. Forbes-Robertson's production of Hamlet, will be given at the New Gallery Kinema, Regent-Street, tonight, at 8.30. Sir J. and Lady Forbes-Robertson left for America on Saturday.

Whether coincidental or intentionally causal, the conjunction of these two sentences demonstrates a profound ontological uncertainty about the nature of film. In simultaneously asserting Forbes-Robertson's dramatic presence and material absence, the announcement underscores and undermines the fundamental difference between the theatre and the film: the presence of the actor. As André Bazin writes, the technology of cinema means that "it is no longer as certain as it was that there is no middle stage between presence and absence".[23] In the ensuing media interest in the new film of *Hamlet*, the narrative of its critical reception and its tour, and the concurrent progress reports on the Forbes-Robertsons' transatlantic journey run in an uneasy but apparently inseparable parallel.

At the gala premiere of the film on September 22, filmgoers were treated to a message from the actor himself, as reported in the "Theatrical Gossip" column of *The Era* magazine on September 24, 1913:

> News of Sir Johnston Forbes-Robertson now on his way across the sea, came in a novel manner on Monday. "Hamlet", in which he acted the chief part, was presented by the New Gallery, and in the course of the evening a Marconigram, despatched from the Mauretania in mid-Atlantic, was thrown upon the screen. It ran as follows:-'It is with infinite regret that I cannot be with you to-night; the call of work leads me to America, and after that rest. I hope your audience will enjoy our pictorial representation of "Hamlet", and in bidding you au revoir I am not saying good-bye. My wife and colleagues join with me in this message. - Forbes-Robertson.'[24]

The words of the telegram recall Forbes-Robertson's speech to the audience at his last stage performance: "it is really my farewell. And yet I will not say that now". His hint at a return in the stress on *au revoir* is particularly suitable for the replayable film, which can, quite literally, be reseen at will. Emphasising return rather than goodbye is reminiscent of his reluctance to say farewell to his audience. What is striking is that in taking up cinema acting, Forbes-Robertson is, of necessity, saying farewell to his audience. One of the differences between acting on stage and in front of the camera to which Walter Benjamin draws attention in his essay "The Work of Art in the Age of Mechanical Reproduction" is the actor's relationship with the audience:

> The film actor lacks the opportunity of the stage actor to adjust to the audience during his performance, since he does not present his performance to the audience in person.[25]

When Forbes-Robertson chooses *au revoir* rather than goodbye, his words are an appropriate description not of the position of the actor, but of the audience, who can see him again, by returning to the New Gallery during the film's run. Forbes-Robertson, on the other hand, by committing his performance to film, has distanced himself from the audience and is able, as the marconigram uneasily attests, to be distanced from his own representation. His "infinite regret" draws on a vocabulary of apologetic indisposition from the theatre, and is a courtesy irrelevant to the new medium, which projects the same image of his presence whether he is in the cinema auditorium or in the middle of the sea. His tour to America is itself redundant, now that the film can travel instead of the acting troupe. The recorded performance is independent of what Walter Benjamin describes as the aura, that which must be relinquished by the film actor, "for the aura is tied to his presence; there can be no replica of it".[26] Forbes-Robertson has surrendered his aura, the presence which was the prerequisite of his stage career.

The first night marconigram is an appropriate figure for this alienation, as a technology almost exactly contemporaneous with the cinema, and transmitting the same illusion of presence. In the words of Benjamin, "even the most perfect reproduction of a work of art is lacking in one element: its presence in time and space, its unique existence at the place where it happens to be".[27] Thus Forbes-Robertson's address to the first audience of the film captures a double illusion of presence - the actor is neither on the stage nor present in the auditorium to see his recorded performance. The first-night telegram draws attention to the absent actor, but denies its own reproducible status by being attached to the premiere only. Forbes-Robertson's well-publicised departure for America was timed to exploit the particular qualities of film and to mark this enterprise as different from the stageplay which had been in regular repertory for fifteen years. The film's unique selling point is subtly emphasised by the media juxtaposition of the New Gallery presentation and the Forbes-Robertsons in mid-Atlantic, while at the same time this uniqueness seems to be a source of anxiety in the film's reception. It cannot throw off completely the interest in the physical presence of the actor, despite its irrelevance to the filmic medium. The simultaneity of Forbes-Robertson's passage on the Mauretania and his first film appearance is a powerful analogy for the alienation which Benjamin sees as the condition of the film actor. Benjamin quotes Pirandello: "... the film actor feels as if in exile - exiled not only from the stage but also from himself" - an appropriate image for Forbes-Robertson *en route* to America while his film plays without him in London.

In his memoirs, Cecil Hepworth, who supervised the production of *Hamlet*, described it as "one of my first important pictures".[28] He is at pains to point out, however, that "the making of a successful film from an existing stage-play is very far from being a mere photographing of the various scenes as they have appeared on the stage".[29] The relation of the film to the stage production is an interesting one. The two shared cast, costumes and, where possible, Hawes Craven's stage scenery. Both were, of course, centred on Forbes-Robertson's portrayal of Hamlet. In his book *Dramatic Values* (1911) C.E. Montague singles out this rendition for particular kind of praise which, he admitted, "you might wholly describe [...] by negatives". Forbes-Robertson's style "may not take your breath away, or send a momentary wave of coldness across your face, or elicit whatever your special bodily signal may be of your mind's amazed and sudden surrender to some stroke of passionate genius", it never approaches "inflation, feverishness, turbidity", "it is not in his art to trouble; rather to tranquillize".[30] A fellow actor, J.H. Barnes, who played Polonius to Forbes-Robertson's Hamlet from 1897 to 1913, described him as "*the* Hamlet of our time - graceful, feeling, pathetic, scholarly, lovable",[31] and similar epithets recur in Richard Findlater's account of his technique in *Six Great Actors*.

What was, however, continually reiterated in appreciations of Forbes-Robertson was the force of his delivery of Shakespearean verse. Montague characterised it in the "great tradition without that booming that infested it".[32] George Bernard Shaw declared that Forbes-Robertson was "the only actor I know who can find out the feeling of a speech from its cadence". His capacity for "wonderful music" in speech was cited as compensation for his sometimes histrionic gestures.[33] Thus *The Times*' review found the film most disappointing in this respect: "it was not only that Sir Johnston Forbes-Robertson's voice had gone, but that no other voice was left to take its place, and that for all the majesty of Shakespeare's verse there were only cold snippets thrown on the screen".[34] The *Pall Mall Gazette* was equally scathing: "to most people it will be obvious that to essay the representation of *Hamlet* without the words is to attempt the impossible".[35] One of the peculiar legacies of the theatrical production was the decision to leave Forbes-Robertson's speeches largely intact in the film, and the effect of this exaggerated and mute mouthing is curiously unsettling. The absence of speech from the film, which was accompanied by specially commissioned music, is emphasised by the presence of the camera's focus on the silently speaking actor.

Other elements of the stage production were translated to meet the particular demands of film. As Hepworth recalled, "it was necessary to interpolate all sorts of scenes, visualising episodes which are merely described in the play",[36] and he made particular mention of the additional scene of Ophelia gathering flowers as described in the play by Gertrude in Act 4, scene 7. Hay Plumb, credited as the film's director, recalled that the addition of this scene was initially opposed by Forbes-Robertson.[37] As Kliman has pointed out, this scene is the most cinematic and visually interesting in the film,[38] and it makes use of cross-cutting and panning techniques used sparingly elsewhere, particularly in the interior scenes. Hepworth's habitual resistance to editing - he asserts that "... none of my films had ever been 'edited' [...] when I went on the floor, I knew exactly what I wanted"[39] ensures that this scene is anomalous in its explicit extra-textual constructedness. Other adaptations were made. In his review of the production in the theatre, Shaw had been generally favourably impressed, but his comment on the ghost was caustic: "... that nice wooden beach on which the ghost walks would be the better for a seaweedy looking cloth on it, with a handful of shrimps and a pennorth of silver sand".[40] The film shot the scene at the favourite Hepworth location of Lulworth Cove in Dorset, and its producer recalled the new realism this allowed: "the 'ghost' had real rocks to walk upon, which he said hurt his feet badly, though he looked much too transparent to care for anything so concrete as that - when he has [*sic*] portrayed by double photography".[41] *Moving Picture World* considered the ghost to be a highlight of the film: "the scene on the battlements, where the ghost of Hamlet's father appears, is a veritable *chef d'oeuvre*, and will cause boundless wonder from audiences in every part of the civilized globe".[42] The ghost was described as "thrilling" by the Liverpool *Evening Express* and the same adjective was used in an otherwise hostile review in the *Pall Mall Gazette*.[43]

Marjorie Garber's suggestive remarks on the phenomenology of ghosts in *Shakespeare's Ghost Writers: Literature as Uncanny Causality* offer a way of reading the stress on the representation of the ghost in the contexts of textual reproduction and proliferation. Garber discusses how "the effect of uncanniness produced by the appearance of a ghost is related simultaneously to its manifestation as a sign of potential proliferation or plurality and to its acknowledgement of the loss of the original - indeed, to the loss of the certainty of the concept of origin".[44] The recognition that "the ghost is a copy, somehow both nominally identical to and numinously different from a vanished or unavailable original"[45] is analogous to the contradictory relationship of the film to the stage production. Publicity for the film suggests that it is a record of the stage production, and Kliman speculates that Forbes-Robertson's silence in his autobiography on his entry into cinema was because he considered the film identical to the stage production.[46] Nominally identical to the theatre production but different from it in its reiterability, its fixed and multiple existence in copies independent of its actors, the film itself has a ghostly quality which is peculiarly appropriate to the preoccupations of *Hamlet*. Preoccupied by its memory of its theatrical progenitor, the film is enmeshed in perpetual nostalgia for its origins. So, it might be argued, are Hamlet and *Hamlet*.

Hamlet is clearly preoccupied with questions of memory. Its relation to its imagined predecessors, such as the spectral *ur*-Hamlet, and to its extant forebears, such as Kyd's *The Spanish Tragedy* cast it as a play looking into the past. John Kerrigan argues that its hero is "continually recoiling from revenge into a 'remembrance of things past'".[47] The words memory, remember, and remembrance echo through the play. Often these activities are prompted or urged by the ghost, Old Hamlet. In the opening scene, Horatio recalls the past glories of Old Hamlet's reign, and Claudius' first words describe how "yet of Hamlet our dear brother's death/The memory be green" (1.2.1-2).[48] Hamlet's first soliloquy equates the memory of his dead father with pain: "Heaven and earth,/Must I remember?" (1.2.141-2). Polonius advises Laertes to lodge his paternal counsel "in thy memory" (1.3.58). and Laertes himself tells his sister "remember well/What I have said to you" (1.3.83-4). The ghost instructs Hamlet "remember me" (1.5.91), and it is striking that Hamlet's response is to avow not the revenge that the ghost entreated, but the remembrance:

> Remember thee?
> Ay, thou poor ghost, while memory holds a seat
> In this distracted globe. Remember thee?
> Yea, from the table of my memory
> I'll wipe away all trivial fond records ... (1.5.95-9)
>
> Now to my word:
> It is 'Adieu, adieu, remember me'.
> I have sworn't. (1.5.111-3)

Memory is associated with the theatre of the Players. Hamlet recalls Aeneas' speech on the death of Priam and urges the First Player, "if it live in your memory, begin at this line" (2.2.449-50). "The Murder of Gonzago" is itself a staging of nostalgia in its recapitulation of the dumb show and stylised rhetoric of earlier dramatic forms. During the play Hamlet's "there's hope a great man's memory may outlive his life half a year" (3.2.125-6) suggests that one function of the inset entertainment is memorial. Catching Claudius' conscience through visual representation, like catching his wife's in showing her the pictures of her two husbands, is a prompt to remembrance. Ophelia returns to Hamlet his "remembrances" (3.1.95), and this is echoed in her madness: "there's rosemary, that's for remembrance. Pray, love, remember" (4.5.175-6). Gertrude welcomes Rosencrantz and Guildenstern's visit with "such thanks/As fits a king's remembrance" (2.2.25-6). As Kerrigan argues, however, "the play's most important link with bygone things [is] Hamlet's memory of his father"[49].

Hamlet's memory haunts the film, and the ghost of Old Hamlet gives visual representation to this fixation. In his repeated "remember me", the ghost is both a function and symbol of memory, like the technology of film. Like the film actor, the ghost is at once absent and present, and as *Hamlet* the play is absorbed in the theatre of memory, *Hamlet* the film is absorbed in the memory of theatre. The reception of Forbes-Robertson's *Hamlet* is significant not only in tracing the relationship between theatre and cinema at a founding moment of Shakespearean film, but in its remarkable echoes of the themes of Shakespeare's play.

The Gaumont-Hepworth *Hamlet*

Notes

1. Robert Hamilton Ball, *Shakespeare on Silent Film: A Strange Eventful History* (London: Allen & Unwin, 1968), p. 199.

2. Harry Furniss, *Our Lady Cinema: How and Why I Went into the Photo-play World and What I Found There* (Bristol: J.W. Arrowsmith, 1914), p. 36.

3. Rachel Low, *The History of the British Film 1906-1914* (London: Allen & Unwin, 1949), p. 16.

4. See David Atwell, *Cathedrals of the Movies: A History of British Cinemas and their Audiences* (London:Architectural Press, 1980) and Allen Eyles and Keith Skone, *London's West End Cinemas* (Sutton: Keystone, 1991).

5. *The Cinema* 8th January 1913, pp. 29-31.

6. *The Times*, 29th April 1913, p. 5.

7. *The World* 6th May 1913, p. 646.

8. All quotations are from intertitles to *Masks and Faces* (1917), produced by Fred Paul for the Ideal Film Company. A viewing copy of the film is available at the British Film Institute, Stephen Street, London.

9. Furniss, p. 39.

10. Susan Sontag, "Theatre and Film" (1966), in *Styles of Radical Will* (London: Secker & Warburg, 1969), p. 115.

11. Johnston Forbes-Robertson, *A Player under Three Reigns* (London: T Fisher Unwin, 1925), p. 287.

12. Unattributed press cutting in the file on "Johnston Forbes-Robertson's *Hamlet*", Theatre Museum, London.

13. *Punch*, 25th June 1913, p. 493.

14. *The World*, 10th June 1913, p. 866.

15. *Kinematograph and Lantern Weekly*, 12th June 1913, p. 16.

16. *Kinematograph and Lanntern Weekly*, 24th July 1913, p. 21.

17. Bernice W. Kliman, *Hamlet: Film, Television, and Audio Performance* (London and Toronto: Farleigh Dickinson UP, 1988), p. 259.

18. *Shakespeare's Hamlet: The Story of the Play Concisely Told* (London: Stanley Paul & Co, 1913).

19. *The Times*, 23rd September 1913, p. 10.

20. *Literary Digest* 18th October 1913, p. 683.

21. Reviews quoted by Ball, pp. 192-3.

22. Sontag, p. 100.

23. André Bazin, *What is Cinema?* transl. Hugh Gray (Berkeley and Los Angeles: California UP, 1967), p. 97.

24. *The Era* 24th September 1913, p.16.

25. Walter Benjamin, *Illuminations* ed. Hannah Arendt (London: Fontana, 1973) p. 222.

26. Benjamin, p. 223.

27. Benjamin, p. 214.

28. Cecil M. Hepworth, *Came the Dawn: Memories of a Film Pioneer* (London: Phoenix House, 1951), p. 116.

29. Hepworth, p. 118.

30. C.E. Montague, *Dramatic Values* (London: Methuen, 1911), p. 62.

31. J.H. Barnes, *Forty Years on the Stage: Others (Principally) and Myself* (London: Chapman and Hall, 1914), p. 215.

32. Montague, p. 60.

33. Richard Findlater, *Six Great Actors* (London: Hamish Hamilton, 1957), p. 188. The other five great actors in this study are Garrick, Kemble, Kean, Macready, and Irving.

34. *The Times* 23rd September 1913, p. 10.

35. Ball, p. 192.

36. Hepworth, p. 118.

37. Ball, p. 190.

38. Kliman, p. 259.

39. Hepworth, pp. 136-7.

40. George Bernard Shaw, *Shaw on Shakespeare: An Anthology of George Bernard Shaw's Writings on the Plays and Productions of Shakespeare* ed. Edwin Wilson, (Harmondsworth: Penguin, 1961), p. 92.

41. Hepworth, p. 117.

42. *Moving Picture World* 30th August 1913, p. 109.

43. Ball, pp. 192-3.

44. Marjorie Garber, *Shakespeare's Ghost Writers: Literature as Uncanny Causality* (New York and London: Methuen, 1987) p. 15.

45. Garber, p. 16.

46. Kliman, p. 259.

47. John Kerrigan, "Hieronimo, Hamlet and Remembrance", *Essays in Criticism*, 31 (1981),pp. 105-26, here p. 106.

48. All references to the play are to *William Shakespeare: The Complete Works* eds. Stanley Wells and Gary Taylor (Oxford: OUP, 1986).

49. Kerrigan, p. 115.

HAMLET AS A WOMAN: ASTA NIELSEN'S SHAKESPEARE FILM OF 1921

Thomas Koebner (University of Mainz)
Translated by Deborah Hooper (Salzburg)

Hamlet as a silent movie - this means walking a particularly thin tightrope. It is necessary to sacrifice all monologues, which bring the ingenious, morbidly witty, Weltschmerz-filled, grumbling hero close to us; to reduce the dialogues; to pare down to their basic external action the scenes and thereby both to accelerate and simplify them. The producer Asta Nielsen accepted all of these restrictions when, following her return to Germany from her native Denmark after the end of the First World War, she wanted by means of a cycle of 'classic' film productions to win for this medium recognition as an art form among an educated audience. Because she also planned to develop for herself in these productions new roles as a much admired, virtuoso mime, it was inevitable that she took on the main part in *Hamlet* - perhaps inspired by the example of the French stage goddess Sarah Bernhardt, who had already 'portrayed' Hamlet in trousers. The medium of film forced Nielsen and her screen play author Erwin Gepard to make far-reaching changes in the Shakespeare text. In order to legitimize the changes introduced they referred to an obscure study by an American scholar, Edward Vining, who, in his *The Mystery of Hamlet* (1881) claimed to have discovered that Hamlet could only be understood if one supposed that the Danish prince was really a woman. Thus Nielsen did not intend to play a male role as convincingly as possible, but rather to portray a woman who was accepted as a man in her environment.[1]

With this aim in mind the film begins with battle scenes on barren hills, on which the Norwegian and Danish men are fighting. The Norwegian king falls, the Danish king is wounded. The rumour that he is also dead reaches Elsinore just as his wife gives birth to a daughter. For dynastic reasons the wet nurse advises passing the child off as a male heir to the throne. When the king returns home he learns of this intrigue, which, it appears, cannot be undone - once you have lied to the people you cannot go back on it. Hamlet therefore grows up in seclusion, in the picture: in an isolated garden behind the castle, in order to hide the fact that 'he' is actually a woman. When Hamlet is sent to Wittenberg to study, it is believed that his/her capacities of dissimulation are so developed as to remove the fear of any unwelcome discovery. The meeting with Horatio, a fellow student, develops, on the surface, into a warm male friendship between young people; under the surface love takes root in Hamlet, which she may not betray, but must hide, while Horatio appears only rarely to wonder about his intense feelings towards Hamlet.

Hamlet's uncle Claudius does not murder his brother, the king, Hamlet's father, mainly out of the lust for power. We are shown that it is the unmistakeable affection of the queen for him which makes him, with her consent, fetch a poisoned-tongued snake from the walled-in snake pit located in the deep dungeons (obviously this belongs to the standard equipment of medieval castles) in order to get rid of his rival. When he and his heart's queen, now retrieved from widowhood, celebrate his criminally acquired royal dignity with a lavish banquet, the funeral baked meats do indeed furnish forth the marriage tables. They closely embrace, apparently without remorse.

Hamlet has at one and the same time lost his father and his mother. But she only grieves for her father, not just because he has been taken from her once and for all, but because an affectionate relationship united her with him: in the only scene in which the two appear together the older man takes her lovingly into his protective arms, while her mother is already returning the covetous looks of the brother who forces his way into the family.

Only at first glance is Hamlet's dilemma in Nielsen's film a political one. She was brought up as a man and may not admit to being a woman, if she did she would clearly lose her claim to the throne. Her father, who embraced her like a mother, has been taken from her by an act of violence, she may not admit her love for her friend Horatio, let alone follow its promptings. Early isolation and diverse denials and failings of others shape this Hamlet figure. Strong feelings build up within her which cannot be expressed outwardly in a natural way. Being a woman proves to be of no advantage to Hamlet - other than the fact that the unbroken affection of the young gentlemen Horatio and Fortinbras finds a plausible explanation, viz. that both feel attracted to the hidden woman in Hamlet. Their solidarity supports Hamlet in the tests of strength with the ruthless Claudius. The almost total world-refusing withdrawal of Hamlet and her prompt, tactical madness prove to be understandable and obvious reactions to a seemingly insoluble and highly oppressive inner tension; she must not and cannot be who she is, and how she wants to be. The renunciation demanded of her and her constant self-concealment also express themselves in her ascetic black habit, which in some scenes even covers her neck. She already wears it in Wittenberg as a clever covering of her female body. In Elsinore the garment assumes the character of a complete mask signifying mourning while allowing for elegant movement.

Nielsen's Hamlet does not hesitate and delay particularly long her act of revenge; pensive self-doubt and brooding speculation are unknown to her. The subtitle of the film version is simply 'A Revenge Play'. The greatly accelerated action of a silent movie, which gets by without extensive speeches, allows the character of the main figure to appear in a different light: Hamlet is no longer a waverer. From the very beginning she is informed about her uncle's crime by an old man who was almost an eye witness. A ghost does not appear, but merely believes she hears her father's voice from the coffin, urging her to wreak vengeance - but we shall come to this later. She feigns lunacy to gain certainty. And her antic disposition both awakens and dispels suspicion. A first assassination attempt fails because she discovers her uncle embracing her mother, even though cup-bearers stand in attendance around the bed. Apart from the fact that this intimate situation makes her flinch, she complains about her weakness - the 'weakness' of a woman who has to carry out a task which calls for a man - and a firmly determined one at that.

However, after this scene Hamlet misses no opportunity to convict the culprit. The travelling players have hardly arrived when Hamlet presses for a presentation of *The Murder of Gonzago*, in order closely to observe the usurper, who is clearly distraught during the performance. When Claudius, caught out, remorsefully prays to God, he escapes Hamlet's sword - for the well-known theological reason that he should not fare better in heaven than he deserves. Subsequently the unscrupulous king, in a ready move of counter-attack, sends his adversary Hamlet with two companions and a 'Uriah's letter' to Fortinbras of Norway. Hamlet eavesdrops on the conversation between the two henchmen and from this point onwards acts consistently and in cold blood: she fakes the letter so that her companions are sent to the scaffold (she takes her leave from the two doomed men as mockingly and as mercilessly as she stabbed Polonius through the curtain quickly and unmoved.) Fortinbras accompanies her with his troops in order to place her on the Danish throne.

At dawn, Hamlet rides on ahead and surprises the king and his followers during a drinking bout, in which she feigns to take part, but sets fire to the hall, in which her opponents burn or suffocate. Only Horatio's despair over Ophelia's death causes Hamlet unease and confusion, for the first time her black dress becomes a little loose, baring the merest hint of her breasts - as if some inner compulsion forced her to reveal her true sexual identity to her friend, with whom she had earlier on so jealously quarrelled over his flirtation with Ophelia. Finally the 'order of the day' asserts itself, there follows the duel with the enraged Laertes; moreover, her mother, bent on revenge, attempts to kill Hamlet with all sorts of poison. There is no question of gentle feelings in Gertrude, who shows solidarity exclusively with her seducer, Hamlet's covetous and brutal uncle. When her mother drinks from the poisoned cup, which a servant had unwittingly pushed her way, and utters her fearful cry "I am dying" (link title), Hamlet, who before had fenced bravely and with flashing eyes, is distracted. She mimes the expression of a daughter still able to be shocked and compassionate. At this moment the unscrupulous Laertes plunges his rapier into the side of his opponent, who is rendered defenceless by her feelings. Hamlet dies quickly, and Horatio, who opens her jerkin and places his hand on her chest, realises, only too late, that she was a woman. He can now understand the passion which drew him to her in such a special way. A first and final kiss, then he covers her body with a black cloak, thus safeguarding the secret from the public. Hamlet's body, lifted up on a shield, is solemnly carried out.

The guiding idea of this production - Hamlet is a woman, while those around her believe she is a man - tempted neither Nielsen (whose influence on the conception and structure of her films must have been considerable), nor Gepard, the screenplay author, nor the director, Svend Gade (at times also Heinz Schall is mentioned as second director) to develop further extravagant or fantastic possibilities. On the contrary, Nielsen's Hamlet film endeavours to maintain laconic objectivity; only for brief moments does it borrow visual compositions from contemporary Expressionism (for instance, the view of the dungeon with the snake pit). In its avoidance of emotive formulas the film is a far cry from the ornamental artificiality and extreme stylization of Caligarism (so called after Robert Wiene's *The Cabinet of Dr. Caligari*, 1920),which secured for the Expressionist post-war film an internationally recognised special position. This *Hamlet* follows no trend, therefore, but in the discreet realism that largely predominates and its attention to the *aside*-acting of the main character, the film has closer links to Nielsen's melodramas of the prewar period and, at the same time, points forward to the sober objectivity which became the new formula of the twenties. Thus it could appear to the audience of 1921 both as *vieux jeu* and modern. One may assume that not only traditionalist inertia but also dramaturgic calculation prompted the decision to adopt a non-contemporary style. In order to cover up the most improbable - Hamlet is not recognised by those around her as a woman - the film suppresses all other action that might be regarded as improbable, it subjects all elements of the Shakespearean drama to a 'rationalist' examination. Consequently no ghost appears, eavesdropping scenes are staged as naturally as possible, the duel with Laertes turns out much more violent than is normal on the stage, the battle and the ride to Norway obviously take place in the open air. Hamlet's return at dawn to Helsingör provides the two cameramen, Curt Courant and Axel

Graatkjer, with the opportunity to capture beautiful, atmospheric *chiaroscuro* pictures without any further poeticizing of the actual lighting conditions.

The conception and casting of the roles was not carried out with the same care. Ophelia appears as a clumsy and stupid maiden with thick blonde pigtails. She is spared from going mad and even as a drowned body is not a touching sight. Gertrude, Hamlet's mother, in the embraces of her gallant, creates the impression of an electrified matron. Alongside Nielsen no actress gets beyond a roughly sketched, cursory and unattractive outline of her role. Horatio (Heinz Stieda) and Fortinbras are at least allowed, as steadfast young men, to appear solemn or candid. Laertes impresses as an uncontrolled, moody muscle-man, while his father, Polonius, shuffles like a degenerate mandarin through the corridors of the castle as a comical old man, half bald and with a goatee - one thinks one can hear his high-pitched, bleating eunuch's voice: a mere caricature. In this group of players Hamlet has only one partner, Horatio, whose noble manliness is, without doubt, to be rated more highly than his astuteness. And he has one opponent: Claudius, the regicide (Eduard von Winterstein), in whose furrowed face, heavy, fleshy and compressed one may indeed read traces of evil passions.

Hamlet is assigned the position of centrality and the role of cynosure to an extent that can only be explained by Nielsen's extraordinary prestige with audiences and critics. She develops subtle nuances which make the acting of the others appear crude and unpolished in comparison. First of all:[2] Nielsen as Hamlet never hides from the audience that she is a woman who has enjoyed the education of a prince. There is the aristocratic gait, the ease of free movement, always moderate and subdued. No gesture is jerkily executed, no movement begins or ends abruptly. Hamlet appears to be controlled by a gentle discipline. And Nielsen avoids exaggerated masculine posturing. The first meeting with Horatio is playful: as they bend over they knock their heads together; then, while Horatio keenly listens to the professor's speech, Hamlet sits back, casually passes one hand under her knee and watches the man at her side, with the curiosity of a young emancipated woman. Nielsen's method of acting seems exemplary even today:

Asta Nielsen's Shakespeare Film 131

without setting heavy emphases she flows, as it were, weightlessly from one attitude and position to the next clearly defining each one. An example of this is the death scene: she sinks onto the steps (a position that is certainly uncomfortable), her head moves once or twice, no message reaches Horatio, who is bending over her. This is the end. No sentimental aria of lament, no additional light on the dying heroine. In next to no time life has fled the body with almost shocking suddenness.

Straight to the point, sparing with gestures, 'untheatrical', this method of dramatic presentation is not always persuasive. Precisely when she has to translate inner chains of thought into body language, Nielsen makes too short thrift. She touches her forehead with her finger - and the title link just about reveals that she is planning to pretend to be mad. Without a title link she changes the letter which demands her death. When she dismisses tiresome people with annoying requests, she mechanically waves her hand from the wrist, even when the travelling actor exaggeratedly raises his hand to the sky. Such small deictic 'pointings', typical of the early phase of silent films, are repeated, they belong to a stereotypical grammar of gesture and do not appear to be adapted to the specific dramatic character. Unusual, on the other hand, is Nielsen's idea of having Hamlet crawl on the floor twice, particularly during the performance of *The Murder of Gonzago*: like a black, lurking snake pursuing its prey (this time a snake that wants to bring perdition to the uncle, who is well versed in vipers). Scenes of such metaphorical clarification and emphasis only appear occasionally. They are demonstrative insets. So are the few close-ups of Hamlet's and Claudius' faces, which show moments of pain or morose rage. Nielsen closes and opens her large eyes. Here we are dealing with insets displaying the dominant emotion in the manner of posters.

Admirable though somewhat surprising is the aristocratic sovereignty of this Hamlet. Her afflictions of an unrealised existence, of the enforced dissimulation, of her renunciation and her being orphaned are only rarely manifested - as she despairingly flees to her father's coffin, sees, standing in the background, Horatio feelingly dallying with Orphelia, is prepared to give up her disguise before Horatio at Ophelia's grave. One more look at Nielsen's rites of mourning. She embraces the massive coffin which contains the corpse of her dead father, presses her body against the outer casing, her head on the dead material. This is the only time in the film when she can give free rein to her otherwise consistently repressed, tender and erotic feelings - normally she is forbidden to get into close touch with another person's body. Her father's shrine becomes a surrogate object. Suppressed love, which never reaches its goal. This key scene brings to light the insoluble conflict which within the soul of a female Hamlet is superimposed on the task of revenge.

Perhaps it is a weakness of this Hamlet film that it is unable to link, continously and with increasing suspense, both components: the existential tragedy of Hamlet and the drama of revenge. The tragedy results from a life-lie, which could only be abandoned at the cost of her life (and not just the claim to the throne). The punishment of the fratri- and regicide is, by contrast, radically carried through by the talionic law of 'an eye for an eye'. The balance is toppled repeatedly in favour of the external action, the punishment plot. But it is particularly the Ibsenite and Strindbergian side of Nielsen's version of Hamlet: the woman to whom as a man it is not granted to live and love in truth, the construction of a subjective dilemma, which leaps to the eye of a contemporary observer, rather than the repetition of a power struggle for legitimate rule in Elsinore or elsewhere. Nielsen has privatised Hamlet - she could even have given him another name.

Notes

1. See my study of Asta Nielsen in *Theater Avantgarde*, ed. Erika Fischer-Lichte (Tübingen and Basel: Francke, 1995), pp. 89-122. See also Jan Berg, "Asta Nielsen: Darstellung von Weiblichkeit und Weiblichkeit als Darstellung" in *Idole des deutschen Films*, ed. Thomas Koebner (Munich: Edition Text und Kritik, 1997), pp. 54-74. See also Dimiter Daphinoff, "Hamlet, Hamletta, Telmahs und der Hamletismus", *Shakespeare Jahrbuch* 133 (Bochum: Kamp, 1997), pp. 310-21.

2. Some of the sentences that follow are taken from my commentary on Nielsen's *Hamlet* film in *Filmklassiker*, ed. Thomas Koebner (Stuttgart: Reclam, 1995), Vol. I, p. 60ff.

A MICROCOSM OF ART: OLIVIER'S EXPRESSIONIST *HAMLET* (1948)

Lawrence Guntner
(Technical University of Braunschweig)

"The Microcosm of Art" vs Neo-Realism

In 1945 Europe lies in ruins: politically, spiritually, aesthetically. By 1948 the reconstruction of the factories and the houses has begun, but the rubble in the minds of the people, conditioned by Fascism, the Holocaust, and World War Two, is not so easily cleared away. This crisis in social, political, and cultural values also troubles western European film directors, and they begin to direct serious questions at a culture that had provided little resistance to Fascism or the catastrophes it had wrought on human civilization. In Italy Neo-Realists, like Luchino Visconti, Robert Rosselini or Vittorio de Sica, point their cameras at the everyday realities of contemporary post-war Europe and the social and political forces at work there. In England and France directors such as David Lean and Jean Cocteau turn their backs on this kind of realism and try to revitalize the great pre-war European traditions in art and literature with the help of the popular medium of film. With his film adaptations of *Great Expectations* (1946) and *Oliver Twist* (1947) Lean returns to the familiar world of Charles Dickens' England and the British pre-war tradition of the costume romance. With *Beauty and the Beast* (1946) and *Orphée* (1949) Cocteau turns to a pan-European myth to create his own private cinematic universe with the stylistic techniques of pre-war French Poetic Realism. These films resemble "microcosms of art", i.e. artificial universes in miniature that imply that the true nature of things cannot be grasped through their "realistic" representation as they appear on the surface, including pressing social and political problems.

No film exemplifies this development better than Laurence Olivier's adaptation of Shakespeare's *Hamlet* (1948), an allegory of modern European man caught up in forces beyond his will and command, unable to act decisively because he cannot differentiate between illusion and reality, truth and misconception. Hamlet's predicament seems to capture the mood of the times as none other: Hamlet, the European Everyman. Together with screenwriter Alan Dent, Olivier radically abbreviates the play, cutting text, characters and even whole scenes, to emphasize Oedipal neurosis as the source of Hamlet's hesitation: "a nearly great man – damned by lack of resolution as all but one in a hundred are."[1]

In his "Essay in Hamlet" Olivier masterfully blends elements from the German Expressionist film – the darkly oppressive settings, *chiaroscuro* lighting, the psychological atmosphere, and the subjective camera work – and the American *film noir* – the black-and-white film, low-key lighting, and deep-focus photography – to break down the "fourth" wall characteristic of most film adaptations of theater before then. He creates a shadowy and claustrophobic cinematic psychogram on the screen that corresponds to the fears and anxieties of Hamlet's interior universe. Any direct references to social or political dimensions in the play that might allow the audience recourse to their own reality in the play are carefully avoided.

Hamlet/Telmah, or The Beginning is also the End

The opening credits begin with the classical Greek theater masks representing tragedy and comedy plus the text from a theater bill: "Laurence Olivier presents *Hamlet* by William Shakespeare". In the background we hear the orchestra tuning their instruments. Credits appear over waves pounding on a rocky shore at the foot of a distant hulk of a castle in swirling mists. From a bird's-eye perspective the camera boom moves slowly in on the castle ramparts surrounded by fog while Olivier's voiceover recites the "one vicious mole" soliloquy: "So, oft it chances in particular men, / That for some vicious mole of nature in them,/.... Carrying, I say, the stamp of one defect, [....] His virtues else, be they as pure as grace, [....] Shall in the general censure take corruption, / From that particular fault." (1.4.23-36)[2] Hamlet's reverie ends with Olivier's own censure: "This is the tragedy of a man who could not make up his mind." With a long pan from above the camera boom closes in on a tableau of four solitary guardsmen keeping watch over Hamlet's dead body on the ramparts of a tower, as if someone were keeping watch over them as well. From Olivier's sudden vision of this shot arose his whole conception for the film.[3] This shot establishes the atmosphere in Hamlet's private world and introduces us to Olivier's narrative strategy for the rest of the film. The first shot of the film is also the last shot of the film. It suggests the cyclical nature of the story we are about to see, or have just seen (again, Hamlet as Everyman), in which all actions are only symbolic, determined by menacing forces beyond Hamlet's (or our) control.[4] It is a technique also employed by Orson Welles in his adaptations of *Macbeth* (1946) and *Othello* (1952) and by Akira Kurosawa in *Throne of Blood* (1957), his adaptation of *Macbeth*.

The plot begins with a six-minute sequence on High Tor (cf. film protocol) in which the Ghost appears to Horatio (Norman Wooland), Bernardo, and Marcellus. Whereas the narrative frame (scene 1) begins with a long pan from above, the action on the ramparts (scene 2) begins with a low-angle shot of Bernardo climbing the winding stairs to the tower. Ascending the stairs with Bernardo we enter a world of physical danger and foggy ramparts in which spirits walk by night. The night is cold and threatening, and the watchmen know they are on their own. A throbbing heartbeat signals the approach of the Ghost. Wrapped in mist he stands in front of them for only a moment before a rooster crows to signal that it is time for him to disappear. The first words of the film, as in the play, are: "Who's there?" It is a call in the dark that sets the mood and the theme for the rest of the film.[5]

The scene shifts to Great Hall (Scene 3). To arrive there the camera takes us down murky, twisting stairways, past two empty chairs and the portrait of a knight on horseback in a hall, now dark and deserted, along empty corridors past Ophelia's apartment, to linger finally in front of Gertrude's empty, oversized canopy bed. It is the same route that Hamlet's corpse will take at the end of the film when it is borne by four soldiers to the ramparts. The symbolic props and sets (the bed, portrait of the knight, the empty chairs, the stairs and corridors, the empty hall) will come to represent the anonymous forces that are steering him toward his tragedy. This melancholic reverie is suddenly interrupted by a dissolve to a close-up of Claudius (Basil Sydney) in the festively illuminated Great Hall. A fanfare of trumpets, a cannonade (heard in the background), the King drinks his chalice of wine, and the play begins. There follows a brief full shot from behind so that we can see the trumpeters from the perspective of Gertrude (Eileen Herlie) and Claudius, followed by a full shot of the royal couple from the front. Through the use of deep-focus photography, the shot develops into a long shot with a *mise en scène* reminiscent of an Italian Mannerist painting.[6] The costumes refer to a historically undefined past: Claudius and Gertrude wear costumes similar to those found on playing cards, the court reminds us of a painting by Hans Holbein, while Ophelia's clothes seem Victorian. The composition, the black-and-white photography and the *chiaroscuro* lighting with its dark gray and black tones combine to create for us the impression of an old engraving rather than a colorful painting, however.[7]

In the first seven minutes (cf. film protocol) of the film Olivier has introduced the cinematic codes that will determine our view of Hamlet's microcosm: the narrative frame to establish the literary source, cavernous sets and *chiaroscuro* lighting that evoke an atmosphere of claustrophobia and confinement, subjective camera work with extreme camera angles and deep-focus photography to evoke Hamlet's view of things and his estrangement from his environment. And lest we miss the point, the obvious symbolic props and William Walton's dramatic musical accompaniment provide an interpretative commentary.

Olivier's Expressionistic Film World
Olivier's debt to the German Expressionist film tradition and its *Dramatik der Bildstruktur* (Schmidt-Rottluf) is substantiated by Alan Dent's review of the film, entitled "*Hamlet* and *Caligari*".[8] Dent, co-author of the filmscript, begins, "Let me begin with *Caligari*." He has noticed that Robert Wiene's Expressionist

masterpiece and Jean Renoir's *The Rules of the Game* are on the same bill at his neighborhood cinema. Then he jumps "to another film about insanity. I mean *Hamlet* by Laurence Olivier." Expressionism gave aesthetic form to the helplessness felt by German artists and intellectuals after World War I. The subjectivity of their view of the world manifested itself in the decor, lighting, and camera activity in the German films of the 1920s.

In the Expressionist film the entire film is designed to convey mood, emotion, and atmosphere. "The cinematic image must become graphic" (*Das Filmbild muß Graphik werden*) was a guiding principle of Expressionist film artists, who rejected naturalistic representations of reality in favor of inner experience. For them the outer world described by the film mirrors the inner world of the characters, a world dominated by *Angst*, insecurity, and a feeling of being at the mercy of exterior forces. Expressionism claimed to express the inner truth of things, i.e., the black depths of human nature and the irrationality of the world we inhabit.[9] Low-key *chiaroscuro* lighting becomes the central stylistic element of a "light-and-shadow" dramaturgy. Often in conjunction with stairs, shadows foreshadow doom. The shadow does not have its source in the lighting itself but in the fate of the person climbing or descending the stairway. Dark and somber lighting is amplified by extremely low-angle shots to create an atmosphere of confinement and oppression, or extremely high-angle shots to communicate an impression of being small and helpless. The ever-shifting camera angle suggests an unstable world with no fixed point.

The cinematic techniques we associate with *film noir* were developed in Hollywood during the 1940s primarily by the German exile directors Fritz Lang, Robert Siodmak, Otto Preminger, Billy Wilder, and Max Ophüls.[10] The atmosphere of Olivier's Elsinore would remind his audience more readily of a nighttime American city from Hollywood's *film noir* than Fritz Lang's German *Metropolis* of 1926. Hamlet, the alienated hero, would call to mind Raymond Chandler's sleuth Philip Marlowe or Dashiell Hammet's Sam Spade, who struggle on their own against all odds to solve a murder in a strange, dark and threatening world in which the real and the unreal are very close to each other. Above all, Oliver's debt to *film noir* is visible in his penchant for deep-focus photography that emphasizes the significance of the background in order to stress the insignificance of the persons at its mercy. Olivier's choice of this tradition implies his rejection of any Neo-Realistic claims to comprehend the reality of the world simply with the help of film.

Set Decor as Psychogram

The parameters of the action in the first third of the film are determined by High Tor and Great Hall. Until the arrival of the Players (scene 10), which provides Hamlet with the idea of capturing Claudius with the help of "The Mousetrap", the action is divided almost equally between these two places (28 minutes and 30 seconds). The ramparts on the upper edge of the Kafkaesque castle enclothed in swirling mist is the place where Hamlet will confront the ghost of his murdered father and his responsibility to revenge him. Great Hall, with its Norman columns and arches, its Byzantine frescoes, its gallery and long banquet tables, is the place where Hamlet will have to challenge Claudius, the King – his uncle and his father's murderer. Great Hall is simultaneously theater stage and arena, and Hamlet will have to climb down into this arena, to do battle with the King. High Tor and Great Hall are at once point of departure and climax. They define Hamlet's task as well as his radius of action, they function as his backdrop as well as a mirror of his own frame of mind. In a Freudian interpretation of the film Great Hall stands for Hamlet's subconscious into which he must descend to do battle with Claudius, who is seated there on Hamlet's throne.[11]

Roger Furse's dream-like, cavernous sets correspond to the shadowy labyrinths of Hamlet's psyche and continually remind the viewers that Denmark is a prison. In Olivier's microcosm there is no escape from the forces of destiny symbolized by the set decor, and no relief can be expected from outside. The young Norwegian king Fortinbras, who could represent a political solution, has been cut.

Olivier's Expressionist *Hamlet*

The seemingly endless, dark hallways and twisting stairways provide simultaneously performance spaces for the actors and actresses and an architectural commentary on the action. After his first soliloquy ("O that this too too sallied flesh would melt," end of scene 3) the camera prowls with Hamlet through seemingly endless dark, empty corridors in search of "Who is there."

This sequence ends with a deep-focus long shot with Ophelia (Jean Simmons) in the background and Hamlet in the foreground, in reality about fifty yards apart. This shot is repeated at the beginning of scene 5 after Laertes and Polonius have warned Ophelia to avoid Hamlet. Hamlet, seated in a chair sees her through a long series of arches. Seeing Polonius (Felix Aylmer), her father, behind a pillar, Ophelia turns aside, but to Hamlet and the audience it appears as if she is avoiding him purposely. As Olivier himself quipped: "the longest distance lovescene on record."[12] After Ophelia has lost her mind she enters the interior of the castle (scene 15) through a long passageway of columns and arches, similar, perhaps identical, to the columns mentioned above. (Furse had the columns mounted on wheels so that he could alter them at will.) As in the Expressionist film the dark, shadowy corridors emphasize Hamlet's and Ophelia's isolation and separation from each other as well as from their environment.

Stairways, of course, provide Olivier the actor with plenty of opportunity to display his own physical agility, and he is forever vaulting up and down them. However, stairways also have symbolical significance. In both the Expressionist film and *film noir* the stairway serves frequently as a bridge between appearance and reality, bourgeois normalcy and the unexplored depths of the human soul, the conscious and the subconscious. Significantly, the plot in Olivier's *Hamlet* film begins with Bernardo mounting the winding stairs to the tower. In decisive moments, Olivier, the director, has his actors and actresses climb or descend stairways, often preceded by a shadow, a foreboding omen of the impending catastrophe. Hamlet, for example, follows the Ghost up the tower stairway, his own overbearing shadow accompanies him on his way up his mother's bedroom (the thematic center of the film). For the dramatic highpoint of the film, Hamlet races to the top of the stairs in Great Hall to spring, like an avenging angel, upon Claudius, and thrust his sword through him again and again. (In the process Olivier knocked the stuntman playing Claudius unconscious and broke two of his teeth.)[13] Psychologically, of course, it is a symbolic fall into his own subconscious where he kills his own father. Olivier also uses stairs to suggest estrangement. Hamlet abandons Ophelia crying on a stairway in the "nunnery scene" (scene 8), and the subjective camera work underlines Ophelia's sense of being cast out with a crane shot that pulls up and back from her. After Hamlet has confronted her in the "closet scene", Gertrude and Claudius leave a hall, both reading a letter, both using separate stairways.

A Dramaturgy of Light and Shadows

In the Expressionist film the lighting steps out of the background as a frame for the action and into the foreground as commentary on the action. It defines the relationships of the characters to each other and to their environment, and it draws the audience into the story. It creates the kind of atmosphere we associate with Olivier's *Hamlet* as well as with films like Robert Wiene's *The Cabinet of Dr. Caligari* (1920), Fritz Lang's *Destiny* (1921), or Friedrich Murnau's *Nosferatu* (1922). The shadows suggest danger but also provide a place to hide. In the dark Hamlet is protected – on the Tower, at the banquet or during "The Mousetrap". In the light things seem clearer but that is where the danger lurks. Claudius' call for light that ends "The Mousetrap" (scene 11) leads to his confession of the fratricide, but in the darkness of his chamber he is protected, even though Hamlet stands behind him, sword drawn and ready to put an end to him. When a character attempts to flee the night-time interior of the castle, he or she is doomed: Hamlet's meditation on suicide – "To be, or not to be" – is delivered by daylight at the top of the tower above the pounding surf; Ophelia, the character in the film most closely connected with daylight (she has the only apartment with windows), goes insane and drowns when she attempts to leave; Hamlet's voyage to England that is supposed to end in his execution, is shown as a tableau in daylight; Hamlet returns by daylight to the graveyard – a sign that he has come to accept his own certain death. Even Claudius is finally killed in Great Hall brightly lit with torches.

The Wandering Camera

Besides the Expressionistic decor and the *chiaroscuro* lighting, it is above all the wandering camera, the deep-focus photography, and the dazzling camera angles that make up Olivier's cinematic style. In the dizzying opening shot the camera shows us Hamlet's dead body on the ramparts. Then it travels down the stairway and through the castle to Great Hall where deep-focus photography reveals Hamlet's isolation, even when he is surrounded by the entire court. The camera, and with it the viewer, accompanies Hamlet on his searchings through seemingly endless corridors, up and down winding stairways on an endless expedition to his own Self. It is primarily the camera work that links Hamlet's disturbed state of mind and his environment.

An unfixed camera also implies a continually shifting point of view. On the one hand, it helps us empathize with Hamlet and his situation, on the other, we are distanced by the ever-changing camera perspective; it disturbs the process of empathy. For example, in scene 6 we see the Ghost first from Hamlet's perspective. Back-lighted, in the fog, from below, he seems like an eerie threatening creature from another world. This shot is followed immediately by a shot from above, the Ghost's perspective, to emphasize Hamlet's helplessness. For the takes of "The Mousetrap", the camera was mounted on a rail and circled the action to provide continually shifting perspectives of the events. With the court we sit in the audience. Then the camera moves slowly in a semi-circle behind the spectators so that we view the events from the perspectives of Hamlet, Horatio, Ophelia, Claudius, Gertrude, Polonius, and finally the courtiers. The meandering camera evokes Hamlet's meandering frame of mind, but at the same time it communicates a significant message: fixed points of view in a continually changing world are impossible.

From dizzying heights we become voyeurs peering down at human beings isolated and helpless, like pawns on a chessboard at the mercy of anonymous players: Hamlet alone in Great Hall (scene 5), Ophelia interrogated by Polonius and Claudius (scene 8), Ophelia rejected and left weeping on the steps (scene 8), Hamlet facing the Ghost on the tower (scene 6) and later in his mother's chamber (scene 13), the King and Laertes plotting Hamlet's murder (scene 20). Often we have the impression that it is Hamlet himself who is eavesdropping on what is being said below. For example, he observes the king's wassail from the tower (scene 6), he overhears from a gallery Polonius and Claudius plot to use Ophelia as a decoy to snare him (scene 8), or he watches from the gallery as the court enters in procession for his duel with Laertes (scene 21). This underlines Hamlet's moral distance to the corrupt society of Elsinore.

The camera angle from high above sets up a code of expectations. When Claudius and Laertes plot Hamlet's murder in scene 21, Olivier employs the same high angle shot he used in scene 8 when Claudius and Polonius eavesdrop on Hamlet and Ophelia. This creates the impression that Hamlet overhears Claudius and Polonius, even though this may not necessarily be the case. Although Jean Renoir and others criticized Olivier's idiosyncratic stylistic mannerisms,[14] they are justifiable as intrinsic to the theme of Hamlet's personal disorientation and his aspirations to transcend the world of deception and compromise embodied by the court at Elsinore.

Relationships via Deep-focus photography

Olivier's choice of black-and-white film not only favors subdued colors – black, gray, sepia – it also makes longer shots through deep-focus possible. This is a great advantage for a filmscript that consists of blank verse.[15] The audience is not diverted from Shakespeare's poetry by shifting camera angles or perspectives while long passages of blank verse are being recited. Olivier resorts to montage only at dramatic highpoints, for instance, when Hamlet meets the Ghost (scene 6) or when pandemonium breaks out after Claudius screams, "Give me some light!" (scene

11). An especially successful example of deep-focus photography occurs in the first scene in Great Hall (scene 3). As mentioned above, the scene begins with a close-up of Claudius drinking wine, followed by a full shot of the royal couple and a long shot of Laertes. After a reverse-angle shot sequence between Claudius, Polonius, and Laertes, there is a brief deep-focus photography long shot from Hamlet's perspective. Then there is a medium shot of Polonius rising that develops into a deep-focus long shot tableau of the whole court with Hamlet in close-up in left foreground. It makes visible Hamlet's perspective of what is going on and establishes his personal isolation and estrangement from his immediate environment in which he is more or less a prisoner.

Through deep-focus photography the characters are brought into a symbolic relationship with props, for example, the empty chair in Great Hall that reminds us at once Hamlet's of murdered father and his own delayed succession to the throne of Denmark (scene 3), his mother's gigantic bed with its opened canopy suggesting a huge womb from which he sprang or into which he secretly wishes to return (scene 13), or the columned hall which reminds Hamlet of the kingly power that keeps him from Ophelia (scene 4-5). On the other hand, deep-focus photography robs human beings of their significance. It reinforces the impression evoked by the extreme-angle shots that all are simply pawns in an anonymous game called fate in which they have but their entrances and exits to make before disappearing into oblivion.

Musical Symbolism

Olivier's metaphors - the oversized bed, the empty chair, and the theater masks – are obvious. The same can be said of William Walton's music. *Hamlet* was Walton's third Shakespeare film (preceded by *As You Like It* in 1936 and *Henry V* in 1944); it was his second with Olivier. For Walton, "the form and content of the music is governed absolutely by the exacting requirements of the pictures on the screen".[16] It is primarily functional, it accompanies the action and monologues, links scenes, identifies characters with individual themes, and creates atmosphere.

144   Olivier's Expressionist *Hamlet*

For example, scene 3 ends with Hamlet's soliloquy, "Oh, that this too too sallied flesh would melt", with a slow and heavy string accompaniment that develops into Ophelia's bright *leitmotif* as the camera meanders through the hallways to her apartment. During "The Mousetrap" there is a minimum of dialogue, and the soundtrack consists primarily of music. A sarabande accompanies the court procession, a sinister melody the poisoner, and a Renaissance instrumental ensemble the Players. During the interlude the camera circles the audience while the musical accompaniment evokes the changing moods of the audience, especially the king. The sixty-piece London Philharmonic Orchestra picks up the poisoner's melody and then drowns out the soft sounds of the cello, oboe, and harpsichord in the Players' theme, and builds to a tremendous final chord when the King screams: "Give me some light!"[17] However, for the critical viewer of today, the musical accompaniment occasionally seems exaggerated and can even provoke an unintended chuckle, e.g. the pounding surf accompanied by clashing cymbals or people rushing up stairs to the accompaniment of musical scales.

"A Theater-infused Film"
Despite his considerable repertoire of cinematic techniques Olivier reminds us continually that the source of this film is a play and that all the world actually is a stage. At the outset of the film we are shown the masks of classical Greek comedy and tragedy, and the first as well as the final shot reminds us of a pageant on stage: Hamlet's bier on High Tor, guarded by four soldiers. At the end of the film, Horatio, speaking the words of Fortinbras, commands: "Let four captains, / Bear Hamlet like a soldier to the stage." As in theater the entrances and exits of each actor and actress at the beginning and end of a scene have been carefully prepared, and they often stand framed in an illuminated doorway, as, for example, at the beginning of the "nunnery" sequence (scene 8), or they climb or descend a stairway to use the gallery as a stage, for example, in the "fishmonger" sequence (scene 8). These theatrical entrances and exits are often framed by a "wipe" or a "fade out" suggesting a theater curtain. On occasion, Olivier employs spots to suggest a

lighting effect. A good example of this is the scene immediately preceding "The Mousetrap" (scene 20) when Olivier jumps onto the stage and announces with theatrical gestures: "The play's the thing / Wherein I'll catch the conscience of the King."

The motif of "the play within the play" is picked up repeatedly: Hamlet is the spectator as the court applauds Claudius's opening performance with gloved hands (scene 3) and when Claudius's confesses his guilt (scene 12). Polonius is an eavesdropping spectator for Hamlet's "performances" with Ophelia and Gertrude (scenes 8 and 13). The court is audience to the final deadly "performance" between Hamlet and Laertes as they act out a grisly "play" the outcome of which has been determined before it begins.

Frequently the *mise en scène* is so intentionally theatrical in style and gestures, the posturing and pictorial blocking in such contrast to the naturalistic scene of the action, that it almost borders on comic relief. For example, the romantic theatrics of the "to be, or not to be" soliloquy on High Tor (scene 9) high above the pounding surf, Ophelia's floating down the stream in a direct "quote" of Millais' famous painting (scene 18), or Hamlet meditating on death in the graveyard with Yorick's skull in hand (scene 19). The use of spots to highlight the entrance of the Players (scene 10), Claudius at prayer (scene 12) or Hamlet and Claudius waiting for the duel to begin (scene 21) are certainly in the tradition of Expressionist *chiaroscuro* lighting, but also owe much to Olivier's theater experience. They remind us of the hybrid nature of Olivier's achievement, located somewhere between Hollywood and the Old Vic. Bernice Kliman has called Olivier's *Hamlet* "a film-infused play", but I would argue that "a theatre-infused film" would be equally as valid.[18]

The Critics

The critical response went from enthusiastic praise to angry rejection. Some objected to the idosyncratic cinematography, others to the lack of a political or social dimension, and others to the omission of familiar characters (Rosencrantz,

Guildenstern, Fortinbras) and textual passages.[19] Predictably, Olivier reaped the scorn of a whole generation of scholars for reducing the complexity of the play to Hamlet's Oedipal neurosis.[20] Yet Olivier's portrayal of Hamlet remains the most influential Shakespeare performance of the twentieth century, certainly the most influential *Hamlet* interpretation.

Until recently almost all discussions have concentrated solely on the question of whether or not Olivier interpreted Shakespeare's play correctly. With few exceptions, cinematic qualities have not been discussed.[21] We still do not have a complete structural analysis of the film, nor a description of its roots in film tradition, even though Roger Manvell, a prominent German-English film critic, has written: "Of the three Shakespearean films directed by Laurence Olivier, *Hamlet* is possibly the one which most repays detailed examination."[22] Olivier's great achievement is that with his *Hamlet* he became the first to succeed in making a Shakespeare film and not filmed theater. To this effect he has borrowed generously from the German Expressionist film and the American *film noir* traditions, which, in addition to specific cinematic techniques, share the conviction that the role of film should not be limited to a naturalistic reflection of the surface reality of everyday life.

The similarities between Olivier's *Hamlet* and David Lean's *Great Expectations* are readily apparent: a popular literary source, a narrative frame, a self-enclosed set design, a penchant for pictorializing in the *mise en scène*, self-consciously interpretive camera activity, the recurrence of stairways, steps, and corridors, the central themes of what is real and what is unreal, human estrangement, parent-child relationships, and last not least the young Jean Simmons playing both Estella and Ophelia. (Oliver engaged her to play Ophelia after seeing her in *Great Expectations*).

Similarities between Jean Cocteau's *Beauty and the Beast* and *Orphée* and Olivier's *Hamlet* lie in the recourse to a literary source, the interpretive camera, the artificial set, the pictorial *mise en scène*, symbolically suggestive props, and above all the question of what is real and what is unreal. Whereas the "microcosms" of

Olivier's Expressionist *Hamlet* 147

Olivier and Lean are basically conservative, invoking the national tradition of Shakespeare and "the good old days" of Dickens as a common denominator for national unity and purpose, Cocteau's explorations of a fairy tale past in *Beauty and the Beast* and a surrealistic present in *Orphée* are radical departures from literary tradition.

Fifty years later films like Olivier's *Hamlet*, Lean's *Great Expectations*, or Cocteau's *Beauty and the Beast* and *Orphée* still impress us with their cinematic mastery. Each bears the unmistakable handwriting of its director, and the images remain etched in our memories: Hamlet on the tower, young Pip alone in the eerie graveyard, Orphée in front of the mirror. Each of these directors returned to earlier film traditions to provide classical models with a new cinematic form. These earlier film styles were also an answer to a specific social reality, thus the decision for a particular style was simultaneously an imminently political decision. For Olivier, Lean, and Cocteau, as for Hamlet, the world is more complex than it appears to be on the surface of things. Only through "microcosms of art" – literary, graphic, theatrical, cinematic – can the reality, the true nature of things be grasped. However, the renunciation of a confrontation with social reality also implies a rejection of any hope of changing this reality by political means. Thus Olivier's Expressionistic *Hamlet* is not only a microcosm of art but also an expression of his political consciousness of his day.

Notes

1. Laurence Olivier, "An Essay in Hamlet", in Brenda Cross, ed., *The Film HAMLET* (London: Saturn, 1948), 15; a commentary on the cuts is provided by Olivier in the "Foreward" and by Alan Dent in "Text-Editing Shakespeare with particular reference to *Hamlet*", in Alan Dent, *HAMLET: The Film and the Play* (London: World Film Publications, 1948). The book also contains the complete filmscript. On the relationship between the Dent-Olivier filmscript and Shakespeare's play, see Sandra S. Singer, "Laurence Olivier Directs Shakespeare: A Study in Film Authorship", Ph.D. Dissertation (Northwestern University, 1979), 100-118. See also Bernice Kliman, "A Palimpset for Olivier's HAMLET", *Comparative Drama*, 11 (1983): 243-53.

2. Filmscript: Dent, *HAMLET: The Film and the Play*.

3. Olivier, "Essay", 11.

4. On the circularity of the plot, cf. Terence Hawkes, "Telmah", in *That Shakespeherian Rag. Essays on a critical process* (London: Methuen, 1986), 92-101.

5. Cf. Hawkes, 96f.

6. Dale Silveira, *Sir Laurence Olivier and the Art of Film Making* (Cranbury, NJ: Farleigh Dickinson UP, 1985), 146f. names Tintoretto's "Last Supper" (1592-94); see also Sabine Laussmann, "Strategien visueller Verrätselung im film noir", in Ludwig Bauer et al., ed., *Strategien der Filmanalyse* (Munich: Schaudig, Bauer, Ledig, 1987), 47-8.

7. Cf. Olivier, "Essay", 12, and Roger Furse, "Design and Costumes", in Cross, 36-42, and "Designing the Film HAMLET," in Dent.

8. *The London Illustrated News*, 15 May 1948.

9. On the German Expressionist film, see Rudolf Kurtz, *Expressionism and Film* (Berlin: Verlag der Lichtbühne, 1926); Siegfried Kracauer, *From Caligari to Hitler* (Princeton UP, 1947), 43-76, Lotte Eisner, *Die dämonische Leinwand* (Frankfurt/M.: Fisher, 1980), 13 f., and Paul Werner, *Film noir: Die Schattenspiele der "schwarzen Serie"* (Frankfurt/M.: Fischer, 1985), 110 f.

10. Cf. Werner, 122f.

11. Olivier himself writes, "Perhaps Dr. Jones is sound in his justification of the Oedipus Complex", in "Essay", 15. See also Laurence Olivier, *On Acting* (New York: Simon and Schuster, 1987), 77-9. The Oedipal interpretation first put forward by Ernest Jones in German in 1910 is expanded and developed in *Hamlet and Oedipus* (London: V. Gollanez, 1949). For Freud's remarks on Hamlet, see "Die Traumdeutung", in Alexander Mitscherlich et al., ed., *Freud-Studienausgabe*, Vol. 2 (Frankfurt/M.: Fischer, 1972), 268-70.

12. See "Essay", 12/15.

13. John Cottrell, *Laurence Olivier* (London: Weidenfeld and Nicolson, 1975), 228.

14. See Raymond Durgnat, *Films and Feelings* (Cambridge, MA: Harvard UP, 1971), 117.

15. See Olivier, "Essay", 12f., and Desmond Dickinson, "Camera and Lighting", in Cross, 29-35.

16. See Muir Mathieson, "Recording the Music", in Cross, 60-4.

17. See John Huntley, "The Music of *Hamlet* and *Oliver Twist*", in *Penguin Film Review*, 8 (1949), 110-13.

18. Bernice Kliman, "Olivier's *Hamlet*: A Film-Infused Play", *Literature/Film Quarterly*, 5 (1977), 305-14.

19. See Andrew McLean's commentated bibliography to the film in Andrew McLean, ed., *Shakespeare: Annotated Bibliographies and Media Guides for Teachers* (Urbana: National Council of Teachers of English, 1980), 150-157; Bernice Kliman, *Hamlet: Film, Television, and Audio Performance* (Cranbury, NJ: Farleigh Dickinson UP, 1987), especially ch. 1; Ken Rothwell and Annabelle Melzer, *Shakespeare on the Screen* (London: Mansell, 1990), 61-2.

20. E.g. John Ashworth, "Oliver, Freud and Hamlet", *Atlantic Monthly*, 183 (May, 1949), 30-33, and the reply by Simon Lesser, "Freud and *Hamlet* Again", *American Imago*, 12 (1955), 207-20.

21. Among the exceptions are Roger Manvell, *Shakespeare and the Film* (London: Dent, 1971), 40-47, Jack Jorgens, *Shakespeare on Film* (Bloomington, IN: Indiana UP, 1977), 207-17, and the work of Bernice Kliman, especially "A Palimpset for Olivier's *Hamlet*", *Comparative Drama*, 17:3 (Fall 1983), 243-53, "The Spiral of Influence", *Literature/Film Quarterly*, 11:3 (1983), 159-66, and *HAMLET*.

22. Manvell, *Shakespeare and the Film*, 44.

Olivier's Expressionist *Hamlet*

Appendix: Film Protocol

Shot	Time	Action	Text

Scene 1: "narrative frame" 3:02 Min.

| 1-6 | 1:46 | Film credits; sea in background |
| 7-11 | 1:16 | "narrative frame"; castle, Olivier's voiceover |

Scene 2: On the ramparts of High Tor 5:44 Min.

| 12-37 | 5:44 | Watchmen; Ghost appears | 1.1. |

Scene 3: In Great Hall 9:55 Min.

38-39	0:51	Camera wanders through stairways and halls, past bed, empty chair and Ophelia's chamber	
40-58	6:23	Claudius' speech before the court	1.2.1-128
59-63	2:41	Hamlet: "O that this too too sallied flesh would melt"	1.2.129-159

Scene 4: Polonius' Chambers 5:19 Min.

64-71	2:07	Laertes warns Ophelia to avoid Hamlet	1.3.1-54
72-75	1:29	Polonius advises Laertes	1.3.55-86
76-77	1:22	Polonius warns Ophelia	1.3.87-135
78-79	0:21	Long shot in deep focus with Hamlet in foreground and Ophelia 50 yards behind in background	

Scene 5: In Great Hall 4:07 Min.

| 80-85 | 3:27 | Horatio and Marcellus tell Hamlet of Ghost | 1.2.160-257 |
| 86 | 0:40 | Camera wanders through the hallways of the castle | |

Scene 6: On High Tor 15:41 Min.

87	0:10	In the background the silhouette of castle in fog; in the foreground the pounding surf	
88-89	0:38	Hamlet and Horatio on the ramparts	1.4.1-6
90	0:38	King's wassail	1.4.7-22
91	1:11	Hamlets: "Some vicious mole of nature"	1.4.23-38
92-98	1:34	Ghost approaches	1.4.39-91
99-104	0:50	Hamlet follows Ghost	
105-114	2:26	Ghost tells about his "unnatural murther"	1.5.1-61

150   Olivier's Expressionist *Hamlet*

115	0:47	Pantomime of murder of Hamlet's father	
116-122	1:16	Ghost:"Remember me!"	1.5.62-91
123-124	1:00	Hamlet swears revenge	1.5.92-112
125-131	3:12	Horatio and Marcellus swear	1.5.113-189

Scene 7: Ophelia's Chamber 1:59 Min.

-132-134	1:59	Ophelia reports of Hamlet's "Madness"	2.1.171-117

Scene 8: In Great Hall 14:22 Min.

-135-146	3:14	Polonius reports Hamlet's "madness" to Claudius and Gertrude and proposes to use Ophelia as decoy to trap Hamlet	2.2.86-158
147	0:24	Hamlet overhears plotting	2.2.159-170
148-163	3:15	"Fishmonger Scene"	2.2.171-216
164-177	5:32	"Nunnery Scene"	3.1.88-186
178	1:17	Claudius suspects Hamlet	3.1.162-188
179	0:40	Tracking shot away from Ophelia weeping on stairs	

Scene 9: On High Tor by daylight 4:07 Min.

180-187	4:07	"To be, or not to be"	3.1.55-87

Scene 10: In Great Hall 2:58 Min.

188-200	2:58	Arrival of the Players	2.2.389-605

Scene 11: In Great Hall 14:26 Min.

201-206	3:33	Hamlet instructs the Players	3.2.1-91
207-213	2:48	Court enters; Hamlet at Ophelia's knee	3.2.92-132
214-225	4:23	"The Mousetrap"	3.2.136-268
226-244	2:38	Claudius:" Give me some light!"; pandemonium	3.2.269-387
245	1:04	Hamlet: "'Tis now the very witching time of night"	3.2.388-399

Scene 12: In Claudius' Chamber 4:03 Min.

-246	0:35	Polonius plans to eavesdrop on Hamlet with the queen	3.3.27-35
247-253	3:28	Claudius confesses fratricide; Hamlet overhears him but does not kill him	3.3.36-98

Olivier's Expressionist *Hamlet*

Scene 13: In Queen's Closet 10:05

-254-256	0:30 Hamlet climbs stairs to his mother's closet	
257-269	2:03 Hamlet stabs Polonius	3.4.1-34
270-285	4:24 Hamlet reproaches his mother	3.4.35-136
286-287	3:08 Hamlet leaves Gertrude's closet	3.4.137-217

Scene 14: In Great Hall 3:28 Min.

288-293	3:28 Hamlet to England	4.3.16-68

Scene 15: River / Interior of Castle 5:38 Min.

294-304	3:38 Ophelia insane	4.5.21-74
305-306	2:00 Laertes returns; Claudius and Gertrude estranged	4.5.75-96

Scene 16: Ophelia's Chamber 1:38 Min.

307-316	1:38 Letter from Hamlet to Horatio; Hamlet's adventures at sea	4.6

Scene 17: In Great Hall 5:07 Min.

317-322	5:07 Ophelia's madness	4.5.131-220

Scene 18: Ophelia's Chamber/River 1:17 Min.

323	1:17 Ophelia drowns in the river	4.7.166-194

Scene 19: In the Graveyard 8:07 Min.

324-337	4:12 Hamlet and the Gravedigger	5.1.61-223
338-348	3:55 Ophelia's Burial; Laertes and Hamlet fight in Ophelia's Grave	5.1.224-296

Scene 20: In Great Hall 5:02 Min.

349-357	5:02 Claudius and Laertes plot to murder Hamlet	4.7.1-162

Scene 21: On the Gallery / In Great Hall 20:07 Min.

358-371	5:17 Osric delivers Laertes' challenge	5.2.81-224
372-373	1:43 Court enters; Hamlet asks Laertes for forgiveness	5.2.224-244

374-377   2:09   Hamlet and Laertes prepare to duel   5.2.244-279
378-381   0:24   Hamlet scores a hit
382-383   0:37   Claudius places poisonous pearl in
                 Hamlet's chalice   5.2.280-283
384-396   1:46   Gertrude drinks from the poisoned chalice   5.2.284-294
397-416   2:17   Laertes wounds Hamlet; Hamlet stabs
                 Laertes   5.2.295-303
317-322   0:38   Gertrude dies   5.2.304-310
323-338   1:39   Hamlet kills Claudius   5.2.311-327
339   0:43   Hamlet and Laertes reconciled   5.2.328-331
340-341   1:49   Hamlets takes leave   5.2.331-360
342-345   1:05   Horatios eulogy for Hamlet   5.2.395-360

Scene 22: Epilogue 2:26 Min.

346-350   2:26   Wandering camera through hallways and up stairways
                 to the ramparts of High Tor

Text: *The Riverside Shakespeare,* ed. G. Blakemore Evans. Boston: Houghton Mifflin, 1974.

ROTTEN STATES: SHAKESPEARE'S *HAMLET* AND KUROSAWA'S *THE BAD SLEEP WELL*

Stephen J. Phillips
(University College of St Mark & St John, Plymouth)

Akira Kurosawa has made three films based on Shakespearean material, two of which are frequently discussed in performance studies of the plays. *Throne of Blood* (1957) and *Ran* (1985), which set *Macbeth* and *King Lear* in feudal Japan have become classics of screen adaptation. However, *The Bad Sleep Well* (1960) which has echoes of *Hamlet* has been neglected.[1] Why has this been the case?

Firstly, in *The Bad Sleep Well* the debt to *Hamlet* does not become apparent until half way through the film. The plots of *Throne of Blood* and *Ran* often follow their Shakespearean counterparts very closely, and a spectator could sit with a copy of Shakespeare and anticipate the order of events in both films. The apparent fidelity to a Shakespearean source has encouraged scholars to regard *Throne of Blood* and *Ran* as cinematic adaptations worthy of study alongside Olivier's *Henry V* or Welles's *Chimes at Midnight*, while *The Bad Sleep Well* could exist independently of its *Hamlet* references.

Secondly, both *Throne of Blood* and *Ran* are examples of the film genre the Japanese call *jidai-geki* - period films - while *The Bad Sleep Well* is an example of *gendai-geki* - films about contemporary life. Modern-dress stage productions of Shakespeare have gained acceptance with academics and audiences but comparable film treatments are still viewed with distrust as 'gimmicky', and consequently marginalized. It seems that an old prejudice in favour of period dress in the theatre has been carried over into our assessment of Shakespeare in a new medium.[2]

Kurosawa has often made it clear in interviews that he only regards *Throne of Blood* as a true 'adaptation' of Shakespeare.[3] The leading English-language authority on Japanese cinema, Donald Richie, records that Kurosawa has never mentioned parallels between *The Bad Sleep Well* and *Hamlet* but once told him that "[*Hamlet*] and *Macbeth* were his favorite Shakespeare". Richie also notes that the genre of revenge tragedy is very accessible to the Japanese.

> Much traditional drama and many Japanese period-films use the formula. If they knew it, the Japanese might make *The Spanish Tragedy* one of their favourite plays. As it is, they have long felt a great affection for *Hamlet*.[4]

In this essay I wish to consider the film's treatment of themes it shares with *Hamlet* and revenge tragedy, and the purpose these allusions may serve. Finally, I want to examine how *The Bad Sleep Well* might enrich our reading of *Hamlet* and so find a place in the canon of Shakespearean film.

The Bad Sleep Well opens with the marriage of Yoshiko, the daughter of Iwabuchi, the Vice-President of a government housing corporation, to his secretary, Nishi. The ceremonies are disrupted by the arrest of the corporation's Assistant Chief, Wada, on charges of corruption, and by the delivery of an enormous wedding cake in the form of a building from which a former Assistant Chief had jumped to his death five years earlier. The police inquiry into the bribery of corporation officials by the Dairyu Construction Company seeking public tenders continues, and they receive anonymous information to help them build their case. One of the suspects, a Dairyu director, commits suicide on orders from his superiors but Wada is saved by Nishi. Nishi uses his position as an insider together with information provided by Wada to weaken the standing of the Chief of the Contracts Department, Shirai, within the corporation. He further undermines the man's sanity by having Wada appear to him as a ghost. Shirai's superiors can no longer trust him when he threatens to go to the police if they pressure him to commit suicide, and Iwabuchi hires a gunman to murder him. Nishi saves Shirai and takes him to the building the wedding cake was modelled on. Here he tells Shirai and Wada that the man who was made to jump from the seventh storey window was his father, Furuya. Nishi's real name is Itakura but he has exchanged identities with an old friend in order to pursue revenge for his

Hamlet and Kurosawa

father's death. He gives Shirai the choice of jumping out of the same window his father fell from or drinking poisoned whisky. Shirai chooses the latter but it is ordinary whisky; he is driven mad with fright and found in the seventh floor office the next day.

Iwabuchi and his Administration Officer, Moriyama, suspect that these incidents are connected with the death of Furuya. Moriyama believes that a relative may be seeking revenge and goes to question Furuya's widow. Not realising his true motives she tells him that Furuya had an illegitimate son by another woman. She produces a photograph of her husband's funeral which shows a man she thinks was Furuya's son watching from a distance; Moriyama recognises Nishi. Yoshiko's brother, Tatsuo, overhears Moriyama reporting to Iwabuchi and, angry that Nishi has deceived his sister for gain, tries to shoot him. Nishi escapes and later succeeds in kidnapping Moriyama. Nishi and his alter-ego, Itakura, hold him hostage in order to obtain the evidence needed to expose the bribery scandal. Wada feels that Nishi's quest for vengeance is pointless as officials never involve their superiors. He reminds Nishi that his new wife will hate him if he exposes her father, and brings Yoshiko to the hideout to persuade her husband to forgive Iwabuchi. He refuses but on her return to her father's house Iwabuchi tricks her into revealing Nishi's whereabouts. Iwabuchi has Nishi and Wada killed, frees Moriyama, and has all the evidence of corruption destroyed. Itakura cannot prove anything and with Nishi's death he has lost his true identity. Yoshiko is driven mad with grief and Tatsuo, now aware of his father's thoroughly evil nature, vows never to see him again. The film ends with Iwabuchi reporting to an unspecified figure who has telephoned him earlier in the film, and who is clearly his superior and equally corrupt.[5]

Such a bald summary might seem to support the argument that there is little value in discussing *The Bad Sleep Well* in relation to *Hamlet*. However, Kurosawa's film makes use of many of the generic features of Revenge Tragedy, and equivalents to most of Shakespeare's *Dramatis Personae* can be found.

Nishi	Hamlet
Telephone Voice	Claudius
Iwabuchi	Polonius
Tatsuo	Laertes
Yoshiko	Ophelia
Itakura	Horatio
Furuya	Old Hamlet
Wada	Ghost

As in *Hamlet* the action centres around the main character's quest for revenge and the guilty party's efforts to avoid exposure. In common with many stage Revengers both Hamlet and Nishi have to resort to trickery in order to discover the individuals responsible for their father's deaths without arousing suspicion. Hamlet's "antic disposition" and Nishi's exchange of identities with Itakura perform the same function, but where Shakespeare first allows Hamlet to unfold his state of mind to the audience in 1.2, Kurosawa keeps Nishi's true motives hidden until he confronts Shirai at the mid-point of the film. Nishi has no equivalent to Hamlet's soliloquies and therefore remains a more distant figure for the audience. When Wada tells him that he is "a terrible man" and that his ruthless treatment of Shirai is inhumane we are forced to scrutinise Nishi's behaviour. Hamlet takes us with him in the early stages of his quest for revenge - we share his dilemmas and uncertainties; our assessment of Nishi's character is abruptly changed when he reveals that Furuya was his father. He has deceived us as well as Iwabuchi in the first half of the film.

When in 2.2. Hamlet decides to use *The Murder of Gonzago* to flush out Claudius he tells the audience "The play's the thing/Wherein I'll catch the conscience of the King". This invites us to scrutinise Claudius as closely as Hamlet and Horatio do during the play-within-the-play, but we are as surprised as the wedding party and the journalists when the second wedding cake arrives at the beginning of *The Bad Sleep Well*. We learn from one of the journalists that the flower projecting from the cake has been placed in the same window as Furuya jumped from; we note the shock on the faces of Shirai and Moriyama, and see Iwabuchi silencing them with a discreet shake of his head but we are not privy to

Nishi's plot. It is only when he tells Shirai that he had arranged for the delivery of the wedding cake in order to judge who was guilty of his father's death that the significance of the opening sequence of the film is fully available to the audience.

By keeping a distance between ourselves and Nishi, Kurosawa makes us question his plan of action. Wada reminds him that Shirai has a wife and family; that Yoshiko will be hurt when she realises that he has used her to expose her father. When Nishi says that he is not only seeking vengeance for his father but for all those who are exploited by corrupt businessmen such as Iwabuchi and the politicians who protect them Wada tells him that he is up against powerful men. The audience is invited to judge whether individual action can effect change in such a society.[6] Like an Elizabethan Revenger Nishi concludes "You can't fight evil by lawful means". As in Revenge Tragedy we are led to ask what are the personal consequences of the thirst for vengeance: does such a task inevitably taint the mind of the Revenger?

By the time we come to share in Nishi's plots Iwabuchi is gaining the advantage. As *Hamlet* proceeds Shakespeare distances us from his protagonist, who is becoming a redoubtable opponent to Claudius. At the mid-point of the film Nishi berates himself because he does not "hate enough". Because he chose to spare Shirai Iwabuchi has been able to buy the newspapers's silence; if he had pushed him from the office window Iwabuchi and Moriyama would be under investigation. Hamlet dismisses any criticism of his ruthless despatching of Rosencrantz and Guildenstern - "They did make love to this employment./They are not near my conscience" [5.2.57-8] - and no longer confides in the audience through soliloquy. He has no moral scruples about acting and is now certain that Claudius has "kill'd my king and whor'd my mother". He has only to find the right opportunity to take his revenge.

Both Hamlet and Nishi come to see themselves involved in more than just a personal vendetta; Hamlet tells Horatio that it would be damnable "To let this canker of our nature come/In further evil" and Nishi tells Wada that he is waging his campaign to expose corruption on behalf of those who are not in a position to fight back. Shakespeare and Kurosawa portray their heroes confronting a rotten state - a common feature of Revenge Tragedy - but both play and film end with them achieving little. Hamlet has begun to acquire the Machiavellian skills which the play demonstrates are a prerequisite for a successful Renaissance monarch but also, perhaps, the source of rottenness. The audience may not find the prospect of the belligerent and opportunistic Fortinbras succeeding to the Danish throne a comforting one. Kurosawa's film ends with Iwabuchi telephoning his superior and reassuring him that all has been resolved satisfactorily. He offers to resign his post - whether to make reparation for his carelessness in allowing Nishi to penetrate the murky world of Japanese business and politics or because he is beginning to develop moral scruples is not clear - but this is refused. He is simply told go abroad. He readily agrees to this and wishes his superior "Goodnight" only to be corrected: it is now morning. Iwabuchi apologises for the mistake; he explains that - unlike his superior - he has not slept all night. He bows low as he replaces the telephone receiver, indicating the higher status of the caller. At the end of both Shakespeare's play and Kurosawa's film the bad still sleep well, as the political system that is the source of corruption is still in place.

In both works women are weak and the tools of the male characters. Hamlet exploits his relationship with Ophelia, performing an elaborate charade of lunacy in her closet to set his plot to expose Claudius in motion; Nishi marries his enemy's daughter in order to penetrate the corrupt corporation. Polonius uses Ophelia to spy on Hamlet; Iwabuchi drugs Yoshiko and tricks her into revealing her husband's whereabouts. Both daughters are driven insane by the murder of a man they love.

Hamlet warns his mother not to let Claudius "ravel all this matter out" [3.4.188]; Moriyama leads Furuya's widow into identifying Nishi by feigning concern for her welfare. The women lack insight into the motives of the men who dominate their societies. Yoshiko cannot believe that her father is such as bad man as Nishi reports him to be, and begs her husband to forgive him. Her promise to "tell father to make up for what he's done" is naive in the extreme. Gertrude finally realises what her new husband is capable of and seeks to defend her son but her new-found awareness comes too late.

Hamlet rages against women in response to his mother's hasty and incestuous marriage, and recites a familiar misogynist's lexicon when confronted by Ophelia. Neither mother nor lover, however, deflect him from his quest for vengeance. In *The Bad Sleep Well* Nishi's resolve is weakened as he finds himself actually falling in love with his wife, and he has to redouble his efforts to maintain his hatred for his father's enemies. His change of attitude is noticed by Wada, however, who brings Yoshiko to the hideout to beg him to forgive Iwabuchi. Her absence from the family home arouses her father's suspicions and he guesses that she knows where Nishi is. Female tenderness nearly destroys his manly resolve to avenge his father's death and is responsible for Nishi's murder.[7]

Neither of the murdered fathers was a saint. Old Hamlet is condemned to purgatory "Till the foul crimes done in my days of nature/Are burnt and purg'd away" [1.5.12-13] while Nishi recognises that his father shared the same values as the bureaucrats he is seeking to punish. Both play and film deal with the corrupt nature of political life and both are the products of societies that did not tolerate direct criticism. The allusions to *Hamlet* allow Kurosawa indirectly to attack the Kishi government that held power in Japan when *The Bad Sleep Well* was first released.

Critics have usually regarded Iwabuchi as the film's equivalent to Claudius[8] but I believe that Claudius remains an off-screen presence. Iwabuchi has a son and a daughter which strongly links him to Polonius; like Shakespeare's character his wife is not mentioned. His daughter is in love with Nishi; his son tries to kill Nishi. Finally, Yoshiko goes mad. Iwabuchi is the servant of a higher political master whom he speaks to by telephone three times during the film: after Wada's funeral ceremony, just before Yoshiko returns from seeing Nishi, and in the final scene. Kurosawa has said that the caller is "someone very high in the Japanese government".

An even worse man is at the end of that telephone line but in Japan if you go any further than that you are bound to run into serious trouble.[9]

This piece of self-censorship he felt weakened the film, and in an interview given in 1986 Kurosawa was more explicit.

> Everyone in the [original Japanese] audience must have deduced that it must be the then Premier Kishi who is the ultimate source of corruption and who is talking at the other end of the telephone. This is why the company has never rereleased the film [...] The company would not have distributed it if this unidentified character had been identified.[10]

Kishi Nobusuke, a former Commerce and Industry Ministry bureaucrat, was Japan's premier between 1957 and 1960. According to Chitoshi Yanaga this government was "a partnership of business representatives and former bureaucrats", and he describes the relations between politics and business in Japan.

> In Japan the power of organised business brings down a government when it concludes that the prime minister has outlived his usefulness and become a definite liability. Once organised business withdraws its support, the collapse of a government follows. There is no way it can be prevented against the will of the business community.[11]

Kishi himself fell from power after losing the support of businessmen. *The Bad Sleep Well* sees the intertwining of business and politics as a major source of corruption. It is Iwabuchi's long-term ambition to go into politics, and when Nishi's efforts to expose him are brought to nothing Itakura exclaims "Now he'll be able to trick the whole of Japan". By echoing the plot and characters of *Hamlet* but not making Iwabuchi the equivalent to Claudius Kurosawa invites the audience to look for this character elsewhere and to make the connection between the telephone caller, Kishi, and Shakespeare's corrupt King, thus circumventing possible censorship. This Oriental Claudius is either unwilling or unable to remove Iwabuchi from his post for fear of alienating the business community upon whom his power depends. Corruption continues to hold sway at the very highest levels of society.

Kurosawa's film can remind Western audiences that *Hamlet* is a political play. Like Kozintsev's Russian screen version (1964) the drama is made more immediate for an English-speaking audience as a consequence of shedding its original language. The "To be or not to be" soliloquy and Hamlet's meditations on mortality as he sighs over Yorick's skull have dominated the play's reception in the Western cultural tradition. Works that have been admitted to the canon of Shakespearean film such as the screen versions of Olivier (1948) and Zeffirelli (1990) have played their part in maintaining the popular emphasis on the characters's individual dilemmas and tragedies at the expense of the tragedy of state. *The Bad Sleep Well* forces us to confront other elements in *Hamlet* that have long been marginalized; elements that may have struck Shakespeare's audience as more pertinent, able as they were to recognise it as belonging to the genre of Revenge Tragedy, and exploring the political and social issues that characterised this dramatic tradition.

Notes

1. John Collick's *Shakespeare, Cinema and Society* (Manchester UP, 1989) contains chapters on Shakespeare in Japan and Kurosawa's treatment of Shakespeare but makes no reference to *The Bad Sleep Well*. Robert Hapgood's essay on Kurosawa's Shakespeare films in Anthony Davies and Stanley Wells ed., *Shakespeare and the Moving Image: The Plays on Film and Television* (Cambridge UP, 1994, pp. 234-49) concentrates on *Throne of Blood* and *Ran* as does James Goodwin in *Akira Kurosawa and Intertextual Cinema* (Baltimore: John Hopkins UP, 1994). Bernice Kliman makes no reference to *The Bad Sleep Well* in her *Hamlet: Film, Television and Audio Performance* (Cranbury: Fairleigh Dickinson UP, 1988).

2. Both the BBC/Time-Life Shakespeare Series 1978-1985 and Kenneth Branagh's Shakespeare films resolutely avoided modern dress, seeking to appeal to a popular audience while Christine Edzard's *As You Like It* (1992) clearly signalled itself as the work of an art-house director by its contemporary setting. David Thacker's *Measure for Measure* transmitted on BBC 2 in November 1994 indicates a new willingness to experiment with modern dress for television Shakespeare.

3. I agree with Hapgood when he observes that Kurosawa's "restriction of the term to a version that is very close to the original is narrower than that in general use" (Davies and Wells, p. 247).

4. Donald Richie and Joan Mellen, *The Films of Akira Kurosawa*, 2nd edn (Berkeley: California UP, 1984), p. 140. The reception of *Hamlet* in Japan is examined by Yasunari Takahashi in "*Hamlet* and the Anxiety of Modern Japan" in *Shakespeare Survey* 48, 1995, pp. 99-111.

5. Several critical studies refer to Iwabuchi as President; I have used the English subtitled version of Kurosawa's film distributed by Connoisseur Video where he is named as Vice-President. Kurosawa wrote the screenplay jointly with Shinobu Hashimoto, Hideo Oguni, Ryuzo Kikushima and Eijiro Hisaita. He was also the film's joint producer with Tomoyuki Tanaka. All Shakespearean quotations in this essay are taken from the Arden editions of the plays.

6. One of Japan's leading film critics, Tadao Sato, goes so far as to claim that "in *The Bad Sleep Well* [...] the main character tries to fight alone against the evil of a bureaucratic structure, and thus degenerates into a shallow terrorist" (*Currents in Japanese Cinema*. Transl. Gregory Barrett. Tokyo: Kodansha International, 1982, p. 122). For Stephen Prince "In his determination to embrace evil, Nishi emerges as one of the darkest of Kurosawa's heroes" (*The Warrior's Camera: The Cinema of Akira Kurosawa* (Princeton UP, 1991, p. 183).

7. The dangers to masculine values posed by female influence is not specific to Japanese culture. Romeo exclaims "O sweet Juliet,/Thy beauty hath made me effeminate" after Mercutio's death in a duel fought on his behalf (*Romeo and Juliet* 3.1.115-16). However, Shakespeare does not treat this issue explicitly in *Hamlet*.

8. Richie and Mellen, pp. 140-1; Marion D. Perret, "Kurosawa's *Hamlet*: Samurai in Business Dress" in *Shakespeare on Film Newsletter*, December 1990, p. 6; Davies and Wells, p. 243.

9. Richie and Mellen, p. 143.

10. Kyoko Hirano, "Making Films for All the People: An Interview with Akira Kurosawa" in *Cinéaste*: Vol. 14: 4 (1986), p. 24.

11. Chitoshi Yanaga, "Big Business in Japanese Politics" in Jon Livingston, Joe Moore and Felicia Oldfather eds, *The Japan Reader. Volume Two: Postwar Japan - 1945 to the Present* (Harmondsworth: Penguin, 1976, pp. 350-1, 348-9). See also Haruhiro Fukui, "Postwar Politics, 1945-1973" in Peter Duus, ed., *The Cambridge History of Japan. Volume 6: The Twentieth Century* (New York: Cambridge UP, 1988), pp. 154-213.

'HIDDEN GAMES, CUNNING TRAPS, AMBUSHES': THE RUSSIAN *HAMLET*

Patrick Burke
(St. Patrick's College, Dublin City University)

Gamlet (*Hamlet*, 1964), directed by Grigori Kozintsev, is the third in line of noteworthy filmed interpretations of the Shakespeare play: preceded by the silent version (National Archive, London, 1913) and that directed by Laurence Olivier (1948), and followed by those of Tony Richardson (1969), Franco Zeffirelli (1991) and, most recently, Kenneth Branagh (1996). The only important foreign-language version, its received critical status, while generally high, has not been undisputed. For James Reid Paris it "is the most cinematic thus far of the several renderings on film of Shakespeare's most popular play and merits our reevaluation and esteem".[1] On the other hand, there is the cryptic comment from Basil Wright in 1972 that the Russian *Hamlet* represents 'an opportunity almost deliberately missed'.[2] The most prestigious source of admiration for the film has probably been the influential stage and film authority, Peter Brook, himself the director of a powerful *King Lear* (1970), who opined in interview with Geoffrey Reeves (1966):

> The strength of the film is in Kozintsev's ablity to realize his own conception with clarity. This is the first Shakespeare film to reflect this form of directorial approach. [... Kozintsev] knows what bars and wood and stone and fire mean to him; he knows the relationship of black to white, of full screen to empty screen, *in terms of content*. ...[3]

Later, however, Brook, out of a concern for what he believes to be the almost untranslatable richness of Shakespearean imagery in all its facets, strongly qualifies that praise: '...[its] limitation lies in its style' (p. 317).

Is it possible, then, to find a focus which will accommodate two critical realities: one, that films such as those listed above have to be addressed primarily in their own defining category as pieces of cinema; two, that they derive from one of the world's great plays, written by the world's greatest dramatist?

I

In his usefully thoroughgoing *Filming Shakespeare's Plays* Anthony Davies succinctly sums up the terms of a recurring artistic dilemma:

> A successful cinematic adaptation of a Shakespeare play must clearly treat the material in *the dramatic terms* of the *cinema itself*, but that should never be taken to imply the elimination of that *theatricality* which is inevitably *embedded in the text* [my emphasis].[4]

In other words, either simply pointing the cameras at a stage production – the method, essentially, of the *Othello* as directed by Stuart Burge in 1965 – on the one hand, or so privileging film as medium, on the other, that the poetic richness of the Shakespeare text is irremediably diluted, makes for the artistically abortive. One of the most illustrative accounts of that dilemma comes from an observation of the producer Michael Birkett, during the filming of the 1967 *Midsummer Night's Dream*, directed by Peter Hall:

> Peter Hall and I found in *A Midsummer Night's Dream* that there were several passages where, looking at the picture on a movieola, without any sound, the cutting pattern would be perfect. Hearing the sound track on its own, the rhythms of the speech also seemed to be fine. *When the two were run together, however*, the result seemed unsatisfactory. We had to evolve a style of cutting which was equally fair to the rhythm of the verse and to the rhythm of the pictures ... [my emphasis][5]

And Kozintsev, the director whose *Hamlet* is the focus of the present essay, intuited from his aesthetic sensibility as film-maker the pressures of that dilemma. What he sought was

> ... the reality and naturalness of a poetic image, not of mundane character. [...] In Shakespeare's plays [...] they are all not only kings, princes,

The Russian *Hamlet*

warriors, but also poets. Poetry is in their blood. Here it seems was the difficulty....[6]

In attempting to overcome that difficulty Kozintsev was richly served by the quality of Boris Pasternak's translation, which manages to avoid both the florid excesses of the nineteenth-century version (which would have transferred to the screen with even greater difficulty than that risked in English-language versions by using Shakespeare uncut) and the flatness of cinematically functional prose: as the director testifies in relation to Pasternak's *King Lear*, "...the natural prosaic quality, the even deliberately unpoetic quality of certain parts is all the voice of a great poet",[7] a poet, moreover, who understood that "Shakespeare's rhythm is the foundation of his poetry. The rhythmic defines the general tone of the drama to a tangible degree".[8]

II

Implicit in any director's attempt to film Shakespeare with integrity will be two partly opposing, partly complementary concerns: one, the optimum realization for the distinctive medium of film of Shakespeare's text; two, the question of what to omit from that text. (Quite a number of even the acclaimed film versions of Shakespeare have cut his texts severely: Olivier's *Henry V* (1944) by one third, his *Hamlet* (1948) by a half, Zeffirelli's *Romeo and Juliet* (1968) by almost sixty per cent, Jarman's *Tempest* (1980) by two thirds. The recently released Hamlet, directed by Kenneth Branagh, is at 242 minutes the first uncut version of the play on film.) If cutting is not to be either reductively arbitrary or merely massaging the vanity of a director who would like to improve upon Shakespeare (a trap not altogether avoided in one or two of the BBC/ Time-Life Shakespeare productions 1979-1985), it follows that its essential justification has to be in the service of a directorial vision consistent with the dramatic truth of the play, its heart, as it were. While I shall be contending that Kozintsev's *Hamlet* (1964) honours such consistency with impressively successful integrity – taking the focus of his interpretation perhaps from the text's reference to Hamlet and the King as "mighty opposites" (5.2.62) – it *is* well to be aware, in honouring his achievement, of what it is, at least in broad outline, that he has chosen to omit, so that he be not accused of failing to do what he never intended to do. That outline will address in particular four aspects of the film: the presentation of Norway, the characterization of the Queen, the treatment of religious awareness and the depiction of human interiority.

Norway

In Kozintsev's film the dramatic standing given by the Shakespeare text to the possibly imminent invasion of Denmark by Norway and to the character of Fortinbras is considerably reduced. Because the play's famous opening scene is cut, we lose the long discussion between Marcellus and Horatio (1.1.73-110) about the paramilitary threat posed by Fortinbras; there can be no ambassadorial going (1.2) or returning (2.2), because Voltemand and Cornelius do not appear at all; when dying, Hamlet does not nominate Fortinbras as his successor (5.2.360-1). In the film the King (Mikhail Nazvanov) simply informs the first meeting of his rather supine court that he has asked old Norway to contain the energies of his nephew, and when we meet Fortinbras for the first time he refers merely to "the conveyance of a promis'd march", not to any "rights of memory" to Danish territory. In narrative terms all of this means that Fortinbras's admittedly dignifed assumption of power at the end of the film is nonetheless a bloodless *coup*, not a matter of due "election"; more significantly, in terms of character, it means that the play's striking parallel between Hamlet and Fortinbras – both princes, both trying to vindicate wronged fathers, both held in check by uncles either physically or morally infirm – virtually disappears: this is most apparent in the elimination of the soliloquy "How all occasions do inform against me ..." (4.4.32-66). This may partly explain also Kozintsev's omission of the description of the murderer-figure of *The Mousetrap* as *nephew* to the King (3.2.239), with the significant political threat to Claudius's *régime* therein implied: the reference would have had less cinematic impact, in the light of the reduced characterization of Fortinbras.

The Queen
While I discuss below the question of the representation of the protagonist's inner life in Kozintsev's *Hamlet*, it is perhaps worthwhile, in the light in particular of what may still be termed the 'Freudian' approach to the workings of that life, the suggestion that Hamlet is inhibited in action by repressed sexual desire for his mother – an approach which, as is well known, influenced the Olivier film of *Hamlet* – to examine briefly the film's characterization of the Queen (Elza Radzin). One way, she is considerably *less* sympathetically portrayed than by, respectively, Eileen Herlie, Glenn Close and Julie Christie in the Olivier, Zeffirelli and Branagh versions: where they are, to varying degrees, all capable of vibrancy, concern (for example, for Ophelia in her madness) and maternal solicitude, the Russian Queen is vainer – spending a lot of time in front of the mirror and a lot of money on clothes – more aloof and, until the scene in her closet, notably less sensitive to her son's plight.

Another way, however, not only is there no hint at all of an 'Oedipus complex' but, more importantly, Kozintsev's Hamlet (Innokenti Smoktunovsky) is considerably less agitated than usual by his mother's behaviour, especially her "o'er-hasty marriage" to Claudius. For example, in what is in any event a severely abbreviated version of the opening soliloquy, "O that this too too sullied flesh would melt ..." (1.2.129-59), there is no reference either to "incestuous sheets" or to the thoughts of "self-slaughter" strongly prompted by them. Similarly, the virtually complete excision of the soliloquy of disorientation, "O all you host of heaven ..." (1.5.92-112) means that we lose not only the directness of "O most pernicious woman" but the harsh ambiguity of "... smiling damned villain" – is it Claudius or Gertrude? Prior to the scene between Hamlet and his mother, after the 'play', Kozintsev deliberately omits those lines from the text (3.2.383-90) which convey at once the prince's heightened emotional temperature and his concern to "speak daggers to her, but use none". Within that scene, after the stabbing of Polonius, only the beginning of the line (3.4.29) "As kill a king ..." is spoken; the remainder, "... and marry with his brother", is suppressed and its dramatic pointing as moral reprimand is lost.

The reduction, in terms of feeling, of the moral relationship between Hamlet and his mother to that of a kind of lay confessor extracting what Catholic idiom sometimes calls 'a purpose of amendment' from a deluded woman living in sexual sin may help to explain why, given the lack of emphasis on a mother's incest and adultery, the 'closet scene' is, in the film, unusually 'tame'. Uniquely, too, the Ghost does not reappear here: instead, by the replaying of the same music which we heard accompany him on his first appearance and by an ingenious close-up on the locket around Hamlet's neck (which contains his father's image), his impact, in filmic terms, is much more that of a powerful memory of Hamlet's than that of a praeternatural presence. That in return reduces a very moving element of the scene, the solicitude of the late husband for his wife – "O step between her and her fighting soul. [...] Speak to her ..." (3.4.112-15) – to the cooler resonance of the earlier "nor let thy soul contrive/ Against thy mother aught" (1.5.85-6).

Religious Awareness

One of the more detectable features both of the text and of many productions of *Hamlet*, especially in its opening and closing sequences, is an emphasis on the religious, on a transcendence recognizably Christian. This is probably most overt in Hamlet's observation in the final scene, "There's a divinity that shapes our ends,/ Rough-hew them how we will" (5.2.10-11). Those lines are omitted by Kozintsev, as are, for example, the oft-quoted "The undiscover'd country from whose bourn/ No traveller returns ..." (3.1.79-80), "Nymph, in thy orisons/ Be all my sins remember'd" (3.1.89-90), "Words without thoughts never to heaven go" (3.3.98), 'There is special providence in the fall of a sparrow" (5.2.215-16). It would seem as if there is inherent in the film a kind of wariness in relation to a sense of the metaphysical as basis either for understanding or behaviour: I see this as manifest in three ways in particular: the denominational allegiance of the Polonius family, the presentation of the King at Prayer and the treatment of mystery.

When Laertes (C. Olesenko) is about to depart for France, his father, Polonius (Yuri Tolubeyev), blesses him with the sign of the cross; when, after her father's death, Ophelia (Anastasia Vertinskaya) is being dressed in black mourning apparel, she dons also a large crucifix while faintly in the background we hear a plain-chant requiem, and when the returned Laertes commits himself to his revenge mission, he does so by solemnly holding aloft a ceremonial sword towards a large picture of the Crucifixion in what appears to be a chapel. I contend, in other words, that in his film Kozintsev wants us to see the Polonius family as Catholics – and rather devout ones. Thus Polonius is at once less prolix and less ridiculous than often portrayed, Laertes is both calmer and duller (and more reasonably motivated than he otherwise would be in the plot he hatches with Claudius: Kozintsev places this scene *after* that of Ophelia's funeral, during which Hamlet had attacked Laertes), Ophelia as dutiful daughter is partly religiously motivated.

It is equally clearly suggested that whatever the denominational allegiance of the other principal characters, it is *not* Catholic: Hamlet and Horatio are 'placed', however imprecisely, by the Lutheran associations of Wittenberg, which each attends; the King I discuss in a moment. Moreover, the often controversial suggestion that the Ghost has come from Purgatory and is therefore to be seen as himself the Catholic father of a student of Lutheran sympathies, is simply evaded in the film by the excision of such apparent clue-supplying lines as "... burnt and *purg'd* away" and "*Unhousel'd, disappointed, unanel'd*" (1.5.13, 77, italics mine). The juxtaposition in the film of Catholic Polonius family and partly Lutheran, partly rationalist, partly agnostic Hamlet family, is, however, subtly tendentious. The dressing-of-Ophelia scene, already alluded to, also includes her being made to wear a kind of heavy metal corselet: this suggests that the formal mourning apparel, including the crucifix, is allied with restriction and physical discomfiture. By extension, Ophelia's religious commitment is seen as one more in a network of protocols – those imposed, for example, by her father or by her slightly sinister dancing teacher – which oppress her and, in tandem with her father's death at the hands of her former lover, push her towards insanity. The Catholicism of this *Hamlet*, then, whatever its decencies, is ultimately repressive, unworthy of seriously thinking people and, as demonstrated by the Priest at Ophelia's funeral, judgementally "churlish".

Kozintsev's King does not "bow [...] stubborn knees" during what is sometimes described as 'the prayer scene' (3.3); instead, he remains standing, looking into a mirror. Taking his cue most probably from Hamlet's definition, when reprimanding his mother, of a mirror as "... a glass/ Where you may see the inmost part of you" (3.4.18-19), Kozintsev unobtrusively establishes the mirror as an image of psychological self-scrutiny in the film. Such self-scrutiny can be superficial, a manifestation of vanity, as noted already in relation to the Queen (who carries her mirror with her!). Claudius, however, looks directly at himself for a long time in a wall mirror; for him, in what is his most vulnerable moment, self-reflection, literal and moral, replaces the process of prayer, even if, in an edited version of the text, some of the idiom of prayer is retained. That may be the reason, too, why Kozintsev, in order to highlight the King's dilemma and dispense with Shakespeare's irony that a character apparently praying is failing to do so, omits completely one of the best-known sequences in the scene – Hamlet's arrival, the "Now might I do it pat..." speech (3.3.72-96), and Hamlet's failure to kill him. That the King is not, however, unrelentingly capable of facing himself the film reveals cleverly in a single late gesture: after he and Laertes have agreed on the double poison plot against Hamlet, Claudius finds himself, goblet of wine in hand, in front of the same mirror as that just referred to, looks at himself for a moment, then suddenly dashes the wine against it. This indicates more than mere self-disgust; it suggests that the very capacity in the King for moral self-examination is being so seriously undermined by his poisonous ways that all he can do, in a self-hating gesture of frustration, is to turn that poison on itself.

For a not insignifcant number of admirers of *Hamlet*, whether we think of text or performance, some sense that there *is* "a divinity that shapes our ends", that

The Russian *Hamlet*

our lives move within the remit of a mysterious but beneficent providence; that there is reality to the notion of cosmic design, that the duplicity of a Claudius, however plausibly presented, can never carry the day, is often experienced as the comforting gift which this major tragedy offers, the reward of a long evening in the theatre or study. Kozintsev deliberately denies us that kind of comfort. In addition to those cited above, he also deletes from that part of the film where the Ghost first appears the "Heaven will direct it" given by the text to the rational Horatio (1.4.91) rather than, as might have been anticipated, the more devoutly orthodox Marcellus; similarly, there is no place for "... even in that was heaven ordinant" (5.2.48) during Hamlet's account of his sea voyage with Rosencrantz and Guildenstern. Missing, too, are the reticent Horatio's oft-quoted lines of elegy, "... Good night, sweet prince,/ And flights of angels sing thee to thy rest" (5.2.364-5).

If it denies us religious solace, this *Hamlet* also denies us religious mystery: the Ghost's "... this eternal blazon must not be/ To ears of flesh and blood ..." (1.5.21-22) is cut as are, as already observed, the references in "To be or not to be" to "the undiscover'd country, from whose bourn/ No traveller returns ..." Because the 'swearing' scene with Hamlet and the sentries (1.5.146-90) is omitted, the Ghost's authority in demanding assent, the identity, possibly malign, of the "fellow in the cellarage", are not offered as matters to reflect upon. The film resolutely eschews metaphysical resonance, most notably in relation to that part of the text in which it is most overt, "...There is special providence in the fall of a sparrow ..." (5.2.215-20). In his dispensing with the specific Gospel echoes of Matthew 10:29, its comforting emphasis on the omniscience of a caring God, we may perhaps recall Kozintsev's 1973 comment, "I am never drawn by biblical associations".[9] He dispenses, too, with the endorsing of "The readiness is all" as something akin to the highest moral wisdom, underlining instead "We defy augury" and switching the final words of the speech, "Let be", from a stage cue for alertness to a whole life stance, arguably a reply in its stoicism to the questioning of "To be or not to be".

Interiority

It is a truism of *Hamlet* criticism, whatever the concerns of critics as different as Eliot, Dover Wilson or Fergusson (to glance at some of the hallowed names), that its action subsumes a double conflict, that between Hamlet and the society presided over by Claudius, in which "something is rotten", and that within Hamlet himself. It is almost equally agreed that the Russian *Hamlet* focusses virtually exclusively on the first conflict, scarcely at all on the second. As David Robinson has put it, "[Kozintsev's] Hamlet owes nothing to any stage tradition of a moody and poetic hero doomed by indecision: as played by Innokenti Smoktunovski [*sic*] he is nervous, virile, positive ..." The film's reluctance to attempt to represent Hamlet's psychic life is reflected most unambiguously in its aproach to Shakespeare's classic device for revealing the dynamics of that life, the soliloquies: three, "O all you host of heaven!" (1.5.92-112), "Now Might I do it pat..." (3.3.73-96) and "How all occasions do inform against me" (4.4.32-66), are omitted completely, and all of the remaining, including "To be or not to be", are so cut and edited that the inner turmoil and self-recrimination of, for example, "O what a rogue and peasant slave am I", are barely present: The Ghost's instructions to Hamlet conspicuously *omit* "Taint not thy mind ..." (1.5.85) and the film sees no need for Hamlet to announce and have kept secret his proposed 'antic disposition', even if, later, the courtiers see his behaviour as peculiar. In general terms, then, Kozintsev has chosen to de-emphasize self-analysis and its often accompanying moral agonizing in his film; moreover, as already noted, we are as likely to be aware of it in the King as in Hamlet.

III

Perhaps the biggest single clue to the intended focus of his film comes from Kozintsev's observation in *King Lear: The Space of Tragedy*: "In *Hamlet* the words about not being a pipe on which the king's men can play whenever they like seemed to be more significant (though of course such comparisons are relative) than the famous 'To be or not to be!'" (p. 50). Implicit in that is a thematic concern

The Russian *Hamlet*

with Hamlet's aloneness as more political than metaphysical: he is profoundly at odds with the King's *régime*, evidenced most directly, at early points in the film, in his absenting himself from the council chamber when Claudius is about to address him for the first time and, more strikingly – by means of a tactic that Kozintsev may have borrowed from David Lean, for example, in *Doctor Zhivago* – in his walking *against* the stream of courtiers while 'thinking' his first soliloquy; in the director's words, "... my own experience taught me that Hamlet's first soliloquy succeeded because it was spoken (like an interior monologue) among crowds of people hurrying to the carnival against a background of noise and music and of faces flitting past". The film imagery by means of which the alien aspects of Claudius's *régime* are most unambiguously conveyed is that of enclosure, confinement, specifically that of imprisonment – "Denmark's a prison" (2.2.243). Since that is a feature of the film that has received much useful critical examination, I restrict my discussion of it on the present occasion, referring in particular to the *resumé* offered by Jack J. Jorgens (1973):

> Kozintsev follows Olivier(?) and earlier stage designers in making Denmark a prison. The deep shadows, drawbridge, portcullis, and moat, the huge doors and staircases, corridors and walls which dwarf people, the ceaseless echoes ... all contribute to this effect ...[10]

Slightly less attention has been given to the use of that imagery as it bears not on Hamlet (whom we see immured within the high castle walls in the opening moments of the film) but on Ophelia, the figure of innocence and vulnerability destroyed by the male-driven forces of Denmark. Thus, when we see her first, she is learning the steps of an over-stately, old-fashioned dance from a rather severe teacher, deferring, physically, to a pattern imposed on her by her elders. She returns to the dance immediately following her father's prohibitions against her seeing Hamlet again, her deference now a moral one. Moreover, at the height of her mental breakdown, after the death of Polonius, she reverts, in conditioned reflex, to the dance when she sees her teacher approach. In the latter scene, too, as already noted, she is literally locked into her mourning apparel, another figure of her enforced deference to social forms: the first indication of Ophelia's madness in the film is her attempt to remove her clothing.

The prison imagery is brought to bear also on the love relationship between Hamlet and Ophelia: at the beginning of 'the nunnery scene' she is *framed*, in a detail which may relate to the issue of her possible Catholicism discussed above, by a stained-glass window (we see her in reverse shot, in shadow, through that window when Hamlet is about to depart for England); the stair rails through which Hamlet first sees her, and clearly prior to his suspecting that they are being overheard by Polonius and Claudius, look like prison bars. This is not a political order in which love can flourish. Ophelia is imprisoned even in death – the dark, heavy coffin lid which is about to cover her when Laertes, in one of the more credible interpretetations of this sequence, intervenes; the oppressive hammering as the gravedigger nails the lid down. It is notable, too, as an element of a sustained imagery pattern, that as Hamlet returns to the castle, right after the funeral scene, the imprisoning portcullis descends.

That the imprisoning claustrophobia of this *Hamlet* palpably intensifies as the action unfolds is most clearly conveyed by Kozintsev's deployment of guards and sentries. Bearing an uncanny resemblance to the visual strategy of Hitchcock's *The Birds* (filmed the previous year, 1963), the film brings sentries more and more noticeably within the screen frame: their vigilance, first apparent when they move along the castle walls, as the Player is giving the 'Hecuba' speech – repressive regimes' stereotypical suspicion of theatre? – sharpens so much when Hamlet is planning *The Mousetrap* with Horatio that he ushers them away. In the ceremonial procession which inaugurates the play scene one sentry, established thenceforth as a favourite and as especially loyal to Claudius (he it is who later announces the threatening return of Laertes), is given centre frame; they are alert and vigilant as 'the play' unfolds. With the killing of Polonius by the prince of Denmark, the threat of Laertes, the beginnings of madness in Ophelia and "...the people muddied,/ Thick and unwholesome in their thoughts and whispers" (4.5.81-2), the camera

The Russian *Hamlet*

indicates growing fear and tension by panning slowly not only across a number of alert sentries but a large salivating dog (a Great Dane, by an 'in joke'!) who had appeared earlier, in the first Ophelia scene, as a companionable, domesticated canine: he is thus a measure, in little, of the distance travelled in the film from reassuring familiarity towards a police state.

IV

The artistic collaboration between Kozintsev and Dmitry Shostakovitch (1906-1975), sometimes neglected in critical analysis, predated the filming of *Hamlet* by almost forty years, extending back to the twenty-two year old composer's score for the silent *The New Babylon* (1929); other films they worked on together included *Alone* (1931) and, memorably, the great *King Lear* of 1971. Theirs was an artistic relationship intuitively based, free of inhibiting dogma or abstraction, as Kozintsev acknowledged:

> ... the vocabulary of aesthetics is alien to [Shostakovitch ....] Elevated words about art inflict on him almost physical pain; an agonizingly fastidious expression comes over his face as if he has come into contact with something disgusting ...[11]

Nonetheless, the composer invariably possessed an unerring sense as to the essential musical requirements of Kozintsev's films, especially the versions of Shakespeare:

> .... I would not be able to make a Shakespearean film without it [the music] just as I would not be able to do without Pasternak's translation What do I think is the main point about it – the tragedy? [...] But not just tragedy [...] philosophy, and a general concept of the whole world? [...] it is another feature which is most important. [...] Goodness, kindness. Mercy.
> However it is a special kind of goodness. [...] In Russian art goodness does not exist without a fierce hatred of everything which destroys a man. In Shostakovitch's music I can hear a ferocious hatred of cruelty, the cult of power and the oppression of justice. ...[12]

Both artists agreed from the outset of their collaboration that the music would be always be integral to the films, never merely decorative, "linked", in Kozintsev's words, "with the inner meaning rather than external action": "His feeling for the image was so much an integral part that probably to have separated the music from it would have been very difficult ..."[13] Thus Shostakovitch seems never to have been attracted by the prospect of marketing, in score or recording form, any of his film music in isolation from the films themselves.

Sometimes the composer will give a film character something like his own signature tune, a process already noted in the representation of the Ghost. It is clearest both to detect as well as to articulate in relation to Ophelia:

> Ophelia's voice [...] took a long time to find. The short piece (the dancing lesson, Polonius' daughter's first appearance) was to have been played on the guitar, then Shostakovitch suggested that it should be played on the violin and piano. Then, a lute was brought from the museum of musical instruments for a new tape-recording. And then one began to hear Ophelia's frailty, her artifciality, her tenderness, doomed to perish.[14]

For purposes of the present essay I wish to focus on the use made in *Hamlet* of two recurring refrains, each of which is inadequately described in a phrase such as 'mood-setting'. One of those I refer to as 'the death music', the other as 'the madness music'.

'The death music' is deployed with impressive artistic tact in the film: we hear it initially as a lament for Hamlet's father, as the black mourning banners are being unfurled in the course of Kozintsev's inserted 'prologue'. It recurs as, in a sense, the final part of a *trio* accompanying the filmically presented leavetaking of Ophelia by Hamlet (the play's 2.1.77-100): the music modulates from a pleasing gentleness, while Ophelia is alone, to a more disturbed idiom, supported by tympani, as the rather alarming Hamlet arrives, to 'the death music', as – "... thrice his head thus waving up and down" – he slowly departs. It is heard next as the significant background to "To be or not to be". Next, aboard ship for England (which the film presents rather than narrates), the music accompanies Hamlet's reading of Claudius's letter demanding his death on arrival, while the treacherous Rosencrantz and Guildenstern sleep: it functions thus as ironic comment on the putative death of Hamlet and as overture to the killing of the other two. We hear this music for the last time, in a kind of militaristic 'up-tempo' version, as Laertes jabs Hamlet with the poisoned rapier during the duelling scene. A noteworthy aspect of almost all of those sequences is that – notwithstanding the conspicuous figure of death (always last) among the figures which appear whenever the castle clock strikes – the deaths evoked by the music are not final: Hamlet's father *has* returned from the dead, Hamlet's love for Ophelia (as he reminds us at her funeral) does not end with his leavetaking, there may equally be "something after death" as not. The 'sting' of death is lessened by intimations of love and memory ("Remember me") as well as by the music, the artefact which, paradoxically, expresses it and denies it.

What I have termed 'the madness music' is less elaborately deployed, being confined to two scenes close to one another in the film, in one of which we see Ophelia in severe mental torment: the music betokening her state is fast, 'driven'. Later, following the *pathos* of her drowning, the camera tracks a long shot of a solitary bird across the sky which, as it hovers near the newly returned, rather ascetic-looking Hamlet, is accompanied by 'the madness music'. I take this to signify that madness is subsumed into whatever it is that links Ophelia and Hamlet, affective in essence, and that this is also why, as Osric and others arrive to invite Hamlet to the duel, the bird reappears: its associations challenge those of death; literally and symbolically, "we defy augury". The bird which Kozintsev presents does philosophic duty, in a sense, for the Gospel sparrows which he omits.

V

The prison which is Elsinore in Kozintsev's *Hamlet* is more than a matter of walls, armour, police-state vigilance: it is intended, in his words, to image "... the state with its armies, police and holidays",[15] to reflect the directorial intuition that "Elsinore is a speculative concept in Shakespeare. It is impossible to translate it directly and completely into plastic form". In specifcally political terms, it presents as the Claudius *régime* to which Hamlet is implacably opposed intellectually and, as conveyed by his obsessive beating of the players' drum and by an agonized cry of frustration as he plans the 'play', emotionally as well. Implicit in his adversarial stance is the question as to how might best be realized those conditions under which Denmark would no longer be a prison, in which the "something rotten" would be extrued from the body politic. I have suggested that embryonic betterment inheres in the film's emphases on the possibility of love, on affectionate memory, on art (the players). Most intriguing in this regard is the relationship of the dramatic action to the realm of such natural elements as water, fire and earth, all of which are strikingly present in the opening of the film – the sea, the torches, the landscape over which Hamlet gallops. As with the prison imagery, that is a topic which, supported by reference to Kozintsev's own comments (themselves acknowledging the influence of the great designer, Gordon Craig), has received much critical comment, which I do not wish to duplicate. It is my belief that, in the essential cinematic strategy which relates, even mutually defines, man and landscape, Kozintsev deliberately opts for ambiguity and uncertainty in closure, rendering at once too abstract and too final evaluations such as Robert Hapgood's: "Kozintsev's *Hamlet* is less of an enactment of Shakespeare's play than a lyric meditation upon it, rendered in visual symbols of stone, iron, fire, sea, earth"[16] – or Anthony Davies's. "It is as though the pattern of a formulative equation were at work here: time (historical period) = value system = spatial features".[17] I suspect that, *mutatis mutandis*, Kozintsev's later comments about notions of the heroic in his *King Lear*, would apply also to *Hamlet*: he refers to his reluctance to "... film a magnificent funeral for Hamlet ..." and to "... the nation's flags unfurled over the body of the dead student", not "prince".[18] In this respect, if no other, Kozintsev is as proletarian in concern as any Soviet realist: Hamlet as prince is at least implicated in a system which keeps ordinary people cowed (the first part of the King's opening speech – "Though yet of Hamlet our dear brother's death ..." – is *read* authoritatively at them), visited by warfare the source of which is never made

The Russian *Hamlet*

clear (the ravaged landscape through which Hamlet walks on his return from sea), harried and driven away by soldiers, as at Ophelia's funeral.

From that complex of social stratification and the relationship of human agent to elemental environment Kozintsev gives qualified endorsement to engagement with and reformation of the social realm. On two occasions Hamlet turns away from the natural elements of the sea and rocks and moves up the pointedly long flight of steps towards the castle, its showiness and its intrigues: once, slowly and with obvious effort, after "To be or not to be"; later, with the kind of *sprezzatura* already noted, after "We defy augury...". Conversely, when about to die, he moves in the opposite direction, out towards the open air, free at last from what Kozintsev terms the 'falsehood' and 'baseness' of the castle. That the kind of decisiveness so signified can be meaningful we may observe from the opening up the Denmark prison as Hamlet's movingly dignified funeral is processing; that it may be ontologically uncertain we can infer from the shot of the boy, one of the people, who stumbles and hesitates as he is about to follow its lead.

The formal elements of the Russian *Hamlet* – its use of space, camera angles, balance of light and shade, integrating of music and soundtrack, editing in the service of rhythm, in addition to the in-depth acting of the Hamlet, the King and, in the best performance on film, the Ophelia – have been intelligently discussed elsewhere, notably by Brook and Jorgens. Those elements enrich and support the coherence of the director's thematic focus on *Hamlet* as a contest of 'mighty opposites': Claudius and Hamlet; capable, courageous but corrupt administration versus personal integrity and idealism free of neurosis or introversion; the possibilities of oligarchy versus those of democracy. In this way what I believe to be the finest film version of *Hamlet* to date speaks with impressive nuance to the Shakespeare text, to the debate on freedom in the Soviet Union of post-Stalinist 'thaw' and to the moral uncertainties of our own threatened time.

Notes

1. James Reid Paris, *Classic Foreign Films* (New York: Citadell Press, 1993), p. 86.

2. Cited in *Halliwell's Film Guide*, 10th edn (London, 1994), p. 466.

3. Geoffrey Reeves, "Finding Shakespeare on Film: From an Interview with Peter Brook" in *Film Theory and Criticism*. ed. Gerald Mast and Marshall Cohen (New York: Oxford UP, 1974), pp. 316-17.

4. Anthony Davies, *Filming Shakespeare's Plays* (Cambridge UP,1988), pp. 23-4.

5. *The Cambridge Companion to Shakespeare Studies*, ed. Stanley Wells (Cambridge UP, 1986), p. 277.

6. Grigori Kozintsev, *King Lear: the Space of Tragedy*, translated by Mary Mackintosh (London: Heinemann, 1977), pp. 67 and 60.

7. *Space of Tragedy*, p. 42.

8. *Space of Tragedy*, p. 174.

9. *Space of Tragedy*, p. 63.

10. Jack J. Jorgens, "Image and Meaning in the Kozintsev *Hamlet*", *Literature and Film Quarterly*: 4 (1975), p. 311.

11. *Space of Tragedy*, p. 244.

12. *Space of Tragedy*, p. 254.

13. *Space of Tragedy*, pp. 243 and 248.

14. *Space of Tragedy*, p. 247.

15. Grigori Kozintsev, *Time and Conscience*, translated by Mary Mackintosh (London: Heinemann, 1967), p. 268.

16. *Cambridge Companion*, p. 282.

17. *Filming Shakespeare's Plays*, p. 21.

18. *Space of Tragedy*, p. 237.

A WORTHY DANE:
RICHARD CHAMBERLAIN'S *HAMLET*

Patrick McCord
(University of Georgia, Athens)

The 1970 Hallmark Hall of Fame *Hamlet*, starring Richard Chamberlain and directed by Peter Wood from John Barton's adaptation, is both a neglected masterpiece and an historical curiosity at the center of a fascinating matrix of intertextual forces.[1] These two issues – the neglect and the intertextual apparatus – interpenetrate each other tellingly.[2] What might be a canonical, or at least an important, interpretation of Shakespeare's most filmed play has instead been confined to the vaults at U.C.L.A., not because of its lack of artistic worth, but because its unusual casting, historical situation, peculiar reception, and challenging aesthetic ambitions have worked together to permit its disappearance before its value was realized. I propose to untangle this matrix of texts by tracing meanings in conventional texts – Shakespeare's playscript, the videotaped record of the Chamberlain/Wood production, and criticism of this production – and also in the 'texts' that inform modes of thought and value embedded in the perceptions of critics, the persona of the star, and the particulars of historical situation. Moreover, the paucity of writing on this *Hamlet*, the perturbing 'neglect', has its own textual value which begs tracing.

The Reception

The immediate critical response to the Chamberlain/Wood production ranged from the ambivalent to the nonexistent. In fact the 'neglect' began here when many national periodicals simply ignored this daring attempt to bring *Hamlet* onto American prime-time commercial television. In 1970, Public Television was not the cultural monolith it is today; the three major commercial networks controlled almost all of television's offerings, and this was the first Shakespeare to be broadcast in years. Yet *The New Republic* spent its ink on *McHale's Navy* that week.[3] Curiously, the perceptions of 1970 critics strongly clashed with the experiences of 1997 viewers.

The few reviews that exist reveal a central textual problem with the reception of the Hallmark *Hamlet*: American reviewers were troubled by the 'text' of Chamberlain. Specifically, they were unable to forget that Chamberlain had been a popular 'heart-throb' actor on American commercial television before he went to England better to learn his craft and returned as Hamlet. The American critics' prejudice about the text of Chamberlain's life tainted their critical perception of the performance. A week before the broadcast, a *Time* article nastily entitled "Kildare as Hamlet" was more actor's biography than criticism: only one paragraph critiqued the production while five detailed Chamberlain's life and career. While informative – even somewhat positive – the essay also assumed a patronizing tone:

> In the early 1960s, when he was MGM Television's Dr. Kildare, Richard Chamberlain got more fan mail than just about anyone on the lot since Clark Gable played Rhett Butler. In 1966, when the TV series ended, Chamberlain decided to start his career all over again.
> He went to England, let his peroxided hair grow brown and long. He took speech lessons, and after a strong performance in a BBC drama, received an offer to play Hamlet with the excellent Birmingham Repertory Theater. [...] He was the first American to dare HAMLET in Britain since John Barrymore, and, premiere night, a full cry of London critics rode to Birmingham for the kill – and for a shock. Wrote the TIMES critic the next morning: "Anyone who comes to this production prepared to scoff at the sight of a popular American television actor playing Hamlet will be in for a deep disappointment."[4]

Such a tone – noting peroxided hair, Gable's fan mail, and a "shockingly" good performance by a TV star – is a peculiar, even anomalous, reaction to a production of *Hamlet*. But so was the appearance of a 'TV actor' in Shakespeare. And although the British critics, well-schooled in live performance, actors, and adaptations, were, apparently, able to overcome their prejudice against an American television actor, American critics were not.

The few words *Time* expended on the production were ambivalent. The production was hailed as a "gratifying surprise" – in other words 'Kildare did not flop' – yet the review continued in more negative terms. Chamberlain's accent was "well east of mid-Atlantic", and his Hamlet was "passionate sometimes to the point of hysteria". Worse, *Time* concluded: "To fit the two-hour time slot [...] more massive surgery has been performed on the Folio than any that Kildare ever did", both a complaint about the extreme cutting of the play and another jibe at Chamberlain's persona. Even before *Hamlet* aired, three textual issues had been raised. Clearly it was difficult to pan 'high art' on television – especially the first Shakespeare to appear in years – but, at the same time, it was equally difficult to credit a television 'personality' with the depth to enact the most challenging of English language role. This ambivalence was focused in a possibly gratuitous complaint about the cutting of the play. Herewith began the travail of the Chamberlain/Wood production.

The day after the national broadcast, *The New York Times* echoed, emphasized, and amplified identical objections. "Chamberlain, Buoyed by English Cast, Portrays Hamlet on N.B.C." was the title of Jack Gould's review, in which he claimed the English thespians "virtually acted [Chamberlain] right off the stage".[5] While Gould did praise Chamberlain's "youthfulness and vigor", he, like *Time*, faulted the American's elocution. Gould, too, was bitter about John Barton's "heartbreaking task of cutting 'Hamlet' in half", calling the production "a midi-thing bound to suffer from the emasculation of so many lines and scenes". Interestingly, Gould contrasted his dislike of the television star Hamlet with special accolades for Ophelia: "...another star was born in the beautiful Ciaran Madden as the rejected Ophelia. Her mad scene was exquisitely delicate artistry".

Cecil Smith in *The Los Angeles Times* was only slightly more generous to the play as a whole, acknowledging that there might be an actual production concept involved in the "opulent and lavish" staging, but he then compromised his insight proclaiming, "Such is the strength of the play that it could be played in loincloths [...] and given a reasonably competent production."[6] Probing slightly deeper than *Time* or Gould, Smith saw Chamberlain as actually having an interpretation, "... less the scholar brooding on the festering sore of his civilization than Prince Valiant sword in hand after dragons and demons in human form." Smith, like Gould, approvingly noticed that Chamberlain "gives a lithe quickness to the man." However, there was still condescension in this "Prince Valiant" diction and the implication that Chamberlain was more athlete than actor. Finally, however, Chamberlain was damned by comparative faint praise. Smith thrilled for ten column-inches over Michael Redgrave's Polonius before concluding with high marks for the rest of "the illustrious cast" stated in specific superlatives: "splendid", "high quality", "special flare" (all the cast, that is, save Ciaran Madden's Ophelia, whom he found "a rather dull character").

Variety, the last of the national periodicals to notice the production, actually mentioned the problem of television-as-text.

> *Hamlet* is probably the least suited of the bard's plays for television. Almost all the other plays can be interpreted in terms of action, but inaction is what *Hamlet* is all about [...] and it suffers badly at the hands of what is probably the most literal of all media, one that serves best in the verities of such actualities as the news and football games.[7]

This last no doubt came as alarming news to the BBC, yet it would seem to endorse the Barton cutting of the play. But *Variety* ignored these implications and harmonized with the other American reviewers:

> ... of Chamberlain's version of the role, it was neither the best nor the worst of the prominent interpretations. [...] Chamberlain's handling of the Shakespearean lyricism and rhythms was adequate but suffered from comparison with the heady competition with which he was working. [...] It was obvious that Chamberlain was laboring with the script, albeit generally successfully, and the others [in the cast] were not.

Variety also concluded by sniping at the adaptation:

> John Barton's excisions from the play were usually adept but often eliminated important buildups to the more famous soliloquies and dramatic byplay. Tinkering with Shakespeare's own dramatic economy is a dangerous game, and Barton more than once fell into the trap of reducing the irreducible.

What is most notable in all these critiques is the strange unanimity of ambivalence as well as a collective critical failure. All the reviewers contrast the Athletic American with the Eloquent English, apparently attempting to praise the production while gainsaying Chamberlain. The focus for the most irritation and the best *bon mots* is the adaptation, yet while critics felt short-changed by the cutting, they seem to have forgotten (or not to have noticed) that the most famous cinematic *Hamlet* to date, and the obvious comparison to Chamberlain's, Laurence Olivier's 1948 version, also cut about half the play.[8]

In at least part of their unanimous perception, these critics were constrained by a specific historical-cultural moment. They were unused to commercially televised Shakespeare enacted by a TV star who had for years been identified as a handsome, if somewhat wooden, M.D. When I screened this production for various audiences in 1997 – audiences whose awareness of the Chamberlain text was informed not by any recollection of *Dr. Kildare*, but by his long and varied career – the response was overwhelmingly positive. His "east of Mid-Atlantic" accent was unnoticed by my audiences, several of whom were English graduate students steeped in BBC Shakespeare, and one of whom was a classically trained actor. One young person had always assumed Chamberlain *was* English. It may be that, when those television critics of the seventies felt discomfited by unexpected forces and references, they 'saw' the text of the 'TV actor' and the text of the script to be at fault. Thus they proved to be disinclined, or were so constrained by the single viewing that they were unable to locate the actual source of disequilibrium, the production's daring originality.

Later Criticism

While commentary on other productions of *Hamlet* is plentiful – including extended remarks on Grigori Kozintsev's Russian Language production – to date, almost nothing has been written about the Chamberlain/Wood version. Among the scholarly appraisals, Jay L. Halio's "Three Filmed *Hamlets*", which appeared in the

Fall 1973 *Literature/Film Quarterly*, is the only essay to treat the production as worthy of serious consideration.[9] In the many books on cinematic or televised adaptation, only J. C. Bulman and H. R. Coursen's 1980 volume, *Shakespeare on Television*, includes more than passing mention of it, and this is in Coursen's chapter, serendipitously entitled "Three Televised *Hamlets*".[10] Neither of these efforts grasped the wealth of meaning in the Chamberlain/Wood production, but they form interesting contrasts to each other and to earlier criticism. And Halio had a rejoinder to the television critics.

Coursen's commentary was more review than close reading. But unlike the seventies reviewers, he uniformly disliked *all* the performances, regardless of the actor's country of national origin, and he surprisingly claimed that Chamberlain "*underplayed* the role, appropriately for TV, but the result was a *bland* performance" (italics mine, p. 104). This is a strange perception given the unanimity of the earlier critics, who all saw Prince Valiant struggling vigorously among the smooth Shakespeareans. But again, there may have been a contextual agenda at work that disposed Coursen to 'see' in a certain way. Perhaps he was inclined to hate the production top to bottom in order to set it up as a straw man for the 1960 Maximilian Schell and 1980 Derek Jacobi vehicles he wanted to praise.[11] He concluded, however, with a phrase that recalled other phobic responses to Chamberlain's past: "Chamberlain's [*Hamlet*] is for those out there in television-land who have no particular opinion about this or any other Dane and who do not wish to be troubled with one" (pp. 106-7). "Television-land" and "no particular opinion" echoe the dismissive diction with which Chamberlain was previously cursed. Coursen, like the earlier critics, was so disposed by his reading of the textuality of television that he was unable to see the very obvious and careful 'opinion' of this production.

In an even briefer essay, which Coursen footnoted but ignored, Jay Halio, like Cecil Smith, sensed the deeper artistic implications of the Chamberlain/Wood version. Halio recalled that, in first-class productions, there are minds and imaginations at work who purpose to make the familiar text resonate with

Richard Chamberlain's *Hamlet*

provocative, and often timely, meanings. In this regard, cutting and design are two important clues to "a particular interpretation of the play that the director has adopted to guide him", a view of the production no critic had heretofore attempted to justify (p. 316). Halio recognized that Chamberlain's was a particularly political and Romantic version of the play, and he began to piece together a rationale for the Regency production design. Nevertheless, he stopped short of what, by his own lights, might have been a full reading, and concluded rather abruptly:

> For Chamberlain's version of the play [...], the sets and costumes are entirely suitable and convincing. We may disagree with the interpretation – Chamberlain's *Hamlet* is not my *Hamlet* – but taken on its own premises as a romantic version of a passionate, sensitive young prince caught up in an intolerable situation not of his making, it works well enough. So does Olivier's. (pp. 319-20)

Halio, however, did deliver an effective riposte to the television critics who had postured as Shakes-purists in their relentless irritation with Barton's adaptation:

> In his own time, Shakespeare frequently revised, cut, added to, and in many other ways altered his plays to meet the changing needs of his company and the changing fashions of the day. It is an error to maintain, as some critics persist in doing, that by altering the text we are somehow violating Shakespeare or doing anything he would not do. [... C]an we seriously hope for anything but "versions" of *Hamlet*? (319)

A Version of *Hamlet*

My claim, that the Chamberlain/Wood *Hamlet* is a neglected masterpiece, is at least partially proven: this version of *Hamlet* has clearly been neglected. That it is a masterpiece, I base on the very original adaptation of the play as well as on Chamberlain's daring and (especially to earlier viewers) disturbing interpretation of the role. Although *Time* typified him as a bleached blond and other critics dismissed his acting as more brio than brain, the best single piece of criticism on the Chamberlain/Wood interpretation was written by Chamberlain himself. His essay, "Why Does an Actor Agree to Do 'Hamlet'?" appeared in *The Sunday New York Times* a few days before the air date and hinted at significant interpretive tropes in the adaptation of the play, all of which were lost on the critics, all of which challenged and used *Hamlet* in a complex and fascinating way.[12] Before reading the essay, I had watched the performance several times and had, from the comfortable perspective of twenty-six years later, remarked on all of the tropes Chamberlain hinted at. It is doubly interesting, then, that the inflections and intertextual references of one of the most ambitious of the recorded *Hamlet*s were invisible at the moment of performance, yet, over time, have become clearer and quite significant.

Chamberlain's most telling statement offered the central premise of the production:

> My Hamlet is, I confess, *against the prevailing fashion.* Contemporary Hamlets from Sir Alec Guinness 20 years ago to Nicol Williamson the other day have been determined anti-heroes, rough figures slouching to their fate.[13] Our version is avowedly and unashamedly romantic, a revival of that earlier and longer lived tradition [...] the prince as a Byronic hero. [italics mine]

Thus, young Hamlet as Byronic hero is a character that differed from the Oedipal-introspective Hamlets that were in fashion, just as Chamberlain differed from the typical TV heart-throb.[14] Chamberlain then articulated more of the rationale behind the cutting and choice of period.

> *Hamlet* in the Regency period [...] becomes more a revenge melodrama, the popular entertainment of the early 19th century. That era was close to our own in its fashions and attitudes, so that the play's contemporary qualities are emphasized.

Here, Chamberlain logically justified the excision of so many lines and also urged his audience to pay close attention to the "fashions and attitudes" of Regency England and 1970 America. This statement sends us back to some teasingly offhand comments with which Chamberlain began:

> [I]t is surprising that someone hasn't pressed the play into service as part of the student protest, with Hamlet as the victim of the generation gap, forced against his will to act according to the violent dictates of his father. Or our more liberal directors might score by transforming Hamlet into one of the boys in the band...(ellipses Chamberlain's).

Obviously, "someone" *had* pressed the play into service as part of the student protest. Chamberlain had obligingly tipped his hand to prepare critics and audiences alike, but none of the critics bothered to notice the complex artistic agenda that was clearly enunciated: a Byronic Hamlet, struggling to overcome a generation gap in an English Regency context that would have direct correlations to 1970s United States social and political issues.

This strategy was yet another example of a textual choice that went against the prevailing tenor of Shakespeare production. The dominant criterion for adaptation – which is still invoked today – was articulated by Jonathan Miller in his 1980 interview regarding *Antony and Cleopatra*: "What details you do introduce *must remind the audience of the sixteenth-century imagination*, not of the archaeologically accurate Egypt and Rome to which the play nominally, and only nominally, refers" (italics mine).[15] The Chamberlain/Wood production simply dispensed with anything like a dubious "the sixteenth-century imagination" in an effort to reinvent *Hamlet* for a contemporary television audience. The result was, again, a *sui generis* approach whose complex justifications were beyond the 1970 critical horizon.

Regency/Denmark/U.S.A.

The triangulation of three historical texts: Regency England, *Hamlet*'s fictional Denmark, and the United States of the late 1960s – emphasizes certain key political issues that sympathetically focused the Chamberlain/Wood interpretation on the contemporary youth movement.

First, there is the theme of illegitimate rule that frames all the periods. The Regency was, literally, the installation of a Regent, George, Prince of Wales, to rule England after George III was declared insane. The causes and ramifications of George III's 'insanity' – like Hamlet's "madness" – are still an issue of debate. Obviously, the Regent correlated to Claudius, who, assuming the throne after a hasty marriage to Gertrude, effectively prevented the rightful king, Hamlet, from his rule. Moving to the 1970 United States, Richard Nixon, installed by less than

44% of the vote, was a minority President, who was disliked by more voters than supported him.

This questionable governance in all three periods exacerbated already difficult international and domestic situations. In 1819 – to pick a Regency year not entirely at random – the memory of recent wars was fresh. The American and French Revolutions had tilted and toppled royals; Napoleon had menaced England. Moreover, there was domestic discontent. English workers had organized to demand parliamentary reform, and under the Regent, harsh repressive measures were taken: *habeas corpus* was suspended, and demonstrating workers were fired on by troops at the infamous "Peterloo Massacre". The younger English Romantics, in this case especially Byron, wrote and lived in reaction against repressive politics both governmental and literary.

In the parallel Denmark of Barton's adaptation, there is also the memory and threat of war personified in bellicose Young Fortinbras. Claudius may have quickly ascended the throne to contain this particular threat – it is his first official act we see – but there is also evidence that domestic problems exist. The underclass is so easily stirred up that the King fears the youngsters Hamlet and Laertes may incite rebellions, and sends one abroad while keeping the other under house-arrest. Indications are of a very rotten Denmark, indeed.

The United States of the late sixties suffered from its own rot as well. The memories of the Second World War and Korean War were used to justify the divisive Vietnam War. The youth movement, in some ways consciously modeled after the English Romantics, sprang up to "make love not war", endorse the civil rights of African Americans and women, as well as question repressive authority in general. Nixon's election was in part a reaction against the "Yippie insanity" at the 1968 Democratic National Convention, when protesters rioted at the very doors of the old-time party bosses, demanded to be heard, and were beaten back. Correlating to Peterloo, the infamous "Kent State Massacre" had occurred in May 1970 when the National Guard – countenanced if not actually encouraged by Nixonian policies – fired on anti-war student demonstrators, killing four.

Many of these correspondences were highlighted or referenced by the Chamberlain/Wood production.[16] Swarthy Richard Johnson was cast and directed like a handsomer, but still dark and unctuous, Nixon. He delivers his first speech as an inaugural address that resembles Nixon's, with Margaret Leighton looking on adoringly, appearing and acting very much like Pat Nixon. In the cutting and characterization, Johnson at first appears to be an appealing King just as Nixon had a gift for charm when he was winning. Yet, as the play progresses, like Nixon, the King grows more paranoid, his manipulations and taste for the clandestine become more apparent, and his posture and gestures more hunched and violent. During "try what repentance can, what can it not?", Johnson actually extends and opens his arms in front of him on the alter in a v-shape that subtly refers to the way Nixon often veed his arms in his characteristic gesture of denial pretending to be victory (3.3.65-6).

Leighton's Gertrude seems to regard Hamlet as less Oedipus and more infant, harkening back to the *in loco parentis* issues that helped precipitate the student movement. Moreover, Michael Redgrave's Polonius, self-infatuated yet understated to the point of abstraction, is more than a little reminiscent of Henry Kissinger, and the role was cut to emphasize a Kissingeresque *realpolitik* of distrust and manipulation. The generation gap is costumed clearly, the young romantics affecting a flamboyant style of dress and hair in contrast to their dour elders and much in the style of 'long-haired, bell bottomed' student protesters. Even Kent State/Peterloo finds a direct corollary when Hamlet is encircled – and nearly killed – by the King's guard's bayonets after he protests to his mother and stabs Polonious. Finally, Nicholas Jones' Laertes easily rallies a revolutionary rabble to storm to the very doors of the royal apartments, an obvious reference to the student protests at the 1968 D.N.C.

Most fundamental, however, to this aesthetic design, is Chamberlain's empassioned Byronic characterization. The Romantics clashed with the repressions of the Regency much as the hippies and Yippies revolted against 'the man in the grey flannel suit'. The choice of an overtly Byronic interpretation aligns Hamlet,

Byron and the youth movement in several significant ways. Byron lived and wrote about his life as an act of rebellion against what he perceived were tyrannical powers. In this rebel role, Byron and his self-identified characters were notorious for spontaneous and extreme reactions. Such a Byronic bent would explain the mercurial acting choices Chamberlain makes: mannerisms that critics (except Coursen, who seemed not to see them) so consistently remarked on but could not praise. Moreover, such impulsive freedom identifies him with Abbie Hoffman's 'revolutionary artistry' and the Yippie slogan "Revolution for the hell of it!". Reading blindfolded to twit Polonius, staging a physical confrontation with his old friends Rosencrantz and Guildenstern, exploding into a temper-tantrum when finding himself observed, playing the child with his mother, jumping into Ophelia's grave with passionate regret after having precipitated her death, even accepting Laertes' challenge against Horatio's wise council – these are all Byronic acting *choices* played intelligently with some relish by Chamberlain. While such acts have no obvious correlation to the youth movement, they suggest an ethos of spontaneity and experimentation that corresponds to the youth movement's radical disruptive politics, drug experimentation, and their disdain for traditional social attitudes and values.

Sweet Prince

But the youth movement of the sixties and seventies was also a sexual revolution. Oedipal-existential Hamlets, once regarded as outrageous in their own way, were able to ride the mid-century Freudian fashion into impassioned closet scenes. The Chamberlain-Byronic persona unbolted the door on another closet altogether. When Chamberlain suggested Hamlet might be one of "the boys in the band", he made a reference that would be obvious to a 1970 audience. *The Boys in the Band* is the title both of the 1970 William Friedkin film and the successful Broadway play it was based on. "The boys" were a group of homosexual men, and both play and film depicted the gay lifestyle of men marginalized by a repressed and repressive society. *The Boys in the Band* signaled a new cultural awareness of homosexuality, fueled in part by the experimental counter culture and the credo: "If it feels good, do it!" The sixties' fixation on free love resulted in more than just male heterosexual liberation, and the ramifications of these attitudes rippled into the women's and gay rights movements. Moreover, a gay Hamlet refers directly to Byron's persona, whose experiments with homosexuality are well known.

The textual evidence in the performance is evident even without Chamberlain's prompting. Hamlet embraces Horatio upon greeting him the first time and throughout the play. This gesture might be rationalized as a possible male greeting in a less homo-anxious culture or attributed to Byronic extravagance, but certain key lines and scenes were blocked, shot, and cut (in both dramaturgic and cinematic senses) to depict the Hamlet/Horatio relationship if not as overtly sexual at least as a powerful, physical, and passionate bond. Hamlet embraces Horatio on key lines: in 1.3 for "Your loves, as mine to you"(259) and is kneeling against him, holding both his hands in 1.5 when he says "With all my love I do commend me to you"(192); both lines seem to be spoken directly to Horatio, and Hamlet clings with more than fraternal feeling.

Most significantly, although this cutting of the play isolated the revenge tragedy, it also focused on Horatio, a character who serves no melodramatic purpose. When the advice to the players was cut, Act 3, Scene 2 began with a different emphasis: "What ho, Horatio!" and the response, "Here sweet lord, at your service" (52-3). Hamlet's next thirty lines are then pared down to a telling ten:

Since my dear soul was mistress of her choice
And could of men distinguish her election,
Sh' hath sealed thee for herself, for thou has been
As one, in suffering all, that suffers nothing,
A man that Fortune's buffets and rewards
Hast ta'en with equal thanks. Give me that man
That is not passion's slave, and I will wear him
In my heart's core, ay, in my heart of heart,
As I do thee ... (62-74)

Clearly, this is not central to the revenge plot but was focused to sound like a declaration of love. The camera style reflects this. The speech is shot in alternating close-ups of the two men, concluding with an extreme close-up of an apparently ardent Hamlet, then a meaningful pause, until "Something too much of this./There is a play tonight before the King" changes the subject (74-5). Such shot/reverse-shot framing of the two men is a cinematic convention of love scenes, and throughout this production, is reserved mainly for Horatio and Hamlet.

The enactment of the end of the play completes this homoerotic motif. Hamlet expires in Horatio's arms, in a *Pietà*-like medium shot which then cuts to a close-up two-shot of Horatio weeping copiously and holding his dead friend's face to his neck as he speaks more intimately than other Horatios:

> Now cracks a noble heart. Good night sweet prince,
> And flights of angels sing thee to thy rest!

Hall of Fame

The *sine qua non* for revered *Hamlet*s has been a remarkable and remarked-upon performance in the title role, but there were no raves or superlatives for the extravagant and possibly gay Chamberlain version. Whether or not Chamberlain deserved better notices is an issue problematized by the ability of 1970 critics to 'see' his performance. The case for the 'masterpiece' status of the Chamberlain/Wood version of *Hamlet*, however, need not be based totally on the performance of the title role, but can be forcefully based on the subtlety, originality, and daring of the production as a whole. It was an interpretation that layered text-on-text at a particular historical moment in an original and a challenging way.

In 1970, the pioneering Hallmark production of *Hamlet* both faced and created a series of complex intertextual challenges that are now visible from a historical distance. First there was the unfamiliar appearance of Shakespeare on television in the first place, complicated by the once-only commercial television broadcast at the moment before videotape recorders became household items.[17] Chamberlain as actor/persona/text was determinedly *sui generis* in his own way. The historical and literary interpretive ambitions of Peter Wood's direction and

John Barton's adaptation were perhaps too subtle or too inventive for the skills of television critics. Finally, the homoerotic overtones were clearly as unfamiliar to prime-time TV as Shakespeare were but even more revolutionary and discursivley challenging. All these 'texts' placed the production beyond the critical horizon of expectation and therefore beyond the full comprehension of viewing critics.

The uneven and occasional reception had a long-term ripple effect on later critics as well as on the availability of this version. The net result has been a tiny amount of rather superficial criticism for a *Hamlet* that can be mined for much, much more. Indeed, of special historical significance is the curious prescience of the selection of the Nixon narrative as congruent to *Hamlet*, since Nixon's Claudius-like cynicism and plotting, abetted by bad advice, imploded with the Watergate burglary, just as the King is poorly advised and makes a nefarious pact with Laertes that leads to calamity. However, the greatest tragedy in this textual *contre temps* is that, like Hamlet himself, the Chamberlain/Wood, Hallmark Hall of Fame version has perished prematurely, and until an act of God (or the Hallmark Company), must remain interred at U.C.L.A. when it might serve as a particularly useful, even inspirational, teaching tool in any number of venues, as well as a wonderfully entertaining text in its own right.

Notes

1. *Hamlet*, Dir. Peter Wood, With Richard Chamberlain, John Gielgud, Michael Redgrave, Richard Johnson, Margaret Leighton (Emmy Award Nominee), Ciaran Maddan. Adaptation by John Barton. Produced by George LeMaire for The Hallmark Hall of Fame; broadcast on N.B.C. 18 November 1970. Errata on this information occur in several texts, including *The New York Times* review. My *deepest* gratitude to Dan Eistein, Television Archivist at U.C.L.A. Film and Television Archive, and Linda Tadic and Linda Elkins of the Peabody Archive, who worked together to permit me to see this *Hamlet* with colleagues and students in Georgia. Normally, viewing is available only on site at the U.C.L.A. Archive: telephone (001)-213-462-4921 for a viewing appointment.

2. I am also indebted to Jack Solomon, California State University, Northridge, Christy Desmet, and Richard Neupert, both at the University of Georgia, for conversations that prompted and helped evolve my sense of historical textualities. Also, a word of thanks to Charles B. Lower, University of Georgia, for asking me to teach Shakespeare and Film on several occasions.

3. It is worth remembering that, with such focused competition, the stakes on 'high art' production were considerably higher than on 1997 programing, and critical interest *should* have been proportionately piqued.

4. Unsigned, "Kildare as Hamlet", *Time,* 16 November 1970, p. 70.

5. Jack Gould, "Chamberlain, Buoyed by English Cast, Portrays Hamlet on N.B.C.", *The New York Times,* 19 November 1970, p. 94.

6. Cecil Smith, "Glitter and Gold in 'Hamlet'", *The Los Angeles Times,* Wednesday, 18 November 1970, Part IV, p 28.

7. Unsigned, *Variety,* 25 November 1970.

8. Jay L. Halio in "Three Filmed *Hamlets*" notes that the Olivier script cut roughly 1900 lines and transposed several scenes and passages, Chamberlain/Wood/Barton cut around 2100 while keeping the structure and sequence of the play almost entirely intact. *Literature/Film Quarterly,* 1:4 (Fall 1973), p. 316.

9. Jay L. Halio, pp. 316-20.

10. H. R. Coursen, "Three Televised *Hamlets*", in *Shakespeare on Television,* ed. J. C. Bulman and H. R. Coursen (Hanover: New England UP, 1980), pp. 101-7.

11. In fairness to Coursen, he reports on "a no-nonsense black and white production", when the videotape I viewed, although shadowed expressionistically, was in vivid color with striking accents of blue, gold, and maroon.

12. Richard Chamberlain "Why Does an Actor Agree to Do 'Hamlet'?" *The New York Times,* Sunday, November 15, 1970. Sec. D, p. 21. A fascinating piece in which Chamberlain takes on T.S. Eliot, modern editors, and famous Freudians.

13. Of course Chamberlain's "slouching toward" is an allusion to Yeats' "The Second Coming"; needless to say, *Hamlet* was to be Chamberlain's 'second coming' to his American audience.

14. Interestingly, Chamberlain, like his critics, doesn't mention Olivier, whose late forties black and white version may have set the trend in existential Danes.

15. Tim Halliman, "Interview: Jonathan Miller on the Shakespeare Plays", *Shakespeare Quarterly,* 32 (1981), pp. 134-45.

16. Chamberlain.

17. On the same page as Chamberlain's *New York Times* essay "Why Does an Actor Agree to Do 'Hamlet'?" is another piece by Gould, "The Great Day Isn't Exactly At Hand", lamenting the confused state of the new technology of "viewer-controlled video" – home video tape machines. *The New York Times,* Sunday, 15 November 1970, sect. D, p. 21.

O THAT THIS TOO TOO SOLID PLAY WOULD MELT: CORONADO'S *ANTI-O(EDI)PUS*

Evgenia Pancheva
(Sofia University)

The critical hue and cry that Celestino Coronado's 1977 shooting of Hamlet barely falls short of killing the play[1] seems to visualize primarily the film's minimalistic reading of Shakespeare's text. A myopic analysis of cutting and glueing practices, however, will show the deeper politics of this textual minimalism – Freudean, Deleuzean, but also truly visual.

Much disputedly, the video version disposes of the "To be or not to be" dramatic highspot. Foregrounded by Kozintsev's and Olivier's classic productions, here it is recycled into the prologue[2] anticipating the identity of the Ghost and Hamlet. (Both a historically 'correct' and a para-generic reading of the play would display the quasi-choric functions of the Ghost.) Not only is this 'prologue' spoken as dispassionately as could be. The speech is demystified even further by the noise of a radio – the words reach us through the nondiegetic noise of changing radio stations.[3] The metaphor is translated into visual terms as the *eye* is assaulted by flashes of light and a momentary picture of a face, the whole ending in darkness and a terrible shriek. This 'translation' – of word into picture, of ear into eye – seems crucial to Coronado's strategy. It is not alien to a Shakespearean aesthetic – the synaesthetic experience is thematized in *A Midsummer Night's Dream*, for instance :

> The eye of man hath not heard, the ear of man hath not seen, man's hand is not able to taste, his tongue to conceive, nor his heart to report, what my dream was (4.1.218-21)

In a theoretical context, this metaphoric substitution is also basically a 'schizoanalytic' procedure :

The mouth of the anorexic wavers between several functions: its possessor is uncertain as to whether it is an eating machine, an anal machine, a talking machine, or a breathing machine (asthma attacks).[4]

Assuming the Shakespearean – and Deleuzean – hint about the reciprocity of various codes makes possible the radical scissoring of the Shakespearean text. Sustained by other episodes (Hamlet's answer to the Ghost, his exchange with Polonius), the automatism of utterance releases tensions in the auditory perception of a text replete with tropes and opens up communicative spaces for the richer presence of non-verbal modes. In this sense Coronado's film is radically opposed to Shakespeare's theatre where acting was conventional and stage pieces sparse, but the word emphatically present. The word's only Elizabethan match was costume, an opaque sign to provide a visual parallel to the untransparent theatrical cue. In Coronado, all the metaphorical opacity goes to the body in a setting communicatively as transparent as Shakespeare's. Speech, on the other hand, seems to assume the function of historical 'costume' – materially gorgeous but as stabilized through monotony as Elizabethan 'costume'.[5] Costume itself is no longer needed – speech assumes its semiotic role, and the body, Coronado's 'speech', can be displayed in all its Protean metaphoricity. The radical opposition of Coronado and Shakespeare melts into the appropriation of 'Coronado's Shakespeare': the *Naked Hamlet* grows into a successful avant-guarde translation of Elizabethan theatre into a different medium.

After an introduction that is both provocation to and tuning of the eye, we are given a long shot of a slit between rocky structures, reminiscent of Stonehenge and ritual sacrifice, but also suggestive of keyhole voyeurism and the primal scene. Anticipating the film's further oscillation between the sacrificial and the phallic, the slit bears a distant resemblance to a crucifix of light, but also to a sexual symbol. The architecture of the scene obviously ironizes Freudean spaces as dramatised by the deep focus of the Olivier *Hamlet*: in Coronado Hamlet *belongs with* the primal space and it is *outwardness* that is inaccessible and voyeuristically conceived. In this sense the film seems to capture the 'claustrophobia' of the text :

Coronado's *Anti-O(edi)pus* 199

The emphasis on locale remains considerably less important here than in most other Shakespearean plays. The play exudes an aura of claustrophobia, as recent film directors have well noted. The convention of unlocalized space [...] here seems to invert itself, to stress the essential sameness of all locality where the philosophical underpinnings of human action, not its Protean texture, are given form. Most of the action in Hamlet takes place within doors. Whether at the home of Polonius or somewhere in the palace, the locales seem largely undistinguishable.[6]

In fact, our expectations are heavily displaced – the torn veil reveals inwardness, the space of the royal bedroom. To the schizo, as Deleuze and Guattari put it, "the self and non-self, outside and inside no longer have any meaning whatsoever."

Later, the camera goes back to 'our own' inner space for a long take of the sleeping Hamlet. His naked body is covered with draperies, whose folds nicely echo the relief of the desert outside and the shapes of the clouds above it. The high-angle shot and the reverse framing lend strangeness to this body, ultimately zooming in on the face. The reversely framed eyes look up at the camera for so long that they seem to acquire an existence of their own, 'dedifferentiating', then re-establishing the whole topography of the face. This deliberate 'defamiliarization' seems to pick up the 'ritual sacrifice' metaphor suggested by the *mis-en-scène*. It totally objectifies Hamlet's body into a tomb effigy, or a would-be 'anatomy' for a Vesalian anatomy-theatre. At the same time, the camera's subjective shooting promotes audiences' anticipatory identification with a Ghost who should be coming from their own off-screen space.

Not quite so. Hamlet's encounter with the Ghost becomes the body's confrontation with its mirroring, but also metamorphic, Other. The seeming passivity of this catatonic body is the delusory passivity of Deleuze's body without organs, the smooth surface of uninterrupted flows of desire upon which anything could be inscribed. The catatonic body is the other side of this all-inviting body whose organs can function as any other organ:

An incomprehensible, absolutely rigid stasis in the very midst of process, as a third stage: "No mouth, No tongue. No teeth. No larynx. No esophagus. No belly. No anus." The automata stop dead and set free the unorganized mass they once served to articulate. The full body without organs is the unproductive, the sterile, the unengendered, the unconsumable.[7]

In Coronado's film this catatonic body has another body materially inscribed upon "its smooth, slippery, opaque, taut surface" (Deleuze) – the Ghost is 'a text' on Hamlet's brow, he is born of it, just as Athene was born of Zeus's head. Inverting the ultimate dream of male autogenesis, the film makes the Father grow out of the Son, and what is more, be physically identical with him: Hamlet and the Ghost are played by the twins Anthony and David Meyer. Replacing the vertical recession of Father-and-Son with the horizontal 'simulacrum' of the twins is not wholly un-Shakespearean either, though it 'flattens' the space of the play. Twins in Shakespeare are a well-established metaphor for wavering identities. Horizontalizing this wavering, Coronado seems to make it part and parcel of a broader 'schizo-project'.

In the long take of the sleeping Hamlet's face[8] (in tune with 'to sleep, perchance to dream', at which the 'prologue' was cut short) grows into a site of human torture: upon the crucifix formed by brows, nose and wrinkle there is the strongly-lit imprint of a pulsating human figure in a moment of agonized – and orgasmic – shriek. The camera frames the face obliquely to accentuate the eye. As he emerges from it, frontally lit in red, the naked Ghost seems to iconographically quote 'accentuated' bodies, tortured or alert - Laocöon, David, Christ on the Cross. Hamlet, on the other hand, is gradually made to look like Andrea Mantegna's *dead* Christ. The sharp cuts from *our* view of the Ghost in central perspective to our identification with *his* view of Hamlet question the spectator's spatial affinities and moral stance. The whole episode is a fine play on bodies' identity and displacement. Hamlet turns his head so that the Ghost does not fit into his crucifix. The play of colours supports the hint - a white Ghost against Hamlet's red face alternating with the glaring red figure supporting a dead-white Hamlet. The motif of this alternation gratually grows into a filmic comment on the uncertainty of bodies – problematizing the distinction between the Meyer twins.

Coronado's *Anti-O(edi)pus*

Coronado's interest in the body is shown in his economical but meaningful selection of text. First comes the Ghost's tale spoken practically above Hamlet's head.[9] After the imposing visual opening its "Hark me!" comes as another demanding shriek. Through long-take close-ups, almost graphically emphasizing the eye, the camera punningly construes Hamlet's *seeing* as harking-fluttering eyelids, eyes gradually opening, the stare – till the body-without-organs seems to appropriate any and every identification of an organ's locale:

> The body without organs is an egg: it is crisscrossed with axes and thresholds, with latitudes and longitudes and geodesic lines, traversed by gradients marking the transitions and the becomings [...] Nothing here is representative [...] Nothing but bands of intensity, potentials, thresholds, and gradiants.[10]

Going to Hamlet's side, the Ghost speaks to his mouth, so that it becomes a listening ear: "Foul, foul, most [...] unnatural." Then, displacing displacement itself, he gently turns Hamlet's head to pour the poison of speech into the actual ear. The two enact the narrative of the murder. At "O, horrible! O, horrible! Most horrible!" Hamlet's body wriggles convulsively. It arches in the agony of a dying man when he hears of his father's deadly metamorphosis:

> Sleeping within my orchard,
> My custom always in the afternoon,
> Upon my secure hour thy uncle stole,
> With juice of cursed hebona in a vial,
> And in the porches of mine ears did pour
> The leperous distilment; whose effect
> Holds such an enmity with blood of man
> That swift a quicksilver it courses through
> The natural gates and alleys of the body,
> And with a sudden vigour it doth posset
> And curd, like eager droppings into milk,
> The thin and wholesome blood; so did it mine,
> And a most instant tetter bark'd about
> Most lazar-like, with vile and loathsome crust,
> All my smooth body. (1.5.59-73)[11]

Like classical metamorphosis, the narrative seems to symbolically exorcise the schizo's fear of bodily fixation. Turned into a tree, as in myth, or covered with a bark that does not allow for the 'smoothness' of the body without organs, the body reaches a deadening finality. The film brings out this phobia of the text, dealing extensively with 'meltings' of the flesh.

Coronado exploits the symbolic positioning of bodies: the red-lit figure of 'old' Hamlet in medium close-up, and its perpendicular extension, the lying white Hamlet, face obliquely positioned close to the Ghost's armpit and Mantegnan feet in extreme close-up. The shot underlines the basic sameness and split of the two - a major paradigm of Shakespeare's play, more Trinitarian (Father, Son, Holy Ghost) than Oedipal.

In this first episode the Ghost actively shapes Hamlet's body, inscribing personal meanings upon it. Thus, at "Horrible, horrible, most horrible" his position behind Hamlet allows him to blow the words into his hair. Dramatising the earlier "make ... each particular hair stand on end", the gesture seems to fashion Hamlet into a Gorgon's head, the ultimate emblem of dangerous *femininity*. When he warns Hamlet against torturing Gertrude, the Ghost presses his hair to the scull, anticipating the Queen's turban in the closet scene. At the same time he quite ambiguously stops up Hamlet's ears with his hands to effect un-hearing as he insists on hearing, to *restore* the catatonic 'closed' body as he explores its orifices to 'open' it. Finally, the Ghost leaves Hamlet in a posture that will be repeated at the film's closure, suggesting perhaps that Hamlet is dead as early as the opening, just as Christopher Marlowe's Faustus was damned even before he wished it. With a grotesque visual pun at "To prick and sting her" he slowly pulls the sheet-shroud covering Hamlet to display the genitals. For a moment, the two share the sheet, then the Ghost walks off sheeted, in the ironic 'full armour' of a dead man.

Coronado's comments on the metamorphoses and splits of the body go on with the superimposition of Hamlet's telescoped lying figure over an extreme close-up of his profile. Thus the naked body is transformed into an ear, with the emphatic genitals gradually emerging as its hole. The film seems momentarily to echo the Lacanian relationship between language, 'poison in the ear', and the phallus, ultimate signifier. The echo is especially appropriate in a circular context where the Ghost is entirely Hamlet-made: *his* 'speech' is a displacement, it seems, of Hamlet's phallic dream.

While omitting *the* soliloquy of the play (3.1), Coronado's adaptation makes much of another famous passage. Spoken off-screen, to the close-up of a perfectly still Hamlet, the 'O that this too too solid flesh would melt / Thaw and resolve itself into a dew' with its leisurely pace and long meaningful pauses orchestrates the film's central construction of the body. The dream of physical self-annihilation, which Shakespeare's hero seems to inherit from Marlowe's Faustus,[12] is given fimlic fulfilment. Two Hamletean faces are slowly superimposed, then severed again to manifest the fluidity of the Face. Eyes are doubled in a brief reference to Picasso, then turn mouths as they 'speak' winking, the nose vanishes. Coronado's editing films the organs' lack of identity, their plurality and mutual substitutions. Hamlet's face is caressed by a hand whose body is hard to identify, a gesture that finely matches the cue of "the hands of heaven / visit her face too roughly". The schizo's feast of meltings and resolutions is cut short by a purely mental act - at 'Let me not think on't' the floating faces all come into focus as *the* face of the protagonist.

The latter part of the speech is enacted by the twinned Hamlets of the film. Throughout it the Ghost takes the prince to the royal bedroom in which the great court scene of the play is transferred. (Similarly, in Tony Richardson's 1969 version Polonius talks to the royal couple as they "lie in a huge, ornate bed, seemingly oblivious to Polonius' s words".[13] And, of course, the earlier Olivier had made much of Gertrude's bed.) An extreme close-up again presents Hamlet's eyes until the features of his face come to reconstruct the rocky slit of the opening. This slit-crucifix displays its erotic affinities as it is obscenely bestriden by the King. A fantastic 'Co*mmm*e, co*mmm*e!' invites the prince right into a surrealist primal scene. The Ghost tears the veil hiding the royal bed and puts the dagger into his hand. The gaze is given full reign.

Claudius's great court speech is located in this bedroom. It is filmed as a movement away from the bed to a kneeling position before Hamlet. The gay touch, though very delicate, is hardly spared. Just as the Ghost, Claudius tries to imprint himself upon Hamlet's body: with "You are the most immediate to our throne" the King presses his palm against Hamlet's brow. (His own forehead betrays a non-human aspect - a nice literalization of the king-sun metaphor, its glittering gold reminds one of the mutant characters of recent fantasy.) This visual 'violence' upon the Other's body is matched by the characteristic diction. The King's emphasis on negative prefixes – *im*-pious, *un*-manly, *in*-correct, *im*-patient, *un*-schooled – distantly reverberate with his erotic 'Co*mmme*! Co*mmme*! Co*mmme*!'.

Quite appropriately to its own staging strategies, Shakespeare's *Hamlet* toys with metaphors of voice and ear. With an equal approriateness to *its* medium, and following the Freudean and Deleuzean tip, Coronado's adaptation offers extreme close-ups of the eye. The most notable of these occur in Hamlet's scene with Polonius, whose whole body is reduced to a monstrous eye, looking through an eye-glass at Hamlet and ourselves.[14] We are never given Polonius's perspective through it – instead, we see the seer as the seen sees him.

A metaphor for both filming and film-watching, the eye on screen has become a topos of the avant-garde. The eye that replaces the lens in Emak Bakia's *Man Ray*, the eyes of Kiki in *Ballet mechanique* (1928), the eye at the keyhole in Cocteau's *Blood of a Poet* (1930), etc., but above all the magnified eye of Willard Maas's *Geography of the Body* (1943) which alludes to "the extremely close and (literally) magnified seeing that is the principal concern of that film"[15] - all these filmic gestures seem to intertextually underlie Coronado's excessive concern with seeing the eye. This confrontation of two eyes, the spectator's and the filmic-screen becoming a mirror up to nature and nature mirroring the screen – circularly consumes space to evoke the claustrophobic original.

Coronado does not hesitate to radicalize the metaphor further. Polonius's whole body is contracted to an eye, just as all Denmark is "contracted to one brow of woe" in the underread but overfilmed text. Showing Hamlet with the book, and the shadow of Hamlet with a book on a screen-wall, Coronado develops the symbolic potential of it on screen – reading a text about old men's eyes grows into a representation of the director coping with "words, words, words" in the Shakespearean text.[16] The Prince reads exhibitionistically, as a film director – he is observed by Polonius, the observer's eye inscribed within the text:

> For the satirical rogue says here that old men have grey beards, that their faces are wrinkled, their eyes purging thick amber and plum-tree gum, and that they have a plentiful lack of wit, ... (2.2.201-5)

Even this magnified eye, however, can hardly escape the flux of energies on the body without organs. It becomes ear, as it 'listens' tensely to Hamlet's double-edged replies, and becomes mouth as Polonius addresses the prince and womb as it, camera-like, 'produces' a 'shot' of Ophelia.[17]

Doublings in the Hamlet-Ophelia scene bring blurrings of selfhood to an extreme. The two Hamlets, Ghost and Prince, alternate in the speech ('I did love you once./ I loved you not'), fighting for the cue. Their alternation is matched by Ophelia's fluid identity, the result of Hellen Mirren's doubling of Gertrude and Ophelia. Thus, when the Ghost, who has won over Hamlet for being *the* Hamlet of the scene, experiments shapes on Ophelia's body, distorting the mouth, smearing her lipstick, and carving a cross at the base of her neck, we are trapped by the essential ambiguity of it. What is unambiguous is the scene's symbolic value, its reaction against the fixed identity of the painted body. Hamlet's horror at bodily fixation- through dressing, painting, playing a conventional role, getting a 'crust', or dying – is pretty obvious. It is part of the body without organs' revulsion with being 'denoted truly':

> 'Tis not alone my inky cloak, good mother,
> Nor customary suits of solemn black,
> Nor windy suspiration of forced breath,
> No, nor the fruitful river in the eye,
> Nor the dejected 'haviour of the visage,
> Together with all forms, moods, shapes of grief,
> That can denote me truly [...]

But I have that within which passes show —
These but the trappings and the suits of woe. (1.2.77-86)

Hamlet himself emerges as the redefiner of the play's body, its own Ghost who seeks to leave an imprint upon its text — to extract a possibility of meaning from it. In the scene with the actors he proposes to introduce 'a speech of 12-15 lines'. This insertion is going to test the 'bodily' reality of a speech in the larger play, of the Ghost's narrative. The moment Hamlet hesitates about its validity, the Ghost emerges behind him with the automatism of the mediaeval stage. He does look like the devil now, but, ironically, his grotesquely overdone lipstick echoes the smearing of Ophelia's: his own body is being redefined for him by Hamlet's 'violent' *speech* until the groaning mouth fades into a stage for the players' performance.

Re-defining the body goes on with *The Murder of Gonzago*. Excess in the inner play (one speech too many) is nicely coupled with economy in the 'outer' — Hamlet's asides to Ophelia are conflated with those to his mother as the two merge into one.

In Coronado's reading *The Murder of Gonzago* meaningfully displaces Shakespeare, just as the Ghost displaces his protagonist. The emblem of this displacement is the false perspectivism of *mise-en-scène* - the distortions of the chessboard floor of Renaissance painting here betray perspective for the *trompe l'oeil* it actually is. The pseudoarchitectonic distances seem to refer tongue-in-cheek to the arches and long-focus shots of Olivier.

Unlike Shakespeare's, Coronado's *Gonzago* has a silent prologue. All performed by the First Player, prologue, queen and murderer embarrassingly merge here. The fictional king and queen obscenely enact the primal scene of Hamlet's dreams. The threat of the play is quite real — the dagger which Lucianus throws cuts the Elizabethan theatrical bladder worn by the Player-King. Blood spurts and taints the hands of Claudius in the audience. The First Player suffers an ironic split, Hamlet's own split, as he seduces the (drag) queen, his other self. The fact that *Gonzago* dramatizes the Ghost's tale is made explicit by casting the Ghost in the lead. He wears a mask so that, peeping through its slits, his eyes look like the jewels on his theatrical crown. When Lucianus throws his dagger, high framing makes us long for the filming of off-screen space – it is quite unclear at whose feet he is actually throwing it. Anyway, Claudius picks it up and tears off the mask to reveal another Hamlet face beneath it. Coronado ventures, it seems, a direct hint at the metatheatrics of the original where Burbage-Hamlet faces his own double.

Hamlet's subsequent soliloquy becomes yet another gesture of self-division: it is filmed as a dialogue of Ghost and Hamlet. As the Ghost begins with 'Tis now the very witching time of night ...', spoken to Hamlet, Hamlet responds with 'Now I could drink hot blood, ...'. Both are present throughout the entire closet scene which makes seeing the Ghost an even more subjective issue.

Hamlet plays for Gertrude the Ghost she chooses not to see: he shapes her into a catatonic body. Objectified through the power structure of the scene – tackled sexually by the 'invisible' Ghost-Hamlet behind her, while reproached and erotically fascinated by the aggressive Hamlet before her – she grows more and more into the Hamlet of the opening. At 'takes off the rose from the fair forehead [...] and sets a blister there' Hamlet mimicks the taking off and the setting on her. Further, he problematises the very representation of bodies – instead of 'counterfeits' he shows her the actual Ghost, as well as what obviously is Coronado's substitute for the prayer scene – Claudius practicing sadomasochistic rites to make his hands bleed. The filmic reality of both images makes effective Shakespeare's questioning of Gertrude's sight: "Have you eyes?" By and by, touching gently Gertrude's body, Hamlet undoes it:

Eyes without feeling, feeling without sight,
Ears without hands or eyes, smelling sans all ... (3.4.78-80)

After her own 'this bodiless creation [...] ecstasy is very cunning in' Gertrude is actually lying in Hamlet's own initial posture, holding his hand. Later a hand – Hamlet's, the Ghost's? - is visible on her breast, obviously making a cross-reference to the unidentifiable hand of Hamlet's Ghost scene. A close-up of the

Queen's face and neck follows at "cleft my heart in twain". Hamlet repeats the Ghost's vigil by his sleeping body, kissing her, letting go her hand. Her face is shown in reversely framed extreme close-up just as Hamlet's was. Like the Ghost, Hamlet occupies the foreground, back to the camera. Gertrude's profile is shown in horizontal close-up, until it, too, acquires a 'defamiliarized' topography.[18] A cut effects the purely visual transition from sleeping Gertrude to drowning Ophelia, whose open mouth is speaking, swallowing water, groaning in orgasm. Grotesquely magnified, it ultimately sings Ophelia's bawdy ballad while the camera offers even more extreme close-ups of facial orifices – nostrils, mouth, ears and eyes.

Conflated on the ground of Hamlet's 'speaking daggers' to both women characters, the two deaths emerge as one – the catatonic closure of the body without organs (Gertrude) alternating with the ex-static openness of the carnivalesque body (Ophelia).

The other conflation of scenes occurs with Hamlet himself: the leaping into the grave is shrewdly blended with the duel scene. In Coronado there is no grave to speak of – indeed, all places are one on the Elizabethan stage, and to the schizo's mind. A deeper probing into the omission, however, would re-pose the question of how alive Hamlet is – 'Why, this is hell nor am I out of it'.[19] (It is hard to distinguish between the living and the dead in the film: Polonius, Claudius and Laertes are never killed, Gertrude is dead, in so far as she is the drowned Ophelia, and still alive, as she watches the fight and its tragic end. Even Yorick's skull is omitted – it is not needed in a film whose 'defamiliarizations' problematize the very reality of faces.

The Laertes of the film is yet another alter ego of Hamlet – he is his father's Ghost, his twin body, himself. The visual pun is projected onto the distribution of cues, as well – Hamlet's speech of "Show me what thou't do" is given to this other self. For the body without organs is by its very nature [...] such eloquent witness of its own self-production, of its own engendering of itself [...] Yes, I have been my father and I have been my son." I, Antonin Artaud, am my son, my father, my mother, and myself.' The schizo has his own system of coordinates for situating himself at his disposal [...] He scrambles all the codes, by quickly shifting from one to another, according to the questions asked him [...] never invoking the same genealogy [...][20]

The film turns Shakespeare's duel into a wrestling match. The furious fight of naked bodies slowly moves towards the embrace as the dying reconciliation is achieved. Gay sensibility grows hilarious as cues "I am satistfied in nature" and "I do receive your offered love like love" are soundtracked against images of half-embracing bodies. Ultimately, death becomes a filming of a Renaissance pun – to die, to reach a sexual climax. Hamlet lies down on the bed-shrine of the opening episode, while the speech of "You that look pale and tremble at this act" is uttered off-screen. The low-angle shot of his face displays the prominent nose, the nostrils, the half-open eyes and mouth, the catatonic body fixed in a carnivalesque openness of orifices. The long shot emphasizes the impression of stasis. On this close-up of the face a high-angle telescoping shot of the entire body is superimposed, to reverse the symbolism of the opening. As "To tell my story" is uttered, the ear seems to produce this lying body, just as it has formerly 'swallowed' it. There is again a figure – two figures – by Hamlet's head, Claudius and Gertrude, who stay there till they gradually vanish into the shape and colour of the Slit. The entire rocky structure is given in a high-angle shot, reminiscent of Olivier's filming of Elsinore. In a bravura of circularity, the film bites its tail.

Coronado's *Hamlet* locates its story in an entirely spiritual dimension. To do so, it utilizes the body, the Deleuzean body without organs. This schizoanalytic body bears all possible inscriptions upon itself, it is dramatised as complex text of desire's network to be deciphered by our desiring selves. It does allow for Oedipal distributions but only as territorial *variants* of a generally deterritorialized flow. Sites of desire waver dizzily from catatonic abstinence and closure ('Leave me in peace') to carnivalesque all-inclusiveness ('I am everything in the world'). Though family romance (mommy-daddy-me) in the Freudian and Olivier vein can briefly have it 'bounded in a nutshell', the desire of the text will still be counting itself 'a king of infinite space'. Critics have described Olivier's *Hamlet* as an Oedipal cinepoem.[21] Coronado, in the post-Freudian episteme, seems to sing 'the body anti-Oedipal'.

Filming the short-circuits of this Deleuzean – and Shakespearean – desire, Coronado's *Hamlet* fulfils the play's dream of self-annihilation. As it translates it into the language of the camera, it makes the text's 'too too solid flesh [...] melt, thaw and resolve itself into a dew' in a remarkably plastic and cinematic way.

Notes

1. Thus e.g. Tony Rayns in *The Time Out of Film Guide*, ed. Tom Milne (Harmondsworth: Penguin, 1991), p. 277). Made impossibly cheaply (shot and mixed on video then transferred to film) this obviously took great effort and dedication. But was it worth it? As a compression of the play, it's initially inventive but all too soon predictable [...] The mysoginist bias puts the film's overall gay camp sensibility in a very questionable light, and preening performances [...] don't help. At worst, offensive; at best, joyless.

2. Of course, Olivier himself takes out a speech to use it 'chorically', but he also, though somewhat redundantly, keeps it as a cue.

3. Compare again Olivier's use of an orchestra tuning up.

4. Gilles Deleuze and Felix Guattari, *Anti-Oedipus: Capitalism and Schizophrenia* (1972, first English edn 1977), repr. London: Athlone Press, 1994), p. 1. The idea of the organs' metaphoric substitution seems to have essentially Freudean origins : "... the familiar prototype of an organ that is painfully tender [...] is the genital organ in its states of excitation [...] Let us now, *taking any part of the body*, describe its activity of sending sexually exciting stimuli to the mind as its 'erotogenicity', and let us further reflect that the considerations on which our theory of sexuality was based have long accustomed us to the notion that certain other parts of the body – the 'erotogenic' zones – may act as substitutes for the genitals and behave analogously to them. [...] We can decide to regard erotogenicity as a general characteristic of all organs...': Sigmund Freud, "On Narcissism: An Introduction", in *On Metapsychology* (Harmondsworth.: Penguin, 1984), p. 77.

5. In this context travesty, or the thematized change of costume in Elizabethan plays would be a semiotic 'detractor', and a proper shell for the Deleuzean body without organs.

6. Robert Duffy, in: Anthony Davies, *Filming Shakespeares Plays* (Cambridge UP, 1994), p. 40.

7. Deleuze, p. 8.

8. The reversely shot face also briefly appears in Olivier's film right after his encounter with the Ghost.

9. This seems to radicalize the spatial power structures of Olivier, whose Hamlet is kneeling before the Ghost.

10. Deleuze, p. 19.

11. Quoted from *The New Penguin Shakespeare Hamlet*, ed. T.J.B. Spencer, London, 1980. All quotations from the play in this article refer to this edition.

12. *Doctor Faustus*, 5.1.

13. H. R. Coursen, *Watching Shakespeare on Television* (London: Assoc. UP, 1993), p 73.

14. In Olivier, it has been noted, the scene is structured theatrically. To use one of Ben Jonson's puns, to understand Hamlet, Polonius under-stands the platform upon which the prince is reading. In Coronado, the metaphor of the medium is rendered appropriately filmic, the lens of the camera quoted directly as Polonius's eye-glass.

15. William C. Wees, *Light Moving in Time. Studies in the Visual Aesthetics of Avant-Garde Film* (Berkeley and Los Angeles: California UP, 1992), p. 14.

16. Matched by Polonius's scroll from which he reads the generic definitions of the players' repertoire. Interestingly, the moment Polonius becomes a reader, he forgets his magnifying glass. As painted as Ophelia, he now *develops an entire body*.

17. Elsewhere in the film it is also the phallic eye, whose winking evokes the pulsating rhythm of sex as pain.

18. Compare Ernest Jones's idea of Hamlet's symbolic identification with Gertrude: 'Hamlet's conscious attitude towards his father was a feminine one, as shown by his exaggerated adoration and his adjuring Gertrude to love such a perfect hero. "The Death of Hamlet's Father", *International Journal of Psycho-Analysis*, 29 (1948), pp. 174-6.

19. Christopher Marlowe, *Doctor Faustus*, 1.3.77.

20. Deleuze, p. 15.

21. Jorgens, *Shakespeare on Film*, 211, in: Davies, *Filming Shakespeare's Plays*, p. 57.

ANTIC DISPOSITIONS:
SHAKESPEARE AND STEVE MARTIN'S *L. A. STORY*

Stephen M. Buhler
(University of Nebraska, Lincoln)

When we first hear Hamlet ruminate alone on the state of Denmark, the embittered prince compares the entire world to a degenerate landscape: "Fie on't, ah fie! 'tis an unweeded garden / That grows to seed, things rank and gross in nature / Possess it merely" (1.2.135-7).[1] When Steve Martin follows the opening credits of his comic film *L. A. Story* with a monologue from the leading character, the expression of discontent is – deliberately – far less eloquent: "My name is Harris K. Telemacher. I live in Los Angeles and I've had seven heart attacks – all imagined. That is to say, I was deeply unhappy but I didn't know it because I was so happy all the time." In the midst of the artificial garden that is L. A., Harris feels unease almost in spite of himself and in spite of the leisure-centered culture of Southern California. Borrowing from Shakespeare helps him to realize his dissatisfaction and to articulate it, however clumsily at first. Despite the initial awkwardness, he perseveres in his identification with Shakespeare's works and characters; unlike Eliot's Prufrock, he resists concluding that he is "not Prince Hamlet, nor was meant to be."[2] What Harris ultimately claims to discover is a truer, more fulfilled identity for himself and for Los Angeles in Shakespeare and in English literary culture more generally.

At the time of its initial release in 1991, *L. A. Story* prompted several reviewers to see the film as enacting a competition between cultural allegiances. In such a view, there are two battles in the film. One struggle, appropriate to a traditional romance, is waged between the U. S. protagonist and his English rival over the object of their contested desire. In the other struggle, over the heart and mind of both the screenwriter, Martin himself, and the character Martin plays, the combatants are what's presented as the Los Angeles variety of United States culture and the kinds of 'Englishness' represented by the other principals in the romantic triangle.[3]

Reviewers who noticed the second contest often went on to decide which side was the victor, sometimes opting for a split decision: as James Cameron-Wilson assessed the outcome, "Steve Martin may love L. A., but he's an Anglophile at heart."[4] Some even attributed this outcome to the influence of having an English director, Mick Jackson, in charge. From the very outset of the film, though, Martin explores a home-grown perception of cultural conflict that masks a deeply rooted identification with the designated Other: this is what makes the film "L. A.'s story." In demonstrating that anglophilia is a pandemic condition of the entertainment industry in Southern California – a condition resulting, in part, from the industry's development in that region – he reminds us how that dream factory appropriates and repackages from English culture many of its fancies and fantasies. Enacting the process, as well as commenting upon it,[5] Martin's screenplay borrows extensively from Shakespeare and especially from *Hamlet*.

L. A.'s own self-image as the earthly paradise resonates with English colonialist takes on the New World as either unfallen or regenerate homeland. The Puritan exiles sought to establish a *New* England, and a sympathetic Andrew Marvell presents "The Bermudas" as Edenic in ways that reflect both on Genesis and the land left behind. Similar refractions occur in Shakespeare's *The Tempest* through the mirrors of 'corrupt' Italy (at the time increasingly dominated by England's imperial rival, Spain) and the temperate isle upon which Prospero and his daughter find refuge.[6] In *L. A. Story* and in much of commercial culture in Southern California, the process comes full circle, as the former colonial territory purportedly finds itself in relation to English culture. Martin's film opens by playfully parodying Angeleno versions of colonial claims to Eden: Los Angeles is established as a temperate refuge from winter's chill and even from age, by quick shots of a man clad in bermuda shorts disposing of his Christmas tree and an elderly, infirm couple roaring off in a high-powered car. Another sight gag begins Martin's more direct engagements with English letters. A vanity license plate reads

"O2B IN LA" in imitation of Robert Browning's expression of longing: "Oh, to be in England / Now that April's there."[7]

The tutelary spirit – and sometime tricksy spirit – of English Literature, though, is Shakespeare. Martin borrows from Shakespeare in the very first voice-over, and the Bard is given full, even excessive credit. After confessing his unhappiness, Harris tells us that Shakespeare once described Los Angeles as "This other Eden, demi-paradise [...] This precious stone set in the silver sea [...] This blessed plot, this earth, this realm, this Los Angeles."[8] This is, of course, taken from John of Gaunt's paean to England in *Richard II* (2.1.42, 46, 50). The slyly bathetic conclusion to Gaunt's *amplificatio* helps to obscure what the selective quotation has omitted – all references to war and to envy. Despite these elisions, the film is predicated upon some Angelenos' envious desire for 'authentic' English culture and their reliance upon it in the face of other cultural threats.

Martin himself plays Harris, who is known as the "wacky, wiggy weatherman", a fixture on a local television news broadcast with an aggressive happytalk style. On camera, he's asked by one of his news anchors if it's true he holds a doctorate in Arts and Humanities. He acknowledges that this is so, only to receive in return the dismissive observation, "A lot of good it did you." Telemacher gains revenge on his former colleagues and the director who fires him when he is later rehired as anchor of a new format, one that parodies the bland old days of BBC newsreaders. George Plimpton's mid-atlantic diction is enough to qualify him as weathercaster for the "Serious News" program. The dream of seriousness apparently has ethnic ramifications as well: the earlier, upbeat format had featured an African-American woman and a Hispanic man as co-anchors; the clip shown of the serious format permits on camera white males only on camera.

The film proposes a conflict between English authoritative speech and American polyglot expression. English speech is portrayed both as dully insular and as happily exempt from cultural chaos: Gaunt's sentiments about the island fortress are transferred to language itself. American expression is felt to be, in comparison, inferior and immature. "I keep thinking I'm a grown-up, but I'm not,"

Harris confides to us in his role as narrator, and the self-assessment also pertains to his speech and to his cultural identity. This tension animates Martin's second direct reference to Shakespeare in the film, one that establishes a recurring pattern. Waiting to leave for a lunchtime gathering on the patio of a trendy California-cuisine restaurant, Harris ruminates:

> Shakespeare once said, "Hey, life is pretty stupid, with lots of hubbub to keep you busy but really not amounting to much." Of course, I'm paraphrasing. He said, "Life is a tale told by an idiot, full of sound and fury, signifying nothing."

Martin consistently contrasts intentionally lame restatements of Shakespearean language with the (more or less) genuine article, just as he contrasts the vapidity of Angeleno Americanese with the style and substance he sometimes associates with RP – Received Pronunciation – accents. At the restaurant, we meet two characters marked as English and played by British-born actors: Sara McDowell (played by Martin's then-wife, Victoria Tennant) and her ex-husband Roland Mackie (played by Richard E. Grant), with whom Sara also shares a town-and-country family background.

Harris is currently in an unhappy relationship with Trudi (played by Marilu Henner), a stereotypical West L. A. career woman who works as a designer-gift consultant. It is probably no accident that Harris' meditations as he waits for her in his car are drawn from *Macbeth*. Trudi's envy of Sara links the interpersonal with the intercultural; she expresses suspicion that Sara's accent is merely an affectation. *Sounding* English is enviable – both desired and resented – in L. A.'s culture of anglophilia. The insubstantiality of Angeleno conversation is contrasted with the vigor of Sara's speech. She announces that she's suffering from jet lag, but no worse than that: it's "nothing a good night's sleep and a good fuck wouldn't help." The shock that registers at the table stems in part from an American inability to connect vulgarity with Englishness, a dissociation that helps to fuel Trudi's suspicion toward Sara. In effect, Californian attempts at elegance are contrasted with country-house ease of manner; the only time that the locals remain unflappable through the lunch is during an earthquake. Ideas and images of transplanted English aristocracy recur: at the restaurant an ice-sculpture swan, water slowly dripping from its beak, echoes a scene from the Granada Television adaptation of *Brideshead Revisited*. Evelyn Waugh's own satire on Southern California, *The Loved One*, is, as we shall see, an important intertext.

A further bit of cultural insecurity and combativeness among Angelenos is signaled by Sara's manner and attire, which are strongly suggestive of Diane Keaton as Annie Hall. Both characters are wonderfully inept drivers, and both *L. A. Story* and Woody Allen's film *Annie Hall* mark driving as a charged cultural term. In the latter film Allen's character, Alvy Singer, has no skill in driving a car and so is completely lost in Los Angeles. In *L. A. Story* Martin's character laughs at Sara's suggestion that they walk anywhere – he even drives to visit his best friend, who lives three houses away – and Sara's difficulty in driving stems from her insistence that she keep to the left-hand side of the road. Using the automobile among other cultural terms, *Annie Hall* sets up a battle between New York and Los Angeles. (The one contribution to civilization Alvy will concede to Southern California is permitting right-hand turns on red lights.) Despite the cultural disadvantages, L. A. and its promises of freedom win Annie away from New York, at least temporarily, and from Alvy. In Martin's film, New York disappears completely, as the struggle is fought between London and L. A. as well as between Roland and Harris over Sara.[9] Her admission, echoing Harris', that "I keep thinking I'm a grown up, but I'm not", marks her as likely Angeleno material. For his part, Roland displays such stereotypical (in the U. S., anyway) 'English' characteristics as an ambiguous, even kinky sexual orientation and a chilly reserve: his and Sara's kisses are, for the most part, decidedly distant; his idea of defying all convention is buying her a hot dog. As the film's Waugh figure, Roland also displays smug contempt for nearly all things "L. A." with the exception of Harris himself, whose manic wit ("verve," Roland calls it) and supposedly sincere relationship with SanDeE* (played by Sarah Jessica Parker) he envies and admires.

Harris, for his part, is deeply enamored of most things English. When the magical aspect of this film is introduced – via a prescient "Freeway Condition" electronic sign – the riddle presented to him takes the form of a English-style crossword puzzle clue and has a solution redolent of the 1960s' 'British Invasion' of American pop music. The answer to the riddle is "SING DOO WAH DIDDY" and refers to the hit recorded by Manfred Mann and frequently played by Sara on the tuba she has brought over from England. (Both complicating and simplifying matters here is the fact that the song was composed by white Americans Jeff Barry and Ellie Greenwich in skillful imitation of African American rhythm-and-blues: generally, such material was much easier to accept coming from the English.) Sara is a journalist, writing a story on the L. A. scene. When she asks Harris for an interview over lunch, Harris asks, "English, French, or Italian?", not really making it clear whether he's referring to cuisines or languages. When Sara wonders if he can speak all those languages, he replies: "No. If I were Italian or French, I'd be out of it." French culture and cuisine are marked as clearly "out of it" themselves, through a send-up of L. A.'s once hyper-fashionable food consciousness. Despite frequent efforts, Harris fails to make a reservation at an incredibly popular, expensive, and contemptuous new restaurant called "L'Idiot". Its tyrannical owner-maître d' – named, in another macaronic pun, Monsieur Pardieu – is played by Shakespearean actor and pop-culture hero Patrick Stewart.[10] Even L'Idiot, however, responds to authentic Englishness: in contrast to the unsuccessful Harris, Roland is able immediately to reserve a table, apparently by virtue of his RP tones.

While L. A.'s responsiveness to French cultural influences strike Martin as purely comic, the city's emulation of English culture receives gentler treatment. During the driving tour Harris takes Sara on, he comments both on the mock "Tudor" style mansions and on what he calls the "Fourdor" mansions, as the automotive motif returns. In a scene very reminiscent of *The Loved One*, Harris and Sara visit a Forest Lawn-type cemetery, where they uncover a monument commemorating Shakespeare's alleged visit to Southern California. Harris recalls that Shakespeare did some writing, apparently in a Hollywood vein, while in the region: he allegedly worked on a continuation of his best-known play, entitled

Hamlet, Part Eight: The Revenge.[11] The monument in the cemetery announces that Shakespeare "Lived in L. A. 1612-1614", placing the Bard on the North American continent at the historical moment of expanding English colonization. Sara later reflects that, while Roland considers Southern California a wasteland, she considers it a place where people have come to make their dreams real. In all this, she does not consider the impact of such dreammaking on other, sometimes earlier arrivals or on original inhabitants. Even Hispanic cultures, with their own complexities and ambivalences regarding the Old and New Worlds, receive minimal consideration. Martin glances at the Spanish language only briefly for comic effect: the name of a resort hotel the major characters visit is *El Pollo del Mar* – that is, chicken of the sea. Here Martin has some fun at the expense of anglophonic Angelenos who resist the language that gave the city its name, a name anglicized generally (and in the film's title) as "L. A."; once again, though, he demonstrates that resistance himself. Asian cultures, reflecting both past and more recent arrivals on the scene, are notably absent; Native American cultures, especially the indigenous ones nearly obliterated over the last two centuries, are perhaps more understandably absent.[12] African-American rap is appropriated only for a waiter's opening spiel at L'Idiot. The tendency toward "erasing all traces of native influence" that Richard Halpern sees represented in Shakespeare's *The Tempest* extends to other arrivals to the Golden State.[13]

But then Martin's idea of L. A. and of its relationship with Englishness predates the resurgence of the Latino community and the development of a "Pacific Rim" sensibility. Martin grew up in the Southern California of the 1950s and 1960s, specifically in Orange County. Interestingly, he has been quoted as describing the area in terms that sum up the attitudes assigned to Roland in *L. A. Story*: "a cultural wasteland".[14] Martin's childhood (like my own) was shaped, to a considerable extent, by the fantasy enterprises which found full expression in the film and television industries and in theme parks such as Disneyland and Knott's Berry Farm. Susan Willis' comments on the attitudes toward culture signalled in the Disney film *Fantasia* and carried into the later attractions are pertinent here:

The desire to incorporate farflung geographic space suggests a society which sees itself bereft of interesting symbols of native culture [... But] the need to incorporate other cultures has less to do with a feeling of lack and more to do with cultural blind spots. *Fantasia* may include everything from Zeus to Satan and Cossacks to Mandarins, but it does *not* include those cultures defeated by the Americanization of America.[15]

Possible and partial exceptions elsewhere in the Disney oeuvre, though, include the versions of English culture both rejected and embraced, both resisted and claimed, in the nation's Revolutionary War and throughout its first centuries. Disney films and television shows of the 1950s and 1960s include, but are not limited to idealizations of the United States' and the North American continent's own past, with examples ranging from Davy Crockett to, both interestingly and disturbingly enough, Zorro – Hollywood's version of a hero for the pre-United States Pueblo de Nuestra Señora Reina de los Angeles de Porciuncula. They also invoke, over and over, English literature for children. Establishing the trend, an adaptation of Kenneth Grahame's *The Wind in the Willows*, narrated by no less a transatlantic figure than Basil Rathbone, was self-consciously paired with Washington Irving's *The Legend of Sleepy Hollow*. That film was followed by *Treasure Island* (one of Disney's last co-productions with RKO), *Alice in Wonderland*, *Peter Pan*, *101 Dalmatians* (now in a live-action version as well), *Mary Poppins*, *The Sword in the Stone*, *The Jungle Book*, and the *Winnie-the-Pooh* short subjects. The campaign continued through *Bedknobs and Broomsticks* (based upon two Mary Norton books)[16] into *The Great Mouse Detective* and the curious echoes of Shakespeare in *The Lion King*. *Pocohontas* presents a Good Brit/Bad Brit schematic, pitting Mel Gibson's post-colonial Australian-American accent for John Smith against David Ogden Stiers mid-atlantic emulation of RP for Governor Ratcliffe, the Jacobean projector (and Ratcliffe's pencil-thin mustache is reminiscent of Uncle Walt's). The programmatic anglophilia may have realized itself most fully in the career of Hayley Mills as the Disney Studio's principal leading lady.

As a teenager, Steve Martin worked at Disneyland, selling souvenirs and eventually demonstrating magic tricks in Merlin's Magic Shop, a marketing tie-in with *The Sword in the Stone*, an adaptation of T. H. White's *The Once and Future King*. His inspiration at the time was a vaudeville-style performer in Disneyland's "Golden Horseshoe Revue" named Wally Boag, who combined delivering comic patter with making balloon animals. (Many of Martin's routines in the 1970s were subversions of Boag's acts: one involved shaping "contraceptive devices" from balloons.) Martin first performed professionally at Knott's Berry Farm, a theme park that at the time presented – much as Disneyland's Main Street, U. S. A., still does – an almost exclusively anglophone version of the American past.

The memory of his days at Disneyland and his own comic magic act for the Bird Cage Theatre at Knott's informs what happens in the "Graveyard Scene" of *L. A. Story*, the film's most sustained direct engagement with *Hamlet*. Harris and Sara meet a gravedigger (played, without credit, by Rick Moranis) taken almost straight out of Shakespeare's play, even if the character's 'Cockney' accent is anything but authentic. Martin's own character makes the allusion overt with an ironic "Finally, a funny gravedigger," but Martin has more than travesty in mind: after first updating the scene as "Churchyard 90210", Martin will allow his own past and Shakespeare's language to return with a romantic vengeance.

The Clown's commentary on the duration of bodies after burial is adapted for the new cultural landscape of Beverly Hills. Instead of tanners' corpses lasting longer, the remains of affluent women who have visited plastic surgeons endure. There is likely a strain of localized misogyny here aimed at the type of California woman represented by Henner's character, Trudi. Of course, all manner of localized misogyny is offered by Hamlet himself, whose "Let her paint an inch think" finds an analogue here. And when the inevitable skull is uncovered and handed to Harris it turns out to be what's left of The Great Blunderman, Harris' mentor in comedy and magic. Harris tries to pay tribute to Blunderman – as Martin honors Wally Boag – in the manner of Hamlet's meditation on Yorick, but requires the help of Sara, who can quote Shakespeare more accurately. She does so, as the Gravedigger encourages her, and Harris falls utterly in love at that precise moment.[17] Harris' adoration is sealed and signalled by a magical breeze that gently disturbs Sara's hair.

Amy Heckerling's 1995 film *Clueless*, itself loosely based on Jane Austen's *Emma*, offers interesting parallels. Since the central character, Cher, is one of the most popular and trend-conscious denizens of Beverly Hills High School, she wants to avoid being perceived as anything so unfashionable as intellectual. So Cher brushes up her Shakespeare in a manner more clearly mediated than Martin's Sara, via commercially-produced study aids (Cliffs Notes) and commercially successful actors/objects of desire (Mel Gibson). Even with such mediation, her ability to quote Shakespeare successfully initiates her campaign to make two teachers fall in love – and, in their joy, raise everyone's grades – and her ability to identify correctly a Shakespearean quote (from *Hamlet*, no less) is what first wins the amused respect of her eventual admirer. In the world of *L. A. Story*, though, Sara's Englishness, rather than market-driven media, seems to provide the desirable access to the Bard.

Repeating the paraphrase gag used with *Macbeth*, Harris reacts to the skull by saying: "The Great Blunderman. I knew him. He was a funny guy; taught me magic." Harris can go no further into Shakespearean territory, despite the Gravedigger's anticipatory echo of the meditation on Alexander the Great: the Great Blunderman is "Not so great now, is he?" Sara is the one who takes off with Shakespearean – if still not quite Shakespeare's – lines.

Sara: A fellow of infinite jest?
Harris: Yeah.
Gravedigger: That's it.
Sara: He hath borne me on his back a thousand times?
Gravedigger: She's knows; she's got it.
Sara: Where be your gibes now? Your flashes of merriment that would
  set the table on a roar?

Sara not only simplifies Shakespeare's language; she also discreetly omits the passages that register Hamlet's physical revulsion at the jester's remains. Steve Martin, as screenwriter, is discreet here as well, because he is building up to the flowering of what is presented as a trans-cultural romance.

In his study of the romance mode in Shakespeare, Howard Felperin reminds us that romance "involves a journey into another world inherently removed from present time and place";[18] Los Angeles' self-image as the place "where dreams come true" – as Sara recognizes – complicates matters by making romance *part* of its "present time and place". Martin has in mind not only popular conceptions of romance but but also the generic meaning of the term: the story of Harris Telemacher resonates with that of Prospero, exiled in the New World. Harris' best friend (played by Susan Forristal) is named Ariel, whose angelic-daemonic name and apparent same-sex orientation guarantee that their relationship will remain Platonic. Ariel is Harris' fellow trickster in a series of performance art assaults on famous galleries, including the Los Angeles County Museum of Art. Not surprisingly, one artist whose work is quite visible during these raids on roller skates is David Hockney, the English-born painter who has made Southern California his home and his primary subject. In fact, Martin physicalizes the cultural collision by having Harris, out of control on his skates, knock Sara down in front of Hockney's famous landscape *Mulholland Drive: The Road to the Studio*. (Roland is an art dealer specializing in English art. Martin, it turns out, is himself an astute collector.)

The Tempest supplies Ariel's name and her function as a benevolent familiar; that play about forms of magic at work in an earthly paradise is further invoked by Harris' occupation, and by the breezes that regularly accompany the Freeway Condition sign's prophecies. During their first encounter, the sign tells Harris that "THE WEATHER WILL CHANGE YOUR LIFE TWICE". First, rain pours down on a weekend that Harris chooses to pretape his forecast, which leads to his director's boat being swamped in the Pacific Ocean and to his being fired. Second, with the sign's help, Harris makes good on his promise to raise a tempest to keep Sara from returning to England: "If I had the power, I would turn the winds around. I would roll in fog; I would bring in storms." This connects with both his erstwhile profession as weatherman but also his name, Telemacher, which connotes not only broadcasting but magic – *doing* and *working* things from afar. Despite his frequent and intentionally disarming ineptitude, this Southern California Prospero is able to arrange things admirably well by conjuring up a storm.

The encounters with *Hamlet*, though, dominate. Much as the Ghost goads and disturbs Hamlet, the Freeway Sign prompts Harris to act; the riddle, after all, involves unscrambling "HOW DADDY IS DOING". Harris also cannot quite get through to his mother, although the problem here is a malfunctioning voice-activated telephone. We understand that, as the "Wacky, Wiggy Weatherman", Harris is merely putting an antic disposition on. When his director (played, without credit, by Woody Harrelson) accuses him of "doing some kind of intellectual stuff" during the broadcast and orders him to be "More wacky, less egghead", Harris sarcastically promises to remember the advice: "Let me make a note of that." This quietly echoes Hamlet's line, "My tables – meet it is I set it down" (1. 5. 107). While torn between his feelings of obligation toward Trudi, amiable lust toward his young admirer SanDeE* (as she insists on spelling her name), and deeper passion toward Sara, Harris writes on his window: "Bored Beyond Belief". This, then, is the L. A. version of "How weary, stale, flat, and unprofitable / Seem to me all the uses of this world" (1. 2. 134). Another version of Hamlet's existential angst can be found in the call letters of the newscast's station, KYOY – why oh why?

Martin continues to use the tensions between source text and paraphrase and between English cultural productions and American mass culture products for comic effect. As the two couples drive, in separate cars, to *El Pollo*, we overhear their conversations: Sara and Roland discuss poetry, philosophy and architecture; Harris and SanDeE* engage in a game of Trivial Pursuit. Roland's ability to quote from Shelley's "Ode to the West Wind" is juxtaposed with Harris' ability to answer the question, "Who was Howdy Doody's friend?" Martin is said to value strongly verbatim quotation. When still married to Martin, Tennant noted his insistence on accuracy:

When I loosely paraphrase something off of one of his comic albums, he corrects me, explaining, "The line has to be read exactly the way it was written, every comma, or it's not funny."[19]

Some of *L. A. Story*'s interest in the relationship between American and English cultures is grounded in Martin's frustration over the 1981 film 'translation' of Dennis Potter's *Pennies from Heaven* from England to Chicago during the Great Depression. (The original television series itself engages with *The Threepenny Opera* as well as with Tin Pan Alley.) Despite Potter's own involvement with the screenplay and Martin's strong identification with the material, the production as directed by Herbert Ross was disappointing both financially and, to a great extent, critically. The dangers of paraphrase and of cultural exchange struck very close to home. Several of Martin's film projects have involved such translation, including *Roxanne* (an Americanized update of *Cyrano de Bergerac*) and *A Simple Twist of Fate* (an adaptation of *Silas Marner*).

In *L. A. Story*, too, Martin does not always insist on exact quotation even in providing the 'right' versions of Shakespeare. Perhaps the most telling revision of a Shakespearean tag occurs in Harris' narration of the events of his and Sara's first night as physical lovers. The cultural differences have been overcome, a point reinforced by the soundtrack at this point, which features Enya's song "On Your Shore". In keeping with the idealization and militant juvenilization that often characterize Hollywood products, the two of them appear as children in a magical garden, after the adult Harris has quietly exclaimed in voiceover: "All I could think was – wonderful, wonderful, wonderful, wonderful, wonderful, and most wonderful, and yet again wonderful." This is loosely adapted from *As You Like It* 3. 2. 191-92: "O wonderful, wonderful, and most wonderful wonderful! and yet again wonderful, and after that out of all hooping!" While Martin's gently ironic view of L. A. as an imperfect (if not unweeded) garden matches that play's presentation of the Forest of Arden, his treatment of love – as well as of language – in this scene is drastically simplified. Not only the text but also the tone has changed from what the source scene presents. The lines are part of Celia's merciless teasing of Rosalind over the identity of the author of verses written in her honor. Celia's mockery of burgeoning pastoral romance, by turns affectionate and resentful, is here transformed into a lover's prayer. At this point in the film Martin allows neither Harris nor Shakespeare ironic distance.

Elsewhere, though, Martin offers deeply comic refractions of recent debates over the sexual and gender politics of Shakespeare's plays and in high culture productions (and presentations) more generally. The Graveyard Scene in *L. A. Story* is preceded by a visit to what is called a "Musicological Museum" but what also enshrines Dead White European Maleness. As part of his attempt to prove to Sara that Los Angeles indeed "has culture," Harris shows her the contents of one display case: Verdi's baton, Mozart's quill, and – completing the phallocentric collection – Beethoven's balls. Testes figure in another bizarre gag, late in the film. The two couples (SanDeE* and Harris, Sara and Roland) discover they have adjacent suites at El Pollo Del Mar only after each couple has made exuberant love and eavesdropped on the other couple in the next room. When they all meet in the hallway immediately after, this realization leads to intense jealousy on the part of Sara and Harris and also to a resolve on Roland's part to spend time with Sara's amusing American friend and his companion. The women go ahead to the hotel's restaurant while Harris notices a clanging sound. He asks Roland about it and Roland replies, "It's a nuisance; it's my damned testicles."

The joke engages with complex cultural attitudes toward virility and, intriguingly enough, toward the sexual identity of Hamlet. The definitive Hamlet for the United States in the early Twentieth Century was John Barrymore; one of the reasons for his success in the role was a calculated attempt to make the character not only vital (in opposition to interpretations holding that Hamlet is unequal to the world of action) but virile. Barrymore reportedly told his producer, Arthur Melancthon Hopkins: "I want [Hamlet] to be so male that when I come out on the stage they can hear my balls clank."[20] In *L. A. Story*, Roland's balls clang because he has just 'proven his manhood' with Sara, though in a way that compromises Barrymore's assertion of uncomplicated male heterosexuality. While the two couples pause in making love, comic-strip-style "thought balloons" make it clear that the lovers have not had their minds on their physical partners: Harris and Sara turn out to be thinking of each other, while SanDeE* and Roland both have been thinking of Mel Gibson, whose work with Franco Zeffirelli on a new film of *Hamlet* was already widely-publicized during the production of *L. A. Story*. In fact, Gibson as Hamlet (who would make such an impact on SanDeE*'s Beverly Hills counterpart, the fictional Cher of *Clueless*) had been in theatres for some months by the time Martin's film was released in early 1991. With his wide-ranging desires for Sara (and for the kind of relationship with her that he believes Harris enjoys with SanDeE*) and for the latest Hamlet, Roland suggests a bisexual version of high cultural virility.[21]

At the film's end, Martin reprises the automotive discourse involved with the opening allusion to Browning. The medium (one might say vehicle) is not, as before, a license plate, but instead the prophetic Freeway Condition sign. When Harris asks, "How did this happen?," the ghost in the machine gives a slightly abbreviated and adjusted Shakespearean quote, again from *Hamlet*. "THERE ARE MORE THINGS N HEAVEN AND EARTH, HARRIS", reads the first message; "THAN ARE DREAMT OF N YOUR PHILOSOPHY", concludes the second. These transcendent sentiments are accompanied by otherworldly but unmistakably British music, as the Pipes and Drums and Military Band of the Royal Scots Dragoon Guards play the traditional tune from the English Methodist hymn, "Amazing Grace"; the sign has informed Harris earlier that it believes it had been bagpipes in an earlier life. Other signs of transcendent affirmation appear when the magical breeze blows more fiercely (through the bagpipes?) and when this prophetic Freeway Condition sign and all others shine out "Condition Clear": the expression suggests channelling, speaking with spirits through a medium, even as it also refers to automotive traffic and meteorology. Through Harris' encounters with cultural inheritances from England, the character is convinced that "romance does exist deep in the heart of L. A." – again, Martin deliberately invokes ideas of genre as well as emotional satisfaction.[22] In exploring this association between personal fulfillment and anglophonic literature, Martin reflects much of the anxiety that has influenced the entertainment industry in Southern California. English literature, especially Shakespeare, can paradoxically serve both as a threat to an ambivalently regarded, jealously guarded cultural innocence and as a means of recovering a supposedly lost cultural identity.

In a groundbreaking study of Los Angeles, Reyner Banham explores connections between the architecture of movie studios and theme parks and the architecture of Southern California communities. This relationship prompts him to consider the 'native' L. A. psyche. There is, Banham claims, a

> special brand of 'innocence' that underlies the purely personal fantasies of Los Angeles. Innocence is a word to use cautiously in this context, because it must be understood as not comprising either simplicity or ingenuousness. Deeply imbued with standard myths of the Natural Man and the Noble Savage, as in other parts of the U. S., this innocence grows and flourishes as an assumed right in the Southern California sun ...[23]

Martin has shrewdly played both the L. A. naif and the self-aware artist, both the 'cultureless' American and the anglophile who comes home to his source culture. In designating England as the soulmate for L. A., he also reflects much of recent politics in California, which appeals to English-speaking culture as a means of avoiding the Others closer to home. Political developments along these lines include Richard Riordan's election as mayor of Los Angeles and intensifying debates over multilingual services and education. They also include California Governor Pete Wilson's attempts to achieve national prominence via immigration issues and moves against affirmative action. The subtext of *L. A. Story* is comprised of such cultural faultlines. These run just below the sunny surface of Martin's satirical tribute both to the region and to what it claims as its cultural patrimony.

Notes

1. For references to Shakespeare's works, I have used *The Riverside Shakespeare*, ed. G. Blakemore Evans (Boston: Houghton Mifflin, 1974).

2. T. S. Eliot, "The Love Song of J. Alfred Prufrock", line 111.

3. Mas'ud Zavarzadeh has commented on how United States mass-market films – even those that offer a "surface of easy charm and humor" – often invoke an ideal of intimacy amidst contestatory situations to elide questions about cultural allegiance and identity; *Seeing Films Politically* (Albany: New York State UP, 1991), pp. 128-38.

4. James Cameron-Wilson in *Film Review 1991-92* (London: Virgin Books, 1992), p. 67.

5. Martin's project, in effect, maps a limited range within the "field of position-takings" that Pierre Bourdieu has proposed as a model for the production of literature and art; *The Field of Cultural Production*, ed. Randal Johnson (Cambridge: Polity Press, 1993), pp. 34-7. While the range may be limited, the observations are often acute, especially of the contradictorily suspicious and adulatory stances possible in the parodic mode.

6. Studies of the multiple mirroring effects in *The Tempest* include Jeffrey Knapp, *An Empire Nowhere* (Berkeley and Los Angeles: California UP, 1992), esp. pp. 220-35, and Richard Halpern, "'The picture of Nobody': White Cannibalism in *The Tempest*", in *The Production of English Renaissance Culture*, ed. D. L. Miller, S. O'Dair, and H. Weber (Ithaca: Cornell UP, 1994), esp. pp. 271-9.

7. "Home Thoughts, from Abroad," lines 1-2.

8. Steve Martin is the only credited writer for *L. A. Story* (Carolco Pictures, 1991); he also served as one of the film's executive producers.

9. Martin may be attempting to supplant Woody Allen as the most thoughtful clown on the United States scene; his recent plays, *WASP* and *Picasso at the Lapin Agile*, owe much to Allen's literary and philosophical pastiches.

10. Martin cannot resist making the reference to U. S. poultry magnate Frank Perdue more explicit. He has Stewart sneer, in faux-French accent, "He can have ze chicken".

11. Another central myth of L. A. culture, one with formidable amounts of truth and fantasy attached to it, is invoked here: Hollywood's corruption of gifted writers who are pressed into screenwriting service.

12. Some of the processes of cultural suppression are surveyed by Tomás Almaguer, *Racial Fault Lines: The Historical Origins of White Supremacy in California* (Berkeley and Los Angeles: California UP, 1994).

13. Halpern, p. 285.

14. Quoted in Peter de Jonge, "Cool Jerk", *New York Times Magazine*, 31 May 1992, p. 46. In the film, Roland calls Los Angeles a "place for the brain dead" and a desert. Martin's send-ups of L. A. culture often agree with Roland's first assessment; his stress on the region's extravagant dependency on water (piped in from elsewhere) acknowledges the literal as well as the figurative applicability of the second judgment.

15. Susan Willis, "*Fantasia*: Walt Disney's Los Angeles Suite", *Diacritics* 17:2 (Summer 1987), 86.

16. On the drastic revision by Disney of women's texts in English children's literature, see Chris Cuomo, "Spinsters in Sensible Shoes" in *From Mouse to Mermaid: The Politics of Film, Gender, and Culture*, ed. E. Bell, L. Haas, and L. Sells (Bloomington: Indiana UP, 1995), pp. 212-21.

17. Linda Charnes has observed how important it is to the scene (and to Harris) that Sara recite "proper lines from the play"; *Notorious Identity: Materializing the Subject in Shakespeare* (Cambridge, MA: Harvard UP, 1993), p. 205, n1.

18. Howard Felperin, *Shakespearean Romance* (Princeton UP, 1972), p. 7.

19. Quoted in de Jonge, p. 48.

20. John Kobler, *Damned in Paradise: The Life of John Barrymore* (New York: Atheneum, 1977), p. 174.

21. On homoeroticism in Zeffirelli's Shakespeare films, see Peter S. Donaldson, *Shakespearean Films/Shakespearean Directors* (Boston: Unwin Hyman, 1990), pp. 165-71, and William Van Watson, "Shakespeare, Zeffirelli, and the Homosexual Gaze", *Literature/Film Quarterly* 20 (1992), 308-25.

22. On intentionality in film, especially the overtly fictional variety, see Christian Metz, *Film Language: A Semiotics of the Cinema*, tr. Michael Taylor (New York: Oxford UP, 1974), pp. 108-10.

23. Reyner Banham, *Los Angeles: The Architecture of Four Ecologies* (London: Penguin, 1971), p. 129.

"A PALPABLE HIT": FRANCO ZEFFIRELLI'S *HAMLET* (USA, 1990)

Chris Lawson,
(The University of the West of England, Bristol)

By casting Mel Gibson, an Australian actor brought to prominence in action film trilogies such as *Mad Max* and *Lethal Weapon*, Zeffirelli establishes Hamlet as a pragmatic, dynamic hero who overcomes doubt with deeds.[1] Far from being an indecisive philosopher, this Hamlet is never static for long, maintaining an animated presence on screen throughout. While Olivier's 1948 *Hamlet* is "the tragedy of a man who could not make up his mind", Mel Gibson's portrayal eschews psychology and extended self-analysis in favour of finding straightforward solutions to difficult questions.[2] Like the heroes of *Mad Max* and *Lethal Weapon*, Gibson's Hamlet is an individualist pitted against the forces of evil (Claudius in this case). His particular brand of hero-figure is essentially a loner who never seems completely comfortable even in the company of family or friends. This is a vital ingredient for any characterisation of Hamlet, whose suspicion of others marks him apart from any group. Bouts of introspection and melancholy are not unusual to the other characters Gibson has played. The burden of revenge for the murder of a father is just as great as that for a wife and child (*Mad Max*), or a lover or colleague (as in *Lethal Weapon*). This *Hamlet* is not the story of a man tormented by hesitation, so much as it is about his struggle to come to terms with a world where "unnatural acts" occur in brutal and unpredictable ways.

The film script is similar in structure to the First Quarto of *Hamlet*, emphasizing themes of betrayal and revenge while minimizing Hamlet's procrastination.[3] Rosencrantz and Guildenstern are retained in this version but Fortinbras is omitted, excluding the sense of an outside threat to Elsinore. A sense of momentum is created in the film by a dramatic re-positioning of scenes and speeches.[4] This rearrangement of the text is striking, with scenes being omitted or radically manipulated in order to emphasize a sense of narrative drive and progression. The director simplifies the drama, using individual episodes in the plot in a strategic way to build and release tension at key points in the film. While lessening the ironies of contiguity between scenes in the original text, this method offers an accessible and exciting approach for those unfamiliar with the play.

The visual symbolism of the film accentuates dramatic themes and issues. Cinematic techniques include colour tinting, which highlights either warm oranges or cold blues, reinforcing the ambient moods of interior and exterior scenes.[5] Additionally, there is the symbolism of Hamlet's sword which is used, at times, as a walking stick or crutch, a crucifix and as a mock headstone.[6] In this way, his sword provides a means not only of physical but also spiritual protection and support. Hamlet's weapon represents a focal point of trust and loyalty, as illustrated when the guards swear an oath upon it, at his request. In a similar way, the placement of characters in their surroundings is another area which can be used to demonstrate emotional states of mind. For example, a degree of separation or dislocation from the court community can be illustrated by placing a character high up on a gallery or battlement, at a closed window or in an open doorway. A sense of entrapment can be created by positioning a character with their back against a wall, as is the case with Gertrude later. Above all, visual symbolism of this kind contributes levels of understanding to the adaptation without overwhelming or displacing the poetry of the play.

Hamlet opens with a view of the castle, shrouded in mist and bathed in a cold, blue light. Subsequent images scan along the silent, still figures of citizens and guards before a dissolve fade takes the viewer into the crypt where Old Hamlet's interment occurs. Here, Zeffirelli establishes a sense of community within the castle, directing attention towards the main characters of the drama. Unlike the castle in Olivier's film, where the characters are dwarfed by a cavernous, seemingly empty shell, the settlement in Zeffirelli's version is inhabited by numerous strata of society, from nobility to ancillary personnel. This interpretation of Elsinore has similarities with Kozintsev's vision of a self-sufficient castle community. A key difference is that the inhabitants of Kozintsev's *Hamlet* are all potential spies or conspirators, whereas the population of Zeffirelli's castle provide a sense of rustic charm, helping to locate the drama in an "Olde Worlde" setting. The importance of these characters also illustrates that the sphere of the court does not exist in isolation from other echelons of society. Zeffirelli includes representatives of the castle community to establish the mutual inter-dependence of this social framework. Any kind of upheaval within the world of the court, such as of Old Hamlet's death, can be seen to have wider ramifications for the population of the settlement as a whole.

Hamlet sprinkles earth on the armour encasing his father's body, to symbolise how much Old Hamlet is a part of Denmark, even in death. This funeral ritual also represents a visual point of connection between Young and Old Hamlet, in addition to introducing Gibson's Prince to the audience. He is first seen with his face shadowed under a large hood. His expression is a visual representation of one "with [...] vailed lids" (1.2.70).[7] The sepulchre is sealed with a stone cover, representing in ceremonial terms the finality of Old Hamlet's mortal influence on the court at Elsinore. Alan Bates' "sensual, ignoble and immoral" Claudius places a broad sword on top of the tomb, symbolising the dormancy of Old Hamlet's military power, while Gertrude appears "Like Niobe, all tears" (1.2.149).[8] After the interment is complete, Gertrude clings to the end of the tomb, weeping uncontrollably. For a while, her grief is openly expressed, but Claudius reprimands her with a stern gaze which immediately pacifies her outburst.

Gertrude's grief for Old Hamlet appears all too real and overwhelming. However, Claudius's ability to censure her emotions with a single glance suggests the level of control he has over his new bride. By placing this brief but significant gesture so early in the film and juxtaposing it with the first appearance of both Young and Old Hamlet, Zeffirelli raises many questions as to the dynamics of the relationships between the court characters. Even before any dialogue has been exchanged, Gertrude's complete subservience to Claudius is evident in no uncertain terms. However, the extent to which this implicates Gertrude in the plot to murder Old Hamlet is not so clear. Her relationship with Claudius seems to be based on a child-like obedience to him, more in terms of a father and daughter bond than that of husband and wife. Of course, Gertrude's alliance with Old Hamlet remains a mystery, both in the text and on film. By his appearance, Paul Scofield's Ghost appears much older than Glenn Close's Gertrude. This perhaps implies that such a father to daughter type of bond may have been a feature of her first marriage. Nevertheless, the question of whether Gertrude continues this role-playing with Bates' Claudius remains ambiguous. As a substitute for the initial scene in the text where the Ghost of Old Hamlet appears to the guards, this inclusion of the funeral highlights the dead King's potent influence upon the court characters. More importantly, this opening scene sets the action to follow firmly in the context of a domestic drama. The immediacy and impact of such a sequence anticipates the conflict to follow between characters, without recourse to the potential excess of a more melodramatic or sensational approach.

The tension which manifests itself in the hostile glances between Hamlet and Claudius in the first scene establishes their rivalry from the outset. Zeffirelli emphasizes the antagonism between the Prince and the King, through this silent, confrontational behaviour. It is ironic that the object which physically separates them, namely the tomb of Old Hamlet, also unites the two in mutual mistrust. Claudius' guilt and Hamlet's grief are both metaphorically contained in this tomb. Suspicion weaves these emotions in an invisible web as the Queen looks silently to Claudius, and Hamlet glances from one to the other. Gertrude is a major cause of jealousy and contention between the two men. To Hamlet she can be the possession of only one person (Old Hamlet, or Hamlet himself, after the death of the father), whereas to Claudius she is the personification of Denmark by which he can legitimately satisfy his unspoken lust for power. With these undercurrents remaining, Hamlet maintains a tacit revulsion towards his step-father with every piercing glance he directs towards the King.

Gertrude is tender and affectionate with both men. There is a manipulative aspect to her use of touching and kissing, which Zeffirelli uses to show that her

affection is not always as genuine as it might appear. Glenn Close's interpretation of Gertrude encapsulates aspects of sexuality as well as a more clinical, calculating side to her nature. Her performance has been described as "electrifying", and like "an ice-goddess".[9] Towards the end of 1.2, Hamlet kneels and embraces Gertrude as he agrees not to return to Wittenberg. He presses the side of his face to her stomach in an act of child-like affection. With this intimate gesture, the Prince displays his feelings of insecurity and subservience to his mother. Hamlet's sense of disappointment and betrayal at Gertrude's "o'er hasty marriage" (2.2.57), is reflected in the conflict of emotions which contort his expression here. Gertrude is seen to reciprocate by dropping to her knees, running her hands through Hamlet's hair and raining passionate kisses on his eyes, forehead and mouth. All the time, she searches his face for the hint of an accepting smile. She needs his compliance and acceptance of her marriage to Claudius to ease her own mixed feelings about the situation. When Hamlet gives a little smile, Gertrude is satisfied and leaves. Her emotional manipulation of Hamlet causes an emotional impasse between mother and son. Hamlet is caught between resentment of Gertrude because of her union with Claudius and a deep affection for her which causes him to remain at Elsinore. It could be argued that she genuinely does not understand the depth of betrayal which Hamlet feels as a result of her marriage to Claudius. Alternatively, Gertrude may choose to ignore the full extent of Hamlet's sadness, considering her marriage to Claudius to be of more importance. Consequently, she may regard her re-marriage as something that Hamlet will have to learn to accept. Thirdly, Gertrude could interpret Hamlet's sombre outlook purely as grief for his dead father which will ease with time. Gertrude's parting comment to Hamlet (transposed from Claudius in the text) is notable as she says:
This gentle and unforced accord [...]
Sits smiling on my heart. (1.2.123-4)

It is the *unforced* nature of the accord which pleases her heart so much. Yet, through the physical intimacy of this scene, Gertrude has used these very persuasive powers over her son which she would seek to dis-associate herself

Franco Zeffirelli's *Hamlet*

from. It is this duality in Gertrude's character that makes her portrayal in the film seem calculating and manipulative.

It becomes clear, then, that the Queen has created more problems than she has solved. Hamlet watches as Gertrude and Claudius depart on horseback to the accompaniment of the hunt. A combination of the huntsman's wailing horn and the barking hounds, together with the image of the couple galloping away, suggests how their consciences are so little troubled by recent events. The extent to which they can indulge in such sport is indicative of their obvious abandon. This image highlights the theme of Hamlet's soliloquy (1.2.129-46), as he contemplates how Gertrude can be so transformed from grief to happiness in such a short space of time. Zeffirelli implies a second level of meaning whereby Gertrude and Claudius adopt the role of calculating and cold-blooded hunters in their attempts to consolidate positions of power. Hamlet punctuates the line: "Frailty, thy name is woman" (1.2.146) by shutting his chamber window against the outside world. With this gesture, he puts a physical, transparent barrier between himself and other characters, especially Gertrude, emphasizing the developing emotional chasm between himself and his mother. His physical and emotional distance from Gertrude will continue until its eventual breakdown during the closet scene later.

A key feature of any performance of *Hamlet* must be the portrayal of Old Hamlet's ghost. The dramatic effect of Paul Scofield's performance relies on the reactions of other characters, who recoil in fear, rather than at the characteristics of the Ghost *per se*. A softly lit and faintly glowing phantom leads Hamlet towards a pool of light at the end of a dark corridor. This light may represent the revelation which Old Hamlet will tell his son concerning his "foul and most unnatural murder" (1.5.25). On a high turret, Hamlet searches for the Ghost, twisting and turning with fear and trepidation. Finally, with an almost visible shiver, he turns to see the Ghost framed by the battlements. Old Hamlet appears as pale and haggard as the moonlit stonework which surrounds him. While the Ghost is on screen, Hamlet is always seen with his face half in shadow. This is a representation of how Hamlet has literally become overshadowed by the knowledge of his father's murder.

Hamlet's enforced role as revenger to that crime is accepted with a combination of anger and disbelief.

While the face of the Ghost is largely impassive, Hamlet struggles against his emotions of grief for, and empathy with, his father. The bond between father and son is illustrated further as, at the close of their first encounter, Ghost and mortal appear almost to merge, dissolving past and present into one instant, when the Ghost approaches a quaking Hamlet. Old Hamlet's face looms over that of his son as he departs with "Remember me" (1.5.91). A reverse image shows the Prince, his arms outstretched and eyes shut, as if anticipating a tender embrace, only to find that the apparition has disappeared. In a shot which lasts only a fraction of a second, the Ghost's arms are seen to rise upward as he exits. Perhaps Zeffirelli subtly hints that this apparition is heaven-sent? This would certainly seem to be the implication here. After the Prince returns to Horatio and the guards, the voice of Old Hamlet exhorts them to swear a solemn oath of secrecy. The group look upwards in response to the Ghost's disembodied voice. Either the Ghost is a heavenly apparition, or it would seem that the other characters compound the suggestion by reacting in the unconscious belief that this must be the case.

One of the most memorable pieces of visual iconography in Zeffirelli's production occurs at the close of this scene, and lasts only for a second or two. As a variation of this image adorns publicity material for the film, including video cassette cases, it has become symbolic for the film as a whole. After Horatio and the guards have sworn themselves to secrecy (1.5), Hamlet's face is seen, half obscured by the upturned hilt of his sword, resembling a crucifix. Here, the side of Hamlet's face which was in shadow in the presence of the Ghost is now hidden behind the sword-crucifix. In this one shot, Zeffirelli shows Hamlet to place his trust in the sword as symbol of revenge and the cross as the Christian symbol of faith. This is such a prominent emblem that, as Van Watson points out, the camera focuses on the sword rather than on Hamlet's face, during this short sequence.[10]

The portrayal of Hamlet's "antic disposition" (1.5.173) is shown to take several courses in the film. From a purely visual re-enactment of Hamlet approaching Helena Bonham-Carter's Ophelia in her chamber (with his "Doublet all unbraced" (2.1.78-85)), to his intellectual word-play with Ian Holm's Polonius (in the scene which takes place in the library during 2.2.175-219), and his confrontation with Ophelia (3.1.91-121 and 132-53), the Prince's displays of madness are complex, provocative and disturbing. During the library scene, a battle of verbal and intellectual dexterity takes place as Polonius' enquiries are met with suspicion, hostility and riddles. By climbing a ladder to try to be nearer to Hamlet, Polonius is part of a visual analogy to this verbal combat. Polonius ascends, trying to understand Hamlet's riddles, while the latter discards pages torn from books, literally bombarding Polonius with words. Unusually in this production, Polonius looks straight to camera when giving his aside: "How pregnant sometimes his replies are-" (2.2.207-8), creating a comic intimacy as he colludes with the audience. Comedy is also the intention in the next occurrence, as Hamlet pushes the ladder away from the wall, with the hapless Polonius still clinging on. Thus Polonius gains an impression of how it feels to go "like a crab [...] backward" (2.2.206).

Later, Polonius hopes that through a deliberate positioning of Ophelia in Hamlet's path, the Prince will reveal the root of his distraction. The Prince quickly realizes that he is being spied upon as he sees the shadows of Polonius and Claudius on an upper gallery. Consequently, he directs most of his words in this direction, especially his: "let the doors be shut on him [Polonius], that he may play the fool nowhere but in's own house" (3.1.134-5). Hamlet's overwhelming sense of betrayal and revulsion leads to an emotionally charged confrontation with Ophelia. As Hamlet circles round Ophelia (3.1.145-50), his anger building moment by moment, the spectator's point of view circles with him, emphasising Ophelia's sense of fear, confusion and disorientation. From Ophelia's point of view, an impression of her entrapment and intimidation is re-enforced by this technique. The soaring vertical space of the room around the characters only adds to this sense of entrapment and dizzying vertigo, as the scene builds to a peak of dramatic tension.

The Prince rejects Ophelia with considerable force, flinging her against a wall during this scene (3.1). Although Ophelia's initial intention had been to return Hamlet's gifts, he takes the line of contention further, stating that the relationship had been no more than a figment of her imagination. By creating a distance between himself and Ophelia, both through aggression and through ambiguous speech and riddles, Hamlet casts doubt and uncertainty upon the future of their relationship. He now links a woman's love with betrayal, after the example laid down by his mother and described in his "Frailty thy name is woman" (1.2.146) soliloquy. With the imposition of this emotional instability, Hamlet hopes to preserve himself and Ophelia from the spiritual corruption which would result from an actively loving partnership. Although he abuses Ophelia, Hamlet's attraction to her is something which, ultimately, he cannot completely suppress.

Zeffirelli keeps the visual narrative pace fluid and restless during Hamlet's "To be or not to be" soliloquy (3.1.58-90) in the vaulted crypt. As Neil Taylor points out, the rapid editing of this scene (encompassing sixteen different shots), could distract audience attention from the content of Hamlet's words here.[11] Alternatively, it could be argued that viewers are fully able to accommodate swift changes on a visual level while still remaining receptive to the spoken words of the scene. After communing with his conscience, we next see Hamlet "commune with nature" as he is shown riding on horseback along a beach.[12] By means of a dissolve fade from gloomy interior to bright exterior locations, the director demonstrates the dynamism of Gibson's Hamlet as a character who is best able to contemplate important issues outside the bounds of the castle community.

Even when Hamlet finds the comparative solitude of this isolated place, he is not left alone for long. The Players provide a physical (with their cart) and conceptual (to put on the "Mousetrap" and indict Claudius) means of return to the court community. While under constant observation from other characters, especially Rosencrantz and Guildenstern, Hamlet feels a common bond with the players who, like him, must adopt different personae according to the demands of a particular situation. Arriving back at the castle, Hamlet is dressed in a cloak of colourful patches. He literally becomes a "king of shreds and patches" (3.4.93) as he faces Claudius and Gertrude, his festive appearance belying a dark desire for revenge. As he turns away, Hamlet casts off his cordial demeanour as he removes his colourful costume. Retreating to the shadow of a darkened doorway, he spies upon Rosencrantz and Guildenstern, who collude with the King out of ear's shot. Hamlet is once again plunged into a mood of doubt and despair as he rails against the all-pervading reach of Claudius. However, the optimism and pragmatism which underpin Gibson's interpretation of the Prince are demonstrated as he physically moves from the gloom of uncertainty to the light of realization during this scene. These visual changes reinforce the sentiments of Hamlet's words, which begin with the introspection of "Am I a coward?" (2.2.573-90), but proceed to determination and resolve as he looks out upon the Players while planning to "catch the conscience of the King" (2.2.591-607).

These plans are brought to fruition during the play-within-the-play scene. As the performance takes place, Hamlet mouths the lines of the play conspiratorially to himself. Sinking low in his seat, he appears mischievous as he bites his thumb, pulls his beard and picks at the fur covering on his chair, in a state of nervous agitation. Unable to sit still for long, Hamlet moves round behind the King and Queen, leaning intrusively between them. He whispers an excited commentary into the King's ear, like a personification of Claudius' guilty conscience. With the King's question of "Have you heard the argument? Is there no offence in't?" and Hamlet's reply of "No, no, they do but jest, poison in jest" (3.2.221-23), Claudius' facial expression becomes visibly more anxious. The "leperous distilment" (1.5.64) of the words which Hamlet metaphorically pours into Claudius' ears combines with a visual re-enactment of the murder, causing the King to become unsettled and alarmed.

As Lucianus poisons the Player King, Claudius stumbles forward, holding his head and laughing. His laughter is forced, an attempt to make light of his behaviour while his inner turmoil refuses to be quelled. Meanwhile, Hamlet clambers through the audience to gain a better view of the King's "Give me some light!" outburst (3.2.257). The actors freeze on stage, as if caught in the beam of the King's imagination. With Claudius and the other spectators leaving in uproar, Hamlet's emotional manipulation of Ophelia resumes with: "Get thee to a nunnery. Why, wouldst thou be a breeder of sinners?" (3.1.121-2). He punctuates this speech with a long, forceful kiss, leaving Ophelia visibly shocked and dazed. To what extent Hamlet's action stems from an antic disposition or genuine love for Ophelia is not certain. While displaying odd behaviour throughout this scene, Hamlet observes Ophelia with fond longing. In this respect, Hamlet's harsh words and actions are at odds with the sensitivity of his gaze. At the end of the scene, Gertrude appears to be torn between Hamlet and Claudius. After Claudius rushes form the room (followed by most of the court), the Queen stays behind witnessing Hamlet's self-satisfied revelry with shock and astonishment. The Queen realizes that the harmony that she so craves between son and step-father is becoming more and more elusive as events unfold. The conflict of doubt which Gertrude displays here serves as a precursor to the traumatic events of the forthcoming closet scene.

After killing Polonius, the Oedipal overtones of this scene (3.4) are visually emphasized with Hamlet mounting Gertrude and punctuating his words "honeying and making love over the nasty sty" (3.4.82-3) in a physical simulation of coitus. However, it is Gertrude who stops Hamlet's mouth with a long and intimate kiss, a gesture that hints at the repressed affection which she feels for him. The appearance of the Ghost causes Hamlet to release his grip of Gertrude and leap from the bed to genuflect in front of the phantom of his father. Framed by a semi-circular stone door way, the Ghost's head and shoulders have the illusion of radiating light, like an angel or divine vision. When Gertrude follows Hamlet's gaze, the "Nothing at all" (3.4.124) which she sees refers to the empty doorway, together with the red and orange glow which infuses the whole room. By contrast, the Ghost's alienation from the domestic setting is re-enforced by means of the blue tint which bathes his appearance. Old Hamlet belongs in a world located beyond the warm comforts of Gertrude's chamber. With the close of this scene, Gertrude is seen in close-up holding a medallion bearing Old Hamlet's image.

Edward Quinn observes that Gertrude undergoes a change in outlook after 3.4, as he states: "Skipping like a schoolgirl early in the film (the Juliet touch), she develops after the closet scene into a pained and conscience-stricken figure."[13] Perhaps it is the effects of weeping which seem to drain Gertrude's face of its previous youthful pallor. She appears to age visibly during this scene, with the "daggers" of Hamlet's words serving to prick her conscience sufficiently that she can no longer disregard her past.

Emotional trauma also affects Ophelia, who gradually begins to show signs of despair as a tide of grief for her dead father gathers within her. Initially, she is determined and forthright, as Jonathan Romney points out: "[Ophelia in this version is] no wilting innocent but a young woman whose obstreperous pique is more than a match for the humours of her father"[14] Indeed, the strong will which was on the verge of rebelling against the authority of Polonius early on in the film (note her terse: "I shall obey my lord" (1.3.136)), crumbles dramatically after his death. Ophelia is overwhelmed by a form of madness which is at once child-like and sexually assertive. A subtle reversal occurs during 4.5, as Ophelia's hitherto humble obedience to Gertrude becomes inverted. She now demands the attention of her Queen by calling: "Where is the beauteous majesty of Denmark?" (4.5.21). Even though Gertrude quickly avoids Ophelia's clutches and runs to Claudius for protection, she is noticeably shaken by the encounter, retreating to the background for the rest of the scene. Claudius realizes that Ophelia's impaired sensibilities could be potentially dangerous to an already unstable political climate at court. In her distracted mental condition, Ophelia commands a fleeting dominance over the royal couple.

Grief, fear and pity are displayed by the other characters as Ophelia later dispenses mementos from Gertrude's throne, in an representation of "madness enthroned".[15] A comparison is made here between Ophelia and Gertrude, indicating that Ophelia might have possessed the throne as Hamlet's wife, if events had been otherwise. By giving out straw and bones as a *memento mori*, a coarse, macabre connection is made whereby the plants and flowers which Ophelia refers to are in fact, dry and lifeless objects. Such behaviour emphasizes her regression to a child-like and unbalanced state of mind, while also linking the mementos with their recipients who are similarly not quite all that they appear. Zeffirelli seems to re-establish the close bond between sister and brother, introduced at their parting (1.3), as Laertes kneels to receive "rosemary" and "pansies" from Ophelia. His reaction, seen from Ophelia's position, is one of grief, anger and dismay. Harold Jenkins argues that Ophelia mistakes her brother for her lover, Hamlet, by symbolically giving him pansies.[16] Jenkins also states that the giving of rosemary for remembrance of the dead equates Ophelia with the Ghost in spurring Laertes to avenge the murder of Polonius.[17] There may be an undercurrent of this in Zeffirelli's interpretation, but it is more likely that Ophelia, unwittingly or not, anticipates her own death.

Before she leaves the castle, Ophelia is shown from the waist up, with the spiral staircase and upper galleries looming over her like "Piranesi's prisons" or an architectural "symmetry of wings."[18] She appears small and vulnerable set against the vast emptiness of the castle interior. A vivid representation of despair is created as Ophelia ventures outside, picking her way along the wet, stony ground with her bare feet. As a wave of grief is seen to grip her, she clings to the cold, flinty exterior wall of the castle, while weeping uncontrollably. Ophelia is denied the love and understanding which she so craves, being offered little instead except hard imperviousness as represented by the castle itself. This emotional gesture serves as a precursor to Ophelia's escape into the natural (as opposed to man-made) hinterlands. Ophelia's suicide (4.7.138-57) starts out as a pastoral interlude, as she runs across a grassy knoll by the castle battlements. Despite the natural beauty of her surroundings, Ophelia's fixed stare gives an indication of her unbalanced emotional state. During this sequence, Gertrude describes Ophelia's drowning in voice over (4.7.138-57). A dissolve fade shows the Queen dressed in mourning black and leaning against a door arch while she relates the rest of the news to Laertes. Gertrude's appearance seems ghostly pale and her voice is strained with grief in this scene. By her physical demeanour, as she leans for support, the Queen seems to suffer acutely with her heavy conscience. At the close of this short sequence, Zeffirelli maintains a sense of pace by linking a view of the lake where Ophelia's body is "pulled [...] to muddy death" (4.7.154-55), to the distant sea (implying Hamlet's absence), followed by the Prince and Horatio returning on horseback, riding unwittingly towards the grave-diggers. Once more, it is part of Gibson's charisma as an "outdoors man" that makes him seem so at ease in this scene. He lies on the grass at eye-level with Yorrick's skull, not so much in admiration, but more with curiosity and almost with a sense of playfulness.[19] If Hamlet communed with nature after his "To be or not to be" soliloquy, here he communes with mortality. In a way, the natural beauty of the location undercuts the sobriety of Hamlet's words (as he recalls the jester), giving his philosophy a double edge which mocks death and is life-affirming. When confronted by the scene of Ophelia's burial, however, Hamlet casts philosophy aside and becomes a man of action once more. After struggling with Laertes over Ophelia's flower-decked body, opposing factions emerge as Hamlet is restrained by Horatio and the royal guards, while Laertes' band of mercenaries placate their leader.

Hamlet has returned from exile a more self-assured figure. With a gesture which re-enforces the high level of intimacy established between Gertrude and Hamlet before his banishment (for the murder of Polonius), the Prince breaks free from his arrest and kisses Gertrude while Claudius looks on, dismayed. The affection which he shows Gertrude here is undeniably passionate but lacks the uncontrolled excess evident during the closet scene. Hamlet's behaviour is tempered by his sense of loss at the death of Ophelia. He realizes that the price of his new-found sense of resolution with fate has been costly. In terms of Polonius' and Ophelia's deaths, the Prince has become an object of revenge with Laertes laying down his challenge. Hamlet returns to the castle confines with a steadfast resolve to encounter his fate without hesitation in the confrontation to come.

Two large doors are swept open, revealing the throne room, now prepared with a raised, wooden stage for the fencing match. The contest has ceremonial overtones, with pieces of protective armour, chain mail and weapons being added and removed at prescribed points during the bout. However, due to the use of cumbersome broad swords rather than rapiers, the combat is highly physical, even brutal in its execution. Although choreographed in structure, the fencing match is unlike the more balletic equivalents in Olivier's *Hamlet* (GB, 1948), and Zeffirelli's *Romeo and Juliet* (GB/It, 1968). Each bout consists of much lashing and swiping of swords, as the combatants try to overcome one another with raw aggression rather than precise technique. A sense of ceremony increases in the second round as Hamlet and Laertes are equipped with shoulder armour, chain mail and head bands, making the contestants appear more "gladiatorial". Hamlet plays the fool in this bout, undermining the sense of ritual. He pretends to struggle under the weight of his sword, feigns a trip and runs around the ring with long, leaping strides, evoking the slapstick humour of Stan Laurel in *Laurel and Hardy*.[20] The Prince enacts this clowning for Gertrude's appreciation as he looks to her, grinning and winking, while turning other characters into his stooges. The Queen and other spectators take delight in this performance, however. Laertes' impatient aside to Claudius: "I'll hit him now" (5.2.248), is partly annoyance at Hamlet's antics, as well as desperation after Gertrude drinks from the poisoned cup. After her fateful sip, Gertrude kneels to offer the cup to Hamlet in a gesture similar to that early on in the film (1.2.120), where Hamlet kneels to embrace Gertrude. A reconciliation between the Prince and the Queen is implied, as Gertrude becomes subservient to her son, while unwittingly offering him the poisoned chalice. Seeing this, both Laertes and Claudius realize that their plan has taken an unforeseen and tragic twist.

For the third and final bout Hamlet and Laertes are armed with two swords each (Laertes' has the envenomed blade). This round is more choreographed and tense, completely lacking the light-heartedness of previous bouts. Osric's exclamation of "Look to the Queen, ho!" (5.2.256), distracts Hamlet momentarily as he struggles with Laertes, the latter seizing the opportunity to slash Hamlet across the arm. This image is juxtaposed with Gertrude grimacing and convulsing,

Franco Zeffirelli's *Hamlet*

as if in reaction to Hamlet's wound and not as a result of the poison taking its effect. By contrast, the Prince does not appear to be in pain, rather a sense of realization dawns that some plot is unfolding against him. In an instant, Hamlet rushes at Laertes and stabs him fatally. After the latter confesses the details of the plot in Hamlet's arms, the Prince runs and kills Claudius, pouring poisoned wine into the King's mouth as he lies gasping. Hamlet struggles against the debilitating effects of the poison and holds his mother's hand to his heart in a fond gesture, as he bids her farewell with: "Wretched Queen, adieu!" (5.2.285).

As Hamlet dies in Horatio's arms, a tableau is created, whereby Gertrude is shown nearest to the two thrones while Claudius lies at the foot of the platform, signifying his dispossession from the seat of power. A final view shows the whole scene with Hamlet's body central in the frame, half obscured by Horatio, who kneels over him. Hamlet perpetuates the sword-crucifix imagery even with his own death pose. An echo to the lines: "The time is out of joint. O cursed spite/ That ever I was born to set it right!" (1.5.189-90) (as dawn breaks over the battlements), is recalled here. Although the weight of revenge has now been lifted from Hamlet's shoulders, the price he pays is his own demise. The film's conclusion is punctuated in such a way as to re-call the theatrical conventions of tragic drama. However, a sense of realism is continued to the end of the film, so that the characters who remain alive (Horatio, the guards and the spectators) stay in their positions, confounding the possibility that the actors may take their curtain-call (as in Zeffirelli's *Romeo and Juliet*). The finality of this image creates an unnerving impression of closure as the actors' performances becomes literally 'petrified' and inseparable from the death of the characters.

Due to the narrative drive of the screenplay, this adaptation has been described as "a fast-food *Hamlet* for the moment, without the stature to make it a *Hamlet* for the ages."[21] However, numerous images serve to embellish the narrative with a rich, visual subtext of meaning. These include the symbolism of Hamlet's sword, interior and exterior location, colour tinting, and the use of sunlight and pastoral settings in contrast to the more sombre stone hues of the castle. While not always immediately noticeable, these aspects serve to heighten an awareness of contrasts that focus attention on key subjects. The final tableau is one of the few occasions (except for Old Hamlet's funeral and the brief freezing of the players at the end of the "Mousetrap"), where Zeffirelli allows the whole scene to remain static for any length of time. While purists may bemoan the undeniably drastic editing of dialogue, the sheer dynamism of Zeffirelli's *Hamlet* makes for an exciting and compelling interpretation of the play onto film.

Notes

1. George Miller (dir.), *Mad Max* (AUS, 1979), *Mad Max II* (AUS, 1981), and *Mad Max: Beyond Thunderdome* (AUS, 1985); Richard Donner (dir.), *Lethal Weapon* (USA, 1987), *Lethal Weapon II* (USA, 1989) and *Lethal Weapon III* (USA, 1992); Ace G. Pilkington, "Zeffirelli's Shakespeare", in Anthony Davies and Stanley Wells, ed., *Shakespeare and the Moving Image* (Cambridge UP, 1994), pp. 163-79 (p. 174).

2. This is the subtitle which Olivier gives his film. A scene-by-scene description appears in Jack Jorgens, *Shakespeare on Film* (Indiana UP, 1977), pp. 296-300.

3. Kathleen Campbell, "Zeffirelli's *Hamlet* - Q1 in Performance", *Shakespeare on Film Newsletter*, 16:1 (1991), 7-8.

4. Kathleen Campbell, ibid., p. 7; Ace G. Pilkington, op. cit., pp. 166-7.

5. David Impastato, "Zeffirelli's *Hamlet* - Sunlight Makes Meaning", *Shakespeare on Film Newsletter*, 16:1 (1991), 1-2; David Impastato, "Zeffirelli's *Hamlet* and The Baroque", *Shakespeare on Film Newsletter*, 16:2 (1992) 1-2.

6. William Van Watson, "Shakespeare, Zeffirelli and the Homosexual Gaze", *Literature/ Film Quarterly*, 20 (1992), 308-325 (p. 319).

7. All references to *Hamlet* are taken from Stanley Wells and Gary Taylor, ed., *William Shakespeare: The Complete Works*, (Oxford: Clarendon Press, 1988; repr. 1994).

8. Victoria Mather, "The Romantic Hero who Turned Ignoble King", *Daily Telegraph*, 18 April 1991, p. 12.

9. David Gritten, "Getting Close", *Telegraph Magazine*, 13 April 1991, 28-31 (p. 30); Desmond Ryan, "Gibson in Zeffirelli's *Hamlet*", *Philadelphia Enquirer*, 18 January 1991, p. 8.

10. William Van Watson, ibid., p. 319. Van Watson also goes on to link the sword-crucifix image with "the Law of the Father" and patriarchal values.

11. Neil Taylor, "The Films of *Hamlet*", in Anthony Davies and Stanley Wells, ed., *Shakespeare and the Moving Image*, op. cit., pp. 180-94 (p. 192).

12. Neil Taylor, ibid., p. 192.

13. Edward Quinn, "Zeffirelli's *Hamlet*", *Shakespeare on Film Newsletter*, 15: 2 (1991), 1-2 and 12 (p. 2).

14. Jonathan Romney, "*Hamlet*", *Sight and Sound*, 5 (1991), 48-9 (p. 49).

15. Bernard Richards, "*Hamlet*", *The English Review*, 2: 1 (1991), 28-9 (p. 28).

16. Harold Jenkins, op. cit., p. 538.
17. ibid., p. 537.
18. Bernard Richards, op. cit., p. 29. David Impastato, "Zeffirelli's *Hamlet* and The Baroque", op. cit., p. 2.
19. Ace Pilkington, op. cit., p. 174.
20. Specific film shorts containing boxing include: *The Battle of the Century* (1927), *Any Old Port* (1932) and *Brats* (1930); From Glenn Mitchell, *The Laurel and Hardy Encyclopedia* (London: Batsford, 1995), p. 51.
21. Geoff Brown, "Yet There is Method in It", *The Times*, 18 April 1991, p.10.

Bibliography

Primary Sources.

Shakespeare, William, *The Complete Works*, ed. by Stanley Wells and Gary Taylor (Oxford: Clarendon Press, 1988; repr. 1994). All quotations are from this edition.
Zeffirelli, Franco (dir.), *Hamlet* (USA, 1990). Distributed by Columbia Tristar Home Video, 1990, on video cassette.

Secondary Sources.

Anon., "Alas Poor Mel", *The Economist*, 27 April 1991, p. 96.
Anon., "*Hamlet*", *Guardian*, 18 April 1991, p. 6.
Biggs, Murray, "He's Going to His Mother's Closet': Hamlet and Gertrude on Screen", *Shakespeare Survey*, 45 (1993), 53-63.
Campbell, Kathleen, "Zeffirelli's *Hamlet* - Q1 in Performance", *Shakespeare on Film Newsletter*, 6: 1 (1991), 7 and 8.
Cart [sic], "*Hamlet*", *Variety*, 24 December 1990, 37-8.
Charney, Maurice, "Analogy and Infinite Regress in *Hamlet*", in *Psychoanalytic Approaches to Literature and Film*, ed. by Maurice Charney and John Reppen (London: Associated UP, 1987).
Church, Michael, "Franco Goes to Elsinore", *Independent on Sunday*, 14 April 1991, pp. 16-17.
Corliss, Richard, "Wanna Be ... Or Wanna Not Be?", *Time*, 137 (7 January 1991), p. 73.
Davenport, Hugo, "Zeffirelli Strips Shakespeare Down to Basics", *Daily Telegraph*, 18 April 1991, p. 9.
De Chick, Joe, "Bard's Oft-Quoted *Hamlet* Called a Film for the Masses", *Arkansas Gazette*, 25 January 1991, p. 7.
Errigo, Angie, "The Italian Job", *Empire*, (May 1991), p. 46.
Errigo, Angie, "The Film's the Thing ...", *Empire*, (June 1991), pp. 44-9.

Errigo, Angie, "*Hamlet*", *Empire*, (May 1991), p. 21.
French, P., "*Hamlet*", *Observer*, 21 April 1991, p. 16.
Geimer, Roger, "Shakespeare Live - On Videotape", in *Shakespeare and the Triple Play*, ed. Sidney Homan (London: Associated UP, 1988), pp. 201-6.
Gritten, David, "Getting Close", *Telegraph Magazine*, 13 April 1991, pp. 29-30.
Hazelton, John, "Mel and Franco Take on Old Bill", *Screen International*, 700 (1989), p. 1.
Impastato, David, "Zeffirelli's *Hamlet* and the Baroque", *Shakespeare on Film Newsletter*, 16: 2 (1991), 1 and 2.
Impastato, David, "Zeffirelli's *Hamlet*: Sunlight Makes Meaning", *Shakespeare on Film Newsletter*, 16: 1 (1991), 1 and 2.
Jenson, Michael P., "Mel Gibson on *Hamlet*", *Shakespeare on Film Newsletter*, 15: 2 (1991), 1, 2 and 6.
Johnston, Sheila, "What a Piece of Work", *Independent*, 18 April 1991, p. 17.
Johnstone, Iain, "Method in His Madness: Max Takes on Hamlet", *Sunday Times*, 14 April 1991, p. 3-4.
Kauffman, Stanley, "*Hamlet*", *New Republic*, 204 (January 1991), p. 24.
King, Andrea, "Warners Going After *Hamlet* Picture With Mel Gibson", *Hollywood Reporter*, 25 July 1990, p. 1 and 20.
Klady, Leonard, "*Hamlet*", *Screen International*, 789 (1991), p. 2.
Kozintsev Grigori (dir.), *Hamlet* (USSR, 1964). Distributed by Russian Classics on video cassette.
Lane Anthony, "Zeffirelli's *Hamlet* Reveals a Prince with Panache but not Poetry", *Independent on Sunday*, 21 April 1991, p. 14.
Marowitz, Charles, "Mad Max Palpably a Hit at Elsinore", *The Times*, 20 December 1990, p. 11.
Marsh, Joss, "To See or not to See ...", *Select*, 11 (May 1991), p. 7.
Mather, Victoria, "The Romantic Hero who Turned Ignoble King", *Daily Telegraph*, 18 April 1991, p. 12.
Muir, Kenneth, "Freud's *Hamlet*", *Shakespeare Survey*, 45 (1993), 75-9.
McFarlane, Brian, "*Hamlet*", *Cinema Papers*, 83 (1991), 55-6.
McGuigan, Cathleen, "*Hamlet*", *Newsweek*, 116 (1990), p. 61.
Nardo, Anna K., "Hamlet, A Man to Double Bound", *Shakespeare Quarterly*, 34 (1983), 181-99.
O'Brien, Ellan J., "Revision by Excision: Rewriting Gertrude", *Shakespeare Survey*, 45 (1993), pp. 27-37.
Olivier, Laurence (dir.), *Hamlet* (GB, 1948). Distributed by Rank Home Video on video cassette.
Peachment, Chris, "A Little Breeze Through Life", *Sunday Telegraph*, 21 April 1991, p. 15.
Pechter, Edward, "Remembering *Hamlet*: Or, How it Feels to go Like a Crab Backwards", *Shakespeare Survey*, 39 (1987), pp. 135-47.
Quigley, Daniel, "'Double Exposure': The Semiotic Ramifications of Mel Gibson in Zeffirelli's *Hamlet*", *Shakespeare Bulletin*, 11: 1 (1993), p. 39.

Quinn, Edward, "Zeffirelli's *Hamlet*", *Shakespeare on Film Newsletter*, 15: 2 (1991), pp. 1, 2 and 6.
Richards, Bernard, "*Hamlet*", *The English Review*, 2: 1 (1991), pp. 28-9.
Romney, Jonathan, "*Hamlet*", *Sight and Sound*, May 1991, pp. 48-9.
Ryan, Desmond, "Gibson in Zeffirelli's *Hamlet*", *Philadelphia Enquirer*, 18 January 1991, p. 8.
Schaltz, Justin, "Three *Hamlets* on Film", *Shakespeare Bulletin*, 11: 1 (1993), pp. 36-7.
Shakespeare, William, *Hamlet*, ed. by Harold Jenkins, The Arden Shakespeare (London: Routledge, 1982; repr. 1990).
Shakespeare, William, *Hamlet*, ed. by G. R. Hibbard, The Oxford Shakespeare (Oxford: Clarendon Press, 1989). All quotations are from this edition.
Skovmand, Michael, "Mel's Melodramatic Melancholy: Zeffirelli's *Hamlet*", in *Screen Shakespeare*, ed. Michael Skovmand (Denmark: Aarhus UP, 1994), pp. 113-31.
Smith, Sheena, "Visualising Elsinore: Visual Design and Symbolism in the Cinematic Productions of *Hamlet* - Olivier, Kozintsev and Zeffirelli". Unpublished MA dissertation, University of Birmingham, 1992.
Travers, Peter, "*Hamlet*", *Rolling Stone*, (10 January 1991), p. 54.

"NEITHER A BORROWER, NOR A LENDER BE":
ZEFFIRELLI'S *HAMLET*

Mary Z. Maher
(University of Arizona)

It was with great trepidation (and a touch of chutzpah) that Franco Zeffirelli announced he would direct film star Mel Gibson in the role of Shakespeare's best known hero in 1991. After all, when an actor decides to play Hamlet, he takes on a canonical role. Acting Hamlet is like earning the Olympic Gold in performance.

In order to sell the movie, Warner Brothers assembled a press packet with a user-friendly brochure and discount coupons sent to 100,000 schools all over the U.S. (Thompson 38). The packet included a 54-minute video, "Mel Gibson – Back to School" showing the star at a high school in Los Angeles talking about his movie: "Look, why don't I just tell you the story of *Hamlet*. It's a great story. There's something like eight violent deaths. There's murder; there's incest; there's adultery; there's a mad woman, poisoning, revenge, sword fights ..." (quoted in Thompson, 39).

The packet further stated that 4000 educators at a National Council of Teachers of English conference gave the film a standing ovation. The scholar Frank Kermode was quoted to add ethos. His comments focused on the problem of accessiblity and making Shakespeare *relevant*:

> [We need to find] contemporary methods of presenting standard curriculum each new semester, especially subject matter as potentially daunting as the works of William Shakespeare [...] we can intrigue these bright young minds and make them more 'Shakespeare-receptive' (quoted in Stivers, 54).

Even the *New York Times* jumped on the bandwagon: "Mel Gibson may not be a Hamlet for the ages but he is a serious and compelling Hamlet for today" (James B1). Thus the case was made that Shakespeare was somehow irrelevant and that violent deaths brought *Hamlet* sharply into twentieth-century focus. Since

I teach a course called "Shakespeare in Performance" (which uses a number of video resources) I closely watched the progress of this film. My college students continued to ask me if I planned to show the film they'd all been shown in high school. Each time I asked why they liked the film, they answered, "Hey, it's Mel Gibson!" When I asked them what they felt about the relationship between Hamlet and Gertrude in the movie, they got vague: "Oh, we just thought that was how they did things in those days."

Now that the fanfare of publicity has quieted and the Zeffirelli film continues to influence students about Shakespeare, it is time for a reappraisal. Although Zeffirelli claimed that Shakespeare was a "hard sell" to film studios (Tibbets, 137), there is a great deal of evidence that his plays are doing well at the box office. Kenneth Branagh's 1990 *Henry V* and 1992 *Much Ado About Nothing* were instant successes, and by the end of 1995, ten full-length Shakespeare projects were in planning or production stages (Cox, 1). Perhaps there were other anxieties about this *Hamlet*.

A feature story in *Premiere* magazine detailed the financial and political agonizing that went on behind the scenes (Stivers, 50-6). The star's agent was ambivalent about his client's decision to play the role of the noble prince, because Gibson, too, had become a kind of movie icon for the little tough guy who battles his way out of drug alleys and triumphs in the end. The budget for the film was low (a moderate $15.5 million) and once Zeffirelli could produce stars of the magnitude of Glenn Close and Mel Gibson, the funding was stitched together (Tibbetts, 136). Yet Zeffirelli clung to his original motivation:

> The critics must understand one thing: I didn't cast Mel because he's a big star. I chose him because in addition to the admiration I have for his work, I felt it important that people be able to identify with the actor I cast because I am trying to lure an indifferent generation to *Hamlet* (Stivers, 56).

Considerable gestures were made in order more comfortably to place the action hero in a Shakespearean context. For example, Gibson's cast was shored up by a retinue of seasoned classical actors, including Alan Bates and Paul Scofield (both of whom had played Hamlet). This scheme gave the impression that Gibson was at least in very good company if he failed at the role, but it also displayed the director's confidence that Gibson could match the acting abilities of experienced British players. Additionally, the play was set in a medieval period slightly earlier than the composition of the play in order to provide "added virility" to the setting of this adaptation (Stivers, 52). In the end, the clincher was Gibson's own: "... I like the story, and it's incredibly difficult, and I wanted to know that I could do it" (Stivers, 51).

There were a number of things to be anxious about. First of all, could Gibson, who had scant stage experience and almost none with Shakespeare, play the role of Hamlet in a creditable way? Secondly, could this movie escape the tremendous influence of the earlier Olivier film and stand as a separate artwork? These were not new questions or concerns. Every actor who plays Hamlet has to face them. In 1948, Laurence Olivier created a film that became a benchmark for the twentieth century. Every aspirant Hamlet knows he will be compared with Olivier and perhaps even yearns for that association. More importantly, every director has to face the cultural and historical baggage the earlier film generated.

There are a great many qualities about the Zeffirelli film that are commendable. It moves quickly, it is engaging, it is beautifully filmed in natural settings selected from three different British castles. There are strong individual performances in the film, character sketches which remained fairly fulsome despite the screenwriter's blue pencil.[1] However, the film offers a conservative and patriarchal point of view which presents a sober, dark Dane shorn of wit and intellect.[2] Furthermore, the text is wildly re-arranged, and Shakespeare's dialogue is re-sorted and re-cycled among various characters. The number of Shakespeare's lines used is approximately 1300 or about 28% of the text.[3] Olivier used slightly under 50%.

Although some cutting of the play is *de rigueur* in Shakespearean films, this screenplay leaves us with a severely truncated text. The major issue of whether Hamlet's madness is real or feigned is simply not one in the movie. Hamlet's relationship with Horatio (a role larger than Ophelia's or Gertrude's) is pruned to a stiff politeness; the two neither share much nor support one another. Ophelia (Helena Bonham Carter) is clearly not Hamlet's love object; in fact, she is not even used on the posters for the film – Glenn Close (as Gertrude) shares Gibson's billing. The Fortinbras plot is edited out completely.

The Zeffirelli film has two additional faults, one of which results from cutting too much of Shakespeare and appropriating too much of Olivier to fill in the blanks, i.e., the sexual attachment of Gertrude to her son. The other results from the director's decision to borrow a role from a non-Shakespearean film and to transport the interpretation wholesale into his version of *Hamlet* – Martin Riggs comes home from graduate school in Wittenberg.

That Zeffirelli does not claim to be doing William Shakespeare's *Hamlet* is subliminally cued to the audience in the opening credits; the disclaimer is barely perceptible, but it is there. At the beginning of the film, the word "Hamlet" shows up in large black print covering the top half of the screen. Each major actor's name is then juxtaposed over this larger title; then a smaller word "Hamlet" emerges, lettered in white over the larger title, and the lesser-known supporting actors' names then appear. The rather elaborated roll of credits means (I think) that Zeffirelli has assumed the role of *auteur* and has created his own work from the inspiration of others.

As most of us know, Olivier's film was intended to convey a number of the ideas of Ernest Jones in his book *Hamlet and Oedipus*. Jones claimed that Hamlet delayed in killing Claudius because he felt guilty about his wish to kill his own father and to replace him in Gertrude's bed. Olivier attempted to adopt this concept early on in his first staged version of *Hamlet* at the Old Vic in 1937. Apparently, no one noticed; reviewers paid little or no attention (Mills, 234-5). Consequently, Olivier was more heavy-handed with the idea when he came to do the film, and we see Gertrude kissing Hamlet lingeringly in the opening scenes. There are also two kisses in the closet scene, and the scene ends with his head in her lap. This psychoanalytic interpretation does not dominate the film; in fact, the result is that the character of Gertrude seems childlike, vague, pathetic and even slightly deranged – not surprising since the lines do not provide motivation for mother and son to be in love with one another.

In contrast, Hamlet and Gertrude are clearly lusting after one another in Zeffirelli's production. Their relationship is given further plausibility by the casting. Glenn Close is the same age as her son Mel Gibson, while both her husbands (the Ghost and Claudius) are easily past 60. The scenes that Close and Gibson share employ lingering eye contact, and the touching and kissing is amorous rather than familial. In the opening scenes, Claudius looks at Gertrude over the coffin of old Hamlet and suddenly a third person intrudes into their mourning, the hooded Hamlet, who threatens their relationship. In an early scene where Claudius tells Hamlet he cannot return to Wittenberg, Gertrude puts her face on Hamlet's chest, her arms around him, and they exchange meaningful looks as she kisses him on the eyes and the mouth. He kneels down and places his head against her abdomen as the scene closes. The acting is suggestive of sexual partnership rather than parental love.

These exchanges continue throughout the film, even at the end, where Hamlet clearly intends to amuse his mother in the duel scene, winking at her and clowning for her benefit. The closet scene carries similar connotations. After Hamlet shouts accusations at Gertrude and villifies her trysts with Claudius, he jumps on top of her, turns her face-up and thrusts his hips into her groin. Glenn Close's dress has fallen off one shoulder, and just as the Ghost appears, she gives her son a long unmistakably erotic kiss. Her behavior is seductive; she is clearly "turned on" by her son. All this renders her dialogue with Claudius shortly afterwards ("Alas, he is mad") very ironic.

Interestingly enough, Derek Jacobi (as Hamlet) also mounts his mother (Claire Bloom) as part of the closet scene in the 1980 BBC version of *Hamlet*, yet there is a distinct difference. Sexual feelings have not been established between mother and son prior to the closet scene, so viewers don't perceive a lustful encounter. The manhandling of Gertrude is brutal and shocking, but it is not a scene between lovers where one or both characters are sexually excited.

In fact, portraying an Oedipal relationship between Hamlet and Gertrude has become one of the filmic anomalies of the twentieth century. Incest is alluded to five times in Shakespeare's text of the play, but each time it clearly describes the relationship between Claudius and Gertrude and refers to the ancient taboo connected with a wife marrying her husband's brother. The Ghost uses the word twice, and Hamlet uses it three times, to describe Gertrude and/or Claudius.

The Oedipal concept in Zeffirelli's film introduces a structural flaw which skews the entire plot. It distorts the character relationships and introduces a fictional red herring by inserting a salacious subplot which has no dialogue to bolster it. Thereafter, the hidden plot becomes so enticing that the play is really about that subject and not about Hamlet's deliberation when faced with the ghost's mandate of revenge. Shakespeare is not an oblique craftsman. He does not by indirections find directions out. In fact, as a master playwright, he often repeats plot information two and three times so the audience will understand the story line. He inserts no statements that Gertrude and Hamlet are attracted to one another. There is interpretative latitude, both in reading and in producing Shakespeare, but an area of universal agreement about the design of the play must obtain.

The Oedipal concept renders certain scenes ludicrous. The point of the closet scene is that Hamlet is attempting to shock his mother into seeing her own iniquity – that she has replaced her husband not only too quickly but with a murderer. If this objective is overlaid with a sexual relationship between mother and son, then both characters are hypocritical and morally obtuse. The omission of any discussion of their own behavior would be too much for an audience to swallow. Gertrude may be the most underwritten part in the play, but there are no dialogue clues that confirm her as the seducer of her son.

Furthermore, Shakespeare has already posited a romance between Hamlet and Ophelia. Although the audience is not given specific information about the nature of the liaison, we do know that Polonius and Gertrude have both considered Hamlet as a potential bridegroom. In the Zeffirelli film, Ophelia and Hamlet have a very peculiar relationship. When Hamlet appears to Ophelia with ungarter'd stockings, he is certainly not a love-sick wooer. Before the nunnery scene, the camera shows Gibson watching Polonius and Ophelia as he catches a glimpse of the stage management of it; he also sees Polonius' shadow on the wall during the scene. Ophelia is hammered verbally and then physically (at one point, he throws her against a stone wall). Not only do the mystery and expectation evaporate, but Hamlet even judges, condemns, and punishes Ophelia for Polonious' plot. In fact, Ophelia is in a quandary throughout the film, like someone plucking on the sleeves of other characters for permission to enter the movie. When Hamlet says to her, "I did love you once", it must have been a long, long time ago – perhaps in *Road Warrior*.

Positing an incestuous relationship between Hamlet and Gertrude also plays havoc with the Ghost's function in the play. Hamlet has been asked by him to avenge a foul murder. Is the Ghost blind to the goings-on between mother and son – after all, he does seem to have remembered every detail of his own murder (indicating that spirits in this play have second sight)? Does the Ghost realize that his command to revenge his own murder will end in Hamlet's replacing both father and uncle in bed rather than in fulfilling the requirements of the revenge pact?

To be fair, the one aspect of the plot that would be enhanced by an Oedipal connection is the relationship between Hamlet and Claudius. If Claudius thinks Hamlet and Gertrude share an attraction, he would be more determined to kill Hamlet and vice-versa. However, Shakespeare has designed Hamlet's motivation already: he has been enjoined to kill Claudius because the king is a murderer, not because Hamlet wants to usurp his place in bed.

Edward Quinn expressed a certain bewilderment about plot and characterization in the film:

> Which is not to say that this production is keyed, like Olivier's, to a now-traditional Freudian interpretation. *Whatever the director's intention* [italics mine], the fact is that you never accept for one moment the notion that Glenn Close's Gertrude and Mel Gibson's Hamlet are mother and son. It's not just the lack of difference in the actor's ages. It's the fact that

there's nothing Oedipal in their straightforward sexuality – unless you want to say that all sexuality is ultimately Oedipal, in which case the Freudian interpretation is a tautology. Perhaps the best way to describe their relationship in this film would be to say that it's a little more than kin and less than kind. (1-2)

Zeffirelli was less roundabout regarding his own interpretation: "[Hamlet] cannot unhook himself from his mother's nipples! Which makes him such an extraordinary contemporary character" (Stivers, 52). (No wonder my students were vague about the mother-son relationship.)

Zeffirelli was not inexperienced in directing Shakespeare. He directed *Romeo and Juliet* on stage in 1960 and *Othello* in 1961. He had to his credit a boisterous film version of *Taming of the Shrew* (1967) which would probably be used more in classrooms had his direction accounted for feminist critics' disapproval of the traditional ending with Kate acknowledging the supremacy of her husband. His 1968 film of *Romeo and Juliet* blew the dust off older interpretations by casting lovers the age and temperament of the teenagers Shakespeare wrote about.[4] Zeffirelli always aimed for widespread commercial success rather than the art film circuit. Zeffirelli claimed that it was Gibson's work in the *Lethal Weapon* action series that inspired him to cast the actor:

> There was a scene in which he has a kind of 'To be or not to be' speech with the gun", Zeffirelli recalls, "but he is not able to pull the trigger. When I saw that, I said, 'Zees ees Hamlet. Zees boy is Hamlet!" Bong!" He mimes a light bulb clicking on in his head. "Bing!" (Stivers, 51)

In the first film in the series, LAPD detective Martin Riggs has lost his wife and is grieving intensely. He contemplates shooting himself while a Bugs Bunny movie is on television in the background. Zeffirelli was so taken with the Martin Riggs character that he reappears in Shakespeare's play. In *Lethal Weapon I*, about a drug ring set up by former Special Forces veterans, detective Martin Riggs acts quickly. He jumps into every fray, and there are several skirmishes throughout the movie. Riggs seems to revel in moments of action. He does not think, he does not contemplate, he does not hesitate, he does not *delay*. He acts. Period.

This is the Hamlet presented to us in the film. We know that there must be emotions inside of the character that we see on screen, but we do not hear what they are. Indeed, the moments of that processing, the soliloquies, are drastically cut. Only about 55% of the soliloquy lines are delivered. No matter. This man of action solves problems with brute strength. He is rarely without his sword in the film. He grabs Guildenstern by the collar and throws him against a stool. He shoves Ophelia into a wall without asking her reasons or finding out circumstances. He assaults his mother in the closet scene. The sequence begins with the famous Gibson roar, a kind of brutish bellow that occurs at least once per movie in the *Lethal Weapon* series.

Indeed, Martin Riggs' edginess is a kind of madness but not the same kind as Hamlet's. Hamlet's makes him consider, think (perhaps too deeply), makes him refrain from action. Riggs' madness makes him leap into action and to immediate performance, now, on the spur of the moment, not shriving time allowed. David Denby concluded that Gibson "never stands outside himself as Olivier did, viewing himself as an actor; he doesn't have the mental agility for that" (Denby, 57).

The diminution of language – not just in the literal sense of an editor having cut lines, but in the interpretative sense, of our knowing as an audience that here is a man who uses speech to define who he is, what his duties and obligations are, what his forebodings are, what his ratiocination leads to – is crucial. Shakespeare's Hamlet is a man of high moral fiber who can invent and shape speech into complexities that resonate with us all, words that are nuanced, measured, wrought – words that are luxuriated in, spoken for the pleasure of speaking them, spoken from the need to speak them. Shakespeare's Hamlet is physical, yes, but at the right moments, at the play-within-the-play, upon hearing Polonius shout behind the arras, upon entering the duel. Zeffirelli's Hamlet is indeed "Hamlet [...] but without the chat" (Corliss, 73). Charles Marowitz complained,

> We are always conscious of a coiled physical energy in his body, but no comparable charge in his brain. It's not that Gibson is stupid – which he

isn't — it's just that when he praises man as being "noble in reason" and "infinite in faculties," the description does not immediately bring to mind Mel Gibson (*Theatre Week*, 17).

There is humor in the Martin Riggs character, and there is a great deal of wit in Hamlet. Yet, the two characters' sense of humor is not the same. Hamlet's wit is borne out of invention, out of punning, out of examining self. The most extensive use of humor in the film is in the duel scene, where Hamlet and Laertes have been handling weapons so large that Gibson begins clowning in a buffoonish way. He is clearly enjoying himself, again the little fast guy with the best aim against the taller fella. The problem is that it is too late to build a character that uses humor. It simply hasn't been prepared for prior to this moment, so we are surprised to see it at the end. It is out of character, given the throughline of action Gibson has chosen to play.

Finally, the performance of this role demands a certain competence in verse-speaking that is not there. The famous "To be, or not to be" speech is badly performed. The actor pumps the iambic pentameter as if he were bouncing a ball. Delicate metaphors are merely shouted and not first seen in the mind's eye, meaning that the actor is not imaging as he speaks but merely generalizing the speech. Much of the time, the verse has been added voice-over in post-production.

What exactly does the film accomplish? The response to it in newspapers and journals was decidedly ambivalent. Some went so far as to accuse Zeffirelli of opportunism (*Economist*, 96). Others panned the work:

> So you get a typical Mel Gibson hero. Rants a lot, roughs up his co-stars, kills people. We even have one of those 'make my day' lines for Mel. He gets hold of his rival and mutters, 'O.K., tough guy, ya wanna be [...] or ya wanna *not* be?' It's a sure $100 million domestic. Whaddaya say? (Corliss, 73)

Still others praised Gibson's "megawatt heartthrob" (McGuigan, 61) performance as a "dignified yet explosive presence" which "speaks easily and directly to our own age" (James, B1). In this second group were mostly parents and teachers who were relieved to be able to take their children or their students to a Shakespearean film which would not bore them. I talked to a great many people about this film because of my continuing interest in it: most of the reactions can be summed up as a sigh of relief – it was better than they thought it would be.

However, how much pedagogical credibility can be given to a film which doesn't cohere as either story or character? In this *Hamlet*, the director has banked on the reputations of two leading actors – one an action-hero known for surviving horrific violence in his films, and the second known for her fatal attraction – and juxtaposting them in a relationship that the playwright did not obviously plot. These choices smack of a kind of exploitation of the unsuspecting, at least in the case of potential student viewers. Teachers were also victims of a very aggressive ad campaign rife with "educational outreach" overtones. The implication was that both would get an exciting Shakespeare movie heavily larded with market value – color and action and scenery, popular movie stars shored up by "real" British Shakespeare actors, violence (much of it directed at women), wrap-around sound (soundtrack album on Virgin Movie Music, cd's and cassettes optional), and lots of close-ups of Mel's hair, Mel's eyes, and Mel's famous buns.

Zeffirelli and Gibson have indeed made a *Hamlet* for the nineties – for they are the abstract and brief chronicles of the time. The film reflects more than they intend, however, of our culture. Stage and film directors have uttered the continuing cry of "making Shakespeare relevant" as an excuse to take whatever liberties they wish in re-vamping Shakespearean scripts. In some cases, the resulting art work sheds light on an old masterpiece. In other cases, the clever overlay of Hollywood public relations tricks is an attempt to hide fundamental weaknesses in the film. For me, Zeffirelli's *Hamlet* falls into the latter category. If one has to distort the story and misrepresent the main character, perhaps the price of relevance is simply too high.

Notes

1. The screenplay was developed by Zeffirelli and Christopher DeVore.
2. For an interesting discussion of Zeffirelli's political stance in juxtaposition to his sexual

orientation, see William Van Watson's "Shakespeare, Zeffirelli, and the Homosexual Gaze," *Literature and Film Quarterly* 20 (1992) 308-325.

3. My line count is approximate since many half-lines were employed, and a number of lines were parceled out to other characters, so these were difficult to count. The screenplay appears to be based on the Folio version, although one cannot exactly discern which version the screenwriters employed.

4. It should be noted that Zeffirelli made two versions of the film, one with nude scenes between the lovers and one without. The first could not be used in schools in 1968.

Works Cited

"Alas, Poor Mel". Unsigned review of *Hamlet*, dir. Franco Zeffirelli. *Economist*, 27 Apr. 1991, p. 96.

Corliss, Richard. "Wanna Be ... or Wanna Not Be?" Rev. of *Hamlet*, dir. Franco Zeffirelli. *Time*, p. 7 Jan. 1991: 73.

Cox, Dan. "H'wood going over-Bard in quest for Will power." *Variety*, 22-8 Jan. 1996, p. 1.

Denby, David. "Monarch Notes". Rev. of *Hamlet*, dir. Franco Zeffirelli. *New York*, 21 Jan. 1991, p. 57.

James, Caryn. "From Mad Max to Prince Possessed". Rev. of *Hamlet*, dir. Franco Zeffirelli. *New York Times*, 19 Dec. 1990: B1.

Marowitz, Charles, "Dane on a Wire". Rev. of *Hamlet*, dir. Franco Zeffirelli. *Theatre Week*, 7 Jan. 1991, pp. 16-18.

Mills, John. *Hamlet On Stage: The Great Tradition*. Westport: Greenwood, 1985.

McGuigan, Cathleen. "Melancholy Mel Goes to Elsinore". *Newsweek* 27 Dec. 1990, p. 61.

Quinn, Edward. "Zeffirelli's *Hamlet*". Rev. of *Hamlet*, dir. Franco Zeffirelli. *Shakespeare on Film Newsletter* Apr. 1991, pp. 1-2.

Stivers, Cyndi. "Hamlet Re-Visited". *Premiere*, Feb. 1991, pp. 50-6.

Thompson, Douglas. "Mel's Class Act". Rev. of *Hamlet*, dir. Franco Zeffirelli. *Radio Times* 13 Apr. 1991, pp. 38-9.

Tibbetts, John. "Breaking the Classical Barrier: Franco Zeffirelli Interviewed by John Tibbetts". *Literature and Film Quarterly*, 22 (1994), pp. 136-40.

MELODRAMA AT ELSINORE: ZEFFIRELLI'S *HAMLET*

By Michael Skovmand
(University of Aarhus)

'I never liked the approach to the character that has been governing the choices and decisions for decades, this kind of wimpy dreamer who is impotent, uncertain in everything sexually, politically, humanly. I never saw Hamlet in those terms. For me, Hamlet is the quintessence of the New Man of the Renaissance.'
And who exactly is that?
'He is the first great modern character ever conceived by a writer,' enthuses Zeffirelli. 'So full of life, full of vitality, zest.'
...

'Shakespeare was looking for popular success. He was talking to a wide world, people of all social conditions and education levels. We have come to this horrendous, *monstrous* division of popular success and artistic success. This is ridiculous. This has been invented by cultivated people who don't like too many people having access to what they consider their own privilege and patrimony.'
(Excerpts from interview with F. Zeffirelli, *Empire*, May 1991.)

On the face of it, the combination of the Italian director Franco Zeffirelli and Shakespeare's *Hamlet* seems an incongruous one. The unwieldy, gloomy study of Danish sexual politics seems far removed from Zeffirelli's other Shakespearean screen productions: the glamourous romp of the Burton/Taylor *Taming of the Shrew* from 1966, his *Romeo and Juliet* from 1968 which fed directly into the Zeitgeist of 'don't trust anyone over 30', and his film version of Verdi's *Otello* from 1986, a lush and spectacular production featuring Placido Domingo and Katia Ricciarelli.

In the following, I shall argue that the Zeffirelli *Hamlet*, whilst offensive to some scholarly traditions, makes interesting, albeit problematic sense. Crucially, the prism through which I read Zeffirelli is the term *melodrama*, more particularly with the inflection given to the term by Peter Brooks in his study from 1976, *The Melodramatic Imagination*.

Hamlet: History, Tragedy, or Melodrama?

Hamlet has always been generically problematic. By origin it is a history play, with its narrative antecedents in Saxo and Belleforest, and is thus on a par with two other Shakespearean plays drawing on murky historical sources: *Macbeth* and *King Lear*.

Belleforest's *Hamlet* was translated into English in 1608 as *The Hystorie of Hamblet*. Shakespeare's play was registered in 1602 as *A booke called the Revenge of Hamlett Prince Denmark;* it was published in 1603 (first Quarto) as *The Tragicall Historie of Hamlet Prince of Denmarke*, and ultimately, in the 1623 Folio edition, it was entitled *The Tragedie of Hamlet, Prince of Denmarke*. The Folio collection operated with only three divisions: (a) histories, (b) comedies and (c) tragedies. These were rough and ready categories, indicating whether the narrative structure of the play in question was dictated primarily by accounts of past events, or was geared towards a happy/upbeat or unhappy/downbeat ending. The ambiguous history of the title of *Hamlet* reflects structural and thematic ambiguities of the play. It can be argued that it is not a history, since historical representation, truthful or otherwise, is not a major concern of the play. Is it a tragedy? A moot point, the intricacies of which cannot be entered into in this essay. Suffice it to say that neither as a classical tragedy nor as a revenge variant is it entirely unproblematic. The notion of the 'flaw' of the protagonist is debatable, the catharsis of the ending equally so. The moral and narrative efficacy of the 'revenge' is dubious, to say the least.

The play, to use T.S. Eliot's famous phrase, is one of *excess*. In the context of his famous formulation of his poetics of the 'objective correlative', the *excess* emotion in *Hamlet* is seen as a major flaw in the play:

> The artistic 'inevitability' lies in [this] complete adequacy of the external to the emotion; and this is precisely what is deficient in *Hamlet*. Hamlet (the man) is dominated by an emotion which is inexpressible, because it is in *excess* of the facts as they appear. And the supposed identity of Hamlet with his author is genuine to this point: that Hamlet's bafflement at the absence of objective equivalent to his feelings is a prolongation of the bafflement of his creator in the face of his artistic problem.[1]

Eliot concludes his critique of *Hamlet* by stating quite baldly that 'We must simply admit that here Shakespeare tackled a problem which proved too much for him'.[2] Had Eliot lived longer, he might have found Peter Brooks' analysis of melodrama as 'the mode of excess' interesting. The term melodrama has traditionally been applied pejoratively to a range of popular literature, and Brooks' *The Melodramatic Imagination* (1976) is a deliberate attempt to rehabilitate the term as a descriptive critical category, and is in the process, an attempt at a revaluation of melodrama in general. Although, historically, Brooks locates the rise of melodrama as coinciding with the development of early Romantic drama, and with the rise of the novel, his general characterization of melodrama illuminates much of the generic confusion which gave rise to Eliot's 'bafflement', and which has persistently created a conceptual mystique in critical and productive approaches to *Hamlet*. Brooks' description of melodrama as the irruption of Modernity with the French Revolution is, *mutatis mutandis*, applicable to the Renaissance Modernity of *Hamlet*:

> This is the epistemological moment which it illustrates and to which it contributes: the moment that symbolically, and really, marks the final liquidation of the traditional Sacred and its representative institutions (Church and Monarch), the shattering of the myth of Christendom, the dissolution of an organic and hierarchically cohesive society, and the invalidation of literary forms – tragedy, comedy of manners – that depended on such a society. Melodrama does not simply represent a 'fall' from tragedy, but a response to the loss of the tragic vision.[3]

In parallel with the idea of 'the liquidation of the Sacred', Brooks points to the 'expressionist' dimension of melodrama – he defines it as 'the expressionism of the moral imagination' (55). Interestingly, he points out how melodrama persists in focusing on *muteness* as an extreme version of the problematics of articulation:

> One is tempted to speculate that the different kinds of drama have their corresponding sense deprivations: for tragedy, blindness, since tragedy is about insight and illumination; for comedy, deafness, since comedy is concerned with problems in communication, misunderstandings and their consequences; and for melodrama, muteness, since melodrama is about expression. (57)

Finally, Brooks couples melodrama and psychoanalysis, a nexus which makes historical sense, but which also accounts for the attractiveness of Oedipal readings of Hamlet's predicament:

> Psychoanalysis can be read as a systematic realization of the melodramatic aesthetic, applied to the structure and dynamics of the mind. Psychoanalysis is a version of melodrama first of all in its conception of the nature of conflict, which is stark and unremitting, possibly disabling, menacing to the ego, which must find ways to reduce or discharge it. The dynamics of repression and the return of the repressed figure the plot of melodrama. Enactment is necessarily excessive: the relation of symbol to symbolized (in hysteria, for instance) is not controllable or justifiable. [cf. Eliot's 'objective correlative']. Psychoanalysis as the 'talking cure' further reveals its affinity with melodrama, the drama of articulation. (201-2)

Zeffirelli's Narrative Choices

Melodrama, historically and etymologically, is drama accompanied by music. The production and direction of opera, the dominant Italian version of melodrama, has been Zeffirelli's primary professional domain throughout his career, and consequently his Shakespearean films have routinely been tagged 'operatic'. In the following analysis of Zeffirelli's *Hamlet*, I shall attempt to demonstrate how the overall approach to the production is melodramatic, occasionally specifically operatic, and how this approach opens up a number of perspectives and shuts out others.

Although the Zeffirelli *Hamlet* cannot be said to represent a *radical* departure from Shakespeare's established text, the text editors, Zeffirelli himself and Christopher de Vore, have made a number of major deletions and transpositions which significantly shift the balance of the play.

The opening scene – a funeral ceremony for Old Hamlet in the vaults of Elsinore Castle, preceded by an establishing shot of the castle and a lengthy take with the camera travelling and zooming its way into the courtyard, past a multitude of immobile soldiers and into the vault itself – is a classic expository scene, firmly anchoring the narrative within the genre of the family melodrama. Indicative of this is the shot of Hamlet, Gertrude and Claudius, the central triangle, placed around the body of Old Hamlet, preceded by the very first diegetic sound of the film, the sound of a woman – Gertrude – sobbing. In many ways this expository device can be compared to the opening scene of Olivier's film *Richard III*, in which the coronation scene – taken from *Henry VI, Part 3* – is given this expository function. In both cases we see a significant triangular pattern of gazes, establishing a field of sympathies and conflicts, and raising our dramatic expectations. However, whereas in *Richard III* this addition makes narrative sense, in that it establishes the historical continuity of the Henriad, a task left in the play to Richard's 'Winter of Discontent' soliloquy, in Zeffirelli's *Hamlet* the opening scene in the vault replaces the entire Scene 1 of the play – an opening scene justly famous within the Shakespeare oeuvre for its haunting creation of an opening mood ("Tis bitter cold, and I am sick at heart')[4] and its establishment of a situation of military alert and spiritual confusion, i.e. an establishment of a far wider range of signification than in the Zeffirelli opening scene. As Jonathan Romney points out, this deletion makes for a far less 'metaphysical' *Hamlet* than usual.[5] Obviously, this is in part due to the deletion of the Fortinbras story in Zeffirelli's *Hamlet*, a deletion which has a whole range of consequences, among which are not only the elimination of that claustrophobic, siege-like mentality we get from Scene 1, but a general reduction of the social and political dimensions of the story. Furthermore, it robs us of the obvious point of comparison between Hamlet and Fortinbras, between the doubter and the doer. Admittedly the Fortinbras story, with all its ramifications (Voltemand, Cornelius, etc.) is an obvious candidate whenever a producer of *Hamlet* has to get down to the inevitable task of cutting. In the 1948 film Olivier, and Alan Dent, the editor, managed to cut out not only Fortinbras but Rosencrantz and Guildenstern (with Polonius taking over some of R and G's lines), leaving us with a *Hamlet* very much focused on the psychology of the protagonist (and giving a lot of screen time to Olivier himself). Zeffirelli, fortunately, kept Rosencrantz and Guildenstern, and the scenes in which they are involved with Hamlet are among the most successful in the film, bringing out as they do a Hamlet who is more interactive and resourceful, and thus better suited to both Gibson as an actor and to the overall concept.

The opening scene, then, is one of several examples of Zeffirelli's essentially *melodramatic* approach in concrete action: situations are, as it were, 'disambiguated' to create a superfluity – or *excess* – of simple signification, in which effects do not work in counterpoint, but in *amplification* of each other.

Another example of 'disambiguation' which, however, is more successful, is the bold shift of the 'nunnery' injunction from the 'nunnery scene' itself to the play within the play. Already Zeffirelli's shift of the 'To be or not to be' soliloquy from before to after the Nunnery scene (a frequent transposition, most famously in the 1949 Olivier *Hamlet*) implicitly interprets the soliloquy as being motivated by the frustrations stemming from Hamlet's exchange with Ophelia. Leaving the nunnery injunction ('Get thee to a nunnery...') out of the Nunnery scene and shifting it to the play within the play - scene, gives it a more logical context, placing this rather definitive statement in what is effectively the last scene with Ophelia and Hamlet together, their only remaining 'encounter' being at Ophelia's funeral.

Crucially, the Chapel Scene (Act 3, sc. 3), our only opportunity to get a sustained inside look at Claudius on his own, bears witness to this strategy of 'disambiguation'. Claudius, the antagonist of the play, must be painted sufficiently black to provide the motivation for Hamlet's quest for revenge. On the other hand,

Zeffirelli's *Hamlet*

a traditional arch villain would make Gertrude's infatuation look unmotivated or perverse, and would make Hamlet's hesitation damning or unintelligible. In other words, Claudius needs to be a *complex* character. In the play, the Chapel Scene provides that complexity, the central dilemma being expressed like this:

> – 'Forgive me my foul murder?'
> That cannot be, since I am still possess'd
> Of those effects for which I did the murder –
> My Crown, mine own ambition, and my queen.
> May one be pardon'd and retain th'offence? (3.3.52-56)

Claudius' 39 lines alone in the chapel, agonizing out this dilemma, are reduced in the film scene to these four:

> O, my offence is rank, it smells to heaven;
> It hath the primal eldest curse upon't –
> A brother's murder....
> O wretched state! O bosom black as death! (3.3. 36-8, 67)

The psychological *complexity* of the full speech is reduced to the *excessive* expressivity of melodrama, giving vent to a *simple* state of mind: 'O, O, O!'

Other major examples of melodramatic simplification occur in the excision of the first half of the soliloquy 'O what a rogue and peasant slave am I' (2.2.544-601) – in the Zeffirelli version the soliloquy starts with the line 'Am I a coward?' (1.566). This excision is a consequence of the excision of practically all of the long scene in which Hamlet meets the players, except for Hamlet's dialogue with Polonius about 'using the players according to their desert' (2.2. 518-528), and the *total* elimination of Hamlet's instructions to the players (3.2. 1-45). This supports the interpretation of a far less *intellectual* Hamlet than ordinary. Add to this the deletion by Zeffirelli/de Vore of 'How all occasions do inform against me', a soliloquy which, though triggered by the chance meeting with Fortinbras, actually contains no direct reference to Fortinbras, which means that if required it can be used in a production in which Fortinbras is cut out.[6]

By the same token, it makes excellent *melodramatic* sense to have the Nunnery Scene plus 'To be or not to be' shifted to before the introduction of the players and Hamlet's resolution to 'catch the conscience of the King'. This creates an unbroken continuity between the arrival of the players and the play within the play.

These transpositions and deletions create an unswerving dramatic trajectory of Hamlet's development, in which he makes his decisive move away from passivity and delay by staging the play. This move is followed up by the Closet scene with Gertrude, which is an acting out of the personal implications of turning to action: the killing of Polonius, and confronting his mother with the 'truth' about Claudius. Then comes the exuberance of at last facing up to Claudius (4.3.); and finally there is the hoisting of Rosencrantz and Guildenstern with their own petard. These are seen as the unambiguous consequences of Hamlet's personal development away from the wimp of the first two acts, into becoming a man of action. From this dramatic trajectory at least two things necessarily follow: one, the difficulty of making Act V anything but anticlimactic, or simply an epilogue, and two, an almost total elimination of the theme of madness. Zeffirelli attempts to counteract the potential anticlimax of Act V by stretching the conspiracy scenes between Laertes and Claudius into Act V, which in Shakespeare consisted only of two long scenes: the gravedigger scene, plus an interior scene which modulates uninterruptedly from Hamlet and Horatio alone through the entrance of Osric the courtier and on to the final fencing scene. The Osric intermezzo traditionally provides comic relief not only through its banter, but also through the overly affected/-homosexual acting of the part of Osric. Not so in Zeffirelli. He probably found the conventional gay-bashing of the scene offensive, but more importantly, comedy at this point would appear disruptive, just as he was setting a sombre mood, with a pensive Hamlet looking at a heavily symbolic setting sun, right after the cross-cut from Claudius and Laertes plotting about the use of poison. Dramatically this is a simplification, but a defensible one, since Hamlet's goading of Osric is little more than a repetition of what he did earlier to Polonius; if kept in full, it might indicate that he had undergone little or no development since early in the play. This is not to say that sombreness reigns for the rest of the scene, and the play. In fact, Gibson/Zeffirelli manage to inject a good deal of hilarious but poignant horseplay into the fencing scene – a scene of grotesque overacting from Gertrude (Glenn Close) and Claudius (Alan Bates), but with predictable gusto and vigour from Gibson.

The idea of 'putting on an antic disposition' – an element inherited from Saxo, where it made sense as a strategy for survival, but in the Shakespearean context always a rather dubious ploy – is practically non-existent in Zeffirelli. This in turn makes it more difficult to build up an atmosphere of hypocrisy, of spying and counterspying, although Zeffirelli attempts to do so through a number of *mise en scène* moves not authorized by the Shakespearean text: Hamlet is seen to overhear Polonius' fatherly injunction to Ophelia to stay away from him, just as Polonius is made to eavesdrop on Hamlet's 'madness scene' with Ophelia (Act II, sc.1); Hamlet overhears Ophelia being 'loosed' on him before the nunnery scene, and Hamlet sees the conspiratorial meeting of Rosencrantz and Guildenstern with Claudius.

The 'disambiguation' approach coincides with, but is separate from, the necessary verbal pruning of a play as long and wordy as *Hamlet*, a process of condensation and visualization of which there are many strikingly creative examples in this film.

One is Hamlet's scene with Ophelia (Act II, sc.1). In the play this is reported to Polonius by Ophelia; in Zeffirelli it is acted without speech, but with Polonius spying – a logical and economical solution. Ophelia's reported speech ('My Lord, as I was sewing in my closet/ Lord Hamlet, with his doublet all unbrac'd'... etc.) cries out for visualisation, and Polonius might as well see the scene for himself. This is a far better solution than that of the Olivier film, in which a silent vignette was accompanied by what was, from the audience's point of view, a redundant report by Ophelia. The other three major examples of reported, offstage action – The Ghost telling of his murder, the undoing of Rosencrantz and Guildenstern, and the drowning of Ophelia (all of which were done by Olivier by means of visual vignettes in an iris framing, all of which were utterly undramatic since they simply added a visual equivalent of the voice-over) – all of these are done simply and effectively by Zeffirelli. He lets the ghost speak without visual aids, since the story is powerful enough on its own (and will in any case be reenacted in 'the play within the play'). He dramatizes the scene on board the ship directly, adding a shockingly effective clip of Rosencrantz and Guildenstern being dragged screaming to the block, and finishing off with the sickening thud of the axe (in the Tower, presumably). The drowning of Ophelia is a special case, however, in that Gertrude, who reports the incident to Laertes and Claudius, cannot have been an eyewitness (or she would at least have tried to save her!). Whereas in the play there are several events (the letter from Hamlet, the conspiring of Laertes and Claudius) occurring between Ophelia's second madness scene and her drowning, in Zeffirelli, through a number of jump dissolves, she runs directly from the castle to the brook, whereupon the voiceover of the queen accompanies a dissolve to the previous interior scene in the castle, with the queen simply *telling* the strikingly visual story of the drowning:

> There is a willow grows askant the brook
> That shows his hoary leaves in the glassy stream
> Therewith fantastic garlands did she make
> Of crow-flowers, nettles, daisies, and long purples... (IV.7. 165-68)

An effective and economical presentation of the scene, the crowning touch of which is the final cut to a high-angle shot of a barely recognisable human form in the river, the camera then rising beyond the surrounding hills, a jump dissolve making the connexion to two riders on horseback – Hamlet and Horatio, on their way to the gravedigger scene, making the theme of death an appropriate tie-in to the final act.

Zeffirelli's Use of Space

At the heart of Zeffirelli's use of space is his sense of Elsinore. Olivier saw Elsinore as a symbolic structure, a *mindscape* in which high and low planes, winding staircases, ever-receding portals, beds, chairs and crucifixes, all interwoven by a wandering, disembodied camera, functioned as symbolic, psychological signifiers, leaving us with very little sense of a concrete historical place called Elsinore. Kozintsev, in his recreation of Elsinore, gave us another kind of symbolic structure: a hyper-historical embodiment of oppression and corruption, in which the brute physicality of stone, fire and servitude became a representation of the ongoing class struggle from the perspective of historical materialism.

Zeffirelli's approach to Elsinore is essentially that of *picturesque naturalism*. That is to say, Zeffirelli represents a sanitized, Italianate version of the average imaginary conception of a Renaissance castle, complete with peasants, soldiers, courtiers and all the clutter of indoor 16th-century activities of scholarship, weaving, embroidery etc., but very little sense of the filth, the physical proximity of people and animals kept inside the castle, the lack of personal hygiene, etc. Pauline Kael's nasty comments on this stagy/operatic aspect of the Zeffirelli mise en scene in *Romeo and Juliet* may to some extent be applied to his *Hamlet*:

Theatricality can be effective in a movie when it is consciously used, but it's very awkward when the director is trying for realism – which Zeffirelli apparently takes horseplay and opulent clutter, and dust, to be. He brings to the screen the filler of opera – all that coarse earthy stuff that comes on when the main singers are off. And Zeffirelli's 'robust' realistic detail is ludicrous; when he throws a closeup of the marketplace onto the the screen and we see peppers and onions, it's like the obligatory setting of the scene in the first act of an opera when the peasant girl walks on with the basket on her arm.[7]

The cinematic strategy with which Zeffirelli approaches Act 1, Sc.2, the court scene, is a good example of how he *narrates* with the spatial dimensions of the story in mind. Whereas Olivier in 1948, and Kozintsev in his 1964 Russian version, grasp the opportunity to foreground the public, representative nature of both Claudius' marriage to the widowed queen and the assumption of power by Claudius, Zeffirelli 'privatizes' the exchanges with Laertes and Hamlet, splitting up the scene into three: the royal proclamation in the great hall, Laertes' petition to go to France in the library (a location to be used later in the 'words, words, words' scene), and the interchange between Hamlet, Claudius and Gertrude in Hamlet's study – a dark, musty room cluttered with books and scientific paraphernalia. Furthermore, this last interchange is rearranged in such a way that, instead of being organized around the triangular tension between Claudius, Hamlet and Gertrude, the King exits, leaving to Gertrude words which in Claudius' mouth are hypocritical ('This gentle and unforc'd accord of Hamlet/Sits smiling to my heart'), thus depriving the scene of much of its irony and ambiguity.

The ensuing soliloquy ('O that this too too sullied flesh...'), is in consequence less motivated than in the play, because it is not a reaction to Gertrude and Claudius *together*, but follows upon Hamlet's exchange with Gertrude alone.

All in all, the rearrangement of the court scene, while creating variety and dynamism in the mise en scene and avoiding the theatrical *blocking* of actors, engenders shifts of emphasis in character relations which appear to be neither consistent nor altogether intentional.

An exceedingly positive, indeed enthusiastic reading of Zeffirelli's use of space (and light) can be found in David Impastato's two articles 'Zeffirelli's *Hamlet* and the Baroque' and 'Sunlight Makes Meaning',[8] in which he identifies Zeffirelli's overall style as the seventeenth-century 'Baroque' style of Rembrandt, Vermeer, Velasquez and Caravaggio, in contrast to the 'Mannerism' of Olivier's 1948 *Hamlet*:

> ... the art of the Baroque is open, fluid, emotionally expansive, sensuously free. A 'naturalism' returns to color, the human form and the physical environment. But above all, Baroque art is distinguished by its quality of light, which moves over and around forms and colors to create a sense of living presence, a nurturing dynamic of action as well as repose [...] The result is no mere 'geo-historical authenticity but a poetic and allusive naturalism ...[9]

Indeed, at its best, the Zeffirelli *Hamlet* moves beyond touristy Technicolour and achieves exactly that – a 'baroque' richness, where the physical details of the setting are transformed from 'clutter' to 'poetic naturalism'. Two striking instances of this are the 'To be or not to be' soliloquy in the crypt, and the outdoor tavern scene with Rosencrantz and Guildenstern, carrying over into the introduction of the players.

The choice of the cavernous crypt, complete with skulls, bones, sarcophaguses and the odd dusty sunbeam for the 'To be or not to be' soliloquy is a happy, if obvious, one. The location is already established in the minds of the audience as the funeral parlour of the opening scene. The place reeks of death, more specifically Old Hamlet's death. There is less need for the theatricality of, for example, a declamatory Laurence Olivier perched on the topmost platform of a tower; the place, as it were, speaks for itself.

The scene from Act 2 between Rosencrantz, Guildenstern and Hamlet, placed as it is in the film immediately after the 'To be or not to be' in the crypt, needs a change of location. Hamlet's reference to 'this most excellent canopy the air, look you, this brave o'erhanging firmament', a tongue-in-cheek reference to the canopy of the Elizabethan thrust stage, in the film context makes the choice of an outdoor location a natural one. Green slopes and the porch of a picturesquely primitive tavern form the backdrop of a dynamically edited scene in which an aggressive Hamlet exposes the double dealings of his former friends. The appearance of the troupe of players takes us logically on to the next location – the vast courtyard of Elsinore Castle, with Hamlet entering merrily in motley dress along with the players. In spite of the deletion of the entire theatrical banter of Acts 2 and 3, we are given an immediate sense of Hamlet's familiarity with the world of acting. As in 1.2 (with Hamlet observing Claudius and his mother kissing from above), the essentially *operatic* space of the courtyard, with its massive flight of steps and windows on high, is used to create a pattern of significant gazes and reaction shots between Gertrude (in the window), Claudius and Polonius (on the steps), Hamlet, and Rosencrantz and Guildenstern (significantly scurrying between Hamlet and Claudius) which speaks volumes.

Ultimately then, place *frames* action in Zeffirelli's *Hamlet*, as in Zeffirelli's films generally. Place does not, as in Brooks' *King Lear*, in Kozintsev's *Hamlet*, or in Kurosawa's *Throne of Blood*, take on special *significance* on a par with character and action. As Pauline Kael puts it, quite simply: '[in Zeffirelli] the realistic locations are used like parts of a stage.'[10]

Zeffirelli's Cinematic Strategies

The 'naturalism', poetic or otherwise, of Zeffirelli's *Hamlet* leaves little scope for heavily foregrounded cinematic features. Characters, actions, and objects are essentially *denotative* rather than connotative, and cinematic features such as camera movement, distance and angle, cutting, lighting and sound track essentially *anchor* or *enhance* already established signification. To give one obvious example: A disembodied, floating camera as used in Olivier's *Hamlet* is inconceivable in this film, because the film offers no scope for a sustained symbolic reading, firmly grounded as it is in the colourful, concrete reality of 'Baroque' naturalism. The flying camera of the opening scene of this *Hamlet* does not present a point of view within the diegesis, but serves simply as a melodramatic enhancement of the imposing orchestration of the scene as a whole. A further example: the neat overlap of the shadow of Hamlet/ Olivier's head with Yorick's skull in the Gravedigger Scene of Olivier's *Hamlet* would be highly unlikely in Zeffirelli – it would be too much of a foregrounding of intentional design to fit into the overall naturalistic approach.

By the same token, the low-angle closeup of Gibson's face as he moves into 'What piece of work is a man ...' (2.2. 295-310) is not a metaphorical composition, and in this I find myself in disagreement with David Impastato, quoted above, who argues that the use of light, and particularly direct sunlight, is the organising metaphor of Zeffirelli's film:

> In his recent production of *Hamlet*, Franco Zeffirelli offers a unique directorial vision that emerges with authority and finds striking cinematic

expression for Shakespeare's theatrical text. A unity of image and idea consistently governs all elements of the film, from costuming and photography to characterization and *mise en scène*. What sets this film apart visually from any previous adaptation of *Hamlet* is the presence of direct sunlight, even in the greater part of the interiors.[11]

There are no *organising* metaphors in Zeffirelli's *Hamlet*, for the simple reason that Zeffirelli does not provide the scope for this type of meta-level of signification. This does not mean that there are no recurrent images or signifiers. Sunlight and darkness, classic Manichaean oppositions of melodrama, figure prominently, as in Hamlet's two major soliloquies, 'O, that this too, too sullied flesh' and 'To be or not to be'.

'O that this too too sullied flesh ...' is spoken in Hamlet's dark, musty study. As he reaches the line: 'Fie on't, ah fie, 'tis an unweeded garden/ that grows to seed' he gets up and walks to the window overlooking the courtyard, from which voices and noise are heard. Half in shadow, half in the sun, he continues his soliloquy, looking down on Claudius and his mother, kissing as they prepare for a ride on horseback. Zeffirelli has him finish off the soliloquy with the phrase: 'Frailty, thy name is woman' – a punch line which sets up a fine match cut to the following scene, with Ophelia in her room, saying goodbye to her brother Laertes. In the 'To be or not to be' crypt scene, the stairway and a skylight grill provide the sunlight. Hamlet meanders about the crypt uttering his famous lines, with sarcophaguses, skulls and bones *enhancing* the mood and theme of mortality. At one point only is there a clear shift between darkness and sunlight, when he moves forward and the light suddenly illuminates his face as he gets to: 'And thus the native hue of resolution/ Is sicklied o'er with the pale cast of thought'. But there is no metaphorical consistency between the light on Gibson's face and the 'sicklying over' of the soliloquy.

The third, and most obvious use of sunlight is in 5.2, with Hamlet and Horatio, immediately before the final fencing scene, watching the setting sun, and Hamlet saying: "If it be now, 'tis not to come; if it be not to come, it will be now; if it be not now, yet it will come. The readiness is all."

A close look at all three examples will yield nothing in terms of sunlight as inscribed in a overriding system of binary signification. Obviously, the early Hamlet in particular is a moody, indoor-type of person, in contrast to the lively, horseback-riding Claudius and Gertrude. But Hamlet in the exterior scenes is not really any different. The sunlight is inhabited equally by everyone in the play. In other words, the chiaroscuro effects are simply *local* intensifiers, making for interesting photography, but essentially 'part of the world' – resolutely *not* foregrounding themselves as an autonomous system of signification. And a setting sun is a setting sun is a setting sun.

Much the same applies to Zeffirelli's use of music. Perhaps with a view to the classically sombre nature of the subject matter, and to avoid the epithet 'operatic', Zeffirelli chose Ennio Morricone, well known for his radically minimalist score of Sergio Leone's *Once upon a Time in the West*, a dramatic departure compared to, for example, the sensuously overblown Nino Rota score of *Romeo and Juliet*. The Morricone music has no pretentions beyond enhancing. Extremely low-key, for long stretches even absent, the music is nevertheless extremely effective as enhancer and moodsetter. The music never competes with, or is contrapuntal to, the words, but it frequently sets in as a particular scene intensifies – often, as in television drama, accompanied by zoom-ins and close-ups. Lyrical passages are often supported by only a single, unobtrusive instrument playing – usually an oboe or a cello. Longer dramatic passages are sustained by a low orchestral ostinato of modulating chords. The only obtrusive use of music in the film is in the opening sequence, when the camera approach to Elsinore is accompanied by 'courtly', early Baroque-like music, blending into the organ music of the crypt scene. And, of course, in the final scene, as the camera is raised upward and away, when we hear the swell not of Baroque but of Romantic orchestral music, underscoring not the catharsis, but the emotional expressivity of the finale.

The only formal cinematic feature of Zeffirelli's *Hamlet* with which an attempt is made to create an overarching formal paradigm of signification is the *tinting*. Zeffirelli works with two special types of coloration: Warm amber tinting (a favourite of his), and a contrastive cold greyish blue. Amber is associated with indoor candle-lit rooms, and the greyish blue with outdoor sombre scenes, e.g. those involving Hamlet and his father's ghost. The contrast is made dramatically in 1.4, with Hamlet outside on the battlements looking down through the skylight at the amber-coloured banquet scene in the great hall of the castle, reflecting:

This heavy-headed revel east and west
Makes us traduc'd and tax'd of other nations –

They clepe us drunkards, and with swinish phrase
Soil our addition; and indeed it takes
From our achievements, though perform'd at height
The pith and marrow of our attribute. (1.4. 17-22)

However, Zeffirelli makes further, and problematic, use of this distinction between amber and greyish blue to create a point of view distinction in the closet scene with the Queen. The appearance of the ghost to Hamlet is presented in greyish blue, whereas the Queen's point of view shot of the doorway where the ghost is supposed to be is presented in the amber tinting in which the rest of the scene is shot. In other words, Hamlet's subjective, potentially deranged vision is identified with the greyish blue tinting, and this is confusing (a) because Zeffirelli's previous use of greyish blue, e.g in the first ghost scene, was not subject-bound and did not indicate any lack of 'reality' in the ghost, and (b) because the use of greyish blue is not restricted to scenes in which Hamlet is present. By the same token, amber tinting has no stable connotations: it is used with the banquet scene, with Ophelia's room, massively with the Queen's closet, and with Claudius sealing letters; and there is an abundance of amber light emanating from the doorway in the outdoor parting scene between Gertrude and Hamlet in Act 4.

The use of tinting is problematic in a way in which the use of sunlight/lack of the same is not, because it is used *both* as a formal system of signification (in the closet scene) and as a general feature of enhancement. As I have pointed out, Zeffirelli really cannot have it both ways without creating what can only be described as an unintentional confusion concerning the nature of both the ghost and Hamlet's grasp of reality.[12]

Casting and Directing

Casting and directing of actors are areas frequently neglected in academic film scholarship. Directing is a collective process of give and take in which the attribution of credit or blame is difficult, even to the people involved. Casting, by the same token, while obviously a manifestation of the governing *vision* of producer/director, involves so much else in addition: availability, budget and box office considerations, existing personal relationships, plus the elusive affective relations between well-known actors and cinema audiences.

> The greatest innovations of this production lay in unifying words and stage-business, and in making the actors' speech as lively and fluent as

their physical action. The result was that the dialogue did not appear the effect of study and care, but the natural idiom of the characters in the particular situations. It is a long time since Shakespeare's text has been so enfranchised.[13]

These words refer to Zeffirelli's theatrical production of *Romeo and Juliet* in 1960 at the Old Vic in London, but they might equally be applied to his *Hamlet*. Zeffirelli's capacity for *naturalizing* Shakespeare is evidenced in all of his Shakespearean work. He is primarily a *communicator* rather than an *interpreter*. Individual direction and a sense of the narrative dynamics of drama are the essential clues to the success of this production. It is the ease and the fluency of execution rather than the profundity of vision which are the redeeming qualities of this *Hamlet*.

Zeffirelli has a track record of spectacular casting, and *Hamlet* is no exception.

The international mix of seasoned Shakespeareans and popular screen personalities in the casting of *Hamlet* makes for a width of appeal which positions the film as a mainstream production rather than an art cinema one. As indicated by my introductory quotation, Zeffirelli clearly wants to *transcend* what he sees as the artificial division between the 'serious' and the 'popular', just as Shakespeare is generally perceived to have transcended this division. The juxtaposition of high Shakespeare and low commercial filming in itself points to this; casting is another, and obvious way of making this point.

The bankability of Mel 'Mad Max' Gibson and Glenn 'Fatal Attraction' Close are balanced against the cultured Britishness of Alan Bates, Ian Holm, newcomer Helena Bonham-Carter and, as Ghost, veteran Shakespearean Paul Scofield, known in particular from the title role of Peter Brook's *King Lear*.

As an ensemble, the cast display a uniformly high professional level of acting in *Hamlet*. Frank Kermode, in his "Commentary on *Hamlet*", puts it even more strongly: 'I don't think I have ever heard the lines of the play spoken by an entire cast with such authority and resource as in this film.'[14]

The casting of Close and Bonham-Carter in particular indicates fresh approaches, Close being cast very much in the role of the sincere, not too clever, foolishly infatuated mature woman, and Bonham-Carter playing an Ophelia with a mind of her own, combined with an intriguing blend of confused innocence and erotic awareness, without the palely loitering quality of, for example, Olivier's Jean

Simmons.

However, the overall quality of any *Hamlet* production hinges on two crucial points: one, the conception and casting of Hamlet himself, and two, a cohesive *vision* of what should be perceived to emerge as happening in the play. Mel Gibson as an actor quite simply has a limited range of expression – you can only roll your eyes and shake your head so many times in the same film. This limited range, however, is largely offset by a surplus of vitality and vigorous movement, and an admirable clarity of diction. The point made by Daniel Quigley,[15] that Zeffirelli *deliberately* builds the 'Mad Max' Gibson known to the audience into the Hamlet role as an 'extra semiotic element into his performance text' I find less than convincing. Obviously Gibson is Gibson, with all the 'semiotic ramifications' of his track record, but beyond that there is no indication of a meta-cinematic dimension to this *Hamlet* – indeed, it would militate against the overall *naturalism* of Zeffirelli's approach.

On the second count, however, Zeffirelli, is found wanting: as instanced above, there is a lack of governing vision in this production. As in *Romeo and Juliet*, Zeffirelli has a sophisticated sense of *texture*, i.e. of mood, decor, costume, setting and staging. But the *structure*, i.e. the developmental dynamics of the play, is unclear. In *Romeo and Juliet* we were given a Romeo whose *development* from superficial courtier and womanizer into a real human being in love was largely ignored in favour of the melodrama of the love plot. In *Hamlet* we are presented with a character whose motives are not complex, but unclear, up against an uncle who is not sufficiently villainous to provide that motivation, and a Polonius who is somehow neither the bureaucratic mastermind nor the loquacious comic relief, but somewhere in between. *Power*, in other words, is diffusely conceived at Zeffirelli's Elsinore. So, as a consequence, is the frustration of *powerlessness* which is such an important ingredient of the central domain of the play: Hamlet's state of mind.

In the final analysis, the Zeffirelli *Hamlet* lacks an overall sense of direction, in every sense of the phrase. Melodrama as a point of entry to *Hamlet* makes interesting sense from a theoretical point of view. However, without an overall sense of the consequences to texture and structure of such an approach, the result, however entertaining and glamorous, remains unconvincing. Laurence Olivier, with becoming if unjustified modesty called his film 'an Essay in Hamlet'.[16] Zeffirelli, in an interview, summarized his approach to *Hamlet* in the following words: 'I simply put the mechanics of popular theatre in motion.'[17]

Notes

1. T.S. Eliot, "Hamlet and his Problems", in T.S. Eliot, *The Sacred Wood* (London: Methuen, 1960), p. 101.

2. Ibid., p. 102.

3. Peter Brooks, *The Melodramatic Imagination* (New Haven: Yale UP, 1976), p. 15.

4. *Hamlet*, ed. Harold Jenkins (London: Routledge, 1989, The Arden Edition). All further references are to this edition and are included in the text.

5. Jonathan Romney, Review of Zeffirelli's *Hamlet*, *Sight and Sound*, May 1991, p. 49.

6. In this Zeffirelli follows the 1948 *Hamlet*, in which Olivier and Alan Dent cut 'How all occasions do inform against me'. In Alan Dent, ed., *Hamlet: The Film and the Play* (London: World Film Publications 1948), Dent notes: 'It proved intractable as cinematic material, and Olivier found it impossibly static in screen terms, though he hated to have to part with it as much as I did' (no pagination).

7. Pauline Kael, *Going Steady* (Boston: Little, Brown and Co., 1968).

8. *Shakespeare on Film Newsletter*, April 1992 and Dec. 1991.

9. David Impastato, "Zeffirelli's Hamlet and the Baroque", *Shakespeare on Film Newsletter*, April 1992, p. 1.

10. *Going Steady*, p. 155.

11. David Impastato, "Zeffirelli's Hamlet: Sunlight Makes Meaning", *Shakespeare on Film Newsletter*, December 1991, p. 1.

12. See Murray Biggs, "He's going to his Mother's Closet: Hamlet and Gertrude on Screen", *Shakespeare Survey*, 45 (1993). Biggs, in comparing the 1980 BBC *Hamlet* with the Olivier and Zeffirelli *Hamlets*, makes the general point: 'It is a weakness of the BBC production that the ghost is presented only from Hamlet's point of view. The camera ought also to show us, as it does under both Olivier's and Zeffirelli's direction, that from Gertrude's perspective there is nothing to see; it is what she says, at line 132. The queen is not simply deprived of her senses here, or lying about what she does or does not see. It is her moral obliquity that obscures her vision, just as Hamlet's enhanced sensibility enables his' (p. 61).

13. John Russell Brown, *Shakespeare's Plays in Performance* (London: Edward Arnold, 1966), p. 170.

14. Kermode, Frank, "A Commentary on Hamlet", *Film Education Study Guide*, (London: BFI, 1992), p. 2.

15. In "'Double Exposure': The Semiotic Ramifications of Mel Gibson in Zeffirelli's *Hamlet*", *Shakespeare Bulletin*, Winter 1993, vol. 11, no.1.

16. *The Film Hamlet: a Record of its Production*, ed. Brenda Cross (London: The Saturn Press, 1948), p. 12.

17. Angie Errigo, "The Italian Job", *Empire*, May 1991, p. 47.

This is a revised and updated version of an earlier article of mine: "Mel's Melodramatic Melancholy: Zeffirelli's *Hamlet*, in *Screen Shakespeare*, ed. by Michael Skovmand (Aarhus University Press 1994).

"SHAKESPEARE IN TOMBSTONE": HAMLET'S UNDISCOVERED COUNTRY

Philip H. Christensen
(SUNY at Suffolk County Community College)

In John Ford's *My Darling Clementine* (1946), Hamlet makes a brief appearance[1] in the person of "that eminent actor, that sterling tragedian" Mr. Granville Thorndyke (played by Alan Mowbray[2]), a third-rate British actor out of his element and down on his luck. Held at gun point by the unsavory Clantons and with a bottle for a prop, the sable-clad Thorndyke attempts to deliver Hamlet's "To Be or Not to Be". That the Danish Prince should appear in a western film is not surprising.[3] Frontier theaters that flourished in cow towns and mining camps west of Chicago, St. Louis, and New Orleans and east of San Francisco demanded the kind of variety that ranged from a Highland fling or sailor's hornpipe to a Shakespeare soliloquy,[4] and audiences, though they looked upon players – especially if English – with suspicion, had a strong appetite for Shakespeare. Professionals, even the renowned Edwin Booth, performed the Bard's works from Cheyenne to Nevada City.[5] Although *Hamlet* was presented before many a "worthy pioner",[6] not all players were delighted with frontier audiences, "young and boisterous men" who might hurl coins upon the stage, if they were pleased, other furnishings, if they were not![7] *Huck Finn*'s "duke" disparages "Arkansaw lunkheads" who cannot "come up to Shakespeare",[8] Granville Thorndyke, the Clantons: "Shakespeare was not meant for taverns, nor for tavern louts".[9]

Since frontier performances were often restricted to select highlights,[10] these bowdlerizations, with reduction in dialogue and concentration on soliloquy, inevitably cast Hamlet as "a statuesque figure who broods apart, who thinks too much, who shies away from the others".[11] This brooding Prince is a not so distant cousin of Dr. John Holliday (played by Victor Mature in *My Darling Clementine*). Dressed in "customary suits of solemn black,"[12] Doc looks more like a clergyman or an undertaker than a gambler and notorious gunfighter whose career Marshal Earp (Henry Fonda) summarizes as "a trail, going from graveyard to graveyard". Moreover, Hamlet and Doc see themselves as prisoners in worlds whose "borders" are seemingly open to all but themselves.[13] Others may come and go, but Hamlet finds a "prison house" at Elsinore,[14] and Doc, despite the almost crippling effects of tuberculosis, tries to outrun the borders of a Monument Valley whose vastness he sees as claustrophobic.

Both Hamlet and Doc seek confirmation of their worth in "counterfeit presentments". For the Prince, it may be the picture of his late father that gives "assurance of a man".[15] For Doc Holliday, it is his own reflection spied in the glass of his framed medical diploma.[16] In both instances, self-scrutiny is closely aligned with art and language. For Hamlet, "Art...is the mirror of nature, designed to provoke self-examination",[17] an introspection that receives shape and substance in the play's towering soliloquies. For Doc Holliday, whose "torments rage in him",[18] the *Hamlet* soliloquy is both theatrical performance and self-examination. Doc "becomes a player in a larger drama, which takes on significance both from the play and from his life".[19]

Wyatt Earp, the principal foil to Doc Holliday, is "a wilderness figure just passing through".[20] As the film opens, he and his brothers are driving cattle, in the vicinity of Tombstone,[21] from Chihuahua to California. The time frame, circa 1881, falls some twenty years after the close of major westward drives from Texas, through Mexico, to California. Into this improbable setting of boundless expanses and towering buttes, Ford places that "Wide-awake, wide-open town, Tombstone".[22] When Wyatt, Morgan, and Virgil Earp see it for the first time, it appears a kind of hellish *Brigadoon*, a cloud of diffused light, laughter, and music. Although the Earps may have convinced themselves that their desire for beer and a shave is innocent enough, they will, in the end, pay dearly for their brief sojourn in this "unweeded garden" where "things rank and gross in nature possess it merely"[23] and for their failure to leave brother James adequately protected.

Wyatt and his brothers have no intention of putting down roots in Tombstone. When the Mayor offers him the marshal's star, Wyatt responds: "Not interested. I'm just passin' through...".[24] After the Earps return to camp and find James dead and their herd gone, Wyatt returns to Tombstone set on taking that "marshalin' job" and avenging the death of James. Despite his grief, Wyatt does not respond hotheadedly. A Westerner, Wyatt is reticent to speak. Nonetheless, he has every confidence in his ability to solve the mystery of brother James's murder:

> For murther, though it have no tongue, will speak
> With most miraculous organ.[25]

After deputizing his surviving brothers Morg and Virg, he looks for likely suspects: cattle drivers and gamblers. Almost from the start, his field is narrowed to the Clantons and Doc Holliday.

Like Wyatt, the Clantons are Westerners. Unlike Wyatt, the Clantons are not *border crossers*. Their inability to see beyond the past or beyond their occupation as cowboys translates into a virulent mean spiritedness. Old Man Clanton (Walter Brennan), the most loquacious member of the family and a "smiling damned villain",[26] speaks in guarded monosyllables. Given to "more matter with less art",[27] he beats his sons for failing to gun down the new marshal; then says: "When ya pull a gun, kill a man".[28]

The two principal women in *My Darling Clementine* are both *border crossers*. Wyatt's first introduction to Dr. John Holliday comes through his establishment – the Oriental Saloon – and his girl, Chihuahua (Linda Darnell). A dark-haired woman "dressed in a low-cut blouse and a Mexican skirt", she openly taunts the new "Tin Star Marshal" while alluding to his recent loss in a song that she performs before all the patrons. When Chihuahua asks for Doc's whereabouts, the Bartender responds that John Holliday's movements are not easily circumscribed: "Tucson...over the border. Who knows where Doc goes?"[29]

The other woman in Doc's life (or at least his past), a nurse from Boston named Clementine Carter (Cathy Downs), is a model of decorum and control. Her name alludes to the very gift she offers Doc, *clemency*,[30] a gift that he adamantly

Hamlet's Undiscovered Country 283

refuses. His frenetic pace is heightened by Clementine's arrival: "Doc has come West to escape his former life and whatever 'slings and arrows of outrageous fortune' plagued him there...he tells [Clementine] he will go further if she will not leave".[31]

At his first appearance, Doc, an Easterner relentlessly driving himself westward – Tucson, the Mexican border, or beyond – sizes up the saloon, as an actor might an attentive house, and the new marshal: "You haven't taken it into your head to deliver us from all evil?"[32] He challenges Wyatt to gun play but backs off when he discovers that the new marshal has support from Deputies Morg and Virg. A violent confrontation avoided, at least for the moment, "music strikes up, and all the patrons, who have moved back away from the bar since Wyatt first went up to Doc, now rush forward".[33] When this music comes to its inevitable "dying fall", a close that is met by the saloon patrons with characteristic "cheers", Granville Thorndyke enters, a man who "seems totally out of place in a saloon".[34] Nonetheless, the actor "comes to a dramatic stop, and acknowledges the crowd by raising his top hat and saying, in highly cultivated tones, 'Thank you'".[35]

This entrance is but the first of several in which Thorndyke uses his craft to his own advantage. While the cheers were clearly directed to the musicians, this seasoned thespian succeeds in turning them to the service of his own *grand entrance*. Both here and later, Thorndyke draws whatever courage he must from well-worn lines delivered without regard to their original dramatic context. After he admonishes the bartender: "Come, come, my good man. Let me have service or I'll take my patronage elsewhere", he handles Wyatt brusquely, ordering him to move his foot from the bar rail and then finishing Wyatt's champagne. When Wyatt identifies this eccentric as "the actor in tonight's show", Doc muses, "Shakespeare in Tombstone", and next thing the Bartender (whether innocently or facetiously is unclear) is addressing him as "Mr. Shakespeare".[36] Wyatt may be no student of the theater. When Doc muses: "It's a long time since I heard Shakespeare", Wyatt responds: "Yeah, fine". However, Wyatt does know that if he does not separate Thorndyke and the bottle, "there won't be any show". He directs Old Dad to take the actor to the Birdcage, but while Thorndyke has been shown the door, he returns one last time to create a perfect exit, with the words: "Drinks on the house!"[37]

A poster outside the Birdcage announces "'The Convict's Oath' starring Granville Thorndyke and Company". In the *shooting script* a scene appears, omitted from the film, that clarifies the circumstances.[38] A drunken Thorndyke has been discovered on the stagecoach; his company, either disgusted with his behavior or taking advantage of the situation, has run out on him. The only thing that Thorndyke has left is one of his props, a skull.[39]

That evening, the Theater Manager must face his audience with a twofold dilemma. Due to circumstances beyond his control (the disappearance of Thorndyke's company), the play "The Convict's Oath" cannot go on. Nonetheless, he had still expected some sort of solo performance from Mr. Thorndyke. He, too, has disappeared. When Wyatt asks the crowd why they are so angry, one responds, "Bird imitators, bird imitators, that's all we get".[40]

When Wyatt and Doc locate the actor, he is wearing "black tights and cape"[41] and has evidently performed several selections from his "very large repertoire". His sables and pendant identify him with the Danish Prince. Ike Clanton's calling him "Yorick" probably suggests that Thornton has already performed excerpts from *Hamlet*, Act Five. Ike, who later cuts Thorndyke off, ironically, at the very point that the Prince is contemplating thoughts of the kinds of dreams that may accompany the "sleep of death", sees no virtue in "them poems". It is likely that he has been expecting more of a variety show with singing and dancing. Wyatt, a man of few words, intends to interrupt this performance and return the actor to the paying customers who are impatiently awaiting his arrival at the theater

Doc, stopping him, confesses: "Wait. I want to hear this". Although Doc is quick to run "tinhorn" gamblers out of town or to draw on those "in opposite camps", he shows remarkable respect for an actor who is down on his luck in Tombstone. For transplanted Easterners like Doc Holliday, "Shakespeare offered an escape, a pleasing reminder of life back east".[42] Absorbed by what he hears, Doc is drawn to language that takes him back to the New England academy. More important, the soliloquy provides an objective correlative to the demon music that has long possessed him, for "the fears expressed in the speech are clearly [Doc's] own".[43]

The performance that follows – the "To be or not to be" soliloquy – is hardly memorable. The lines are delivered in a mannered, oratorical style that denies the power of the verse and the depth of its vision.[44] Moreover, Thorndyke insists on reciting Shakespeare to a saloon player's piano accompaniment! But when Thorndyke breaks down, letting fall his "bare bodkin" and confessing to Doc: "Would you carry on? I'm afraid ... It's been so long", Thorndyke speaks from Doc Holliday's heart as well as his own.

The curious thing about this moment is that it works with remarkable power. This second-rate tragedian in black tights is hardly a credible Hamlet; even his breakdown smacks of the overplay of the worst sort of melodrama. Nonetheless, the soliloquy strikes home: for Holliday and, undoubtedly, for the viewer. Even Wyatt, who has little use for language, is *puzzled* by the impromptu performance of the physician turned gambler and gunfighter. While Doc's dark, impenetrable eyes appear to glimpse shadows of "the undiscovered country, from whose bourn/No traveller returns", Wyatt's response is wide-eyed silence.[45]

On one level, Ford's insertion of this soliloquy into *My Darling Clementine* mirrors, as Gallagher observes, "the advent of culture in the wilderness," an advent that "is both undercut and underscored by staging the soliloquy on a saloon table with a drunken actor...and an uncomprehending savage audience...".[46] On a thematic level as well, Hamlet's appearance is far from "out of place midst [this film's] muddle of duty, vengeance, right, and doubt."[47]

Marshal Earp, John Ford's archetypal western hero, does not "unpack [his] heart with words".[48] He is capable of sweeping to his revenge once he has "the motive and the cue for passion".[49] Schatz writes: "Earp is a natural man who operates on instinct and savvy" and who "is a harbinger not only of law and order but also of civilization".[50] Tombstone shows promise of no longer living up to its name. Civilization is "changing the desert into a garden",[51] the night's "rouse" giving way to the church bell's call to worship and celebration.

Wyatt, unlike *Hamlet*'s Fortinbras, does not claim "some rights...in this kingdom".[52] Gallagher writes: "Like many another Fordian hero, [Wyatt] comes out of the wilderness, rights wrongs, and goes on his way".[53] Nonetheless, things are not quite as neat and simple as what they may appear to be in the *B*, or programmer, westerners. Wyatt and Morg are journeying homeward; however, they must face Pa without the Chihuahua steers and with news of the deaths of brothers James and Virgil. And while Wyatt makes clear, even in his awkward fashion, his affection for Clementine, he leaves without an embrace[54] and with only a promise that he will return some day.

Although Doc and Wyatt share a certain mutual respect and though both are "riding westward", they are fundamentally little alike. Holliday is "a cultivated man seeking refuge in the West from a failed romance and a demanding career".[55] Like Hamlet, Doc is a student of performance. Quick to correct Chihuahua's grammar or to set down "a speech of some dozen lines," Doc, like the Danish Prince, "is defined in a sense precisely as a performer, the consciousness of whose gestures and manner signal the uneasiness of his identity".[56] For Doc, civilization is less a promise than a threat, even as Hamlet sees in Denmark "a dynasty in decay".[57] Like Hamlet, Doc's basic dilemma "is his inability to come to terms with himself and the various aspects of his life".[58] In the end, viewers identify closely with Doc, even as they admire the *western hero* – Wyatt Earp – whose single-mindedness and resolve are possible only because he remains uncorrupted by the introspective turmoils of civilization. Sinclair writes: "Holliday is...made to quote Hamlet's soliloques to emphasize his role between life and death...".[59] As viewers of John Ford's *My Darling Clementine* find, in Dr. John Holliday, symptoms of their own incurable malady, they surely understand that their journey – like Hamlet's and Doc's – must take them inevitably "west of everything".[60]

Notes

1. In Hamlet's first appearance in a John Ford film, *Upstream* (1927), the prince (Earle Fox) appeared briefly, skull in hand, in a play within a film.

2. Ephraim Katz, "Alan Mowbray", *The Film Encyclopedia* in *Cinemania '94* (Microsoft 1992-93), writes that Mr. Mowbray "appeared in nearly 200 films, generally portraying an assortment of pompous or eccentric Britishers". In John Ford's *Wagonmaster* (1950), Mowbray plays another down-on-his-luck showman, "Doctor A. Locksley Hall"!

3. Lawrence W. Levine, *Highbrow/Lowbrow: The Emergence of Cultural Hierarchy in America* (Cambridge, MA: Harvard UP, 1988), p. 20, writes that Shakespeare's plays were frequently performed in frontier towns and mining camps: "makeshift stages in halls, saloons, and churches". Richard A. Van Orman, "The Bard in the West," *Western Historical Quarterly*, 5 (January 1974), p. 29, notes: "Mountain men, soldiers, miners, and cowboys read his works. Theater audiences demanded his plays".

4. Mark Twain, *Adventures of Huckleberry Finn*, eds. Walter Blair and Victor Fischer (Berkeley: U of California P, 1988), p. 178.

5. Keith Wheeler, *The Townsmen* (New York: Time-Life Books, 1975), pp. 178-81, noting that the appeal of Edwin Booth's frontier performances was such that he could earn $25,000 dollars a month, writes: "At least a part of the widespread interest in Shakespeare doubtless resulted from the great desire for cultural improvement that characterized Victorian America".

6. *Hamlet* I.v.163.

7. Richard A. Van Orman, "The Bard in the West", *Western Historical* Quarterly, 5 (January 1974), pp. 31ff.

8. Twain, p. 194.

9. John Ford, *My Darling Clementine*, ed. Robert Lyons (New Brunswick, NJ: Rutgers UP, 1992), p. 58. One recalls Hamlet's own remark (II.ii.423) that a certain play "pleased not the million, 'twas caviary to the general".

10. In Twain, p. 180-81, the duke's play bill promises everything from "The Balcony Scene in Romeo and Juliet" to "Hamlet's Immortal Soliloquy".

11. Harry Levin, *The Question of Hamlet* (New York: Oxford UP, 1959), p. 48, is not writing specifically about frontier performances. Nonetheless, his observations are clearly relevant to all performances of *Hamlet* that are limited, essentially, to the soliloquies.

12. *Hamlet* I.ii.78.

13. Horatio and Laertes have returned from their studies abroad both for a royal funeral and a royal wedding. Hamlet's university "friends" Rosencrantz and Guildenstern arrive from Wittenberg. Fortinbras is preparing to lead his armies through Denmark and on to Poland. And the Ghost, whose nature perplexes Hamlet and whose presence defies the boundaries of life and death, denies the Prince a tale "whose lightest word/Would harrow up [his] soul". (*Hamlet* I.v.16)

14. Mark Rose, "Reforming the Role", in *William Shakespeare's Hamlet*, ed. Harold Bloom (New York: Chelsea House Publishers, 1986), p. 118, writes: "From the first scene in which the prince appears, Shakespeare wishes us to perceive that Hamlet is tethered" and that his "real prison is . . . more a matter of mental than physical space".

15. *Hamlet* III.iv.62.

16. Wyatt also catches a glimpse of himself in a glass. The context and meaning of this double imaging are entirely different. The glass is a mirror, held by the barber, and the marshal's gaze is limited to inspection of his outward appearance.

17. Rose, p. 122. *Hamlet* III.ii.20: Playing's "end , both at the first and now, was and is, to hold as 'twere the mirror up to nature".

18. J. A. Place, *The Western Films of John Ford* (New York: Citadel Press, 1974), p. 69.

19. Place, p. 68.

20. Tag Gallagher, *John Ford: The Man and His Films* (Berkeley: U of California P, 1986), p. 226.

21. The film's setting, Mounument Valley, is actually far removed from the town of Tombstone. For John Ford, the Valley's boundless expanses and towering buttes recalled primordial colossi who themselves were metamorphosed into stone. Jane Tompkins, *West of Everything* (New York: Oxford UP, 1992), p. 71, writes that the setting of western films is "a land defined by absence: of trees, of greenery, of houses, of signs of civilization, above all, of water and shade".

22. Ford, p.28.

23. *Hamlet* I.iv.90.

24. Ford, p. 36.

25. *Hamlet* II.ii.573-74.

26. *Hamlet* I.v.106.

27. *Hamlet* II.ii.95.

28. Ford, p. 59.

29. Ford, p. 43.

30. In the entire Shakespeare canon, this word, and its variants, appears in *Hamlet* alone.

31. Place, pp. 68-69.

32. Ford, p. 49.

33. Ford, p. 50.

34. Ford, p. 51.

35. Ford, p. 51.

36. The following day as Thorndyke prepares to leave Tombstone, he receives much thanks from the mayor for his "wonderful performance" (whatever it may have been!). His parting words to Old Dad, taken from Joseph Addison's *The Campaign*, are delivered with bravura, though they are clearly inappropriate to the old drunk and himself (though they might have applied to Hamlet and Horatio):

> Great souls by instinct to each other turn,
> Demand allegiance, and in friendship burn.

His final words to Old Dad are Horatio's last to the Prince: "Good night, sweet prince". And after autographing the hotel bill, Thorndyke climbs up on the stage next to the driver and with a parting wave to the cleaning ladies *on the balcony*, he delivers Juliet's famous balcony line to Romeo: "Parting is such sweet sorrow".

37. Ford, p. 52. A theatrical gesture, Granville Thorndyke has no intention of honoring the bill!

38. Ford, p. 23. The *shooting script* of *My Darling Clementine*, completed by Samuel G. Engel and Winston Miller, became the basis of the film. Ford, however, did make changes, and these are reflected in the *continuity script* (a transcript from the completed film).

39. This explains Thorndyke's nickname in the film: "Yorick". However, we don't know why the Clanton boys use it.

40. Ford, p. 54.

41. As Hamlet, Thorndyke appears as one of the two characters from English literature who are most easily identified worldwide and who frequently appear out of context or in parody. The other is quite obviously Conan Doyle's Sherlock Holmes.

42. Van Orman, p. 31. Levine, p. 20, writes that Shakespeare's popularity on the frontier rested on people's "need for the comfort of familiar things under the pressure of new circumstances and surroundings".

43. Place, p. 68.

44. Esther Cloudman Dunn, *Shakespeare in America* (New York: Benjamin Blom, 1968), p. 190, points out that *oratorical style* was quite popular on the frontier stage. Thorndyke's performance, whether wittingly or not is uncertain, leaves out a line and a half: "Th' oppressor's wrong, the proud man's contumely,/The pangs of despis'd love..." (III.i.70-71a). Doc Holliday's continuation of the performance stops short of the final seven lines (83-89).

45. In the *shooting script* (Ford, p. 116), Wyatt had been given a far more loquacious response: "First time I heard it. Parts I could understand makes a powerful lot of sense – especially that last about conscience makin' cowards out of all of us".

46. Gallagher, p. 232.

47. Gallagher, p. 227.

48. *Hamlet* II.ii.565 reads: "Must like a whore unpack my heart with words...". Robert Lyons, "Introduction: *My Darling Clementine* as History and Romance," *My Darling Clementine,* p. 13, writes that Ford often demonstrates in his films that "Eastern fluency can never encompass the significant moments in experience".

49. *Hamlet* II.ii.541.

50. Jim Hitt, *The American West from Fiction (1823-1976) into Film (1909-1986)* (Jefferson, N. Carolina: McFarland & Co., Inc., Publishers, 1990), p. 299.

51. Jay Hyams, *The Life and Times of the Western Movie* (New York: Gallery Books, 1983), p. 68.

52. *Hamlet* V.ii.371.

53. Tag Gallagher, p. 226.

54. Ford had wanted Wyatt and Clementine to marry and settle down.

55. Thomas Schatz, *Hollywood Genres* (New York: Random House, 1981), pp. 68-69.

56. Douglas Pye, "Introduction: Criticism and the Western." In *The Book of Westerns*, eds. Ian Cameron and Douglas Pye (New York: Continuum, 1996), p. 17.

57. Kenneth Branagh, "Introduction", *Hamlet: Screenplay, Introduction and Film Diary* (New York: W. W. Norton & Co., 1996), p. xv.

58. Place, p. 68.

59. Andrew Sinclair, *John Ford* (New York: The Dial Press/James Wade, 1979), p. 132.

60. Tompkins, p. 24, reminds her readers that in the western "west of everything" lies death.

THE "HOPE" HAMLET: KENNETH BRANAGH'S COMIC USE OF SHAKESPEARE'S TRAGEDY IN *A MIDWINTER'S TALE*

Park Bucker
(University of South Carolina)

The 1996 big-budget movie spectacle of *Hamlet* featuring the eclectic talents of Derek Jacobi, Julie Christie, Jack Lemmon, Rufus Sewell and Gerard Depardieu, photographed in 70mm format, filmed on location at Blenheim Palace, and premiering on Christmas Day, 1996 at only three theatres on the North American continent, does not represent Kenneth Branagh's first film version of Shakespeare's tragedy. That distinction belongs to his previous feature film venture, *In the Bleak Midwinter*, retitled *A Midwinter's Tale* for American release. This low-budget, black-and-white, domestically-cast comedy recounts the story of an out-of-work actor (Michael Maloney) who attempts to stage *Hamlet* in a deserted country church over the Christmas holidays with only a van-load of props and six other actors. Although the movie does not boast an international cast and opened to little fanfare and less critical attention, it does present a version of *Hamlet* as seen from the perspective of those that have to perform it. The experience of playing the tragedy produces comic results in the film because it fundamentally transforms the characters. While portraying horribly fragmented families, the play simultaneously brings together the actors into a homogeneous, albeit transitory, family unit.

The film's original title, *In the Bleak Midwinter*, refers to the seasonal lyric "A Christmas Carol" by Christina Rossetti in which the phrase occurs as a refrain. Branagh employs a rendition of the hymn for the movie's final sequence and credits. Its suggestion of traditional English Christmases corresponds perfectly to the film's final images of reconciliation and familial devotion. Yet the somber Victorian tone of *In the Bleak Midwinter* does not serve the story well as a controlling impression. The American title, *A Midwinter's Tale*, more accurately describes the film as it carries connotations of both the Christmas season and Shakespearean drama.

Although the title obviously plays off Shakespeare's romance *A Winter's Tale*, the film bears a stronger resemblance to *A Midsummer Night's Dream* in which egotistical and insecure actors gather to stage a famous tragedy as part of a community festival. Branagh's collection of farcical characters could easily be described as "rude mechanicals." A single actor performs both Rosencrantz and Guildenstern; Polonius bears a nose worthy of Jimmy Durante; Laertes insists on performing topless covered with body oil; Ophelia auditions with an *a capella* rendition of Blondie's "Heart of Glass"; Claudius imagines himself as the reincarnation of Henry Irving; and a drag queen appears as Gertrude, or rather "Dirty Gerty" as he calls her. Wheras Bottom and his fellow players distort and burlesque the tragic story of Pyramus and Thisby, the players of *A Midwinter's Tale* amazingly overcome their eccentricities, insecurities and petty rivalries to present an inspired *Hamlet* full of legitimate pity and fear. The success of their production lies in the actors' evolving commitment to the text and each other.

A superficial rendering of the plot and characters would not immediately suggest an homage to such family values as loyalty and selflessness. Suffering from a career crisis, talented but chronically unemployed Joe Harper borrows money from his agent to produce and star in his own version of *Hamlet*. He plans to stage the play as a fund-raiser for the declining community center in his hometown of Hope. As most successful actors already have commitments for the holiday 'panto' season, Joe can only assemble a ragtag group of six actors with varying degrees of talent and experience. Joe's agent, Margaretta, describes them, as "eccentrics, misfits and nutters."[1] Joe's sister, Molly, joins the company as stage manager and Hamlet stand-in, and a suitably bizarre designer, Faoge, provides the settings and costumes. With less than two weeks of rehearsal, and more than their fair share of comic reversals, the troupe manages to find the truth of the play and present it to the townspeople of Hope in a rousing and unexpectedly moving performance.

Would any Shakespearean tragedy have worked as well as *A Midwinter's Tale*'s play-within-play? Obviously, any serious play performed during the Christmas 'panto' season contains great comic potential. Molly complains that no one in Hope will want to "come and watch a four-hundred-year-old play about a depressed aristocrat."[2] Yet *Hamlet* does contain seasonal connections to Joe's production in its supernatural properties; ghosts populate many Christmas stories. As the Ghost of Hamlet's father fades with the coming of morning, Marcellus observes:

> Some say that ever 'gainst that season comes
> Wherein our Saviour's birth is celebrated,
> This bird of dawning singeth all night long:
> And then, they say, no spirit dares stir abroad;
> The nights are wholesome, then no planets strike,
> No fairy takes, nor witch hath power to charm,
> So hallow'd and so gracious is the time (1.1.163-9).

Although *Hamlet* obviously does not take place during the Christmas season, the "wholesome nights" of this time offer a special protection against the despair and danger of tragedy that *A Midwinter's Tale* exploits.

Hamlet offers other qualities that make it a perfect choice for *A Midwinter's Tale*. It holds a unique position in both theatre history and Kenneth Branagh's biography. Branagh's relationship with *Hamlet* began at the age of eleven when he viewed a televised production starring Richard Chamberlain. A few years later he saw Derek Jacobi as the Prince at the New Theatre, Oxford. In the introduction to his screenplay for *Hamlet* Branagh records his first live encounter with the play: "I was convinced as I left the theatre that I had experienced – not just watched, but truly experienced – something unique. The story was gripping, and I wanted at every moment to know 'what happened next.'"[3] Branagh's large-scale film version of *Hamlet* testifies to the actor/director's passion and intellectual devotion for the play for the intimacy and sentiment of *A Midwinter's Tale*. But he reserves his youthful exuberence for the play and personal theatrical experience.

Hamlet also serves as the Mount Everest of the acting profession. As Branagh notes "[i]t represents, for some, Shakespeare's greatest achievement, and for others its meaning is as remote as an ancient civilization."[4] One auditioning actor gropes for an adequate description of the play: "Hamlet is me ... Hamlet is ... Bosnia, Hamlet is ... this desk ... Hamlet is the air, Hamlet is ... my grandmother, Hamlet is everything you've ever thought about sex, ... about ... geology."[5] Branagh deflates *Hamlet*'s popular image as the ultimate expression of human thought, so that he can celebrate its actual power later in the film.

Branagh invests much of his personal theatrical experience and philosophy in the character of Joe Harper. "Harper" is Branagh's mother's maiden name. To answer his sister's complaint on the choice of *Hamlet*, Joe explains his fascination and obsession with the play in terms identical to Branagh's:

> I think if we can do it with humour, passion and reality people will be interested in seeing it. I saw this play when I was fifteen, and it changed my life. You don't forget that, I don't think I was any different then to any of your hormonally confused kids now. All I was ever interested in was girls and wanking. Unfortunately, hardly ever in that order. I saw this play and it spoke to my heart, and my head, and my chief reproductive organ.[6]

Branagh provides the company's triumphant opening night performance as evidence of his belief in the play's accessibility. Much of *A Midwinter's Tale* serves as a recreation of the author's youthful exuberant love of *Hamlet* and its inherent power to inspire both actors and audience.

Hamlet is also perfectly suited to demonstrate Branagh's belief in the emotional bonds formed within theatrical companies. In his introduction to the published screenplay of *A Midwinter's Tale* Branagh explains that "the relationships between actors, directors, stage managers, designers – the ad hoc 'family' that is a theatrical company – becomes very intense. Angry showdowns, love affairs, nervous collapses, philosophical breakthroughs can all occur in a frighteningly short space of time."[7] All these extremities of behavior occur in *A Midwinter's Tale* yet the 'family' does not disintegrate. Branagh presents the text of

Hamlet as the instrument of their unification because it provides him with a model for the intimate emotional commitment demanded of actors.

Although never depicted in *A Midwinter's Tale*, *Hamlet*'s traveling players mark the strongest thematic connection between the play and Harper's fledgling troupe. As demonstrated in his filmed version of *Hamlet*, Branagh perceives the players as a literal family: a mom-and-pop acting company filled out with sons, daughters, and grandchildren. In his published screenplay Branagh describes the arriving players as "a motley troupe who look like the 'Crummles' from *Nicholas Nickleby* – a real family affair. Tatty grand."[8] In his film diary for *Hamlet*, the film's textual consultant Russell Jackson describes his discussions with Charlton Heston and Rosemary Harris (Player King and Player Queen): "Players background discussed: They used to run a theatre, but times are bad, and they have been forced to take the road [...] a sort of ideal alternative family. (The only one we see that is not dysfunctional?)"[9] *A Midwinter's Tale* merely reverses the thematic connection between players and play so that the focus becomes a familial acting troupe reacting to the tragedy around them rather than a tragedy momentarily interrupted by travelling players. Just as Tom Stoppard's *Rosencrantz and Guildenstern Are Dead* presents the play from the perspective of Hamlet's duplicitous classmates, *A Midwinter's Tale* examines the tragedy from the viewpoint of the players. Branagh relies on the audience's familiarity with the play (or with his filmed version of *Hamlet*) to make the sub-textual connection between *A Midwinter's Tale* and Shakespeare's tragedy.

Branagh's reliance on the emotional bond among actors becomes evident to anyone familiar with his films. Many of his casts form a sort of repertory in that they draw from a group of actors with which Branagh has worked for many years. A comparison of cast lists for *A Midwinter's Tale* and *Hamlet* illustrates this association. In the 'Hope *Hamlet*' Michael Maloney plays the Prince, Richard Briers plays Claudius, and Nicholas Farrell plays Laertes. In the posh 'Blenheim Hamlet' the same actors perform in different roles; Maloney plays Laertes, Briers plays Polonius, and Farrell plays Horatio. Patrick Doyle, Branagh's usual film composer (also for *Hamlet*), plays a cameo roll in *A Midwinter's Tale* as an insane ventriloquist. Branagh created many characters in *A Midwinter's Tale* for specific actors. He claims that the screenplay itself benefitted from their previous relationships and became a collaborative process. In the script's introduction he asserts that "[i]t was the cumulative experience of this group that informed and changed the script."[10]

Drawing on his theatrical experience, Branagh uses *A Midwinter's Tale* to illustrate how a performance profoundly affects its performers. The text of *Hamlet*, with its numerous references to acting and dependence on a play-within-a-play plot device, lends itself particularly well to such an examination. Just as many critics perceive Shakespeare's acting philosophy in Hamlet's 'advice to the players', Joe Harper's direction of his eccentric troupe could easily represent Kenneth Branagh's performance. In the film's opening madcap audition montage Joe/Branagh offers advice to actors incapable of benefitting from it. He posits to a Scot actor that Shakespeare could embrace regional accents: "They are vitally important in fact. There is no 'set' voice for Shakespeare."[11] The Glaswegian unintelligibly responds "Noi iz thah wuntre ov r diskantant/Maid glorius summer bai that sun of York," and remains uncast.[12]

Joe initially imagines a revolutionary production in which the actors should "create the period. I mean I don't think it should be Elizabethan, that would be ridiculous." He ignores an actor's pragmatic response "[a]lthough it is an Elizabethan play isn't it?"[13] His idealized concept dissipates when faced with the bare mechanics of staging a five-act tragedy. When an actor portraying many parts differentiates them with wildly inspired accents, Joe identifies their practical failure: "I think you have to be from Pluto not to notice it [...] Unfortunately I also think you have to come from Pluto to understand it."[14] When Joe tries to tone down an over-the-top reading, the actor responds "I like to be bold early on but I get the message chief. It's basically L.C.A. [...] Less Crap Acting."[15]

Joe attempts to chart a middle path of acting between the old-fashioned, formalized presentation and modern colloquial approach. His direction of Terry's drag performance of Gertrude reveals Branagh's personal philosophy on Shakespearean acting.

JOE
Terry, Look I am slightly concerned about the voice. The general movement is fine but the voiced is just a little . . .

TERRY
But it's what they all do darling. All the grande dames. They don't talk like they do in the real world. They put on the old cigarette gravel. The tragic trill. The emotional break in their middle of the line, the operatic credenzas, ... I'm not making this up, they do.

JOE
Sure and sometimes it's very good, and sometimes they're very wrong and give Shakespeare a bad name.
[...]

TERRY
Look that's what I hear love when I go to the classical theatre. I thought that's what you did.

JOE
Have a little think about something more natural. [16]

Like Hamlet, Joe urges his players to be both moderate and sincere in their performance, "to hold, as'twere, the mirror up to nature" (2.3.21-2). Yet Hamlet offers his players advice alone; Branagh extends not only theatrical guidance to his characters, but also consolation, affection and tribute. In his introduction Branagh provides his intent for *A Midwinter's Tale*:

> At the heart of the film I wanted to touch on the personal lives of the characters involved. The actors' melancholy, loneliness and isolation. Their ongoing relationship with failure, rejection and humiliation. Familiar feelings to many people but often concentrated in the lives of actors."[17]

Many film critics find Branagh's unashamed celebration of the acting profession too saccharine for serious consideration. Despite reviews ranging from

A Midwinter's Tale

lukewarm to hostile, the film received the Osella D'Oro award at the 1995 Venice International Film Festival and Branagh received the Filmmaker Excellence award when it screened at the 1995 Boston Film Festival. In reviewing the Toronto Film Festival *Times*-critic Geoff Brown called the movie a "grating comedy."[18] In *The Times* formal review, "Reeling from Charm Offensive", Tom Shone expressed a severely antagonistic reaction to Branagh's characters and their ultimate devotion to each other. Shone criticized the characters' transformation as not leaving the audience "with much to do except hate them as dramatic creations."[19] He ignored the fact that the actors vilify each other for most of the movie. Shone also displays incredulous disdain at a comedy containing a happy ending.

James Wolcott of the *New Yorker* disparages the film for its greatest achievement. He criticizes the company's successful opening night performance: "The production they stage of "Hamlet" blitzes past the text to present a machine-gun opening, sword fights in the aisle, loud declamations and clouds of hokey atmosphere, which are cheered by the audience as if it were a Saturday matinée at the Bijou."[20] This description accurately represents the film's events, yet Wolcott's use of the word "blitz" implies that their performance violates Shakespeare's intention. *A Midwinter's Tale* presents a modern recreation of how Elizabethan audiences responded to and interacted with their plays. The Hope townspeople scream, cheer, boo, comment and ultimately comprehend the "four-hundred-year-old play about a depressed aristocrat."[21] Many critics believe that Shakespeare's contemporary audience enjoyed a more vital and exhilarating theatrical experience than the ones available to most twentieth-century theatre-goers. *A Midwinter's Tale* production serves as Branagh's thesis on how Shakespeare can be and should be accessible to 'working-class' audiences, to which the author belonged at age eleven.

All the critics agreed on Branagh's obvious intent to imitate Woody Allen in his black-and-white photography, autobiographical subject matter, low-budget artsy atmosphere and use of scene titles and vintage music. Yet in the screenplay's introduction Branagh describes his inspiration for *A Midwinter's Tale* as a combination of Hollywood's "heightened reality" typified by the Mickey Rooney/Judy Garland "let's-put-on-a-show" musical, and the British satirical comedies produced by Ealing Studios in the late 1940s and early 1950s.[22] Frequently starring Alec Guiness, these black-and-white comedies exemplified English irreverence and understated humor. Their greatest commercial success came in 1951 with *The Lavender Hill Mob*. Woody Allen's films also fall into this dual cinematic tradition. Unlike Branagh, Allen rarely lionizes actors, a further example of the two prolific filmmakers' differences.

Of all the film's reviewers only David Jays of *Sight and Sound* comments on the thematic connection between *Hamlet* and *A Midwinter's Tale*. He astutely observes that "[p]erforming *Hamlet* shapes (and reflects) these performers' offstage lives and the correspondences made are light and often unexpected."[23] Yet the similarities between player and part emerge as much more comprehensive than Jays allows. Branagh places his characters in potentially tragic circumstances analogous to the characters they portray in Hamlet. The key to their emotional survival, let alone success, lies in their discovery of the familial bond among themselves. This situation dramatizes Branagh's belief (shared by most modern acting teachers) that an actor must explore his/her own emotional memory as an empathic key to a successful characterization.

Following this theory Joe Harper, admittedly on the edge of a nervous breakdown since he was seven-months old, possesses many of the same insecurities, indecisions and predilection for depression exhibited by Shakespeare's Prince. As with Hamlet and Fortinbras, Joe has an external rival in Dylan Judd, an actor who apparently has achieved commercial success by landing a recurring part in a science-fiction trilogy. Although Joe prides himself on his artistic integrity, he secretly covets Judd's financial windfall. Joe attempts his high-concept, low-budget production of *Hamlet* as a last-ditch effort to dredge himself out of a convergence of emotional, financial and professional crises. Although he is gifted with talent and intelligence, Joe's career seems to have stalled in his mid-thirties. He complains that his career has not followed his expectations: "If everything had gone according to Laurence Olivier's book I would have known triumph, disappointment and married a beautiful woman. Instead I've known tedium, humiliation and got shacked up with the psycho from hell. Life has to change".[24] His pragmatic agent (brilliantly portrayed by Joan Collins) underscores the Hamlet analogy by describing his plan as "professional suicide".[25]

Midway through the rehearsal process, the company suffers major financial and logistical problems. During Joe's rendering of the "too-too-solid flesh" soliloquy, text and actor appear to merge. Branagh's screenplay directions call for the other actors to be ignorant of the circumstances. The scene initially appears as a rehearsal as Joe performs "O God! God! How weary, stale, flat and unprofitable, Seem to me all the uses of this world!"[26] Yet it immediately shifts to a business meeting between Joe and his sister Molly (Hetta Charnely). The words "weary, stale, flat and unprofitable" apply directly to the company's bleak financial situation.

The fusion of actor and role becomes complete two days before opening when Joe experiences a crisis of confidence as he delivers a real-life version of the "To-be-or-not-to-be" soliloquy. Inpatient with the company's petty squabbling, Joe abruptly cancels the show. Mounting the stage, he expresses his despair to the assembled cast and crew.

> What is the point? What is the fucking point? I ... look. You're a perfectly decent group of people. A group of actors with all the normal insecurities and vanities. But basically I know you want to be here, we all want to do what's best for the show, but look at us? We argue. We're depressed, we've set ourselves too great a target. It is too personal for us all [...] The Hope *Hamlet* is a loser, led by the chief loser, yours truly, and circumstances just force me to ask myself, not only what is the point of carrying on this meaningless shambles, but as the Yuletide season take us in its grip I ask myself what is the point of going on with this miserable, tormented life? I mean can anyone tell me, please, please, what makes this fucking life worth living?[27]

Unlike Hamlet, who broods over the meaning of life alone in the corridors of Elsinore, Joe poses his cosmic question to an audience of people in similar emotional straights. Joe survives his moment of doubt and despair because he voices it in the presence of others. Also, unlike Hamlet, Joe receives an answer. Vernon, the ex-child star who plays Polonius, supplies Rachmaninov as a reason for living. Although other characters provide more personal answers, the existence of art remains Branagh's first response. Henry, the veteran character actor portraying Claudius suggests that the company try the play one more time in the morning. What Joe perceives as weaknesses among the players, i.e. their interdependence, sensitivity, and heightened emotionalism, emerge overnight as a strength for the company. The morning rehearsal proves a success and the play goes on. The group's disparate depressions and personal involvements allow the hodgepodge group to congeal into a viable acting company.

Like Hamlet, Joe faces a tragic choice between duty and personal desire. Mere hours before the curtain rises, Joe's agent appears explaining that he has been offered the coveted movie contract for the science fiction trilogy. Branagh clearly positions Joe's dilemma between financial success represented by his agent and aesthetic fulfillment symbolized by his burgeoning romance with Nina, the company's Ophelia. She accuses Joe of abandoning his original ideal and denying the personal transformations that rehearsals have wrought:

> Two weeks ago we all met up to start this adventure and much though we didn't care to admit it we were all in our various ways depressed, especially you Joe. We needed this job, this play, this experience. And all through our ups and downs and disagreements we've continued to need it [...] We're with our family. That's what actors do. That's what people do in what's left of Hope. They hang on, they stick it out. Now they're here tonight for us and we have to do the show for them.[28]

Joe does not offer a defense. His agent whisks him away to Hollywood as the company resolves to continue with Molly as Hamlet. Yet he ultimately abandons financial security and returns in time to make a triumphant entrance, illustrating an irrational and romantic proclivity common to most actors. He refuses the tragic, isolated exile to Hollywood in favor of the emotional unity offered by his cast.

As with Joe, the character of Henry Wakefield (Richard Briers) corresponds precisely with his role of Claudius. An Old School leading man, Henry views this production as his last chance to play a Shakespearean king. Like the usurping Claudius, who views himself as cheated out of a throne, Henry feels deprived of the opportunity to attempt classical roles. He resents the financial pressures that forced him "into understudying old men and 'anyone for tennis'."[29] He initially behaves selfishly like Claudius, treating the entire production as a showcase for his portrayal. Whereas Claudius' relationship with Gertrude contributes to his downfall, Henry's evolving affection for Terry, his "Dirty Gerty", leads directly to his success. Overtly hostile toward his queen during the initial read-through, Henry ultimately respects and admires Terry's talent and theatrical acumen.

Terry's revelation of his estranged relationship with his son both initiates his friendly association with Henry and signals his thematic connection with Gertrude. During an intense rehearsal of the 'closet scene' Terry (John Sessions) runs from the rehearsal in tears over his own estranged relationship with his teenage son, stemming from Terry's open homosexuality. Yet Terry is reconciled to with his son after he attends the play's opening night at Henry's invitation. Unlike Claudius and Gertrude, Henry and Terry demonstrate the mutual affection and thoughtfulness necessary for a successful marriage.

As expected, the company's most fragile psyche belongs to Nina (Julia Sawalha), who plays Ophelia. She shares many attributes with her role: problematic relationship with her father, inability to accurately perceive her surroundings (she is terribly nearsighted), and insecurity as to her lover's intentions. She does not go insane as Ophelia does, yet her bad eyesight causes her to fall off the stage and run into walls in a semblance of madness. Whereas Ophelia fragments during the course of *Hamlet*, Nina painstakingly follows Joe's direction and successful builds a believable portrayal. She employs her own sorrow over the death of her husband for Ophelia's sung lament for Polonius, yet suppresses her anger with Joe when it does not fit her performance. She experiences the greatest triumph of the company in that she reaches a reconciliation with her father, enters a romantic relationship with Joe, and emerges as an accomplished actor.

Tom (Nicholas Farrell) also experiences overwhelming success through his performance as Laertes, Fortinbras and various other parts. After the successful performance Tom receives an offer for the same movie contract that Joe rejected. The shallow and vapid Tom displays none of the aesthetic reservations that prohibited Joe from accepting the part. Just as Fortinbras usurps Hamlet's temporal power, Tom commercially triumphs over Joe. Tom similarly succeeds in his performance of Laertes. He takes the simplicity and directness of Laertes to a comic extreme, sincerely viewing himself as a New Age martyr. He agonizes over the many indignities he must endure: "I'm committed to this project 132%, you know that. Everything that I am as a human being is here [...] But all I ever get back from people is ridicule. Let's all have a cheap joke at Tom's expense, well that's fine that really is perfectly all right because my shoulders are broad."[30] Just as Laertes' lack of guile leads him into Claudius' trap, Tom's overt simplicity will allow him to succeed as a movie star. Film roles would probably suit Tom best as he prefers the designer's cardboard audience to a real one because they would never cough.

Superficially, the witty and dependable Vernon (Mark Hadfield) exhibits few similarities with his role, Polonius. He insists on playing the aging advisor to overcome his child-actor past. Yet like Henry and Nina he turns his character's weakness into a personal strength. Among the company members Vernon becomes a 'reverse-Polonius' and plays the role of a sincere and successful advisor. He works tirelessly as a promotional assistant to Joe and serves as a literal chorus by documenting the rehearsal process with his video camera. He admits to Molly "I like being needed. It's a new experience for me".[31] Much of Polonius' treachery could be explained as a misdirected desire to be needed. Vernon succeeds by directing his talents appropriately.

A Midwinter's Tale 303

Vernon offers his most effective advice to Carnforth (Gerard Horan) who plays multiple roles in the production. Carnforth initially appears as the most negligible of the company. His résumé exhorts his variability and facility with multiple disguises. This protean ability lands him the roles of Bernardo, Horatio, Rosencrantz *and* Guildenstern. In the course of the rehearsal process Carnforth exhibits characteristics of all his roles. During the early rehearsals, he demonstrates the terror of Bernardo by recalling his own fear of disappointing his mother. His pathetic attempts to mask his alcoholism recall Rosencrantz and Guildenstern's transparent duplicity. Carnforth assumes the reliability and self-awareness of Horatio after Vernon's cogent advice. In a suitably avuncular Polonius mode, Vernon observes that Carnforth's talent as an actor lies in his inherent affability: "The audience can't help themselves [...] You walk on, they love you. Because you're yourself. You're kind and vulnerable and [...] well [...] nice."[32] Carnforth overcomes his doubts and makes his first entrance serene with self-confidence because "they love me you know."[33]

Carnforth also displays a sophisticated understanding of the text. At the film's lowest emotional depth, when Joe announces that he that must leave for Hollywood, Carnforth tries to assuage the actor's guilt with Horatian fellowship:

> Easy on yourself old chap. I'm afraid we can't all afford the luxury of nourishing our souls. That's the prerogative of the romantics among us, I fear. These things happen. What does he say, "if it be now 'tis not to come, if it be not to come it will be now, if it be not now, yet it will come, the readiness is all."[34]

Placed in this theatrical context, Branagh applies Hamlet's fatalistic lines to the acting profession. Commercial success in show business relies heavily on "being in the right place at the right time." Those that excel in this random environment are the ones who are "ready" when the big break comes.

Joe's sister Molly provides the film with a normal, i.e. non-actor, perspective. Her presence and supportive relationship with her brother emphasize the film's familial theme. Terry, Carnforth and Nina all experience reunions with family members. These reunions contrast directly with the butchered families of Hamlet and Ophelia. Branagh reverses Shakespeare's movement from stability to disintegration and isolation; *A Midwinter's Tale* rebuilds and solidifies families rather than destroying them. Branagh uses *Hamlet* as the basis for a comedy, not only to evoke laughter in a string of jokes, but also in the classical sense to transform and unify characters. In *A Midwinter's Tale* the tragic text of *Hamlet* not only reveals and unifies the players and but also secures a happy ending for them.

In the screenplay's introduction Branagh admits that many will find the ending sentimental. "It is. Actors are sentimental. It's one of our weaknesses. But I believe at times one of the gloriously silly ones."[35] The ending may appear overly saccharin, but only if the audience believes in the permanence of the "theatre family." For all their sincerity, emotional intimacy and good intentions, theatrical relationships remain transitory. The bonds that actors genuinely form for one production often do not last outside the immediate theatrical environment. Many actors dream of forming a permanent repertory, as Branagh has done, but few achieve this. As *A Midwinter's Tale* ends with a post-play celebration on Christmas Eve, the seasonal significance becomes evident. The productive and valid family of players will fade with the new year.

Branagh's film lauds the resilience and inherent nobility of actors. It also illuminates the text of *Hamlet* by focussing on the players' perspective.Similar to Stoppard's explication of Rosencrantz and Guildenstern, Branagh offers an imaginative and affectionate interpretation of *Hamlet*'s traveling players. *A Midwinter's Tale* could be viewed as an explanation of their fate. After a hasty exit in Act Three, the players survive the slaughter of Elsinore, reaffirm their familial commitment, and add what they have witnessed to their repertory. More than likely, they will perform "The Murder of Hamlet" at the Polish Court.

Notes

1. Kenneth Branagh, *A Midwinter's Tale: The Shooting Script*, New York: Newmarket Press (1995), p. 3.
2. *Shooting Script*, p. 28.

A Midwinter's Tale 305

3. Kenneth Branagh, *Hamlet: Screenplay and Introduction*, New York: Norton (1996), p. xii.
4. Branagh, *A Midwinter's Tale: Shooting Script*, p. vi.
5. Branagh, *Shooting Script*, p. 9.
6. Branagh, *Shooting Script*, p. 43
7. Branagh, *Shooting Script*, p. v.
8. Branagh, *Hamlet: Screenplay and Introduction*, p. 64.
9. Russell Jackson, "Film Diary" in *Hamlet: Screenplay and Introduction*, p. 181.
10. Branagh, *A Midwinter's Tale: Shooting Script*, p. vi.
11. Branagh, *Shooting Script*, p. 11.
12. Branagh, *Shooting Script*, p. 12.
13. Branagh, *Shooting Script*, p. 34.
14. Branagh, *Shooting Script*, p. 45.
15. Branagh, *Shooting Script*, p. 53
16. Branagh, *Shooting Script*, p. 47-8.
17. Branagh, *Shooting Script*, p. v.
18. Geoff Brown, "Old Dogs Revel in New Tricks", *The Times* (Nov. 19, 1995), p. 5A.
19. Tom Shone, "Reeling from Charm Offensive," *The Times* (Dec. 3, 1995), p. 3C.
20. James Wolcott, *The New Yorker*, 71 (Feb. 12, 1996), p. 85.
21. Branagh, *Shooting Script*, p. 30.
22. Branagh, *Shooting Script*, p. vi.
23. David Jays, *Sight and Sound*, 5 (Dec. 1995), p. 47.
24. Branagh, *Shooting Script*, p. 2.
25. Branagh, *Shooting Script*, p. 3.
26. Branagh, *Shooting Script*, p. 64.
27. Branagh, *Shooting Script*, p. 74.
28. Branagh, *Shooting Script*, p. 96.
29. Branagh, *Shooting Script*, p. 63.
30. Branagh, *Shooting Script*, p. 72.
31. Branagh, *Shooting Script*, p. 85.
32. Branagh, *Shooting Script*, p. 90.
33. Branagh, *Shooting Script*, p. 102.
34. Branagh, *Shooting Script*, p. 97.
35. Branagh, *Shooting Script*, p. vii.

WORDS, WORDS, WORDS: SEARCHING FOR *HAMLET*

H. R. Coursen
(University of Maine, Augusta)

Hamlet. Castle Rock. 238 minutes. Producer: David Barron, Director: Kenneth Branagh. Camera: Alex Thompson. Music: Patrick Doyle. Design: Tim Harvey. Costumes: Alex Byrne. With: Richard Attenborough (Ambassador), Brian Blessed (Ghost), Kenneth Branagh (Hamlet), Richard Briers (Polonius), Michael Bryant (Priest), Julie Christie (Gertrude), Billy Crystal (First Gravedigger), Judi Dench (Hecuba), Gerard Depardieu (Reynaldo), Reece Dinsdale (Guildenstern), Nicholas Farrell (Horatio), John Gielgud (Priam), Rosemary Harris (Player Queen), Charlton Heston (Player King), Derek Jacobi (Claudius), Jack Lemmon (Marcellus), Michael Maloney (Laertes), John Mills (Norway), Simon Russell Beale (Second Gravedigger), Rufus Sewell (Fortinbras), Timothy Spall (Rosencrantz), Robin Williams (Osric), Kate Winslet (Ophelia).

Branagh's *Hamlet* is a film searching for the 'full play', looking for a way to get all those lines into a film. The words themselves are not easy, indeed are often terribly complicated. Horatio says "And even the like precurse of fear'd events,/ As harbingers preceding still the fates / And prologue to the omen coming on", lines that sound ominous enough, but are probably a bit difficult for the post-modern ear. Laertes tells Ophelia that "nature crescent does not grow alone / In thews and bulk, ..." (1.3.11-12). No doubt she understands, but do we? Claudius' disquisition on "would" and "should" (4.7.113-22), which is not in Folio, might work opposite a better Laertes than the film provides. Still, Branagh would have been forgiven by most for omitting the lines. Hamlet and his "famous ape, / [Who] To try conclusions, in the basket creep[s]" is there to baffle Gertrude and us. "They are sheep and calves that seek assurance in that", Hamlet says in the graveyard and we have no time to ask "What is 'that'." Perhaps we recall Hamlet's "so capital a calf"?

These lines are usually cut, even from stage productions, which can often get away with some fruitfully mysterious language. But the surprising thing about the film is how many of the words *do* work. Some lines get in the way of emphasis, and of the actors, but Shakespeare builds that sense of linguistic labyrinth into the script – as with Polonius, who forgets where he was, and with Player, who remembers ("But orderly to end where I begun..."). A *Hamlet* "presented [...] in its convoluted Machiavellian entirety", as Janet Maslin describes it ("More Things in *Hamlet* ...", C7), permits it to express its "contradictory thoughts and actions" and "its characters' often confused motivations", as Terrence Rafferty says ("Solid Flesh", pp. 80-1). Furthermore, the full text makes connections that edited versions tend to erase. The lawyer's "fine pate full of fine dirt" (5.1.104) links up in this full-text production with Osric, "spacious in the possession of dirt" (5.2.89), for example. Laertes' "Contagious blastments are most imminent" (1.3.42) rubs against Hamlet's "hell itself breathes out / Contagion to this world". (3.2.379-80) It is "the breathing time of day" with him, Hamlet says, not knowing that the point of Laertes' sword will be "touch[ed]" with "contagion" (4.7.147).

If the play is a fictional construct, the 'full play' is another kind of fiction. The script is usually shaped for production as it was, no doubt, in 1601, as Stephen Orgel argues: "Shakespeare habitually began with more than he needed [...] his scripts offered the company a range of possibilities [...] the process of production was a collaborative one of selection as well as of realization and interpretation" (p. 7). The very fact of multiple texts, Orgel suggests, may signal different performances dictated by different audiences and shaped by the variable pressures of politics ("What is a text?", 1991, pp. 83-7). *Hamlet* delivers multiple texts and almost 3800 lines (Kliman, p. 311).

Efforts at getting the words in involve a lot of walking. The camera tracks along with Horatio as he explains the background for the "post-haste and rummage in the land" to Marcellus and Bernardo, and with Laertes as he lectures Ophelia. The camera is stationary at the end of a long corridor as Hamlet approaches with Marcellus and Bernardo, discussing the "one defect" theory. Hamlet's encounter with Rosencrantz and Guildenstern finds them striding around in the crisp snow as the camera tracks and pans and the three discuss "the late innovation". That walking, though, reaches the destination of Hamlet's disappointment, framed in an archway, when Guildenstern admits "We were sent for". (2.2.291).

Branagh seeks the *effect* of language, even language in conflict with its medium. Film is not a linguistic medium. The only one in the film who understands that language is merely an adjunct to unspoken purpose is Fortinbras. The rest wander about/in a pre-Wittgensteinian world of absolutes and essentialist premises, not grasping that concepts change their meanings as the conditions that quiver around them also change. No doubt exists what "rights of memory" means when Fortinbras is seated on the throne with a hundred bayonets at his beck.

The culmination of the film's concentration on language is Hamlet's "How all occasions" soliloquy. As the camera trucks back, it shows Hamlet "isolated, cut off, frozen out, and reduced in filmic terms to making grand gestures of impotent frustration while Fortinbras [...] gets on with the business of doing" (Crowl p. 2). His words fly up and out and lose themselves against a cold sky and a frozen mountain range. The larger point is that he totally misreads Fortinbras. Fortinbras *may* be "puff'd with divine ambition" – that is, with psychic inflation that makes one feel like a divinity – but Hamlet tangles his own subjective state with what he thinks he has observed. That is a trait of intraverts that Hamlet had demonstrated in contrasting himself earlier with the Player's response to Hecuba. Here, he asks "How stand I then?" when he sees Fortinbras finding "quarrel in a straw / When honor's at the stake". Hamlet himself is trapped in a "fantasy, a trick of fame" constructed in the labyrinth of his own psyche. In one of the film's few 'interpretations', Fortinbras will demonstrate that he is not out for honor. Power is his game and it requires an army, after which words can follow. The play's emphasis on sheer language and on the dangers of interchanging phrases for reality or words for essence becomes clear at this moment. As Hamlet constructs self-lacerating myths of his own identity, Fortinbras, like Bolingbroke from a previous play, moves his troops silently. Snow muffles the marching footsteps and fog conceals the troops as they close in, not on a little patch of Poland but on Elsinore. The command is "Go softly on".

The irony that the full text establishes is that Hamlet understands the phoniness of the language of court and courtier, as Branagh demonstrates in 5.2 with virtuoso parodies of each style, first in telling Horatio of the rewriting of the commission to England, then in describing Laertes to Osric. But Hamlet assumes no satiric stance relative to *his* meanings. Both he and Horatio look up words in books – as if the meaning of Ghost were *there*, or as if Osric's affectations were only to be laughed at. The film shows that Osric does well. He gets Hamlet to the duel. Hamlet is only interested in showing his linguistic skill. Osric is willing to take the odd hits if he can maneuver Hamlet into the hallway.

If Hamlet functions in two linguistic traditions – the essential and the satiric and sees no relationship between the two, Claudius is trapped between the essentialist and the utilitarian. "*There* is no shuffling", he says of heaven (3.3.61), but later suggests that the foils may be exchanged "with a little shuffling". (4.7.137) Fortinbras becomes a Claudius free of a brother's murder, and it is Fortinbras, not Claudius, who completes Claudius' work and knocks down the statue of King Hamlet that had stood at the palace gates.

The film meanders meaningfully toward the explosive center of "Gonzago". We get all that walking, steps on steppes in this land of perpetual winter, as the words visibly contact the cold. The Ghost walks not on Elsinore's parapets but on the frozen ground just beyond the iron fence around Blenheim Palace. Snow flicks in front of the faces of Horatio and the guards as they decide to report to Young Hamlet. It is winter inside, too. Gertrude wears a white wedding dress – the large court scene is the reception. After the good-natured discussion with Laertes and Polonius, the disquisition with Hamlet is private, until Claudius says "For let the world take note". Hamlet has been forced to promise to obey Gertrude. Claudius then places the official interpretation on what Hamlet has said. The scene has more of an edge with Jacobi's sneering agreement and Patrick Stewart's suave walking out among the courtiers to tell them what to make of it in the 1980 BBC-TV version. At the end of the scene in Branagh's film, white flowers drop down on the new King and the continuing Queen, leaving Hamlet, who has brought some of the night into the scene, adrift in the blossoms that have also brought images of winter to the scene.

As he pursues the Ghost, Hamlet remembers his father lying in state, which we are shown in flashback ("the sepulchre / Wherein we saw thee quietly inurn'd...", 1.4.48-9). Hamlet's questions are shouted out against a steaming wasteland of leafless trees, where sulfurous flames burst from the earth as in a low-budget combat film. Hamlet's frantic shouts are then contrasted with the Ghost's intense whispering – as if even what he does impart is on the borderline of what can be said to "ears of flesh and blood". Hamlet and the Ghost do not appear in the same frame. Instead we get radical close-ups of their eyes – the Ghost's an intense blue with dark, dilated pupils. At the end of the scene, Hamlet's hand of flesh almost grasps the Ghost's gauntlet. While I prefer the heights for which the lines call: "the dreadful summit of the cliff" and while the scene reminds me of some of the landscape of *Frankenstein*, Branagh is at least reaching here for a cosmic effect, a dimension that most recent versions of the play have not attempted to achieve.

In the full-text Noble production of 1992, in which Branagh played Hamlet, the Ghost (Clifford Rose) emerged from a Pet Sematary and inducted Hamlet into Valhalla at the end – these "bright ideas" marred a splendid production. The best recent Ghost was that in Ron Daniels' RSC 1989. He (Russell Enoch) was in complete steel, which Fortinbras also wore at the end. The anachronistic militarism that King Hamlet represented entered finally to take over. The world was pulled back in time, not permitted to go wherever Hamlet would have taken it had he been "put on". In Branagh's film, the ground heaves as the Ghost walks, as in an uncontrolled chain reaction, until the others swear on Hamlet's sword. Then the earth settles down. But the smoky fissure remains an emblem of damnation, as later, when Hamlet thinks of his father ("'Tis heavy with him", 3.3.84) while Claudius attempts to pray. It may be necessary to use the techniques of the horror film to capture the Ghost for today's audience, but I think we might have been educated to the heights for which the script calls and perhaps to the irony of the Ghost being up *there*. In this film the word "cellarage" becomes a metaphor for below. In the script it is a word for the lower levels of the castle. The Branagh approach contrasts with the Zeffirelli film, its parapets and its quiet, even exhausted, Ghost (Paul Scofield). Here, one almost expects to see the Weird Sisters bubbling up from the dry ice.

Other flashbacks in the Ghost's narrative include Claudius's seduction of Gertrude, first as he instructs her at a version of curling and finally as he is permitted to unlace the myriad strings of her corset, and of the murder of King Hamlet. Even in his orchard it is winter, icicles hanging on the wall, as Claudius' treacherous steps are muffled in the snow. The King awakens, however, and points at Claudius before he tumbles into the snow and dies like one of Napoleon's soldiers on the retreat from Moscow.

Except for the murder of the former King, Branagh avoids the other flashbacks that Olivier provides in his film – one for Hamlet's visit to Ophelia's closet (cf. 2.1.74 ff.) and one for Hamlet's encounter with the pirates (cf.his letter in 4.6), for example. Perhaps Branagh's most effective flashbacks involve Ophelia.

Searching for *Hamlet* 311

As she says "I shall obey, my lord" to Polonius, she thinks of herself and Hamlet making love. The flashback provides a powerful undercutting of the moment of her obedience. I was reminded of Montgomery Clift flashing back to Elizabeth Taylor as George Eastman goes off to die in George Steven's 1952 film *A Place in the Sun* – a terrible counterpull of life and promise against the killing energy that awaits him in that room. Another effective use of flashback occurs with Hamlet's letter to Ophelia. Although prompted by Polonius, Ophelia is unable to read it and rushes away in tears. Polonius continues. A dissolve shows Hamlet and Ophelia together as Hamlet says "O dear Ophelia [...] adieu." (2.2.119-21) Then Polonius concludes. The visualization reinforces the relationship as much more than the tumble that the frequent flashbacks depict and underscores Ophelia's sense of loss. She has not been building castles in air.

In her madness, she comes to believe the official line – that because she has submitted, she has been discarded. She remembers her lovemaking with Hamlet as she mimes the sexual act during her song about "the maid that out a maid / Never departed more." Love has become the stuff of conventional song, has become just sex, just what Laertes and Polonius warned about, when it might have been something more. She thought it was. The film shows vividly that the priggish Laertes and the politic Polonius offer their advice too late. Ophelia needs something else from them. Now her love for Hamlet and his for her suffer, like so much else in Elsinore, a terrible reduction of value. We find out what it might have been in lines that are never cut from a production – those in which Gertrude reveals her hope that Ophelia might have become "Hamlet's wife" (5.1.238).

Hamlet's "To be" (3.2.129 ff.) is delivered with a bare bodkin pointed at one of the many mirrored doors in Elsinore's great hall. Hamlet looks at himself, of course, although Claudius and Polonius are behind one of those mirrors. Later, Hamlet will almost impale Claudius with that blade and will thrust Polonius through. Kate Winslet's colorless Ophelia enters without reading on the book Polonius has given her. That makes Hamlet's line about her "orisons" merely a generalized wish. She has sought him out, it seems, to return his gifts. After kissing her, Hamlet interprets her action in returning the gifts as merely a ploy to re-establish contact with him. A noise alerts him to eavesdroppers. He whispers "Where is your father?" (3.1.130), giving her a chance to tell him the truth. He drags her with him as he opens door after mirrored door and finally presses her face against the two-way mirror behind which Claudius and Polonius lurk. We share their point of view, as Claudius restrains Polonius from intervening. Hamlet shouts "all but one" at the invisible Claudius. (3.1.148) It is a parody of the casket sequence in *The Merchant of Venice*. Hamlet almost catches Claudius behind the door. Polonius' "we heard it all" (3.1.180) is an acknowledgement that Ophelia has been badly used and is excused from further involvement in a stratagem run amuck.

At the "Gonzago" play, Winslet's Ophelia has her one good moment. Her "Still better, and worse" (3.2.249) refers to their lovemaking, which she hopes Hamlet remembers. Hamlet leaps on to the stage to confront both Gertrude and Claudius. He is revenging himself for their having manipulated him from the same space in the first court scene. He takes the vial of poison from Lucianus, as he did in the 1984 Birmingham Repertory production, directed by Jacobi, and narrates the end of the play. It catches Claudius' conscience. He flashes back to the look of reproach his brother had given him after the poisoning. But Claudius does not give way publicly. He demands light and exits. Hamlet attempts to get Horatio to agree with him, but Horatio does not. Hamlet, recognizing Horatio's disagreement, changes the subject and calls for the recorders. The energy generated in this scene sustains itself into the prayer scene (3.3.36ff.), where we actually get Hamlet's imagined pop of a blade through the confessional window and into Claudius's left ear – the same ear into which Claudius poured the poison – and his wish to send Claudius' soul to that place signalled by the crack in the earth where his father is. The film seems to assume, with Hamlet, that King Hamlet is damned. That makes the Ghost's sympathetic appearance later rather odd. But perhaps we are meant to believe that Hamlet reads the Ghost correctly there in Gertrude's closet, that tears are preferable to blood. By then, though, Polonius has bled copiously on to Gertrude's floor and we almost expect her to ask, Who would have thought the old man to have had so much blood in him? Here, Gertrude *almost* sees the Ghost. A shot from behind Hamlet and Gertrude shows them both looking at the place where the Ghost disappears. Gertrude almost shares Hamlet's vision, as she did in John Barton's 1980 stage production.

The film provides an intermission before Act 4, Scene 5 and begins again with Claudius' voice-over narrative which summarizes events. The speech is moved from 4, 5, 77-96, meaning that Claudius already knows of Ophelia's

Searching for *Hamlet*   313

distress. We have seen her scream against the iron gate of the chapel where Polonius has been placed – a verbalization of Hecuba's silent scream in the dramatization of the Player's speech. (2.2.446 ff.) One wonders how Ophelia can be a political danger wrapped as she is in a strait-jacket and locked in a padded cell. Who can "botch the words up fit to their own thoughts" if Ophelia is as isolated in her 'wasteland' as Hamlet is in his? This Ophelia has been driven mad, like the tortured women Rebecca West describes in *The Court and the Castle* (1957). Unlike most recent Ophelias, there is little method in her madness, that is, no intention, no production-informing design to it. That Ophelia is the *jester*, assuming the role vacated by Hamlet and, long before, by Yorick, does not emerge here.

Jacobi's Claudius saves the first mad scene. (4.5.131 ff.) He feels guilt and responsibility at first. Gertrude has untied Ophelia's strait-jacket. Claudius pulls her to her feet. He says "conceit upon her father", thinking that she won't understand him. She breaks from him and runs away. He tries to retie her strait-jacket after she says, meditatively and sanely, "My brother shall know of it". She runs out of the room. Now, Claudius senses danger. The scene is about *him*. Any effort he makes to be *human* is compromised by the fragility of his political position. He is "a man to double business bound". After the killing of Polonius, Rosencrantz and Guildenstern go on and on about kingship. Claudius puts his head in his hands for a moment. Near him, an attendant pours wine. Claudius looks up, startled. It reminds him of the sound of poison in the ear. After a now hardened Claudius says, "I have sent to seek him and to find the body", Rosencrantz reports back that he cannot get from Hamlet "where the dead body is bestowed". Rosencrantz has gotten things out of order. "But where is *he*?" demands Claudius, showing us what the line means. First things first, you idiot! Claudius knows that dead Polonius will stay, but that living Hamlet is dangerous. Jacobi's emphasis illuminates an entire sequence.

The second mad scene (4.5.151 ff.) makes the mistake of centering on Ophelia, as opposed to having her force the center and demand attention. In the Cuilei Arena (D.C.) production of 1978, Ophelia burst in upon a state dinner party. In the Lyth film of 1984, she breaks into a formal garden party for visiting diplomats. In each case, she is an embarrassment and a danger and, in each case, other agendas are at work on stage. *Conflict* between the outer politics of Elsinore and its inner disturbances is vividly depicted. Here, we get Ophelia's final song "And will a not come again" excruciatingly slow and closed-up upon. It is like waiting through an NBC time-out. Surely, as she sings away in the background, Claudius could begin to temper Laertes between thumb and forefinger. Or, the camera could flash back to "Ryan's Daughter" – anything but this wan Ophelia singing on and on. It does not help that Michael Maloney plays a drama-school Laertes, a few variations in intensity but all on one-note. True, Laertes is a "foil" to Hamlet, but here we never sense anything but an actor playing a role. Why couldn't he appal Claudius with a smiling "To cut his throat i' th' church", showing Claudius a dimension very far beyond the "bounds" that the King himself would set and suggesting that Claudius has gone beyond any point of return to normality? Why couldn't Laertes at least have been to Paris? I kept wondering how Depardieu would have been as Laertes. Ironically, the stereotype does deliver one interesting moment. "Drown'd? [...] O [...] Where?" (4.7.166) The "O" takes in the information. The "Where?" suggests that he is expected to say something, to ask a question at least. For him, Ophelia is not important anymore. It is feeding time at the zoo of revenge. Instead of giving Claudius a pause to think ("Now out of this –" 4.7.105-6), Laertes just blurts "What out of this, my lord", stepping on the beat that would create a convincing impatience in contrast to Claudius' calculation.

Early on we get shots of Fortinbras (Rufus Sewell) sharking up his resolutes, being admonished by Old Norway, and marching as to Poland. The only one paying any attention is Horatio, who stands outside the gates of Elsinore reading in a newspaper about Fortinbras' army. This moment occurs between "Madness in great ones" (3.1.188) and "Speak the speech." (3.2.1 ff.)The inner world is circling in on itself and getting ready for the ambiguous climax, the understandings and misunderstandings of "Gonzago". Horatio is aware of some force gathering out there in the desert places beyond the gates. We learn, step by step, that Fortinbras' request for "quiet pass through [Denmark's] dominions" (4.4.3-4) is a pretext for a surprise attack. Wherever Elsinore may be, Fortinbras is very much in a world where flags of truce mean nothing, as in the Hungarian uprising of 1956. As Crowl aptly says, Fortinbras is "closing in on a world crumbling from within" (p. 3). An explosion from inside meets implosion from outside. We know, though he does not, that Fortinbras is closing in on a "sight [that] becomes the field". It is not as if one movement of plot could forestall another, as in the classic cross-cutting of separate but simultaneous converging actions that E. W. Griffith perfected in "Birth of a Nation". Fortinbras is launching his final attack as Hamlet apologizes to Laertes. Will Fortinbras get there in time to kill Claudius and Hamlet or will they die before his troopers break through the windows? How will Denmark be destroyed? It is a question of timing. The reality of a new world, the twentieth century, rushes toward a comic opera court.

Osric, who has been given an honorary medal for possessing dirt, attempts to escape his complicity in the matter of the foils. He gets nailed by one of Fortinbras's men but survives to misidentify the "warlike volley" and hold out his bloodcovered hand as a dying warning to the court below. He earns his medal posthumously as Fortinbras steps in to a *fait accompli* and the gaudy uniforms of Elsinore flee in search of Nelson Eddy. While Fortinbras is ready for battle, he doesn't even need a mopping-up operation. Inner Denmark has destroyed itself. As Claudius and Polonius look in through the mirror on Hamlet, only a few eyes are looking outward. As Fortinbras moves, events conspire to assist him. Finally, he and his troops move through those mirrored doors. Again, he is Bolingbroke loosed within the script of *Hamlet*.

Crowl (p. 1) likens Branagh's approach to a Russian novel, specifically *War and Peace*. Borodino, that novel's battle, on 7 September 1812, was inconclusive, but its conclusion was Napoleon's retreat from Moscow, beginning on 19 October, and the destruction during that long agony of withdrawal of the Grande Armee. In the twists and coils of the complete script, revenge or lack of it is diminished as an issue. The weight of the narrative takes on an independent status, as Kutusov, the Russian general, knew that history would, regardless of Napoleon, and as Fortinbras knows his army will, regardless of vows to the contrary and words like "honor" and "quiet conveyance". Ironically, Fortinbras' army *is* quiet, muffled in snow and fog, any telltale clink of equipment drowned out by the tumult inside the Danish throneroom.

Some smaller moments are superbly realized. Among the Players' props is the head of an ass. Their courtly repertory includes other plays than "Gonzago". But it is in the outer play that its main character says, "Why, what an ass am I!" (2.2.578) Branagh's is the first production I have seen in which Hamlet *should* recognize Yorick. The skull has the same buck teeth as the Yorick in the flashback that accompanies Hamlet's apostrophe.

One of the more difficult moments for any Hamlet is his outburst at Ophelia's grave. (5.1.249 ff.) Branagh's graveyard scene comes alive at this point. In the best filmed version of the scene – Ragnar Lyth's 1984 production – Horatio knows whose funeral is approaching through the mud. He would like to get Hamlet away from there! Here, he is merely a passive recipient for Hamlet's commentary. Branagh, however, translates "Hamlet the Dane" into a powerful statement of the love he *did* have for her, expressed here in hyperbolic o'ertopping of Laertes, but, in its excess, showing all the retrospective regret for what he did not do or could not do at the time he loved her. One signature of a Branagh film is a male figure pinioning another male figure, as Branagh's Henry did Scroop in the 1989 *Henry V*. Here, Laertes throws his prayer book at Hamlet – one of the few overtly anti-sacramental actions in the film – then jumps on top of him, shouting at him a few inches away from his face. It is perhaps the only moment when the *relationship* between the two young men is expressed beyond the words ("For by the image of my cause I see / The portraiture of his", 5.2.77-8).

For some reason, Branagh eschews facing the camera directly, an approach that served his Iago well in the Parker *Othello*, where Iago's sense of humor, however warped, coerced our own uneasy laughter. Perhaps because he does not look at us, Branagh's film Hamlet has no sense of humor. In the Noble stage version, Branagh's Hamlet did address the audience with a quiet authority that pulled us in. The stage Hamlet also acknowledged the audience, making an unforgettable gesture towards us with his right hand, palm upward, as he said "guilty creatures sitting at a play". As we are not inhabiting the same space, Branagh's film Hamlet, played as detached and isolated, comes off as remote. But that is not bad, since the approach decenters Hamlet and helps the film to become a coherent sequence of multiple narratives. It is not just Hamlet's story. Even Horatio's eulogy, often a final statement of closure, as in Olivier's film, emerges here, we know, a moment before Fortinbras will burst in.

Some parts of the film do not succeed. When Hamlet says "Well, God-a-mercy" to Polonius (2.2.171), Hamlet is wearing a skull. Where did that come from? In Jacobi's Old Vic and BBC performances, he had borrowed a skull from the Players' prop chest and donned it before "Gonzago", superbly playing the role of jester and

Searching for *Hamlet*

anticipating his later meeting with Yorick. Here, it is just a localized effect, with neither motive, opportunity, nor resonance. When Hamlet greets the boy actor, saying "Pray God your voice, like a piece of uncurrent gold, be not cracked within the ring" (2.2.423-4), he hopes that the boy's voice has not changed. What can that mean when the person addressed *is* a young lady, daughter of one of actors? How did Branagh's academic advisors let him make so obvious a mistake? Here is an instance of the historical moment Branagh has selected for his film colliding with one of the conventions of Shakespeare's stage. The script is a victim of Branagh's decision to play "Gonzago" as a post-Restoration vehicle. One of the actor's wives looks confusingly like Ophelia, so for a moment one may wonder how she got in among them. The boy actor in the Olivier film *did* look like Ophelia once Hamlet put a blonde wig on the lad. The resemblance disconcerted Olivier's Hamlet.

The star turns – *Hamlet* as vaudeville – work out pretty well. Jack Lemmon is awful as Marcellus. I expected him to break into the march of the wooden soldier at any moment. Gerard Depardieu is a splendid Reynaldo. He pulls Polonius' Danish tart to his lap, considers taking her to Paris with him, then realizes that France has willing dames enough and flings her from him. Here was a case where one wished the script longer, so that it could incorporate Reynaldo's report. Rosemary Harris and Charleton Heston bring a naturalistic style to the couplets of "Gonzago" and create a sense of humanity in their characters and of love between them. Billy Crystal is fine as First Digger, but Simon Russell Beale as a somewhat slow-witted but good-hearted Second Digger is even better. Robin Williams stays within the role of Osric and demonstrates its importance.

Richard Briers, one of Branagh's regulars, shows that Polonius does not like to be insulted or ordered around by Hamlet. He conveys a sense that he outranks Hamlet – or *should* – by dint of his position as Claudius' prime minister. He makes it clear as well that, while it's a man's world, he loves Ophelia. He recognizes, too late, that he has wronged her by involving her in state matters. Briers' is a complicated and interesting performance, but he gets nothing from Ophelia or Laertes to create the family dynamic that is often a fascinating subplot in the performance of this script. That such a study is intended is suggested by the strange glitch in continuity that finds Polonius, Ophelia, and Laertes suddenly in the chapel for Polonius's advice to Laertes, a scene meant to parallel the earlier conversation between Claudius, Gertrude and Hamlet as the full court looks on.

The final scene, always difficult to orchestrate, goes reasonably well in the film. The full script permits the unnamed Lord (here, a bastard brother of Laertes, we assume) to be implicated with Osric, Laertes and Claudius. The Lord adds a sinister dimension. So much is aligned against Hamlet at the end! The duel itself is so violent that further violence, like Laertes' tumbling from a balcony, is hard to respond to. In the Noble production, Hamlet threatened Osric with his sword, on "I'll play this bout first" (5.2.276), revealing a dangerous side that critics were reluctant to credit to Branagh's performance. Get away from here, sirrah, Hamlet was saying. You are likely to be hurt. Here, when Horatio tries to help him after Laertes's treacherous thrust, he pushes Horatio roughly away. No "sweet prince" here! This late and uncharacteristic action made me wish that Branagh's Hamlet had lost control from time to time earlier, as Jacobi's Hamlet did, often sneering at himself, verging on madness and realizing it, and as Mark Rylance's very antic and nasty and often very funny Hamlet did in the 1989 RSC production. That pushing of Horatio suggested a dimension that Branagh's Hamlet might have explored.

A small, but strange instant, occurs when Laertes wounds Hamlet and *then* says "Have at you now" (5.2.294). The textual cues are not absolute here, but surely the line precedes the action. In the Folio, when Hamlet "Hurts the king." (s.d.), "All" cry "Treason, treason." (5.2.315) Here, treason is mentioned, tentatively by one lady in waiting and then by another, after Laertes says "the King's to blame". Such a change very much rebalances the power relations at the end. This is confusing, not because anyone is likely to recognize the transposition, but because a) Claudius has the political retinue here, not Hamlet, even if Claudius's Switzers are still AWOL, and b) because Claudius' immediate crimes, as Laertes outlines them, do not constitute treason.

Since Branagh looks down at the end from a balcony, we may anticipate the Olivier leap. Instead, Hamlet tosses his sword, impaling Claudius and then pendulums a chandelier down on Claudius and swings down himself, like Robin Hood or Scaramouche. Earlier, Hamlet and Claudius had confronted each other face to face in a brilliant rendition of the "so my mother" sequence. (4.3.53) The two are alter egos there, as they had been when Hamlet threatened his own mirrored image *and* Claudius' hidden body with the bodkin. This is where the Freudian interpretation finds its point in the film, in Hamlet's relationship with his "father", Claudius, not in his desire for Gertrude. The final confrontation of King and Prince promised closure to this process, but it was not forthcoming. Claudius lies pinioned beneath the chandelier and Hamlet uses his gloved hands to lap wine into Claudius' mouth. In the 1960 Austrian production, Maximilian Schell holds the chalice to Claudius' lips. The latter (Hans Caninenberg) accepts the wine as his due. The moment reflects its sacramental premises, however distorted by Hamlet into an anti-Eucharist, and captures the relationship between Hamlet and Claudius, which is finally reciprocal and recognized. It is a quiet moment when the play needs one. Branagh's production builds towards that possibility and wastes it.

The large effects – the tossed sword and swinging chandelier – implicate *Hamlet* in a film tradition far removed from the issues of the play and rob the scene of the intimacy that might have circled around the antagonists and of the power that might have resonated from their final shared moment. Hamlet's "union" is "there" too. Here that moment is predictable, not surprising for all of its high jinks, and not particularly interesting. It is scripted, not interpreted.

"Sorrow" comes easily to Fortinbras' lips. These are obligatory words after goals have been accomplished. In the 1994 Ashland, Oregon production, Hamlet (Richard Howard) and Fortinbras (Michael Behrens) had met, although Fortinbras did not know who that young man had been near the fjord until he saw Hamlet at the end. At Ashland, Fortinbras' "sorrow" was motivated by his recognition of the dead prince. In the Branagh film, Fortinbras sets up against one wall of the throne room. His will be a narrower view than that which previous kings of Denmark have assumed. They enjoyed the long vista down the expanse of the room of court, but they did not see much from there. Fortinbras will not see into the distance, but he won't have to squint to control what he does see. Ceremony will be a corollary of power. Horatio's warnings at the end about "men's minds [being] wild" (5.2.386) is pro forma. There's no fear of further outbreak. Fortinbras' troops have everything covered. Horatio, who saw Fortinbras coming in *his* mind's eye, now conducts a charade of negotiation with the new king. The Ambassador from England, recognizing that he has no further business here and may himself be in danger for having carried out a bogus command, slips out.

As I said, the film occurs in winter. Fall, however, according to Northrop Frye incorporates "The sunset, autumn and death phase. Myths of fall, of the dying god, of violent death and sacrifice, and of the isolation of the hero. The archetype of tragedy and elegy" ("The Archetypes"; see also the *Anatomy*, pp. 206-23). As Wallace Stevens says

> Life contracts and death is expected,
>   As in a season of autumn.
>   The soldier falls.   ("The Death of a Soldier")

Fall is the time of "the sere, the yellow leaf." It is cold on the parapets, but it is not near Christmas, if Marcellus' take on the supernatural is accurate. It has to be autumn in Elsinore for Gertrude's narrative about Ophelia's drowning to be plausible. That is, unless Gertrude is lying. We are shown, a couple of times, a river wandering the mist below the palace, but in this wintry landscape, nettles would be the only available foliage. Crow-flowers, long-purples and daisies cannot be growing nearby, although Gertrude scrounges up a few daisies for Ophelia's funeral. We could be led to believe that Ophelia's cold dousing – apparently an effort to freeze the insanity out of her – causes her death, and that Gertrude's narrative is an official metonymy invented to cover this event. Laertes would be seen to accede to this version in spite of its palpable impossibility. The problem in the film is that Ophelia is shown to have secreted a key in her mouth. Thus are we asked to believe that she *did* escape the cold showers and somehow gathered flowers in the winter waste beyond the gates before her cruise down the river.

The music tends to be a vague theme searching for a melody. It occasionally reinforces action, as with Ghost, or when someone practices Bach in the Chapel, lending an ironic liturgical tone to the script (as is effectively done in the Trevor Nunn Thames Television version of *Macbeth*), or in the slightly dissonant cello and viola that signal Claudius' confusion as he tries to pray. (3.3.) It is mostly "irritating muzak", as Crowl says (p. 7), a seemingly obligatory set of strings, perhaps an occasional horn or tympany, that slither in behind "what a piece of work is a man" (2.2.391) or halfway through "To be or not to be" (3.1.56 ff.) and play on, with the abandon of a metronome, regardless of the radical variations in tone of the Nunnery and Graveyard scenes, as if to normalize all of this into the experience of the aisles of a supermarket. The music is particularly unfortunate when the lines are spoken so superbly by Branagh and Jacobi, who have 55% of the complete script. Furthermore, there are cues for the music in the script – Claudius' "kettle drum and trumpet" (5.2.267 f.) and Hamlet's "recorders" (3.2.336 ff.) The songs of Ophelia and the Gravedigger could weave a Bahktinian counterpoint to the high rhetoric and hidden politics of the court. Instead we get the annoying repetition of a theme that Tchaikovsky discarded over a century ago. I look at my notes and find the plea, "No music, please!" but find the hope ignored over and over again. Natural sounds – Hamlet striding into the nunnery scene, for example – or soundlessness – the boots of an army muffled into silence by the snow – make their points brilliantly here. After the music stops in the graveyard scene, Claudius's cold line "Good Gertrude, set some watch over your son" (5.1.290) brilliantly conveys its subtext of alienation – partly because no music rides under to muffle it.

The interior of the palace is supposed to suggest an illusory zone of comfort and safety. But that effect goes too far. Branagh does nothing with the setting. It is just background. What is being discovered in and around this world? It is post-Darwinian, it seems, in that religious issues are subdued. It is a Catholic world, with a crucifix and a confessional, but ritual is hardly brought to the fore. The production takes its cue from Claudius's decision for the funeral of Polonius. Michael Bryant's Priest makes it clear with a nod that what enlargement of Ophelia's obsequies is by command of the King. It is a time after the invention of the photograph, as the miniatures of Claudius and King Hamlet show and as a fraternity composite – that probably contains pictures of Rosencrantz and Guildenstern – on the wall of Hamlet's room also shows. The film, though, does not implicate itself in the texture of its times. One does not want a script buried in detail – the Papp-Antoon *Much Ado* and the Loncraine *Richard III* translate each script into narratives about America in 1910 or Great Britain in 1937. One of the few good moments in the former shows a bust of Shakespeare on Don Pedro's mantlepiece. One of the few good moments in the latter shows the royals watching a newsreel of Edward's coronation, a sudden shift in point-of-view that also captures a way of life that, as Fitzgerald said, is "very different" than our own.

In Branagh's film, it is cold outside. Breath flows visibly and nostrils click in the ice. Fires burn and coal smolders in braziers. Inside there is no sense of cold. It is all quite snug. No fireplaces seem to exist. We can almost hear the central heating purring in the cellarage, and, in spite of the ubiquitous candles, there have to be other sources of light in these bright interiors. A spotlight shows incongruously behind Horatio as he prepares to watch Claudius, and is turned on as Hamlet, master of ceremonies, takes the stage before "Gonzago." It may seem that I am asking a question like "where is the music coming from?" but film allows a world to be implicated in the stuff of its historical moment. What Frederic Jameson calls "the cultural logic of late capitalism" surely has its analogue in the cultural logic of late nineteenth-century Europe. This film does not reveal that cultural logic, though Horatio does show surprise as he read "pirates" – we don't have pirates anymore, do we? One of the few exceptions to what I am saying is the arrival of Rosencrantz and Guildenstern on a narrow-gage engine. Rather than seeking Hamlet out, they have been playing with the royal toys. In the Noble production they arrived at Elsinore on a train. This odd moment in the film seems to have been borrowed without effect from the stage production. Elizabeth Wheeler, in discussing Stoppard's film of *Rosencrantz and Guildenstern Are Dead*, argues that Stoppard "revels in the detailed physicality of place missing from theatrical production" ("Light it up and Move it Around", p. 5). Mirrors exist in the world of Branagh's *Hamlet*, but few shadows. The only scene that *looks* candlelit is the one for Hamlet's "witching time of night" (3.2.387) soliloquy. For the rest of the time, the light is like the music – bland, accommodating, predictable, unchanging. What happened to the winter so effectively imitated in the white blizzard that fell on the exit of Claudius and Gertrude from the first big scene? It was a localized effect, almost accidental, it seems, certainly incidental. The film has brilliant backgrounds but little sense of people actually living in its depicted world.

One can object that genre films, as Leo Braudy says, "concentrate not on the reality of a society or the reality of the past, but on an individual's perception of those superhuman orders and what they mean" (*The World in a Frame*, p. 122). One could further object that *Hamlet* is a good example of this subjective vision. Olivier's film, with its stairways, corridors, and dizzying heights, is certainly a good example of "a world that must be read as a projection by the character rather than as objective reality", according to Kathy Howlett (*Shakespeare Framed an Reframed*, p. 13). "Hamlet's difficulty, like that of the artist", she says, "is the problem of determining the aesthetic shape of this performance within the limits of the frame" (p. 20). Branagh's film, like Zeffirelli's sun-drenched version, is more of an "open form" film than Olivier's. In the open form, the character finds that "possibilities of the self to be a freedom rather than a prison" (Braudy, p. 225). A character discovers who he or she is through an "interplay between artifice and the reality that refuses control" (p. 66). The way a play works on the 'reality' of a specific spectator, for example, varies from spectator to spectator, as "Gonzago" and as *Hamlet* prove. The full script grants perceptions to others beside Hamlet. Certainly Branagh's film does. The Ghost's subjective vision fixates on his own murder and Gertrude's betrayal, both imaged in flashbacks. Claudius glimpses the murder just as the Ghost had described it. Claudius' horror at what he has done is captured in both the Ghost's *and* Claudius' memories of the poisoning. Ophelia reverts to the most important events in her young life, her making love with Hamlet.

Gertrude is granted neither flashbacks nor the ability to see the Ghost in her very chamber, but that lack is an aspect of her characterization. What I hoped for here was not an absolutely objective reality surrounding these events, but some sense of 'thingness', like that of the peasants coming out of hiding to salvage their belongings after the final battle in Kozintzev's film of *King Lear*, or children skating on a pond at the edge of the woods, oblivious to the superhuman orders and not caring what they mean. I wanted more of the interplay between the real surfaces of the world and the constructed psyches inhabiting those surfaces.*

This production is based on the First Folio, with additions like the disquisition on drunkards-and-defects and some of Hamlet's lines to Gertrude in the Closet scene, added from the Second Quarto. So we hear "landless resolutes", "solid flesh", "our philosophy", "a god kissing carrion", "blood and judgment are so well commingled", "advise me", "most royally", but not "Rosincrane" or "politician" for "pelican." The choice of the Folio culminates in Fortinbras' command for "the body" of Hamlet, as opposed to Q2's "bodies" of those littering the throne room floor. (5.2.403) Fortinbras makes a ceremony of transition out of Hamlet's funeral, using Hamlet's "dying voice" to confirm the changing of the kings. Fortinbras understands the cues given him by Horatio. Whatever he believes, Fortinbras knows that the world requires its rites of passage. The camera tracks back past Hamlet, stiff and holding a sword in a much better coffin than Ophelia's ill-constructed pine box, and continues until it stops on the head of the statue of King Hamlet, an icy tear in his cast-iron eye.

The music that does work in the film is the intentionally pretentious and over-blown "In Pace", sung by Placido Domingo. It is the 'official word' on Hamlet, no doubt commissioned by Fortinbras for that occasion. A thousand soldiers have stood at attention for the final orchestral chorus, a hundred muskets have risen for a last volley, and, at the gates, the statue of King Hamlet comes tumbling down. The new king's men pull the head into the wreckage of its body. The tear of ice bounces from the decapitated face. King Hamlet becomes Ozymandias, Lenin, Ceausescu. The credits roll and Domingo sings on.

This is finally a romantic *Hamlet*. Elsinore, for all of its corruption and espionage, is a world of student kings and princes. I was reminded of that great musical comedy star, Alfred Drake, presiding delightedly over his new dispensation in the Gielgud-Burton version of 1964. But beyond Branagh's Elsinore are Fortinbras and fascism. The nineteenth century surrenders to the twentieth and anything of value lies back there as the new century swings in on a steel hinge.

* For a contrasting approach, see Trevor Nunn's autumnal *Twelfth Night*, where setting and season contribute to tonality and meaning. Another example of inner and outer weather and their interactivity is Branagh's tiny and wonderful film, *A Mid-Winter's Tale*, where the inside of the abandoned church does not forget that the lakes outside are cold as iron.

Works cited

Braudy, Leo. *The World in a Frame: What We See in Films.* Chicago UP, 1976.
Crowl, Samuel. "*Hamlet*". *Shakespeare Bulletin* (forthcoming).
Frye, Northrop. "The Archetypes of Literature". *Fables of Identity.* New York: Harcourt, Brace & World, 1963.
Anatomy of Criticism. Princeton UP (1957), pp. 206-23.
Howlett, Kathy. *Shakespeare Framed and Reframed* (forthcoming).
Jameson, Frederic. *The Cultural Logic of Late Capitalism.* London: Verso, 1991.
Kliman, Bernice. *Hamlet: Film, Television, and Audio Performance.* Madison, N. J.: Fairleigh Dickinson UP, 1988.
Maslin, Janet . "More Things In *Hamlet* Than Are Dreampt Of In Other Adaptations." *New York Times.* 25 December, 1996, C7.
Orgel, Stephen. "The Authentic Shakespeare". *Representations* 21, 5-25.
"What is a Text?" in *Staging the Renaissance: Reinterpretations of Elizabethan and Jacobean Drama.* Ed. David Scott Kastan and Peter Stallybrass. New York: Routledge, 1991, 83-7.
Rafferty, Terrence. "Solid Flesh". *The New Yorker.* 13 January, 1997, 80-1.
Wheeler, Elizabeth. "Light It Up and Move It Around". *Shakespeare on Film Newsletter* 16:1 (December, 1991), 5)

SUITING THE WORD TO THE ACTION: KENNETH BRANAGH'S INTERPOLATIONS IN *HAMLET*

David Kennedy Sauer
(Spring Hill College)

Kenneth Branagh has made the first postmodern film of *Hamlet*, picturing the title character as a swashbuckling hero swinging from the chandeliers, instead of the usual brooding melancholic: "Our Hamlet is not presented as a man predisposed to melancholy. His usual character, described so often in the play, is vibrant, curious, positive."[1] Critics are confused by this radical departure from the conventional modernist Hamlet who is usually the center of the play.[2] Branagh decenters the play, spreading the story to other characters, so that Hamlet's story becomes one among many. Indeed, the film does not end with the death of Hamlet; two more stories are concluded after he dies. Fortinbras assumes the crown, and his soldiers occupy Elsinore; Norway has conquered Denmark. Then Old Hamlet, the statue with which the film opens, and which becomes the Ghost, is destroyed by Fortinbras's men. Its destruction depicts the end of the Ghost's control of the narrative of Denmark. Such a radical re-thinking of the cultural icon *Hamlet* requires analysis of Branagh's design and conception.

In some ways, this *Hamlet* has more in common with Henry Irving, as described in a review of 1874, than any twentieth-century interpreter:

> The scene changes to a dazzling interior, broken in its artistic lines and rich with architectural beauty: the harps sound, the procession is commenced. The jewels, and crowns, and sceptres dazzle, and at the end of the train comes Hamlet [...] a man and a prince in thick robed silk and a jacket, or paletot, edged with fur, a tall, imposing figure so well-dressed that nothing distracts the eye from the wonderful face.[3]

This sounds like Branagh's film, except that Claudius and Gertrude are the resplendent ones. Rather than upstaging Claudius and Gertrude in the midst of their wedding celebration, this Hamlet is discovered by the camera standing alone, in the wings, in black, as if he does not want to appear at all.

In this opening scene Hamlet is no hero ready to confront Claudius and Gertrude, but rather a solitary peripheral character. By contrast, Claudius is decked out in a red military uniform with gold braid while Gertrude is in wedding dress, white gloves, and veil. The scene concludes with the newlyweds running out through confetti. The atmosphere of celebration resembles Branagh's triumphant ending to *Much Ado About Nothing* – but now the celebration is illegitimate, undercut by the initial appearance of the Ghost.

In his first soliloquy, Hamlet is clearly the one who does not fit in, the spirit of anti-celebration at the wedding. This production presents the political/social world of the others as real, and Hamlet's problem is that he cannot join in with the others. So Hamlet's view does not relegate everyone else to minor roles as they fit into his dilemma as he is in the conventional unified production.

Branagh's approach follows the three main lines of postmodernism which Grady delineates.[4] The first is the "abandonment of organic unity as an aesthetic value and practice" (207). The argument is taken from Jameson: "The former work of art has now turned out to be a text, whose reading proceeds by differentiation rather than by unification" (208). The differentiation, in this case, is shown in the treatment of the minor characters, whose stories are as valid and central to them as Hamlet's own is to him. Secondly, there is an "anti-hierarchical impulse and practice" (208), which is reflected in the privileging of minor characters over major ones. The published film script, *Hamlet by William Shakespeare: Screenplay* does not distinguish between high and popular art, as indicated by casting and by including intertextual references to Laertes and Hamlet as if "it's *High Noon*" (167), and to Francisco as "the Gert Fro[e]be character in *The Longest Day*" (154).[5] And cinematically there are allusions, notably to Eisenstein and Olivier.[6] Linked with this is the obvious corollary, the third characteristic, "a 'fragmentation' and decentering of subjectivity" which is reflected both in the decentering of the story to tell every other character's story, as well as in the abandonment of

Hamlet's consciousness as the focus of the play. That kind of a subjectivity which dominated modernist Hamlets will not do for a postmodern one.

Of course, Branagh's is not a fully postmodern version which would attack the authority of the text as do Goddard's *Lear* or Müller's *Hamletmaschine*. They deconstruct, reorder, and reassemble the text in the director/playwright's new vision. Branagh, however, follows the Folio text faithfully, and unifies the production in its costuming and setting in the late nineteenth century.[7] Even the choice of period reflects the postmodern convention usually seen on stage,[8] but rarely in film until the latest productions, which also take place in alternative times from the conventional Renaissance setting: Ian McKellan's *Richard III*, Baz Luhrmann's *Romeo and Juliet,* and Trevor Nunn's *Twelfth Night*.

Such an approach requires a wholly different understanding of minor characters – to start with, they are cast with major popular stars in lesser roles. At the New York showing, a program was distributed which pictured only the ten top stars: Branagh, Derek Jacobi as Claudius, Julie Christie as Gertrude, Jack Lemmon as Marcellus, Billy Crystal as First Gravedigger, Rufus Sewell as Prince Fortinbras, Gérard Dépardieu as Reynaldo, Robin Williams as Osric, Charlton Heston as Player King, and Kate Winslet as Ophelia. The effect of this is to diminish the role of Hamlet, as, Anthony Dawson argues, happened in the first modern dress *Hamlet*, Barry Jackson's Birmingham Repertory production of 1925:

> One of the keys to the anti-Romantic presentation was to reduce Hamlet's importance, both his stature and his appeal, turning him into one of a group of concerned participants. [...] Here was a Hamlet who was neither famous nor old, not one luminary in a company of nonentities, but simply an actor among many. (88)

The difference here is that the cast includes so many stars that Branagh is one star among many. As in the earlier production, the story that each has to tell is seen as important, so that each gets a full characterization, rather than simply a cameo appearance reacting to the leading actor's lines.

This is clear from the opening of the play, where Jack Lemmon's exceedingly badly acted Marcellus steals his scenes – even from the Ghost.

Lemmon tries to be serious, but seems only comic. Pushing his nose into scenes between Hamlet and Horatio to show Marcellus's serious interest in following their discussion about Hamlet's father, Lemmon becomes a parody of the major actor trying to play a minor character with diligence. Nevertheless, he is riveting, even as a scene-stealer, giving one the sense that Marcellus is important to this story.

A similar minor role is performed by Gérard Départdieu as Reynaldo. His character is a man of few words, but whose reaction to Polonius's suggestions of how to spy on his son gives the sense of a whole character. No stereotypical message-sender to the audience, neither of disapproval of Polonius nor of obsequious acceptance of commands, he sits back in his chair, smoking a cigar, a character in control. He accepts Polonius's excessive suggestions with calm reflection and confidence in his own abilities (both as character and as actor), without Lemmon's editorializing or overacting.[9]

Russell Jackson, *dramaturg* of the production, kept a "Film Diary" which is published at the end of the filmscript. His account of Départdieu is itself a mini-short story. His narration of the final rehearsal is revealing for the Branagh approach:

> At first, Polonius seems to be ordering Reynaldo around too firmly, and a less servant/master approach is suggested: more 'two men of the world'. Polonius' 'Fare you well' must not be too dismissive, and for a moment Dickie [Richard Briers, as Polonius] is saying 'Observe his inclination in yourself' as though he were warning Reynaldo (who in our version probably runs a chain of whorehouses) not to be naughty. Eventually the scene seems like part of (lost) Balzac novel. Depardieu is able to be evil, amusing, vulnerable all at once. He has Polonius' number. (183)

Remarkable is the sense of time taken for rehearsals and openness to explore where the scene might go. When the first attempt yields too masterful a Polonius, then a whole back history of the characters is invented: Reynaldo is no mere servant, but a master in his world of whorehouses. None of this is occasioned by the text directly; it is simply invented to redefine what did not work in a rehearsal when the relationship was too one-sided. The point about many of the minor

Branagh's Interpolations in *Hamlet* 329

characters is that they are equals to the major characters – both in performance, and as box-office stars. This creates a delightful doubleness to the performances. [10]

The acting/directing technique ultimately derives from the Stanislavski method of filling in the full pre- and post-history of a character. It is taken to extraordinary lengths to be incorporated into this film which, by my count, features 45 interpolated moments which are not in the Folio text that was used. Some of these are flashbacks; others are establishing shots for the next scene; more often they are of an interpolated time or place intercut into the present moment of the text, usually with a voice-over. These scenes, are often used as if filling in visually some key point of an actor's improvisation or sense of self just before or after an entrance.[11]

Since the Folio is followed faithfully, the interpolations added to the text are all visual; no new lines are added. Most of these sequences use a voice-over technique showing shots which may illustrate, or elaborate, or even invent new material. At other times the shots may not be implied by the lines at all, as is the case with the freely invented invasion of Elsinore by Fortinbras's troops at the end of the play.[12]

The most complete back story and forward story is that of Fortinbras. His history is recalled in "**flashbacks**" in 1.1 when Horatio narrates the past and in 1.2 when Claudius instructs Voltemand to go to see Old Norway. Fortinbras is shown in simultaneous action in 2.2: as Voltemand reports back to Claudius we see Rufus Sewell look on Blenheim Palace (Elsinore), then Norway (John Mills) summons him for rebuke. At the end of the film, eight interpolated sequences of Fortinbras and his troops are intercut throughout the duel scene, concluding with Fortinbras's coronation, the carrying out of Hamlet's body, Fortinbras's troops outdoors guarding the casket of Hamlet, and their destruction of the statue of Old Hamlet.

This shows how far Branagh goes to fill in the stories of minor characters who are treated as more than mere foils. The interpolation of the invasion of Elsinore at the end of the play is unexpected and not even implied by the text. Like

Ian McKellan's *Richard III*, this is a fantasy of the takeover of the kingdom by an obsessed dictator.

Why make this substantial change to a script otherwise regarded as sacrosanct? It is possible that a fictive Fortinbras might invade Denmark and so defy his sickly Uncle to win more worthwhile territory. Doing so makes sense of Fortinbras's life, as all of these interpolations do for their characters. This approach to Fortinbras presents a theoretical problem: the usual understanding is that Fortinbras is hot-headed, too unthinking, a pure warrior. By contrast he makes the reflective Hamlet seem more sane. But that contrast does not quite work here. For one thing, his ambition knows no limits; Fortinbras seems over the top entirely; the brooding eyes of Sewell imply that he is a driven, single-track thinker. This could hardly be said of Hamlet in Branagh's rendition. What is fascinating is that Branagh does not relegate Fortinbras to a minor reflective role, but gives him a full story of his own, one that even rivals the story of Hamlet.

This is the approach to each of the characters, most of whom are given complete stories. Here Osric is not presented conventionally as effete and gay (e.g. by Peter Gale in both the Richardson/Nicol Williamson and the BBC/Derek Jacobi versions). Instead, as Russell Jackson describes Robin Williams, the approach to the role is to create a whole history: "He is careful to see Osric as a person – a landowning upstart, but with his own sense of place and purpose. Details: he looks round the room nervously (but with only a brief glance) while waiting for Hamlet to answer him" (179). Osric's story in the interpolation is tragic, as we discover at the end of the movie when Fortinbras's troops stab him in the back as they invade Elsinore. So the only speaking character other than Horatio who does not die in this scene joins in the tragedy – another complete change to the playscript that gives finality to the story of Osric.

These interpolations are more than mere acting exercises carried to extremes, however. They are also complex commentaries on the present action. Hamlet and Laertes's swordfight, through intercutting, is made to resemble Fortinbras's invasion of Denmark and conquest of Elsinore. Both fights are motivated by revenge for past wrongs (real or imagined). It is only the scale, and the openness of the assault that are different.

The most obvious place where this commentary is evident is in the seven shots of Hamlet and Ophelia together in her bedroom. The first occurs with Ophelia's voice-over as she responds to Polonius's "Do you believe his 'tenders' as you call them?" Ophelia responds, "utterly panicked and embarrassed" (27), "I do not know my lord, what I should think." Then the filmscript gives the editing cue for the interpolated scene: "**Flash cut to: Interior/BEDROOM Night** Close on HAMLET and OPHELIA as they make tender love" (28). The obvious implication is that this seems to be her memory, and the cause of her "embarrassment" in speaking to Polonius.

There has been more controversy about these shots than any other. Unlike Fortinbras' invasion of Elsinore, the affair between Hamlet and Ophelia is a possible implication of the text, as the many jokes which surround it indicate ("Did Hamlet sleep with Ophelia?", "In my company, always", etc.). Anthony Dawson quotes Olivier as saying "Hamlet is not just imagining what is beneath Ophelia's skirts, he has found out for himself – country matters – for certain" (111). Controversy regarding Branagh's use of the motif has obscured the real issue: from whose point of view is the affair presented? Are these scenes flashbacks? Fantasies? Memories or dreams?[13]

Twice more on the page of the filmscript there are similar cuts to this bedroom sequence: in the first "both naked", and the second "as they make love". Both occur with Polonius's voice-over. Are the cuts meant to suggest that this is the father's imagining of what has happened between Hamlet and Ophelia? Or could they be her recollections, spurred by his words, with no visual clue to the audience. The fourth such cut occurs as Polonius exits the chapel with a "Flash cut to: .... [the lovers] lying together in bed, entwined" with Ophelia's voice-over "I shall obey, my lord." Then "**Cut to: Interior/Chapel day** Ophelia closes her eyes in despair" (29). Here clearly we begin with Polonius's exit, and the cut can only be in Ophelia's mind, made more explicit by returning to her for the final shot and using her voice-over. Again, the sequence has the feel of filling in what the actress imagines or uses for motivation in playing Ophelia in the scene.

Interestingly, Kenneth Branagh, director and star, does not use the same cut/memory to motivate any of Hamlet's speeches. Indeed, we do not know for sure whether this is an Ophelia fantasy or memory. The only other two uses of the bedroom scenes are even more problematic. The first comes when Hamlet's letter is read to Claudius and Gertrude. Ophelia runs out of the scene unable to read the letter, and instead, Polonius picks up the reading, and then "**Cut to ... (Flashback)** HAMLET, undressed, and OPHELIA in her nightgown are sitting at the piano" (54). Hamlet reads the rest of the letter – the verse and the apology, then "**We cut to**" Polonius reading the conclusion to the letter. The problem with the sequence is: whose head is the camera inside of? It cannot be Ophelia's flashback, she has already exited. Is it Polonius's fantasy? The final use of the same memory occurs, appropriately, in Ophelia's mad scene where she sings, "By Cock they are to blame" (127). Here it seems to be in Ophelia's mind, but since she is deranged, is it delusion or reality?

Ophelia's other interpolations reflect Elaine Showalter's study of Ophelia's use in the nineteenth century as a model for madness in women, and both her stage history and the photographic depiction of real madwomen became interconnected.[14] Thus we see Ophelia straightjacketed, and later Horatio opens the spy hole to see her doused with a firehose.

The next time she is seen is after Gertrude has told Claudius and Laertes of her death, and at the end of the scene:

> Dissolve to:
> **Exterior/WILLOW WEIR Day**
> Close on the drowned Ophelia as she lies under the surface of the water. A beautiful, ghostly corpse.
> Dissolve to:
> **Exterior/ELSINORE Day**
> OPHELIA'S watery home in foreground and back, away from the lake, the shimmery evening presence of Elsinore. (141)

Branagh's Interpolations in *Hamlet*

This sequence is a strange one. It does not occur in anyone's head. It occurs after Gertrude's revelation of the death and just before the graveyard scene. Again, it gives completeness to Ophelia's life by picturing her death as the classic Pre-Raphaelite painting of John Everett Millais appropriate to the nineteenth-century setting. But who is seeing her? The cuts could have come during Gertrude's description as voice-over, but they do not. Here is the first clear indication of an outside narrative presence. The only character who might see all, know all, is the Ghost. The peculiarity of the last cut, to show Elsinore from the perspective of the dead Ophelia, implies that something of the perspective of the dead is at work.

Certainly the Ghost is the focal character in his own set of interpolated scenes. In his scene with Hamlet (1.5) Branagh intercuts nine sequences of flashback to Old Hamlet being poisoned by Claudius. At the Washington preview gala, John Andrews objected to the use of the poisoning sequences in 1.5, contending that they are too explicit:

> I took issue with the kudos Michael Kahn lavished on the use of flashbacks, and I argued not only that the Ghost's description of the poison's effect upon him is far more "horrible" than any visualization of it on film could possibly be, but that when we see Claudius (Derek Jacobi) do the deed the Ghost narrates we are led to believe in the spirit's "honesty" at the moment when the dramatist appears intent on keeping theater patrons, if not Hamlet, in doubt about "some necessary question of the play."[15]

However, a close analysis of the use of these shots shows much more ambiguity than Andrews notes. The implication of his comments is that merely showing a picture of Claudius poisoning Old Hamlet makes it true. Why are pictures any more reliable than words, if they emanate from a voice-over? As with Ophelia and Polonius, one wonders whether what we see emanates from within Hamlet's imagination, the Ghost's memory, or both?[16]

Consider the first sequence of cuts:

                                                              We cut to:
Close on THE GHOST'S mouth.
THE GHOST
Revenge his foul and most unnatural murder.

                                                    Cut to:
         An ear receiving poison
         HAMLET
         Murder?
                                                    Cut to:
         The skin of the ear expanding
         HAMLET seems overcome.
         THE GHOST
         Murder
                                                    Cut to:
         Blood, pus, awfulness
         THE GHOST (continuing)
            most foul, as in the best it is,
            But this most foul, strange and unnatural. (35)

The interpolations seem at first to be in Hamlet's mind, since they come before and after Hamlet's speech. But the last one comes in the middle of the Ghost's speech. Soon after, the Ghost speaks as a voice-over, while we are shown "OLD HAMLET asleep in his wintry orchard" (35). When Hamlet responds, "*O, my prophetic soul! My uncle?*" there is a cut to "The man himself. CLAUDIUS. Smug – self-satisfied. Eyes on the QUEEN" (36) and the Ghost responds, "*Ay, that incestuous, that adulterous beast*" and continues as a voice-over while we see two sequences of Gertrude and Claudius "in a curling competition." In both cases it is confusing as to whether the imaginings are Hamlet's, the Ghost's, or whether they alternate between them. What is fantasy and what is real flashback/memory?

This question is further complicated by an unusual series of cuts at the end of the sequence Andrews noticed. We see the "sleeping peaceful monarch", then "a Figure walks towards" him, "a very close shot of poison entering the ear", "A Jump-cut rhythm of the King's convulsions," concluding with "CLAUDIUS moves away, removing his footprints" (37). For Andrews, the pictures are taken to be real, and in his view all ambiguity is removed for the audience. But at the end of this sequence, not quite indicated in the filmscript, there are close-ups of the eyes of the Ghost, in an effervescent blue, intercut with Hamlet's eyes, as if they had exchanged this vision. The script only says, "We are now Close on the distorted face, a picture of pain [...] The two faces are close together now" (37-38). As the rest of the film implies, Hamlet accepts the vision of the Ghost from this point forward.

The final use of the shots of the poisoning, however, still blurs the boundaries of fiction and reality, as Hamlet intervenes in the play-within-a-play, interrupting Lucianus as he is about to pour the poison in the king's ear:

> HAMLET grabs the poison phial from the actor, and turns on CLAUDIUS. Through the following we track faster and faster towards HAMLET and the KING. Flash cuts of the poisoning. The courtiers reacting. CLAUDIUS's mind reeling. HAMLET possessed. (93)

Again it is unclear whether this is fantasy or reality, a vision conjured up by the play-within-a-play, or by Hamlet's imagining based on the Ghost's words, or by Claudius's own guilty flashback which sets his "mind reeling".

A comparable ambiguity exists in the other extended series of interpolated sequences: those depicting the Ghost's effect either on the earth or in Hamlet's mind. The first occurs after Hamlet leaves Horatio and Marcellus. Instead of merely following the Ghost, this Hamlet is running through the woods, "exploding with terror" (33), apparently searching for the Ghost:

> On and on through the woods we race with our Camera. Explosions through the trees, cracks in the ground, the very earth itself shaking, but still no GHOST.
> HAMLET V/O (continuing)
> *I'll call thee Hamlet,*
> *King, father, royal Dane. O answer me!*
> *Let me not burst in ignorance,*
> Flash cuts of his dead father sear through his mind as his urgent thoughts continue in voice over. (33)

Fires, explosions, and smoke are intercut with pursuit of the Ghost through woods. Are these blasts from Hell as Hamlet runs through the woods? The earth opens – to let a spirit out of Hell? Is this a Hell-driven spirit? All one can conclude about the sequence with certainty is, again, that it resembles an actor's rehearsal improvisation of what images go through Hamlet's mind before he is able to speak with the Ghost. This is the closest that Branagh's Hamlet comes to madness, as well as a rare moment where we are shown an interpolation clearly from Hamlet's perspective.

Once he meets the spirit, the interpolation is more like an illustration of the Ghost's speech than a fantasy/reality sequence. But the pictures start to show what the Ghost says that he is precisely forbidden to tell *"the secrets of my prison-house"*:

> He looks to the ground, where we track across the floor. It cracks open to reveal an ominous gateway to hell. Agonized voices from beyond pierce the night's dull ear. (34)

So even here, in the most seemingly literal of interpolations, the words and the pictures both illustrate and yet subvert each other's reliability.[17]

This duality is further evident in the 'Swear' sequence. The first time the Ghost says "Swear", "Without warning the ground under HORATIO's foot splits apart, smoke rising from the depths" (41). Continually after this, as they move to the different locations of the Ghost, "the earth explodes," "trees still shaking," "ground moving under their feet" and [Hamlet] "brings them to their knees amid the earth-moving chaos" (42). Watching the sequence on film, however, I wondered if this were all Hamlet's sensation, while Horatio and Marcellus did not see it. Part of the problem is due to Lemmon, who seems to ignore all the (later added?) special effects, and just watches Hamlet. Only once did Lemmon turn around, though the whole screen, and all the trees were shaking while they knelt. Horatio (Nicholas Farrell) looked more concerned, but it seemed to me as though his concern was for Hamlet's sanity rather than that the world around him split open and shook violently. Once they both swear, the filmscript simply says, "At last, all is quiet", but in the film the halves of earth slide back in place together on "Rest, perturbed spirit." In this whole sequence the film comes closest to making the interpolated scenes illustrative of the text instead of adding a new possibility to it.

Branagh's use of this filmic convention of interpolation to illustrate is nicely handled at the end of 1.2 as Hamlet goes to his bookshelf and pulls down an

Elizabethan book "on demons and demonology" (23). This Hamlet immediately questions whether the Ghost is a spirit from heaven or from Hell. He does research to try to help him resolve the issue, but does not seem to be in any doubt after meeting the Ghost. This is not a "tale of a man who could not make up his mind", as Olivier's version announces at the outset, but rather of a man who quickly is resolved after the meeting with the Ghost.

In the first of the rebukes-himself-for-not-taking-action soliloquies ("O, what a rogue and peasant slave am I", 2.2.550 ff.), Branagh's Hamlet returns to his room. He closes the door and sags against the doorsill. "Now I am alone." Hamlet is relieved to escape minor characters like Rosencrantz and Guildenstern, who have become frustrating obstacles to be negotiated or eliminated. This is not an introspective, self-torturing Hamlet; instead, in this speech, he is full of anger. Some of the anger is directed at himself but there is none of the usual self-rebuke. Instead: "he rushes to the window, eager to shout to the heavens, "*O vengeance!*" (73).

The difficulty of Hamlet's negotiating his way through the obstacles is demonstrated in two sequences which occur just after the play-within-a-play. The first is the brilliantly staged scene of Claudius in the confessional (3.3). What is extraordinary in the filming of the sequence is the fantasy sequence of stabbing Claudius:

> HAMLET V/O
>
> *Now might I do it pat, now he is praying,*
> *And now I'll do it.*
> He puts the long thin dagger through one of the grill holes and moves it very slowly to a centimetre away from CLAUDIUS's ear. He puts the palm of his hand against the hilt ready to hammer it into CLAUDIUS's skull.
> HAMLET V/O (continuing)
> *and so he goes to heaven,*
> *And so am I revenged.*
> And he does! We see the blood spurt before an abrupt **cut** we are back in real time as before – CLAUDIUS is still praying – HAMLET fine-tuning his revenge. (102)

There was an audible gasp from the audience during this sequence. It is quickly evident that this is totally Hamlet's fantasy. The sequence is the only one in the film which is purely imagined, with no possibility of being real. It comes as a total shock because the other interpolations were at least ambiguously real/or imagined. Later in the same sequence there are cuts of "The Entrance to Hell" and of "The gates to Hell shut fast" as Hamlet decides to delay killing Claudius until he is sure that Claudius will die in a state of sin.

In the next scene we begin to grasp the grammar of this kind of camera work when the Ghost appears in Gertrude's closet, and Hamlet sees it while Gertrude does not. The first shot is a lovely echo of a telling moment in 1.2 when Hamlet is framed between Claudius and Gertrude just before they parade out. This time it comes on "*A king of shreds and patches":* "Suddenly his [HAMLET's] eyes open wide, the atmosphere has changed. He slowly pulls away from his mother and we see THE GHOST, with them by the window" (108). What "we see" is shown from Hamlet's point of view. Moreover, though the filmscript does not indicate it, the Ghost's make-up changes from the supernatural deathly blue of the first act, to more natural skin tone in this appearance, emphasizing the family togetherness. Right after this, when Hamlet asks the Ghost "*What would you, gracious figure?*": "GERTRUDE sees nothing of the spectre. Only her son responding with sheer lunacy [...] to [...] nothing" (108). In this case, the camera first shows us Hamlet's view of the Ghost by the window, then, after his line to the Ghost, a shot of the same window with nothing there. It is for us to realize that the camera has switched perspectives from Hamlet's to Gertrude's.

Another point of view emerges here, not Hamlet's, not Gertrude's, and not even the Ghost's, but ours: "We see all three close. The complete family, now all unable to reach each other and all heartbroken by the frustration of the attempt" (109). Thus, more than just an echo of the ironic family portrait of 1.2, this shot is designed to give us the impression of a simultaneously joined, and yet tragically separated family.

The most fascinating part of Branagh's use of the interpolations, therefore, is the perspective from which they are generated. In the example above, clearly Branagh gives first Hamlet's, then Gertrude's perspective on the Ghost, then a perspective outside of all of them. It is unusual for any director to take multiple perspectives on a play, especially on *Hamlet*, and all the more rare that the star/director shares focus with the other players. As I have tried to argue, Branagh uses these interpolations to broaden the context, and thereby to show other characters' views, imaginings, stories. He seldom uses them to amplify his own perspective or presence. Even in the most obvious instance where an interpolation might appear, in Act 4 when the sailors bring Hamlet's letter to Horatio, the letter would work as voice-over, while pictures could show Hamlet swinging from ship to ship, à la Errol Flynn. But Branagh never resorts to such a cliché; instead, the interpolations usually add something interpretive, not merely illustrative to the next.

By the end of Act 4, however, this Hamlet is totally transformed, and to swelling Patrick Doyle music reminiscent of *Henry V*, Branagh reveals super-Hamlet, one who is now resolved to be, and is, heroic. The camera on the soliloquy over Fortinbras and his 20,000 men moves back, as Olivier's did with soliloquies (he thought the soliloquies too powerful for a close camera)[18] – and so Branagh becomes the hero from this point to the end of the play, even swinging on chandeliers in the sword-fighting scene. This Hamlet changes radically after meeting the Ghost again.

Once he has made the change, Branagh de-emphasizes the reflective side of Hamlet. Osric's challenge to the duel with Laertes might have shown him debating whether to die or not, but instead presents a new, confident recognition as Hamlet walks with Horatio that "There is a special providence in the fall of a sparrow" and "There's a divinity that shapes our ends,/ Rough hew them how we will". There is a direct line from these sentiments to a heroic: "The readiness is all". No more interiority for this Hamlet; once he has decided to be heroic, he is that entirely!

Thus the interpolated scenes give weight to the lesser characters against whom Hamlet must struggle to fulfill the Ghost's commands. Instead of the obstacles being all internal, his own doubt and inadequacy, this Hamlet's struggle is to work his way around external obstacles – the characters of the court of Denmark. Trying to read and understand them is the new source of uncertainty for Branagh's *Hamlet*.

The result of Branagh's approach is that Hamlet's story becomes one among many. This certainly conforms to postmodern Shakespearean production practice.[19] By the end of the film his personal struggle to assassinate Claudius seems less significant when the whole kingdom is lost to a monomaniacal Fortinbras of Norway. One wonders if this diminishing of significance does not apply to all the interpolations, which are so visually arresting and often unexpected that they have the power to throw the whole work out of balance. What Branagh tries to do is give us a heroic model of Hamlet – not the tortured melancholy Dane, but an active avenger. To do this, however, requires giving substance to the external characters, obstacles, which Hamlet must negotiate, and letting them tell their own stories. But these stories are not always fully revealed in the text and so require interpolation to be completed. And when Branagh revises Shakespeare in order to tell all those stories, Hamlet can be upstaged, and Branagh must press hard to present the heroic Hamlet to keep the play in balance.

Another way to consider this use of interpolations is to reexamine again the question of point of view. Throughout the film, there is an emphasis on eyes, and on point of view. Ophelia describes Hamlet as the "th'observed of all observers" after the magnificently set "To be or not to be" scene in the Hall of Mirrors. In that scene Claudius and Polonius watch Hamlet with Ophelia through a two-way mirror, even as he pushes her face against the glass and we see their reaction. Soon after, Horatio watches Claudius with opera glasses from his box at the play-within-a-play. All of the ceremonial scenes continually emphasize that there is an audience for every royal act, not to speak of spies like Rosencrantz and Guildenstern.

It is arresting, at the start of the movie, to be given "THE GHOST'S POV" (5). Once the Ghost's POV has been exchanged with Hamlet in the intercutting of the eyes at the end of 1.5, it seems as if Hamlet sees, to some extent from the Ghost's point of view. The exterior shots of Elsinore/Blenheim, used sometimes between scenes, are another continual reminder that this is the world seen from the perspective of the statue – the Ghost. In a discussion sponsored by the theatre after the film's opening in New Orleans, Andrew Horton, a scholar specializing in film adaptations, speculated that the use of the continually, slow moving camera is a means of conveying something of the Ghost's eye view of the world of Elsinore. A similar point is made by Jack Jorgens of Olivier's similar use of the camera:

> A moving camera implies a shifting point of view, and *Hamlet* is above all a play of ambivalent and shifting points of view. We become the ghost drifting down into the castle or sweeping behind a pillar in the closet scene. [...] The moving camera, taken by many as a gimmick to make a stagey work seem filmic, is a symbol of the impossibility of fixity in a world of flux.[20]

Considering Branagh's film from the Ghost's POV would also explain why so many different stories are told. If the perspective is not Hamlet's but the Ghost's, then the overview of all the stories as perceived from an eternal perspective makes sense. So too does showing the dead Ophelia, not when Gertrude reports her death, as an intercut scene, but between the end of Act 4 and the start of Act 5, followed by a shot of "OPHELIA's watery home in foreground and back, away from the lake, the shimmery evening presence of Elsinore." Again, this seems to be the distant vision of the Ghost.

The strongest indication that the Ghost's POV may be the controlling vision is that the film ends with a final interpolation: the destruction of the statue of Old Hamlet which became the Ghost. As the soldiers dismantle it with sledge hammers, reminding us of the fall of Lenin's statue at the demise of the Soviet Union, there is the implication that the Ghost was as controlling a figure as Lenin himself, and that the destruction of this statue may be all to the good.

In the postmodern world of Branagh's *Hamlet*, the ending appropriately deconstructs the very heroism it seems to posit. Urged on by the Ghost himself, Hamlet gets his private revenge for his father's death, but while he does, the whole kingdom falls into the hands of Norway. It seems as if the Ghost were taking down the whole kingdom with him, through his son. The massacre inside the Hall of Mirrors, the destruction of all the members of the Polonius and Hamlet families, is the family tragedy. But a much larger tragedy is implied in the takeover of Denmark by the black-cloaked troops of Fortinbras.

So the tragedy of Hamlet becomes, in Branagh's construction, one of taking private vengeance by a prince who then ignores the larger issues facing his country. This particular Hamlet's tragedy presents no Aristotelian recognition and reversal in the main character, who never sees or knows the consequences to his actions. But the viewer is given those final interpolations to see the destruction of the statue as the destruction of the Ghost of Denmark, the very Ghost whose story Hamlet accepted so completely at the outset that he became blind to any larger national concerns.

Notes

1. Kenneth Branagh, "Liner Notes" to *Hamlet, Original Motion Picture Soundtrack*. Similarly, John Andrews, "Kenneth Branagh's *Hamlet* Launched at Air and Space Museum", *The Shakespeare Newsletter* 46:3 (Fall 1996) notes that in response to Susan Stamberg's question about Hamlet as "a depressed man in tights" Branagh "went on to observe that in fact the hero we meet in the opening scenes of Shakespeare's play is not a melancholic by nature. He is deeply disturbed, of course, but there are good reasons for what his elders regard as an antisocial disposition" (p. 62).

2. The newness of the approach is indicated by reading the initial reviews which were mostly positive, but not too sure what to praise, or what to query. Matt Wolf, the *Village Voice* London reviewer, was the most negative in longing for the old Hamlet in "At the Movies", *London Theatre News* 10:1, Feb./Mar. 1997:

> It's as if Branagh were so far inside the play that he can no longer communicate what once excited him about it: his obsession, oddly, has served to dim the play's lasting fire. [...] the actor presents a ceaselessly bitter, vengeful prince at some remove from the metaphysician who has moved theatregoers for centuries. [...] He's an angry, even degrading Hamlet, whose treatment of Ophelia is noticeably shocking, but there's scant soul or passion in which to root his thirst for revenge. There was more genuine ache, not to mention sex appeal, in a single soliloquy of Daniel Day Lewis's ill-fated 1989 National Theatre Hamlet than exists in Branagh's entire screen marathon. (p. 3)

By contrast, Terrence Rafferty in the *New Yorker*, "Solid Flesh: The Prince of Denmark and the king of sleaze" (13 Jan. 1997) had a much more positive, if initially baffled response:

> Branagh yields to that temptation ['to act it and make physical sense of its contrariness' – Kenneth Tynan] with wholehearted intensity of someone who does not know that his task is impossible. Maybe it is not after all. In this *Hamlet* Branagh himself plays the unhappy Prince, and so lucidly that every shift in the volatile character's mood seems perfectly natural. He's a startlingly normal Hamlet: neither a madman nor a neurotic, self-absorbed egghead. (p. 81)

Janet Maslin's *New York Times* review, "More Things in *Hamlet* Than Are Dreamt Of In Other Adaptations" (25 Dec. 1996) similarly goes back and forth:

> Kenneth Branagh's fine, robust performance as Hamlet is the bright centerpiece of his lavish new version of the play. This "Hamlet" takes a frank, try-anything approach to sustaining its entertainment value, but its gambits are most often evidence of Mr. Branagh's solid showmanship. His own performance is best evidence of all. (p. B1)

But in *Time* ("The Whole Dane Thing", 13 Jan. 1997, p. 72) Richard Corliss, positive about the movie, was not about the star:

> If there's a lapse, it's in the central performance. Spurning his lines with catarrhal intakes of breath punctuating the bolts of rhetoric, Branagh is a whiz at making the poetry colloquial and intelligible. He spits out the 400-year-old verse like a rapmaster. But he can't so easily make it poetic. [...] What's lacking in this merchant of culture is Olivier's danger, the preening beauty and sweet delirium that makes an actor a star. (p. 72)

3.   J. C. Trewin, *Five and Eighty Hamlets* (1987; rpt. New York: New Amsterdam Books, 1989), p. 9.

4.   Hugh Grady, *The Modernist Shakespeare* (1991; repr. Oxford UP, 1994).

5.   The page references are to the Branagh filmscript *Hamlet by William Shakespeare: Screenplay* (New York and London: Norton, 1996).

6.   A similar view of the popular culture references in Branagh's first film is given by Michael Pursell in "Playing the Game: Branagh's *Henry V*", *Literature and Film Quarterly* 20:4 (1992), pp. 268-76.

7.   The filmscript notes:

> The screenplay is based on the text of *Hamlet* as it appears in the First Folio. [...] Nothing has been cut from this text, and some passages absent form it (including the soliloquy "How all occasions do inform against me...") have been supplied from the Second Quarto. [...] We have also incorporated some readings of words and phrases form this source and from other early printed texts, and in a few cases emendations by modern editors of the play. (p. 174)

8.   Branagh's film was preceded by a stage version at the Royal Shakespeare Company in 1992 of which Anthony Dawson observes in *Shakespeare in Performance: Hamlet* (Manchester and New York: Manchester UP, 1995) :

> Of course, the practical purpose in [director Adrian] Noble's version was not paramount; it arose from the decision, in keeping with the post-modern fondness for allusion and pastiche, to 'quote' Victorian/Edwardian staging techniques; the idea was not simply to allude to them, but to conjure them in order to resist them. This strategy

allowed the production to place itself in relation to tradition and simultaneously to stage a subversion of that tradition" (p. 14).

9. Norman Holland's review, on the SHAKSPER Listserv, notes Dépardieu's performance as one of the best. Janet Maslin in *The New York Times*, however, thought "Some of the star turns are here for blatant marquee value and stand out as gratuitous. (Gerard Dépardieu and Jack Lemmon, as Reynaldo and Marcellus respectively, are here only briefly and look understandably adrift.)" (B1). On that point, Holland observed: "Yes, there are box office stars in small parts, Billy Crystal, Robin Williams, Gérard Dépardieu, but I thought they were directed with discretion, indeed, following Hamlet's recommendations on clowns. (I laughed with delight at Dépardieu's Reynaldo)." (31 Dec. 1996 from NNH@nervm.nerdc.ufl.edu). Maslin misses the point. First, as a director, taking major stars in lesser roles can only upstage the star – so he has little to gain by it unless his purpose was to give prominence to roles usually overlooked, or taken for granted.

10. Branagh did something similar in *Henry V*, which cast the old stars against the new, Paul Scofield and Derek Jacobi in one realm, and the new young players, Branagh and Brian Blessed, on the other. This suited the fiction in which the youthful Henry was intruding on the old and settled feudal order of France.

11. Alan Dent, "Text-Editing Shakespeare with particular reference to 'Hamlet'", in *Hamlet: The Film and the Play*, ed. Alan Dent (London: World Film Publications, 1948, no page numbers; p. 4 of essay):

All the same, it was not without some trepidation on my part – and some hesitation on Laurence Olivier's – that those two whole lines of Marlowe ["Is it not passing fair to be a King/And ride in triumph through Persepolis?"] presented to Pistol and inserted into the filmscript of *Henry V*. What happened? When the film was duly presented, we noted, with a surprise amounting to mortification, that not a single critic appeared to have detected – much less resented – the interpolation."

The Random House Unabridged Dictionary (2nd ed. 1993) defines "Interpolate: 3) to alter (a text) by the insertion of new matter, esp. deceptively or without authorization. 4) To insert (new or spurious matter) in this manner."

12. The forty-five interpolations arranged chronologically, with act and scene (from *The Riverside Shakespeare*), and page number from the filmscript at the end of the entry.

1) Part One: Before the dialogue begins:
    1. **Exterior/MONUMENT Night.** The base of plinth, winter's night, camera pans to Elsinore. (1)
    2. **Exterior/SENTRY POST Night.** Cuts to FRANCISCO's POV of unending darkness. (1)
    3. **Exterior/MONUMENT Night.** The immense statue of OLD HAMLET. (1)
    4. **Exterior/SENTRY POST Night.** Tight on FRANCISCO, terrified. (2)
    5. **Exterior/MONUMENT Night.** We see the statue's hand pull the sword from the scabbard with a savage rip. (2)
    6. **Exterior/SENTRY POST Night.** FRANCISCO frozen in terror. (2)
2) 1.1.40 INTERPOLATION: "The statue come to life! They run for their lives! We are way above them in the night air. THE GHOST'S POV as the Camera rushes from a great height, swooping down on the retreating figures racing across the snow. We almost reach them, but no! Just in time they fling themselves behind a pillar" (4).
3) 1.1.80 ff. Horatio's voice-over to Marcellus and Bernardo about the post:
    Flashback Fortinbras. "We see but cannot hear the dark, wild young man, as he leans yelling" over a table of "military flags and toy soldiers" "ferocious young man" (*Back to real time*). (8)

Branagh's Interpolations in *Hamlet* 345

4) BETWEEN 1.1 and 1.2: "They move off as, we move towards the Danish Royal Crest, atop the gates. The dawn light starts to appear" (11).
5) 1.2.29 ff. Claudius' voice over to Voltemand – is this in Claudius's mind?
   Flashback "wizened frightened old man" (Old Norway) and "surly young Fortinbras" "Tearing up the map" (*Back to real time*) (12).
6) 1.2.257. INTERPOLATION. "He goes back to the ancient tome [...] A heavily bound treatise on demons and demonology" (23).
7) BETWEEN 1.2 and 1.3: **Exterior/PALACE GROUNDS Day.** "We pan down the great South Front of the Palace to find a horse and carriage with luggage being packed aboard" (23).
8) 1.3.99 ff. INTERPOLATION Ophelia Voice-over:
   1. Cuts to Hamlet and Ophelia "as they make tender love" (28)
   Polonius Voice-over:
   2. then "both naked [...] They touch lightly, beautifully" (28)
   3. then "as they make love" (28)
   4. "then, together in bed, entwined" (29). As Polonius leaves, and Ophelia's voice over is heard. Then **Cut to:** OPHELIA closes her eyes in despair" (then cut to Armory with Horatio) (29)
9) 1.4.8 ff INTERPOLATION: HAMLET V/O: "CLAUDIUS AND GERTRUDE [...] With "carousing courtiers" moving to "bridal bed" (30)
10) 1.4.39 ff. INTERPOLATION. HAMLET V/O *"Angels and Ministers of Grace"* (33):
    1. We pan and track with HAMLET as he runs through a wood exploding with terror.
    2. On and on through the wood we race with our Camera. Explosions through the trees, cracks in the ground, the very earth itself shaking, but still no GHOST.
    3. Flash cuts of his dead father sear through his mind as his urgent thoughts continue in voice over.
11) 1.5.25 ff. INTERPOLATION. INTERCUT: HAMLET AND GHOST (35) with:
    1. An ear receiving poison
    2. The skin of the ear expanding
    3. Blood, pus, awfulness
12) 1.5.35 ff. **Exterior/ORCHARD Day (Flashback)** Ghost V/O: OLD HAMLET asleep in his wintry orchard. (35).
13) 1.5.40 ff. FLASHBACK/INTERPOLATION. While HAMLET speaks in V/O, *"O, my prophetic soul"* (36) **Cut to:**
    1. The man himself. CLAUDIUS. Smug – self satisfied. Eyes on the QUEEN. THE GHOST *"Ay, that incestuous, adulterate beast".*
    2. We see the Royal party in a curling competition. GHOST V/O continues:
    3. "CLAUDIUS moves to GERTRUDE and she throws a disk, they embrace"
14) 1.5.59 ff. INTERPOLATION. Cut to **real time**, "Panic in the Ghost's voice" then intercut w. V/O (37):
    1. sleeping monarch
    2. figure walks up
    3. Very Close Shot of the poison entering the ear.
    4. A Jump-cut rhythm of the King's convulsions
    5. Claudius moves away, removing his footprints as he goes
15) 1.5.148 ff. INTERPOLATION. the Swear sequence (41-42):
    1. CUT TO: "The ground [...] Splits apart"
    2. The earth explodes
    3. The earth explodes as
    GHOST O/S *Swear*
    4. Trees still shaking
    5. Ground moving under their feet
    6. Their knees amid the earth-moving chaos.

7. NOT IN TEXT but in the film, "At last, all is quiet" = ground slides back in place together.
16) BETWEEN 1.5 and 2.1: Exterior/PALACE Night. "Meanwhile . . . people are still at work" (43)
17) BETWEEN 1.5 and 2.1: Exterior/PALACE Day. "Elsinore, serene and majestic" (48)
18) 2.2.60 ff. INTERPOLATION. Voltemand reports: with intercuts of Fortinbras and old Norway (51):
  1. Young Fortinbras on horseback
  2. Old Norway reads the news
  3. **Exterior/ELSINORE Night (Flashback)** "Yes. This is what the Norwegian Prince wants."
  4. Old Norway turns and Fortinbras, head bowed
  5. Fortinbras on knees asking for forgiveness
19) 2.2.208 ff. INTERPOLATION: HAMLET'S letter (after Ophelia runs out of the room: **Flashback:** HAMLET, undressed, and OPHELIA in her nightgown are sitting at the piano. Hamlet reads the rest of the letter – in verse – Then back to Polonius reading the conclusion to the letter. (54)
20) 2.2.497 ff. INTERPOLATIONS: **Exterior/TROY Night** OLD PRIAM AND HECUBA
  1. OLD PRIAM, battling in blood and gore to stay alive. (68)
  2. We see the action in violent, gory detail, amid the smoke and flames. (68)
  3. We see PRIAM dying. (69)
  4. To find the distracted and hysterical HECUBA running amidst the debris. (70)
  5. We track her face as she sees the savage murder of her husband. (68)
21) BETWEEN 3.1 and 3.2: Exterior/ MONUMENT Day "HORATIO reading a newspaper detailing YOUNG FORTINBRAS's ongoing incursions across Northern Europe" (83).
22) 3.2.260 ff. INTERPOLATION. LUCIANUS on stage and Hamlet takes over narration with "Flash cuts of the poisoning" (93).
23) 3.3.73 ff. INTERPOLATIONS. The confessional HAMLET V/O: *"And now I'll do it."* (102):
  1. He puts the long thin dagger through one of the grill holes
  2. "We see the blood spurt before an abrupt cut we are back in real time as before – CLAUDIUS is still praying"
  3. Still with v/o: Old Hamlet in the garden, "clutching his ear in pain ... collapsing on the floor—dead"
  4. "The Entrance to Hell"
  Cut to: Claudius's eyes closed and praying. Hamlet (continuing)
  5. "quick cuts of CLAUDIUS drinking, arguing with POLONIUS, in bed with GERTRUDE, kissing GERTRUDE, talking, hiding" (103. going with HAMLET V/O: drunk asleep, or in his rage," etc.
  6. The gates to Hell shut fast. – voice over of Hamlet continues
24) 4.3.68 ff. INTERPOLATION. The body of POLONIUS as it is carried to the Chapel. OPHELIA being restrained by GUARDS. A great primal yell and then she flings herself at the body etc. (119):
25) BETWEEN 4.3 and 4.4. INTERPOLATION. Then: "We see a distant Elsinore, we are reminded once again of its massivity, its loneliness. Still moving, we Dissolve again, to grey misty dawn" (119).
26) BETWEEN 4.4 and 4.5, PART TWO: **Exterior/ELSINORE Day** "A windswept Elsinore looks bleak in the winter light" (123).
27) 4.5 INTERPOLATIONS: Part TWO'S FLASHBACKS TO PART 1 plot review (123) at start of scene with Claudius's voice over from 78 ff.:
  1. POLONIUS's horrific stabbing
  2. Hamlet dragged away to England
  3. gaggle of gossiping courtiers

Branagh's Interpolations in *Hamlet* 347

    4. body of blood stained Prime Minister bundled away
    5. noble features of young LAERTES
28) 4.5.1 INTERPOLATION. **CUT to**: "OPHELIA straitjacketed runs around the room banging herself against walls" observed by GERTRUDE, HORATIO, and the DOCTOR (124).
29) 4.5.20 ff. INTERPOLATION. "She pushes her squashed face along the floor, unable to get up, still in the straightjacket" (125).
30) 4.5.65 ff. FLASHBACK. As OPHELIA does "By Cock they are to blame" there is **flashback** to HAMLET and OPHELIA together (127).
31) 4.5.77 ff. INTERPOLATION. **Interior/ PALACE CORRIDOR Day**
    1. "Many bodies rushing past. Running along the corridors – weapons in hands" (127).
    2. "A great tide of rebellion sweeps away everything in its violent wake – Guards included" (128).
    3. "The rebels charge towards the doors, along the corridor" (128).
32) BETWEEN 4.5 and 4.6: **Exterior /PALACE Day.**
33) 4.6.4 INTERPOLATION. HORATIO opens the spy hole and we see OPHELIA being doused down with a hose (133).
34) 5.1 INTERPOLATION. OPHELIA lies under the surface of the water (141).
35) 5.1 INTERPOLATION. Dissolve to "OPHELIA'S watery home in foreground and back, away from the lake, the shimmery evening presence of Elsinore" (141).
36) 5.1.187 ff. **Flashback.** Two shots of Yorick with Hamlet's voice over (149):
    1. mobile face of this classic clown
    2. YORICK in full swing as OLD HAMLET, GERTRUDE, CLAUDIUS, and YOUNG HAMLET roar with laughter"
37) B4 5.1 and 5.2. INTERPOLATION. "FRANCISCO back in place as formal sentry by the gate" (154).
38) 5.2.194 INTERPOLATION FRANCISCO Again: "but there is nothing there, between Osric and Lord coming to HAMLET" (160-61).
39) 5.2.232 INTERPOLATION FRANCISCO surprised from behind [seeing the invasion coming] with HAMLET'S voice over "*I here proclaim was madness*" (162*).*
40) 5.2.285 INTERPOLATION. HAMLET: "*Come*" Cut to Quick Cuts of FORTINBRAS's Army taking complete control back to Second bout, masks off (165-66.).
41) 5.2.322 INTERPOLATION. The death of OSRIC (169).
42) 5.2.331 INTERPOLATION. **Cut to** The Palace secured [by Fortinbras' men] (170).
43) 5.2.390 INTERPOLATION. The crown is placed on Fortinbras's head (172)
44) 5.2.403 INTERPOLATION. Carrying out Hamlet's body, display of his body in courtyard, surrounded by Fortinbras's troops (173)
45) End INTERPOLATION. "FORTINBRAS's men tear at the great statue, hitting it continually with hammers, until with a mighty crash it falls. Our final frame is the legend on the plinth . . . great broken pieces of stone come falling into shot, the great head first, and gradually obliterate the name HAMLET. For ever" (p. 173).

These scenes can be grouped another way: by character.
Fortinbras: 3, 5, 18, 37, 38, 39, 40, 41, 42, 43, 44
Elsinore exterior: 4, 7, 16, 17, 21, 25, 26, 32, 35
Killing of Old Hamlet: 11, 12, 13, 14, 22
Ghost/Statue: 1, 2, 10, 15, 45
Hamlet and Ophelia: 8, 19, 30
Ophelia: 28, 29, 33, 34
Claudius and Gertrude: 9
Death of Polonius: 24, 27
Hamlet: 6
Player King: 20
Confessional Claudius: 23

Yorick: 36

13. Jackson's "Film Diary" (p. 177) recounts this approach as what seems to be more back history of the "Polonius family":

> Polonius (Richard Briers) was promoted by new king. Laertes (Michael Maloney) is in Paris getting the gentlemanly accomplishments (N.B. not at Wittenberg). Ophelia (Kate Winslett) and Hamlet have been having an affair (yes, they have been to bed together, because we want this relationship to be as serious as possible) since the death of Hamlet senior. (Effect of a surge of feeling in time of bereavement and crisis?)

14. Elaine Showalter, "Representing Ophelia: Women, Madness, and the Responsibilities of Feminist Criticism", in *Case Studies in Contemporary Criticism: Hamlet*, ed. Susan L. Wofford (New York: Bedford/St. Martin's, 1994), pp. 220-40.

15. Andrews, p. 62.

16. Andrews writes of the panel discussion with Branagh and Jacobi accompanying the film's preview: "[Susan] Stamberg mentioned that objections had been raised to some of the flashbacks. In defense of the one that occurs in 1.5 Branagh said: 'Because the Ghost's narrative is so long, it seemed to cry out for illustration.' The director noted that he also thought some visual aids would help the audience 'feel the urgency of Hamlet's mission'"(p. 62). However, I think these interpolated moments are more than mere "illustration".

17. I do not want to give the impression that there are no merely decorative or illustrative interpolations. There are a few. For example, Guildenstern pulls out a newspaper to verify that children's companies are all the rage. That is not quite an interpolation. And there are two strange ones both of Priam (John Gielgud) and two of Hecuba (Judi Dench) to illustrate the Player King's speech. There are not many of these.

18. See Olivier's critique of Cuckor's use of film close-ups for soliloquies in *Romeo and Juliet* in *On Acting* (New York: Simon and Schuster, 1986), pp. 279-81. He concludes: "If Shakespeare has a flourish and a big speech, bring the camera back" (p. 280).

19. Peter Brook began this trend with his production of King Lear. Brook argues that Goneril should not be seen as merely Lear's antagonistic wicked daughter, but rather a character in her own right, whose opening speech should not, indeed could not, be twisted into ironic wickedness without destroying the whole nature of the speech. But once her first speech is taken as sincere, then Goneril becomes evil, rather than being evil throughout as she was usually depicted. The result of this insight is the recognition that all the characters are separate and individual and develop in their own ways, not just the title character. See *The Empty Space* (New York: Atheneum, 1968), pp. 13-14.

20. *Shakespeare on Film* (Bloomington: Indiana UP, 1977), p. 213.

ALL THE WORLD'S A SCREEN: TRANSCODING IN BRANAGH'S *HAMLET*

Anny Crunelle Vanrigh
(University of Valenciennes)

It seems we are in a rich period for Shakespeare on film again after a fallow phase spanning nearly 20 years between the early 70s and the late 80s, which saw only three major productions: Roman Polanski's *Macbeth* (1971), Derek Jarman's *The Tempest* (1980), Akira Kurosawa's *Ran* (1985).

The ebb and flow of Shakespearean films seems to have been ruled so far by the moods of big-money producers who deemed Shakespeare a soft option after the commercial success of Zeffirelli's 1968 *Romeo and Juliet* until, that is, the commercial failure of Roman Polanski's otherwise excellent *Macbeth* spelt the death (or dearth) of Shakespeare on film for a while. Kenneth Branagh revived their interest with *Henry V,* filmed on a shoestring budget in 1989. Excited by the sweet smell of lucre they consented to remember that Shakespeare had an unmatched flair for a good story and a healthy habit of supplying not just one but two plots where a Hollywood scriptwriter nowadays proves barely capable of putting a single flimsy one together. This has resulted in the current flurry of Shakespeare productions: Branagh's *Henry V* was followed by his own *Much Ado About Nothing* (1993) and Richard Loncraine (1996) filmed an inspired version of *Richard III* based on Richard Eyre's production at the National Theatre. Zeffirelli had a go at a short version of *Hamlet* under the combined umbrella of an all-star cast and an all-cut text. *Romeo and Juliet* emigrated to Miami. Even seasoned stage-directors jumped on the bandwagon: Adrian Noble filmed his own stage version of *A Midsummer Night's Dream,* and Trevor Nunn a disappointingly low-key *Twelfth Night* (1996). It seems reasonable to hope that this unprecedented surge will not abate, as films have now two commercial careers and can recoup their initial investment over the years in video sales. *Henry V* is now showing a profit. Can Branagh's big-budget version of *Hamlet* (1996) prove as good an investment for producers with its uncut, four-hour text? A bold gamble indeed, though a shorter version was simultaneously released for financial safety.

This version will probably not be remembered as one of the great *Hamlet*s of all time, whether on stage or film. As Quentin Curtis suggested in his review for the *Daily Telegraph*, Branagh is "an intelligent layman behind the camera". This "friendly dismissal" of the film's artistic merit (some were decidedly less friendly) I will use to advantage. A layman he may be behind the camera, but a layman he is not when it comes to drama. A practitioner of both, he has reflected on the passage from stage to film. Yet *Hamlet* raises questions which *Henry V* and *Much Ado About Nothing* do not. Film thrives on the kind of realism which a History or a Comedy can accommodate. This is not the case with *Hamlet*. Of all plays this is most abstract and, as Anthony Davies noticed, "the director has very little spatial material to work with", which may result in "a major adaptive problem for film".[1] It is moreover an intensely theatrical piece of drama, using the play as a ploy "to catch the conscience of the king". For these two reasons at least, no screen adaptation can expect simply to "dissolve the play into film"[2] unless it merely retains the story line as Zeffirelli did in his *Hamlet* without the play. Branagh's film is a reflection on the passage from stage to screen, a constant dialogue between their respective conventions in which he occasionally comes up with challenging concepts.

"There can be no doubt that the full-scale spoken poetry of Shakespeare's stage and the continuous visual imagery of the cinema can be oil and water", Manvell once wrote.[3] At the other end of the spectrum André Bazin thinks that the opposition between the inherent artificiality of drama and the realism of film can be reconciled by paradoxically reinforcing through film techniques the theatricality of the original, as Olivier did in *Henry V* and Jean Cocteau in *Les Parents Terribles*. Commenting on Cocteau's film Bazin writes:

> Rather than attempt, like so many others, to dissolve [the play] in the film format, he uses the flexibility of the camera to highlight, accentuate,

confirm stage structures and their attendant psychology. Film contributes here what can only be defined as more, not less, theatricality.[4]

This is what Branagh constantly attempts and at times achieves. His camera moves may occasionally be unsure and tentative, they always bear witness that he has constantly in mind the aesthetic issues arising from the transposition of Shakespeare's plays to the screen: the oral-aural character of the stage as opposed to the visual nature of film, the necessity to find cinematic analogies for such specific conventions as the soliloquy, the dumb-show, the play-within-the-play that are so much part of the structure, plot and technique of the original that they simply cannot be bypassed, and finally the handling of a limited, as opposed to a potentially boundless space.

Shakespeare's original public was called an 'audience', modern spectators are 'viewers', a significant shift in language recording a major cultural shift from the ear to the eye. Elizabethan ears were not only trained, but hungry for words, as evidenced by the intricacies of Shakespeare's puns, now largely lost on modern ears. Elizabethan eyes were treated to a meager diet of sets, costumes and props. These priorities were gradually inverted over time: nineteenth-century stages created the sort of brass-button hyper-realism that makes today's cinema look like the natural offspring of melodrama. Such swinging of the pendulum suggests that aural and visual signs cannot coexist and that one must always give way to the other:

> On the stage all the other signs are subordinated to speech (in monologue, dialogue or aside), while on the screen words are secondary, the dialogue follows the image. [...] The screen addresses its public through pictures which often replace words, so much so that words may seem out of place and too much speech may be prejudicial to the effect of a film.[5]

Film calls for the striking of a new balance between speech and image. Some kind of translation from one mode to the other is required, almost inevitably at the expense of the text. In Kosintsev's words, "the aural has to be made visual. The poetic texture has itself to be transformed into a visual poetry, into the dynamic organization of film imagery".[6] A case in point – an extreme case admittedly – is Zeffirelli's substitution of visual correlatives for words, which enabled him to prune the four-hour play down to a two-hour film, in so drastic a way that one critic complained that "Frankly, Franco, that ain't cutting; it's a play" while another quipped: "It's not *Hamlet* without the Prince that I mind so much as *Hamlet* without the words".[7] Hamlet's visit to Ophelia's closet in Zeffirelli's film is an exact visual translation of the gestures and attitudes described in the text, making any verbal accompaniment all but superfluous. Zeffirelli has the Prince, doublet all unbraced, no hat upon his head, as pale as a healthy Mel Gibson will ever look, taking Ophelia by the wrist, holding her at arm's length while, his hand o'er his brow, he looks at her in a way that no amount of imagination might call "such perusal of [her] face / As a would draw it". The eerie poetry of the passage is lost as is, more crucially, its status as the report of a past episode to a present audience, one of the many plays-(or dumb-shows) within-the-play.

To this conception of a Shakespeare reduced to the dimensions of a postcard (or the stamp on it), Bazin opposes due respect of the text. To Zeffirelli's view – smacking of the proud man's contumely – that "with the cinema, you have to make up your mind whether you do a film for a small number of people who know it all – and it's not very exciting to work for them – or really make some sacrifices and compromises to bring culture to a mass audience",[8] he opposes the idea that the text cannot be ignored, as it is the very essence of drama:

> Whichever way one looks at it, a play, whether classical or modern is irrevocably protected by its text. One cannot "adapt" it without at the same time repudiating the original work for another which, though possibly superior, is of a different nature. This only holds, moreover, for minor or contemporary playwrights, as strict adherence to the text must be regarded as a given when working on time-honoured works.[9]

He then goes on to note how film pays increasing respect to the dramatic text:

> The first proccupation for filmmakers of the past was to conceal the dramatic origin of their material, to adapt it, to dissolve it in the film format. This not only appears now to be a thing of the past but today's filmmakers increasingly emphasize the theatricality of their material. This

Branagh's *Hamlet* 353

is inevitable with uncut texts. The playtext, originally written with a view to its dramatic potentialities, contains them all. It determines representational modes and styles; it is always already drama. One cannot both decide to be faithful to the text and divert it from the course of its natural expression.[10]

Still, Branagh's decision to retain the full text in its conflated form[11] was bound to create a major crisis. This is more than film, not to mention the average spectator, can tolerate. Branagh's opening is provocatively clear. There are no credits for adaptation, cast or direction, nothing but the name "Hamlet" on the plinth of the Old King's statue, an inscription which serves as the film's title. This is unmediated drama. Branagh outdoes Olivier here. Olivier had inserted the "dram of evil" speech as a written prologue to his 1948 version, a signal that *Hamlet*, even on film, remained a theatrical construct. Focusing on the name carved in stone, Branagh symbolically displays the whole text on the screen.[12] The script's description of the name as a "screen-filling legend carved deep in the stone: HAMLET"[13] moreover discloses, in a programmatic *double-entendre*, the text's challenge to the filmmaker. The vast expanses of snowy landscape repeatedly seen through the windows of Elsinore are a metaphor of the screen to be filled with the written signs of the play. The passage from the page (or the stage) to the screen is thus a central question for the director.[14] The blank spaces of page and screen must be made to merge.

To merge, not to overflow. Keeping the full text in, Branagh rules out visual correlatives, an unsatisfactory option, for another, possibly just as precarious: illustration. "Branagh seems terrified that the Elizabethan language might sail over heads. [...] And if the text offers the chance for an illustrative glimpse or flashback, [he] leaps in," Geoff Brown reported in the *Times*.[15] Illustration is at its weakest when, trying to match Shakespeare's "morn in russet mantle clad", all the camera conjures up is postcard prettiness. It adds visual variety to long speeches which today's spectators in a non-aural culture might wish to send to the barber's. It is user-friendly when Denmark's Norwegian diplomacy is made accessible by intercut shots of Fortinbras and Old Norway. Branagh occasionally breaks away from mere illustration when words are belied by images. Shots of a couple in bed give the lie to Ophelia's demure protestations of chastity (1.3), adding weight to Polonius's quibble: "Tender yourself more dearly [...] or you'll tender me a fool." The acid test is the reporting of past events, one of the main features of the play. Refusing to go the Zeffirelli way and substitute images for words, Branagh has but two alternatives: concentrate on the narration or on the thing narrated, complete with images *and* comment. He chooses the former - to disastrous effect - in the graveyard scene, raising Yorick from the dead as Ken Dodd. He favours the naked word for Gertrude's report of Ophelia's death, refraining from the Millais effect and, more surprisingly perhaps, for Hamlet's encounter with the pirates related in the letter to Horatio in 4.6. In both cases he seems eager to steer clear of the choices of his predecessors. Though the use of flashbacks and illustration wanes as the film goes on, the overall effect is of a film dying in its own too much.

Yet mere illustration may give way to metacinematic comment. Marcellus's enquiry about military preparation in Denmark (1.1) is a case in point. "Good now *sit down*, and tell me that he knows" is changed to "Good now *look here*, and tell me", acknowledging the nature and requirements of the film format. Here an arresting visual addition makes a further point: Marcellus shows Horatio the current military preparations through a spy-flap which he pulls back to reveal an arms factory working overtime. This is the first of a long list of secret doors, large and small. As the camera moves forward, the frame of the spy-flap becomes that of the screen itself and we are made privy to the "post-haste and romage of the land" from Marcellus's point of view. The spy-flap thus becomes an instance of the fourth wall, taking us to a privileged space of representation which ambiguously belongs both to theatre and film.

This deliberate blending of stage and film is emblematic of Branagh's attempt to "fill the screen with a stage-legend", and one particularly famous for its theatricality. The theatre is the mode, the subject, the driving force and the central metaphor of the play. Failing to come up with proper cinematic analogies would turn the whole enterprise into a mere instance of what Jorgens terms the "theatrical mode", which has "the look and feel of a performance worked out for a static theatrical space and a live audience."[16] This would not be a play while never achieving the status of a film. If the film-maker is not to wander in a no art's land he must strike a balance between realism and convention, drama and film. In this he is bound, in Kenneth S. Rothwell's words, to broaden "the ancient trope of the world as stage to include the world as screen. As the idea of the screen as screen takes its place alongside the idea of play as play, so 'meta-cinema' inevitably emerges alongside metadrama."[17]

The opening scene of Branagh's *Henry V* was striking as it took the spectator on a set cluttered with theatrical props and film equipment, the joint signs of both film and theatre. This became the place for a reflection on the passage from the dramatic to the cinematic medium, the cross-pollinating of film and drama superimposed on Shakespeare's own metadramatic reflection, so that the Chorus's opening words, now emphasizing the parallel between theatre and film, playwright and director, acquired additional resonance and new relevance. The doors opening and closing the film were a visual metaphor of the framing of the play by a prologue and epilogue taking us into, then out of the world of dramatic/cinematic fiction, the way Feste's song takes us out of the Carnival world of Christmas festivities back into the extra-dramatic, everyday world of Lent complete with "hey ho, the wind and the rain" and this unmistakable Monday morning feel.

As *Hamlet* offered no such opportunity for a reflection on framing, Branagh provided it with a sort of Prologue in the form of his small-budget, black-and-white film venture, *In the Bleak Midwinter* (1995),[18] which featured an improbable group of would-be, has-been or might-have-been actors choosing a derelict church as a venue for an even more derelict Christmas production of *Hamlet*. The film, a highly entertaining turn in four acts, is a behind-the-scenes view of the various stages of a theatre production, from casting and initial read-through to rehearsal and first night. *Midwinter* is to Branagh's *Hamlet* what Pyramus and Thisbe is to Shakespeare's *Romeo and Juliet*.

That *Bleak Midwinter* was meant as a sort of apologetic Prologue to the four hours' traffick of Branagh's own film-to-come is made evident by a number of self-referential hints (some actually smacking more of self-appraisal than self-reflexivity): the opening shot of *Hamlet* sets the action on a bitter, cold, very bleak midwinter night indeed which looks back as much to the 1995 film as to the 1601 play – a critic quipped that Old Hamlet "would have died from hypothermia, never mind poison in his earhole"[19] – ; the director-cum-leading actor (Michael Maloney, cast as Laertes in *Hamlet*) is offered what looks like a promising career in the United States. But beyond such topical considerations *Midwinter* more seriously sets the metacinematic agenda for *Hamlet*, inasmuch as it features a long "play-within-the-film" the way *Hamlet* repeatedly offers "films-within-the-play".

Film thrives on realism, the theatre on convention,[20] and *Hamlet* is a meditation on the multiple uses of theatrical conventions. *Hamlet* on screen is apparently a contradiction in terms as there can be no *realistic* equivalent to the soliloquy, the dumb-show or the play-within-the-play. One way out is, as Davies suggests Olivier did, to refuse "to abandon the aesthetic oscillation between theatre and cinema."[21] Branagh settles on another option and endeavours to recover the conventions, theatrical and otherwise, at the root of cinematic realism, establishing that film and drama are "a little more than kin". To do so the camera uncovers a series of analogies between stage and screen, as in the Graveyard scene. The camera first lingers on the classic image of Hamlet holding Yorick's skull, deliberately filmed in the most traditional way, i.e. as an icon of drama. It then proceeds in shot and reverse-shot of Prince and skull engaged in a sort of "one-way dialogue". While Shakespeare dramatized the *memento mori*, passing from the two-dimensionality of the image to the three-dimensionality of the stage representation, Branagh moves one step further, to its "cinematization", passing from a fixed to a changing point of view. Conversely he shows how drama can accommodate and actually contain genres that are thought to pertain specifically to the cinema, e.g. war film and action movie, as in his treatment of Fortinbras's coup "in SAS style",[22] the swashbuckling fencing match or simply the choice of 70mm photography. Explicit references are made in the synopsis to war film or western. "It's *High Noon*" all over again as Hamlet and Laertes stand facing each other before the fencing match. Francisco first catches sight of the invading army "like the Gert Froebe character in *The Longest Day* [...] who sees the massive flotilla coming across the Channel at him".[23] Still, one is left to feel that Birnam Wood moving up to Dunsinane might have been just as relevant. The choice of the cast (Derek Jacobi, Judy Dench, John Gielgud, Simon Russell Beale alongside Robin Williams and Julie Christie) also bridges the gap between the two media with a particular mention for Charlton Heston, of Ben Hur memory, who directed his own version of *Antony and Cleopatra* in 1972. It is all but impossible to see Depardieu (Reynaldo), Heston (the Player King) or Lemmon (Marcellus) without being aware of the film types they represent. Sir Richard Attenborough may well make an appearance in 5.2. less as the English ambassador than as a man knighted for his achievements in the British film industry. This refers the audience to a different fictional world, emphasizing Branagh's determination to blend the two formats. Hamlet's plea for naturalistic acting in his advice to the Players (3.2) takes on additional relevance as a sly comment on the difficult shift from stage to film delivery, a point previously made in the Pyrrhus speech, where the screen actor Heston takes over from the stage actor Branagh.

These are but minor points. Two passages are of greater importance in Branagh's treatment of the analogies between stage and screen: the play-within-the-play and Hamlet's third soliloquy.

"To be or not to be" is spoken by Hamlet standing in front of a two-way mirror behind which Claudius and Polonius hide as "lawful espials". We see at first a full-length reflection of him in the mirror while he stands on the left, his back to the camera. Then the figure on the left disappears from view and we are left with just the reflected image in the mirror, whose gilded frame, reminiscent of a proscenium arch, coincides with the limits of the screen. The shot seamlessly simulates the passage from the stage to the screen and the substitution of the photographic image for the real presence of the actor. This is all the more impressive because Bazin uses the mirror as a metaphor to discuss the issue of the presence – or rather pseudo-presence – of the actor on the screen. The screen, he claims, recreates the presence of the actor "as a mirror might [...] but one whose silvering would be able to retain images and display a deferred reflection".[24] The mirror in Branagh becomes the metaphor of the transcoding of play into film. It is also very adequately a cinematic, visual transposition of the dramatic, aural convention of the soliloquy. As the image of Hamlet slides off-screen, we are made to see his reflection from his own point of view. Wondering who's there, we stand and unfold ourselves. The mirror is now held up to us, a visual demonstration of the mechanisms of identification at work in the soliloquy, while Branagh shows how Shakespeare's definition of the function of drama in 3.2 ("to hold, as 'twere, the mirror up to nature") holds for film as well.[25] It does so all the more successfully perhaps because film, unlike drama, is an isolating experience as a result of the lack of interaction between actors and spectators.[26] Branagh's use of the mirror in this soliloquy capitalizes on such isolation. Hamlet's long journey into night and detachment is bound to find an echo in the spectator exiled in the dark, whereas the communal enjoyment of a festive Comedy is somehow hampered by the film format.

The play-within-the-play effect is notoriously difficult to achieve on screen. It requires a prior exploration of the geography of the space in which the drama is to take place, so that we might be constantly aware of what is theatrical space and what is not. Branagh achieves this by contrasting a flat horizontal stage with a dizzyingly vertical space for the auditorium, stretching up from the floor to the top gallery.[27] Superimposed on these initial landmarks, another, more fluctuating code is set up through the director's insistence on gazes which determine what is stage space and what is not, according to who is actually watching whom. Horatio's spying gaze, his stage-glasses trained on Gertrude, Claudius, or Ophelia, together with fascinated gazes from the audience turning in alarm to an uproarious, scandal-mongering Hamlet commenting fiercely on the stage action, serve as a substitute eye and a guide for the cine audience.

Hamlet moves constantly between stage and audience, cleverly blurring the limits between the two spaces even before the show starts. He is first seen not among the courtiers but on stage, a clear signal of his twofold role as actor and director (and a metacinematic comment by the film-maker on himself). The spotlights turn to him while the Court begins to cheer. His dialogue with Polonius ("My lord, you played once i' t' university you say" 3.2) is spoken from the stage. It is returned to its original function as a comic duologue, a double-act, with Hamlet dragging the old man on stage as his designated stooge. Here again Elizabethan conventions and modern references meet, as Hamlet is both the Jester (and Lord of Misrule as well perhaps) and the evening's M.C. and warm-up man.

He then carries on his foolery in the audience, the stand-up comedian turned heckler, to the great embarrassment of the Court. The stage is thus gradually transferred to, or rather a twin stage is opened in, the midst of the audience. Hamlet's final move from the stage up to the Royal box makes the decisive connection between onstage and offstage events and reveals where the real stage lies, for all to see, redirecting the audience's gaze to the place of crime and incest, from the image in the mirror to the thing itself.

The passage from the metadramatic to the metacinematic is explicit on the screen and in the synopsis, which describes Hamlet arranging the details of *The Mousetrap* as a "very bossy writer, director". The re-decoration still taking place shortly before the show begins makes the improvised theatre as cluttered a space as is a film set. "We see the magic of theatre happening before our very eyes", Branagh comments.[28] The magic of theatre and of film, too. One almost misses, as a metacinematic touch, the primitive camera recording for future reference this evening of light-hearted entertainment at Elsinore.

Branagh is aware that there is more to metadrama in *Hamlet* than just *The Mousetrap*. A great deal of the action is recognized as insets. They take place in the State Hall conceived as a sort of huge auditorium with a "gallery" and "balconies".[29] The language of the script is openly theatrical, referring to the courtiers as an "audience" and to Claudius as a consummate actor.[30] The play's initial confrontation between Hamlet and Claudius (1.2) is filmed as a show taking place on the royal dais as on a stage. Ophelia's report to Polonius of Hamlet's strange behaviour (2.1) is conceived as a dumb-show where Ophelia acts as a mime and chorus performing to a one-man audience. Branagh later departs from tradition the better to make a similar point. Polonius's business with Hamlet's letter to Ophelia, which he proffers to support his diagnosis of the Prince's madness (2.2) has been variously staged, usually with Polonius, the impresario, holding his royal audience in suspense, then reading the letter with zest as one who was once accounted a good University player. But whatever his tone or mood, accent or manner, he is invariably the performer, occasionally supported by Ophelia whom he may have brought along with him "as a prop".[31] Branagh's Polonius calls out to Ophelia to have *her* read aloud Hamlet's letter. There is metadramatic method in it: she enters on cue, through a hidden door, as from the nowhere that lies beyond the stage. She delivers to an audience a written text, Hamlet's play, directed and reviewed by Polonius, who finds fault with the language, deeming "beautified" a vile phrase. Where the play allowed only one reader, Branagh has three. The reading is begun by Ophelia and completed by Polonius, after she runs out in distress. The third protagonist is Hamlet, who is heard and seen in a flashback to speak the words of the letter. This is again Branagh commenting on the various ways in which stage and film can deal with the same material and turn words into acting. It is a visual demonstration of the process of cine/dramatization.

In this perspective the many silent flashbacks of the play appear as much more than mere naive visual illustrations of the words. They are Branagh's cinematic equivalent of Shakespeare's dramatic insets, i.e. films-within-the-film in dumb-show, a homage of the silent screen to the silent stage. The flashback supporting the complex diplomatic manoeuvering of Claudius, Voltemand and Cornelius in 2.2 is a significant instance of this technique blending together elements of film and drama. The editing underlines a five-act arrangement similar to that of the dumb-show preceding *The Mousetrap*: Old Norway finds out about Fortinbras's real plans; has him summoned; rebukes him; forgives him; eventually

Branagh's *Hamlet* 361

gives him permission to redirect his steps toward Poland. The same flashback technique is used for the Dido speech on Priam's slaughter later in 2.2. The point is not to provide a helpful visual comment on complex action but to respond to the text's hypotyposis, its vivid description of Pyrrhus, "total gules, horridly tricked / With blood of fathers, mothers, daughters, sons", "With eyes like carbuncles", of Priam's "milky head", of a powerless Hecuba "threat'ning the flames / With bisson rheum, a clout upon that head / Where late the diadem stood." Hypotyposis as defined by Fontanier "is so vivid and dramatic as to actually show what is depicted, turning a tale or a description into an image, a picture or even a *tableau vivant*",[32] a nineteenth-century definition which suggests a sort of natural continuity between words and images. Images come to life at the crossroads where the playwright's language and the audience's imagination meet. "Think when we talk of horses that you see them", the Chorus suggests in *Henry V*. Such an awareness of the connection of words and images in the age of Shakespeare Branagh finds directly applicable to, and exemplified by, modern technology. The film-within-the-film of Priam's slaughter moreover suggests its theatrical origin by its very cast: two major actors with stage-legend status, John Gielgud and Judy Dench.[33]

Drama thrives on convention, and cinema on realism. The handling of convention by film is crucial. So is the handling of space by drama. Bazin, quoting Sartre, suggested that "in the theatre the drama proceeds from the actor; in the cinema it goes from the décor to the man".[34] Jorgens distinguishes between three modes in Shakespearean film, one of them being the "realistic mode" specific for its handling of space, "shifting the emphasis from the actors to actors-in-a-setting".[35] Zeffirelli is a case in point. Influenced by his debut as a stage-designer he takes the opposite view to Bazin, claiming that "an actor cannot hold the stage alone; he needs to be helped by [...] a beauty around him. [...] It becomes a kind of additional character".[36] The result is a play swamped in its setting, justifying Bazin's point. The handling of space is thus the stumbling block of drama on film.

Bazin warns against the illusion that the cinema is the answer to the limitations of a constricted stage:

> If film means absolute freedom from the limits imposed by the stage space both to the action and the point of view, adapting a play to the screen mainly consists in granting to the text the kind of realistic, extensive décor that the stage cannot offer. It also consists in emancipating the spectator from a fixed, frontal point of view, so as to set off the performance of the actor. [...] Yet this is not *mise en scène* but merely the forcible infusion of "film" into drama. The original action inevitably finds itself out of place and the word loses its priority and is thrown off balance by the extra dramatic status conferred upon the setting.[37]

Film making up for the deficiencies of drama is a gross misconception because the artificiality of the stage does not result from technical shortcomings, some "vicious mole of nature" or "effect defective" for a Polonius-like film-maker to pinpoint and make good. Broadening the perspective does not provide a wanted breath of fresh air to a choking world, it merely robs it of its life and blood, i.e. the primacy of man and the word. The cinema is not the providence of the stage, the bounty of a rich uncle from Hollywood to some destitute distant relative:

> The real gamble for the film director is to transform a space turned inward to the theatre of the mind, i.e. the enclosed, conventional space of play-acting, into a window opening out onto the outside world. [...] The film-maker's predicament is to restore dramatic density to his décor while respecting its innate realism. Once he has solved this conundrum, the director, no longer fearing merely to import into film the conventions of drama and the demands of the text, is free to capitalize on them.[38]

Despite an alarming prefatory statement: "My film-maker's instincts made me long [...] to take the play into the cinema in its fullest form. I longed to allow audiences to join Fortinbras on the plain in Norway".[39] Branagh's stage instincts prevailed. His choice of Blenheim Palace for Elsinore may look odd, because the place is too familiar for certain lines to sit comfortably, such as, for instance, Horatio's warning to Hamlet to steer clear of "the dreadful summit of the cliff / That beetles o'er his base into the sea" (1.4). There is no way you can hear the ocean "roar beneath" in

Blenheim or conjure up an image of the shores of Oxfordshire. Yet it is true to Kozintsev's perception of Elsinore's Court life:

> The theatre sometimes takes too literally the words "Denmark's a prison", and proceeds to construct a set reminiscent of a dungeon. The tragedy is in something else. Court life is comfortable. The external trappings are beautiful. But for a person of ideas and feelings this can constitute a prison.[40]

Bleinheim is such a one. It is easy to connect Hamlet's description of the macrocosm as a "goodly frame" with "excellent canopy" and "majestical roof" to what the Bleinheim microcosm can offer.

The film's bid for realism and the outside world is confined to flashbacks, i.e. something less real, with sepia photography, than the brightly lit State Hall of Elsinore/Bleinheim with its endless vista of mirrored doors. One keeps returning to the State Hall as to some oversized prison cell crushing its prisoners by its very magnitude, a place as inhuman as the mad Ophelia's dimly-lit padded cell. The whole action is encapsulated within the confines of the Palace where characters are so many flies thumping against the mirrored doors in a vain attempt to escape. Spatial variety is limited to moving the action to a new place (weapons room, courtyard, gallery etc.) for each sub-section of a long scene.[41] The resulting syntax is more dramatic than filmic, a visual version of the division into acts and scenes. This creates a bleak sense of claustrophobia. The woodland setting for the so-called "Platform" and Graveyard scenes is possibly even more claustrophobic, with its dark, bare, low trunks. There is little sense of 'a world elsewhere' existing beyond the frame of the screen, as required by film realism. The miniature steam train on which Rosencrantz and Guildenstern arrive for their first meeting with Hamlet is a mere toy of the new king, a theatrical prop notoriously incapable of connecting the inside and the outside worlds. The key to Ophelia's cell takes her nowhere but into the brook. Branagh is closer to Olivier than Kosintzev in this. As Neil Taylor suggested: "Beyond Olivier's Elsinore there is nothing, but beyond Kosintsev's there is everything else."[42] Beyond Branagh's, there are limitless expanses of white snow besieging the Palace, the blank screen of the cinema closing in on the self-contained space of the stage. This conveys a sense of threat, the awareness that there is no life for drama in the open, that it just cannot survive in the open. Oxygen and green fields are lethal to it, "nature and drama cannot merge without drama melting away into non-existence."[43] The plains of Norway moving on to Denmark, Fortinbras's army closing in on Elsinore, the outside on the inside world, may be read as a metaphor suggesting that the attempted coexistence of film and drama is potentially destructive for the stage.

In an image reminiscent of the grey cyclorama of Adrian Noble's 1993 production of the play with the army in grey uniforms snaking through the snow, Fortinbras's men prepare to invade Denmark. The camera moves away as Hamlet delivers his final soliloquy (4.4) from the top of a promontory standing out against a snowy expanse where the soldiers, now tiny figures in the vast landscape, look increasingly like signs beginning to crowd on a blank page, ominous shadows looming out of the blank screen. The camera, pulling back in a high-angle shot, gradually dwarfs Hamlet to the dimension of a mere dot as the screen fades to black for the interval. This shot is a turning point. So far the stage has prevailed in (and over) the film, with the excitement, hustle and bustle of the Play scene filmed in glowing reds and golds. From now on, the stage world dwindles to nothingness as film takes over. Branagh's parable on the transcoding from one medium to another becomes increasingly bleak. When film eventually bursts into the space of the Palace it dissolves the fabric of the play, brings its action to an end on a funeral oration, the closure of all closures.

Before he comes to this grim outcome, Branagh retains a continuously theatrical focus, with the State Hall the central area of action. Its theatricality is given constant emphasis. Claudius stage-manages events from the throne dais as a natural-born actor and director (1.2) for the benefit of an audience of courtiers sitting on either side of this version of the apron stage, while Hamlet stiffly waits behind black drapes as a player waiting backstage for his entrance cue. The Hall is easily turned for the *Murder of Gonzago* into the auditorium it has never quite ceased to be, with its bleachers, gallery, balconies. All action, all movements converge on it. Like the stage of a theatre but unlike the screen, it is a centripetal space. The side rooms behind the mirrored doors are dressing-rooms where actors ready themselves for their entrances. Claudius and Gertrude are being "dressed, combed and spruced" in their private apartments by attendants in the early part of 2.2 before they move down to the State Hall for yet another official performance. So does Hamlet, dressing for the Play scene. There is a definite sense of backstage activity in the side rooms behind the State Hall's mirrored doors. The screen actor, off camera, is still a participant in the action, unlike the stage actor, who, when offstage, goes to the "green room" or to his dressing-room or simply waits in the wings for his next entrance cue. We are well aware that

> These few square feet of light and illusion are hemmed in by machinery and coulisses. Though aware of the presence of these unseen mazes, the audience plays along with the game, its pleasure never spoilt.[44]

Branagh's Elsinore is such a place. Its corridors do not, as in Olivier, take us through the convolutions of the Prince's tortuous mind, but on a backstage tour of a theatre. The dazzling light of the central stage contrasts with the dimness beyond its frame. Its mirrored doors form one huge mirror, that which the theatre holds up to nature. It reflects the boundlessness of the human soul, the only infinite space that drama will ever need.

Branagh's *Hamlet* is filmed as an attempt to span the whole development of the performing arts from the origins to the present day and examine their final compatibility. Starting with a (fairly awkward) representation of Hell (1.5) reminiscent of the Mystery Plays, with smoke rising, geysers spurting, cracks opening in the ground,[45] he then pays a passing tribute to the Commedia dell'arte, whose masks are everywhere on display in Hamlet's environment. For the Fishmonger scene, he appears to Polonius from behind a pillar wearing a grotesque mask of a skull, reminiscent of the representations of "Death the Antic" leading the medieval Dance of Death. This image (perhaps borrowed from the BBC production) is rooted more deeply in the dramatic tradition of the Jester turned sour than is Olivier's head-shadow falling over Yorick's skull in the 1948 version. It is an abridged statement of each director's priorities, dramatic or psychological. Branagh's choice of a stage for the Play-scene is distinctly Elizabethan. He visually reminds the audience that all the world is a stage when musing over a toy theatre which looks like the main State Hall, or meditating over a G/globe for "O what a rogue and peasant slave", his most metadramatic soliloquy. Then film references gradually take over, until the final showdown in Erroll Flynn style, with a mad chase, Laertes falling to his death over the balustrade, Hamlet throwing the poisoned rapier like a javelin across the Hall, and swinging down a rope. Fortinbras's invasion is like the irruption of cinematic into theatrical space, dismantling it. The three codes of page, stage and screen, "the triad of Shakespearean incarnation"[46] are constantly present in the film-maker's mind. Drama pays homage to film, and film to drama when Fortinbras the outsider has soldiers' music and the rites of war film speak loudly for Hamlet ... and *Hamlet*. But one shudders as the soldiers take the Old King's statue down, hammering it to pieces until it falls, its head-piece "obliterating the name HAMLET for ever. As we fade to black."[47]

Notes

1. Anthony Davies, *Filming Shakespeare's Plays* (Cambridge UP, 1988), p. 40.
2. André Bazin, *Qu'est-ce que le cinéma?* (Paris: Editions du Cerf, 1975), p. 149. My translation.
3. Roger Manvell, *Shakespeare and the Film* (London: Dent, 1971), p. 15.
4. (Bazin, p. 148). "Au lieu de tenter après tant d'autres, de dissoudre [la pièce] dans le cinéma, il utilise au contraire les ressources de la caméra pour accuser, souligner, confirmer les structures scéniques et leurs corollaires psychologiques. L'apport spécifique du cinéma ne se pourrait définir ici que par un surcroît de théâtralité".
5. Michèle Willems, "Verbal-visual, Verbal-pictorial or Textual-televisual? Reflections on the BBC Series", in *Shakespeare and the Moving Image: The Plays on Film and Television*, ed. Anthony Davies and Stanley Wells (Cambrige UP, 1994), p. 70.
6. Grigori Kozintsev, "*Hamlet* and *King Lear*: Stage and Film" in *Shakespeare 1971*, ed. Clifford Leech and J.M.R. Margeson (Toronto, 1972), p. 191.

7. Respectively Lewis Grossberger and James Bowman, quoted in Davies and Wells, p. 165.

8. Quoted in Davies and Wells, p. 168.

9. (Bazin, p. 137). "De quelque biais qu'on l'aborde, la pièce de théâtre, classique ou contemporaine, est irrévocablement défendue par son texte. On ne saurait "adapter" celui-ci qu'en renonçant à l'oeuvre originale pour lui en substituer une autre, peut-être supérieure mais qui n'est plus la pièce. Opération fatalement limitée du reste aux auteurs mineurs ou vivants, les chefs-d'oeuvre consacrés par le temps nous imposant le respect du texte comme un postulat."

10. (Bazin, p. 138). "Naguère, la préoccupation première du cinéaste semblait être de camoufler l'origine théâtrale du modèle, de l'adapter, de la dissoudre dans le cinéma. Non seulement il paraît maintenant y renoncer, mais il lui arrive d'en souligner systématiquement le caractère théâtral. Il n'en peut guère être autrement dès l'instant que l'essentiel du texte est respecté. Conçu en fonction des virtualités théâtrales, le texte les porte déjà toutes en lui. Il détermine des modes et un style de représentation, il est déjà, en puissance, le théâtre. On ne peut à la fois décider de lui être fidèle et le détourner de l'expression vers laquelle il tend".

11. See Kenneth Branagh, *Hamlet, by William Shakespeare: Screenplay, Introduction and Film Diary* (London: Chatto and Windus, 1996), p. 175.

12. He made a similar statement about the importance of the text in the opening shot of *Much Ado About Nothing*, displaying the words of Balthazar's song for audiences to see. It was read in voice-over by Beatrice, from a *book*, as discovered in the first scene.

13. Branagh, p. 1.

14. An incidental note in the script (p. 64) compares the Players with "the Crummles from *Nicholas Nickleby*". The reference is both to Dickens's novel and to the RSC's stage adaptation, i.e. yet another example of what Willems calls "transcoding" (in Davies and Wells, p. 72).

15. *The Times*, 13 February 1997, 41.

16. Jack J. Jorgens, *Shakespeare on Film* (Bloomington: Indiana UP, 1977), p. 7.

17. "Representing *King Lear* on Screen: From Metatheatre to 'Meta-cinema' " in Davies and Wells, p. 211.

18. For a complete analysis of this film as a Prologue to *Hamlet*, see Danielle Berton's forthcoming paper: "*In the Bleak Midwinter* de Kenneth Branagh: Le Miracle de Noël ou le cinéma, le théâtre et la religion en interaction", *Cahiers du CIEREC* (Saint-Etienne University).

19. Alexander Walker, *The Evening Standard*, 13 February 1993, 26-27.

20. See Willems's analysis in Davies and Wells, p. 71.

21. Anthony Davies: *Filming Shakespeare's plays* (Cambridge UP, 1988), p. 44.

22. Branagh, p. 171.

23. Branagh, pp. 167, 154.

24. Bazin, p. 152: "Il le fait à la manière d'un miroir [...] mais d'un miroir au reflet différé, dont le tain retiendrait l'image."

25. From a psychoanalytic perspective, the scene is an unsettling comment on the father-son relationship in the play. Hamlet, tottering on the brink of annihilation, delivers his meditation on suicide to the very mirror behind which Claudius and Polonius are concealed, i.e. which stands as yet another instance of the father's destructive gaze. The paternal gaze was first established as

paramount in a close-up shot of the Ghost's face and a succession of high-angle shots dwarfing the son under the father's eyes in the opening sequence.

26. Peter Holland, "Two-Dimensional Shakespeare: *King Lear* on Film," in *Shakespeare and the Moving Image*, ed. Davies and Welles, p. 52.

27. The auditorium is reminiscent of Bob Crowley's set for Adrian Noble's production of the play with Branagh in the title role (RSC, London and Stratford, 1992-3). The set proper is similar to Olivier's.

28. See Branagh, p. 83 for both examples.

29. Branagh, p. 14.

30. Branagh, p. 13.

31. See Marvin Rosenberg, *The Masks of Hamlet* (London and Cranbury: Associated University Presses, 1992), pp. 377-87.

32. "L'hypotypose peint les choses d'une manière si vive et si énergique, qu'elle les met en quelque sorte sous les yeux et fait d'un récit ou d'une description, une image, un tableau, ou même une scène vivante." Fontanier, *Les Figures du discours, 1827-1830* (Paris: Flammarion, 1977), p. 390.

33. The artistic merit of the technique is beyond the scope of this paper.

34. Bazin, p. 156-7: "Au théâtre le drame part de l'acteur, au cinéma il va du décor à l'homme".

35. Jorgens, p. 10.

36. Quoted in Ace Pilkington, "Zeffirelli's Shakespeare," in Davies and Wells, p. 104.

37. Bazin, p. 139: "Si par cinéma, on entend la liberté de l'action par rapport à l'espace, et la liberté du point de vue par rapport à l'action, mettre au cinéma une pièce de théâtre, ce sera donner à son décor l'ampleur et la réalité que la scène ne pouvait matériellement lui offrir. Ce sera aussi libérer le spectateur de son fauteuil et mettre en valeur, par le changement de plan, le jeu de l'acteur. [...] Mais il ne s'agit précisément pas de mise en scène. L'opération a seulement consisté à injecter de force du "cinéma" dans le théâtre. Le drame original s'y trouve fatalement dépaysé et la primauté dramatique du verbe est décalée par rapport au supplément de dramatisation prêté au décor par la caméra."

38. Bazin, p. 166: "La gageure que doit tenir le metteur en scène est celle de la reconversion d'un espace orienté vers la seule dimension intérieure, du lieu clos et conventionnel du jeu théâtral en une fenêtre sur le monde [...] Le problème qui se pose au cinéaste est donc de rendre à son décor une opacité dramatique, tout en respectant son réalisme naturel. Résolu ce paradoxe de l'espace, le metteur en scène, loin de craindre de transporter à l'écran les conventions théâtrales et les servitudes du texte, retrouve au contraire toute liberté de s'appuyer sur elles".

39. Branagh, p. vii.

40. Quoted in Davies and Wells, p. 53. The problem is there is no sense of the numinous in Blenheim Palace.

41. Act 1, scene 3, for example, was shot in two different locations, the Grounds for Ophelia and Laertes's leave-taking, the Chapel for Polonius's homily to his son and the following confession extorted from Ophelia. The setting is used as a comment. Polonius closes the gates to the chapel for his cross-examination of his daughter and shoves her into a confessional on "Give me up the truth". The increasing constriction of space points forward to the padded cell where

Branagh's *Hamlet*

Ophelia is later seen straightjacketed and banging herself at the walls and that in which she is blasted with a high-pressure hose, a reference to nineteenth-century treatment of (female) madness. The face of the dead Ophelia is then seen in close-up under water as in a glass case. The final image of her is in her coffin.

42. Neil Taylor: "The Films of *Hamlet*", in Davies and Wells, p. 187.

43. Bazin, p. 158: "Le théâtre ne peut par essence se confondre avec la nature, sous peine de s'y dissoudre et de cesser d'être."

44. Bazin, p. 158: "Ces quelques mètres carrés de lumière et d'illusion sont entourés de machinerie et de coulisses dont les labyrinthes cachés, mais connus, ne gênent nullement le plaisir du spectateur qui joue le jeu".

45. "[The ground] cracks open to reveal an ominous gateway to Hell. Agonized voices from beyond pierce the night's dull ear" (Branagh, p. 34). Whatever the effectiveness of the final result, this can be read as a reference to an early form of drama and a cinematic equivalent of the Elizabethan "cellarage".

46. K.S. Rothwell, in Davies and Wells, p. 213.

47. Branagh, p. 173.

REFORMATTING *HAMLET*:
CREATING A Q1 *HAMLET* FOR TELEVISION

Hardy M. Cook
(Bowie State University, Maryland)

I have argued that television is a medium that has unique qualities which demand particular televisual and theatrical styles. Additionally, I have stressed the flexibility that television provides to us to analyze these productions in depth.[1] However, I had not until the summer of 1995 considered using video technology physically to re-edit an existing 'full-text' version of a play into a shorter Q1 (so-called 'bad' quarto) version. Since the publication of *The Division of the Kingdoms*, many have investigated the "bad" quartos. A quality common in many of the seemingly disparate approaches to the transmission of these printed scripts is that they might provide us with insights into actual performances. Operating under the premise that the first printed edition of *Hamlet* may indeed supply such theatrical insights, I re-edited *The BBC TV Shakespeare Hamlet* from its little more than three-and-a-half-hour-long, roughly full-text version into an approximately three-hour version, following the scene structure of Q1. Having completed my reconstruction, I now propose to describe my method and to explore some of the insights I have gained from this exercise.

After my initial background reading of Kathleen Irace's *Reforming the 'Bad' Quartos: Performance and Provenance of Six Shakespearean First Editions* and the essays in Thomas Clayton's collection *The Hamlet First Published (Q1, 1603): Origins, Form, Intertextualities*, I prepared my working script. Using the Bertram and Kliman *The Three-Text HAMLET* and the Allen and Muir facsimile of the Q1 *Hamlet* from *Shakespeare's Plays in Quarto*, I marked up the *The BBC TV Shakespeare Hamlet*[2] in four colors, corresponding roughly to passages in the BBC production with Q1 equivalents, to passages in the BBC production with no

Creating a Q1 *Hamlet* for TV 371

Q1 equivalents, to passages cut from the BBC production with Q1 equivalents, and to passages cut from the BBC production with no Q1 equivalents. Because I was re-editing a production based on a conflated Q2/F1 text,[3] my interest was primarily in the theatrical impact of Q1's scene structure and of the resulting shortened playtext; I obviously could not be concerned with the issues that have been raised about the poetical merits, or lack thereof, of the Q1 text. However, even with this limited scope, I was faced with many choices of my own that were complicated by what I identified above as "Q1 equivalents" – in that the corresponding Q2/F1 passages were inevitably longer than those in Q1. Further, my reading of Q1 and of commentaries on it led me to conclude that the Q1 Gertrude appears less complicit and problematic than her Q2/F1 counterpart, that the Q1 Claudius appears even more the principal evil presence (one might say 'typical' revenge-play villain) than his Q2/F1 counterpart, that Ophelia appears even more used and victimized than her Q2/F1 counterpart, that the Q1 Laertes appears less complicit than his Q2/F1 counterpart, and that the Q1 Hamlet appears more like a revenger than his more problematic Q2/F1 counterpart.[4] I knew that as I edited the BBC production I would have not only to follow Q1's scene structure but also to delete some sections within scenes in order to try to replicate the spirit of Q1.

I needed some operating assumptions because, for one, attempting a line-for-line deletion strategy within scenes would surely result in a disjointed, incoherent video. I determined that my bottom line would be to strive to delete as many passages as possible that I identified as being in the BBC but as having no Q1 equivalents, especially those Q2/F1 passages that increase Gertrude's role over that portrayed in Q1. These particular deletions would include some of her speeches (such as her early lines in 1.2) and some of the references to her (such as the Ghost's 1.5.47-53: "O Hamlet, what a falling off was there").

My task was further complicated by Q1 passages for which there are no Q2/F1 equivalents or for which there exist significant theatrical differences. The most obvious of these is Q1's Scene 15.[5] Additionally, I identified four other passages from Q1 that, to me, so significantly altered the theatrical dynamics that I felt they should also be included, but how – that was the question. What I finally decided to do was to have my teenage daughter (and aspiring Shakespearean actress) and myself read the line while I showed on the screen images of the appropriate passages from the Q1 text. With these decisions being made, I proceeded to re-edit the *BBC Hamlet.*

For my Q1 Scene 1 (7:50), I retained the *BBC Hamlet* 1.1 as it was. I confess that as I began preparing my working script I color-coded much more scrupulously than I did later on. What became obvious to me was that line-by-line comparisons for specific echoes between the texts were less important than investigating how equivalent Q1 passages, which, as I have said, are inevitably shorter than parallel passages in Q2/F1, were captured in spirit in Q2/F1. In this scene, I also determined that the *BBC Hamlet* included approximately twenty lines that had no Q1 equivalents and cut fourteen lines that did. These discoveries extended throughout my investigation.

My Q1 Scene 2 (11:30) presented much more interesting choices than Scene 1 had. The King's opening speech is notably shorter in Q1 than in Q2/F1. It begins with "Lordes, we here haue writ to *Fortenbra[s][s]e*", and thus omits much of the exposition of Q2/F1. I began the scene with "young Fortinbras, / Holding a weak supposal of our worth" (1.2.16b-ff), retaining the Fortinbras exposition while omitting the Old King Hamlet exposition. I also retained "to suppress / His further gait herein; in that the levies, / The lists, and full proportions, are all made / Out of his subject" (1.2.30b-33a) and "You cannot speak of reason to the Dane" to "What wouldst thou have, Laertes?" (1.2.44-50) for smoothness. I deemed it necessary, according to my operating principles, to delete Gertrude's first and second speeches and move from Hamlet's "Not so, my lord; I am too much in the sun" to his "'Tis not alone my inky cloak, good mother" to try to replicate Q1's not having Gertrude speak until she delivers her Q1 "Let not thy mother loo[s]e her praiers *Hamlet*" (1.2.118's "Let not thy mother lose her prayers, Hamlet"). I also omitted

Creating a Q1 *Hamlet* for TV

Claudius's "But to persever / In obstinate condolement" to "Do I impart toward you" (1.2.92b-112a) because these lines have no Q1 equivalents and did not appear to me to be necessary.

I made few changes in my Q1 Scenes 3 to 6. I left my Q1 Scene 3 (6:20) as it was in the *BBC Hamlet*, but I deleted Hamlet's lines 17 to 38a in my Q1 Scene 4 (3:10): they had no Q1 equivalents, and I wanted as much as possible to strive for a more rapid pace in my re-edited version than existed in the original production. In my Q1 Scene 5 (11:05), I deleted the Ghost's "O Hamlet, what a falling off was there" (1.5.47-52) because these lines make Gertrude appear more culpable than she appears in the Q1 version. After considering cutting some of Polonius's[6] lines from my Q1 Scene 6 (5:40), I let the scene stand as it was in the *BBC Hamlet*.

Of course, the first substantial change in scene structure between the Q1 version and the Q2/F1 versions occurs in Q1's Scene 7 – where the "To be, or not to be" speech is located. I began my Q1 Scene 7 (40:50) with the first 167 lines of the *BBC Hamlet*'s 2.2. Both Q1's Scene 7 and Q2/F1's Act Two, Scene Two, open with the King and Queen welcoming Rosencrantz and Guildenstern.[7] However, when Polonius enters in Q1, he is accompanied by Ophelia, something that is not the case in Q2/F1. This was a Q1 theatrical dynamic that I could not reproduce by re-editing the *BBC Hamlet*, and one that I find quite interesting. Having Ophelia present when her father offers his theory of Hamlet's madness and reads the letter Ophelia received from the prince further emphasizes her being used and victimized. When Hamlet enters the scene in Q1, he is reading just as he is in Q2/F1's 2.2 although the line – "[s]ee where hee comes poring vppon a booke". – is given to Claudius and not to Gertrude: "But look where sadly the poor wretch comes reading." At this point, I cut to the *BBC Hamlet*'s 3.1.43, where Polonius instructs Ophelia: "Ophelia, walk you here." I cut 3.1.45-55, resuming the scene with the "To be, or not to be" speech and continuing the scene until Claudius says, "There's something in his soul / O'er which his melancholy sits on brood" (3.1.165). From there, I returned to 2.2.170, where Polonius begins to question Hamlet – "How does my good Lord Hamlet?" and followed this with all of the remainder of 2.2. Even though my edited Q1 Scene 7 is somewhat rough, it does replicate the structure of Q1. The relocation of the "To be, or not to be" speech to this point in the play makes much dramatic sense to me. Having Hamlet's meditation on suicide before the arrival of the players, the initial interrogation by Rosencrantz and Guildenstern, the hatching of the plot to present "The Murder of Gonzago", and the reciting of the "O, what a rogue and peasant slave am I!" soliloquy, I believe, makes dramatic sense. I find it appropriate that Hamlet would have such thoughts at this point and that having them later, after he has resolved "to haue [s]ounder proofes" (Q1) – the Q2/F1 "grounds / More relative than this" – appears less plausible. Other directors have also felt this way; one example that immediately comes to mind is the 1969 Tony Richardson filmed version of the Round House Theatre *Hamlet* with Nichol Williamson. One could, of course, argue that the Q2/F1 placement further problematizes Hamlet, showing an intellectual struggling with a conflict between his individual will and his concern for divine providence (Lull, 137), but for me the Q1 placement works and works well.

My Q1 Scene 8 (2:10) was the first place I considered it necessary to include an insert from Q1.[8] I began with the first twenty-eight lines of the *BBC Hamlet* 3.1, in which the King and Queen discuss with Rosencrantz and Guildenstern what they have learned from Hamlet just as they do in Q1. The next sixteen lines of 3.1 set up Claudius's and Polonius's spying on Hamlet and were obviously not necessary, so I omitted them; my insert, however, continues the momentum of Q1 as Claudius, Gertrude, and Polonius discuss attending the play that Hamlet has arranged.

Although I considered some cuts in both my Q1 Scene 9 (20:10) and Scene 10 (4:50), the only actual parts I deleted were the opening thirty-six lines of 3.3 in Scene 10, for which there are no Q1 equivalents.

My next insert came in my Q1 Scene 11 (9:10). I used the first 159 lines of 3.4. At Hamlet's "but go not to mine uncle's bed" (3.4.159), I decided that the Q1 conclusion of the scene could not be replicated by attempting deletions to the *BBC*

Hamlet version. In the eleven lines of the Q1 insert, Hamlet asks his mother to assist him in his revenge, and she agrees: "I will conceale, con[s]ent, and doe my be[s]t, / What [s]tratagem [s]oe're thou [s]halt deui[s]e." The Q2/F1 lines are plainly not as direct or unambiguous as these are.

My Q1 Scene 12 (4:05) too required some careful decisions. I started it at 4.1.6 just as Q1 begins – "What, Gertrude? How does Hamlet?" (*BBC Hamlet*) – Q1's "Now Gertred, what [s]ayes our [s]onne, how doe you finde him?" After Gertrude's response (4.1.7-12a), I cut both Claudius's and Gertrude's next speeches (4.1.12b-27), included Claudius's "O Gertrude, come away!" and his instructions to Rosencrantz and Guildenstern. The scene in Q1 then includes a speech in which Claudius announces to Gertrude that he plans to send Hamlet to England, but this information is conveyed later in my Q1 Scene 12, so I did not add an insert here. I next deleted all of 4.2, Hamlet's exchange with Rosencrantz and Guildenstern, and the first sixteen lines of 4.3, picking up the action with Hamlet's entrance at 4.3.17 and continuing the scene to the end of 4.3. This compression of three Q2/F1 scenes into one replicates Q1, emphasizes the rapidity of the activities after the death of Polonius and, to me, supports Gertrude's pledge to her son in Scene 11 that she will assist him. This Gertrude appears less ambiguous than her Q2/F1 counterpart, who could be played to illustrate the saying "love the one you're with".

My Q1 Scene 13 (0:35) includes only Fortinbras's few lines and follows Q1 in not having Hamlet's discussion with the Captain or his "How all occasions do inform against me" soliloquy.

I began my Q1 Scene 14 (9:00) with an insert in which Claudius and Gertrude discuss Hamlet's leaving and Laertes's arrival. I did not include 4.5.1-34, moving after my insert to Claudius's entrance at 4.5.35. I omitted 4.5.75-107 to capture the Q1 abruptness of Laertes's entrance after the departure of Ophelia and ended my Scene 14 with the remainder of 4.5, which, even though it is longer than its Q1 equivalent, does capture the same spirit.

As I indicated above, Q1's Scene 15 is the only complete Q1 scene for which there is no single Q2/F1 equivalent. In this scene, Horatio informs Gertrude that Hamlet has safely returned to Denmark, that Hamlet found Claudius's instructions to the King of England ordering Hamlet's immediate execution, that Claudius will surely be displeased by these events, and that Rosencrantz and Guildenstern go on to England and their imminent deaths. This thirty-six line scene obviates the need for all of 4.6 and parts of 4.7 and 5.2, thus clearly affecting the rhythms of my attempt at replicating the theatrical impact of Q1.

For my Q1 Scene 16 (5:20), I also determined that the first 163 lines of 4.7 did not convey the sense of Q1, so I did not include them and instead used another insert. In this Q1 insert, Claudius hatches the plot to dispatch Hamlet with Laertes. In it, Claudius suggests that Laertes's sword will be both unbated and envenomed and that he will in addition have the poisoned chalice ready. Q1 here clearly portrays Claudius as the complete instigator of all phases of the plot and, thereby, reduces somewhat Laertes's complicity in Hamlet's death. Scene 16 then picks up with Gertrude's arrival and her announcement of Ophelia's death.

I let the *BBC Hamlet*'s 5.1 remain intact for my Q1 Scene 17 (15:35). I had considered making some cuts but concluded that they were not necessary. For my Q1 Scene 18 (20:15), I deleted the first seventy-five lines of the *BBC Hamlet*'s 5.2, because they had no Q1 equivalents and let the rest of the BBC's last scene stay as it was.

In conclusion, I believe there was some value to the experiment I undertook. Video technology provided me with my first opportunity to act as a director, and therein lies both the source of my satisfaction and disappointment with my project. My resulting video does capture some of the spirit of the Q1 text and, therefore, of the Q1 performance dynamics. However, my biggest disappointment was that I was not able to create a production of what I would estimate to be the two-hour playing time of Q1 (thus replicating the rapid pace of Q1), something that Ralph Alan Cohen did accomplish in his recent Shenandoah Shakespeare Express's *Hamlet* based on the Q1 scene structure. When I saw this

Creating a Q1 *Hamlet* for TV 377

production in Harrisonburg, Virginia, on August 12, 1995, it lasted two hours and five minutes. This particular performance was not the one the SSE had toured with earlier in the season; instead it was re-edited and re-blocked for the first time in preparation for the SSE's upcoming trip to the Fringe Festival in Edinburgh, Scotland, for which the company was allotted two-hour time slots. Nevertheless, after the show, Cohen expressed his confidence that he would be able to reduce the production time by at least those five minutes, and I have no doubt that he did. The difference, of course, was that he was working with "live" actors and I was working with a video production.

What I did accomplish was to replicate some of the dynamics of Q1, especially involving differences between many of the Q1 characters and their Q2/F1 counterparts. I discovered that I could not realize all of the differences I found in Q1; most notably, I could not have Ophelia present when her father talked with Claudius and Gertrude about Hamlet's "madness", a presence that implies her character is portrayed as being even more victimized in Q1 than in the conflated text. Through my deletions and reordering of the *BBC Hamlet*, I was able, however, to suggest some of the other differences, but I found it necessary to include five inserts to do greater justice to these differences in the Q1 portrayals. My re-editing in combination with these inserts reveals a more determined Hamlet and a more evil Claudius, as well as a less complicit Gertrude and Laertes.

Appendix

Insert One: Q1: Scene 8

King	Thanks to you both: Gertred you'l [s]ee this play.
Queene	My lord I will, and it ioyes me at the [s]oule
	He is inclin'd to any kinde of mirth.
Cor.	Madame, I pray be ruled be me:
	And my good Soueraigne, giue me leaue to [s]peake,
	We cannot yet finde out the very ground
	Of his di[s]temperance, therefore
	I holde it meete, if [s]o it plea[s]e you,

	El[s]e they [s]hall not meete, and thus it is.
King	What i'[s]t *Corambis?*
Cor.	Mary my good lord, this [s]oone when the [s]ports are (done,
	Madam, [s]end you in ha[s]te to [s]peake with him,
	And I my [s]elfe will [s]tand behind the Arras,
	There que[s]tion you the cau[s]e of all his griefe,
	And then in loue and nature vnto you, hee'le tell you all:
	My Lord, how thinke you on't?
King	It likes vs well, Gerterd, what [s]ay you?
Queene	With all my heart, [s]oone will I [s]end for him.
Cor.	My [s]elfe will be that happy me[s][s]enger,
	Who hopes his griefe will be reueal'd to her. *exeunt omnes*

Insert Two: Q1: Scene 11

Ham.	Idle, no mother, my pul[s]e doth beate like yours,
	It is not madne[s][s]e that po[s][s]e[s][s]eth Hamlet.
	O mother, if euer you did my deare father loue,
	Forbeare the adulterous bed to night,
	And win your [s]elfe by little as you may,
	In time it may be you wil lothe him quite:
	And mother, but a[s][s]i[s]t mee in reuenge,
	And in his death your infamy [s]hall die.
Queene	Hamlet, I vow by that maie[s]ty,
	That knowes our thoughts, and lookes into our hearts,
	I will conceale, con[s]ent, and doe my be[s]t,
	What [s]tratagem [s]oe're thou [s]halt deui[s]e.
Ham.	It is enough, mother good night:
	Come [s]ir, I'le prouide for you a graue,
	Who was in life a fooli[s]h prating knaue.
	Exit Hamlet with the dead body.

Insert Three: Q1: Scene 14

King	Hamlet is [s]hip't for England, fare him well,
	I hope to heare good newes from thence ere long,
	If euery thing fall out to our content,
	As I doe make no doubt but [s]o it [s]hall.
Queene	God grant it may, heau'ns keep my *Hamlet* [s]afe:
	But this mi[s]chance of olde *Corambis* death,
	Hath pier[s]ed [s]o the yong *Ofelines* heart,
	That [s]he, poore maide, is quite bereft her wittes.
King	Alas deere heart! And on the other [s]ide,

Creating a Q1 *Hamlet* for TV 379

Qu. We vnder[s]tand her brother's come from *France*,
And he hath halfe the heart of all our Land,
And hardly hee'le forget his fathers death,
Vnle[s][s]e by [s]ome meanes he be pacified.
O [s]ee where the yong *Ofelia* is!

Insert Four: Q1: Scene 15

Enter Horatio and the Queene.
Hor. Madame, your [s]onne is [s]afe arriv'de in *Denmarke*,
This letter I euen receiv'd of him,
Where as he writes how he e[s]cap't the danger,
And [s]ubtle trea[s]on that the king had plotted,
Being cro[s][s]ed by the contention of the windes,
He found the Packet [s]ent to the king of *England*,
Wherein he [s]aw him[s]elfe betray'd to death,
As at his next conuer[s]ion with your grace,
He will relate the circum[s]tance at full.
Queene Then I perceiue there's trea[s]on in his lookes
That [s]eem'd to [s]ugar o're his villaine:
But I will [s]oothe and plea[s]e him for a time,
For murderous mindes are alwayes jealous,
But know not you *Horatio* where he is?
Hor. Yes Madame, and he hath appoynted me
To meete him on the ea[s]t [s]ide of the Cittie
To morrow morning.
Queene O faile not, good *Horatio,* and withall, com-(mend me
A mothers care to him, bid him a while
Be wary of his pre[s]ence, le[s]t that he
Faile in that he goes about.
Hor. Madam, neuer make doubt of that:
I thinke by this the news be come to court:
He is arriv'de, ob[s]erue the king, and you [s]hall
Quickely finde, *Hamlet* being here,
Things fell not to his minde.
Queene But what became of *Gilderstone* and *Rossencraft?*
Hor. He being [s]et a[s]hore, they went for *England,*
And in the Packet there writ down that doome
To be perform'd on them poynted for him:
And by great chance he had his fathers Seale,
So all was done without di[s]couerie.
Queene Thankes be to heauen for ble[s][s]ing of the prince,
Horatio once againe I take my leaue,

Horat.	With thow[s]and mothers ble[s][s]ings to my [s]onne. Madam adue.

Insert Five: Q1: Scene 16

King.	Hamlet from *England!* is it po[s][s]ible? What chance is this? they are gone, and he come home.
Lear.	O he is welcome, by my [s]oule he is: At it my iocund heart doth leape for ioy, That I shall liue to tell him, thus he dies.
king	Leartes, content your [s]elfe, be rulde by me, And you [s]hall haue no let for your reuenge.
Lear.	My will, not all the world.
King	Nay but Leartes, marke the plot I haue layde, I haue heard him often with a greedy wi[s]h, Vpon [s]ome prai[s]e that he hath heard of you Touching your weapon, which with all his heart, He might be once tasked for to try your cunning.
Lea.	And how for this?
King	Mary Leartes thus: I'le lay a wager, Shalbe on *Hamlets* [s]ide, and you [s]hall giue the oddes, The which will draw him with a more de[s]ire, To try the mai[s]try, that in twelue venies You gaine not three of him: now this being granted, When you are hot in midst of all your play, Among the foyles [s]hall a keene rapier lie, Steeped in a mixture of deadly poy[s]on, That if it drawes but the lea[s]t dramme of blood, In any part of him, he cannot liue: This being done will free you from [s]u[s]pition, And not the deere[s]t friend that *Hamlet* lov'de Will euer haue Leartes in [s]u[s]pect.
Lear.	My lord, I like it well: But [s]ay lord *Hamlet* [s]hould refu[s]e this match.
King	I'le warrant you, wee'le put on you Such a report of [s]ingularitie, Will bring him on, although against his will. And le[s]t that all [s]hould mi[s][s]e, I'le haue a potion that [s]hall ready [s]tand, In all his heate when that he calles for drinke, Shall be his period and our happine[s][s]e.
Lear.	T'is excellent, O would the time were come! Here comes the Queene. *enter the Queene.*

Notes

1. See: (1) "Two *Lears* for Television: An Exploration of Televisual Strategies". *Literature-Film Quarterly* 14 (1986), 179-86. Repr. in *Shakespeare on Television: An Anthology of Essays and Reviews*. Eds. James C. Bulman and H. R. Coursen. Hanover, NH: New England UP, 1988 and in the Appendix to James P. Lusardi and June Schlueter. *Reading Shakespeare in Performance: King Lear* (Rutherford: Fairleigh Dickinson UP, 1990); (2) "Reading Shakespeare on Television." Dissertation. University of Maryland, 1988; and "Jane Howell's BBC First Tetralogy: Theatrical and Televisual Manipulation." *Literature-Film Quarterly*, 20 (1992), 326-31.

2. *The BBC TV Shakespeare Hamlet* uses Peter Alexander's text in *The Works* (London: Collins, 1951). It further includes notations from the BBC Television camera scripts to indicate new locations (changes of sets) with descriptions of the set location and time setting, variations of characters in scenes that do not coincide with the start of a scene in the printed text, cuts in the printed text, and occasional notes of a character's movement when that movement is necessary for the comprehension of the action (32).

3. Alexander does not even include the Q1 stage direction *"Enter the ghost in his night gowne"*. (3.4).

4. "In this regard", Janice Lull asserts, "the Q1 text affirms the ethics of the postfeudal honor culture, especially the value of heroic individualism, whereas the F text shows Hamlet accepting the newer Protestant ethic by subordinating his individual will to divine providence" (137).

5. In numbering scenes in Q1, I followed the convention of a new scene's beginning after all of the characters present in the previous scene have left the stage.

6. I have decided to designate Q1's Corambis as Polonius throughout this paper.

7. I will also refer to these two characters by their more familiar Q2/F1 names rather than as Rossencraft and Gilderstone as they are in Q1.

8. I have included transcriptions of all the inserts I used in an appendix to this paper.

Works Cited

Allen, Michael J. B., and Kenneth Muir, eds. *Shakespeare's Plays in Quarto: A Facsimile Edition of Copies Primarily from the Henry E. Huntington Library*. Berkeley: California UP, 1981.

The BBC TV Shakespeare Hamlet. Literary Consultant John Wilders. London: BBC, 1980. (The text used for this volume is the Peter Alexander, *The Works*. London: Collins, 1951).

Bertram, Paul, and Bernice W. Kliman, eds. *The Three-Text HAMLET: Parallel Texts of the First and Second Quartos and First Folio*. New York: AMS Press, 1991.

Bulman, James C., and H. R. Coursen, eds. *Shakespeare on Television: An Anthology of Essays and Reviews*. Hanover, NH: New England UP, 1988.

Clayton, Thomas, ed. *The Hamlet First Published (Q1, 1603): Origins, Form, Intertextualities*. Newark: Delaware UP, 1992.

Cook, Hardy M. "Jane Howell's BBC First Tetralogy: Theatrical and Televisual

Manipulation". *Literature-Film Quarterly,* 20 (1992), 326-31.
---. "Reading Shakespeare on Television". Dissertation. University of Maryland, 1988. Director: Maynard Mack, Jr. Readers: Jane Donawerth and Neil Isaacs.
---. Two *Lears* for Television: An Exploration of Televisual Strategies." *Literature-Film Quarterly,* 14 (1986), 179-86.
Irace, Kathleen O. *Reforming the 'Bad' Quartos: Performance and Provenance of Six Shakespearean First Editions.* Newark: Delaware UP, 1994.
Lull, Janice. "Forgetting *Hamlet*: The First Quarto and the Folio." In Clayton 137-50.
Lusardi, James P., and June Schlueter. *Reading Shakespeare in Performance: King Lear.* Rutherford: Fairleigh Dickinson UP, 1990.
Taylor, Gary, and Michael Warren, eds. *The Division of the Kingdom: Shakespeare's Two Versions of 'King Lear'.* Oxford UP, 1983.

SOME POETIC AND DRAMATIC USES OF COOKERY IN SHAKESPEARE'S PLAYS

Patricia L. Cornett
(Lawrence Technological University, Southfield, Michigan)

Introduction

The everyday world of eating and drinking and food and cooking, encompassing what G. Wilson Knight (in his commentary on the symbolic importance of the feast in Shakespeare's plays) called the "fundamentals of human existence,"[1] informs Shakespeare's plays like a subtle infusion of spirits. So commonplace is this domestic world that critics usually take it for granted or glance at it only perfunctorily even if they acknowledge that references to food and drink rank high on any list of topics surveyed for the frequency of their appearance in Shakespeare's plays. The purpose of this paper is to explore that domestic world, chiefly from the perspective of social and culinary history, and, through selected examples, to show how Shakespeare uses it for a wide variety of poetic, dramatic, and thematic purposes.

Definitions of Cookery and Culinary History

Two definitions will help orient the reader to my approach. Firstly, I use the term 'cookery' to mean the preparation and consumption of food and drink as described in period cookery books, household account books, books of domestic management, dietaries, herbals, diaries, and journals.[2] Secondly, culinary history, a form of social history, involves the study of the domestic world of cooking, eating, dining, and drinking, with emphasis on: (1) types of food and drink and their consumption, (2) cooking techniques and equipment, and (3) the settings and social occasions, both private and public, that reveal the eating and drinking habits of the period in their social and historical contexts.

Shakespeare's plays contain a deliciously wide variety of examples of this domestic institution, but I will concentrate in this paper on examples from the English histories and comedies. From an early comedy like *The Comedy of Errors* to the late tragicomedies, such as *The Winter's Tale* or *The Tempest*, references to cookery are abundant. Louis Marder, for example, has compiled a list of culinary terms in Shakespeare's gastronomic vocabulary. The list contains 335 terms, from ale to wort, but is "far from complete".[3] Some of these terms, such as 'eringoes', appear for the first time in English in Shakespeare's plays.[4]

Poetic and Rhetorical Uses of Cookery

Shakespeare's poetic, rhetorical, dramatic, theatrical, psychological, and thematic uses of cookery are numerous. To start with possibly the best researched use, the world of cookery provides Shakespeare with a well-stocked storehouse of images, comparisons, and other poetic and rhetorical devices, as Caroline Spurgeon painstakingly recorded in *Shakespeare's Imagery and What It Tells Us*.[5] However, few readers today would be so foolhardy as to believe that these culinary images and gastronomic vocabulary tell us about Shakespeare's own tastes, or to conclude, as Spurgeon does, that Shakespeare

> seems to dislike stale or dry tasteless things, dry biscuits, dried pears, stale dry cheese, musty or tainted meat, ill-baked doughy bread, sodden or greasy food, a carelessly boiled egg or an over-roasted joint; that he appreciates green salad and the sharp savoury tang of herbs, the sweet kernels of nuts, the taste of honey, well-baked crusty bread, and looks on beefsteak and fried potatoes as a luxury. If we add to this, what we all know, that skim milk struck him as a poor drink, while cakes and ale seemed good to him, that ginger and cordial appeared to him of more comfort than cold porridge, it is but one more proof of how completely he shared in the tastes and weaknesses of our common and suffering humanity (124).[6]

Also in the same well-stocked culinary storehouse are proverbs and hornbook commonplace sayings, some of which were undoubtedly stale in Shakespeare's day, some of which are his own creation and have become stale only later as they passed into common use. In the former category are "Unquiet meals make ill digestions" (*CE*, 5.1.74) or "Our cake's dough on both sides" (*TS*,

1.1.108). In the latter are Pistol's "Why then the world's mine oyster" (MWW, 2.3.3). Epithets and insults, as well as terms of endearment, also draw on the storehouse of cookery lore. The many culinary epithets used to describe Falstaff perhaps come most readily to mind: "Sir John Sack and Sugar" (*1HIV*, 1.1.113-14); "my sweet beef" (*1HIV*, 4.1.177); "gross wat'ry pumpion" (*MWW*, 3.3.41).

Dramatic and Theatrical Uses of Cookery

But Shakespeare's use of cookery goes far beyond the rhetorical and poetic surface of the plays, however rich and sometimes strange that surface may be. The figurative language of eating and drinking, dining and feasting has its dramatic counterpart in the theatrical language of visual stage metaphor, what David Bevington calls the "presentational language of the theater".[7] Often, Shakespeare stages a meal or feast to dramatize social relationships and a sense of community and order, or, alternatively, to comment on the need for, or absence of, social order and spiritual well-being. As John Mahon points out:

> Meals affirm human community; when they are abortive, they fail because community has failed. Indeed, Shakespeare uses meals more often than not to dramatize the *absence* of good fellowship and a sense of community. He seems deliberately to manipulate audience expectations of happy meals in order to emphasize the disorder and hostility in a given situation. [...] Most of the meals are interrupted. A pattern, then, emerges, in which Shakespeare uses meals to dramatize conflict rather than conviviality (237).[8]

Like Mahon, Bevington also argues that ceremony in Shakespeare's plays is a "focus of dramatic conflict. We learn much about the visual nature of ceremony on Shakespeare's stage from the manner in which it is interrupted or violated" (137). The rituals surrounding the daily meal, as well as the feast that celebrates social and religious occasions or holidays, are "part of a rich vocabulary expressing contractual obligation, obedience, homage, submission, fealty, petition, hospitality..." (136).

Such ceremony, both social and religious, infused all but the most casual and informal meals for all but the lowest social orders in Elizabethan society.[9] Daily meal-times, especially for the upper 'estates', were wellregulated, often elaborate affairs with numerous courses and customs governing all aspects of behavior and service. Rules dictated the behavior of hosts and guests, and order and rank were observed at table. Good manners reflected one's station in society and were instilled in young children through etiquette books. Hosts and guests were expected to be hospitable and gracious to friends and strangers alike.[10] In addition, the daily meal, which began and ended with a prayer, had religious overtones, and Mahon suggests that "Elizabethans would readily associate meals with liturgy" (235). Hospitality and grace were inextricably intertwined. To say grace at the meal was to invoke the blessing of the divine Giver. Dining and feasting, therefore, are imbued with a rich complex of social and religious values. With this view in mind, the Shepherd's scolding of Perdita at the beginning of the sheep-shearing feast in Act Four of *The Winter's Tale* resonates at several levels of meaning:

> Fie, daughter, when my old wife liv'd, upon
> This day she was both pantler, butler, cook,
> Would sing her song, and dance her turn; now here,
> At upper end o' th' table, now i' th' middle;
> On his shoulder, and his; her face o' fire
> With labor, and the thing she took to quench it
> She would to each one sip. You are retired,
> As if you were a feasted one and not
> The hostess of the meeting. Pray you bid
> These unknown friends to's welcome, for it is
> A way to make us better friends, more known.
> Come, quench your blushes, and present yourself
> That which you are, mistress o' th' feast. Come on,
> And bid us welcome to your sheep-shearing,
> As your good flock shall prosper.
> (4.4.55-69)

Perdita's role in these Act Four scenes is complex and ambivalent because she is not to the country manner born, no more than is Autolycus, the out of-favor courtier, who is Perdita's antithesis throughout Act Four. Thus, when she shows a dainty reluctance to serve as hostess at the feast, the Shepherd, her spiritual father, chides her and instructs her in the true meaning of grace and gentleness.

It would be a mistake to think that because Elizabethans took the daily meal seriously meal-times were solemn, ponderous occasions. From all contemporary accounts, quite the opposite was true. Elizabethans loved to eat and drink and were famous throughout Europe for their lusty appetites, their "large tabling and bellycheer". Harrison's justification for the hearty English appetite is especially attractive:

> The situation of our region, lying near unto the north, doeth cause the heat of our stomachs to be of somewhat greater force; therefore our bodies do crave a little more ample nourishment than the inhabitants of the hotter regions are accustomed withal, whose digestive force is not altogether so vehement, because their internal heat is not so strong as ours, which is kept in by the coldness of the air that from time to time (especially in winter) doth environ our bodies (123-4).

Comments about the English appetite were not always flattering, however. Elizabethans were often called gluttons and drunkards and were criticized for their excessive gourmandizing by foreign visitors as well as by Puritans like Philip Stubbes.[11] Puritan reformers preached moderation in diet as in other aspects of daily living, and they inveighed incessantly against the gluttonous excesses of their countrymen. As a result, prosperous Puritan households in the early 17th century undoubtedly practiced more restraint and moderation in their dining and drinking than did the Elizabethan gentry a generation earlier.

In Shakespeare's plays, there are numerous examples of the feast, banquet, or meal used as a visual theatrical metaphor to dramatize and comment on social relationships and religious values, from the "gossip's feast" that harmoniously closes *The Comedy of Errors* to the spectacular vanishing banquet in *The Tempest*. Mahon describes nine such occasions, but limits his analysis to fully-staged meals.[12] I would add to Mahon's list the sheep-shearing feast in Act Four of *The Winter's Tale*. If his definition is expanded to include meals that take place off stage or are referred to in on-stage dialogue or stage directions, then we can add the gossip's feast at the end of *The Comedy of Errors*, the menu-specific invitation to dinner in Act One of *The Merry Wives of Windsor* ("Come, we have a hot venison pasty to dinner", 1.1.195), and the off-stage supper of Duncan and his retinue in Act 1, Scene 7 of *Macbeth* ("Enter sewer and divers servants with dishes and service over the stage"). Knight's discussion of feasts in *The Crown of Life* (215-16) cites additional examples from *Romeo and Juliet*, *Antony and Cleopatra*, *Pericles*.

Other Dramatic Uses of Cookery

Besides the explicit staging or near-staging of the feast or banquet, more general applications of cookery are one of Shakespeare's favorite dramatic methods. He uses this domestic world, for example, to hold the dramatic structure of the stage action together. The insistent, repeated references to dining and to dinnertime (the mid-day meal) in *The Comedy of Errors* are not only the means to reinforce the classical unity of time being observed in the play; they are also the dramatic heartbeat of the action urging the characters and the audience relentlessly toward the end of the day and the end of the play.[13] Dining and food are analogues for the passage of time: "The capon burns, the pig falls from the spit;/The clock hath strucken twelve upon the bell" (*CE*, 1.2.44-5). It is altogether fitting that this play should conclude with a "gossip's feast" that reunites the family into a harmonious social unit. In the words of Joseph Candido, this feast is a "baptismal banquet at which the whole family assembles to welcome with joy a new member into a social and religious community".[14]

The domestic setting and details of the cookery world are also used for dramatic counterpoint and thematic contrast. More than merely layering on descriptive details to particularize a specific stage setting or location, references to cooking, eating, and drinking create an imaginatively realized, richly detailed world that serves various dramatic and thematic purposes. The mercantile and domestic worlds of the so-called middle-class comedies are good examples, so it is not surprising that *The Comedy of Errors*, *The Taming of the Shrew*, *Twelfth Night*, and *The Merry Wives of Windsor* contain many references to cookery and related domestic activities.

However, this use of cookery is hardly limited to the middle-class comedies. One of the most notable uses is the contrast in the two *Henry IV* plays between the worlds of the court and the tavern. As Herschel Baker notes in his Introduction to the Riverside Shakespeare, "this continual oscillation [between the two worlds] is the most conspicuous feature of these plays" (844). Shakespeare enriches the particularity of the Boar's Head tavern scenes to intensify the dramatic counterpoint of Prince Hal's movements between the two worlds and to heighten the dramatic tension of his choice. The gross, earthy world of Eastcheap and the Boars Head tavern involves more than cookery as such, but dining and drinking are its defining features, as Falstaff is its chief exemplar.

These scenes, such as 2.1. in *1 Henry IV,* give us a vivid, memorable picture of an Elizabethan public house in an undesirable lower-class neighborhood of London. Eastcheap was a disreputable, dangerous commercial district known as much for its butcher shops and meat markets, appropriately enough, as for being a haven for petty criminals like Bardolph. Shakespeare undoubtedly chose the Boar's Head Tavern, "the most villainous house in all London road for fleas" (*1HIV*, 2.1.14), for the porcine associations of its name. This was a fairly common name for an inn in Elizabethan times, and at least six actual inns of this name have been identified as the possible site of Shakespeare's Boar's Head tavern.[15] Significantly, in *The Merry Wives of Windsor*, Falstaff inhabits a more innocuous, less dangerous tavern world, just as he himself is a reduced, shrunken shadow of his former Rabelaisian self.

The sheepshearing feast in Act IV of *The Winter's Tale* is another example of cookery used to provide dramatic contrast between separate but complementary worlds. After the court tragedy of the first three acts, Father Time introduces us to the pastoral countryside of Bohemia, where in quick succession we meet, first, Autolycus singing of the "white sheet bleaching on the hedge" and "a quart of ale is a dish fit for a king" and then the Clown, whose shopping list for the feast includes: "Three pounds of sugar, five pound of currants, rice. [...] I must have saffron to color the warden pies; mace; dates, none – that's out of my note; nutmegs, seven; a race or two of ginger, but that I may beg; four pounds of pruins, and as many of raisins o' th' sun" (4.3.37-49). The transition from tragedy to comedy, from court to country, from the religious mystery and enigma of Apollo's Oracle to a country girl's shopping list of fruits and spices is swiftly accomplished with dramatic economy and freshness. Perdita, the "queen of curds and cream" (5.4.161), is the emblematic exemplar and generative force of this pastoral world, just as Falstaff, in his tavern world, holds forth as the Old Vice at the Boars Head Tavern and is, metaphorically, the "old boar [who doth] feed in the old frank" (*2HIV*, 2.2.145).

The Use of Cookery to Define Character

Shakespeare also uses cookery to define character. Who can forget the kitchen wench Nell in *The Comedy of Errors* who is "all grease" (*CE*, 3.1.)? So synonymous is she with her domestic role that Shakespeare even coined the verb "kitchen'd" to describe her behavior (5.1.416).[16] Nell is the first of a long line of "fat friends", Shakespearean characters defined by their association with, and most often, their love of food and drink. Among Nell's companions are Sir Toby Belch, the drunken Porter, and Caliban.[17]

The most notable and complex example, however, is Falstaff, chiefly, in the two *Henry IV* plays. Falstaff at once energizes and exemplifies the tavern world at its best and worst. More than any other topic (even whoring and wenching), food and drink are used to establish Falstaff's character. The constant, comical litany of references to his gargantuan capacity for eating and drinking – along with sex the basest and most basic of human needs – defines his fleshly grossness, his earthbound sensuality, and identifies him as the emblem for the world, the flesh, and the devil. Symbolically, he is identified with the boar's head because gluttony is traditionally associated with swine. Falstaff *is* the sin of gluttony, and his punishment at the end of *2 Henry IV*, in Prince Hal's famous rejection, is couched in culinary terms with a grave pun on Falstaff's girth: "Make less thy body (hence) and more thy grace,/Leave gormandizing, know the grave doth gape/ For thee thrice wider than for other men" (*2HIV*, 5.5.52-4).

There are, however, worse sins in the canon than gluttony. Falstaff's base physical needs and his comically excessive, almost infantile appetite also make him inherently human and appealing. Falstaff's expansive persona embodies and embraces all of humanity: "banish plump Jack, and banish all the world" (*1 HIV*, 2.4. 479-80). Moreover, fatness is, by its nature, associated with feasting, plenty, and the earth's bounty (Cf. Juno's speech in the masque of Ceres in *The Tempest*, 4.1.110-17:

> "Earth's increase, foison plenty,
> Barns and garners never empty;
> Vines with clust'ring bunches growing,
> Plants with goodly burthen bowing [...];
> Scarcity and want shall shun you
> Ceres' blessing so is on you."

just so, antithetically, leanness is associated with hunger, famine, and things vaguely threatening: "Yon Cassius has a lean and hungry look" (*Julius Caesar*, 1.1.194). Because of his corpulence, a continual source of jokes, sometimes by him, sometimes about him, Falstaff is the visual icon of the earth's abundance and of the round earth itself. He is not only of the earth, he is the earth. He is at once gross and gluttonous, but also vital and life-engendering: "Falstaff sweats to death,/And lards the lean earth as he walks along" (*1HIV*, 2.2.108-9). The complexity and duality of Falstaff's fleshly nature are not neatly resolved, despite Prince Hal's harsh rejection at the end of *2 Henry IV*. The audience is left with a "rounded" character, a multi-dimensional creation whose vitality escapes the confines of the dramatic conventions. Prince Hal may have to choose between the court world and the tavern world, but the audience does not: the two *Henry IV* plays are expansive enough to hold them both in tension and paradox.

Conclusion

The world of cookery is pervasive throughout Shakespeare's plays, as this brief excursion into that domestic arena suggests. Whether drawn upon for imagery and dramatic speech, used to reinforce dramatic structure, to expand the symbolic and metaphorical limits of the stage action through visual icon and tableaux, or adapted to define character, food and drink, dining and drinking, meals eaten or abandoned, are all important elements of Shakespeare's poetic and dramatic methods.

Notes

1. G. Wilson Knight, *The Crown of Life: Essays in Interpretation of Shakespeare's Last Plays* (London: Methuen, 1948), p. 215.

2. There are five definitions of cookery in the *OED* for this listing: 1) the art and practice of cooking and preparation of food (1393); 2) cooking apparatus and materials (1613); 3) a product of the cook's art (1734); 4) cooking establishment (1598); 5) action or method of cooking or dressing up or falsifying. The first four definitions are applicable here, and three of the four were in use in Shakespeare's day. For the first definition, the OED cites, among several examples, *Antony and Cleopatra*, 2.6.63-4: "your fine Egyptian cookery/Shall have the fame." Also under the first definition, the second earliest listing from 1450 is contained in the title of *Two Cookery Bookes.*

All quotations from Shakespeare's plays are taken from *The Riverside Shakespeare*, ed. G. Blakemore Evans (Boston: Houghton Mifflin, 1974).

3. Personal correspondence, April 10, 1994.

4. 'Eringoes' are mentioned in *The Merry Wives of Windsor*, 5.5.18-20: "Let the sky rain potatoes; let it thunder to the tune of 'Green-sleeves', hail kissing-comfits, and snow eringoes." Eringoes are the candied roots of the sea-holly and were commonly supposed to have aphrodisiac properties.

Gerard's *Herball* (1597) contains the second English reference to them: "The rootes condited or preserued with sugar [...] are exceeding good to be giuen vnto old and aged people that are consumed and withered with age, and which want naturall moisture: it is also good for other sorts of people that haue no delight or appetite to venery, nourishing and restoring the aged, and amending the defects of nature in the yoonger." Since *MWW* was probably first performed in April, 1597, Shakespeare's play takes the honor for having the first published reference to eringoes, beating out Gerard's *Herball* by a less than a year. See Mats Rydén, *Shakespearean Plant Names: Identifications and Interpretations*, Stockholm Studies in English XLIII (Stockholm: Almqvist and Wiksell International, 1978), p. 48.

5. Chap. VII (London: Cambridge UP, 1971), pp. 117-24. Spurgeon's chart in Appendix VII on the frequency of food, drink, and cooking images in Shakespeare's plays is less helpful that it might at first appear. For example, based on her chart, *The Comedy of Errors* would seem to have fewer such images than any other play except *1 Henry VI*; but, in fact, *The Comedy of Errors* is pervaded by food references, more so than many other plays. See Joseph Candido, "Dining

Out in Ephesus: Food in *The Comedy of Errors*", *SEL* (1990) 30, pp. 217-41.

6. The fried potato referred to here is not, despite Spurgeon's implication, the white potato and certainly bears no resemblance to American French fries or even to English chips. Shakespeare refers to the potato at least twice, once in the lines quoted above from *The Merry Wives of Windsor* and again in *Troilus and Cressida*, and his references are among the earliest recorded uses of the word. However, he is referring to the sweet potato, not the white potato. See Madge Lorwin, *Dining With William Shakespeare* (New York: Atheneum, 1976), p. 41 and Mats Rydén, *Shakespearean Plant Names: Identifications and* Interpretations. Stockholm Studies in English XLIII (Stockholm: Almqvist & Wiksell International, 1978, pp. 48, 89). The latter is a New World plant brought back to Europe at the end of the Sixteenth century by explorers but not in widespread cultivation in England and elsewhere until the Seventeenth century. Only in Ireland was the white potato a staple crop by 1625. See Henry Hobhouse, *Seeds of Change: Five plants that transformed mankind*, Cambridge, MA: Harper & Row, 1985, pp. 191 f.

7. *Action is Eloquence: Shakespeare's Language of Gesture* (Cambridge, MA: Harvard UP, 1984), Chap V. See also Peter Farb and George Armelagos, "The Meal as Metaphor", in *Consuming Passions: the Anthropology of Eating"* (Boston: Houghton Mifflin, 1980), pp. 97-111. The ritual of the daily meal as a means of bringing the family together in social community and harmony remains a potent metaphor even in today's fast-food world; it is, for example, the dominating metaphor of Ann Tyler's novel *Dinner at the Homesick Restaurant*.

8. "For now we sit to chat as well as eat': Conviviality and Conflict in Shakespeare's Meals", *"Fanned and Winnowed Opinions": Shakespearean Essays Presented to Harold Jenkins*, ed. John W. Mahon, Thomas A. Pendleton (London and New York: Methuen, 1987), p. 237. See also Daryl W. Parker, "Entertainment, Hospitality, and Family in *The Winter's Tale*", Iowa State Journal of Research 59 (1985), pp. 253-61.

For a detailed discussion of meal-times and manners in Shakespeare's day, see Lorwin, pp. 151-8; 241-6.

9. William Harrison's rather dismissive comment at the end of the chapter on the food and diet of the English in his 1577 *Description of England* (Ithaca: Cornell UP for The Folger Shakespeare Library, 1968) is revealing in this regard: "As for the poorest sort, they generally dine and sup when they may, so that to talk of their order of repast it were but a needless manner" (144).

10. See "Manners Maketh Man," in Bridget Ann Henisch's *Fast and Feast: Food in Medieval Society* (University Park and London: Pennsylvania State UP, 1976), pp.190-205.

11. Lorwin's Introduction (3-7) discusses the lusty English appetite for food and

drink and quotes numerous contemporary travelers' accounts to support this attitude.

12. Mahon defines these as "scenes in which tables are set and people actually sit down, or attempt to sit down, to a meal, and not all of these are elaborate feasts" (232). The plays in which these scenes are found are *Titus Andronicus*, *The Taming of the Shrew*, *As You Like It*, *Timon of Athens*, and *The Tempest*.

13. For example, the *Harvard Concordance to Shakespeare* (Cambridge: Harvard UP, 1973) lists 25 references for the verb "dine": 9 of the 25 (36%) are from *The Comedy of Errors*. Similarly, 7 of 17 (41%) references for "din'd" are from this play, as are 21 of 83 (25%) references to "dinner".

14. Joseph Candido, "Dining Out in Ephesus: Food in *The Comedy of Errors*", *SEL* 30 (1990), pp. 217-41.

15. O. J. Campbell, *The Reader's Encyclopedia of Shakespeare* (New York: Crowell, 1966), p. 75.

16. The *OED* labels this verbalization of "kitchen" a rare, obscure usage and cites Shakespeare's line from *The Comedy of Errors* as its only example.

17. See Knight's discussion (note 1 above, pp. 217 f.) of the drunken anti-trinity of Stephano, Trinculo, and Caliban in *The Tempest*.

HAMLET AND PHARAOH'S DREAM

Will and Mimosa Stephenson
(Texas State Technical College; University of Texas at Brownsville)

In Act 3, Scene 4 of *Hamlet,* the protagonist scolds Queen Gertrude for transferring her affections from his father, King Hamlet, to the dead king's brother and successor, Claudius:

> This was your husband. Look you now what follows:
> Here is your husband, like a mildewed ear,
> Blasting his wholesome brother. Have you eyes?
> Could you on this fair mountain leave to feed
> And batten on this moor? (3.4.64-8)[1]

Edward A. Armstrong observes of this scene, "Almost every word arouses a group of linked images and each group is linked with each other group by interpenetrating meanings".[2] In the passage quoted above, Hamlet's impassioned words are rich in allusion and word play, as, to heighten the contrast between Claudius and his predecessor, Hamlet resorts to a metaphor of two ears of grain, the one "mildewed", the other "wholesome". The comparison is an accusation of murder, as the diseased ear *poisons* the healthy one by contaminating it with the toxic mildew. The punning synecdoche reveals Hamlet's knowledge that Claudius murdered King Hamlet by pouring poison into his *ear.*

Hardin Craig[3] has pointed out that the "mildewed ear" in line 65 refers to Genesis 41:5-7: "Again [Pharaoh] slept, and dreamed the seconde time: and beholde, seuen eares of corne grewe vpon one stalke, ranke and goodlie. And, lo, seué thinne eares, & blasted with the East winde, Sprang vp after them: And the thinne eares deuoured the seué ranke and ful eares. [T]hen Pharaóh awaked, and lo, it was a dreame".[4] Critics have explicated one aspect or another of these lines, but we are not aware that anyone has yet related Hamlet's angry speech in his mother's closet to the entire story in Genesis 41:1-32 of Pharaoh's dreams of approaching famine.[5] Associating the story of Joseph with the actions and predicament of Hamlet – an association invited by Hamlet's biblical allusion –

enriches our understanding of Gertrude, Claudius, the Ghost, Hamlet, and the nation of Denmark itself.

The allusion to Claudius as "a mildewed ear, / Blasting his wholesome brother" recalls the seven thin ears of grain "blasted with the East winde", with the dead king represented by the "goodlie" ears. The ears of grain may reasonably be thought of as brothers, with the destruction of the good by the bad corresponding to Claudius's murder of his brother. In Shakespeare's allusion to Pharaoh's dream, the withered ears passively "blasted" by the east wind become active, with Claudius "blasting his wholesome brother". Recognition of this image from Genesis shapes our response to the next two lines, which relate Queen Gertrude to Pharaoh's first dream: "Could you on this fair mountain leave to feed / And batten on this moor?" In verses 17-21 of Genesis 41, Pharaoh narrates to Joseph his earlier vision of seven fat-fleshed kine emerging from the river, followed by seven evil-favored kine that devour the fat kine but remain as emaciated as before. Though the most obvious connection between the Joseph and Hamlet stories is to associate the fat and the evil-favored kine with the past and present kings, in the lines from the play the tenor of "this fair mountain" is King Hamlet, and of "this moor" is Claudius. According to the *O.E.D.*, a *moor* is "A tract of unenclosed waste ground" or "A marsh". The contrast here is between King Hamlet, a beautiful high mountain, and King Claudius, a low wasteland or a swamp. In an unflattering bovine image, Gertrude has left grazing on the heights and sunk to the depths to glut her appetites.[6] Having been consort both to King Hamlet (the wholesome corn/fair mountain) and Claudius (the mildewed corn/moor), Gertrude with King Hamlet becomes the equivalent of the fat kine, and with Claudius of the evil-favored kine of Pharaoh's disturbing dream: the good wife has been eaten up by the "euilfauoured" wife, and Hamlet would add with Pharaoh, "I neuer sawe the like in all the land of Egypt, for euilfauoured" (Gen. 41:19).

We should not leave the *kine* metaphor without noting that the word *batten* admirably fits the motifs and themes Shakespeare develops throughout the play. According to the *O.E.D.*, *batten* means "To grow better or improve in condition; *esp.* (of animals) to improve in bodily condition by feeding, to feed to advantage, thrive, grow fat". Gertrude and Claudius have attempted to better their physical condition, to thrive, at the expense of their souls. Within the metaphor Gertrude is a cow, but the word *batten* metaphorically suits both Claudius and Gertrude as animals, in line with the pattern of animal imagery found in the play (i.e., fox, rat, adders, worms, dogs, bat, ape, and numerous others). The Ghost calls Claudius "that incestuous, that adulterate beast" (1.5.43). The *O.E.D.* also says *batten* means "To feed gluttonously *on,* glut oneself; to gloat or revel *in".* The word seems especially appropriate in the light of Claudius's fondness for sex and drink, which makes him seem a creature of appetite in contrast to his nephew/stepson, who ponders. Hamlet wants to kill Claudius

> When he is drunk asleep, or in his rage,
> Or in th' incestuous pleasure of his bed,
> At game, a-swearing, or about some act
> That has no relish of salvation in 't. (3.3.89-92)

After his allusion to the story of Joseph, Hamlet tells Gertrude that she lives "In the rank sweat of an enseamèd bed, / Stewed in corruption, honeying and making love / Over the nasty sty! (3.4.94-96). Claudius, who was, we may assume, having an affair with her before the murder, says that Gertrude is his very life:

> My virtue or my plague, be it either which –
> She is so conjunctive to my life and soul
> That, as the star moves not but in his sphere,
> I could not but by her. (4.7.14-17)

Figuratively *batten* means "To thrive, grow fat, prosper (*esp.* in a bad sense, at the expense or to the detriment of another); to gratify a morbid mental craving". This sense seems especially apt in *Hamlet,* where Claudius has murdered his brother because he coveted his brother's wife and throne. A final definition is "To grow fertile (as soil); to grow rank (as a plant)". This definition adds to the motif in the play of "an unweeded garden / That grows to seed. Things rank and gross in nature / Possess it merely" (1.2.135-7). In the scene under discussion, Hamlet tells his mother not to "spread the compost on the weeds / To make them ranker" (3.4.158-9). Thus *batten* is an apt verb to describe the actions of Claudius and Gertrude.

In the biblical story to which these four lines in Act 3, Scene 4 allude, Joseph tells Pharaoh, "Bothe Pharaohs dreames are one: God hathe shewed Pharaóh, what he is about to do" (25), and Hamlet plays on the oneness of two in addressing Claudius as "My mother". He explains, "Father and mother is man and wife, man and wife is one flesh, and so, my mother" (4.3.55-6). His references to corn and kine are also one. The tenor of "wholesome brother" and "fair mountain" is King Hamlet. The "mildewed ear" and "moor" on which Gertrude battens is King Claudius. Gertrude has chosen a mildewed ear over a wholesome one, a marsh over a mountain, a satyr over Hyperion (1.2.140). Joseph tells Pharaoh his two dreams are one and gives them one interpretation, a prophecy for Egypt: "All the plentie shalbe forgotten in the land of Egypt, and the famine shal consume the land: Nether shal the plentie be knowé in the land, by reason of this that shal come after: for it shalbe exceeding great" (Gen. 41:30-1). The story of Claudius and Gertrude has a similar import. When Claudius gained his brother's throne and his brother's wife a month later, the harvest seemed abundant indeed, but the guilty pair's joy is brief, for they soon reap the weeds they have sown. At the end of Act 3, Scene 3, immediately preceding the scene under discussion, Claudius vents his grief, the guilty aftermath of his deed:

> O, my offense is rank! It smells to heaven.
> It hath the primal eldest curse upon 't,
> A brother's murder. [...]
> O wretched state, O bosom black as death,
> O limèd soul that, struggling to be free,
> Art more engaged! (3.3.36-8, 67-9)

And Gertrude is also miserable as a result of her choice of a mildewed ear over a wholesome one. As Hamlet points out the difference between the two brothers, she responds, "Thou turn'st mine eyes into my very soul, / And there I see such black and grainèd spots. [...] These words like daggers enter in my ears. [...] O Hamlet, thou hast cleft my heart in twain" (3.4.91-2, 98, 163). In Pharaoh's dream the scrawny cattle and the scanty ears destroy the abundant ones yet remain ravenous. That picture holds for the king and queen in Shakespeare's play. They betrayed and destroyed their brother and husband, but they are worse off than before, not better. Sadly, Claudius says near the end of the play, "Howe'er my haps, my joys were ne'er begun" (4.3.72). Claudius accepts the psalmist's view that "The statutes of the Lord are right and reioyce the heart: [...] and in keeping of them there is great rewarde" (Ps. 19:8, 11), but as his actions are contrary to his values, he remains discontented though his plans have succeeded.

Hamlet concludes the speech in question by saying that Gertrude must have been demon-possessed to make the choice she did: "What devil was 't / That thus hath cozened you at hoodman-blind?" (3.4.77-8).[7] He has previously considered the possibility that the Ghost was demonic. Hamlet suggests that demons enticed Claudius and Gertrude and then entrapped them in their folly. The actions of Claudius are based on a theory of scarcity, the idea that there is not enough for everyone and that each man must undo his neighbor to ensure his own prosperity. The Joseph story in Genesis teaches that there is enough if it is shared, though not if each person hoards at his neighbor's expense. Joseph, as Pharaoh's prime minister, saves of the abundance of the seven plentiful crops to provide for the seven years of famine. There is enough food and to spare for neighbors, such as Joseph's brothers, who come to Egypt during the second seven years. But as long as people live with a theory of scarcity, they must grab as much as they can to ensure their future, and the most grasping will waste far more than they need, while others are in want. At the court Prince Claudius, as brother to the king, could have chosen from the most desirable maidens in the kingdom. Living with a philosophy of scarcity, he insisted on stealing what his brother had. Demanding a superfluity of abundance, he loses all.

The fourth significant agent in Hamlet's "mildewed ear" allusion, after Gertrude, Claudius, and the dead king, is Hamlet himself. Joseph's appearance before Pharaoh is a threshold event in the story of a young man who narrowly survives a struggle for dominance in a ruthless family, a struggle which includes an attempted fratricide, a related cover-up, and the protagonist's unfair fall from power. Hamlet's parallels with Joseph are imperfect, as Joseph rather than his father is the attempted murder victim, and the murder is not actually carried out. Nonetheless, Hamlet's situation is similar to Joseph's in significant ways: he feels confined, stating that all of Denmark is a prison, while Joseph spends years in prison unjustly condemned; like Joseph sold into slavery by his kin, Hamlet falls to a lower position in his uncle's accession to power; he is troubled by visions; he is ambivalent about pursuing revenge; and he would like to become as powerful as Joseph does.

Joseph's story ends with his attaining power over his brothers, while Hamlet dies rather than becoming king. And rather than seek revenge Joseph forgives his brothers when he is satisfied that they have repented. At their father's death the brothers tremble for fear Joseph will kill them, but he tells them, "When ye thoght euil against me, God disposed it to good, that he might bring to passe, as it is this day, and saue much people aliue" (Gen. 50:20). The most significant factor in the differing outcomes of the two stories is that Hamlet takes revenge and Joseph forgives. Joseph trusts God to provide abundantly for him and does not need to deprive his brothers in order to have enough. Hamlet is unwilling to share the air he breathes with his uncle, who has wronged him. Even the Ghost insists on his rights – an eye for an eye and a tooth for a tooth. Considering the outcome, we conclude with Roy W. Battenhouse that the Ghost is a pagan from hell.[8] Neither the Ghost nor Hamlet is willing to let God take care of Claudius, though both should be familiar with St. Paul's admonition, "Dearly beloued, auenge not your selues, but giue place vnto wrath: for it is written, Vengeāce is mine: I wil repaye, saith the Lord" (Rom. 12:19). As Eleanor Prosser points out, it may be "that Hamlet's real duty is *not* to kill Claudius."[9] Because King Hamlet's Ghost must have revenge, his whole family is annihilated, and he leaves no descendants. In contrast, Joseph and his brothers have left millions of descendants, for Joseph left the injustice for God to deal with. His brothers did bow down to him as his dreams said they would, and he ruled the land. In tragic contrast, Hamlet and those he loves all die violent deaths.

As a final point, the comparison of Gertrude and her two husbands to the ears of corn and the kine is also apt when we consider the ramifications that Pharaoh's dream holds for the entire kingdom. The succession from good seed to bad seed and from healthy cattle to sickly cattle augurs evil for all of Egypt, and we must remember that Hamlet considers Claudius's succession and his marriage to Gertrude a curse to Denmark. Claudius is "a vice of kings, / A cutpurse of the empire" (3.4.101-2) and "A king of shreds and patches" (3.4.106). This reminder of the larger importance to the nation of these domestic sins is a final achievement of Shakespeare's biblical metaphor, but unfortunately, Hamlet does not benefit by applying the lesson. Joseph has chosen forgiveness instead of revenge, and he proves a blessing not only to his family but also to the entire land of Egypt, saving all by storing up grain during the seven years of plenty. At the end of *Hamlet* Denmark is in a worse state than it was at the beginning. With an elderly Claudius on the throne, Denmark could yet hope in its young prince, who would assume the throne at the death of Claudius. Instead, the dying Hamlet names as the next king Fortinbras, a young man who has distinguished himself by leading his troops into battle and death, "Exposing what is mortal and unsure / To all that fortune, death, and danger dare / Even for an eggshell" (4.4.52-4). Fortinbras will fight for a shadow of honor, leading Denmark into wars that gain nothing. His troops will be slaughtered that he may make his name known. Ultimately the allusion to Joseph and Pharaoh in Hamlet's railing speech to his mother leads the reader to see that revenge is destructive not only to the victim and the avenger, but also to those whose lives touch theirs.

While penning a drama which revolves around fratricide, Shakespeare would naturally have turned his thoughts to the book of Genesis, with its tale of the "primal eldest curse" brought upon Cain by his murder of Abel. But in addition to several allusions to Cain and Abel, we also find in *Hamlet* a significant reference to a second story from the Book of Beginnings in which the deadly rivalry of brothers causes chaos and sorrow. Though superficially less relevant to *Hamlet*, the story of Joseph, taking place as it does in a more mature society and involving the fate of a nation, becomes in Shakespeare's hands a portentous emblem of the fate of Hamlet, his kin, and his nation.

Notes

1. *Hamlet. The Complete Works of Shakespeare,* ed. David Bevington, 4th edn. (New York: Harper/Collins, 1992), p. 1096. All quotations from the play are taken from this text.

2. Edward A. Armstrong, *Shakespeare's Imagination* (Lincoln: Nebraska UP, 1963), p. 114.

3. *The Complete Works of Shakespeare* (Chicago: Scott, Foresman, 1951), p. 927n.

4. Biblical quotations are from the Geneva Bible. According to Lloyd E. Berry (Introduction, *The Geneva Bible: A Facsimile of the 1560 Edition* [Madison: Wisconsin UP, 1969], p. 20), this was the version that Shakespeare used primarily (from 1596 on (*Hamlet* is 1601-4).

5. Avi Erlich points out that "mildewed ear" in this passage refers both to an ear of corn and to the part of the body and that "King Hamlet is re-established as a powerful 'mountain' [...] whose picture levels Claudius to a flat 'moor'", in *Hamlet's Absent Father* (Princeton UP, 1977), p. 83; and Roland M. Frye notes the "mildewed ear" phrase as part of the "Physical ridicule" Hamlet uses to disparage his uncle, in *The Renaissance 'Hamlet': Issues and Responses in 1600* (Princeton UP, 1984), p. 294. Ronald G. Shafer lists biblical allusions from this scene, even from this speech, but does not mention the Joseph reference, in "Hamlet: Christian or Humanist?" *Studies in the Humanities*, 17.1 (June 1990), p. 23. Finally, Theodore Lidz sees that the sibling rivalry in *Hamlet* is like that of Joseph and his brothers, in *Hamlet's Enemy: Madness and Myth in 'Hamlet'* (New York: Basic Books, 1975), p. 215, but does not mention this speech of Hamlet.

6. Shakespeare wrote *Hamlet* and *Othello* within a short period, and the possible conjunction of ideas from both plays suggests an additional pun on *moor,* appealing to racial prejudice such as that evidenced by Iago and Desdemona's father.

7. It is interesting to note that in the companion play *Othello,* Brabantio insists that some witchcraft or potion must have coerced Desdemona to marry Othello:

> She is abused, stol'n from me, and corrupted
> By spells and medicines bought of mountebanks;
> For nature so preposterously to err,
> Being not deficient, blind, or lame of sense,
> Sans witchcraft could not. (*Othello* 1.3.62-6)

8. Roy W. Battenhouse, "The Ghost in 'Hamlet': A Catholic 'Linchpin'?" *Studies in Philology,* 48.2 (April 1951), p. 190.

9. Eleanor Prosser, *Hamlet and Revenge* (Stanford UP, 1967), p. xii.

ISSUES OF KINGSHIP AND GOVERNANCE IN *RICHARD II, RICHARD III* AND *KING JOHN*

Ian Ward
(University of Dundee)

In *Shakespeare and History* (1995) I presented the thesis that Shakespeare's constitutional thought, as presented in the Histories, could be charted along two axes. The first is the axis of constitutional politics, from absolute to mixed monarchy. The second is the axis of constitutional philosophy, from theories of providence to English humanism. In this article I want to develop this thesis by applying it to three of Shakespeare Histories, *Richard II, Richard III* and *King John*.

Richard III

By all contemporary accounts Richard III was a good king. Recent historical scholarship has reinforced the view that he was a good administrator, a good politician, a good soldier and a devout man of God. In short, he was precisely the godly monarch that the Tudors were so keen to applaud. Moreover, his claim to the throne was at least as viable as any at the time, and certainly not exceptional in the often uncertain world of medieval monarchial succession.[1] Yet the Richard who emerges from Shakespeare's portrayal is infamous as the archetypal tyrant and villain. Shakespeare could have portrayed Richard in the same way as was to portray Henry V, but instead he chose to make life difficult for himself. The reason, of course, is that Shakespeare was rewriting a story which had already been told by previous Tudor propagandists, most notably More and Hall, in which Richard was already typecast.[2] According to Tillyard, his fate was determined by the grand design which lay behind the entire first tetralogy. Richard was visited upon, and symptomatic of, the sinful and unnatural state of fifteenth century England. His tyranny and evil were part of God's design, and only Providence would remove him, as it did in 1485, when Henry Tudor restored law and order to the dislocated realm. The Tudors were thus God's chosen dynasty. In suggesting this theme, Tillyard concludes that Richard is thus "the vehicle of an orthodox doctrine about kingship."[3]

A complementary reason for the portrayal of Richard which Shakespeare presented in *Richard III*, was the genus of the character which emerged from the *Henry VI* plays, primarily in Part 3, and at the same time, the intensification of a particular theme which has pervaded all three parts - that of insufficient kingship.[4] It is quite clear that Shakespeare was increasingly interested by this, and all of the Histories to varying degrees, and indeed many of the tragedies, question the validity of the central thesis in medieval and Tudor kingship, of the "kings two bodies". The ideal monarch was ideal in both personas. Such monarchs were Henry V and Henry VIII. But every other king portrayed in the Histories is in some way deficient in one or other of the two bodies. Richard is particular in being defective in both, and it is this, ultimately, which makes Shakespeare's job, constitutionally at least, easier. Richard is a plain tyrant, and can thus be treated as such.[5] It has been suggested that in his desire to effect a more subtle approach to the problems of politics, Shakespeare realised the need to concentrate upon the development of key characters. *Richard III* thus represents an evolutionary stage on the way to the greater complexities of *Richard II*.[6]

As a number of commentators have noted, the Richard III described thus tends to be a more one-dimensional figure, and one familiar to Shakespeare's audiences. The 'stage Machiavel' was certainly familiar in Elizabethan literature, and provided Shakespeare with a ready-to-hand and popular character with which he could portray the Richard which Tudor culture demanded. At the same time, Richard could thus be represented, as by More, as the antichrist. He could also represent 'Vice', another figure familiar to audiences from the Morality Plays, which was synonymous with decayed public morality.[7] Richard's Machiavellian persona was introduced in the final scenes of *3 Henry VI*, where his "dreams" of sovereignty betray a raw and evil ambition and a determination to achieve all by subverting God and nature, by setting "the murderous Machiavel to school" (3.2.124-95). Later Richard urges Edward to be a pragmatic King, and to ignore constitutional niceties in favour of a raw politics of power (4.7.58-9). Monarchy, he advises Edward, must be absolute and unprincipled. In other words, it must be tyrannical. At the close of *Henry VI*, as he murders God's anointed King, Richard's unnatural character, having "neither pity, love, nor fear", has already been laid (5.6.68).

In declaring himself to be Machiavellian Richard is declaring himself self-determinative and not determined by providence. At the same time, the route which he maps for himself in his very first soliloquay in *Richard III* is a contradiction of nature and good government. Richard is "determined to prove a villain" (1.1.1-41).[8] He is a wholly ungodly and unnatural prince, but, for a while, a thoroughly effective one.[9] Subsequently, having established his ambition, the realization of it reveals to Richard himself the tenuous nature of unnatural government, standing as it does on "brittle glass" (4.2.61).[10] The hypocritical puritanism with which Shakespeare colours Richard's speech reinforces the presentation of a man and a King deceitful towards both his subjects and his God, as Richard is himself only too well aware.[11] He thus denounces Edward's excesses as King, and sends Hastings to his death in a fit of puritan rhetoric.[12]

Yet Anne knows that Richard acknowledges "no law of God nor man", and thus, of course, potentially could be a King in neither of his two bodies (1.2.70). Clarence, at the moment of his death, makes precisely the same observation (1.4.174-81 & 184-9). Similarly, Margaret, too, appeals to providence to reveal the dishonesty of Richard's puritanism (1.3.216-33). Because Richard is so evil, God strikes him down. This is achieved by Richmond, whom Shakespeare very carefully portrays as the hand of God. Richmond works with heaven and the angels. His men go forward in "God's name" (5.2.14-16 & 156-7). In sharp contrast to Richard, Richmond is a barely developed character.[13] He does not need to be. His function is merely to serve as the mouthpiece of good and Godly princely government. He is, by his own reckoning, merely the "captain" of God (5.3.109).

The orthodox providential theme here is, as Tillyard saw, pervasive in *Richard III*.[14] This has its advantages, and certainly makes Shakespeare's task easier. It does not, however, tackle the crux of contemporary early modern constitutional debate. Rather it serves to deflect it. By unambiguously describing God's vengeance upon an equally unambiguously evil and insufficient Richard,

Shakespeare was able to negate the need for anyone else to remove him. There is no need for rebellion, at least not a self-determined rebellion. This, perhaps, is the central constitutional message in *Richard III*.[15] Conversely, the problem of what to do with the more ambiguously insufficient Kings, John and Richard II, catalyses much deeper constitutional themes in the subsequent Histories.

However, despite the fact that *Richard III* is very much more about providentialism than the niceties of constitutional debate, of mixed and absolute monarchy, and is a play about the character rather than kingship, yet, as providentialism was a necessary constituent of constitutional theory, there are certain more obviously constitutional issues in the play which warrant our attention. The first issue has already been suggested. Tyrants were subject to providence. Although Shakespeare could graphically portray the misery which tyrants visited upon their realms, it was not for subjects to rebel, unless so instructed by God.[16] This was Tudor orthodoxy.

A second, and not unrelated, constitutional issue is the question of legitimacy. Richard is consistently conscious of the issue of legitimacy, and it has been recently claimed that this is the dominant constitutional issue in the play.[17] Of course, Shakespeare ensures that Richard does not appear to be legitimate, and moreover, that Richard realises this. Yet, here Shakespeare was presented with an unavoidable dilemma. Although he is quick to reject Richard's legitimacy, his approach to Richmond's is more ambivalent.[18] Tudor orthodoxy was itself ambivalent here, championing a long dynastic genealogy right back to Cadwallader, yet at the same time concentrating far more on Henry Tudor as the unifying force above the dynastic struggles and claims of legitimacy which characterized fifteenth-century England. As the ghost of Henry VI says, it is the invasion of the King's "anointed body" which serves to condemn Richard, not merely the insufficiency of his genealogy. Richmond, in contrast, is the epitome of the godly prince (5.3.124-33). Interestingly, in his oration to his soldiers in Act 5 Scene 3, Richmond makes no particular claim to genealogical legitimacy, appealing instead to God and justice as his right:

Yet remember this:
God, and our good cause, fight upon our side;

The prayers of holy saints and wronged souls,
Like high-rear'd bulwarks, stand before our faces. (5.3.236-71)

Richard's appeal, which follows, conspicuously makes no mention of any form of legitimacy, save for possession (5.3.315-42). However, in the final scene, Shakespeare overtly refers to legitimacy, but then again only to strengthen the more important theme of inter-dynastic unity, and moreover as an adjunct to divine providence:

And then, as we have ta'en the sacrament,
We will unite the white rose and the red.
Smile, heaven, upon this fair conjunction,
That long have frown'd upon their enmity...
...
O now let Richmond and Elizabeth,
The true succeeders of each royal House,
By God's fair ordinance conjoin together,
And let their heirs, God, if Thy will be so,
Enrich the time to come with smooth-fac'd peace,
With smiling plenty, and fair prosperous days. (5.518-21 & 529-34)

It is the 'divine' right of the king which seals his legitimacy. Elizabeth's long litany of Richard's wrongs in 4.4, concludes by asserting the "greatest" wrong of usurpation is not against the usurped, but against God (4.4.377-87).[19]

A related question is Richard's relation with his subjects. Shakespeare portrays his attempt to secure the throne by popular acclamation as a reflection of his insufficient legitimacy, something about which Richard and his followers seem to be only too aware.[20] At the same time as trying to stress his legitimacy, in 3.7, Buckingham and Richard also make much of Richard's godliness. Richard knows what a king should be, and knows the extent of his own insufficiency. Shakespeare appears to make two particular observations here. Firstly, that Richard is himself deceitful in his claim to be a desirable monarch. Indeed, Richard is advised by Buckingham to be deceitful, and Catesby deliberately lies in his description of Richard's holiness (3.7.46-50 & 60-3). As Richmond later emphasises, Richard has been a suitably unnatural and thoroughly destructive King (5.2.1-16). A second observation seems more ambiguous. As he suggests elsewhere, most obviously in his treatment of Cade's rebellion, in *2 Henry VI*, the people are fickle, and certainly not the wise counsel which the godly prince requires. Popular democracy is not favourably portrayed in Shakespeare.

Yet, this is not to say that all the people are so incapable. Buckingham's attempt to woo the people, in 3.7, is met in silence, and only the Mayor urges Richard to take the Crown (3.7.1-3, 24-43 & 200). Moreover, in the scene immediately preceding Richard's appeal to the common people, the Scrivener wisely emphasises the wrongness in perjuring the law (3.6.1-14). The common Englishman can understand right and justice, but he can also, as a few are by Buckingham, be misled by rhetoric.[21] Ultimately, Shakespeare seems to indicate, it is a matter of both principle and good government. Kings should not seek approbation from their subjects, only from God. Richard's desire to be, in effect, crowned by the populace, as McNeir has commented, makes a mockery of the sanctity of legitimate coronation, something which will not have been lost on an Elizabethan audience.[22] Neither would have been Richard's loss of control at the end of his own coronation in 4.2.[23]

Richard III, then, though a less obviously constitutional play than either *King John* or *Richard II*, should not be too lightly dismissed as such. A treatise discussing the merits of providentialism is to some degree always a constitutional treatise. The approbation of providentialism does not, however, itself however tell us whether mixed or absolutist monarchy is more desirable. Although it tended in Shakespeare's day to sit more neatly with absolutist theory, the 'consensus' which characterised Tudor absolutism, could just as well align providence with mixed monarchy.[24] Certainly in its portrayal of the dangers of the tyrant, *Richard III* presents Shakespeare at his most anti-absolutist in constitutional terms.[25]

Despite its relatively restricted and rather one-dimensional approach to constitutional issues, concentrating almost exclusively on the question of legitimacy, *Richard III* has a virtue in beginning an examination of the much more subtle constitutional problems which develop in the subsequent Histories. In a sense *Richard III* opens the constitutional debate, for a retreat from the tidy orthodoxy of Tudor providentialism and a reopening of the question of humanism that characterizes Shakespeare's treatment of things constitutional in the next two plays.[26] *Richard III* proved, and continues to prove, to be one of the most enduringly popular plays of Shakespeare's corpus. Yet it might reasonably be suggested that we can detect a Shakespeare who is, if not actually dissatisfied, certainly is not entirely satiated by the neat and tidy providential theory of kingship which he inherited in the Tudor myth of Richard III.[27]

King John

The thesis that *King John* is the natural development of *Richard III*, and the natural precursor of *Richard II*, at least as a political play, has attracted growing support. Despite one or two lingering doubts it is now generally suggested that *John* was composed between the two *Richards*.[28] Similarly, although for so long one of the more neglected plays, in recent years *King John* has been perceived as representing a crucial stage in the development of Shakespeare's politics.[29] It is certainly the first place where Shakespeare addresses overtly constitutional political themes.[30]

Once again it is important to begin with the origins of Shakespeare version of the story of *King John*. John was treated variously by different Tudor chroniclers, but the dominant influence was undoubtedly the anonymous play, *The Troublesome Raigne of John King of England*, which had set the scene for a thoroughly incompetent and wicked king.[31] What is remarkable about Shakespeare's characterization of John, in sharp distinction with his characterization of Richard III, is the extent to which he modifies this image. In *King John*, Shakespeare is trying to create ambiguity.[32] At the same time, the most striking similarity between *King John* and *Richard III* is the development of the Machiavellian theme. Compared to the two *Richards*, there is no one dominating character in *King John*. That role is shared by John himself, whose character declines as the play progresses, and the Bastard, whose role correspondingly rises. Both are to some degree Machiavellian, but at the same time, neither are so patently evil or tyrannical as Richard III.[33] For this reason, Shakespeare's ambition is greater, and his task more difficult. Tyrants such as Richard were easier to deal with.

Although there is, of course, the matter of his right to the throne, John's wickedness really only emerges in an unambiguous form in his decision to kill

Arthur. Even then, in sharp contrast to Richard's treatment of the Princes, he shows remorse. In his discourse with Philip, the French King makes much of John's unnaturalness as king, but there is not, at least initially, any evidence of his unnaturalness as a person (1.2.94-8). However, by 3.2, as well as ordering Arthur's murder, he is also ordering the Bastard to "skin the fat ribs of peace", but even here, given that John refers to "hoarding abbots" it might be inferred that the audience would treat such a command with sympathy (3.2.16-21). Indeed, John's presentation as the champion of England against the Papacy was perhaps the greatest ambiguity of his character.[34] Again, it is one which Shakespeare inherited from the chronicles, but it was also one which he was careful to exacerbate. In his defiance John suggests that the Pope is a usurper of the realm (3.1.73-4). His resulting excommunication, of course, takes John and his subjects outside the law of God (3.1.89-110). Yet, once again, the audience could just as well read this as a victory for the law of the realm.

Constance suggests that heavenly justice is always superior to civil justice, but then Constance is the mouthpiece of Popery, and the prime example of such supremely godly law is French absolutism (3.1.1-5-16, 150-79 & 235-8). However, it is after his order to murder Arthur in the following scene that John's fortunes, and indeed his importance in the play, decline. By 4.2, he is figure of indecision and inconstancy, belatedly seeking, but still failing to execute the advice of his counsellors (4.2.40-105). It is significant that, as in *Richard III*, Shakespeare chooses to reveal the pretender's inadequacies at the moment of his coronation. As a king without ceremonial trappings of kingship John is presented as the king with "one body", devoid of the divinity which "doth hedge a king". His survival thus depends purely upon his success as a politician.[35] Later in the same scene he is advised that a considerable French army is already approaching. Ultimately he merely tries to escape responsibility for his own insufficiencies, both as a person and as a King (4.2.208-14).

The Machiavellian monarch, the supreme pragmatist, depends on the constant enforcement of his possession. He must be the man of action. In 5.1, in contrast to his earlier patriotic defiance of the Pope, John is a humble supplicant resigning his realm to Rome, under the threat of deposition by the French king, and his own nobles. As the Bastard notes, he now appears as wholly unfit to rule and incapable of action (5.1.1-4 & 43-61). Later, in 5.7, John dies, symbolically as sick as his realm, burnt up by "tyrant fever" (5.3.3-4 & 14 and 5.7.35-43). His is a tyranny bred, not just of illegitimacy, but of incompetence and weakness.

As John declines, from 3.2 his place is taken by the Bastard. Recent scholarship has championed the character of the Bastard as pivotal, although opinions as to what that character is vary enormously.[36] Some see him as the high priest of "Commodity", a direct evolution of Richard III, and the precursor of Henry V.[37] Others say that in his presentation of the Bastard, Shakespeare is making his first tentative critique of the 'king's two bodies' thesis, a critique which emerges as central in *Richard II*.[38] The Bastard's character announces itself with force as early as the first scene. Aligning himself with John's "strong possession", the Bastard declares himself for power in politics, as well as bastardy in lineage, and his ensuing ridicule of the trappings of form and ceremony strikes echoes of certain of Richard's early comments in *Richard III* (1.1.182-219). Reacting to John's incompetence, the Bastard reflects on the chaos brought by a usurped and ineffective monarchy (4.2.141-52 and 4.3.140-9). His 'conversion' in Act 3 is one of the most important turning points in the play. Though the epitome of illegitimacy, he increasingly emerges as an ideal kingly figure.[39] When John resigns himself to the will of Rome, it is the Bastard who appreciates the unkingliness of this act and its subversive effect on the realm (5.1.65-76). In 5.2, again the Bastard voices the English repost to Lewis and the invading army (5.2.17-58).

Thus, it is the Bastard who assumes the mantle, and the rhetoric, which John had earlier worn, as England's champion (5.7.110-18). In his final act of fealty to the new King, Henry, he completes his conversion, and with it marries 'Commodity' to honour and duty (5.7.100-5).[40] It was, of course, his Machiavellian capabilities as a politician and soldier that secured Henry's crown. The Bastard is the supreme exponent of politics in a world without absolutes. More than that, he is successful and ultimately loyal. In creating the Bastard, Shakespeare is thus creating a figure for the new world, as opposed to the old medieval one.[41] If this is so, then the Bastard can be seen as the prototype of Bolingbroke in *Richard II*. If anything, John, too, is akin to Bolingbroke. At times, certainly in the opening scenes, John and the Bastard appear to be complementary characters.[42] As Machiavellians and pragmatists, though one more competent than the other, they often think alike. Both abandon legitimacy as a creed, in favour of power. Both thus agree to abandon constitutional debate before the citizens of Angiers, and instead attack the town (2.1.373-96). They both also decide to bleed England in order to finance further warfare (3.2.16-26). It is only following the Bastard's conversion that their character and roles divert.

Shakespeare's ambivalence in his portrayal of less obviously tyrannical Machiavellianism in *King John* than in *Richard III* has the inevitable result of casting a shadow across the role of providence, which had, of course, been the essential gear of *Richard III*. Constance and Eleanor exchange divine curses, but neither with the avowedly holy conviction of the female characters in *Richard III* (2.1.167-90). Constance continues intermittent cursing of "perjur'd kings" such as John, and to the extent that John dies, her appeal is successful (3.1.34-7). Yet they do not effect the fortunes of Arthur. Whilst the fortunes of the illegitimate and similarly "perjur'd" Machiavellian Bastard improve those of the only character of undoubted virtue, Arthur, decline. Nature is on Arthur's side, but providence abandons him in much the same way as it abandoned the Princes in *Richard III* (2.2.52). Of course, order is restored, both to the country and to the succession, with Henry, and the Bastard's submission to him. But if God has engineered Henry's unifying succession, as he did Richmond's, he has chosen the supreme Machiavellian as his instrument.[43]

Other constitutional themes, along with the issue of providence and humanism, are the same in *King John* as in *Richard III*.[44] Firstly, there is the question of legitimacy and rights of succession.[45] The play opens with Chatillon's comment on John's "borrow'd majesty" (1.1.5). John himself is inclined to stress his "strong possession", whilst Eleanor replies that it is "Your strong possession much more than your right" (1.1.39-40).[46] It has been noted that in John's time, lineal descent was not such a recognised necessity of succession, but it is reasonable to assume that Shakespeare was writing less about medieval problems of succession and more about those which were troubling Elizabethan audiences in the 1590s.[47] The matter of legitimacy is immediately reinforced by the ensuing discussion about the Bastard. Although it is perhaps significant that John is correct in law in his pronouncement, and thus is well aware of the legal repurcussions of illegitimacy, what is really important about this episode is the Bastard's conscious decision to renounce legal legitimacy in the cause of John's political legitimacy of 'possession' (1.1.116-252). In his discourse with Philip in 2.1, John certainly speaks the rhetoric of legitimacy, together with a somewhat unconvincing appeal to providence (2.1.85-8). It is, however, Philip of France, a truly legitimate monarch, who is able to furnish a convincing appeal to divine right legitimacy (1.2.89-109 & 112-17). In reply, John can only seek recourse to the reality of his "authority" (1.2.118). As we have noted, France was recognised in the 1590s as being the archetypal absolutist monarchy, and of course, Shakespeare effects a dilemma by making John appear to be the patriot in his, and the Bastard's, defence against the Papist French. The audience is to support "strong possession" against Catholic absolutism, no matter how legitimate. John may have committed "rape/Upon the maiden virtue of the crown", but at least he is not French or Catholic (2.1.97-8). Once again, in the scene before Angiers, whilst Philip discourses richly on Arthur's divine right to the throne, John concentrates on his "lawfulness" and his military strength. "Doth not the Crown of England prove the king ?", he asks (2.1.236-66 & 273). The answer is much less certain than in *Richard III*.[48] It just might.

Given the diminished certainty with which Shakespeare presents providence, there is also the problem of disposing of tyrants. This introduces one theme in particular which is central in *King John*, that of oaths. Subjects' oaths, are constantly being compromised, not least by John's insistence on demanding new ones to abrogate former. Thus, ultimately, John undermines his own legitimacy a king.[49] The dilemma that repeatedly faces various subjects in the play is that there are clearly times when it is worse to keep an oath than to break it.[50] It has been suggested that Shakespeare creates ambiguity with regard to the status of oaths in an attempt to undermine the "capstone" of divine right theory, and is thus a further critique of absolutism. Particularly in a Machiavellian world of politics, oaths themselves can no longer be taken as guarantees of obedience, unless they enjoy an independent rational force.[51]

Although there is a greater ambiguity with regard to the issue of obedience, as in *Richard III* it is clear in *King John* that Shakespeare recoils from the idea that subjects should really be trusted with the task of selecting monarchs. The scene before Angiers when the rival Kings, John and Philip, bid for the throne of England would have seemed disturbing to the Elizabethan audience. More unsettling still would have been the citizens' resolution, that until they could make their minds up, there would be no king at all (2.1.281-2).[52] The Kings, not surprisingly, merely go off to fight. This might seem to be all very providential, because after all God would grant victory to the righteous. Indeed, Hubert suggests that a "greater power than we" can thus resolve the issue (2.1.368-72). The problem is that, unlike in *Richard III*, nothing really is resolved. Moreover the Bastard seizes the opportunity to recommend "wild counsel", and suggests the joined assault on the impertinent and chronically indecisive citizens (2.1.373-96). He, at least, appreciates the unnaturalness of allowing subjects to select monarchs. This applies, too, to noble subjects. Thus Salisbury muses on the dilemma of whether to support the French in order to enforce what he perceives to be right (5.2.8-39).[53] The error of his reasoning can be best seen when compared to York's attitude in *Richard II*. Salisbury's inability to act positively sums up the inadequacies with which Shakespeare portrays the treasonous nobles hoodwinked to such a degree that they almost fight to ensure their own destruction, saved only at the last by the Bastard.[54]

Providence might be a weaker force in *King John*, but it is far from clear as to who else should take the responsibility of effecting good government. It certainly is not for the subject to decide. The role of the perfect subject is played, ultimately, by the Bastard, and he recoils from the horror of rebellion, but only because he rationalizes that John is not a tyrant. As Womersley suggests, it is not the decision that the Bastard makes which threatens constitutional orthodoxy, it is the manner in which he reaches it which is heterodox.[55] This, of course, is the essential dilemma which Shakespeare has added to his drama - the problem of the incompetent king who is not a tyrant, and who cannot safely be left to the whim of divine providence.[56] The Bastard thinks for himself. Some think, therefore, that *King John* is a much more subversive play, and is questioning the very foundation of English constitutionalism.[57] Certainly *King John* represents a more overt turn

Kingship and Governance

towards the peculiar characteristics of English humanism, but as we have noted this was not in itself a challenge to English constitutional orthodoxy. Indeed, English mixed monarchy theory deliberately evolved to accommodate it. Thus, more moderately, and I would argue, more persuasively, Hamilton suggests that in its particular treatment of oaths, and its complementary critique of absolutism, in *King John* Shakespeare is confirming his allegiance to mixed monarchy theory.[58] The play does, then, operate within the boundaries of constitutional orthodoxy, revealing a conscious shift in Shakespeare's thinking towards a more mixed and balanced polity.

Richard II

Richard II is Shakespeare most compelling investigation into constitutional thought. Like *Richard III*, *Richard II* is a play around one dominating character. Indeed, such is the depth and subtlety of that character, that the play has been seen as a precursor of the tragedies which were shortly to follow.[59] As with *King John*, Shakespeare took a common history and transformed it. Shakespeare disdained a one-dimensional approach, presenting a substantive discourse on the nature of the constitution, employing all the concepts which he had been developing in *Richard III* and *King John*.[60] Moreover, as with *King John*, he did so whilst at the same time clothing the debate in the dilemmas made inevitable by the weakness of human nature.[61]

The character of Richard represents the epitome of an absolutist monarch, or at least one who harboured such absolutist ambitions.[62] Recent scholarship has emphasised that Richard's reign was indeed noteworthy for its attempt to introduce a continental absolutist style of monarchy, in place of the kind of mixed polity which Fortescue had observed half a century later.[63] The ambitions which Shakespeare's Richard holds are evident from the very first scene. His court is defined by its ceremony and formality. Indeed, the entire scene is an enactment of ritual.[64] It is Richard's consciousness of what a divinely ordained monarch must do which forces him to permit, against his better judgment, the trial by combat of Bolingbroke and Mowbray. As becomes clear in the following scene, it is Richard who has caused Gloucester's death, and so recourse to divine justice, though a kingly duty, is likely to be counter-productive for him (1.4.196-205). Here is the first example of many which see Richard as kingly in status but not in person.[65]

Richard's ambitions are not only absolutist, they are portrayed as being ultra-medieval.[66] Thus, the Elizabethan audience would also have been struck by this first example of Richard's championing of divine justice over the natural course of the law. The legality of Richard's decision to halt the combat in 1.3 is much contested. It is unorthodox, and can only be justified, at best, as an extreme exercise of royal prerogative. It would certainly have appeared to the audience as an indication of such a monarch's inclination to override judicial form in order to achieve his personal ambitions.[67] The abruptness of Richard's behaviour is emphasised when compared with his earlier commitment to the immanent rightfulness of such a combat. Gaunt, very much a symbol of the old order, immediately appreciates that Richard's actions have rejected Gaunt himself, and the constitutional theory for which he stands. Moreover, as Gaunt suggests, Richard's extra- or, at best, quasi-legal behaviour serves to condemn the King himself and his reign. The denial of justice to his subjects is the most serious abrogation of monarchial responsibility.[68] It is Richard, Gaunt notes, who is exiled, not Bolingbroke who now goes to a "fresher clime" (1.3.216-24, 236-46, and 275-94).

Gaunt's doubts with regard to Richard's kingliness are quickly confirmed, as we learn of his reckless extravagance, his determination to "farm" his realm, his propensity for continental fashions, and his determination to follow his will, regardless of reason and good counsel. Richard, indeed, has consistently sought bad counsel, from favourites and not from his barons - the mark of the absolutist and the tyrant.[69] He is, as even his Gardeners are aware, a thoroughly incompetent monarch (3.4.29-71). Ultimately Richard seeks Gaunt's death so that he can seize his estates (1.4.42-52 & 59-64, and 2.1.17-30 & 190-210). These related events will cause the return of Bolingbroke to exact justice, and the arrival of a new political order. Berated by Gaunt, Richard is well aware that he is abandoning his inheritance, and in "farming" out his own realm, subjecting himself to the vicissitudes of the common law. As Gaunt says, "Landlord of England art thou now, not King/ Thy state of law is now bondslave to the law." (2.1.13-14)[70] As soon as Gaunt dies, Richard himself abandons his realm to fight the Irish

(2.1.155).[71] Richard is very conscious that he is moving into fresh political waters. Indeed, as neither he, nor of course Bolingbroke, espouse the constitutionalism represented by Gaunt, Shakespeare makes a different polity inevitable.

Richard appreciates the novelty, and weakness, of his position in 3.2, when the bishop of Carlisle, whilst approving his confidence in his position as God's anointed ruler, suggests that in the real world of politics, that alone is not always enough. Clinging to his quasi-divine status, reassures himself that:

> Not all the water in the rough rude sea
> Can wash the balm off from an anointed king;
> The breath of worldly men cannot depose
> The deputy elected by the Lord...
> God for his Richard hath in heavenly pay
> A glorious angel: then, if angels fight,
> Weak men must fall, for heaven still guards the right. (3.2.54-7, 60-2)

Angels are all Richard has, for the whole country, he is told, has turned against him. As the seriousness of his position, and his misapprehension with regard to the nature of kingship, sinks in, Richard temporarily loses his reason, to be followed by the complementary realization that he is ultimately just a human being, and then, finally, the acknowledgement of despair. Rather than defend his realm, Richard decides instead to "sit upon the ground/ And tell sad stories of the death of kings" (3.2.83, 129-34 & 144-77).

This reversal, and growing self-awareness emerges as the dominant characteristic of Richard during the closing Acts. Like Richard III and John, before him, Richard is left to muse upon his own question, "How can you say to me, I am a King ?" (3.2.177). It is Carlisle who immediately replies by suggesting that he will only be a secure king if he can win battles (3.2.178-85). Richard's despair, however, pervades through 3.3. Initially his rhetoric is that of God's anointed, demanding of Northumberland, "show us the hand of God/ That hath dismiss'd us from our stewardship" (3.3.77-8). But he is quick to submit to Bolingbroke's demands.

It is only now that Bolingbroke can emerge as a major character. Though for the most part overshadowed by Richard, Bolingbroke, "the silent king", is presented as an equally unambiguous figure. He is the Machiavel first introduced in the character of Richard III, and then developed in a non-villainous, and thus more ambiguous, guise in the Bastard.[72] His first appearances, however, reveal little other than his disillusionment that Richard refuses him the justice to which he was entitled under either divine or civil law. Indeed much of what we learn about Bolingbroke in the early scenes is hearsay. Richard fears his "courtship to the common people", and his political abilities (1.4.24-36). Bolingbroke reappears in 2.3, seeking, he maintains, merely the legal restoration of his estates. It is Richard's refusal to effect the law of the land which has prompted his return (2.2.112-35). His ambition for the crown only becomes apparent in 3.3, where he threatens rebellion if Richard fails to effect justice 3.3.35-61).[73]

There are three occasions in *Richard II* where the two figures Richard and Bolingbroke interact, and each goes to the heart of the issues of kingship and obedience. The first is protracted matter of the combat between Bolingbroke and Mowbray. The second is in 3.3 when Bolingbroke effectively takes power. Bolingbroke begins by demanding the return of the estates, and ends by being hailed "King Bolingbroke" by Richard, and by ordering his King's return to London (3.3.209).[74] The command contains only four words, but it signals the triumph of power over rhetoric.[75] The Machiavel has finally usurped the old order.

The third occasion is the ceremony of deposition. It is noteworthy that, unlike similar ceremonies concerning Richard III and King John, Bolingbroke's is the first such ceremony to be effected with the active approval of Parliament. The occasion gives rise to a direct confrontation between alternative theories of monarchy. Carlisle voices the divine right of the monarch, whilst Bolingbroke typically stays silent (4.1.114-49). He espouses no constitutional theory. Events have spoken for Bolingbroke, and others have chosen to 'crown' him, most notably and most literally Richard, who assumes the role of both "priest and clerk" (4.1.173). Throughout the scene which was to represent his triumph, Bolingbroke is kept to occasional one-line orders. Such is the depth of his new-found appreciation of kingship and its demands, that Richard quite steals the scene from Bolingbroke. Paradoxically, this is to be Richard's greatest moment. The ceremony of kingship is still his, and ill suits Bolingbroke.[76]

As with Richard's coronation, and John's, Shakespeare choses this moment to re-emphasise Bolingbroke's illegitimacy, at least as an anointed ceremonial monarch. Revealing the falsity of an abdication effected by duress, Richard berates the new king and his supporters. When Northumberland demands of him a confession of his guilt, he responds by reemphasising the constitutional nakedness of their actions:

> If thou wouldst,
> There shouldst thou find one heinous article,
> Containing the deposing of a king,
> And cracking the strong warrant of an oath,
> Mark'd with a blot, damd'd in the book of heaven. (4.1.232-6)

Following his deposition, Richard continues to muse, with far greater insight, the paradoxes of kingship, and particularly of the 'king's two bodies'. At the moment of his abdication and his 'crowning' of Bolingbroke, Richard comments that, though Bolingbroke might now be king of his realm, he is still "king" of his own "griefs" (4.1.191-3). His smashing of the mirror symbolises the destruction which he has effected of his own kingship, and, he also realises, that of kingship itself (4.1.276-91).[77] It is he, ultimately, who has served:

> T'undeck the pompous body of a king;
> Made glory base, and sovereignty a slave;
> Proud majesty a subject, state a peasant. (4.1.250-2)

It is this presentation of Richard which, Kantorowicz suggested, represented the classic portrayal of the 'king's two bodies'.[78] What is Richard without a crown, and what is the crown without Richard? (4.1.201-22).

The nature of Bolingbroke's kingship can only emerge once Richard has departed. As Richard suspected, Bolingbroke proves to be a popular king, capable of wooing the commons (5.1.7-21). He also displays other suitable kingly abilities, revealing the quality of mercy in his treatment of Aumerle, and revealing his instinct for swift action in the defence of his realm (5.3.129 & 135-143 and 5.6.2-29). At the same time, in wishing for Richard's death, he also reveals the darker side of the competent Machiavellian (5.6.39). As the play closes, he further reveals a sense of guilt and responsibility, and a coming to appreciate the "burdens" of kingship which Richard had suggested would be his (5.6.49-50). Whereas Bolingbroke remains the man of action rather than words, Richard achieves new poetic heights. The rhetoric of nobility is still his. In the soliloquay before his death, Richard continues to muse on the nature of kingship, and the inadequacies of absolutism and divine right alone. A king, he realises, must be so much more than a symbol or a ceremony:

> Thus play I in one person many people,
> And none contented. Sometimes am I king,
> Then treasons make me wish myself a beggar,
> And so am I. Then crushing penury
> Persuades me I was better when a king;
> Then I am king'd again, and by and by
> Think that I am unking'd by Bolingbroke,
> And straight am nothing. (5.5.31-8)

In a final act of self assertion and understanding, Richard refuses to take poison, and with previously undisplayed vigour attempts to defend himself against his murderers (5.5.102-12).[79]

Although Richard and Bolingbroke, and the interaction between them, provide the heart of the play, three other characters play an important supporting role. The first of these is the Bishop of Carlisle, who consistently articulates the theory of divine right, even when Richard himself comes to doubt it. Carlisle is thus the mouthpiece of providentialism, advising Richard, "Fear not, my lord. That Power that made you king/ Hath power to keep you king in spite of all." (3.2.27-8) It is he, alone, who defends Richard's position in the deposition scene (4.1.114-49). It is noteworthy that, as in *King John* especially, the representatives of the church appear to be particularly subversive and duplicitous ones. It is the Abbot of Westminster, along with Carlisle and Aumerle, who hatches a plot to oust Bolingbroke. Men of the church should not be entrusted with affairs of state, or given the opportunity to meddle (4.1.321-34). The two other characters both represent the old order, and are essentially Shakespeare's inventions.[80] The first of these is Gaunt, who consistently articulates the medieval providential approach to kingship. He thus refuses to act against "God's substitute", even though he knows him to be responsible for Gloucester's death. It is for heaven to effect "revenge" (1.2.37-41). Providence, however, can no longer be relied upon. Gaunt dies, and with him dies the culture of medievalism, bled dry by Richard.[81]

Gaunt's role is, however, taken up by other characters of the old order, including Northumberland, who ferments rebellion in his desire to throw of the "slavish yoke" which Richard has introduced, and by York, whom Richard entrusts with government of the realm whilst he is in Ireland, and who in constrast to Northumberland, agonises over the question of obedience (2.1.238-45, 262-6 & 285-98). York's is the classic dilemma:

> If I know how or which way to order these affairs,
> Thus thrust disorderly into my hands,
> Never believe me. Both are my kinsmen:
> Th'one is my sovereign, whom both my oath
> And duty bids defend; th'other again
> Is my kinsman, whom the king hath wrong'd
> Whom conscience and my kindred bids me to right. (2.2.109-14)

The dilemma is reinforced in the following scene when Bolingbroke again forces York to acknowledge his right (2.3.139-41).

York indeed, emerges as a key figure constitutionally, because it is his character which serves to describe the changing role of the obedient subject.[82] Prior to deposition, York, like Gaunt, had obeyed the anointed monarch. Such a monarch might be wholly inadequate, like Richard, but, despite constant misgivings, ultimately there was no question with regard of disobedience. Thus, York warns both Bolingbroke and his supporters that they are "rebels all", if they support an attempt to force justice upon the King (2.3.139-46). York only switches his allegiance when Richard conveys his intention to abdicate; until then, he determines to remain "neuter" (4.1.107-12). Despite his appreciation that it is not providence, but power which has effected Richard's deposition, York becomes Bolingbroke's most dutiful subject, to the extent that he is prepared to reveal his own son's involvement in fomenting rebellion (5.2.23-40 & 72-110). York is the ideal Hobbesian subject, content to serve whoever is monarch, regardless of their achievement of that position, and equally regardless of the capabilities.[83] Rebellion, against either Richard or Bolingbroke, is not to be contemplated.

The story of the performance of *Richard II* on the eve of Essex's rebellion is familiar. Upon subsequently hearing of the event, Queen Elizabeth is reported to have said: "I am Richard II. Know ye not that?"[84] But was Shakespeare himself a subversive and dangerous constitutional thinker? The ever-sensitive Elizabethan authorities thought not.[85] Having said that, it is a fact that the deposition scene was cut, either by the censors or by Shakespeare, from the 1597 and 1598 quartos.[86] Did the written word matter more than the performance ?[87] Certainly, both Elizabeth and an Elizabethan audience would have appreciated that *Richard II* was a play with a political message.[88] But it was also a piece of tragic drama. The extent to which the constitutional debate would have fomented or effected civil unrest must remain doubtful. The inconsistencies of the play's treatment by the authorities probably simply reflect the inconsistencies of confidence which characterized government during the 1590s.

This should not, however, detract from the importance of *Richard II* in helping us to access Shakespeare's understanding of matters constitutional. In this it remains, by a considerable margin, his most important play. By the end of *Richard II* it is quite clear that Shakespeare has committed himself to a thoroughly anti-absolutist stance in constitutional thinking. Absolutism represents the past, the medieval world of Gaunt. The new world is that represented by Bolingbroke.[89] This does not, of course, necessarily make Shakespeare a subversive thinker, although it does confirm his increasing uncertainty with regard to certain of the fundamental tenets of earlier quasi-absolutist Tudor thought, most obviously providence and divine right.[90] Neither does his more ambiguous portrayal of providentialism necessarily make him ungodly.[91] What it does reveal is Shakespeare's growing sympathy with a position more akin to that taken by the English humanists, and to the type of mixed monarchy to which Queen Elizabeth herself subscribed, absolute to a degree, but subject to the common law of the realm, and limited by the common law determination of kingship. It is Bolingbroke who rules in accordance with Parliament, who exercises the prerogative propitiously, and determines to subject himself to the law of the realm. This, as Holderness notes, makes Bolingbroke's victory a victory against constitutional innovation, and marks the 'return' to pre-Tudor mixed monarchy.[92] Shakespeare's constitution, at least that presented by the close of *Richard II* was certainly not subversive. Though not thoroughly providential, or absolutist in the strict continental or Ricardian sense, it was entirely orthodox in that it remained unquestioningly godly and monarchic. Shakespeare's was the constitution which reflected the evolving redefinition of constitutionalism in the England of the 1590s. The redetermination of mixed monarchy, and the accommodations with absolutist themes, such as divine right, was a tortuous task, which took decades, and two seventeenth-century rebellions, to work through. The fact that its thematic evolution proved, at times, to be difficult in Shakespeare's Histories, and that doubts and dilemmas clearly remained, only serves to reinforce the impression that Shakespeare shared, and articulated, many of the uncertainties of his time.

Notes

1. For a general account of Richard's reign, see P. Sacchio, Shakespeare's English Kings: History, Chronicle and Drama, (Oxford UP, 1977), pp. 157-86, stressing how much of the Shakespearean Richard is without foundation. For more substantive revisionist accounts of Richard, see C. Ross, Richard III, (London: Methuen, 1981), and A. Sutton, "A Curious Searcher for our Weal Public': Richard III, Piety, Chivalry and the Concept of the 'Good Prince', in Richard III: Loyalty, Lordship and Law, ed. P.Hammond (London: Alan Sutton, 1986), pp. 58-90.

2. For an interesting discussion of More's The History of Richard III, see R. Warnicke, 'More's Richard III and the Mystery Plays', Historical Journal, 35 (1992), pp. 761-78. See also Hammond's edition to the Arden Shakespeare Richard III, (London: Routledge, 1981), pp. 97-119.

3. See E.Tillyard, Shakespeare's History Plays, (Penguin, 1966), pp. 205-18. For a review of this thesis, see W. McNeir, 'The Masks of Richard the Third', Studies in English Literature, 11 (1971), pp. 168-86.

4. See A. Rossiter, 'The Structure of Richard the Third', Durham University Journal, 31 (1938), pp. 44-75, for the suggestion that the structure and themes of Richard III must be approached from 3 Henry VI.

5. The plainest of all Shakespeare's tyrants. See M.Prior, *Drama of Power* (Chicago: Northwestern UP, 1973), pp. 131-2.

6. See L. Champion, *Perspective in Shakespeare's English Histories*, (Athens: Georgia UP, 1980), pp. 54-69. Although his fate was in accordance with Tudor orthodoxy, certainly the character of Richard was Shakespeare's own invention, and different again from that portrayed in earlier Richard plays. See J. Candido, 'Thomas More, the Tudor Chronicles, and Shakespeare's Altered Richard', *English Studies*, 2 (1987), pp. 137-41, and E. Pearlman, 'The Invention of Richard of Gloucester', *Shakespeare Quarterly*, 43 (1992), pp. 410-29.

7. As, for example, used by Marlowe in *Barabas*. See Hammond, pp. 74-119. For a discussion of Richard as 'Vice', see Pearlman, pp. 421-2. The ghosts scenes in Act 5 would also have been familiar to audiences from the Morality plays. See Tillyard, p. 214. It has been suggested that in portraying such an unambiguously evil tyrant, Shakespeare was in fact merely redescribing a common caricature. See Prior, pp. 283-4 and 288-95. See also M.Reese, *Cease of Majesty*, (London: Edward Arnold, 1961) p. 98 and pp. 208-10, saying that Shakespeare's portrayal of Richard is the only "vulgarisation" of a type in the Histories, and that the character has "less of Cesare Borgia, than of Captain Hook". The idea that Richard, at least in the first part of the play might be viewed as a comic character has gained some support, see H.Richmond, *Shakespeare's Political Plays*, (New York: Random House, 1967), pp. 76-79 and 96. For the suggestion that Richard can be seen as a derivative of the Biblical Herod, see S. Colley, *'Richard III* and Herod',

Shakespeare Quarterly, 37 (1986), pp. 451-8.

8. See also H.Kelly, *Divine Providence in the England of Shakespeare's Histories*, (Cambridge, MA: Harvard UP, 1970), p. 277, and G. Day, "Determined to prove a villain': theatricality in *Richard III*', *Critical Survey*, 3 (1991), pp. 149-56.

9. According to Kiernan, the "first real master" of the "technique of politics" in Shakespeare's plays. See V.Kiernan, *Shakespeare Poet and Citizen*, (London: Verso, 1993)), pp. 90-1.

10. For an interesting discussion of this particular metaphor and the use of mirror imagery as a symbol of falsity and the unreal see M. Neill, 'Shakespeare's Halle of Mirrors: Play, Politics, and Psychology in *Richard III*', in *Richard III: Modern Critical Interpretations*, ed. H.Bloom, (New York:Chelsea House, 1988), pp. 15-43.

11. And Richard himself, of course, appreciates the hypocrisy of puritanism, unlike, we are led to believe, the self-evident truth of Anglican protestantism (1.3.318-19 & 334-8).

12. See Kelly, p. 282.

13. See A. French, 'The World of *Richard III*', *Shakespeare Studies*, 4 (1968), pp. 31-2 discussing the bare portrayal of Richmond.

14. See also Kelly, p. 295, and Prior, pp. 34-35, and 43 arguing that, "*Richard III* is more thoroughly permeated by suggestions of a providential order and the operations of divine retributive justice than any of the other history plays."

15. See Reese, p. 212 and R.Ornstein, *A Kingdom for a Stage*, (Cambridge MA: Harvard UP, 1972), p. 81 noting the convenience of Richmond's providential role. See also P. Sahel, 'Some Versions of Coup d'etat, Rebellion and Revolution', *Shakespeare Survey*, 44 (1991), pp. 26-8, and R.Burkhardt, 'Obedience and Rebellion in Shakespeare's Early History Plays', *English Studies*, 55 (1974), p. 116, suggesting that Shakespeare is not altogether convincing in his treatment of rebellion in *Richard III*.

16. For a discussion of the idea that Shakespeare wrote *Richard III* as a particular response to 'tyranny' in late sixteenth century government, see M. Hotine, '*Richard III* and *Macbeth* - Studies in Tudor Tyranny ?', *Notes and Queries*, 236 (1991), pp. 480-6.

17. See W. Carroll, 'Desacralization and Succession in *Richard III*', *Deutsche Shakespeare-Gesellschaft West Jahrbuch* (1991), pp. 82-96, stressing Richard's concern with legal formality and legitimacy.

18. For Shakespeare's problem here, see Prior, pp. 121-3 and 134-8. The problem is exacerbated, Prior suggests, because Richard's claim to lineal legitimacy is at least as strong as Richmond's.

19. For the suggestion that Richard's greatest failure was his failure to establish his legitimacy, see Carroll, pp. 82-96.

20. See Ornstein, p. 73. For the suggestion that Richard's wooing of the crowd in fact shows his greater awareness of the importance of popular support in times of civil disturbance, see A. Gurr, '*Richard III* and the Democratic Process', *Essays in Criticism*, 24 (1974), pp. 39-47.

21. For the significance of Richard's rhetorical capabilities as part of his overall deceitful character, and the suggestion that such an ability is always a mask of danger, see Pearlman, p. 414, and R. Berry, '*Richard III*: Bonding the Audience', in *Mirror up to Shakespeare*, ed. J.Gray (Toronto UP, 1984), pp. 114-27.

22. McNeir, pp. 181-2.

23. See Ornstein's observations, p. 75.

24. This conclusion seems to be implied by French who stresses that Shakespeare markedly refuses to introduce any conception of divine right into the play, at pp. 33-4.

Kingship and Governance

25. Reese, p. 128-9.

26. See Prior, pp. 8 and 51-3. Prior suggests that Shakespeare moves from a providentialist position in *Richard III*, to a more skeptical humanism in the second tetralogy. He also suggests that the fate of the two princes reveals Shakespeare's own doubts with regard to providential justice.

27. For the contemporary popularity of *Richard III*, see Ornstein, p. 62. For the idea that *Richard III* was simply not disturbing enough and demanded of Shakespeare a thematic revision in subsequent plays, see French, p. 38.

28. See Ornstein, pp. 83 and 101, Richmond, p. 96, J. Simmons, 'Shakespeare's *King John* and its Source: Coherence, Pattern, and Vision', *Tulane Studies in English*, 17 (1969), pp. 53-72, and E. Grennan, 'Shakespeare's Satirical History: A Reading of *King John*', *Shakespeare Studies*, 11 (1978), p. 21. The famous exception here is Honigmann, who suggests a very early dating of the play, to around 1591, which would thus have it preceding both *Richard*s. See 'Introduction', *King John*, (London: Routledge, 1967), pp. xliii-xliv. Honigmann does however join the chorus in stressing similarities with *Richard II* in particular.

29. See Reese, p. 263, P. Rackin, *Stages of History: Shakespeare's English Chronicles*, (London: Routledge, 1991), p. 66, and Champion, referring to its "pivotal" position in the Histories, at pp. 92, 94 and 110. For the neglect of *King John*, see E. Waith, '*King John* and the Drama of History', *Shakespeare Quarterly*, 29 (1978), pp. 192-211.

30. See D. Womersley, 'The Politics of Shakespeare's *King John*', *Review of English Studies*, 40 (1989), pp. 497-8, disputing Tillyard's dismissal of the play as a failure.

31. For the origins, and the various Johns, see J. Elliot, 'Shakespeare and the Double Image of King John', *Shakespeare Studies*, 1 (1965), pp. 56-72, and C. Levin, 'The Historical Evolution of the Death of John in Three Renaissance Plays', *Journal of the Rocky Mountain Medieval and Renaissance Association*, 3 (1982), pp. 85-106.

32. See Simmons, pp. 53-72, and Grennan, p. 29.

33. It has been suggested that Shakespeare was describing a character closer to the 'real' Machiavelli, that the stage Machiavel. See Elliot, pp. 76-7.

34. For the importance of Shakespeare's presentation of John as an anti-Catholic figure, and the response that would have generated amongst his audience, see R. Battenhouse, 'King John: Shakespeare's Perspective and others', *Notre Dame English Journal*, 14 (1982), pp. 191-215, and Rackin, p. 11.

35. See B. Traister, 'The King's One Body: Unceremonial Kingship in *King John*', in *King John: New Perspectives*, ed. D. Curren-Aquino (Newark:Delaware UP, 1989), pp. 91-8.

36. According to Manheim, the Bastard, as the transitional figure between the two tetralogies, emerges as the most important figure in Shakespeare's Histories. See 'The Four Voices of the Bastard', in Curren-Aquino, pp. 126-35. See also D. Kastan, '"To set a Form upon that Indigest": Shakespeare's Fictions of History', *Comparative Drama*, 17 (1983), pp. 11-15, and J. van de Water, 'The Bastard in *King John*', *Shakespeare Quarterly*, 11 (1960), pp. 137-46.

37. See Tillyard, p. 239, Champion, pp. 99-100 and Grennan, pp. 30-1. For the thesis that the Bastard preshadows Henry, see Reese, p. 285.

38. Levin, p. 105.

39. Thus, according to Levin, implying a preliminary critique of the 'king's two bodies' thesis. See p. 105. See also van de Water, pp. 142-5, and Tillyard, p. 226.

40. See J. Calderwood, 'Commodity and Honour in *King John*', *University of Toronto Quarterly*, 29 (1960), pp. 341-56, and Simmons, pp. 68-9. See also van de Water, p. 144 and Battenhouse, p. 204, for the Bastard's role as the ideal subject.

41. Womersley, pp. 501-15.

42. See Richmond, pp. 102-3 and 108, suggesting that both characters can thus be seen as developments of Richard III.

43. See L. Champion, "Answere to this Perillous Time': Ideological Ambivalence in *The Raigne of King Edward III* and the English Chronicle Plays', *English Studies*, 69 (1988), p. 128. For the suggestion that the Bastard shares Hubert's conversion, see Battenhouse, p. 208. For an attempt to restore a partially providentialist commentary, see D. Kehler, "So Jest with Heaven': Diety in *King John*', in Curren-Aquino, pp. 100-13, suggesting that Shakespeare, rather than dismissing providentialism, deliberately creates ambiguity by granting it certain successes, balanced by certain conspicuous failures.

44. See Tillyard, p. 227.

45. The crucial theme according to Champion, p. 103, and Rackin, p. 186.

46. See Richmond, pp. 110-11, emphasising John's own appreciation of his situation.

47. For a general discussion, see Sacchio, pp. 190-1.

48. See Richard's similar question, in *Richard III*, 4.4.469-473. See also Richmond's commentary, p. 99. It is also less certain than it was in the *Troublesome Raigne*, where John's usurpation was much more clearly condemned. See Simmons, pp. 59-60.

49. See Champion, p. 105, and D. Hamilton, *Shakespeare and the Politics of Protestant England*, (Louisville: Kentucky UP, 1992) pp. 56-7.

50. See Simmons, pp. 66-7.

51. The strongest line here is taken by Hamilton, at pp. 30-58, who says that Shakespeare was not merely attacking absolutism in general, but more precisely the absolutist pretensions of the ecclesiastical courts in late Elizabethan England. In jurisprudential terms, she adds, Shakespeare was aligning himself with the arguments of the common lawyers.

52. See V. Vaughan, '*King John*: A Study in Subversion and Containment', in Curren-Aquino, pp. 68-9.

53. See Simmons, pp. 66-7, stressing the extent to which Shakespeare has created a dilemma which was less evident in the *Troublesome Raigne*.

54. See Elliot, p. 81, and Battenhouse, pp. 206-7.

55. See Womersley, pp. 514-15. According to Tillyard, it is the Bastard who appreciates that although John is both a bad person and a bad king, he is not a tyrant, and so there is no question of rebellion. See Tillyard, p. 231.

56. See Champion, p. 128, Simmons, pp. 67-8, Burkhart, pp. 112-13, and Hamilton, pp. 49-58.

57. See Manheim, pp. 126-35 discussing the idea that the Bastard can thus be seen as the most subversive character in the Histories, and also the crucial transitional character between the two tetralogies. See also Grennan, pp. 34-5, and a similar implication in Kastan, pp11-15. For a moderate discussion of subversion and its containment in *King John*, see Vaughan, pp62-75.

58. See Hamilton, pp. 42-9.

59. Ornstein sees similarities with Lear. See Ornstein, p. 108. See also J. Elliott, 'History and Tragedy in *Richard II*', *Studies in English Literature*, 8 (1968), pp. 253-71, Champion, pp. 70-1 and 90-1, and Prior, pp. 156-82. For a refutation of this idea, see Richmond, at p. 123, emphasising that the play is rather, Shakespeare's purest and most sophisticated study of political thought.

60. See Tillyard, pp. 250-1, and Reese, pp. 116-19, for its derivation.

61. See Prior, pp. 141-2, suggesting the Richard emerges as the "ideal protagonist" for such a venture.

62. See Prior, pp. 141-3, and also J. Gohn, 'Richard II: Shakespeare's Legal Brief on the Royal Prerogative and the Succession to the Throne', *Georgetown Law Journal*, 70 (1982), pp. 955-9.

63. See A. Tuck, *Richard II and the English Nobility*, (London: Edward Arnold, 1973), and most recently B. Bevan, *King Richard II*, (London: Rubicon Press, 1990).

64. See Richmond, p. 124, and also, G. Lanier, 'From Windsor to London: The Destruction of Monarchial Authority in *Richard II*', *Selected Papers from the West Virginia Shakespeare and Renaissance Association*, 13 (1988), p. 1.

65. See H. Kantorowicz, *King's Two Bodies: A Study in Medieval Political Theology*, (Princeton UP, 1967), pp. 24-41 suggesting that Richard is the classic portrayal of such a monarch.

66. See Tillyard, pp. 258-61, and P. Phialas, 'The Medieval in Richard II', *Shakespeare Quarterly* 12 (1961), pp. 305-10.

67. See D. Bornstein, 'Trial by Combat and Official Irresponsibility in *Richard II*', *Shakespeare Studies*, 8 (1975), pp. 131-41, and M. Ranald, 'The Degradation of *Richard II*: An Inquiry into the Ritual Backgrounds', 7 *English Literary Renaissance*, 7 (1977), pp. 170-83.

68. See Gohn, pp. 959-65, Hamilton, p. 15, and Bornstein, pp. 131-41.

69. His failure to heed good counsel is a crucial failing, as Northumberland observes at 2.1. 238-45. Bolingbroke subsequently refers to Richard's unsuitable counsel as the "caterpillars of the commonwealth", at 2.3. 165, and admonishes them at 3.1.1-30. See also P. Gaudet, 'The 'Parasitical' Counselors in Shakespeare's *Richard II*: A Problem in Dramatic Interpretation', *Shakespeare Quarterly*, 33 (1982), pp. 142-54. For a discussion of whether or not this really makes Richard a tyrant, see Prior, p. 150, and Kelly, pp. 205-6, who is particularly doubtful. Certainly Richard's 'tyranny' is portrayed in very much more ambiguous manner that Richard III's.

70. For a discussion of the 'farming' of the realm, see D. Hamilton, 'The State of Law in *Richard II*', *Shakespeare Quarterly*, 34 (1983), pp. 5-17, suggesting that it is symbolic of Richard's subjecting himself to the law.

71. See also the Captain's comments at 2.4.7-17, saying that Richard in abandoning the country has left it to run wild.

72. See Elliott, pp. 264-5, and Richmond, pp. 123 and 133-6.

73. For a discussion of Bolingbroke's rather shadowy appearances, and the almost secretive portrayal of his ambition, see B. Stirling, 'Bolingbroke's "Decision"', *Shakespeare Quarterly*, 2 (1951), pp. 27-34.

74. Richard acknowledges that his earthly realm is lost and, in his physical descent from the battlements of Flint castle, analogizes himself to be Phaeton at 3.3.178-9. For a discussion of this analogy, see S. Heninger, 'The Sun-King Analogy in *Richard II*', *Shakespeare Quarterly*, 11 (1960), pp. 319-27, and R. Merrix, 'The Phaeton Allusion in *Richard II*: The Search for Identity', *English Literary Renaissance*, 17 (1987), pp. 277-87.

75. See Lanier, p. 3, and Stirling, pp. 30-4.

76. Lanier, pp. 5-7.

77. See Kantorowicz, at p. 39, suggesting that the mirror scene represents the final dissolution of the 'two bodies thesis'.

78. See Kantorowicz, pp. 24-41. For a commentary on Kantorowicz's appropriation of Richard, see J. Drakakis, 'The Representations of Power in Shakespeare's Second Tetralogy', *Cosmos*, (1986), pp. 111-18.

79. See P. Jensen, 'Beggars and Kings: Cowardice and Courage in Shakespeare's *Richard II*',

Interpretation, 18 (1990), pp. 137-8, suggesting that, in fact, this presents Richard at his most majestic.

80. For Shakespeare's development of the two characters, see Ornstein, p. 123.

81. For a discussion of the symbolism of England's decline as 'paradise', see C. MacKenzie, 'Paradise and Paradise Lost in *Richard II*', *Shakespeare Quarterly*, 37 (1986), pp. 318-39.

82. See M. Kelly, 'The Function of York in *Richard II*', *Southern Humanities Review*, 6 (1972), pp. 257-67. For the counter-position, see P. Rackin, 'The Role of the Audience in Shakespeare's *Richard II*', *Shakespeare Quarterly*, 36 (1985), pp. 273-81, suggesting that York is merely the symbol of the degeneracy of the old order and its theory of obedience.

83. Hobbes constructed such a theory of obedience in *Leviathan* in order to provide a theoretical means by which disaffected royalists could subscribe the Engagement Oath to the new Commonwealth authorities in 1650. For a commentary on this theory, see I. Ward, 'Thomas Hobbes and the Nature of Contract', *Studia Leibnitiana*, 25 (1993), pp. 90-110. For the suggestion that York has been made aware of the need to subscribe to a new theory of obedience, see Richmond, p. 136, and Kelly, pp. 257-67. See also S. Zitner, 'Aumerle's Conspiracy', *Studies in English Literature 1500-1900*, 14 (1974), pp. 242-3 and 253-6, suggesting that the manner of the York-Aumerle scenes, degenerating at times almost into comedy, has tended to detract from the importance in introducing a new understanding of obedience.

84. Ure expresses doubts with regard to the authenticity of the entire episode. See his 'Introduction', *Richard II*, (London: Routledge, 1966), p. lxii. For a revisionist discussion of Lambarde's account, see A. Kinney, 'Essex and Shakespeare versus Hayward', *Shakespeare Quarterly*, 44 (1993), pp. 464-6.

85. If they did feel that a play was at all subversive they were quick to act. Two years earlier, Sir John Hayward's book on Henry IV had been quickly suppressed, and Hayward himself imprisoned.

86. For a discussion of this, see C. Greer, 'The Deposition Scene of *Richard II*', *Notes and Queries*, 197 (1952), pp. 492-3, and 'More about the Deposition Scene of *Richard II*', *Notes and Queries*, 198 (1953), pp. 49-50, and J. Clare, 'The Censorship of the Deposition Scene in *Richard II*', *Review of English Studies*, 41 (1990), pp. 89-94.

87. See D. Kastan 'Proud Majesty Made a Subject: Shakespeare and the Spectacle of Rule', *Shakespeare Quarterly*, 37 (1986), pp. 468-73, suggesting that it was the fact that the ceremony of kingship was being revealed as merely a piece of theatre which was potentially subversive, but that the authorities in late Elizabethan England were, if anything, keen to support the enactment of such ceremony. See also D. Bergeron, '*Richard II* and Carnival Politics', *Shakespeare Quarterly*, 42 (1991), pp. 33-43.

88. See Gohn, pp. 953-955, and A. Potter, 'Shakespeare as Conjuror: Manipulation of Audience Response in *Richard II*', *Communique*, 6 (1981), pp. 1-9.

89. See Richmond, pp. 139-40, and Kiernan, pp. 37-8 and 77-81.

90. For a convincing argument that Richard's invocation of divine right is consistently compromised by Shakespeare, see Kelly, pp. 208-9. See also G. Holderness, *Shakespeare Recycled: The Making of Historical Drama*, (London: Harvester Wheatsheaf, 1992), at pp. 8-9, suggesting that *Richard II* signals Shakespeare conversion to humanism. For the implication that *Richard II* is more subversive, at least in fact that it suggests a degeneracy of kingship itself, see A. Leggatt, *Shakespeare's Political Drama*, (London: Routledge, 1988), p. 72.

91. See Champion, pp. 72-3.

92. Kiernan, pp. 77-81 and Reese, pp. 128-141 stressing the anti-absolutist message of the play. For the suggestion that what Shakespeare was presenting, as a kind of mixed monarchy thesis, can be identified with its accommodation half a century later with absolutism in a 'social

contract', see H. Coursen, 'Theories of History in *Richard II*', *Upstart Crow*, 8 (1988), pp. 46-8. The alternative is articulated by Gohn, at pp. 971-2, suggesting that the deposition scene is a 'vindication' of absolutism, and that Bolingbroke merely becomes an alternative absolutist monarch ruling by divine right. I would suggest, particularly given Shakespeare's presentation of the deposition scene, and in the light of the tenor of the whole play, that this is mistaken. See R. Sandler, *Northrop Frye on Shakespeare*, (Yale UP, 1986), pp. 55-67 for Frye's perceptive observation that in separating the two bodies, Richard as symbolic king, and Bolingbroke as king in person, Shakespeare realises the essential dilemma in medieval kingship, and thus suggests the necessary accommodation of medieval and post-medieval constitutional theory, in mixed monarchy.

"AND YET A MAIDEN HATH NO TONGUE BUT THOUGHT": SHAKESPEARE'S SUBVERSION OF THE *QUERELLE DES FEMMES* IN *THE MERCHANT OF VENICE*

Julie D. Campbell
(Texas A & M University)

The Merchant of Venice, one of Shakespeare's most provocative problem plays, is frequently the subject of scholarly debates concerning Shakespeare's perspectives on anti-Semitism, Christianity, and interpretation of law, to mention only a few topics from which rhetorical commonplaces often arise.[1] In fact, this controversial play appears to be as much about debates as it is about comedy and romance. Lee Jacobus, echoing such scholars as Stanley Cavell, Margaret Wiley, and Sukanta Chaudhuri, argues that Shakespeare was clearly aware of developments in sixteenth- and seventeenth-century dialectic concerning epistemology, and he contends that "Shakespeare's plays reveal a careful consideration of the chief intellectual controversy of his day: the question of the reliability of human knowledge."[2] Building upon Cavell's theory that "scepticism was central to Shakespeare's thinking from the time of the great tragedies," Jacobus, too, emphasizes Shakespeare's sceptical tendencies and states, "On reflection, it seems clear that Shakespeare was concerned with epistemology much earlier and not only in the tragedies" (1). He also writes,

> Disputes in the 16th and 17th centuries between the dogmatists, who believed certain knowledge to be attainable, and the sceptics, who held that all knowledge was vain, must have interested Shakespeare. Their implications figure in all his plays, although the epistemological issues are treated with more and more care from The Taming of the Shrew (1593-94) to him much later The Tempest (1611), appearing at first the proper matter to wit but at last penetrating to the most important issues relative to being human. (4)

Although Jacobus does not include *The Merchant of Venice* (probably written in 1596 or 1579)[3] in his study, it is clearly a play ripe for analysis in light of his theory. One could analyze Shakespeare's sceptical approach to any number of controversial debates presented in the play; however, the primary focus for this study will be Shakespeare's application of the sceptic's view to elements of the *Querelle des femmes*, or "the formal controversy over women."[4]

As will become evident, Shakespeare incorporates aspects of this debate into *The Merchant* with a subversive twist. Instead of dogmatically presenting characters who clearly embody the positive or negative exempla typically used in *querelle* literature, one finds that, especially in the story line concerning Portia and Bassanio, he presents an amalgam of the issues frequently argued by attackers and defenders of women.[5] For example, stock figures of women used by attackers of women, such as the opinionated shrew, the deceitful wife, and the greedy seductress are combined in Portia, along with the characteristics cited frequently by defenders of women as those most redeeming, including obedience, chastity, and piety.[6] Additionally, Portia exhibits characteristics such as the ability to reason clearly, an adventurous spirit, and heroic bravery that are considered typically masculine virtues. To complicate matters further, Shakespeare deflects some questions normally raised about women in the *querelle* onto the men in the play. For instance, the questions usually raised by attackers of women concerning their lack of capacity for fidelity and their inability to reason clearly and logically are especially directed toward Bassanio.[7] Antonio, too, has difficulty knowing his own mind and acts irrationally: he goes into debt to aid Bassanio, who has already squandered a fortune. In general, Shakespeare juxtaposes *querelle* issues such as unquestioned patriarchal decree, idealized appearances, and idealized behavior with antics, plots, and revealed thought processes that belie (and make the audience question) the stereotypes presented in the *querelle*.

First, of course, one must acknowledge that a fundamental reason for creating complex characters so richly layered is for the comic effect produced. One such example would be when Portia, in the midst of a long speech, observes, "And yet a maiden hath no tongue but thought ..." (3.2.8),[8] then continues with her speech, beseeching Bassanio to stay for a few days before choosing a casket. The observation is also ironic because only a short while earlier, the audience has heard her express her thoughts on the subject of her suitors at great and bawdy length (1.2). However, the incorporation of such a distinct echo of traditional instruction for women's behavior would be certain to sound a familiar note for those among Shakespeare's audience who were followers of the literary attacks on and defenses of women in the pamphlet wars that flourished throughout the period.[9] Thanks to the rise of printing, there was a wide dissemination of such treatises to both the upper- and middle-class population of London, who, not inconsequently, were often play-goers (Henderson and McManus 11). Additionally, the debate over women, which began in the middle ages with such arguments as the *Querelle de la Rose*, the literary battle over representation of women in Guillaume de Lorris's and Jean de Meun's *Roman de la Rose* (1236 and c. 1276) taken up by Christine de Pizan in her *Epître au Dieu d'Amours* (1399) continued throughout the Renaissance, surfacing in conduct books, sermons, and popular literature (Kelly 69-79). Therefore, Shakespeare's inclusion of issues and character references from the debate would be recognizable and significant to his audience who would appreciate their comic value, but who would also be interested in the commentary on the debate itself taking place on stage.

Initially in *The Merchant* there is the issue of obedience to patriarchal decree, which triggers Portia's action in the play and provides a frame for the story as a whole. Within this traditional frame, Shakespeare includes elements that would elicit responses from both sides of the debate. To begin, Portia's father has decreed that her future husband must choose the correct casket in order to marry her. This game of chance sets the scene for the circumstances in which the audience first meets Portia (1.2.29-33). Within these circumstances, she manipulates and controls what she can, but on the surface, it seems she has control over very little. She says,

> O, me the word choose! I may neither choose who I would nor refuse who I dislike; so is the will of a living daughter curb'd by the will of a dead father. Is it not hard, Nerissa, that I cannot choose one, nor refuse none? (1.2.22-6)

Ultimately, she is not even given the choice of remaining unmarried. Patriarchal decree seems to win this round from beyond the grave, as well it should, some defenders and attackers of women would agree. Carroll Camden notes that according to the laws and general opinions of the time, Elizabethan girls were "to be under the strict authority of their fathers at all times."[10] In one skirmish during the pamphlet wars, a defender of women declared that for women, "Obedience is better than Sacrifice, for nothing is more acceptable before God than to obey."[11] However, some would disagree and would consider the casket gambol a game of chance, an appropriate symbol of a woman's chances for happiness with a man of her father's choosing (Camden 85-6).

Unhappy arranged marriages were a point of contention in the *querelle*, and protests against them surfaced in a variety of literary works. In Shakespeare's *The Merry Wives of Windsor*, Master and Mistress Page promise their daughter Anne in marriage, and Fenton, the man she prefers, laments, "I see I cannot get thy father's love ... " (3.4.1). He later protests her arranged marriage in a discussion with Mrs. Page, stating, "You do amaze her [...] You would have married her most shamefully, / where there was no proportion held in love ..." (5.5.220-30).[12] The motif of characters rebelling against arranged marriages appears in some of Shakespeare's other plays, too, such as *Romeo and Juliet* and *A Midsummer Night's Dream*. In these plays, the arranged marriages are protested before they occur, and the stories end in a desired marriage or tragedy, depending upon the situation; but in a woman's writing from the period, arranged marriages are attacked both before and after they take place. One finds especially colorful protests in Lady Mary Wroth's prose romance *Urania*, which includes the stories of Orilena, whose father forced upon her a "loathed match" and Lisia, whose father married her to a "churlish" and "dull piece of flesh."[13] Also in Wroth's play, *Love's Victory*, Musella flees a marriage arranged in her dead father's will.[14] However, no matter what the outcome of an issue involving parental decree, writers on both sides of the debate agreed, at least publicly, that unquestioning obedience was a key trait for the "good" Renaissance woman. In spite of feelings of protest, her ultimate duty was to bow to patriarchal will.[15]

Portia's obedience to her father in carrying out the trial of the chests is an act that most *querelle* writers would applaud. Indeed, the play ends with the story neatly framed by marriage, a marriage arranged more or less how Portia's father had intended. However, in *The Merchant,* Shakespeare sides concretely with neither those in favor of arranged marriages nor those who argue for the right to choose. Instead, he combines patriarchal decree with the woman choosing her own mate, as Portia sets her sights on Bassanio. Scholars who choose to argue either that Portia is in control of the action of the play, and her own destiny, as well as those who say that she is never actually entirely in control of either find evidence to support both claims.[16]

Jacobus notes that "[t]he sceptic, according to Pyrrho, does not trust appearances and 'must not assume that what convinces [...] is actually true. For the same thing does not convince everyone, nor even the same people always'" (6). He also brings up Sir Walter Raleigh's translation of Sextus Empiricus which begins with the headnote: "The sceptic doth neither affirm, neither deny any position; but doubteth of it, and oposeth his reasons against that which is affirmed or denied, to justify his not consenting" (7). Admitting that "[a]lthough we cannot link Shakespeare with either Oxford or Cambridge University, it is clear from his plays that he was aware of what went on in them, Jacobus indicates, as mentioned above, that Shakespeare wove elements of the debates discussed by those who frequented the universities into his work (4). Shakespeare's stance, or non-stance, as it were, on arranged marriages clearly reflects the sceptic's practice of neither affirming nor denying any position. Shakespeare also combines other issues from the *querelle* in thought-provoking ways in this play. Especially in the character of Portia, one finds a complex mingling of *querelle* concerns, and, in the first addressed below, Shakespeare emphasizes the importance of questioning appearances.

Shakespeare first introduces Portia to his audience via Bassanio's idealizing description of her for Antonio. His speech, replete with Petrarchan imagery, is one that leads the audience to believe that they are about to meet a character who embodies all the virtues that *querelle* writers attributed to a "good," that is, defensible, Renaissance woman. Bassanio tells Antonio,

> In Belmont is a lady richly left,
> And she is fair and, fairer than that word,
> Of wondrous virtues. Sometimes from her eyes
> I did receive fair speechless messages
> [...]her sunny locks
> Hang on her temples like a golden fleece,
> Which makes her seat of Belmont's Colchis' strond,
> And many Jasons come in quest of her. (1.1.161-72)

One learns that Portia's outward appearance and public comportment reflect Renaissance ideals of feminine beauty. Her fair skin, golden locks, and her "speechless messages", which indicate her virtuous silence, testify that she is, at least on the surface, a Renaissance male lover's dream, the ideal beloved.[17] In the following scenes, however, this paragon of virtue soon crumbles before the audience's eyes.

Through her exchanges with Nerissa, the audience sees her as anything but silent and virtuous. Instead, she is witty, bawdy, irreverent, and prejudiced, especially in passing judgment on her suitors (1.2.36-121). Of the Neapolitan prince, she suggests that perhaps "my lady his mother play'd false with a smith," (1.2.43-4) and she reviles the melancholy disposition of the County Palentine, emphatically stating, "I had rather be married to a death's-head with a bone in his mouth ... " (1.2.50-2). She eschews routine piety in her criticism of the French lord when she says, "God made him, and therefore let him pass for a man. In truth, I know it is a sin to be a mocker," then continues to mock away with barely a pause for breath (1.2.56-7). In fact, she has a derogatory word for each of her suitors. When the Prince of Morocco chooses incorrectly and must leave, she comments to Nerissa with undisguised bigotry, "A gentle riddance. Draw the curtains, go. / Let all of his complexion choose me so" (2.7.78-9). Additionally, in 3. 4. deceit and irreverence converge when Portia lies, telling Lorenzo and Jessica that she has "toward heaven breath'd a secret vow / To live in prayer and contemplation" (3.4.27-8) and thus must make a pilgrimage to a nearby monastery. Of course, Portia is bawdy in the extreme in the last scene of the play as she takes Bassanio to task for his carelessness with the ring she has given him. She cries, "By heaven, I'll ne'er come in your bed / Until I see the ring!" (5.1.190-1). *Querelle* writers would have much to say about these aspects of Portia's character.

The author of the *Schoolhouse of Women* (c. 1541)[18] rails against deceitful, shrewish women who "[h]ave tongue at large, voice loud and shrill", (138) and reminds his readers that, as Teiresias testified, "the woman is far more lecherous" than the man (146). Then he provides a catalogue of evil female exempla from classical and Judeo-Christian history, including Eve, the wives of Socrates, and Jezebel. If one judges Portia for her defiance of traditional Renaissance virtues for women, one realizes that she, too, could be categorized as an evil, or at least negative, exemplum; however, it is necessary to note that there are *querelle* writers who, although they would not condone her behavior, would insist that it was not really her fault. They would say that her father or Bassanio made her do it. For example, in *Mulierum Paean* (c. 1542),[19] Edward Gosynhill (thought also to be the author of *Schoolhouse*) gives examples of men's coercion of women to act deceitfully, and in her *Protection for Women* (1589)[20] Jane Anger argues that men's behavior directly influences women's. She counters arguments about deceitful women with a sharp discussion of deceitful men, contending that "[d]eceitful men with guile must be repaid" and that "[women's] behaviors alter daily, because men's virtues decay hourly" (176; 179). From these defenders' points of view, if women are deceitful, it is because men, with all *their* faults, cause women to be so. Certainly when Bassanio avoids revealing his whole purpose for seeking Portia's hand in marriage, insisting he is "on the rack" (3.2.25) but not fully elaborating the reasons (i. e., he is tortured by his desire for her money and his fears for Antonio), he is acting in the manner *querelle* writers such as Anger abhorred.

Yet, the issue is further complicated by the fact that Portia also exhibits virtues typically found in the good female exemplum, virtues that exceed even the surface ones that Bassanio points out to Antonio. For example, the audience witnesses that Portia is ultimately chaste in her marriage and obedient to her father's will. Furthermore, the tone of her speech on "the quality of mercy" (4.1.184-205) arguably suggests that she harbors at least a degree of sincere piety, even though she plays fast and loose with religious conventions and turns of speech in other parts of the play. Clearly, paradox abounds as Portia triumphs in the legal match of wits at the trial scene and in the sexual match of wits in marriage as she wins Bassanio and secures the terms of marriage with which she is willing to live. She accomplishes these goals with what *querelle* writers would consider virtuous motives: She desires a faithful husband, and she wishes to prove her loyalty to him -- and secure his indebtedness -- by saving his best friend's life. However, some critics argue that in the process of fulfilling these mostly virtuous goals, her motives become skewed. René Girard suggests that, greedy for power, Portia's vanity about her abilities causes her to eschew her own words about mercy. He writes that "feeling her claws in Shylock's flesh, she drives them deeper and deeper in order to exact her own pound of flesh."[21] Harold Goddard hypothesizes that, at the beginning of the play, Portia symbolizes the leaden casket with the spiritual gold within, but, by the end, her greed for power obliterates such a possibility.[22] Ultimately, both critics' opinions about Portia's character inadvertently illustrate personality characteristics attributed to evil female exempla and contribute further to the inevitable paradox one confronts when exploring the may facets of Portia's personality.

As the play progresses, it becomes evident that Shakespeare mingles positive and negative female characteristics in Portia's persona until it is ultimately impossible to categorize her according to the traditional standards of behavior for Renaissance women. He begins with a reference to the appearance of a traditionally "good" female exemplum with all her attendant virtuous traits, but he swiftly allows this image to erode as the audience gets to know the lady herself, yet she is ultimately the heroine. In the trial scene, she appears eminently wise and resourceful as she takes on her masculine disguise and argues Antonio's case successfully, with artful logic (4.1.167-420). In fact, her abilities to reason logically, to travel alone (except for another woman) into adventure, and to engineer circumstances to save, not a damsel in distress, but a young gentleman, are all attributes typically considered masculine in nature; actually, they are the traits of a positive male exemplum. Clearly, Shakespeare's sceptical tendencies are evident as he presents his audience, conversant in female types portrayed in the *querelle*, with the hybrid character of Portia who does not easily yield to analysis. He presents issues from both sides of the debate, then steps back, leaving his audience to wrangle with the dilemma.

Further complications are presented by Jessica, who, in many ways serves as Portia's foil. She both disobeys and deceives her father in order to marry Lorenzo, the man of her own choosing (2. 5); however, the Elizabethan audience could conceivably forgive her because she is escaping Shylock, a character Elizabethans would view as non-christian and villainous father; but in terms of moral and social debate, much more is at stake. A kind of situational ethics arises in the play, and Shakespeare plays the devil's advocate as he poses the question, "When is it justifiable for a woman to deceive and disobey?" Again, Shakespeare's multi-layering of opposing issues in the *querelle*, as well as in other debates, compels his audience to think far beyond their initial reaction to the comic elements of the play.

Diogenes Laertius wrote that the sceptic Pyrrho (fourth century B. C.) "denied that anything was honourable or dishonourable, just or unjust. And so, universally, he held that there is nothing really existent, but custom and convention govern human action ..." (in Jacobus 5). In *The Merchant*, Shakespeare poses question after question about what is honorable or dishonorable, and, as Portia and Jessica's motives and actions illustrate, he turns custom and convention upside down. Under the auspices of comedy, Shakespeare tests the boundaries of popular opinion concerning women's behavior, yet he does not stop there. His line of philosophical questioning takes on more profoundly gender-related undertones as he engages other controversial issues debated in the *querelle*, those of masculine women, feminine men, and cross-dressing.

Shakespeare's use of boy actors who portray women who pretend to be men would have particular resonance for *querelle* opponents. In *querelle* discussions, Baldassare Castiglione's *The Book of the Courtier* (1528) is frequently cited by both attackers and defenders of women. George Bull suggests that Shakespeare's familiarity with the English translation by Sir Thomas Hoby (1561) may be seen in his renewal "of the jokes and puns recommended by Castiglione",[23] but it may also be seen in his manipulation of masculine and feminine traits in his characters. When describing the ideal lady at court, Castiglione has Giuliano de'Medici state:

> ... above all, I hold that a woman should in no way resemble a man as regards her ways, manners, words, gestures and bearing. Thus, just as it is very fitting that a man should display a certain robust and sturdy manliness, so it is well for a woman to have a certain soft and delicate tenderness, with an air of feminine sweetness in her every movement, which, in her going and staying and whatsoever she does, always makes her appear a woman, without any resemblance to a man. (Castiglione 211)

And Count Ludovico says of the proper courtier that he should not "appear soft and feminine as so many try to do, when they not only curl their hair and pluck their eyebrows but also preen themselves like the most wanton and dissolute creatures imaginable ..." (61). Instead, the courtier should be "well built, with finely proportioned members, and [...] good at all the physical exercises befitting a warrior" (61). Further, "his first duty is to know how to handle expertly every kind of weapon", and he is to be "enterprising, bold, and loyal to whomever he serves" (57). In *The Merchant*, Shakespeare plays havoc with these ideals.

First, Portia's cross-dressing escapade to expedite her trip to Venice to save Antonio is the sort of behavior critics of women decried. Linda Woodbridge points out that "although masculine disguise gives [the heroine] certain unwonted freedoms [...] like Portia in The Merchant of Venice [who] must adopt male dress to practice a profession barred to women," the dramatists "insistently remind us that such behavior, however necessitated by emergency circumstances, is unnatural" (153). Merry Wiesner explains that real women who cross-dressed in the early modern period usually did it "to gain the greater opportunities and mobility available to men, and were discovered serving as soldiers, sailors, or explorers."[24] Opponents in the pamphlet wars of the early seventeenth century were outspoken on the subject. In 1620, the author of *Hic Mulier* argued that masculine style of dress for women is unnatural and blasphemous; also, it shows that women are trying "to usurp masculine aggressiveness, authority, and sexual freedom" (Henderson and McManus 17-18). (One cannot help but wonder how behavior viewed on stage affected behavior in real life, just as today there is much speculation about the effects of television on viewers.) Portia, however, seems blithely unconcerned about what people will think. She explains to Nerissa,

> [...] they shall think we are accomplished
> With what we lack. I'll hold thee any wager,
> When we are both accoutered like young men,
> I'll prove the prettier fellow of the two,
> And wear my dagger with the braver grace, [...] (3.4.61-5)

Portia also describes how she will "turn two mincing steps / Into a manly stride; and speak of frays / Like a fine bragging youth, and tell quaint lies" about "honorable ladies" who "fell sick and died" for love of him/her (3.4.67-71). In this speech, Portia gleefully describes her plan to defy all the conventions of a respectable woman. She will deceive, dissemble, and connive; further, she will dress and disport herself like a man, and a pretty one, at that. She will employ the "quaint lies" about women which Jane Anger deplores in male behavior. Although Castiglione's Count Lodovico would approve the "manly stride" and the dagger worn with "brave grace" if she really were a man, Portia's pretty, feminine countenance would win his disapproval. However, the fact that she is a woman dressed as a man would appall Castiglione's Giuliano de'Medici. Thus, the tenets of Renaissance idealism concerning masculine and feminine behavior and appearance are especially intricately layered at this point in the play. One realizes the depth of such a ploy by Shakespeare only when one remembers that the Elizabethan audience is watching a young male actor portray a beautiful young woman who is pretending to be a pretty young man. At the point, the audience's sense of what is right, wrong, or ideal in any sense must have been shifting rapidly.

Leaving aside a very masculine Portia for the moment to focus on the would-be hero Bassanio, one notices that if Shakespeare temporarily turns Portia into a resourceful, adventurous young man, he does something quite the opposite with her male counterpart. As mentioned above, Shakespeare directs some questions usually raised about women in the *querelle* to the men in the play, especially to Bassanio, and one finds in his nature negative traits that women are usually accused of having, including a weak intellect, a mercenary nature, and a lack of fidelity or loyalty.

First, the audience is led to believe that his powers of reasoning are weak, a characteristic typically labeled feminine (Wiesner 147). For example, early in the play, Bassanio tells Antonio that when he was a child and had lost one of his arrows, he would send another flying after it, in hopes that one would guide him to the other. According to such logic, he plans to risk more money to regain that which he has squandered (1.1.140-85). The scheme is that Antonio will go into debt, risking his life in the process, to provide Bassanio, a man known to be inept with finances, enough money to travel to Belmont where he will further gambol by attempting to win a rich bride in the Renaissance equivalent of a shell game. Neither of these men comes across as particularly logical or rational. In fact, the intensity of their emotions for each other crowds out rational behavior in a way that could be considered feminine by *querelle* standards. Incidentally, Bassanio's story about the arrows not only suggests weak intellect, it also brings to the audience's attention the fact that he is not particularly proficient at arms – a serious flaw in the makeup of a courtier. Fortunately, Bassanio is attempting to make himself welcome at Belmont instead of Castiglione's court at Urbino.

Second, as Bassanio is the male romantic lead, one might expect him to be the hero who saves Antonio's life, but he does not. He only takes Portia's money, hoping to buy off Shylock (4.1.84). However, one soon sees that he is no match for Shylock and the letter or the law or for Portia's intellect. Concerning Portia's money, Shakespeare makes clear from the start that it, as much, if not more than her beauty, attracts Bassanio. The allusions to Jason and the golden fleece in Bassanio's first description of Portia (1.1.161-72) and Gratiano's return to this theme later as he notes that "We are the Jasons, we have won the fleece" (3.2.241) confirm Bassanio's mercenary intent. Girard, too, underscores Bassanio's mercenary instincts as he points out the "parallel between the amorous venture of Bassanio and the typical Venetian business of Antonio, his commerce on the high seas" (Girard 92).

The mercenary lover is a stereotype *querelle* writers frequently used in attacks upon women. Of course, the motif of the mercenary male lover is a familiar one in Renaissance literature, one which Shakespeare also uses in *The Taming of the Shrew*; however, it is the mercenary female lover most often disparaged in *querelle* literature. According to the author of the *Schoolhouse of Women*, women are greedy and marry only for money and position. He suggests that for men, of the choices "[t]o hang or wed," hanging is the better option because it is over more quickly than marriage. Wives are far too expensive, demanding costly apparel and jewelry, then cuckolding a man for his trouble (in Henderson and McManus 138; 144-7). Joseph Swetnam writes, "women are proud without profit, and that is good purgation for thy purse; and when thy purse is light, then will thy heart be heavy."[25] In *The Merchant*, however, it is Bassanio who schemes to marry for money. After he chooses the correct casket, Portia responds with what might be considered the wording of her half of a *de praesenti* espousal in which she acknowledges the importance of money to Bassanio.[26] Portia, unlike the *querelle* writers who scorn signs of greed in a lover, is clearly willing to utilize this knowledge about Bassanio as she endeavors to seduce him. Her speech is full of accounting imagery as she states,

> [...] yet for you,
> I would be trebled twenty times myself
> A thousand times more fair, ten thousand times more rich,

> That only to stand high in your account,
> I might in virtues, beauties, livings, friends,
> Exceed account. But the full sum of me
> [...]
> Commits itself to [you] to be directed
> As from her lord, her governor, her king.
> Myself, and what is mine, to you and yours
> Is now converted. (3.2.152-67)

She seals her vow with a ring; however, the ring is her trump card, a carefully planted sign (3.2.171-4). Although her persistent desire for a man whose greedy nature she comprehends is difficult to explain, Portia continues to seek a commitment from him. However, just as attackers of women in the *querelle* are suspicious of a wife's ability to keep her vows, Portia is suspicious early on of Bassanio's capacity for fidelity.[27]

As for his part in the rather one-sided *de praesenti* espousal, Bassanio responds vaguely,

> Only my blood speaks to you in my veins,
> And there is such confusion in my powers,
> As after some oration fairly spoke
> By a beloved prince, there doth appear
> Among the buzzing pleased multitude,
> Where every something, being blent together,
> Turns to a wild of nothing, save of joy
> Express'd and not express'd. But when this ring
> Parts from this finger, then parts life from hence;
> O then be bold to say Bassanio's dead! (3.2.176-85)

This reveals the "confusion" of his thoughts and his senses, and his references to "a wild nothing" of joy both "express'd and not express'd" hints at his divided motives and loyalties. Only at the end of his speech does he pull himself together enough to allude to the cliché of death before dishonor. However, when his loyalty to Portia is put to the test, Bassanio falters, betrays his vow about the ring, and lets Antonio persuade him to give it to Portia, disguised as Balthazar (4.2.449-54). In a mirroring sequence, Nerissa, also disguised as a man, easily persuades her betrothed, Gratiano, to give her the ring she has entrusted to him (5.1.147-50). Both men acquiesce rather quickly. When confronted with his misdeed, Bassanio considers lying, saying in an aside that it would be "best to cut my left hand off, / And swear I lost the ring defending it," (5.1.177-8) but Gratiano confesses, reporting what he thinks is the truth, that they gave their rings to a lawyer and a clerk who would not be refused (5.1.179-83). In *The Merchant*, the men, with their faulty schemes and bumbling antics, bear little resemblance to Castiglione's intelligent, loyal, and heroic ideal courtiers. Ironically, the women in the play do.

At the end of the play, the women clearly have the upper hand. They have remained chaste and faithful to their lovers, in spite of their deceitful and occasionally shrewish behavior, and Portia is ultimately obedient to her father's will. Defenders and attackers of women would be somewhat mollified, but puzzled. As for the men, their honor is questionable since their vows are swiftly broken, and their loyalty is easily divided. Additionally, there is the issue of mixing traditionally assigned gender traits in the characters. Portia has the forethought to consult her cousin, the learned Bellario, for legal advice, then to argue Antonio's case successfully, with cunning logic (4.1.167-420), abilities typically considered masculine. In the end, she saves Antonio's life. Bassanio, with his general air of incompetence and his mercenary motives, is more a rescued victim, a position usually reserved for a female character, than a hero. Put simply, if Bassanio were a woman, she would be a slow-witted, greedy, untrustworthy female exemplum, and if Portia were male, he would be a quick-witted, adventurous courtier. Ultimately, Shakespeare turns gender-based Renaissance character ideals upside down and presents his audience with multifaceted individuals whose behavior and appearances change from scene to scene.

The question remains, of course, with which side of the *Querelle des femmes* did Shakespeare most sympathize? Wiesner points out that

> Writers of poetry, drama, and fiction [...] expressed their position in the debate through the female characters they created and the relationships between women and men they portrayed, but the best authors, such as Shakespeare, Milton, or Cervantes, recognized the complexity of the issue and so did not unambiguously support one side or another. (20)

However, another possible reason for Shakespeare's ambiguous treatment of the *querelle* is that he incorporated this debate into the play in the same manner in which he incorporated others, such as those concerning Christianity and Judaism, interpretation of law, and justice and mercy -- with a larger debate in mind -- one which encompasses all of these smaller debates and more: that of the debate over epistemology, or the reliability of human knowledge. If this conclusion is true, then he clearly approaches the smaller debates in the context of the larger debate with a sceptic's eye for seeing snags in dogmatic argument and pointing out problematic oversights in accepting ideals at face value.

Jacobus recounts Sextus Empiricus's Pyrrhonist view of reasoning, which argues that "the sensibles and the intelligibles are equally fallible" and that the "end goal of the sceptic is to suspend judgment" (7). Additionally, he records that Sextus stated, "Whenever the Sceptic says 'I determine nothing', what he really means is 'I am now in such a state of mind as neither to affirm dogmatically nor deny any of the matters now in question'" (8). Quite possibly, Shakespeare presents the numerous debates in *The Merchant* without providing definitive proof of his own beliefs on the subjects because his sceptical views are best served by doing so. One may argue that, along with Cornelius Agrippa, Shakespeare believes that truth

> can not be perceiued, with the speculations of any Science, nor with an straite iudgement of the Sences, nor with any argumente of the Arte of Logike, nor with any discourse of mans reason, but with Faithe onely; [...] (in Jacobus 51)

Hence, he leaves undetermined many disturbing questions raised in his plays. Jacobus points out that, like many sceptics, Agrippa "proclaimed the impossibility of knowledge while praising its worth" (in Jacobus 4). The paradox inherent in this idea underscores what is most likely the *raison d'être* for the for the open-ended debates carried on in *The Merchant*. The scholarly arguments about the issues raised in the play are never entirely resolved; thus, *The Merchant* retains its status as a problem play, but, from the sceptic's point of view, the continuation of the debates is what really matters. Suspended judgment leaves the door open for further questing after moral certainty, and, whether or not moral certainty can be attained, there is much to be learned through the process of debating itself, no matter what the question. Shakespeare's desire to push issues from the *Querelle des femmes* to the limit, exploring the multifaceted nature of human personalities as opposed to the flat, good or evil exemplary models used by writers in the debate illustrates how the sceptic's insistence on the suspension of judgment calls certain aspects of Renaissance idealism into question.

Notes

1. See *The Rhetorical Tradition: Readings from Classical Times to the Present*, ed. Patricia Bizzell and Bruce Herzberg (Boston: Bedford-St. Martin's, 1990) p. 298, note 6.

2. Lee A. Jacobus, *Shakespeare and the Dialectic of Certainty* (New York: St. Martin's, 1992) p. 1.

3. See *The Riverside Shakespeare*, ed. G. Blakemore Evans (Boston: Houghton Mifflin, 1974) p. 51.

4. For general overviews of the *Querelle des femmes*, or the formal controversy, see Linda Woodbridge, *Women and the English Renaissance: Literature and the Nature of Womankind, 1540-1620* (Urbana: Illinois UP, 1984) pp. 1-113; Katherine Usher Henderson and Barbara F. McManus, *Half Humankind: Contexts and Texts of the Controversy about Women in England, 1540-1640* (Urbana: Illinois UP, 1985) pp. 3-130; and Joan Kelly, "Early Feminist Theory and the *Querelle des Femmes*, 1400-1789," *Women, History, and Theory: the Essays of Joan Kelly* (Chicago UP, 1984) pp. 65-109.

5. Woodbridge (p. 14) notes that "[a]ll works of the formal controversy use *exempla*historical and/or literary examples, usually biblical and classical in origin, of good women or bad."

6. Woodbridge (pp. 15-18) discusses some of the most influential collections of *exempla*: Giovanni Boccaccio's *De Claris Mulieribus*, Christine de Pizan's *Le Livre de la Cité des Dames*, Henry Cornelius Agrippa's *De nobilitate et praecellentia Foeminei sexus*, and Baldassare Castiglione's *Il Cortegiano*. In *Redeeming Eve: Women Writers of the English Renaissance* (Princeton: Princeton UP, 1987) pp. xiii-xxiv, Elaine Beilin discusses implications of silence, patience, chastity, and piety as key virtues for women of the Renaissance.

7. In Portia's ring trick conspiracy to test Bassanio's fidelity, there is a comic reversal of the conceit from domestic tragedy in which the male characters plot to catch unfaithful female characters, as occurs, for example, in Thomas Heywood's *A Woman Killed with Kindness* (1607).

8. All quotations and references from Shakespeare's plays are from *The Riverside Shakespeare* (see note 3 above).

9. Beilin (p. 7) points out that one influential source advocating women's silence is Juan Luis Vives's *Instruction of a Christen Woman* (1523), translated into English in 1529 by Richard Hyrde. She notes that in Chapter 4, Vives states "As for eloquence I have no great care nor a woman nedeth it nat. . . . It is no shame for a woman to hold her peace. . .".

10. Carroll Camden, *The Elizabethan Woman* (Mamaroneck, NY: Appel, 1975) p. 39.

11. Ester Sowernam, *Ester Hath Hanged Haman* ..., 1617, in Henderson and McManus, p. 225.

The Merchant of Venice

12. Also discussed in Camden, p. 86.

13. See Carolyn Ruth Swift's "Feminine Identity in Lady Mary Wroth's Romance *Urania*", *Women in the Renaissance: Selections from English Literary Renaissance*, ed. Kirby Farrell et al. (Amherst: Massachusetts UP, 1988), pp.166-67, in which she compares the fathers of Orilena and Lisia to Egeus in *A Midsummer Night's Dream* and Lord Capulet in *Romeo and Juliet*.

14. Mary Wroth, *Love's Victory: The Penshurst Manuscript*, ed. Michael Brennan (London: Roxburghe Club, 1988), Act 5, lines 11-16.

15. Lawrence Stone, in *The Family, Sex, and Marriage in England 1500-1800*, abridged ed. (New York: Harper, 1979), notes that "[a]lmost all children until the end of the sixteenth century were so conditioned by their upbringing and so financially helpless that they acquiesced without much objection in the matches contrived for them by their parents" (p. 128) and "[o]nly a handful of children resisted parental dictation before the end of the sixteenth century, and their rebellion was soon crushed" (p. 130).

16. See Peter Erickson's *Rewriting Shakespeare, Rewriting Ourselves* (Berkeley: California UP, 1991) p. 23, and Susan Radtke Tong, "Portia's Power and Sexual Politics in Shakespeare's *The Merchant of Venice*", Ph. D. thesis, U of Texas at Dallas, 1989.

17. Woodbridge (p. 77) discusses the importance of women keeping silent because of associations attackers of women would make with the "biblical reflection that 'a Harlot is full of words' . . . ".

18. *Schoolhouse of Women*, in Henderson and McManus, pp. 137-55.

19. *Mulierum Paean*, in Henderson and McManus, pp. 157-70.

20. *Protection for Women*, in Henderson and McManus, pp. 173-88.

21. René Girard, "To Entrap the Wisest," *William Shakespeare's 'The Merchant of Venice'*, ed. Harold Bloom (New York: Chelsea, 1986) p. 101.

22. Harold C. Goddard, "Portia's Failure," in Bloom p. 36.

23. George Bull, introduction, The Book of the Courtier, by Baldassare Castiglione (New York: Penguin, 1976) p. 14.

24. Merry E. Wiesner, Women and Gender in Early Modern Europe (Cambridge: Cambridge UP, 1993) p. 54.

25. Joseph Swetnam, *The Arraignment of Lewd, Idle, Froward, and Unconstant Women*, in Henderson and McManus, p . 196.

26. See explanation of two types of espousals, in *verbis de futuro* and in *verbis de praesenti* in Camden, pp. 86-7. The *de praesenti* espousal uses verbs in the present tense, i. e. "I do take thee"; thus, when Portia tells Bassanio, "the full sum of me / ... commits itself to [you] ...," (3. 2. 157-64) she is enacting her part of a *de praesenti* espousal, but Bassanio's response is more vaguely stated.

27. The author of the *Schoolhouse of Women* argues that not even Satan himself can guarantee a woman's chastity (in Henderson and McManus, p. 150).

VERBAL ENERGY IN SHAKESPEARE'S *MUCH ADO ABOUT NOTHING*

Peter Cummings
(Hobart and William Smith Colleges, Geneva, NY)

> They that dally nicely with words may quickly make them wanton. – *Twelfth Night*, 3.1.14-15[1]
>
> *Much Ado* is a base camp that secures the approaches to the peaks [of *Hamlet* and *Othello*]. - Ralph Berry[2]
>
> Like honesty, [the word nothing] had developed shadings just closely enough related to one another to prevent easy distinction. In its combination of one covert meaning with several respectable meanings - enough to make it permissible, but never securely so - Shakespeare must have recognized one of his favorite opportunities. - Paul A. Jorgensen[3]

1

With these passages in mind, and as a further orientation to the critical tack taken here, let me at the outset call up the axioms of Shakespeare's unique mastery of rhetorical skills from apostrophe to zeugma, his persistence in punning – even in the most somber dramatic moments[4] – and the primacy of his verbal, or better yet, his etymological imagination. The purpose here will be to frame a critical corollary or two to such principles, at both the microlevel of language and at the macrolevel of theme-fabric reading in the text of *Much Ado about Nothing*. For, after reviewing the most prominent recent readings of the play, in connection with teaching it in the college classroom, it seems crucial to me to notice the insufficient attention currently paid to the linguistic sophistication of Shakespeare's title-word dissections, puns, and wordplays. As a direct consequence of these microlevel oversights, too little emphasis falls where it should in reading the general conceptual structure of the play. This, in turn, could of course lead to decisions affecting staging and acting the play; and, while pragmatic direction on these matters is not my purpose here, they are of the first importance.

As early as Richard Grant White's edition of *Much Ado* in 1857[5] the pronunciation of "nothing" as rhyming with "doting" (see Sonnet 20, *Much Ado*, 2.3.57, etc.) is established in modern criticism. Important confirmation comes in Helge Kökeritz's authoritative *Shakespeare's Pronunciation* in 1953,[6] although the pedantry of his excluding "eavesdropping" as a possible meaning of "noting" in Shakespeare's time is a critical fault. It is simply undeniable that noting things that others say – whether they know it or not – is part of any human noticing. A. R. Humphreys duly gives a page to the title in his 1981 Arden edition, saying "The play's title is, in fact, teasingly full of meanings."[7] That he stops too soon at that point, teases the reader into wanting some fuller detail. Dorothy Hockey supplies some of that detail,[8] stressing the persistence of Shakespeare's puns on nothing / noting throughout the play, and Paul A. Jorgensen truly widens the horizon of implications for the word "nothing" in his study of Shakespeare's language, *Redeeming Shakespeare's Words*.[9] With a fine case of historical contextualizing, Jorgensen locates *Much Ado* in a decade of very high-stakes religious and philosophical debate about *ex-nihilo* creation and the ontology of nothingness in both cosmos and culture. It was a time of "much ado" in several writerly circles about the idea of "nothing." We can think of Lear's "nothing comes of nothing" here, which, in the light of Christian doctrine and debate makes him an Aristotelian miscreant.

Add to this Jorgensen's acknowledgement of the "covert meaning" that he says "nothing" could have in the period, a bawdy reference (as of course the word "thing" itself still is to both genders' private parts) to the vagina, as in Ophelia's "nothing"[10] – what Hamlet calls "a fair thought to lie between maids' legs" (3.2.118), and the word "nothing", as we sound it today, takes on an in fact universally wide range of meanings and innuendos. If we make the apparently optional phonetic change to "noting", as Jorgensen does not really do, then it takes on yet another set of layers and associations that make it a very formidable word – perhaps 'phonemic container of semantic culture signals' might be a more suggestive term – over which Shakespeare could gather some very fine wool.

2

What Martha Craig did almost single-handedly for the critical understanding of Spenser's etymological imagination in the subtle wordplay of his character and place names,[11] several others have done for Shakespeare's language. One might here cite, apart from those already mentioned, G. L. Brook's *The Language of Shakespeare*,[12] Ralph Berry's *The Shakespearean Metaphor*,[13] John and Ann Thompson's *Shakespeare: Meaning and Metaphor*,[14] and most recently, W. F. Bolton's *Shakespeare's English*[15] as works which document Shakespeare's significant wordplay around key themes. It seems necessary to me, however, to connect several disparate principles and points from such works to the partial and fragmentary business of noticing microlevel wordplay in *Much Ado*. One metaphor that might be apt here would be to see criticism as a process of connecting some as yet unattached links in a kind of drive chain of separate observations about Shakespeare's language poetics, and the text of *Much Ado*. When we do this, the parts of the critical chain may cohere to form a kind of energy-transfer system from the force fields of Shakespeare's individual key words, and their several available phonetic and dramatic puns, to the systemic textual power of the play as a whole.

Much Ado about Nothing is a perennially satisfying, mature Shakespearean romantic comedy that the theater-going and reading public has never been able to ignore. This is so not only because of the powerful moral clarity of the comedic human experience captured in this intricate story of misperception and confusion, but also because, in the language of a critical corollary deduced here, *Much Ado about Nothing* is a poetic masterpiece of language notes and queries about the deep structure of some very fundamental human practices: perception (notation), language, knowledge, and error. As such, it is Shakespeare's richest language-game play apart from *Hamlet*, which it precedes by only a year. Ralph Berry is cited in a preface passage here as seeing *Much Ado* as a "base camp that secures the approaches to the peaks [of *Hamlet* and *Othello*]", and I would like to reassert that sense of the crucial historical importance that *Much Ado* may have as an index of Shakespeare's most sophisticated wordplay, and his most subtle language-theme coherence. We may, I think, read the play as a kind of Shakespearean challenge to notice just how much can be done with words. "Words, words, words", Hamlet will soon say, and find less matter than madness in them. But here the mood is, if not festive, then fully comedic, and there is much matter and a clear healthful sanity in the method of the words of *Much Ado*.

3

Phonetically speaking, and with Elizabethan spoken and written contraction practices in mind, to "note" is to "know't". That which we take notice of, we say we know. Shakespeare frequently toys with this idea in the play, and so a direct sound-pun connection between seeing and knowing, or at least believing, is often made. In the crucial, and physically middle scene 3.2., conversation in the first half of the scene turns on noticing changes in Benedick's appearance and dress, and so on what others can now know about him. In the second half of the scene, Don John the bastard gives us a fine instance of the idea when he tricks Claudio and others into believing that Hero is a whore. Drawing out their curiosity he says, "I know not that, when he knows what I know" (91), and later,

> If you dare not trust that you see, confess not that you know. If you will follow me, I will show you enough, and when you have seen [noticed] more, and heard [the notes] more, proceed accordingly. (3.2.119-22)

That is to himself: "I know something that I say I noticed, and when I trick your eyes, you too will believe my lie." Seeing is believing, as we say, but seeing may be flawed; one's noticing may be tricked, or changed, and so the believing may be in error. About this, as every reader and audience knows, there is much ado in the play.

From this easy pun, however, several other branches quickly seem to develop. The problem is to try to follow them all as they do. The play is, of course, much about the idiosyncratic noting of one person by another, from Claudio of Hero, to Benedick of Beatrice and vice-versa, to the watchmen seeing the suspicious dress, the "notes of apparel" [*OED note*, sb2, II.9][16], and furtive behavior of Conrade and Borachio; it is about the written notes that figure in the gulling of Benedick and Beatrice, about various informational letters, Dogberry's interrogation notes, etc., and of course musical notes are both sounded in the play as songs, talked about by the singer, Balthasar, and punned on openly in several ways. The notes of the pipers end the play.

In the main plot, of course, the misnotation of the truth – the failure to notice Don John's trickery – threatens to ruin the wedding, and in the subplot the noticing of strategic written notes radically "changes the tune"[17] regarding the opposite sex that is so confidently sounded by both Benedick and Beatrice, who make much ado of noticing that the other one has the good taste to notice him or her. The energy of the notion that noticing something creates the belief that it is known drives the play at all levels. The idea that to *note* is to *know't* comes face to face with the idea that what we notice may be *nothing*.

On the covert level, to take that option for instance, there is no thing [*thing*, 11c *euphem.*], no male "privy part" in the picture, as Don John wants others to think there is, and about which many make so much ado. This in turn makes much ado about Hero's private *nothing*, her *no-thing* (perhaps in more than one sense: not a thing, and a *no-no* thing?). Hero's shamefastness, and her being especially notable in Acts 4 and 5, here comes up against the rough innuendo of Don John's slander [*note*, v. 7a, and sb2, II.8] of her reputation [*note*, sb2, IV.19], and the text pays particular attention to the way in which more careful reading of signals in Hero's being is her rescue. The Friar speaks after silent "noting of the lady":

> I have marked
> A thousand blushing apparitions
> To start into her face; a thousand innocent shames
> In angel whiteness beat away those blushes,
> And in her eye there hath appeared a fire
> To burn the errors that these princes hold
> Against her maiden truth. (4.1.158-64)

Here we have the semiotics of what we have come to call "body language." The generous and virtuous "reading" of Hero by the Friar sees evidence of some "biting error" (16) in the princes' opinion of her, and he sets about the "practice" [*note*, sb1, 2] of feigning her death, and winning back her reputation as a noteworthy young woman. The Friar's interpretive aesthetic is the only thing that works to erase what Leontes, Hero's father, calls "the story that is printed in her blood", because she has "fall'n / Into a pit of ink" (4.1.122, 140). We notice that the metaphors work to suggest the idea of the inked *nota*, as a mark or sign of shame. Only a refined clerical cognition seems capable of erasing the marks of stigma [*note*, sb2, II.8] by correcting false perceptions.

Meanwhile, much ado is made in the play about clothing, again as "notes of apparel", a usage now lost to modern readers, which causes much to go unnoticed in the text. Clothing makes, or does not make, the man or woman, as we know – depending on one's point of view – and the play turns on the idea of reading and misreading details of dress. There is, for instance, the business of purposeful disguises at the masked ball, the changes of clothing that Benedick's romance brings with it, and the mistaking of Margaret in Hero's clothing. Indeed, the watchman scene in 4.3. contains a virtual essay on clothing fashions and how much they denote shifting identities, in Borachio's often overlooked speech on the matter:

> Seest thou not, what a deformed thief this fashion
> is, how giddily 'a turns all the hot-bloods between
> fourteen and five-and-thirty, sometimes fashioning
> them like Pharaoh's soldiers in the reechy painting,
> sometime like god Bel's priests in the old church-

> window, sometime like the shaven Hercules in the
> smirch'd worm-eaten tapestry, where his codpiece
> seems as massy as his club. (2.3.130-38)

Our images would be quite different (ranging from, say, Michael Jackson to Arnold Schwarzenegger), but we are all no doubt still fairly vulnerable to wardrobe mania from age 14 to 35. There are, after all, some things to be said for being over 40. Here, and virtually everywhere in the play, Shakespeare's dramatic interactions are driven by his thinking about aspects and innuendoes of the word *noting*, as in both reading signals and sending them, in the various fabrics of our lives, from those that clothe us to those we create in the language notations that we make as perceivers and speakers. It is possible to call *Much Ado*, from this perspective, Shakespeare's most profoundly semiotic play. For the sake of the meaning of the larger issues, its small signs must simply not be missed.

As we think of these puns and watch them connect the several usages of nothing and notation, from simple bawdy naughtiness to complex mistaking in perception and flawed denotation in language, and on to comedic parody of the *ex-nihilo* debate, the play seems to be fixed on the project of tracing how wide a net a single word and its linked phonetic and etymological associations can cast over, and indeed both capture and entangle, the social projects of living and interacting in the world of ambiguous human signs.

Interestingly enough, the connection Shakespeare repeatedly makes between noticing things and knowledge, whether intellectual or carnal, is in fact made in the very word *note* itself. It could easily have been known to Shakespeare, and as such it can be seen as a corollary here of his careful curiosity about language roots and usages, that the word *nota* itself in Latin derives from the Greek γιγνωσκω, to observe, make judgment, come to know, and is thus cognate with the *gno*-root of such words as *gnomon*, *gnosis*, and *gnostic*. What this etymology says, from early on in western language, is that any sign, any mark or *nota*, is the signal of a knowledge claim. Our marks for what we remark is what we presume to know. What is clear, both from word counts (in one of which Ralph

Berry finds 84 usages of forms of the verb *to know*),[18] and from reiterations of the word-idea, is that knowing is the conceptual theme of the play. What the etymology does *not* say, however, until Shakespeare leaks the notion of error into language, is that either the sign, the signer, or the sign-reader may be wrong.

In this sense, to carry the puns of the title yet further, the play is much ado about *not*-ing, that is negating, or *no*-ing one thing or another. We find in the concordance not only a greater number of no's, not's, and never's in this play than in any other,[19] but a kind of choral refrain of soundplays on the words:

> *Claudio*: Benedick, didst thou note the daughter of Signor Leonato?
> *Benedick*: I noted her not, but I looked on her.
> *Claudio*: Is she not a modest young lady?
> [...]
> *Benedick*: Why i' faith; methinks she is too low for high praise [...] I do not like her. (1.1.160ff.)

Or again, as in many instances throughout the play,

> *Benedick*: ... but till all graces be in one woman, one woman shall not come in my grace. Rich she shall be, that is certain; wise, or I'll none; virtuous; or I'll never cheapen; fair, or I'll never look on her; mild or come not near me; noble, or not I for an angel. (3.3.26ff.)

4

"If you will follow me, I will show you enough." (3.2.119) What else can we notice here? When I issue this question as a challenge to my students, they have a field day finding instances and repetitions of the above puns and wordplays, and I find it a compelling way to interest them in virtually sifting every speech for cases in point. Naturally they discover many other things along the way, and are continually amazed. Suffice it to say that every scene in the play in many ways flirts and plays with the language details we have noted so far. What might be more interesting here on this matter, however, is to list some few additional minute particulars of the language Shakespeare uses which to my knowledge have not yet been noticed in print. These are observations and notations, not proofs of course, and I would sooner encourage others to add to the list than to subscribe to it. We must I think try to notice as much as possible in this play about noticing – as Shakespeare seems almost to dare us to do. When Shakespeare says 'Much I Do' we have 'much to do'.

1. The play is much ado about the word "ado" (I do, he do) as well: note the wartime "doings" of Claudio, the sexual "doings" of Benedick (we notice the suggestive spelling and hybrid etymology of his name at this point) as a ladies' man in scene one, the bawdy "doing" that Beatrice wishes to avoid in 2.1., and the "doing" that Hero is charged with. There is the "doing in" of Claudio that Beatrice requires of Benedick in 4.1., the written epitaph on Hero as being "Done to death by slanderous tongues" (5.3.3), and much more too. More than we can track down here. That the reader can "do".

2. In the middle scene of the play, 3.2., that crucial chiasmic scene where subplot and plot cross in rising and falling actions, respectively, there is some quite literal language play involved in the exchange on Benedick's supposed toothache. When Benedick, attempting to explain his melancholy appearance, says "I have the toothache", the others urge him either to "Draw it" or "Hang it", or "hang it first, and draw it afterwards" (3.2.21ff.). Aside from the often footnoted allusion here to the methods of executing traitors, let me suggest that the remedy for the toothache, pronounced "tooth-*aitch*" (i.e. "h") in Shakespeare's time, can be noticed as a pun on the idea of pulling out the "h" in nothing. Here I suggest that nothing may be assumed to be too small a feature to carry signals in this play. This may be seen as a literal (letteral) meaning.

3. With regard to the crucial miniplot involving Dogberry, Verges, and the Watch, we can start by noticing names. The Watch is, of course, the group responsible for official noticing of suspicious activity in the community, and as such they are the play's official noters. Verges's name suggests the *verge* (Latin, *virga*, stick or rod), the baton or nightstick of authority, but perhaps also the "male intromittent organ of [...] various invertebrates," simple tool that Verges is. Dogberry's name, as the inferior or unfit dogwood berry, if not the "dog turd" that

more than one student suggests, by analogy to "dingleberry", is a metaphor of inferior social status or mental acuity. But what Shakespeare would have us notice, I think, is that for all his blundering malapropism, it is Dogberry, that honest, proud, and tediously consequential constable, who brings Borachio to justice, and so saves the day. As Borachio, the villain himself says, "What your wisdoms could not discover, these shallow fools have brought to light" (5.1.332 ff.). What we owe sometimes to the simpletons; they are "Gifts that God gives" 3.5.43), says Dogberry. They may not often solve things, but they notice them. By the skin of its teeth the play thus rescues itself from the potential tragedy of erroneous observation, wrong words, mistaken identities, misreading, malapropism, and human error of the most pervasive sort. As such it works wonders as a comedic cautionary tale of how much ado is commonly made in social practices of all sorts about what we do, know, imagine, and make mistakes about. As Claudio, exclaims, even as he is making the biggest mistake of the play, and of his life,

> O, What men dare do! What men may do!
> What men daily do, not knowing what
> they do! (4.1.20)

4. To close, we can return to the word "giddy" cited above in Borachio's speech on fashion. People are giddy about fashion, he says, which causes Conrad to ask, "But art not thou thyself giddy with the fashion too, that thou hast shifted out of thy tale into telling me of the fashion?" In a third instance of the word in the play, Benedick uses it in his defense of falling in love and marrying:

> In brief, since I do purpose to marry, I will think nothing to any purpose
> that the world can say against it, and therefore never flout at me for what
> I have said against it; for man is a giddy thing, and this is my conclusion.
> (5.4.104-9)

The word is of Anglo-Saxon origin in *gydig*, insane, but in the etymological sense of A.S. *gyden*, goddess, where to be *gydig* is to be possessed by a supernatural female power. "Man is a giddy thing," says Benedick, once again at a dramatic point, as in the church when Hero is wronged, taking the side of the female perspective and finding in that change a note of consolation for our mad and silly errors, and changes of mind. What the play says about this is that, given how often we are wrong, it is a saving grace that we can giddily change our tunes, that something larger and more loving can possess us, correct our errors, and change our minds and hearts.

Notes

1. All quotations of Shakespeare are from *The Riverside Shakespeare*, ed. G. B. Evans et al. (Boston: Houghton Mufflin, 1974).
2. *The Shakespearean Metaphor: Studies in Language and Form* (New Jersey: Rowman & Littlefield, 1978), p. 174.
3. "Much Ado about Nothing", *Shakespeare Quarterly*, V (1954), p. 289.
4. See M. H. Mahood, "The Fatal Cleopatra: Shakespeare and the Pun", *Essays in Criticism*, I (1951), p. 198.
5. *The Works of William Shakespeare* (Boston: 1857), Vol. III, pp. 226-7.
6. (New Haven: Princeton UP, 1953), p. 132.
7. (London and New York: Methuen, 1981), p. 5.
8. "Note Notes, Forsooth..." *Shakespeare Quarterly*, III (1957), p. 354.
9. California UP: Berkeley and Los Angeles, 1962.
10. See Thomas Pyles, "Ophelia's Nothing", *Modern Language Notes*, XLIV (1949) pp. 322-3. Here the word is found to have "yonic symbolism" in its "anatomical localization of sexuality." It is found to be a "shape metaphor", the nothing, the "naught" (and "naughty") of the female *pudendum* in what Pyles calls the "venereal vernacular" of Shakespeare's time.
11. "The Secret Wit of Spenser's Language", in *Elizabethan Poetry: Modern Essays in Criticism*, ed. Paul J. Alpers (New York: Oxford UP, 1967), pp. 447-72.
12. London: Andre Deutsch, 1976.
13. *Op. cit.*, footnote 2.
14. Brighton, Sussex: Harvester Press, 1987.
15. Oxford and Cambridge, MA: Blackwell, 1992.
16. Subsequent italics, in or out of brackets, indicate references to entries in the *OED Second Edition*, where sb. indicates substantive, and v. verb usages.
17. Here I sense a necessary correction of the *OED*, sometimes in error regarding first usages, as we know, which has, at sb2 I.5, "To change (one's) note: to alter (one's) way of speaking or thinking", with a first usage in George Herbert's *The Temple* (1633). Clearly, in the light of the central recurrent significance of fundamental changes in habits of thought and speech in this play, we can move first usages back to at least the 1590s.
18. *Op. cit.*, p. 155-74.
19. Marvin Spevak, *The Harvard Concordance to Shakespeare* (Cambridge, MA: Harvard UP, 1973).

HELENA'S TRICKS: TRANSGRESSION AND NEGOTIATION IN *ALL'S WELL THAT ENDS WELL*

Hee-Won Lee
(Seoul National Politechnic University)

In the exchange on virginity, Helena asks Parolles, "How might one do, sir, to lose it [virginity] to her own liking?" Helena's question is shocking and provocative partly because Helena dares to express female sexual desire: she actively longs to have sex with the man she likes ("to lose it to her own liking") and she occupies a masculine position to seek a practical strategy of satisfying her desire ("How might one do"). Helena not only articulates a distinct female desire in terms that betray a patriarchal fantasy to urge a girl to keep a feminine virtue, virginity, but also practically tries to surmount obstacles to get what she desires. In her arrangement of her own wooing and wedding through her ingenuity, she has close affinities with such male heroes as Richard Duke of York, Bolingbroke, Henry V, Petruchio, Hamlet, Duke Vincentio, and Prospero. Recognizing this, we can easily agree with Honigmann who, in the critical line of Bernard Shaw,[1] calls the play a feminist play, seeing Helena as "an unconventional woman" or "the New Woman" who has a professional skill (79).[2]

However, it is worthwhile to note that although Honigmann's observation is not completely wrong, it neglects the complexities lurking in Helena's question. That question, which introduces the issue of sexual desire and anticipates the two explicitly sexual plots that Helena will manipulate, is how to adapt the claim of sexual instincts to the demands of society. As the action proceeds, the question Helena asks underscores the central concern highlighted in "the healing of the King" and the bed-trick: Helena's attempt to legitimize sexual desire. As a desiring subject and manipulative heroine, she transgresses the patriarchal boundary of gender and advances beyond the limit of class. But as a girl who desperately wants a legal husband as well as a sexual partner, Helena serves the interests of patriarchy and thus situates herself safely within its structures. Helena attempts to legitimize the patriarchal culture as much as challenge it; she is subversive only in the "name, and not the thing" (5.3.308).

All's Well That Ends Well dramatizes the complex, ambivalent relation of Helena to the patriarchy that the question, "How might one do, sir, to lose it to her own liking?" excellently illustrates. This essay confronts this ambivalence, a contradiction arising from the gaps between Helena's sexual desire (which poses a threat to patriarchal order) and her accommodation to the patriarchy, between the effective manipulative power Helena exercises and the nominal power given to patriarchal institutions.

1

Although the nostalgic opening introduces a patriarchal social system centered on the King of France and based on patrilineal descent, the Kingship and the father-son relationship are critically jeopardized. Actual fathers are dead; the King is sick. The heroic past to which the dead fathers belong cannot be recovered in the present. Bertram seems to lack his father's morality, as expressed in the desires of his mother and the King that he be like his father in moral parts as well as in shape (1.1.61-2;1.2.21-2). The generational tension between fathers and sons is more clearly visible in the unstable mood created by the King's nostalgic admiration of Bertram's father and his critique of the younger generation. The noble past is in sharp contrast to the present when the young lords are preoccupied with "levity in honor" (1.2.35). Anxiously criticizing the young son's interest in "new things", "garments", "fashions" (1.2.61,62,63), the King desires them to be "goers backwards" (1.2.48) who revere the values found in the generation of the fathers, the values of the patriarchy. In making Bertram a ward, a son, the King tries to repair the broken father-son relationship and by this mediation to transmit the values of the father's generation to the son's generation. But utterly lacking physical energy because of his illness, the King is ready to relinquish some authority to the young sons ("To give some labourers room" [1.2.67]). The political impasse created by the King's ailment gives the young sons room to threaten the patriarchy. As the bond of father and son is diluted, so the link to form social relationships and continuity is shaken.

The King's political weakness is well demonstrated in his handling of the Florentine-Sienese war. The King's refusal to send official aid to Florence because of warning from his "cousin Austria" (1.2.5) reveals his lack of political judgment. Confronted with the political business that requires complicated diplomatic talent, the King totally depends on the pre-judgement of his cousin and tries to avoid becoming involved. In a moment, however, he quickly switches his initial decision of non-involvement into the policy of private actions, a policy that gives the young soldiers freedom to fight on either side (1.2.14-15). The second decision further raises doubt about the King's leadership because it is a policy that comes from his political uncertainty and contributes to the young men's random activity rather than their brave soldiership, one of his ideal virtues. And the King's lack of coherence and judgement corresponds to the sickness found in the present young men, whose "judgments are / Mere fathers of their garments" and whose "constancies / Expire before their fashions" (1.2.61-3; Erickson, 61-6).

If male authority becomes weakened and precarious within a debilitated patriarchy, a feeling of loss and sadness broods over the Countess's and Helena's personal life. Bertram is departing for the King's court, leaving Helena and his mother behind. The King's wardship means personal deprivation for Helena and the Countess. The King acts the role of father at the cost of the Countess's maternal care. Helena's personal sadness, however, is more painful than the Countess's sense of loss. In the context of the Countess and Lafew's public grief at the death of Helena's father, Helena shockingly reveals a lover's sorrow for the departure of her beloved rather than a daughter's mourning for the dead father:

> I think not on my father,...
> I have forgot him. My imagination
> Carries no favor in't but Bertram's
> I am undone, there is no living, none,
> If Bertram be away.... (1.1.79-85).

As Asp recognizes, Helena here becomes "the subject of her desire, not the object of another" (49), asserting her passionate, wholly sexual love for Bertram and concerning herself only with Bertram's physical beauty (his "arched brows, his hawking eye, his urls" and "every line and trick of his sweet favour" [1.1.94,96]). But Helena is crying less for Bertram's departure than for his "inaccessibility as a love object" (Asp, 52). Her lament is mainly founded on the difference in social status between her and her beloved. In fact, she becomes "a Petrarchan lover" (Neely, 66) who accepts the futility of her love and the unattainability of her beloved, idealizing Bertram as a religious idol she can worship in her fancy only. Here it seems that Helena passively accepts her social inferiority and acquiesces in her own helplessness as defined by the patriarchal code. Yet, her sexual desire remains strong enough for her to feel frustration of love as "plague" (1.1.90,92). For Helena to love a man of a different class is painful enough to question the power of divine authorities. While complaining about the powerlessness of Fortune, Love, and Diana, Helena delivers "in the most bitter touch of sorrow" (1.3.117) utter disillusionment at her society, a society in which fortune "had put such difference" between her and Bertram, in which love is allowed "only where qualities were level", and in which a maiden's sexual desire remains in captivity "without rescue in the first assault or ransom afterward" (1.3.112,113,115-6). Helena is deeply torn between her sick desire and her social situation.

Yet, decisive action to overcome both political sickness and personal (sexual) predicament comes from Helena. The King's physical and political weaknesses make Helena's control of patriarchal power possible. Helena asserts her intellect and force of personality to offer the healing solution: "Our remedies oft in ourselves do lie, / Which we ascribe to heaven" (1.1.216-7). While seeking in the King's disease and Bertram's lustful desire a practical means of overcoming her personal dilemma, Helena boldly decides to disrupt the normal gender role attributed to a woman and to transgress the social barrier, the "mightiest space in fortune" (1.1.222), between her and Bertram. She needs to mold political events and invade male space for her own sexual satisfaction.

In achieving her subversive goal of marrying herself to the aristocratic Bertram, however, Helena chooses to protect patriarchal order rather than disrupt it. Helena's transgressive purpose and her submissive ways have made many critics uncomfortable. Calderwood ("Mingled Yarn", 64), Neely (67), Dreher (136), Cohen (185), Hodgdon (66), Snyder ("Shakespeare's Helens", 66-7), Jardine (12), and Zitner (106-7) have recognized in Helena's character the strange combination of activity and passivity, transgression and submissiveness, but they do not observe Helena's manipulative use of a submissive mask to mitigate her disruptiveness. Combining Nakayama's and Asp's analysis,[3] I would suggest that, to reorder her world both psychologically and socially within the patriarchy, she pretends to accept the patriarchal conventions of womanly submissiveness and powerlessness. She hides her subversive desires and plans, and her power before figures of authority.[4]

In front of Lafew and the Countess, Helena, at the beginning, adopts the role of a silent, submissive and modest girl. To both, Helena appears to be a shy maiden who blushes at being praised and a dutiful daughter who mourns the death of her father. Even during the personal interview with the Countess, Helena hesitates to speak openly about her intentions. Contrary to her willful determination to seek out Bertram, she first assures the Countess that she "follow[s] him not / By any token of presumptuous suit" (1.3.190-1), admitting her inferior status and characterizing her love for Bertram as that of a humble worshipper for an idol. After realizing that the Countess was informed of her passion and project, she denies her own healing power, attributing her power to her "father's skill" or "the luckiest stars in heaven" (1.3.236, 239).

Such capacity for role-playing makes possible Helena's success in the King's court. She dares to set her skill against that of the learned doctors. As the Countess points out, Helena, "a poor unlearned virgin" (1.3.240), who is capable of employing medical skill customarily confined to men, faces the King's serious objections. But Helena can gradually nullify the objections against her socially disruptive force (a woman's learned skill) by adopting a language of weakness and obedience. Helena introduces herself as a dutiful daughter who can humbly continue her father's skill, not as a rebellious female doctor:[5]

> ... wherein the honor
> Of my dear father's gift stands chief in power,
> I came to tender it and my appliance,
> With all bound humbleness. (2.1.111-14).

When confronted with the King's further refusal, she then appeals to God. Describing herself as God's "weaker minister" or His holy "babe" (2.1.137,138), she presents herself as merely an instrument of providential power:

> But most it is presumptuous in us, when
> The help of heaven we count the act of men,
> Dear sir, to my endeavors give consent;
> Of heaven, not me, make an experiment. (2.1.151-4)

By claiming the power of heaven, that is, by disclaiming what she asserts earlier ("Our remedies oft in ourselves do lie, / Which we ascribe to heaven"), Helena succeeds in persuading the King. Her long plea to the King that God might intervene in her medical process is shared by the King's court. The King answers her: "Methinks in thee some blessed spirit both speak / His powerful sound within an organ weak" (2.1.175-6). Lafew also interprets Helena's work as something supernatural, "a showing of a heavenly effect in an earthly actor" (2.1.23). Although Susan Snyder sees the miraculous talk as the patriarchal rationalization (or mystification) of a woman's personal success in a male province ("Displacement", 26), it is Helena herself (not the patriarchy) who mystifies her personal power, giving all credit to Heaven. By using patriarchal rationalization as a technique, Helena beguiles the King and the court into believing that she is a powerless girl and that her success is due to God's intervention.

Helena also convinces the King of her medical confidence, appealing in her oath to the patriarchal form of "defamations of a woman's reputation" (Jardine, 10), a denigration of female honor: she will take the name of a whore in case of failure ("Tax of impudence, / A Strumpet's boldness, a divulged shame / Traduced by odious ballads" [2.1.170-2]). Here Helena acquiesces to Lafew's erotic definition of her medical skill, which recalls the Renaissance charge of witchcraft and its demonising of transgressive women into impudent whores.[6] Lafew articulates the patriarchy's mistrust of female sexuality. To him, Helena the female healer is eroticized as a "medicine" (2.1.72) to "araise King Pepin" and "To give great Charlemain a pen in 's hand, / And write to her a love line" (2.1.76-8). Lafew calls her "Doctor she" (2.1.79), a name implying, as Rutter rightly points out, that "female achievement [...] is inscribed within her sexual 'doing'" (117).

Helena challenges the traditional masculine power even more in wanting to use (to adapt Bertram's term) "the help of mine own eye" (2.3.108) in the selection of love, by demanding the right to choose her husband. Yet in her aggressive action, Helena again uses a language of meekness and moderation and tries to mitigate her power. Helena's action threatens the patriarchal marriage system itself, but her language is that which patriarchy assigns to women. Once again emphasizing the power of heaven ("Heaven hath through me restor'd the King to health" [2.3.64]) and describing herself as "a simple maid" (2.3.66), Helena plays out the role of a shy girl with the "blushes in her cheeks" (2.3.69). In designating Bertram as a husband, she manages to be a powerless, moderate bride who is willing to serve her future husband: "I dare not say I take you, but I give / Me and my service, ever whilst I live, / Into your guiding power. This is the man" (2.3.102-4). Through her attempt to mask the subversiveness of her intervention in a male sphere, Helena becomes Bertram's wife, but only in a legal sense.

A legal marriage without consummation is not Helena's ultimate goal. In order to be a legitimate wife sexually as well as legally, Helena continues to take up a strategy of ostensible submission to Bertram's will. Helena appears to be the "most obedient servant" (2.5.72) to Bertram when she accepts Bertram's rejection without a complaint. In contrast to the Countess, who responds to Bertram's betrayal of Helena with contempt, Helena becomes a passive female who tearfully shows sympathetic understanding for, and continuous devotion to, Bertram. She blames herself for the potential danger and the supposed death Bertram will face in the wars. But behind her apparent humbleness lies her ambitious action of capturing her reluctant husband. Helena assumes the role of a humble pilgrim, a sinner who repents of her "Ambitious love" (3.4.4) begging forgiveness from God. Yet the purpose of her disguise is to invade Bertram's military space, Florence.

In the bed-trick, Helena ascends to the position of sexually desiring subject through the manipulation of Bertram's lust. Having chosen Bertram as a legal husband, Helena continuous to pursue her chosen husband to his bed. Her dominance becomes obvious when she imposes the restrictions, "darkness and silence" that "deprive him [Bertram] of the two patriarchal capacities that define him as (masculine) subject: the gaze and speech", as MaCandless suggests (463). It is in the bed-trick that Helena reaches the climax of her disguise strategy. In the impossible conditions Bertram set up ("When thou canst get the ring upon my finger, which shall never come off, and show me a child begotten of thy body that I am father to, then call me husband" [3.2.57-60]), Helena finds a trap to capture him: she uses the bed-trick, following the very language of his directions literally (apparently), but subverting their actual message of refusal. The ruse, which is designed to serve the interests of women and humiliate Bertram, priviliges the patriarchal codes in love-making. Helena disguises herself as Diana, a penniless virgin who is forced to satisfy Bertram's sensual pleasure. It is with such seeming powerlessness that she traps Bertram's lustful desires and "cozen'd thoughts" (4.4.23) to lure him into consummating the legal bond.

Both Helena's cure of the ill patriarch and her trick against Bertram rely on her devious manipulation of male sexuality. In her medical treatment of the ailing King, Helena utilizes the masculine mentality that finds male assertiveness (political potency) in sexual potency. Though Helena introduces herself as a physician's daughter and heavenly minister, her treatment is focused on rejuvenating the King's sexual potency rather than curing his disease, "a fistula" (1.1.34). As Lafew comments on the newly healed monarch, the King's renewed potency is first shown in his lusty dance: "Lustick! [...] Why, he's able to lead her a cornato "(2.3.40-2), a leaping dance that symbolizes a sexual arousal with its sudden upward leaping. The same image of sexual erection informs the angry exchange between the King and Bertram:

> King: Thou know'st she has raised me from my sickly bed.
> Bertram: But follows it, my lord, to bring me down
>   Must answer for your raising? (2.3.111-3)

By repeating the King's metaphor of erection, "raise", Bertram expresses both his revulsion for Helena's seductive power which rekindled the King's phallic desire and his rebellion against being "his surrogate father's imagined sexual partner" (Adelman, 156; Wheeler, 40; Snyder, "Displacement", 25-6).

In the overtly sexual bed-trick, Helena, along with Diana and her mother, traps Bertram by observing and manipulating patriarchal values and structures in sexuality and marriage. The virginity discussion Helena has with Parolles epitomizes the patriarchal concept of virginity as a medium of procreation and a commodity, the concept which is then used to make Bertram trade his family honor for Diana's virginity and make Helena yield Bertram's offspring. Parolles, a man of "[c]old wisdom" (1.1.105), delivers the male world's views that looks to female sexuality in terms of profit – either children or money. Parolles insists that a virgin is a "desperate offender against nature" (1.1.140-1) because "[l]oss of virginity is rational increase" (1.1.126-8), and that to keep virginity "against the rule of nature" is to "accuse your mothers, which is most infallible disobedience" (1.1.135, 137-8). Parolles emphasizes a woman's sexual need to perpetuate the race, her need to be a mother who continues the male heritage. But he transforms the natural medium of male continuity into a medium of exchange. Virginity is, Parolles argues, also a commodity which is vendible in the male traffic of women, and it is profitable for a maiden to sell virginity when she is vendible at the highest price: "'Tis a commodity will lose gloss with lying: the longer kept, the less worth. Off with't / While 'tis vendible" (1.1.152-4). Parolles summarizes the misogynist view, widespread in the Renaissance, that defines female sexuality according to biological and economic relationships to men, quite apart from human intimacy. The loss of virginity was important for men because it promised biological continuity by means of male offspring. At the same time, the Renaissance males accorded market value to virginity. (King, 29-31; Camden, 62; Calderwood, *The Properties of 'Othello'*, 19-37).

Parolles's views of sexuality as a medium of procreation and a commodity reflect or support Bertram's. Bertram accuses Diana's virginity of unnaturalness, of wanting youthful passion, of being "cold and stern" (4.2.8) and declares the virgin a traitor to her mother (4.2.9). Bertram's commercial bargain for Diana's virginity is parodied in Parolles' sonnet letter, which urges that Diana be paid in advance for her loss: "When he swears others, bid him drop gold, and take it; / And I had that which any inferior might / At market price have brought" (5.3.217-9). Diana, instructed by Helena, beguiles Bertram by using the very power that her virginity has as a medium of exchange for men, that is, by selling her chastity, "the jewel of our house, / Bequeathed down from many ancestor" (4.2.46-7) at the high price of Bertram's family ring, which is similarly "bequeathed down from many ancestors" (4.2.43).

In the bed-trick, Helena and Diana also unmask and exploit men's polarized attitudes to sexuality: fear of domestic sexuality and desire for the illicit. In an early conversation with the Countess, Lavatch, "a foul-mouth'd and calumnious knave" (1.3.56), cynically parodies this masculine attitude in regard to marriage. According to Lavatch, marriage not only gives a man sensual satisfaction but also leads to cuckoldry. He seeks to marry to satisfy his own sexual needs and to produce progeny: "My poor body, madam, requires it. I am driven on by the flesh" (1.3.28-9); "I think I shall never have the blessing of God till I have issue of my body" (1.3.24-5). But Lavatch also emphasizes the disastrous aspect of marriage, cuckoldry: although "your marriage comes by destiny", cuckoldry is inevitable because "your cuckoo sings by kind" (1.3.62-3). Exaggerating male solidarity created by men's common experience of cuckoldry transcending religion and age, Lavatch expresses his fear of sexual impotence: "if men could be

Helena's Tricks 469

contented to be what they are, there were no fear in marriage ..."(1.3.50-1). To Lavatch, the marriage bed is a fearful place where he has no choice but resign his power to adultery, to unmanageable female sexuality (Adelman, 174; Snyder, "Displacement", 23).

Male fear of domestic sexuality is also articulated when Parolles encourages Bertram not to "spend" his "manly marrow" by bedding (2.3.280). Although Parolles does not mention the fear of cuckoldry, he introduces the threat of emasculation in marriage, voicing the fear that a man will lose manliness in the arms of the woman. While fearing their loss of masculinity by being overwhelmed by the wife, men usually pursue lust and wantonness outside the family. Hence the King's warning to the departing French nobles against seductive foreign women: "Those girls of Italy, take heed of them [...] beware of being captives / Before you serve" (2.1.19-22). Bertram's horror of marital sexuality and his seduction of Diana briskly conform to this dual masculine view. Bertram never connects his "dark house and the [detested] wife" (2.3.291-2) to cuckoldry, as Lavatch does. But the fear of emasculation that Lavatch and Parolles describe is hinted at when he complains about his staying at home, which, in an effeminized subjugation to a woman, will deprive him of military action and insult his manhood.

> I shall stay here the forehorse to a smock,
> Creaking my shoes on the plain masonry,
> Till honor be bought up, and no sword worn
> But one to dance with! By heaven, I'll steal away. (2.1.30-33)

Distinguishing compelled marital sexuality from free sexuality governed by "love's own sweet constraints" (4.2.16), Bertram escapes from the duty he owes to his wife in order to sport with Diana, by which action he not only enjoys the sensual pleasure of maleness but also asserts male autonomy frustrated in the enforced marriage to Helena.

Mariana's distrust of men's seduction, "their promises, enticements, oaths, tokens, and all these engines of lust are not the things they go under" (3.5.18-20), and Helena's expectation of Bertram's amorous pursuit of Diana (3.5.68-69) are well-founded, as Bertram seduces Diana just as her mother expected "how he would woo" (4.2.69), makes sweet use of his lust (4.4.21-5), and later vilifies her as a dangerously seductive whore (5.3.210-9). As Helena, along with Diana, cozens Bertram's "sick desires" (4.2.35) for their own desires in the sexual trick, she reverses the patriarchal sexual traffic. Not Diana but Bertram becomes a commodity, a victim. As Dreher, a defender of Helena and her transgressive power, points out, by "excelling in a man's world, by outperforming men" (139), Helena and the Florentine women violate the patriarchal convention of objectifying women and reverse gender stereotypes.

Helena's control of patriarchal gender values in sexuality and marriage allows her to take a masculine position, performing tasks which seem to be impossible for a woman in patriarchy. With the aid of the female friends, she reduces the King to an instrument of her marriage and Bertram to a commodity, the object of her desire, and rises from servant to Countess. Yet her assertive desire locates itself within the patriarchal order; her control preserves rather than disrupts the patriarchal system and its values. Helena's two (masculine or assertive) projects are performed to ensure patriarchal marriage, to continue male heritage with the child in her womb and to protect a virgin's chastity.[7]

The purpose of Helena's first project is to settle a bargain with the King, to restore the King's power and in return get from him "honor and wealth" (2.3.144), a title that validates her eligibility for marriage to the aristocratic Bertram and a dowry that transforms her virginity into a commodity.[8] The King's royal hand enhances Helena' status, just as her medical skill lends new power to his authority. Helena boldly enters into the political arena, displaying her feminine (medical or sexual) power, not because she wants to get involved with male politics but because she needs the "Kingly hand" (2.1.193) in demanding Bertram as her marriage partner. Helena's radical demand to choose her own husband according to her desire does not really upset the established order because she provides the listless patriarch with energy enough to exercise "sovereign power and father's voice" (2.3.54). In restoring the King's political ability that can make her "this good gift" (2.3.150), an object of exchange in the marriage market, Helena supports the patriarchal marriage system whose primary concern is the preservation of wealth (King, 32; Cook, 120). In plotting the bed-trick, Helena, along with the Widow, again participates in the male traffic of women against Diana's claim that she will "live and die a maid" (4.2.74). Helena offers the Widow a "purse of gold" (3.7.14) and "After / To marry her, add three thousand crowns ..." (3.7.34-5).

The bed-trick's complicity with patriarchal values is clearly seen in its enforcement of a wife's licit sexuality and its maintenance of a virgin's chastity, which were tied to the reputation of the family in the Renaissance patriarchy. Helena and Diana maintain patriarchal responsibilities placed on women, the wife's duty to produce legitimate male heirs and the maiden's to ensure the purity of male line. Helena's possession of Bertram's patriarchal ring and his legitimate heir also ratifies her social position as a wife and mother in a patriarchal culture. In fulfilling Bertram's stipulations, Helena consents to be the medium for a male link between fathers and sons.

2

Helena's final project is to break up the arranged marriage between Bertram and Maudlin, Lafew's daughter. The noble match that the old generation desires and the King orders (for Helena has reportedly died) is interrupted by Diana's suit on Helena's behalf. In her bold (but false) claim that Bertram is legally contracted to her, Diana replicates Helena's artful manipulation, introducing herself as a seduced, deceived woman, a "poor maid [...] undone" (5.3.146). Bertram attempts to defame Diana as a cunning and experienced whore, characterizing his liaison with Diana as prostitution, and the King and Lafew join Bertram in their accusations of Diana: "This woman's an easy glove, my lord; she goes off and on at pleasure" (5.3.277); "I think thee now some common customer" (5.3.286). Diana, like Helena before her, must accept the title of whore if she fails to tell where she got Helena's ring. But Diana boldly provokes and mystifies the King by revealing the bed-trick in a riddle and by presenting the pregnant and presumedly dead Helena to the King and the court. The King is awed to recognize the mysterious power of the trick (play) that leads Helena to fulfill Bertram's seemingly impossible conditions and to rise from the dead:

> Is there no exorcist
> Beguiles the truer office of mine eyes?
> Is't real that I see? (5.3.304-6)

Helena (and Diana's) cunning enactment of mystery and surprise has certain power to tame Bertram into a submissive husband as well as to disrupt the traditional arranged marriage. While Diana relentlessly exposes Bertram's undignified lies with the aid of Parolles, Bertram is totally helpless. All he can do is to cover himself with lies and he is finally forced to confess the truth, and discards his former fantasies which divide women in two roles – a whore who serves men's sexual satisfaction and a wife whose domestic duty confirms procreation – reconciling at last the roles of sexual partner and wife in his marriage to Helena. Bertram quickly asks pardon and acknowledges her as his wife in both the legal and sexual sense ("Both, both, O pardon!" 5.3.308). And Helena accepts Bertram's plea by altering her view of him in their sexual encounter from "a strange man" (4.4.21) propelled by primitive lust to a sophisticated man of "wondrous kind" (5.3.310). However, we should note here that Helena's strategy is to place Bertram in the position of the sinner in order for her to become the powerful savior rescuing him from the humiliating posture. Here Helena's strategy has close links with the benign policy Prospero uses when he decides to make Antonio and the other enemies the sinners, to forgive their sins, and then elicit their feelings of indebtedness to him. This is a form of "pastoral power", a type of salvation-oriented power that Michel Foucault elaborates in his "The Subject and Power" (783-4). By adopting a role of benign ruler and husband, Helena clearly reverses the normal relationship between husband and wife in the Renaissance patriarchy.

Yet, the completion of Helena's marriage to Bertram is made possible not only by the women's trick but also by the re-establishment of the King's political authority. In order to humiliate Bertram and elicit his pardon, Helena needs to seek the King: "fore whose throne 'tis needful, / Ere I can perfect mine intents, to kneel" (4.4.3-4). Helena needs the authority of the King to legitimize her marriage to Bertram and to punish Bertram before the court. Helena contains her power in the patriarchal structure, submitting to the King's authority, while the King succumbs to her power, satisfying her individual desire. Such a relation is an uneasy negotiation, both "corrupt and restorative" (Neely, 81).[9] In the bargain, Helena and the King totally disregard Bertram's feelings, transforming Bertram into her object of desire and his medium of exercising royal power.

The marriage between Helena and Bertram completed in the end of the play is, thus, not a climactic completion of all conflicts but a mutually satisfying bargain grounded on payment and receipt. Bertram's and Helena's vows, which are put in the conditional, describe their marriage in terms of a contract or bargain: Bertram will love Helena "dearly, ever, ever dearly" (5.3.316) only if her fulfillment of the tasks is proved; Helena swears that if Bertram proves untrue, "Deadly divorce [will] step" between her and Bertram (5. 3.318). Bertram and Helena strike a contract rather than surrender to each other's sexual attraction and to mutual commitment. As Bassnett-McGuire states, their marriage is "far away from a marriage as a union of equal minds" idealized in Milton's vision of marriage (101). Helena's marriage to Bertram is a negotiation by which he moderates his prime concerns to satisfy her and she cooperates with him to promote patriarchal ideology. Considering that marriage in the Renaissance was viewed as an economic and political bargain between families (Cook; King, 32-5; Stone, 127-36), the marriage contract between Helena and Bertram in a form of bargain effectively reflects culturally shared expectations about the proper marriage. In healing the patriarchal King as a female doctor and boldly fulfilling Bertram's conditions in the bed-trick (in producing progeny and continuing the patriarchal family), Helena does her feminine duty to the patriarchy.[10] In a sense, Helena, who manipulates and challenges the patriarchy's deepest structures within its own institutions, mirrors her creator Shakespeare, who is, according to Greenblatt, "as dutiful servant, content to improvise a part of his own within its orthodoxy" embodying in that improvisation "an almost boundless challenge to the culture's every tenet" (253).

Notes

1. Bernard Shaw's praise of Helena's character is famous. He finds the power of *All's Well That Ends Well* in "the sovereign charm of the young Helena and the old Countess of Roussillon" (7) and admires Helena: "the heroine is a lady doctor, and [...] no lady of any delicacy could possibly adopt a profession which involves the possibility of her having to attend cases such as that of the king in this play" (8).

2. Carol Rutter also sees this play as a feminist play, but in the sense that it reveals the limits of the patriarchy rather than Helena's subversiveness.

3. Both Nakayama's analysis of Helena's two languages, a language of deference and a language which she speaks to herself (130-6), and Asp's discussion of Helena's mask suggest Helena's manipulative use of patriarchal language as a mask.

4. In this sense, I am close to McCandless' position that "Helena is consistent throughout the play in mitigating her audacity with displays of "femininity" (453) and against Jardin's view that Helena is transformed from the sexually transgressive girl in the play's first part to the passive wife in the second. But where McCandless sees Helena's performance of femininity as a successful internalization of "a culturally imposed image of Woman" (454), I stress her manipulative power to shape the self and see the manipulation as a strategy. I argue that for her own purposes, Helena adopts, as a strategy, a persona acceptable in the patriarchal circumstance.

Helena's manipulation and mobility remind us of the concept of self-fashioning developed in Greenblatt's *Renaissance Self-Fashioning*. Greeblatt analyzes the formations of the self in the Renaissance under the assumption that man has power to shape his own self and to move out of a narrowly circumscribed social sphere into a different realm. Her manipulative strategies also recall Foucault's technologies of the self, a genealogy of how the self constituted itself as subject ("Technologies of the Self"). In his historical study of the Greco-Roman and the early Christian practices in relation to that constitution of the self, Foucault suggests such various techniques of the self as self-knowledge, meditation, training, memory, writing letters, disclosure of self, examination of self and conscience, recognizing one's self as a sinner, confession, etc. Helena's managerial skills can be examples of such techniques of the self.

5. Helena is rebellious in the sense that she appropriates male medical skills. She is totally different from the female lay healers who were considered as rebellious and accused of witchcraft. "While the female lay healer operated within a network of information-sharing and mutual support" (Ehrenreich and English, *For Her Own Good*, 34), Helena achieves her professional medical skills from her father and concentrates the skills within the court, as Countess observes that "I have those hopes of her good that her education promises her dispositions [which] she inherits" (1.1.39-40).

6. Despite the radical difference between Helena and the Renaissance female lay healer, we can find a similarity between them in the fact that both Helena's medical skill and that of the female lay healer are associated with female sexuality (both are accused of or considered as

having magical, sexual powers of healing). From the fourteenth to the seventeenth century, Ehrenreich and English argue, witches are accused of female transgression – female sexuality and the possession of medical skills and "in the eyes of the church, all the witches' power was ultimately derived from her sexuality" ("Witches, Midwives, and Nurses", 9, 10).

7. Runyan, Nakayama, Adelman, and Zitner have argued that Helena works for the patriarchy because her main purpose is to ensure the validity of her marriage (Cox also recognizes Helena's alliance with the apex of power in his concern with her as a benign trickster [147-80]), while Dreher, Asp, Jardine, Erickson, and Snyder ("Shakespeare's Heroines") have emphasized Helena's transgression of gender stereotypes.

8. In *Renaissance Self-Fashioning* Greenblatt points out that "self-fashioning for such figures involves submission to an absolute power or authority situated at least partially outside the self-God, a sacred book, an institution such as church, court, colonial or military administration" (9). I think that Helena becomes one of "those figures" in her submission to the King.

9. Neely and Bassnett-McGuire see the entire play in terms of bargain. Neely, concentrating on the bed-trick, traces the circulation of all the bargains, from the one between Helen and the King, through the several contracts between the King and Bertram, Bertram and Helena, Helena and the Widow, to the bargain between Bertram and Diana (81-2); and Bassnett-McGuire characterizes the play's major structure as a contract and relates Helena's marriage contract to the political contract between the King and Bertram with reference to historical debate about divorce (100-1).

10. But it does not mean that Helena is a character of redemptive force or a mythic figure as Knight and R. G. Hunt suggest. According to Knight, Helena's spiritual power shown in her performance of miracle and her humble character is the redeeming power of sainthood and all-embracing love. Hunter sees Helena as an instrument of heaven "through which the grace of God can be communicated to man" (130).

Works Cited

Adelman, Janet. "Bed-Tricks on Marriage as the End of Comedy in *All's Well That Ends Well* and *Measure for Measure*." In *Shakespeare's Personality*. Ed. Norman N. Holland, Sidney Homan, and Bernard Paris (Berkeley: California UP, 1989), pp. 151-74.

Asp, Carolyn, "Subjectivity, Desire, and Female Friendship in *All's Well That Ends Well*." *Literature and Psychology* 32:4 (1986), pp. 48-63.

Bassnett-McGuire, Susan. "An Ill Marriage in an Ill Government: Patterns of Unresolved Conflict in *All's Well That Ends Well*." *Shakepeare-Jahrbuch* 120 (1984), pp. 97-102.

Bergeron, David M. "The Mythical Structure of *All's Well That Ends Well*". *Texas Studies in Literature and Language* 14 (1973), pp. 559-68.

Calderwood, James L. "The Mingled Yarn of *All's Well*." JEGP: *Journal of English and Germanic Philology* 62 (1963), pp. 61-76.

-------. *The Properties of Othello*. Amherst: Massachusetts UP, 1989.

Camden, Carroll. *The Elizabethan Woman*. 1952, rev. ed., NY: Appel, 1975.

Cohen, Eileen Z. "Virtue Is Bold": The Bed-Trick and Characterization in *All's Well That Ends Well* and *Measure for Measure*." *Philological Quarterly*, 65 (1986), pp. 171-86.

Cook, Ann Jennalie. *Making a Match: Courtship in Shakespeare and His Society*. Princeton UP, 1991.

Cox, John D. *Shakespeare and the Dramaturgy of Power*. Princeton UP, 1989.

Dreher, Elizabeth Diane. *Domination and Defiance: Fathers and Daughters in Shakespeare*. Lexington: Kentucky UP, 1986.

Ehrenreich, Barbara, and Deidre English. *For Her Own Good: 150 Years of Experts' Advice to Women*. London: Pluto Press, 1979.

-----. *Witches, Midwives, and Nurses: A History of Women Healers*. Glass Moutain Pamphlet No. 1. Oldwestbury, NY: The Feminist Press, 1973.

Erickson, Peter. *Rewriting the Renaissance, Rewriting Ourselves*. Berkeley: California UP, 1991

Foucault, Michel. "Technologies of the Self." In *Technologies of the Self: A Seminar with Michel Foucault*. Ed. Luther H. Martin, Huck Gutman, and Patrick H. Hutton (Amherst: Massachusetts UP, 1988), pp. 16-49.

-----. "The Subject and Power". *Critical Inquiry*, 8 (1982), pp. 777-95.

Greenblatt, Stephen. *Renaissance Self-Fashioning: From More to Shakespeare*. Chicago UP, 1980.

Hodgdon, Barbara. "The Making of Virgins and Mothers: Sexual Signs, Substitute Scenes and Doubled Presences in *All's Well That Ends Well*." *Philological Quarterly*, 66 (1987), pp. 47-71.

Honigmann, E.A.J. "*All's Well That Ends Well*: A "Feminist Play?" In *Shakespearean Criticism Yearbook* 13 C (1989). [Detroit: Gale Research, 1991], pp. 77-83. Originally in his *Myriad-Minded Shakespeare: Essays, Chiefly on the*

Tragedies and Problem Comedies. (London: Macmillan, 1989), pp. 130-46.

Hunter, R.G. *Shakespeare and the Comedy of Forgiveness*. New York: Columbia UP, 1965.

Jardine, Lisa. "Cultural Confusion and Shakespeare's Learned Heroines: These Are Old Paradoxes." *Shakespeare Quarterly*, 38 (1987), pp. 1-18.

King, Margaret L. *Women of the Renaissance*. Chicago: Chicago UP, 1991.

Knight, G. Wilson. "The Third Eye: An Essay on *All's Well That Ends Well*." In *The Sovereign Flower* (London: Methuen, 1958), pp. 93-160.

McCandless, David. "Helena's Bed-Trick: Gender and Performance in *All's Well That Ends Well*." *Shakespeare Quarterly*, 45 (1994), pp. 449-68.

Nakayama, Randall Shige. "Divided Duty: Gender Identity and Marriage in *Much Ado About Nothing, All's Well That Ends Well, Troilus and Cressida, and Othello*." Diss. University of California, 1986.

Neely, Carol Thomas. *Broken Nuptials in Shakespears's Plays*. New Haven: Yale UP, 1985.

Runyan, William R. "The Healing of Hierarchy in *All's Well That Ends Well*." *Shakespeare and Renaissance Association of West Virginia: Selected Papers*, 5 (1980), pp. 49-55.

Rutter, Carol. "Helena's Choosing: Writing the Couplets in a Choreography of Discontinuity (*All's Well That Ends Well* 2.3)" In *Shakespearean Criticism Yearbook*, 19 (1991), pp. 113-21. Originally appeared in *Essays in Theatre* 9:2 (1991), pp. 121-39.

Shaw, Bernard. "*All's Well That Ends Well*." *Shaw on Shakespeare: An Anthology of Bernard Shaw's Writings on the Plays and Production of Shakespeare*. Ed. Wilson Edwin (London: Cassell, 1961), pp. 5-12.

Snyder, Susan. "*All's Well That Ends Well* and Shakespeare's Helens: Text and Subtext, Subject and Object." *English Literary Renaissance*, 18 (1988), pp. 66-77.

-----. "The King's Not Here: Displacement and Deferral in *All's Well That Ends Well*." *Shakespeare Quarterly*, 43 (1992), pp. 20-32.

Stone, Lawrence. *The Family, Sex, and Marriage in England 1500-1800.* Abridged edn. New York: Harper Colophon, 1979.

Wheeler, Richard P. *Shakespeare's Development and the Problem Comedies: Turn and Counter Turn.* Berkeley: California UP, 1981.

Zitner, Sheldon P. *All's Well That Ends Well.* Boston: Twayne, 1989.

BRADLEY'S ENDING OF *KING LEAR*

Edward M. Moore
(Grinnell College)

Numerous commentators have remarked that the ending of *King Lear* is essential to an understanding of the whole action; in a recent article, Arthur Kirsch goes so far as to say that Lear's death "is not merely the conclusion of the action of the play, it is its recapitulation, the moment in which the whole of it is crystallized."[1] In view of the work on the text(s) of *King Lear* over the last fifteen years or so, one has to ask, which ending? for the Folio and Quarto texts differ markedly. Since Rowe (1709), and since the first use of the Quarto by Pope (1723) and Theobald's full collation (1733), editors and commentators, with few exceptions, have based editions and interpretations of the play on the Folio text. There, Lear's death comes as he gazes at the corpse of Cordelia.

> *Lear.* And my poore Foole is hang'd: no, no, no life?
> Why should a Dog, a Horse, a Rat haue life,
> And thou no breath at all? Thou'lt come no more,
> Neuer, neuer, neuer, neuer, neuer.
> Pray you vndo this Button. Thanke you Sir,
> Do you see this? Looke on her? Looke her lips,
> Looke there, looke there. *He dies.*
>   *Edg.* He faints, my Lord, my Lord.
>   *Kent.* Breake heart, I prythee breake.
>   *Edg.* Looke vp my Lord.
>   *Kent* Vex not his ghost, O let him passe, he hates him,
> That would vpon the wracke of this tough world
> Stretch him out longer.
>   *Edg.* He is gon indeed.
>   *Kent* The wonder is, he hath endur'd so long,
> He but vsurpt his life.[2]

The Quarto, however, does not have Lear's last two lines, and has him die with the line given in the Folio to Kent.

> *Lear.* And my poore foole is hangd, no, no life, why should a dog, a horse, a rat of life and thou no breath at all, O thou wilt come no more, neuer, neuer, neuer, pray you vndo this button, thanke you sir, O, o, o, o. *Edg.* He faints my Lord, my Lord.
> *Lear.* Breake hart, I prethe breake. *Edgar.* Look vp my Lord.
> *Kent.* Vex not his ghost, O let him passe,
> He hates him that would vpon the wracke,
> Of this tough world stretch him out longer.
> *Edg.* O he is gone indeed.
> *Kent.* The wonder is, he hath endured so long,
> He but vsurpt his life.[3]

Since 1904, commentary has been overwhelmingly dominated by A. C. Bradley's interpretation of the lines from the Folio. As is well known, Bradley believed that "though [Lear] is killed by an agony of pain, the agony in which he actually dies is one not of pain but of ecstasy [...] an unbearable *joy*" in the belief that Cordelia lives; indeed, we may accurately call "this poem *The Redemption of King Lear*".[4] Bradley was too good a scholar to ignore the Quarto text, but he glosses over the problem it raises here. He refers to the lines 'Do you see this ...' as "represented in the oldest text by a four-times repeated 'O'" (p. 291) and mentions only in a footnote (p. 293) that the Quarto gives Lear the line 'Breake hart, I prethe breake.'

Certainly an actor could do almost anything with 'O, o, o, o,' and the exclamation has even been called "an actor's interpolation" or "the printer's formula for a death cry",[5] but it is difficult to reconcile Bradley's reading with the Quarto text; and as far as I can discover, no critic or editor before Bradley interpreted even the Folio reading as he does, nor did any actor so act it. Bradley was a frequent playgoer, and he specifically complains of "all the actors I have ever heard" in the role (p. 293, note). He thinks the Folio stage direction *'He dies.'* comes "a few lines too soon"; his interpretation, he says,

> may be condemned as fantastic, but the text, it appears to me, will bear no other. [...] To make Lear during this interval [from the Messenger's confirmation of the killing of Cordelia's hangman] turn continually in anguish to the corpse is to act the passage in a manner irreconcilable with

the text, and insufferable in its effect. I speak from experience [...] (pp. 291-2, note).

Bradley's "experience" was probably dominated by Henry Irving's production which opened at the Lyceum Theatre in November of 1892 and ran for 76 performances. Irving cut the play by almost half, rearranged scenes, and played the title role primarily for pathos. Shaw called the production "an impertinent intrusion of a quite silly conceit of his own into a great play",[6] and a recent adulator of Irving admits that "*King Lear* became a pathetic melodrama [...] a dull and ill-constructed melodrama." Here is the latter's reconstruction, quoting contemporary reviews, of Irving's ending. As "the sun was symbolically setting, its slowness keeping time with the 'slow loosening, one by one, of the cords of life,' ...

> With his last words he bent to kiss Cordelia, then fell back gently in Kent's arms, 'pointing his gaunt fingers to her dead body as he ... gently expired'. Around him 'the crowd of barbaric warriors lowered their spears pointing to the dead king'.[7]

Certainly no ecstasy here, and from his final entrance Irving displayed much anguish over the corpse. Other major productions Bradley may have seen were two famous Italian Lears: the first, Ernesto Rossi, with an all-English cast at Drury Lane for six performances in 1876 (Bradley was 25 and a Fellow at Balliol at the time) and again at Her Majesty's for five performances in 1882, the year Bradley took a Chair at Liverpool (until 1889); the second, Tommaso Salvini with an all-Italian cast at Covent Garden for two performances in 1884, and whose tour that year included Liverpool.[8] There was also Edwin Booth's Lear at the Princess's Theatre in 1881. Both Rossi and Salvini played for pathos (Irving, apparently, in large part modeled his Lear on theirs). Rossi's ending was described by a contemporary as "too painful to contemplate for harmonious effect, or for leaving on the mind of the spectator the final sense of great sorrows ended in peaceful rest."[9] The more famous Salvini also died in despair at Cordelia's death. He "looked wildly about" at 'This feather stirs,' but

When this last illusion passed, his face grew grey [!], his grizzled head drooped, and whispering "Look there, look there!" he fell, face downward, over Cordelia's body.[10]

Henry James, who saw the production in Boston in 1883, reported that "Nothing can be more touching than the way in which, after he has ceased to doubt that Cordelia has ceased to live, he simply falls on his face on her body."[11] Booth, after he abandoned Tate's version in the 1870's, died "a man afraid, exhausted by suffering, confronting Cordelia at the end with a dreadful terror, as if in fear not only of what was, but what was to come."[12]

Earlier Lears also died in despair. Before Edmund Kean (1823) and William Macready (1834 and after), of course, Lear's death was not seen on the English stage; Lear and Cordelia lived happily in an adaptation by or after Nahum Tate (1681). When Shakespeare's (Folio) ending was restored by Kean, Lear died "Stupified with grief and years, [...] dead to all but the corpse before him, and to this the last glimmerings of sense and feeling were directed." His biographer specifically mentions "his last pointing to her lips with his trembling fingers in death."[13] Macready, Samuel Phelps (1845), and Charles Kean (1858) all died in despair.[14] The Continental tradition does not differ from the English and American. There is no indication that any of the Devrients or other German Lears of the nineteenth century died differently,[15] and French productions (when not after Tate) at least through André Antoine's famous one in 1904 seem to have followed the stage direction of the first French translation in having Lear "succombe d'aliénation, de doleur & dépuisement sur le corps de sa fille."[16]

Actors and directors of the last generation have done almost anything to the play, but I believe a survey of productions before 1962 would show a preponderance of attempts, at least, to show that Lear dies in ecstasy, such as Gielgud's famous performance in 1940, in which Harley Granville-Barker had a strong hand.[17] Twentieth century commentators have differed in emphasis, but the remarkable thing in the critical tradition is the dominance of Bradley's reading of the last lines. Kenneth Muir, for example, in his influential Arden edition (1952, frequently revised and reprinted) gives Bradley's interpretation as a gloss. It is only since about 1960 that many critics have argued against *The Redemption of King Lear*, but very few of these have disputed Bradley's interpretation that Lear dies in the belief (illusion or delusion) that Cordelia lives.[18] There have been many versions of the meaning of Lear's belief, and a definite swing against redemption, but that he does so believe has been almost unquestioned. Even W. R. Elton's full-length study, perhaps (leaving aside Jan Kott) the bleakest reading since Swinburne, assumes Bradley's interpretation of Lear's final lines. Elton does not explicitly discuss 'Do you see this ...' but he sums up "this dark world of the tragedy" as one

> in which man's chief joy is to be removed from the rack of this tough world and in which man's pathetic solace is – ultimate irony! – the *illusion* that that which he has most loved still breathes: 'Look on her, look, her lips,/ Look there, look there!' No redemption stirs at this world's end; only suffering, tears, pity, and loss – *and* illusion.[19]

So dominant has Bradley's reading of the Folio been, that most of the recent scholars acutely conscious of the difference between the Folio and Quarto texts have not disputed it,[20] even though it is not difficult to imagine an actor delivering 'Do you see this ...' in despair because Cordelia does not live. And in fact all before Bradley did.

II

As with actors, so with critics. Except for two possible foreshadowers, I have found no editor or commentator who interpreted the ending of *King Lear* as Bradley does; critical and theatrical traditions reflect each other. In his essays on *King Lear* Bradley singles out two previous critics of the play, Swinburne and Dowden. He calls Swinburne "the greatest of Shakespearean critics since the days of Coleridge, Hazlitt and Lamb" (p. 276), but he brings up Swinburne in part specifically to deny the contention that Gloucester's lines "As flies to wanton boys are we to the gods,/They kill us for their sport", "strike the keynote of the whole poem, lay the keystone of the whole arch of thought." For Swinburne, in *King Lear*

> we look [...] from the roots that no God waters to the stars which give no man light; over a world full of death and life without resting-place or guidance [...] Requital, redemption, amends, equity, explanation, pity and mercy, are words without a meaning here.[21]

Bradley says that Dowden influenced him most in interpreting King Lear, and calls him the best "guide" to Shakespeare (p. 330, note), and Dowden is sometimes referred to as propounding something close to Bradley's redemption.[22] Dowden speaks of "the awful and purifying ordeal through which Lear is compelled to pass"; but the context here is of Lear's loss, not redemption:

> To be thrown out of this passionate wilfulness, to be made a passive thing, to be stripped first of affection, then of power, then of home or shelter, last, of reason itself, and, finally, to learn the preciousness of true love only at the moment when it must be forever renounced – such is the awful and purifying ordeal through which Lear is compelled to pass.[23]

And whereas Bradley draws a parallel of Lear's death to Gloucester's (p. 294), Dowden contrasts them: Gloucester is "restored to spiritual calm and light [...] in a rapture of mingled gladness and grief", while Lear "expire[s] in the climax of a paroxysm of unproductive anguish."

> And though he is in part delivered from his imperious self-will, and learns, at last, what true love is, and that it exists in the world, Lear passes away from our sight, not in any mood of resignation or faith or illuminated peace, but in a piteous agony of yearning for that love which he had found only to lose forever.[24]

Of other commentators before Bradley, all use the Folio text for the ending, but none that I have found see any joy in Lear at his death. In reading pre-Bradleyean commentary on *Lear*, one is struck with how little attention is, in fact, paid to the final scene. *King Lear* is discussed fairly frequently during the eighteenth century, as a glance through Brian Vickers's collection will show,[25] but the emphasis is on Lear's curses, his madness, the storm scenes, and the reconciliation with Cordelia; there can be little doubt that Garrick's powerful playing in these scenes (in an adaptation based on Tate) is largely responsible for much of this emphasis later in the century. When the ending is alluded to, the assumption is that he dies in despair, as in Theobald's summary in 1715 that Cordelia "is hang'd in the Prison, and [Lear] breaks his Heart with the Affliction of it", or Joseph Warton's comment (1754) that Cordelia's death "is so severe and intolerable that it again deprives [Lear] of his intellect, which seemed to be returning."[26] Discussions in the nineteenth century are fuller, but the emphases are the same, except that the Fool gains in prominence (he had been restored to the stage by Macready in 1838). In Germany, Schlegel (1808) contrasts the main plot with the Gloucester sub-plot: "all the circumstances are so different, that these stories, while they each make a correspondent impression on the heart, form a complete contrast to the imagination", and he goes on to say that "After surviving so many sufferings, Lear can only die; and what more truly tragic end for him than to die from grief for the death of Cordelia."[27] The sentiment is similar to a famous passage in Lamb's "On the Tragedies of Shakespeare" (1811): "as if at his years, and with his experience, anything was left but to die!"[28]

Coleridge's extant writings never directly mention the last scene of *King Lear*. H. C. Robinson's record of an 1812 lecture mentions "a vindication of the melancholy catastrophe."[29] Hazlitt (1817), like eighteenth-century commentators, emphasizes the first three acts and the reconciliation scene with Cordelia; he states that "Lear dies broken-hearted, lamenting over her", and quotes Lear's last speech, but, interestingly, ends the quotation at "Pray you undo this button: thank you sir!" and ends his essay by quoting Lamb.[30] Keats, who thought Hazlitt's lectures on Shakespeare one of the three great things of the age, speaks in a famous sonnet of "the fierce dispute/Betwixt damnation and impassioned clay." Victor Hugo (1864) elaborates a little more than Hazlitt: "The old man is stunned; he no longer understands anything; and, embracing her corpse, he expires";[31] I have already mentioned Swinburne's even bleaker reading. Closer to Bradley's time, a very influential study by the Danish scholar Georg Brandes, published in English in

1898, is the same: "He can feel nothing but Cordelia's death: "And my poor fool is hanged! No, no, no life!" He faints and dies.[32] R. J. Moulton has (for my purposes at least) an extremely interesting essay in 1885, for it demonstrates how relatively little attention was paid to the ending of the play before Bradley's interpretation and how basic the assumption that Shakespeare's ending was unrelieved by any joy. Moulton's subject is the play's structure, especially how the plot is set up and worked out up to the 'climax' of the scenes on the heath, with some reference to the sub-plot. But he says *nothing* about acts four and five, for either plot. There is only a passing reference to the ending:

> there is no longer sharp suffering, but the whole mind is wrecked, gleams of coherence coming at intervals to mark what a fall there has been; the strain on our emotions sinks into the calm of hopelessness.[33]

But there was during the century a less despairing reading of the play's ending, especially notable in German commentaries. Between 1849 and 1862, G. G. Gervinus published a series of commentaries on the plays, best remembered today for their use of metrical tests for dating the plays and tracing Shakespeare's development. But his English translator (1862) had special praise for Gervinus's unfolding "one ruling idea pervading every play", following the example of Goethe's reading of *Hamlet*.[34] Gervinus has no discussion of the final scene of *Lear*, and he tends to be vague, but he does state that Lear finds peace, and that "The death of his child forcibly retains him in that peace and gentleness in which he is to depart to a better life. [...] He recognized in her the martyr and saviour – the precursor of a better time. This was Shakespeare's meaning in her death."[35] Hermann Ulrici, in the later editions of *Shakespeare's Dramatic Art* (originally published in 1839; 3rd edn, 1876), cites Gervinus in his pages on *Lear*, and elaborates on his own earlier interpretation of a peaceful end: "Lear's deranged mind, the contradiction in his love, terminates in a mortal sigh for Cordelia's loss", but that loss is "cleared of the dross of its earthly existence, and ascends to heaven purified and glorified." With his death, as with "Gloster's death in Edgar's arms [...] the tragic pathos loses its depressing influence, and changes into the elevating feeling of a gentle death and blissful peace."[36] We are not yet to Bradley, but the movement is there – and beyond.

III

H. H. Furness's *New Variorum* edition of 1880 has no note on Lear's final words. He prints them as follows:

> Do you see this? Look on her, – look, – her lips, –
> Look there! – look there!

Except for the dashes, this is substantially the way all modern editors print them and derives from Johnson (1765). I am more skeptical than some about making much of Folio's punctuation, but it is worth noting that the Folio has no exclamation marks;[37] editors from Pope to Johnson printed a dash after the final "look there." No editor, until very recently (and few of them), made anything of the variation from the Quarto reading, though all since Pope have used the Quarto to some extent.[38] The adoption of exclamation marks would seem to indicate that editors thought something extra happened at the moment of Lear's death, but before Bradley none except Capell and Delius made any mention of what Lear sees as he dies.

Edward Capell published an edition of Shakespeare in 1768, and in 1774 a volume of *Notes and Various Readings to Shakespeare*, expanded to three volumes in 1779-80 (published posthumously, 1783). In a note to Albany's 'O see, see,' he writes:

> The last words of his [i.e., Albany's] speech are occasion'd by seeing Lear exert himself to embrace the body he lay upon once more, and pour his agonies over it: his expression about the "*lips*" of that body might proceed from an imagination of motion in them; or else from some actual convulsive appearance, for such is said to have happen'd to bodies in that circumstance.

But it does not occur to Capell that Lear might think Cordelia lives, for he says that Lear falls into a stupid and senseless apathy: out of which he awakes in his last minutes, and gives vent to some other piercing exclaims; is suffocated almost by a rising of new grief, and, in the burst of it, dies.[39]

In 1792 Ambrose Isaac Eccles paraphrased Capell's suggestion about the lips, only to reject it: "Perhaps he points to the pale colour of the lips in death"; and he also paraphrased Steevens's gloss (1773 and after) that Lear "dies away while he is searching for life there."[40] Neither Capell's nor Eccles's suggestions are noted by Malone's edition of 1790 or by Boswell's Malone of 1821. Furness at "Oh, see, see" cites only the first clause of Capell's note, "These words are occasion'd by seeing Lear exert himself to embrace the body he lay upon once more, and pour his agonies over it."

The only other pre-Bradleyean editor I have found who makes any suggestion about Cordelia's lips is Nikolaus Delius, who published an edition of Shakespeare's works in English with notes in German in 1854; it went through many editions (Furness collated the first and third) and became the text, without the notes, of the Leopold Shakespeare (1877) and the Royal Shakespeare (1880-84), both with an introduction by F. J. Furnivall. At Lear's last lines (following Johnson's punctuation), Delius cryptically notes, "Lear glaubt noch immer, dass Cordelia die Lippen bewege."[41] Perhaps he is following Capell. I have found no editor or commentator who picks up this note; Furness cites Capell, Eccles, and Delius in his collation and notes to the final scene; the note to "my poor fool is hang'd!" cites Steevens that "fool" refers to Cordelia, "on whose lips he is still intent, and [he] dies away while he is searching there for indications of life" (by this time a standard gloss).

Bradley uses Furness, of course, but he was thoroughly familiar with the editorial tradition in England and Germany at first hand; he may well have developed the suggestion of Capell and Delius – he regularly cites both in passing (e.g., in the notes to *Lear*, pp. 453, 455). But the crucial interpretation that Lear believes that Cordelia lives is certainly his own.[42] In the hands of some of Bradley's followers, we have an ending even happier than Tate's, all grief and despair redeemed in a final (sometimes even Christian) vision. But Bradley is not so extreme. *King Lear* is "certainly the most terrible picture that Shakespeare painted of the world" (p. 273), and Bradley speaks of "those sufferings which made us doubt whether life were not simply evil, and men like the flies which wanton boys torture for their sport" (p. 285). The reference is to Swinburne, but Bradley's next sentence is the important one: "Should we not be *at least* as near the truth if we called this poem *The Redemption of King Lear*" (emphasis added). At Lear's death, the joy is only a part: "though he is killed by an agony of pain, the agony in which he actually dies is one not of pain but of ecstasy" (p. 291). For Bradley tragedy must include evil, waste, and suffering, but also good and ultimately reconciliation. In an essay on "Hegel's Theory of Tragedy", three years before *Shakespearean Tragedy*, he states that Hegel underrates the roles of fate and moral evil in tragedy, and that

> the element of reconciliation in the catastrophe is strengthened by recognition of the part played by evil in bringing it about; because our sense that the ultimate power cannot endure the presence of such evil is implicitly the sense that this power is at least more closely allied with good.

There must be an "affirmative aspect in the catastrophe."[43] He specifically mentions *Lear* as a case in which the "pain" of the ending "is mingled not merely with acquiescence, but with something like exaltation."[44] And he must find this "affirmative aspect" in the tragedy itself; by the time of *Shakespearean Tragedy*, it is found in Lear's last two lines. In a review, "Eighteenth Century Estimates of Shakespeare", the same year as *Shakespearean Tragedy*, he praises that century's critics for eliminating judgments of Shakespeare by standards external to the plays (the unities, for example), and beginning interpretation by what Schlegel and Coleridge called "organic form".[45] In *King Lear*, the "catastrophe, unlike those of all the other mature tragedies, does not seem at all inevitable", and the "dramatic sense" calls for a "'happy ending'" (*Shakespearean Tragedy*, p. 252). He recognizes that this desire "is a heresy and all the best authority is against it" (p.

253). He quotes Lamb and Schlegel. But Lear's last two Folio lines accord him this 'happy ending', though when he explicates them he is compelled to add in a footnote: "This interpretation may be condemned as fantastic, but the text, it appears to me, will bear no other" (p. 291).

But as far as I have been able to discover, no twentieth-century critic, until very recently, thought his reading "fantastic", even when Bradley was most unfashionable in some critical circles. His reading, in fact, went unnoticed in contemporary reviews, and then quickly became the standard interpretation.[46] Granted that there was a lot in *Shakespearean Tragedy* for reviewers to talk about, it is still remarkable that no one took notice of this new ending. Tate's happy ending had held the stage for almost a century and a half, and though Johnson approved, critics since Addison (*Spectator* 40, 1711) had objected; by 1904 Shakespeare's ending had been restored to the stage for almost a century. One must conclude that, in conjunction with the Gervinus-Ulrici escapist readings, the world was ready for a new, less bleak ending for what was becoming more and more to be described as "Shakespeare's greatest work" (*Shakespearean Tragedy*, p. 243).

Bradley was a man of his time, though certainly its greatest Shakespearean critic, and some contemporary responses to movements in the theory of evolution made for a very bleak world indeed. Several writers on Bradley have stressed his rejection of his spiritual background (his father was an Evangelical minister), his finding meaning in the Idealist philosophy at Oxford, his need to defend the cosmos in the wake of nihilistic doctrines of the survival of the fittest.[47] Bradley takes his "courage in both hands and say[s] boldly" that the "dramatic sense" of *King Lear* calls for a happy ending (p. 252). The eighteenth century had not been an age for tragedy; Tate prevailed. Nor is it any wonder that an upsurge of pessimism in the late twentieth century has seen a return to a very bleak *King Lear*. Shakespeare wrote for all time, and others abide our question; there is nothing new in the observation that each age reads Shakespeare as its own. It is not difficult to see that Bradley is guilty of the charge that he makes against Schlegel, that he "takes us beyond the strictly tragic point of view" (p. 254).

Bradley's reading of Lear's last words still holds its own – with whatever further elaborations. The difference between the Folio and Quarto texts remains. As long ago as 1910, R. H. Cunningham thought that in the Quarto Shakespeare "may not have intended" the joy at the end; he assumes Bradley's reading of the Folio. In 1931 Madeleine Doran suggested that Lear's final Folio lines "may be a brilliant afterthought."[48] Quite an afterthought! I myself have seen an actor (in 1962) throw in a few "she lives" at the end, presumably because he did not think the words in the text sufficient to make the point. The provenance of the texts is still in question; the New Oxford editors agree that the Quarto is from foul papers and the Folio from a marked-up copy of Q2 involving the prompt book, or perhaps from a manuscript involving the two, but "a confident solution still eludes us."[49] The question of a revision of *King Lear*, by Shakespeare himself or by others, so much discussed recently, was debated much earlier, especially among nineteenth-century German editors.[50] As far as I know, no one has suggested that Shakespeare shaped a revision toward Lear's final belief that Cordelia lives. Perhaps most scholars presently agree that the text of the Folio represents in some way a revision by Shakespeare. Whether that means he added the conclusion that Lear dies thinking that Cordelia lives is not a question resolved by textual studies alone; nor by the critical and theatrical traditions.

Indeed, Bradley's interpretation of the ending may come to be seen as a twentieth century interlude in the play's critical history, as was Tate's ending for some century and a half in its theatrical history. It shares with Tate's an attempt to take away the despair of Lear's death. But, as moving as Bradley's reading is, it is difficult to see how Lear's final two lines, only in the Folio text, can carry the weight Bradley and his followers would give them. While many critical readings continue to reflect Bradley's interpretation, many do not, and recent editors have not so glossed the lines[51] (as Muir's Arden had done); nor do productions of the last thirty years or so that I am familiar with attempt to show joy at Lear's death. Quite the contrary.

Perhaps the most celebrated production of *King Lear* in the last half-century – Peter Brook's in 1962 – followed Jan Kott's notably unBradleyan interpretation, "*King Lear* or *Endgame*"; both Kott and Brook were indebted to the drama of Samuel Beckett to the point of distorting the text of the play far beyond anything Bradley's 'new reading' had done in his day.[52] We at the end of the twentieth century, no less than Bradley, can be victims of our times, and there is always the tendency to believe that nobody before us knew how to read Shakespeare.

Notes

1. "The Emotional Landscape of *King Lear*", *Shakespeare Quarterly*, 39 (1988), p. 156.

2. *The Norton Facsimile: The First Folio of Shakespeare*, ed. Charlton Hinman (New York: Norton, 1968), TLN 3277-97, p. 817.

3. *Shakespeare's Plays in Quarto*, ed. Michael Allen and Kenneth Muir, (Berkeley: California UP, 1981), p. 703. The only modern edition I know of that uses Quarto for copy text, M. R. Ridley's New Temple (1935), prints both the Q's O's and the Folio's "Do you see this ..."; Ridley gives "Breake hart ..." to Lear and has him die after Kent's "... stretch him out longer."

4. *Shakespearean Tragedy*, (1905; 2nd ed. London: Macmillan, 1937), pp. 291, 285. Subsequent references are in parentheses in the text.

5. J. K. Walton, "Lear's Last Speech," *Shakespeare Survey*, 13 (1960), p. 17 (citing G. I. Duthrie's edition [Oxford, 1949], p. 44); Derek Peak, "'And that's true too'", *ibid.* 33 (1980), p. 45; J. S. Bratton, ed., *King Lear* (Bristol: Bristol Classical Press, Plays in Performance, 1987), p. 213.

6. "Henry Irving", (1905), in *Pen Portraits and Reviews* (London, Constable, 1932), p. 163.

7. Alan Hughes, *Henry Irving, Shakespearean* (Cambridge UP, 1981), pp. 138-9, 136-7.

8. Marvin Carlson, *The Italian Shakespeareans* (Washington: The Folger Shakespeare Library, 1985), pp. 190-1, 200-1. Bradley's movements are from Katherine Cooke, *A. C. Bradley and his Influence in Twentieth-Century Shakespeare Criticism* (Oxford: Clarendon Press, 1972), pp. 18-30.

9. *The Academy*, 6 May 1876, pp. 445-6 (signed May Thomas). Partially quoted by Carlson, p. 153.

10. Carlson, p. 105.

11. *The Scenic Art*, ed. Alan Wade (New Brunswick: Rutgers UP, 1948), p. 180. Bradley had seen Salvini act; he refers to him in connection with *Othello* (p. 434).

12. Marvin Rosenberg, *The Masks of King Lear* (Berkeley: California UP, 1972), p. 320. There are references to productions at Stratford in 1883 by Elliot Galer's Company and in 1890 by

Osmond Tearle; F. R. Benson played Lear in 1902 and 1904. I have found no indication that any of these departed from the traditional ending of despair.

13. F. W. Hawkins, *The Life of Edmund Kean* (London, 1869), Vol. II, pp. 214-15.

14. See Rosenberg, pp. 318ff.; Bratton (cited above, note 5).

15. See Marvin Rosenberg, "*King Lear* in Germany, France, and Italy", *Theatre Survey*, 9 (1965), pp. 1-10.

16. Pierre Le Tourneur, *Shakespeare Traduit de L'Anglais* (Paris, 1776-82), Tome V. Antoine's version is printed in *L'Illustration Théatricale*, 17 Dec. 1904.

17. John Gielgud, *Stage Directions* (New York: Capricorn Books, 1966), pp. 51-5, 121-33, esp. p. 129; Rosenberg, *Masks*, p. 319.

18. There are a number of surveys that deal with responses to Bradley's reading, among them W. R. Elton, *'King Lear' and the Gods* (San Marino, CA: Huntington Library, 1966), pp. 3-8; Katherine Cooke (cited note 8), esp. pp. 166-78; Joseph H. Summers, "'Look there, look there!': The Ending of *King Lear*", *English Renaissance Studies Presented to Dame Helen Gardner*, ed. John Carey (Oxford: Clarendon Press, 1980), pp. 74-93, slightly revised in *Dreams of Love and Power* (Oxford: Clarendon Press, 1984), pp. 95-114; G. R. Hibbard, "*King Lear*: A Retrospect, 1939-79", *Shakespeare Survey*, 33 (1980), pp. 1-12. There were some relatively early dissenters from Bradley's "redemption", if not specifically from his reading of the last two lines, e.g. L. L. Schücking, *Character Problems in Shakespeare's Plays* (New York: Henry Holt, 1922), pp. 185ff.

19. Elton, p. 334. Prof. Elton does not mention Swinburne in his summary of earlier readings. He also associates Lear's death with Gloucester's, pp. 271, 282. Jan Kott, "*King Lear* or *Endgame*," in *Shakespeare, Our Contemporary*, tr. Boleslaw Taborski (Garden City, NY: Anchor Books, 1966), pp. 127-68.

20. For example, all of the relevant contributors to *The Division of the Kingdom*, ed. Gary Taylor and Michael Warren (Oxford: Clarendon Press, 1983). John C. Meagher does suggest that 'Do you see this ...' is uttered in despair, perhaps not even directed toward Cordelia's lips [!], "Vanity, Lear's Feather, and the Pathology of Editorial Annotation", in *Shakespeare 1971*, ed. Clifford Leech and J. M. R. Margeson (Toronto UP, 1972), p. 259, note 13.

21. "A Study of Shakespeare" (1880, internally dated 1864), in *Complete Works*, ed. Sir Edmond Gosse and T. J. Wise (London and New York: Bonchurch Edition, 1928), Vol. XI, pp. 122-3.

22. For example, Cooke, p. 165.

23. *Shakespere: A Critical Study of His Mind and Art*, (1875; 3rd edn. (New York: Harper and Brothers, n.d. [1881]), p. 234.

24. *Ibid.*, pp. 238, 242-3. Hughes (cited note 7) refers to an article by Dowden in *The Illustrated London News*, 12 Nov. 1892, "timed to accompany [Irving's] Lyceum production" which seems 'softer' on Lear's death: "even in his agony it is love that delivers over the afflicted old man to the great calm of death" (p. 121). See Gervinus and Ulrici below.

25. *Shakespeare: The Critical Heritage*, 6 vols (London and Boston: Routledge & Kegen Paul, 1974-81). Ian J. Kirby's statement that "Criticism ancient and modern alike has concentrated on Lear's final speech in the attempt to determine exactly what happened at the end of the play" is simply not true. "The Passing of King Lear", *Shakespeare Survey*, 41 (1988), p. 153.

26. Vickers, Vol. II, p. 304; Vol. III, p. 82.

27. *Lectures on Dramatic Art and Literature*, transl. J. Black, 2nd rev. edn (London: George Bell & Sons, 1894), pp. 412, 413.

28. *Dramatic Essays*, ed. Brander Matthews (New York: Dodd, Mead, 1891), p. 187. Apparently, there is no indebtedness to Schlegel, whose lectures were not translated into English until 1815. Lamb mentions them as a new book in that year, see *The Letters of Charles and Mary Lamb*, ed. E. W. Marrs, Jr. (Ithaca: Cornell UP, 1978), Vol. III, p. 175.

29. *Coleridge's Shakespearean Criticism*, ed. T. M. Raysor (Cambridge, MA: Harvard UP, 1930), Vol. II, p. 219.

30. *Characters of Shakespeare's Plays*, in *Complete Works*, ed. P. P. Howe (London: J. M. Dent & Sons, 1930), Vol. IV, p. 270.

31. *William Shakespeare*, transl. Melville B. Anderson (Chicago: A. C. McClurg, 1911), p. 248.

32. *William Shakespeare: A Critical Study*, transl. William Archer, Mary Morison, and Diana White (New York: Macmillan, 1899), p. 459. Whether 'my poor fool' refers to Cordelia or the Fool was much discussed in the late eighteenth and nineteenth centuries – H. H. Furness has almost three pages of commentary in the New Variorum edition (Philadelphia: J. B. Lippencott, 1880), and Furness himself "very reluctantly" agrees with the majority of commentators that the phrase refers to Cordelia. The first French translation (cited note 16) has the Fool's corpse brought on stage with those of Goneril and Regen, and translates, "O! vois, vois, mon pauvre serviteur aussi étranglé."

33. *Shakespeare as a Dramatic Artist*, 2nd edn (Oxford: Clarendon Press, 1888), p. 215.

34. Shakespeare Commentaries, transl. F. E. Burnett, 6th edn (London: Smith, Elder & Co., 1903), p. vi.

35. *Ibid.*, pp. 640, 641.

36. Transl. L. Dora Schmitz (London: G. Bell and Sons, 1876), Vol. I, p. 457.

37. The Folio also has a question mark after "Looke on her." Editors from Rowe to Johnson (and some after) adopted the later Folios' "look(e) on her lips."

38. Capell, Malone, and some others note the difference in Quarto (and usually cite five "O"s from Q2), but without comment.

39. (London, printed 1779-80, pub. 1783), Vol. I, p. 189. The first part (only) of the quotation is pr. by Vickers, Vol. VI, pp. 230-l, and is cited in Philip Hobsbaum, "*King Lear* in the Eighteenth Century", *Modern Language Review*, 68 (1973), pp. 494-506.

40. *The Tragedies of 'King Lear' and 'Cymbeline'* (London: C. Dilly, 1792), pp. 447, 444. Hobsbaum mistakenly implies that Eccles supports Capell.

41. *Shakespere's Werke* (Elberfeld: 1854), Band I. I have also checked the 2nd (1864), 3rd (1872), and 5th (1882) editions, which all agree. Delius makes much use of Boswell's Malone (1821), referred to as Steevens and Malone. Furnivall's introduction to the Leopold and Royal editions obviously ignores this note: Lear's death comes "at last, when the eye catches the tokens of mortality in the dead, snapping the chords of life in an agonized horror." *Leopold Shakespeare* (London: Cassell and Co., 1877), p. lxxx; *Royal Shakespeare* (London: International Bibliographical Society, 1880-84), Vol. XII, p. lxxxviii.

42. It is perhaps worth noting that in *The Shakespeare Story-Book* (New York: Barnes & Co., n.d. [bibliographies give 1902]), with an introduction by Sidney Lee, Mary MacLeod, in paraphrasing the story quotes Lear's "Look there ..." and relates that "with a strange cry of mingled joy and anguish King Lear fell dead on the body of his dear child Cordelia" (p. 359).

Perhaps she picks up the phrase from Edgar's description of Gloucester's death (which is not given); perhaps she is extending the Gervinus-Ulrici interpretation. In Charles and Mary Lamb's *Tales from Shakespeare* (1807), Lear just dies, offstage, as it were (Everyman Edition, p. 148).

43. In *Oxford Lectures on Poetry* (Bloomington: Indiana UP, 1961), pp. 82-5, 91.

44. *Ibid.*, p. 84.

45. A review of D. Nicoll Smith's *Eighteenth Century Essays on Shakespeare*, *Scottish Historical Review* (1904), pp. 291-5.

46. Cooke's summary, (pp. 164-78), mentions several commentators who have not recognized that the reading originated with Bradley (she is not always accurate). In her report of reviews of *Shakespearean Tragedy* (p. 191) she is oddly mistaken in saying that the reviewer for *The Spectator*, 28 Jan. 1905, pp. 140-1, cites Bradley's interpretation of Lear's death.

47. For example, G. K. Hunter, "A. C. Bradley's *Shakespearean Tragedy*," *Essays and Studies*, NS 21 (1968), pp. 101-17; Peter Alexander, "Critics Who Have Influenced Our Time, XV: A. C. Bradley", *The Times*, 11 July 1963, repr. in *Critics Who Have Influenced Taste*, ed. A. P. Ryan (London: Geoffrey Bles, 1965), pp. 67-9; Cooke, esp. pp. 19-42; Terence Hawkes, *That Shakespeherian Rag* (London: Methuen, 1986), pp. 27-50.

48. "The Revision of King Lear", *Modern Language Review*, V (1910), p. 452; *The Text of 'King Lear'*, Stanford University Studies in Language and Literature, IV (1931), p. 68. Various possibilities of what happens on stage during the last few lines are discussed at length by Philip C. McGuire, *Speechless Dialect: Shakespeare's Open Silences* (Berkeley: California UP, 1985), pp. 97-121.

49. *William Shakespeare: A Textual Companion*, ed. Stanley Wells and Gary Taylor (Oxford: Clarendon Press, 1987), p. 531.

50. Cunningham, pp. 445-53. See also Furness, pp. 359-73. P. W. K. Stone, who believes the Folio is a revision by another hand, perhaps Massinger, thinks that "Do you see this ..." was added by the reviser who "misunderstood the drift of the scene" and, "unable to supply anything original, reverts to an idea that has already been exploited to moving effect." See *The Textual History of 'King Lear'* (London: Scholar Press, 1980), p. 247.

51. Eg., *The New Cambridge Shakespeare*, ed. Jay Halio (1992), *The New Penguin*, ed. G. K. Hunter (1981).

52. See Alfred Harbage, *Conceptions of Shakespeare* (Cambridge, Mass.: Harvard UP, 1966), pp. 71-5; Maynard Mack, *'King Lear' in Our Time* (Berkeley and Los Angeles: California UP, 1965), pp. 30-2, 38-40, 74-5. For Kott, see note 19.

REVIEWS

The World Shakespeare Bibliography, 1990-1993, on CD-ROM [with booklet], ed. James L. Harner. Cambridge: Cambridge University Press in Association with the Folger Shakespeare Library, 1996. ISBN 0-521-565421

In ten years' time people will undoubtedly be asking what all the fuss is about. At present, however, in what one day may well come to be dubbed the incunabula age of electronic information retrieval, the development of the greatly respected bibliography regularly published in the *Shakespeare Quarterly* into a CD-ROM, *The World Shakespeare Bibliography,* is an event in literary scholarship that merits a report and a review as well as a welcome.

The disk under consideration covers the period from 1990 to 1993. The plan for the future is not simply to update the *Bibliography* annually but also to move back successively three more years each time. In other words, the next issue will list materials from 1987 to 1994, and progress will continue like this, one step forward and three steps back, until coverage is complete from 1900 to the report year. Pricing is a rather complex business, with special arrangements for what is in effect taking out a subscription for the next few issues. If, as seems likely to be the case, the CD-ROM is networked, there is a sliding charge according to the number of terminals; the stand-alone price is increased by 50% for any number between two and one hundred and doubled for the next four hundred.

The present CD-ROM comprises an impressive total of no fewer than 12,000 individual items. These are further complemented with several thousand reviews, many of which, if not all, are themselves of considerable value as criticism and constructive comment. The compilers' grasp is international, involving seventy-five languages, and help is given by transliterating non-roman alphabets and by translating into English all titles except those in French, German, Italian and Spanish.

As well as comprehensive listings of details of books, individual chapters, articles, dissertations and computer software entirely or substantially concerned with Shakespeare and of professional and semi-professional stage, screen and electronic productions, once again with reviews as appropriate, the *Bibliography* provides selective coverage not only of non-professional performances but also of those books and articles with shorter references to Shakespeare that are deemed to have some significance despite their brevity. It is good to see that space is made too for reminiscences, obituaries and other appreciations of notable Shakespearean scholars and performers. A certain amount of material of only peripheral value to Shakespeare studies is excluded, and few apart from the bit-part players themselves are likely to complain about the decision to pass silently over the names of actors taking non-speaking roles. Though the line evidently has to be drawn somewhere, it might, none the less, be thought a little harsh to make a principle of omitting abstracts and summaries of unpublished conference papers. If, on the one hand, there is some truth in the oft-repeated assertion that the best of them will no doubt be published in due course, it is, on the other, arguable that this is not, in fact, the case in every instance and that there may, besides, be real advantages in having the earliest possible notice of trends, no less to spur further thought than to prevent undue reduplication of effort, even to promote co-operation and to prompt editors and learned presses to make contacts. Despite this minor reservation, there is no denying that coverage is impressive in its scope. Long-term users of the Bibliographies in the *Shakespeare Quarterly* will also be glad to find that the material that has been collected largely, if not totally in accord with established policies has then been classified in familiar categories.

The question that at once arises concerns, of course, ease of access through a CD-ROM. The technical requirements of what is presented as a DynaText electronic book are by no means onerous in IT terms. The *Bibliography* has been designed so that, to quote the booklet on a matter on which potential purchasers will wish to be precisely informed, it can be used either on a Macintosh (System 7 or later; 4 Mb of RAM) or a PC (386 or later; Windows 3.1+; 8 Mb of RAM); a double-speed CD-ROM drive is also required. Installation is a perfectly simple operation, even for a computer duffer like the present reviewer, and perhaps some readers will understand my feeling of relief on being given an assurance that pressing the wrong key or whatever cannot do any harm to the disk. Experimenting is safe, but there is really very little need for a trial-and-error session. The booklet is clear and helpful, despite some computer speak and a few unsettling trade names. Consulting the records, located essentially under the rubrics General Shakespeareana, Play Groups, Individual Works and Indexes, is, at least in the first instance, a matter of no more than the usual routines of mouse-clicks on items in the Indexes or typing key words in a box helpfully labelled 'Find'. Scroll bars can also be used to move from one part of the List of Works or the Index to another. The text that comes up on screen is easy to read, with all the information presented in a clear, immediately accessible format. Brief comments are added where necessary to elucidate the content of the various items, and keywords that are taken up in the Index are also clearly indicated.

Basic cross-referencing, in response to a neatly indicated invitation, is a simple matter of mouse-clicking on an icon in the margin. More complex searches are possible, linking potential areas of interest. A simple technique makes it possible to locate, for example, instances of listing of the word 'Falstaff' in conjunction with 'Wives', or, alternatively, to isolate references to 'Falstaff' that are *not* linked with 'Wives'. I must admit to being a little puzzled, however, by the question I am invited to pose in some dual searches. In a concordance, where the textual issues are of fundamental significance, enquiring whether a certain adjective occurs within, say, ten words of a given noun makes good sense. Asking, as the booklet suggests, whether 'Lear' occurs within ten words of 'economics' appears to have less validity, and it does not really help to know that the number of words can be varied between one and twenty. It may be naive to say so, but simply knowing which items in the *Bibliography* contain both terms would appear an adequate response to most users' needs. However this may be, many are bound to be grateful for the 'wild card' and asterisk facilities that make it possible to light on the right information even if the detail of, say, the spelling of a surname has not been remembered quite correctly. Equally useful are techniques for noting down and printing out information. The days of peering at a screen and trying not to make too many mistakes as you jot down details while holding the mouse in the other hand have gone. It is also possible for users to add their own annotation, so that they can, in the course of time, produce their personal version of the *Bibliography*. Without seeking to lay any claim to expertise that, possibly like a number of other potential users, I must regret not yet possessing, I feel at liberty to report my relief, not say delight in finding *The World Shakespeare Bibliography* user-friendly. Familiarity will no doubt add respect for the potentialities of the retrieval technology; mere beginners will be able to profit from it within minutes and save hours of research time.

So we must thank the editor, Professor James L. Harner, his technical editor, Priscilla J. Letterman, and all their team, saluting them on their fine achievement in bringing forth, in a form that will not take up scarce library space and that cannot be regarded as particularly expensive, this electronic offspring of the invaluable Bibliographies that have appeared in the *Shakespeare Quarterly* over the decades. Using the CD-ROM is not going to be difficult at a technical level; the problem will lie rather in making best use of all it provides so abundantly at such high speed. Retrieving information, for instance, about Erpingham is one thing, with decisions about what to discard straight away and what to retain for future investigation causing no headaches. With Hamlet things will never be so easy. But that, notoriously, is not a new problem, and no one can complain when enumerative bibliographers do their job better by making it a good deal easier and less tedious for us to discover what they have so assiduously gleaned and garnered. Winnowing the grain from the chaff is a different field of scholarly endeavour.

The World Shakespeare Bibliography is bound to become an indispensable tool, and it certainly will not be long before the researchers of the next generation learn to handle it with practised expertise and start wondering how people ever managed without it. Meantime even the digitally inept can, however, do something to assist the editor and his dedicated team of collaborators. However advanced its technology, this *Bibliography* can, like any other computer system, only be as good as the information it contains. So we ought to be scrupulous in heeding Professor Harner's call to send copies of our publications to him (at the Department of English, Texas A & M University, College Station, TX 77843-4227, USA); he undertakes to return them if asked. It would also plainly be helpful if authors would take particular pains to select for our books and articles titles that reflect their contents accurately and readily yield as much precise information as possible.

University of East Anglia, Norwich   Christopher Smith

JOSEPH CANDIDO, ed. *Shakespeare: The Critical Tradition: 'King John'*. London and Atlantic Highlands, NJ: Athlone Press, 1996. pp. xvi + 415. ISBN 0-485-81001- (hb).

This volume marks the inception of a new series of the Critical Heritage, following in the wake of Brian Vickers's six-volume anthology, *Shakespeare: The Critical Heritage, 1632-1801*. *King John* is the first of three new anthologies devoted to a single play (the others being *Richard II* and *A Midsummer Night's Dream*), and concentrating on the period 1790 to 1920. The Critical Heritage series itself began in the late 1960s, with volumes devoted to Tennyson (1967), Thackeray (1968), Fielding and Trollope (1969). It ranges chronologically from Chaucer to Beckett and Nabokov, the latter being the only living writers honoured so far. A few writers (Arnold, Chaucer, Joyce, Milton) qualify for two volumes, but Shakespeare is unique in his six. In fact, in Volume 1 Vickers promised "to offer a more detailed account of the progress of Shakespeare criticism" after he had completed the projected six volumes, a huge task of valuable historical scholarship published over seven years; and since nearly two hundred further years of criticism remained to be covered, it was clearly necessary to find some way of proceeding. This new series suggests that Vickers has decided to change tack; and rather than continue with an anthology of materials relating to Shakespeare's work as a whole, to embark on a series devoted to the criticism of separate plays, which takes over chronologically from where his sixth volume ended.

It is good that the series has taken on a new lease of life in this way, because it is a valuable one, despite the many limitations placed on the selection of material, which, in the case of the Shakespeare volumes, means the exclusion of contemporary allusions, because, in Vickers's view, "none of these amount to sustained criticism of any great value". Luckily not all the editors of early writers take this stern attitude. The arbitrariness with which Vickers stopped his anthology at 1801, because, as he says, there was too much material to permit him to continue to 1832 (why 1832?), is of a piece with a certain lack of consistency in the aims and methods of the series as a whole. This is not necessarily something to complain of; obviously, however one defines a 'critical heritage' or a 'critical tradition', the materials of which it consists will be very different in the case of recent writers such as Sylvia Plath or Evelyn Waugh from that of canonical greats such as Chaucer and Milton. The Critical Heritage must be responsive to the varied nature of its materials.

Brian Southam, in his preface as General Editor of the whole series, makes modest claims for it, based on the value to the student of literature of a knowledge of 'the reception given to a writer by his contemporaries and near-contemporaries'. But in many cases, notably those of Shakespeare and other early writers, the usefulness of the series lies elsewhere, since little or no material is provided to illustrate "the tastes and literary thought of individual readers of the period". Southam takes account of this lacuna, noting that for pre-eighteenth-century writers "the historical period has been extended [...] in order to show the inception and growth of critical views which were initially slow to appear". The period is often not extended much, if at all, into the twentieth century for these writers, so that in many cases the bulk of the materials come from critics of the nineteenth century, thus causing a disproportionate emphasis to fall on a particular type of criticism. Although Southam refers to "private comments in letters" as possible material from which a writer's critical heritage might be built up, these are likely to create a negligible impact beside the contributions of professional scholars, editors, and journalists.

This volume devoted to *King John* consists of materials published between 1790 and 1919, the period which is to be the main focus of the new series. Even within these limits the aim is not completeness of coverage, and major Romantic critics, whose work is already familiar, will be marginalized in favour of lesser-known nineteenth-century writers. This might be disappointing to a student who consults the volumes in the hope of gaining an overall perspective on the development of a particular play's reputation, only to find that if s/he wants to know what Keats or Lamb, for example, has to say about it, then s/he must look elsewhere. There is further delimiting of the scope of Candido's selection, in that he excludes continental criticism not translated into English at the time; and also writing that deals mainly with theatrical history, although luckily he is flexible enough to retain some lively accounts of Sarah Siddons's portrayal of Constance.

What, then, do we get in this expensive book? The extracts are preceded by a useful introduction pointing out general trends in nineteenth-century criticism of *King John*, and, somewhat frustratingly, concluding with a summary of critical trends from 1920 to the present, none of which is of course represented. Candido takes the view that *King John* has finally 'arrived' in the late twentieth century, but we must look for evidence of this elsewhere. He does help us with the provision of a decent bibliography. There are 75 extracts from figures familiar to the world of professional Shakespeare scholarship, such as Ritson, Furnivall, Furness, and E. K. Chambers, as well as a host of more shadowy writers now largely confined to Victorian obscurity. There are a few names unexpected in this context, such as that of Frank Harris, who opines that Shakespeare modelled Constance on his wife, "so bad-tempered, such a wordy termagent", and a number of completely unfamiliar ones. Vickers praises Candido for recovering three in particular: J. Lytelton Etty, Charlotte Porter, and John Munro. Etty, one of the few examples of a general reader, writes well enough in Bradleian mode about John's character as "an incomplete hypocrite"; Porter, who sounds interesting, an American editor of Browning, writes character-criticism in the vivid, incisive style that one sometimes hankers after today: "despite the glamor of John's first bold successes, his mongrel coarseness, neither straightforward nor astute, traps him into crookedness." Munro, a collaborator of Furnivall's, compares *King John* with *The Troublesome Raigne of King John* as its source play, and makes some good points about Shakespeare's methods as an adaptor.

The range of topics covered by these critics is not wide, and there is a repetitiveness about the material. This is largely due to the limitations of *King John* as a play; but in any case the anthology is designed for selective reading. It is nonetheless disheartening to find so many accounts of a play written by people who clearly regard it as second-rate, and draw particular attention to its failure to deal with those major events we associate with King John's reign, the signing of Magna Carta, and the activities of Robin Hood. George Henry Calvert is exceptional in his praise for the play as "this tumultuous prophetic prologue to the grand series of Shakespeare's historic dramas", but Barrett Wendell typical in his reference to it as "queerer, more archaic, more puzzling" than Shakespeare's other chronicle histories. For the late twentieth century, these qualities might make the play more attractive, but it was not so in the nineteenth. The topics most often discussed, apart from John's character, are Constance (thought by a physician, John Charles Bucknill, to be a study in the psychology of madness), the Bastard, the play's relation to Elizabethan politics, the masterly scenes between John and Arthur, and between Hubert and Arthur, and hints of Shakespeare's own religious views to be gathered from the play. George Wilkes, in one of the zanier pieces, entitled "Shakespeare from an American point of view", thought him to be writing from a distinctively Roman Catholic perspective. Feminist scholars may find useful material in the many discussions of the play's female roles, though only three of the authors cited in the anthology are women. As a whole, this volume gives us a good sense of the growth of the Shakespeare industry in Europe and North America in the nineteenth century, and by default, in taking 1920 as its cut-off point, makes us aware of how much Shakespeare criticism has moved on since then.

Birkbeck College, University of London   Sandra Clark

Andrew Gurr, *The Shakespearean Playing Companies* (Oxford: Clarendon, 1996). pp. xi + 483. ISBN 0 19 812977 7

Andrew Gurr's book is an up-to-date history of the playing companies of London in Shakespeare's time and up to 1642. It is divided into two parts. The first is a general account of acting in London from the 1560s up to the closure of the theatres. The second deals with the known playing companies one by one; a short but comprehensive history of the company concerned is followed by a summary of what is known about it: plays associated with the company, its playing sharers and hired men and boys, London venues, appearances at court and details of travelling outside London. The result is a compendious volume which significantly updates the relevant sections of E. K. Chambers's *Elizabethan Stage* and G. E. Bentley's *Jacobean and Caroline Stage*. Gurr's knowledge of the stage-history of the time would be hard to rival, and he is fertile in conjecture, something very necessary when there is so much that is obscure, as is the case here. He has also had access to nineteen unpublished volumes of the *Records of Early English Drama* at Toronto; these have provided much new information about travelling, both the distances covered and the rewards ("Bath 1602 'Bestowed uppon the Quenes men for their Kytchinge bread beare wyne & sugar' 8s., 'paid for their horsemeate' 3s.2d." [p.217]). All this makes *The Shakespearean Playing Companies* a book which editors and historians in the field will have to consult for some time to come.

The book's first part, the general history, covers such topics as the use of London as a base, travelling, the role of the Master of the Revels, usual practices in the Shakespearean theatre (there is nothing on the nature of the structures themselves), the changes following the advent of James and the subsequent development of companies and repertory up to the time of the Civil War.

There are plenty of good things here. The chapter on travelling, for example, deals with patronage and patents and plague, all predictable topics, but there is also some calculation of journey-times; in 1613, Queen Anne's Men executed a journey of more than two hundred and thirty miles, from Leicester to Hythe in Kent, in eighteen days, which seems very good going. Perhaps it had been a dry summer and the roads were good. Gurr speculates very reasonably that on some occasions companies must have had recourse to the sea: "several companies show a notable rapidity of transit between Dover and Norwich, or Plymouth and Dover. A visit to a port is a regular prelude to the next recorded visit appearing a hundred or more miles away, often in another port" (pp.46-7). We know from their continental travels (touched on only incidentally in this book) that players were not averse to sea-travel. One of the new pieces of information from REED to be found here is that in 1589 the Queen's Men went to Dublin. When the Queen Anne's Men went from York on 13 September 1607 via Ipswich to Dunwich in Suffolk by 14 October, it seems likely that they would have gone by sea part of the way, if not from York, then from Hull as far as Ipswich.

The chapter on "Settled Practices" is broken up into a number of heads, including "The Times of Day for Performance", "The Length of Performances", "Changes in Play-runs in the Shakespearean Repertory" and so on. This is a very useful chapter, but it brings to the surface a problem which is present throughout the book. It is this: the book never solves satisfactorily the conflict between its desire to be a repository of information and its aspiration to be something more. Gurr is well equipped to write about the practices of the Shakespearean stage, but doing so in this fashion inevitably affects the dynamic of his history. He is in some ways too scrupulous a scholar. He refuses to be downright when the evidence does not warrant it. Writing a history does require him to be downright; he tends, honourably, to duck out, and his book suffers for it. Time and again he enters into a form of argument that suggests a conclusion and then concludes that a conclusion cannot be reached. On the times of day at which performances started, for example, he mulls over the possible hours – two o'clock, three o'clock, four o'clock – with great care, but leaves the reader still pretty much up in the air. "A 3 p.m. start must [...] have been standard at the Fortune by 1614"; "it may be best to conclude that the different companies had different starting-times, and that the Globe company's normal starting-time was 2 p.m." (p. 79). This is sober, but not as enthralling as one would wish. Gurr is more positive on the length of performances, citing the experimental performances of the Shenandoah Shakespeare Express; the usual length was between two and three hours. But he does not address the question of long plays like *Hamlet* and whether they were performed in full or not. There is at times a rag-bag feel about the book and it is hard to imagine a reader without specialized professional interest going straight through it.

That is a pity, because this is the work of someone with a real love of the theatre – as you would expect in someone closely associated with London's new Globe Theatre as Gurr is. He points to an important difference between his own work and that of Chambers and Bentley. "They give minimal attention to the plays and the distinctive repertory traditions that led the different companies to stage them", he says; his own book, by contrast, "shifts the focus back to the plays and to their highly mobile social and political contexts" (p.v). This is felt in several ways, for example, in the emphasis he places on references to the Globe theatre in Shakespeare's first two plays for that theatre, *As You Like It* and *Hamlet*, or in the way he draws attention to parallels between the repertories of the Lord Admiral's and the Chamberlain's Men:

> The Chamberlain's Men had Shakespeare's history plays, so the Admiral's followed suit with a *Richard Crookback* and a *Henry V*. The Admiral's introduced humours comedy, and the Chamberlain's copied them. The Admiral's rubbed in their rivals' Oldcastle/ Falstaff mistake by taking up the Oldcastle story from Foxe's *Book of Martyrs*, and then developed the idea with a run of plays based on stories from Foxe. (p.287)

This has something of the boldness of history. Gurr is good on this side of things, though often he is, of course, taking up ideas that have been in circulation for a while. He is strong on the significance of the Chamberlain's Men using the Blackfriars in winter and the Globe in the summer as an indication both of their confidence and the conservatism also reflected in their repertory. At the same time he does much to dispel the notion that the Lord Admiral's Men came a poor second to the Chamberlain's. Throughout the sense of social context is strong.

The book's second part suffers from a certain amount of necessary repetition from chapter to chapter; the idea is obviously that it will serve as a reference tool. But the individual histories themselves are well done. Gurr obviously wants to go along with the idea that Shakespeare was a member of Lord Strange's company, largely because he is so struck by the prominence given in the first Henriad and *Richard III* to Lord Strange's ancestors, Talbot, Derby and Stanley. This presents him with a difficulty, because, whilst *1 Henry VI* stayed with Strange's, the other two plays went to Pembroke's and Sussex's on their way to the Chamberlain's Men. It does not seem to me that this difficulty, which has to do with the companies that Shakespeare himself played with prior to his arrival with the Chamberlain's in 1594, is ever clearly resolved. Nor is the question of whether Strange's and the Lord Admiral's companies amalgamated for a while in 1591 dealt with clearly. The reader can deduce from the very title of Gurr's own oft-cited article, "The Chimera of Amalgamation", that he is against it, but his text fails to be lucid on his reasons for this. Indeed, in his summary of the Lord Admiral's court performances and Strange's he marks the performances of 27 December 1590 and 16 February 1591 as being by both companies, adding a question mark in respect of the December performance only in the Lord Admiral's account. This is puzzling in itself and also fails to match in any certain way with what he has to say about the court records that give rise to the problem.

But of course it is possible to gripe about any scholarly undertaking on a scale as large as this. That does not mean that for many years to come students will not bless Gurr for his great feat of synthesis and original insight.

Royal Holloway College, University of London Martin Dodsworth

Gordon Williams. *Shakespeare, Sex and the Print Revolution.* London and Atlantic Highlands, NJ: Athlone Press. pp. ix + 274. ISBN 0-485-11495-X (hbk); 0-485-12121-2 (pbk)

Shakespeare's interest in the relationship between a growing book culture and social inequality is palpably illustrated in Caliban's recognition of the role Prospero's books played in his self-appointed authority:

> CALIBAN: There thou mayst brain him,
> Having first seized his books; or with a log
> Batter his skull, or paunch him with a stake,
> Or cut his weasand with thy knife. Remember
> First to possess his books, for without them
> He's but a sot, as I am, nor hath not
> One spirit to command. They all do hate him
> As rootedly as I. Burn but his books. (3.2)

The ambivalent position of print in the processes of liberating and restricting free-thought, if not social freedom, is further indicated in Stephano's joyous anticipation of power: "Flout 'em and scout 'em,/Thought is free." Newly available writing from contemporary Europe and the classical past as well as Counter-Reformation propaganda fuelled debates on the church, war, the New World discoveries and marriage: "the new print age was one of redefinitions, and theories about sexual roles and behaviour and about family structures poured off the presses." In *Shakespeare, Sex and the Print Revolution*, Gordon Williams sets out the paradox that the printed word had the potential for greater political democracy through making the new theories into general currency - "print was responsible for the first shockwave of cultural pluralism" - but the mediators of knowledge, the Church and state, exercised tight control over publishing during Elizabeth I's reign.

'Shakespeare', 'Sex' and 'Print Revolution' are best understood as umbrellas which go up and down in Williams' investigation of the ways in which the Shakespeare plays recorded and contributed to the new thinking about socio-sexual systems and values. Part I, "Shakespearean Images and the Paradox of

Print" sketches the transformation of playscripts from collaborative works-in-progress to printed texts; the obvious implications for the question of authorship - what is meant by 'Shakespeare'? - are introduced but not pursued, largely because "the obvious possibilities of comparing printed and manuscript playscripts are impeded by the lack of Shakespeare's manuscripts". However, Williams refers to a handful of near-contemporary plays to illustrate how bawdy and erotic references would have been censored. The umbrellas of 'sex' and 'print revolution' allow Williams scope for his specialist study of Shakespeare's "sexual elements", by which he means the sexually coded terms of evasion, replacement words and the fools' quasi-nonsense rhymes, as outlined in more detail in his two other books, *A Dictionary of Sexual Language and Imagery in Shakespearean and Stuart Literature* and *A Glossary of Shakespeare's Sexual Usage*.

The uncomfortable questions about Shakespeare's appropriations of "print-impelled stereotypes", such as the sexually irresponsible madman, the silent woman, Jews, Moors and the underclasses, are invoked in the hit-and-run conclusion: "serious critical interest in Shakespeare's collaborations is one of two major developments in recent years. The other is the recognition that Shakespeare is not always giving expression to views of which we may approve." Williams further suggests that the future agenda for directors and academics will be "can bad values generate good art?" The implication of 'bad values' is puzzling in the context of a loose notion of authorship, and, in reading the plays as comments on current social and cultural shifts, Williams seems to be defending Shakespeare against the charge of wrong attitudes.

The organizing structure of Part II, "Shakespeare and the Classics" is the new access to the classical world: "While [the printing press] brought into easy reach the ancient preachers of heroic virtue - it also led to a critical scrutiny of their values. Print gives a measure of permanence, but at the same time exposes the illusion of stability which is the basis of classicism." Here we have another paradox in that the mythologized classical ideals at the heart of Renaissance thought were undermined by approximation; new translations exposed the complex nexus of power, sex and war in ancient civilization. Shakespeare drew out the controversial and gruesome elements for dramatic effect and deflated the cultural elitism attached to familiarity with classical languages and literature. The sexually charged comic sequence when Catherine learns English in *Henry V* also exemplifies the play's deflations of the spreading influence of French court culture.

The strongest evidence against wrong attitudes is Shakespeare's participation in the new debates illustrated in Williams' wide-ranging references to European literary and political texts and to visual art. The chapters in Part III, "The Sexual Reformation", tackle Shakespeare's dramatizations of how his "society theorized extensively about the subordination of women". The chapter "Othello, Cuckolding and the Doctrine of Gentility" proposes that the disappearance of mixed public baths from Germany was a consequence of the spread of an acute form of sexual jealousy in Europe during the fifteenth century and that print mediated "the process by which southern European paranoia became naturalized in Britain and print opened up secular debate about the complexities of sex and marriage". In "Honest Whore, or the State as Brothel" Shakespeare's treatment of the "tangle between legal power and sexual disorder" in *Measure for Measure*, *2Henry IV*, and *Pericles* is historicized in relation to the re-energised debates about prostitution and capital punishment for sexual offences.

Williams' avowed refusal to endorse Shakespeare as our contemporary - Shakespeare speaks *to* not *for* us - is the only clue to a theoretical position. Apparently, the book grew out of his university courses in Renaissance Literature in History, and although he does not directly address the intersections of new historicism and the key contemporary concerns of race, gender and power, Williams approaches the plays in the context of these concerns. The stimulating combination of historical and text criticism places it with other historically situated studies such as Lisa Jardine's *Reading Shakespeare Historically* (1996), Louis Montrose's *The Purpose of Playing: Shakespeare and the Cultural Politics of the Elizabethan Theatre* (1996) and Patricia Parker's *Shakespeare from the Margins: Language, Culture, Context* (1996). It is also refreshing in its close readings of less often discussed works like *Timon of Athens*, *The Rape of Lucrece*, *Venus and Adonis*, *Anthony and Cleopatra*, *Troilus and Cressida*, and *Titus Andronicus* as well as the obvious sites for discussing economic structures, family values and sex roles like *Hamlet* and *Much Ado*.

De Montfort University, Leicester   Jane Dowson

ANNOUNCEMENTS, ETC.

'There Are More Things ...':
The Romanian Shakespeare Miracle

Holger Klein (University of Salzburg)

Sometimes one is lucky in life. This was my lot in 1997, when I was invited to participate in the "Third Students' National Shakespeare Symposium", jointly organised, under the able leadership of Eugenia Gavriliu, by the Galati branch of the Romanian Society of English and American Studies and the Galati University Students' Union. I did not quite know what to expect, but whatever it was, the actual experience was overwhelming.

What happened – for the third time now – was that in all Romanian universities students were invited to write papers on some aspect of Shakespeare's work. Members of staff working in the numerous English departments selected what they thought the best entries locally. The students whose papers had been chosen were eligible for a travel grant and assembled in Galati for a three-day symposium. Their stay at Galati University was funded by the British Council, which also sent a representative. Nearly all groups (consisting of between 3 and 10 students each, save for one solitary but heartily welcomed guest from neighbouring Bulgaria) were accompanied by a member of their department. The entire enterprise corresponded to the professional symposia and congresses held by national and international bodies the world over, only this time it was not – as usual – the teachers who held forth (saving very brief statements in the opening plenary session), but their students.

Papers had been assigned to sections: "Recurrent Patterns in Shakespearean Dramatic Structures", Degrees of Referentiality in Shakespearean Drama", The Recourse to Shakespeare" (a comparative literature section), "Shakespeare and the Stage Convention", "Mythical and Archetypal Dimensions in

Shakespearean Drama", "Shakespeare and Gender", and "Explorations in Shakespearean Discourse". The sections met for one or more sessions, each session uniting some 4-5 twenty-minute papers followed by brief discussions the pattern looks familiar, of course – we have all experienced it ourselves in various context. The difference to an ordinary congress was, however, that at the end the members of staff involved (who had also chaired the sessions) had the pleasant task of handing out prizes. Another difference was that the prize ceremony was followed by a wild night's dancing, with the teachers dropping out, dragging themselves home one by one, while the main body of participants continued unwearied till nightingale or rather lark time. I can remember one or two academic gatherings ending with a dance – the XIIIth ICLA Congress in Paris, for instance, but in general this does not happen often enough.

And yet high spirits are not incompatible with high intelligence – of this the Romanian students showed ample proof. And that they could also act was demonstrated in three theatre performances, one a Shakespearean scenes sequence (in Romanian) done by fourth-year students of the Iasi Arts Academy, the other two by English department drama groups, one from Baia Mare, presenting Reni Drew's *Shakespeare and Me* (a thoughtful and provocative women's lib piece) the other from Galati itself, presenting *Of Royalty, of Marriage and ... of Shakespeare*, written by Tina Britten, a highly enjoyable spoof in form of a pageant partly inspired by *1066 And All That*, but including some very recent expoits – if that is the word – of British royalty.

The most astounding feature of the entire occasion was, however, the quality of the papers presented. Comparisons are odorous, Dogberry is perfectly right for once. There were more whiff's here of the true flowers of rhetoric, scholarship and criticism than at many gatherings of established academics I have attended. This is all the more remarkable as the material conditions of study at Romanian universities are not exactly ideal. Having since perused a typical Romanian first degree curriculum I am less amazed than I was at Galati. The vast quantity of contact hours alone, however, cannot explain such signal success as these student papers, with some few exceptions, showed in 1997. The real explanation must be the commitment on the part of the students, the dedication of their teachers and the enthusiasm for their subject which teachers and students share. The Bard is well loved and well served along the lower reaches of the Danube. Romanian Shakespeareans are setting a wonderful example of what may be achieved if people really want to.